Moving from C to C++

Discussing Programming Problems, Why They Exist, and How C++ Solves Them

Arunesh Goyal

Apress·

Moving from C to C++: Discussing Programming Problems, Why They Exist, and How C++ Solves Them

ISBN-13 (pbk): 978-1-4302-6094-3

ISBN-13 (electronic): 978-1-4302-6095-0

President and Publisher: Paul Manning
Lead Editor: Saswata Mishra
Editorial Board: Steve Anglin, Ewan Buckingham, Gary Cornell, Louise Corrigan, Morgan Ertel, Jonathan Gennick, Jonathan Hassell, Robert Hutchinson, Michelle Lowman, James Markham, Saswata Mishra, Matthew Moodie, Jeff Olson, Jeffrey Pepper, Douglas Pundick, Ben Renow-Clarke, Dominic Shakeshaft, Gwenan Spearing, Tom Welsh, Steve Weiss
Coordinating Editor: Anamika Panchoo
Copy Editor: Mary Behr
Compositor: SPi Global
Indexer: SPi Global
Artist: SPi Global
Cover Designer: Anna Ishchenko

Distributed to the book trade worldwide by Springer Science+Business Media New York, 233 Spring Street, 6th Floor, New York, NY 10013. Phone 1-800-SPRINGER, fax (201) 348-4505, e-mail orders-ny@springer-sbm.com, or visit www.springeronline.com. Apress Media, LLC is a California LLC and the sole member (owner) is Springer Science + Business Media Finance Inc (SSBM Finance Inc). SSBM Finance Inc is a Delaware corporation.

For information on translations, please e-mail rights@apress.com, or visit www.apress.com.

Apress and friends of ED books may be purchased in bulk for academic, corporate, or promotional use. eBook versions and licenses are also available for most titles. For more information, reference our Special Bulk Sales–eBook Licensing web page at www.apress.com/bulk-sales.

Any source code or other supplementary materials referenced by the author in this text is available to readers at www.apress.com. For detailed information about how to locate your book's source code, go to www.apress.com/source-code/.

For Maa, Paa, & Pals! :~

Contents at a Glance

Contents

About the Author

Arunesh Goyal is serving as the honorary director of the ISMRSC (Institute for Studies in Mathematics & Related Sciences in Computers), Delhi. He actively participates as a freelance writer/author for different projects. He has a master's degree in computer application from the University of Delhi. He has worked as a computer analyst/consultant on programming and systems development at St. Stephen's Hospital, Delhi for more than 10 years. In the past, he was also associated with two projects on intelligent databases for Comtech International Ltd., Noida, and The Times of India, New Delhi. He has authored several books including The *C Programming Language, See Thru C++*, and *Systems Analysis and Design*.

Acknowledgments

I would like to laud the role played by each and every one who came into interaction with me during the course of writing this book, nay the whole cosmos, as otherwise this work may perhaps would never have been possible.

In particular, I take this opportunity to thank and acknowledge my publisher, Apress Media LLC, for making this work see the light of the day. But, above all, I would like to put on record the role played by my SadGuruDev, Shri Siddheshwar Baba (formerly Sh. B.S. Goel, M.A., Ph.D.; founder of the Third Eye Foundation of India, Regd.) for constantly encouraging me whenever my spirits were down and out. It is indeed, rightly said,

> *"Gurura Brahma, Gurura Vishnu, Gurura Devo Maheshwara!*
> *Gurura Sakshat Para_Brahma, Tasmai Shri Guruvey Namah!!"*

Finally, this section would remain incomplete without mentioning the extremely sincere and benevolent part played by my parents, Smt. Sita and Shri Rabinder Nath Goyal, whenever I looked to them for support!!!

—Arunesh Goyal

Introduction

Like any human language, C++ provides a way to express concepts. If successful, this medium of expression is significantly easier and more flexible than the alternatives as problems grow larger and more complex.

However, you can't just look at C++ as a collection of features; some of the features make no sense in isolation. You can only use the sum of the parts if you are thinking about design, not simply coding. And to understand C++ this way, you must understand the problems with C—and with programming in general. This book discusses programming problems, why they are problems, and the approach C++ has taken to solve such problems. Thus, the set of features I explain in each chapter is based on the way that I see a particular type of problem being solved with the language. In this way I hope to move you, a little at a time, from understanding C to the point where the C++ mindset becomes your native tongue.

Throughout, I'll be taking the attitude that you want to build a model in your head that allows you to understand the language all the way down to the bare metal; if you encounter a puzzle, you'll be able to feed it to your model and deduce the answer. I will try to convey to you the insights that have made me start "Moving from C to C++".

Prerequisites

I have decided to assume that someone else has taught you C and that you have at least a reading level of comfort with it. My primary focus is on simplifying what I find difficult: the C++ language. Although I have added a chapter that is a rapid introduction to C, I am still assuming that you already have some kind of programming experience. In addition, just as you learn many new words intuitively by seeing them from their context in a novel, it's possible to learn a great deal about C from the context in which it is used in the rest of the book.

Learning C++

I clawed my way into C++ from exactly the same position I expect many of the readers of this book are in: as a programmer with a very no-nonsense, nuts-and-bolts attitude about programming. I discovered later that I wasn't even a very good C programmer, hiding my ignorance of structures, malloc() and free(), setjmp() and longjmp(), and other "sophisticated" concepts, scuttling away in shame when the subjects came up in conversation instead of reaching out for new knowledge.

Goals

I had several goals that guided the writing of this book. The following list describes them.

1. Present the material one simple step at a time, so the reader can easily digest each concept before moving on.

2. Use examples that are as simple and short as possible. This often prevents me from tackling "real world" problems, but I've found that beginners are usually happier when they can understand every detail of an example rather than being impressed by the scope of the problem it solves.

3. Carefully sequence the presentation of features so that you aren't seeing something you haven't been exposed to. Of course, this isn't always possible; in those situations, a brief introductory description will be given.

4. Give you what I think is important for you to understand about the language, rather than everything that I know.

5. Keep each section relatively focused.

6. Provide readers with a solid foundation so they can understand the issues well enough to move on to more difficult coursework and books.

7. I've tried not to use any particular vendor's version of C++ because when it comes to learning the language, I don't think that the details of a particular implementation are as important as the language itself.

Chapters

C++ is a language in which new and different features are built on top of an existing syntax. (Because of this, it is referred to as a hybrid object-oriented programming language.) This book was designed with one thing in mind: to streamline the process of learning C++. Here is a brief description of the chapters contained in this book.

1. **Introduction to Objects:** When projects became too big and too complicated to easily maintain, the "software crisis" was born, with programmers saying, "We can't get projects done, and if we can, they're too expensive!" This precipitated a number of responses that are discussed in this chapter, along with the ideas of object-oriented programming (OOP) and how it attempts to solve the software crisis.

2. **Making and Using Objects:** This chapter explains the process of building programs using compilers and libraries. It introduces the first C++ program in the book and shows how programs are constructed and compiled.

3. **The C in C++:** This chapter is a dense overview of the features in C that are used in C++, as well as a number of basic features that are available only in C++. It also introduces the make utility that's common in the software development world.

4. **Data Abstraction:** Most features in C++ revolve around the ability to create new data types. Not only does this provide superior code organization, but it lays the groundwork for more powerful OOP abilities.

5. **Hiding the Implementation:** You can decide that some of the data and functions in your structure are unavailable to the user of the new type by making them private.

6. **Initialization and Cleanup:** One of the most common C errors results from uninitialized variables. The constructor in C++ allows you to guarantee that variables of your new data type will always be initialized properly. If your objects also require some sort of cleanup, you can guarantee that this cleanup will always happen with the C++ destructor.

7. **Function Overloading and Default Arguments:** C++ is intended to help you build big, complex projects. While doing this, you may bring in multiple libraries that use the same function name, and you may also choose to use the same name with different meanings within a single library. C++ makes this easy with function overloading, which allows you to reuse the same function name as long as the argument lists are different. Default arguments allow you to call the same function in different ways by automatically providing default values for some of your arguments.

8. **Constants:** This chapter covers the const and volatile keywords, which have additional meaning in C++, especially inside classes.

9. **Inline Functions:** Preprocessor macros eliminate function call overhead, but the preprocessor also eliminates valuable C++ type checking. The inline function gives you all the benefits of a preprocessor macro plus all of the benefits of a real function call.

10. **Name Control:** Creating names is a fundamental activity in programming, and when a project gets large, the number of names can be overwhelming. C++ allows you a great deal of control over names in terms of their creation, visibility, placement of storage, and linkage. This chapter shows how names are controlled in C++ using two techniques, the static keyword and the namespace feature.

11. **References and the Copy-Constructor:** C++ pointers work like C pointers with the additional benefit of stronger C++ type checking. You'll also meet the copy-constructor, which controls the way objects are passed into and out of functions by value.

12. **Operator Overloading:** In this chapter, you'll learn that operator overloading is just a different type of function call and you'll learn how to write your own, dealing with the sometimes-confusing uses of arguments, return types, and the decision of whether to make an operator a member or friend.

13. **Dynamic Object Creation:** How many planes will an air traffic control system need to manage? How many shapes will a CAD system require? In the general programming problem, you can't know the quantity, lifetime, or type of objects needed by your running program; here, you'll learn how C++'s new and delete elegantly solve this problem by safely creating objects on the heap.

14. **Inheritance and Composition:** Data abstraction allows you to create new types from scratch, but with composition and inheritance, you can create new types from existing types. With composition, you assemble a new type using other types as pieces, and with inheritance, you create a more specific version of an existing type.

15. **Polymorphism and Virtual Functions:** Through small, simple examples, you'll see how to create a family of types with inheritance and manipulate objects in that family through their common base class. The virtual keyword allows you to treat all objects in this family generically.

16. **Introduction to Templates:** Inheritance and composition allow you to reuse object code, but that doesn't solve all of your reuse needs. Templates allow you to reuse source code by providing the compiler with a way to substitute type names in the body of a class or function.

17. **Exception Handling:** Error handling has always been a problem in programming. Exception handling is a primary feature in C++ that solves this problem by allowing you to "throw" an object out of your function when a critical error happens/occurs.

18. **Strings in Depth:** The most common programming activity is text processing. The C++ string class relieves the programmer from memory management issues, while at the same time delivering a powerhouse of text processing capability.

19. **iostreams:** One of the original C++ libraries—the one that provides the essential I/O facility—is called iostreams. It is intended to replace C's stdio.h with an I/O library that is easier to use, more flexible, and extensible.

20. **Run-time Type Identification:** Run-time type identification (RTTI) finds the exact type of an object when you only have a pointer or reference to the base type.

21. **Multiple Inheritance:** This sounds simple at first: a new class is inherited from more than one existing class. However, you can end up with ambiguities and multiple copies of base class objects. That problem is solved with virtual base classes.

All the best, then, for your "Moving from C to C++"!

—Arunesh Goyal

14th May, 2013, New Delhi

CHAPTER 1

■ ■ ■

Introduction to Objects

The genesis of the computer revolution was in a machine. The genesis of our programming languages thus tends to look like that machine.

But computers are not so much machines as they are mind amplification tools ("bicycles for the mind," so to say) and a different kind of expressive medium. As a result, the tools are beginning to look less like machines and more like parts of our minds, and also like other expressive mediums such as writing, painting, sculpture, animation, and filmmaking. Object-oriented programming is part of this movement toward using the computer as an expressive medium.

This chapter will introduce you to the basic concepts of object-oriented programming, including an overview of OOP development methods. This chapter, and this book, assume that you have had experience in a procedural programming language, although not necessarily C.

This chapter is background and supplementary material. Many people do not feel comfortable wading into object-oriented programming without understanding the big picture first. Thus, many concepts are introduced here to give you a solid overview of OOP. However, many other people don't get the big picture concepts until they've seen some of the mechanics first; these people may become bogged down and lost without some code to get their hands on. If you're part of this latter group and are eager to get to the specifics of the language, feel free to jump past this chapter; skipping it at this point will not prevent you from writing programs or learning the language. However, you will want to come back here eventually to fill in your knowledge so you can understand why objects are important and how to design with them.

The Progress of Abstraction

All programming languages provide abstractions. It can be argued that the complexity of the problems you're able to solve is directly related to the kind and quality of abstraction. ("Kind" refers to *what* you are abstracting.) Assembly language is a small abstraction of the underlying machine. Many so-called *imperative languages* that followed are abstractions of assembly language. These languages are big improvements over assembly language, but their primary abstraction still requires you to think in terms of the structure of the computer rather than the structure of the problem you are trying to solve. The programmer must establish the association between the machine model (in the *solution space*, which is the place where you're modeling that problem, such as a computer) and the model of the problem that is actually being solved (in the *problem space*, which is the place where the problem exists). The effort required to perform this mapping, and the fact that it is extrinsic to the programming language, produces programs that are difficult to write and expensive to maintain, and as a side effect created the entire *programming methods* industry.

The alternative to modeling the machine is to model the problem you're trying to solve. PROLOG casts all problems into chains of decisions. Languages have been created for constraint-based programming and for programming exclusively by manipulating graphical symbols. Each of these approaches is a good solution to the particular class of problem they're designed to solve, but when you step outside of that domain they become awkward.

The object-oriented approach goes a step farther by providing tools for the programmer to represent elements in the problem space. This representation is general enough that the programmer is not constrained to any particular type of problem. We refer to the elements in the problem space and their representations in the solution space as *objects*. (Of course, you will also need other objects that don't have problem-space analogs.) The idea is that the program is allowed to adapt itself to the lingo of the problem by adding new types of objects, so when you read the code describing the solution, you're reading words that also express the problem. This is a more flexible and powerful language abstraction than what we've had before. Thus, OOP allows you to describe the problem in terms of the problem, rather than in terms of the computer where the solution will run.

There's still a connection back to the computer, though. Each object looks quite a bit like a little computer; it has a state, and it has operations that you can ask it to perform. However, this doesn't seem like such a bad analogy to objects in the real world; they all have characteristics and behaviors.

Some language designers have decided that object-oriented programming by itself is not adequate to easily solve all programming problems, and so advocate the combination of various approaches into *multiparadigm* programming languages.

There are five characteristics that represent a pure approach to object-oriented programming.

1. **Everything is an object.** Think of an object as a fancy variable; it stores data, but you can "make requests" to that object, asking it to perform operations on itself. In theory, you can take any conceptual component in the problem you're trying to solve (dogs, buildings, services, etc.) and represent it as an object in your program.

2. **A program is a bunch of objects telling each other what to do by sending messages.** To make a request of an object, you "send a message" to that object. More concretely, you can think of a message as a request to call a function that belongs to a particular object.

3. **Each object has its own memory made up of other objects.** Put another way, you create a new kind of object by making a package containing existing objects. Thus, you can build complexity in a program while hiding it behind the simplicity of objects.

4. **Every object has a type.** Using the parlance, each object is an *instance* of a *class*, in which "class" is synonymous with "type." The most important distinguishing characteristic of a class is the messages you can send to it.

5. **All objects of a particular type can receive the same messages.** Because an object of type circle is also an object of type shape, a circle is guaranteed to accept shape messages. This means you can write code that talks to shapes and automatically handles anything that fits the description of a shape. This *substitutability* is one of the most *powerful* concepts in OOP.

An Object Has An Interface

The idea that all objects, while being unique, are also part of a class of objects that have characteristics and behaviors in common was used directly in the first object-oriented language, Simula-67, with its fundamental keyword class that introduces a new type into a program.

Simula, as its name implies, was created for developing simulations such as the classic bank teller problem. In this, you have a bunch of tellers, customers, accounts, transactions, and units of money—a lot of *objects*. Objects that are identical except for their state during a program's execution are grouped together into *classes of objects* and that's where the keyword class came from. Creating abstract data types (classes) is a fundamental concept in object-oriented programming. Abstract data types work almost exactly like built-in types: you can create variables of a type (called *objects* or *instances* in object-oriented parlance) and manipulate those variables (called *sending messages* or *requests*; you send a message and the object figures out what to do with it). The members (*elements*) of each class share some commonality: every account has a *balance*, every teller can accept a deposit, etc. At the same time, each member has its own state, each account has a different balance, and each teller has a name. Thus, the tellers, customers, accounts, transactions, etc. can each be represented with a unique entity in the computer program. This entity is the object, and each object belongs to a particular class that defines its characteristics and behaviors.

So, although what we really do in object-oriented programming is create new data types, virtually all object-oriented programming languages use the class keyword. When you see the word "type" think "class" and vice versa.

Since a class describes a set of objects that have identical characteristics (*data elements*) and behaviors (*functionality*), a class is really a data type because a floating point number, for example, also has a set of characteristics and behaviors. The difference is that a programmer defines a class to fit a problem rather than being forced to use an existing data type that was designed to represent a unit of storage in a machine. You extend the programming language by adding new data types specific to your needs. The programming system welcomes the new classes and gives them all the care and type-checking that it gives to built-in types.

The object-oriented approach is not limited to building simulations. Whether or not you agree that any program is a simulation of the system you're designing, the use of OOP techniques can easily reduce a large set of problems to a simple solution.

Once a class is established, you can make as many objects of that class as you like, and then manipulate those objects as if they are the elements that exist in the problem you are trying to solve. Indeed, one of the challenges of object-oriented programming is to create a one-to-one mapping between the elements in the problem space and objects in the solution space.

But how do you get an object to do useful work for you? There must be a way to make a request of the object so that it will do something, such as complete a transaction, draw something on the screen, or turn on a switch. And each object can satisfy only certain requests. The requests you can make of an object are defined by its *interface*, and the type is what determines the interface. A simple example might be a representation of a light bulb in Figure 1-1 and the code would be

```
Light lt;
lt.on();
```

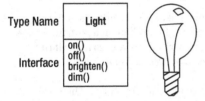

Figure 1-1. *Type and interface for a light bulb*

The interface establishes *what* requests you can make for a particular object. However, there must be code somewhere to satisfy that request. This, along with the hidden data, comprises the *implementation*. From a procedural programming standpoint, it's not that complicated. A type has a function associated with each possible request, and when you make a particular request to an object, that function is called. This process is usually summarized by saying that you send a message (*make a request*) to an object, and the object figures out what to do with that message (*it executes code*).

Here, the name of the type/class is Light, the name of this particular Light object is lt, and the requests that you can make of a Light object are to turn it on, turn it off, make it brighter or make it dimmer. You create a Light object by declaring a name (lt) for that object. To send a message to the object, you state the name of the object and connect it to the message request with a period (dot). From the standpoint of the user of a pre-defined class, that's pretty much all there is to programming with objects.

Figure 1-1 follows the format of the Unified Modeling Language (UML). Each class is represented by a box, with the type name in the top portion of the box, any data members that you care to describe in the middle portion of the box, and the *member functions* (the functions that belong to this object, which receive any messages you send to that object) in the bottom portion of the box. Often, only the name of the class and the public member functions are shown in UML design diagrams, and so the middle portion is not shown. If you're interested only in the class name, then the bottom portion doesn't need to be shown, either.

The Hidden Implementation

It is helpful to break up the playing field into *class creators* (those who create new data types) and *client programmers* (the class consumers who use the data types in their applications). The goal of the client programmer is to collect a toolbox full of classes to use for rapid application development. The goal of the class creator is to build a class that exposes only what's necessary to the client programmer and keeps everything else hidden. Why? Because if it's hidden, the client programmer can't use it, which means that the class creator can change the hidden portion at will without worrying about the impact to anyone else. The hidden portion usually represents the tender insides of an object that could easily be corrupted by a careless or uninformed client programmer, so hiding the implementation reduces program bugs. *The concept of implementation hiding cannot be overemphasized.*

In any relationship it's important to have boundaries that are respected by all parties involved. When you create a library, you establish a relationship with the client programmer, who is also a programmer, but one who is putting together an application by using your library, possibly to build a bigger library.

If all the members of a class are available to everyone, then the client programmer can do anything with that class and there's no way to enforce rules. Even though you might really prefer that the client programmer not directly manipulate some of the members of your class, without access control there's no way to prevent it. Everything's naked to the world.

So the first reason for access control is to keep client programmers' hands off portions they shouldn't touch— parts that are necessary for the internal machinations of the data type but not part of the interface that users need in order to solve their particular problems. This is actually a service to users because they can easily see what's important to them and what they can ignore.

The second reason for access control is to allow the library designer to change the internal workings of the class without worrying about how it will affect the client programmer. For example, you might implement a particular class in a simple fashion to ease development, and then later discover that you need to rewrite it in order to make it run faster. *If the interface and implementation are clearly separated and protected, you can accomplish this easily, and it requires only a relink by the user.*

C++ uses three explicit keywords to set the boundaries in a class: `public`, `private`, and `protected`. Their use and meaning are quite straightforward. These *access specifiers* determine who can use the definitions that follow. `public` means the following definitions are available to everyone. The `private` keyword, on the other hand, means that no one can access those definitions except you, the creator of the type, inside member functions of that type. `private` is a brick wall between you and the client programmer. If someone tries to access a `private` member, they'll get a compile-time error. `protected` acts just like `private`, with the exception that an inheriting class has access to protected members, but not `private` members. *Inheritance* will be introduced shortly.

Reusing the Implementation

Once a class has been created and tested, it should (ideally) represent a useful unit of code. It turns out that this reusability is not nearly so easy to achieve as many would hope; it takes experience and insight to produce a good design. But once you have such a design, it begs to be reused. Code reuse is one of the greatest advantages that object-oriented programming languages provide.

The simplest way to reuse a class is to just use an object of that class directly, but you can also place an object of that class inside a new class. We call this "creating a member object." Your new class can be made up of any number and type of other objects, in any combination that you need to achieve the functionality desired in your new class. Because you are composing a new class from existing classes, this concept is called *composition* (or more generally, *aggregation*). Composition, illustrated in Figure 1-2, is often referred to as a "has-a" relationship, as in "a car has an engine."

Figure 1-2. *Showing a composition (the "has-a" relationship)*

(This UML diagram indicates composition with the filled diamond, which states *there is one car*. I shall be typically using a simpler form: just a line, *without the diamond*, to indicate an association.)

Composition comes with a great deal of flexibility. The member objects of your new class are usually private, making them inaccessible to the client programmers who are using the class. This allows you to change those members without disturbing existing client code. You can also change the member objects at runtime, to dynamically change the behavior of your program. Inheritance, which is described next, does not have this flexibility since the compiler must place compile-time restrictions on classes created with inheritance.

Because inheritance is so important in object-oriented programming it is often highly emphasized, and the new programmer can get the idea that inheritance should be used everywhere. This can result in awkward and overly-complicated designs. Instead, you should first look to composition when creating new classes, since it is simpler and more flexible. If you take this approach, your designs will stay cleaner. Once you've had some experience, it will be reasonably obvious when you need inheritance.

Inheritance: Reusing the Interface

By itself, the idea of an object is a convenient tool. It allows you to package data and functionality together by *concept*, so you can represent an appropriate problem-space idea rather than being forced to use the idioms of the underlying machine. These concepts are expressed as fundamental units in the programming language by using the `class` keyword.

It seems a pity, however, to go to all the trouble to create a class and then be forced to create a brand new one that might have similar functionality. It's nicer if you can take the existing class, clone it, and then make additions and modifications to the clone. This is effectively what you get with inheritance, with the exception that if the original class (called the *base* or *super* or *parent* class) is changed, the modified "clone" (called the *derived* or *inherited* or *sub* or *child* class) also reflects those changes.

(The arrow in the UML diagram in Figure 1-3 points from the derived class to the base class. As you will see, there can be more than one derived class.)

Figure 1-3. *Showing inheritance (derivation of subclass from superclass)*

A type does more than describe the constraints on a set of objects; it also has a relationship with other types. Two types can have characteristics and behaviors in common, but one type may contain more characteristics than another and may also handle more messages (or handle them differently). Inheritance expresses this similarity between types using the concept of base types and derived types. A base type contains all of the characteristics and behaviors that are shared among the types derived from it. You create a base type to represent the core of your ideas about some objects in your system. From the base type, you derive other types to express the different ways that this core can be realized.

For example, a trash-recycling machine sorts pieces of trash. The base type is trash, and each piece of trash has a weight, a value, and so on, and can be shredded, melted, or decomposed. From this, more specific types of trash are derived that may have additional characteristics (a bottle has a color) or behaviors (an aluminum can may be crushed, a steel can is magnetic). In addition, some behaviors may be different (the value of paper depends on its type and condition). Using inheritance, you can build a type hierarchy that expresses the problem you're trying to solve in terms of its types.

A second example, illustrated in Figure 1-4, is the classic Shape example, perhaps used in a computer-aided design system or game simulation. The base type is Shape, and each shape has a size, a color, a position, and so on. Each shape can be drawn, erased, moved, colored, etc. From this, specific types of shapes are derived (*inherited*): Circle, Square, Triangle, and so on, each of which may have additional characteristics and behaviors. Certain shapes can be flipped, for example. Some behaviors may be different, such as when you want to calculate the area of a shape. The type hierarchy embodies both the similarities and differences between the shapes.

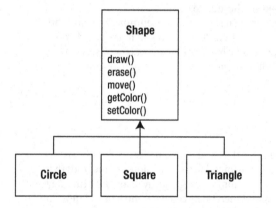

Figure 1-4. *Showing a type hierarchy of shapes*

Casting the solution in the same terms as the problem is tremendously beneficial because you don't need a lot of intermediate models to get from a description of the problem to a description of the solution. With objects, the type hierarchy is the primary model, so you go directly from the description of the system in the real world to the description of the system in code. Indeed, one of the difficulties people have with object-oriented design is that it's too simple to get from the beginning to the end. A mind trained to look for complex solutions is often stumped by this simplicity at first.

When you inherit from an existing type, you create a new type. This new type contains not only all the members of the existing type (although the private ones are hidden away and inaccessible), but more importantly it duplicates the interface of the base class. That is, all the messages you can send to objects of the base class you can also send to objects of the derived class. Since you know the type of a class by the messages you can send to it, this means that *the derived class is the same type as the base class*. In the previous example, a Circle is a Shape. This type equivalence via inheritance is one of the fundamental gateways in understanding the meaning of object-oriented programming.

Since both the base class and derived class have the same interface, there must be some implementation to go along with that interface. That is, there must be some code to execute when an object receives a particular message. If you simply inherit a class and don't do anything else, the methods from the base class interface come right along into the derived class. That means objects of the derived class have not only the same type, they also have the same behavior, which isn't particularly interesting.

You have two ways to differentiate your new derived class from the original base class. The first is quite straightforward: you simply add brand new functions to the derived class. These new functions are not part of the base class interface. This means that the base class simply didn't do as much as you wanted it to, so you added more functions. This simple and primitive use for inheritance is, at times, the perfect solution to your problem. However, you should look closely for the possibility that your base class might also need these additional functions. This process of discovery and iteration of your design, illustrated in Figure 1-5, happens regularly in object-oriented programming.

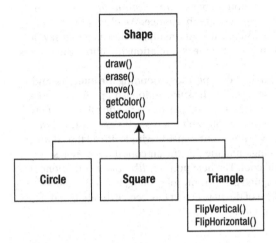

Figure 1-5. *Showing an iteration in OOP*

Although inheritance may sometimes imply that you are going to add new functions to the interface, that's not necessarily true. The second and more important way to differentiate your new class is to *change* the behavior of an existing base-class function. This is referred to as *overriding* that function and is shown in Figure 1-6.

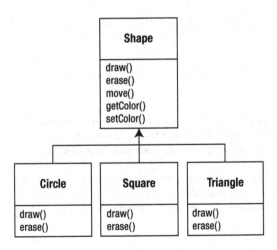

Figure 1-6. *Showing overriding of functions in OOP*

To override a function, you simply create a new definition for the function in the derived class. You're saying, "I'm using the same interface function here, but I want it to do something different for my new type."

Is-a vs. is-like-a Relationships

There's a certain debate that can occur about inheritance: should inheritance override *only* base-class functions (*and not add new member functions that aren't in the base class*)? This would mean that the derived type is *exactly* the same type as the base class since it has exactly the same interface. As a result, you can exactly substitute an object of the derived class for an object of the base class. This can be thought of as *pure substitution*, and it's often referred to as the *substitution principle*. In a sense, this is the ideal way to treat inheritance. We often refer to the relationship between the base class and derived classes in this case as an *is-a* relationship, because we can say "a circle *is a* shape." A test for inheritance is to determine whether you can state the is-a relationship about the classes and have it make sense.

There are times when you must add new interface elements to a derived type, thus extending the interface and creating a new type. The new type can still be substituted for the base type, but the substitution isn't perfect because your new functions are not accessible from the base type. This can be described as an *is-like-a* relationship; the new type has the interface of the old type but it also contains other functions, so you can't really say it's exactly the same. For example, consider an air conditioner (illustrated in Figure 1-7). Suppose your house is wired with all the controls for cooling; that is, it has an interface that allows you to control cooling. Imagine that the air conditioner breaks down and you replace it with a heat pump, which can both heat and cool. The heat pump *is-like-an* air conditioner, but it can do more. Because the control system of your house is designed only to control cooling, it is restricted to communication with the cooling part of the new object. The interface of the new object has been extended, and the existing system doesn't know about anything except the original interface.

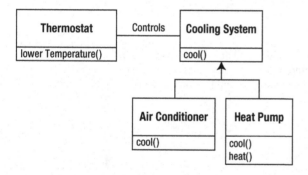

Figure 1-7. *Cooling system vs. temperature control system*

Of course, once you see this design it becomes clear that the base class `Cooling System` is not general enough, and should be renamed to `Temperature Control System` so that it can also include heating—at which point the substitution principle will work. However, the diagram in Figure 1-7 is an example of what can happen in design and in the real world.

When you see the substitution principle it's easy to feel like this approach (*pure substitution*) is the only way to do things, and in fact it *is* nice if your design works out that way. But you'll find that there are times when it's equally clear that you must add new functions to the interface of a derived class. With inspection, both cases should be reasonably obvious.

Interchangeable Objects with Polymorphism

When dealing with type hierarchies, you often want to treat an object not as the specific type that it is but instead as its base type. This allows you to write code that doesn't depend on specific types. In the shape example, functions manipulate generic shapes without respect to whether they're Circles, Squares, Triangles, and so on. All shapes can be drawn, erased, and moved, so these functions simply send a message to a shape object; they don't worry about how the object copes with the message.

Such code is unaffected by the addition of new types, and adding new types is the most common way to extend an object-oriented program to handle new situations. For example, you can derive a new subtype of Shape called Pentagon without modifying the functions that deal only with generic shapes. This ability to extend a program easily by deriving new subtypes is important because it greatly improves designs while reducing the cost of software maintenance.

There's a problem, however, with attempting to treat derived-type objects as their generic base types (Circles as Shapes, Bicycles as Vehicles, Cormorants as Birds, etc.). If a function is going to tell a generic shape to draw itself, or a generic vehicle to steer, or a generic bird to move, the compiler cannot know at compile-time precisely what piece of code will be executed. That's the whole point! When the message is sent, the programmer doesn't *want* to know what piece of code will be executed; the draw function can be applied equally to a Circle, a Square, or a Triangle, and the object will execute the proper code depending on its specific type. If you don't have to know what piece of code will be executed, then when you add a new subtype, the code it executes can be different without requiring changes to the function call.

Therefore, the compiler cannot know precisely what piece of code is executed, what does it do? For example, in Figure 1-8 the BirdController object just works with generic Bird objects, and does not know what exact type they are. This is convenient from BirdController's perspective because it doesn't have to write special code to determine the exact type of Bird it's working with, or that Bird's behavior. So how does it happen that, when move() is called while ignoring the specific type of Bird, the right behavior will occur (a Goose runs, flies, or swims, and a Penguin runs or swims)?

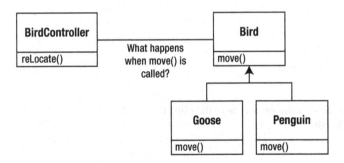

Figure 1-8. *Early binding in non-OOP vs. late binding in OOP*

The answer is the primary twist in object-oriented programming: *the compiler cannot make a function call in the traditional sense.* The function call generated by a non-OOP compiler causes what is called *early binding*, a term you may not have heard before because you've never thought about it any other way. It means the compiler generates a call to a specific function name, and the linker resolves this call to the absolute address of the code to be executed. In OOP, the program cannot determine the address of the code until runtime, so some other scheme is necessary when a message is sent to a generic object.

To solve the problem, object-oriented languages use the concept of *late binding*. When you send a message to an object, the code being called isn't determined until runtime. The compiler does ensure that the function exists and performs type checking on the arguments and return value (a language in which this isn't true is called *weakly typed*), but it doesn't know the exact code to execute.

To perform late binding, the C++ compiler inserts a special bit of code in lieu of the absolute call. This code calculates the address of the function body, using information stored in the object (this process is covered in greater detail in Chapter 15). Thus, each object can behave differently according to the contents of that special bit of code. When you send a message to an object, the object actually does figure out what to do with that message.

You state that you want a function to have the flexibility of late-binding properties using the keyword `virtual`. You don't need to understand the mechanics of `virtual` to use it, but without it you can't do object-oriented programming in C++. In C++, you must remember to add the `virtual` keyword because, by default, member functions are *not* dynamically bound. Virtual functions allow you to express the differences in behavior of classes in the same family. Those differences are what cause polymorphic behavior.

Consider the Shape example. The family of classes (all based on the same uniform interface) was diagrammed earlier in the chapter. To demonstrate polymorphism, you want to write a single piece of code that ignores the specific details of type and talks only to the base class. That code is *decoupled* from type-specific information, and thus is simpler to write and easier to understand. And, if a new type—a Hexagon, for example—is added through inheritance, the code you write will work just as well for the new type of Shape as it did on the existing types. Thus, the program is *extensible*.

If you write a function in C++ (as you will soon learn how to do):

```cpp
void doStuff(Shape& s) {
  s.erase();
  // ...
  s.draw();
}
```

this function speaks to any Shape, so it is independent of the specific type of object that it's drawing and erasing (the & means "Take the address of the object that's passed to doStuff()," but it's not important that you understand the details of that right now). If in some other part of the program you use the doStuff() function

```cpp
Circle c;
Triangle t;
Line l;
doStuff(c);
doStuff(t);
doStuff(l);
```

the calls to doStuff( ) automatically work right, regardless of the exact type of the object.

This is actually a pretty amazing trick. Consider the line

```cpp
doStuff(c);
```

What's happening here is that a `Circle` is being passed into a function that's expecting a Shape. Since a `Circle` *is* a Shape, it can be treated as one by doStuff(). That is, any message that doStuff() can send to a Shape, a `Circle` can accept. So it is a completely safe and logical thing to do.

We call this process of treating a derived type as though it were its base type *upcasting*. The name *cast* is used in the sense of casting into a mold and the *up* comes from the way the inheritance diagram is typically arranged, with the base type at the top and the derived classes fanning out downward. Thus, casting to a base type is moving up the inheritance diagram; upcasting is shown in Figure 1-9.

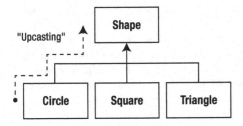

Figure 1-9. *Moving up the inheritance diagram, also called "upcasting"*

An object-oriented program contains some upcasting somewhere, because that's how you decouple yourself from knowing about the exact type you're working with. Look at the code in doStuff():

```
s.erase();
 // ...
  s.draw();
```

Notice that it doesn't say "If you're a Circle, do this, if you're a Square, do that, etc." If you write that kind of code, which checks for all the possible types that a Shape can actually be, it's messy and you need to change it every time you add a new kind of Shape. Here, you just say "You're a shape. I know you can erase() and draw() yourself, so do it, and take care of the details correctly."

What's impressive about the code in doStuff() is that, somehow, the right thing happens. Calling draw() for Circle causes different code to be executed than when calling draw() for a Square or a Line, but when the draw() message is sent to an anonymous Shape, the correct behavior occurs based on the actual type of the Shape. This is amazing because, as mentioned earlier, when the C++ compiler is compiling the code for doStuff(), it cannot know exactly what types it is dealing with. So ordinarily, you'd expect it to end up calling the version of erase() and draw() for Shape, and not for the specific Circle, Square, or Line. And yet the right thing happens because of polymorphism. The compiler and runtime system handle the details; all you need to know is that it happens and more importantly how to design with it. If a member function is virtual, then when you send a message to an object, the object will do the right thing, even when upcasting is involved.

Creating and Destroying Objects

Technically, the domain of OOP is abstract data typing, inheritance, and polymorphism, but other issues can be at least as important. This section gives an overview of these issues.

Especially important is the way objects are created and destroyed. Where is the data for an object, and how is the lifetime of that object controlled? Different programming languages use different philosophies here. C++ takes the approach that control of efficiency is the most important issue, so it gives the programmer a choice. For maximum runtime speed, the storage and lifetime can be determined while the program is being written by placing the objects on the stack or in static storage. The stack is an area in memory that is used directly by the microprocessor to store data during program execution. Variables on the stack are sometimes called *automatic* or *scoped* variables. The static storage area is simply a fixed patch of memory that is allocated before the program begins to run. Using the stack or static storage area places a priority on the speed of storage allocation and release, which can be valuable in some situations. However, you sacrifice flexibility because you must know the exact quantity, lifetime, and type of objects while you're writing the program. If you are trying to solve a more general problem, such as computer-aided design, warehouse management, or air traffic control, this is too restrictive.

The second approach is to create objects dynamically in a pool of memory called the *heap*. In this approach you don't know until runtime how many objects you need, what their lifetime is, or what their exact type is. Those decisions are made at the spur of the moment while the program is running. If you need a new object, you simply make it on the heap when you need it, using the new keyword. When you're finished with the storage, you must release it using the delete keyword.

Because the storage is managed dynamically at runtime, the amount of time required to allocate storage on the heap is significantly longer than the time to create storage on the stack. (Creating storage on the stack is often a single microprocessor instruction to move the stack pointer down, and another to move it back up). The dynamic approach makes the generally logical assumption that objects tend to be complicated, so the extra overhead of finding storage and releasing that storage will not have an important impact on the creation of an object. In addition, the greater flexibility is essential to solve general programming problems.

There's another issue, however, and that's the lifetime of an object. If you create an object on the stack or in static storage, the compiler determines how long the object lasts and can automatically destroy it. However, if you create it on the heap, the compiler has no knowledge of its lifetime. In C++, the programmer must determine programmatically when to destroy the object, and then perform the destruction using the delete keyword. As an alternative, the environment can provide a feature called a *garbage collector* that automatically discovers when an object is no longer in use and destroys it. Of course, writing programs using a garbage collector is much more convenient, but it requires that all applications must be able to tolerate the existence of the garbage collector and the overhead for garbage collection. This does not meet the design requirements of the C++ language and so it was not included, although third-party garbage collectors exist for C++.

Exception Handling: Dealing with Errors

Ever since the beginning of programming languages, error handling has been one of the most difficult issues. Because it's so hard to design a good error-handling scheme, many languages simply ignore the issue, passing the problem on to library designers who come up with halfway measures that can work in many situations but can easily be circumvented, generally by just ignoring them. A major problem with most error-handling schemes is that they rely on programmer vigilance in following an agreed-upon convention that is not enforced by the language. If programmers are not vigilant, which often occurs when they are in a hurry, these schemes can easily be forgotten.

Exception handling wires error handling directly into the programming language and sometimes even the operating system. An exception is an object that is "thrown" from the site of the error and can be "caught" by an appropriate *exception handler* designed to handle that particular type of error. It's as if exception handling is a different, parallel path of execution that can be taken when things go wrong. And because it uses a separate execution path, it doesn't need to interfere with your normally-executing code. This makes that code simpler to write since you aren't constantly forced to check for errors. In addition, a thrown exception is unlike an error value that's returned from a function or a flag that's set by a function in order to indicate an error condition—these can be ignored. An exception cannot be ignored so it's guaranteed to be dealt with at some point. Finally, exceptions provide a way to recover reliably from a bad situation. Instead of just exiting the program, you are often able to set things right and restore the execution of a program, which produces much more robust systems.

It's worth noting that exception handling isn't an object-oriented feature, although in object-oriented languages the exception is normally represented with an object. Exception handling existed before object-oriented languages. (You may note that Chapter 17 covers exception handling thoroughly).

Analysis and Design

The object-oriented paradigm is a new and different way of thinking about programming, and many folks have trouble at first knowing how to approach an OOP project. Once you know that everything is supposed to be an object, and as you learn to think more in an object-oriented style, you can begin to create "good" designs that take advantage of all the benefits that OOP has to offer.

A *method* (often called a *methodology*) is a set of processes and heuristics used to break down the complexity of a programming problem. Many OOP methods have been formulated since the dawn of object-oriented programming. This section will give you a feel for what you're trying to accomplish when using a method.

Especially in OOP, methodology is a field of many experiments, so it is important to understand what problem the method is trying to solve before you consider adopting one. This is particularly true with C++, in which the programming language is intended to reduce the complexity (compared to *C*) involved in expressing a program. This may in fact alleviate the need for ever-more-complex methodologies. Instead, simpler ones may suffice in C++ for a much larger class of problems than you could handle using simple methodologies with procedural languages.

It's also important to realize that the term "methodology" is often too grand and promises too much. Whatever you do now when you design and write a program is a method. It may be your own method, and you may not be conscious of doing it, but it is a process you go through as you create. If it is an effective process, it may need only a small tune-up to work with C++. If you are not satisfied with your productivity and the way your programs turn out, you may want to consider adopting a formal method, or choosing pieces from among the many formal methods.

While you're going through the development process, the most important issue is this: *don't get lost*. It's easy to do. Most of the analysis and design methods are intended to solve the largest of problems. Remember that most projects don't fit into that category, so you can usually have successful analysis and design with a relatively small subset of what a method recommends. But some sort of process, no matter how limited, will generally get you on your way in a much better fashion than simply beginning to code.

It's also easy to get stuck, to fall into *analysis paralysis*, where you feel like you can't move forward because you haven't nailed down every little detail at the current stage. Remember, no matter how much analysis you do, there are some things about a system that won't reveal themselves until design time, and more things that won't reveal themselves until you're coding, or not even until a program is up and running. Because of this, it's crucial to move fairly quickly through analysis and design, and to implement a test of the proposed system.

This point is worth emphasizing. Because of the history we've had with procedural languages, it is commendable that a team will want to proceed carefully and understand every minute detail before moving to design and implementation. Certainly, when creating a DBMS, it pays to understand a customer's needs thoroughly. But a DBMS is in a class of problems that is very well-posed and well-understood; in many such programs, the database structure *is* the problem to be tackled. The class of programming problem discussed in this chapter is of the wild card variety, in which the solution isn't simply re-forming a well-known solution, but instead involves one or more wild card factors—elements for which there is no well-understood previous solution, and for which research is necessary. *Attempting to analyze thoroughly a wild card problem before moving into design and implementation results in paralysis of analysis because you don't have enough information to solve this kind of problem during the analysis phase.* Solving such a problem requires iteration through the whole cycle, and that requires risk-taking behavior (*which makes sense, because you're trying to do something new and the potential rewards are higher*). It may seem like the risk is compounded by "rushing" into a preliminary implementation, but it can instead reduce the risk in a wild card project because you're finding out early whether a particular approach to the problem is viable. *Product development is risk management.*

It's often proposed that you "build one to throw away." With OOP, you may still throw *part* of it away, but because code is encapsulated into classes, during the first iteration you will inevitably produce some useful class designs and develop some worthwhile ideas about the system design that do not need to be thrown away. Thus, the first rapid pass at a problem not only produces critical information for the next analysis, design, and implementation iteration, it also creates a code foundation for that iteration.

That said, if you're looking at a methodology that contains tremendous detail and suggests many steps and documents, it's still difficult to know when to stop. Keep in mind what you're trying to discover.

1. What are the objects? (How do you partition your project into its component parts?)

2. What are their interfaces? (What messages do you need to be able to send to each object?)

If you come up with nothing more than the objects and their interfaces, then you can write a program. For various reasons you might need more descriptions and documents than this, but you can't get away with any less.

The process can be undertaken in five phases, and a phase 0 that is just the initial commitment to using some kind of structure.

Phase 0: Make a Plan

You must first decide what steps you're going to have in your process. It sounds simple (in fact, all of this sounds simple) and yet people often don't make this decision before they start coding. If your plan is "let's jump in and start coding," fine. At least agree that this is the plan.

■ **Note**   Sometimes that's appropriate when you have a well-understood problem.

You might also decide at this phase that some additional process structure is necessary, but not the whole nine yards. Understandably enough, some programmers like to work in *vacation mode* in which no structure is imposed on the process of developing their work; in other words, "It will be done when it's done." This can be appealing for a while, but *having a few milestones along the way helps to focus and galvanize your efforts around those milestones instead of being stuck with the single goal of "finish the project."* In addition, it divides the project into more bite-sized pieces and makes it seem less threatening (plus the milestones offer more opportunities for celebration).

The Mission Statement

Any system you build, no matter how complicated, has a fundamental purpose—the business that it's in, the basic need that it satisfies. If you can look past the user interface, the hardware- or system-specific details, the coding algorithms, and the efficiency problems, you will eventually find the core of its being, simple, and straightforward. Like the so-called *high concept* from a Hollywood movie, you can describe it in one or two sentences. This pure description is the starting point.

The high concept is quite important because it sets the tone for your project; it's a mission statement. You won't necessarily get it right the first time (you may be in a later phase of the project before it becomes completely clear), but keep trying until it feels right. For example, in an air traffic control system you may start out with a high concept focused on the system that you're building: "The tower program keeps track of the aircraft." But consider what happens when you shrink the system to a very small airfield; perhaps there's only a human controller or none at all. A more useful model won't concern the solution you're creating as much as it describes the problem: "Aircraft arrives, unloads, gets serviced and reloaded, and then departs."

Phase 1: What are we making?

In the previous generation of program design (called *procedural design*), this is called "creating the *requirements analysis* and *system specification*." These, of course, were places to get lost; intimidatingly-named documents that could become big projects in their own right. The intention was good, however.

The requirements analysis consists of making a list of the guidelines to use to know when the job is done and when the customer is satisfied. The system specification is a description of *what* the program will do (not *how*) to satisfy the requirements. The requirements analysis is really a contract between you and the customer (even if the customer works within your company or is some other object or system). The system specification is a top-level exploration into the problem and in some sense a discovery of whether it can be done and how long it will take. Since both of these will require consensus among people (and because they will usually change over time), it's often best to keep them as bare as possible—ideally, to lists and basic diagrams—to save time. You might have other constraints that require you to expand them into bigger documents, but by keeping the initial document small and concise, it can be created in a few sessions of group brainstorming with a leader who dynamically creates the description. This not only solicits input from everyone, it also fosters initial buy-in and agreement by everyone on the team. Perhaps most importantly, it can kick off a project with a lot of enthusiasm.

It's necessary to stay focused on the heart of what you're trying to accomplish in this phase: determine what the system is supposed to do. The most valuable tool for this is a collection of what are called *use cases*. Use cases identify key features in the system that will reveal some of the fundamental classes you'll be using. These are essentially descriptive answers to questions like:

- "Who will use this system?"
- "What can those actors do with the system?"
- "How does this actor do that with this system?"
- "How else might this work if someone else were doing this, or if the same actor had a different objective?" (to reveal variations)
- "What problems might happen while doing this with the system?" (to reveal exceptions)

If you are designing an auto-teller, for example, the use case for a particular aspect of the functionality of the system is able to describe what the auto-teller does in every possible situation. Each of these situations is referred to as a *scenario*, and a use case can be considered a collection of scenarios. You can think of a scenario as a question that starts with: "What does the system do if...?" For example, what does the auto-teller do if a customer has just deposited a check within 24 hours and there's not enough in the account without the check to provide the desired withdrawal?

Use case diagrams, illustrated in Figure 1-10, are intentionally simple to prevent you from getting bogged down in system implementation details prematurely.

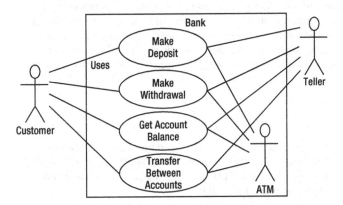

Figure 1-10. *Use case diagram for an auto-teller (ATM)*

Each stick person represents an *actor*, which is typically a human or some other kind of free agent. (These can even be other computer systems, as is the case with the ATM.) The box represents the boundary of your system. The ellipses represent the use cases, which are descriptions of valuable work that can be performed with the system. The lines between the actors and the use cases represent the interactions.

It doesn't matter how the system is actually implemented, as long as it looks like this to the user.

A use case does not need to be terribly complex, even if the underlying system is complex. It is only intended to show the system as it appears to the user. For example, Figure 1-11 shows a simple use case diagram.

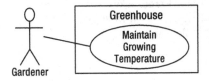

Figure 1-11. *Showing a simple use case diagram for an underlying complex system*

The use cases produce the requirements specifications by determining all the interactions that the user may have with the system. You try to discover a full set of use cases for your system, and once you've done that you have the core of what the system is supposed to do. The nice thing about focusing on use cases is that they always bring you back to the essentials and keep you from drifting off into issues that aren't critical for getting the job done. That is, if you have a full set of use cases you can describe your system and move onto the next phase. You probably won't get it all figured out perfectly on the first try, but that's okay. Everything will reveal itself in time, and if you demand a perfect system specification at this point, you'll get stuck.

If you get stuck, you can kick-start this phase by using a rough approximation tool: describe the system in a few paragraphs and then look for nouns and verbs. The nouns can suggest actors, context of the use case (e.g., "lobby"), or artifacts manipulated in the use case. Verbs can suggest interactions between actors and use cases, and specify steps within the use case. You'll also discover that nouns and verbs produce objects and messages during the design phase (and note that use cases describe interactions between subsystems, so the noun-and-verb technique can be used only as a brainstorming tool as it does not generate use cases).

The boundary between a use case and an actor can point out the existence of a user interface, but it does not define such a user interface. You now have an overview of what you're building so you'll probably be able to get some idea of how long it will take. A lot of factors come into play here. If you estimate a long schedule, the company might decide not to build it (and thus use their resources on something more reasonable—that's a *good* thing).
Or a manager might have already decided how long the project should take and will try to influence your estimate. But it's best to have an honest schedule from the beginning and deal with the tough decisions early. There have been a lot of attempts to come up with accurate scheduling techniques (like techniques to predict the stock market), but probably the best approach is to rely on your experience and intuition. Get a gut feeling for how long it will really take, then double that and add 10 percent. *Your gut feeling is probably correct; you can get something working in that time.* The "doubling" will turn that into something decent, and the 10 percent will deal with the final polishing and details. However you want to explain it, and regardless of the moans and manipulations that happen when you reveal such a schedule, it just seems to work out that way.

Phase 2: How will we build it?

In this phase you must come up with a design that describes what the classes look like and how they will interact. An excellent technique in determining classes and interactions are the *Class Responsibility Collaboration* (CRC) cards. Part of the value of this tool is that it's so low-tech: you start out with a set of blank 3" by 5" cards, and you write on them. Each card represents a single class, and on the card you write the following:

1. **The name of the class**. It's important that this name capture the essence of what the class does, so that it makes sense at a glance.

2. **The "responsibilities" of the class—what it should do**. This can typically be summarized by just stating the names of the member functions (since those names should be descriptive in a good design), but it does not preclude other notes. If you need to seed the process, look at the problem from a lazy programmer's standpoint. What objects would you like to magically appear to solve your problem?

3. **The "collaborations" of the class: what other classes does it interact with?** "Interact" is an intentionally broad term; it could mean aggregation or simply that some other object exists that will perform services for an object of the class. Collaborations should also consider the audience for this class. For example, if you create a class Firecracker, who is going to observe it, a Chemist or a Spectator? The former will want to know what chemicals go into the construction, and the latter will respond to the colors and shapes released when it explodes.

You may feel like the cards should be bigger because of all the information you'd like to get on them, but they are intentionally small, not only to keep your classes small but also to keep you from getting into too much detail too early. If you can't fit all you need to know about a class on a small card, the class is too complex (either you're getting too detailed, or you should create more than one class). The ideal class should be understood at a glance. The idea of CRC cards is to assist you in coming up with a first cut of the design so that you can get the big picture and then refine your design.

One of the great benefits of CRC cards is in communication. It's best done real time, in a group, without computers. Each person takes responsibility for several classes (which at first have no names or other information). You run a live simulation by solving one scenario at a time, deciding which messages are sent to the various objects to satisfy each scenario. As you go through this process, you discover the classes that you need along with their responsibilities and collaborations, and you fill out the cards as you do this. When you've moved through all the use cases, you should have a fairly complete first cut of your design.

Before I began using CRC cards, the most successful consulting experiences I had when coming up with an initial design involved standing in front of a team that hadn't built an OOP project before, and drawing objects on a whiteboard. We talked about how the objects should communicate with each other, and erased some of them and replaced them with other objects. Effectively, the CRC cards were being managed on the whiteboard. The team (who knew what the project was supposed to do) actually created the design; they "owned" the design rather than having it given to them. All that needed doing was guiding the process by asking the right questions, trying out the assumptions, and taking the feedback from the team to modify those assumptions. The true beauty of the process was that the team learned how to do object-oriented design not by reviewing abstract examples, but by working on the one design that was most interesting to them at that moment: theirs.

Once you've come up with a set of CRC cards, you may want to create a more formal description of your design using UML. You don't need to use UML, but it can be helpful, especially if you want to put up a diagram on the wall for everyone to ponder, which is a good idea. An alternative to UML is a textual description of the objects and their interfaces, or, depending on your programming language, the code itself.

UML also provides an additional diagramming notation for describing the dynamic model of your system. This is helpful in situations in which the state transitions of a system or subsystem are dominant enough that they need their own diagrams (such as in a control system). You may also need to describe the data structures for systems or subsystems in which data is a dominant factor (such as a database).

You'll know you're done with Phase 2 when you have described the objects and their interfaces. Well, most of them—there are usually a few that slip through the cracks and don't make themselves known until Phase 3. But that's okay. All you are concerned with is that you eventually discover all of your objects. It's nice to discover them early in the process but OOP provides enough structure so that it's not so bad if you discover them later. In fact, the design of an object tends to happen in five stages, throughout the process of program development.

Five Stages of Object Design

The design life of an object is not limited to the time when you're writing the program. Instead, the design of an object appears over a sequence of stages. It's helpful to have this perspective because you stop expecting perfection right away; instead, you realize that the understanding of what an object does and what it should look like happens over time. This view also applies to the design of various types of programs; the pattern for a particular type of program emerges through struggling again and again with that problem. Objects, too, have their patterns that emerge through understanding, use, and reuse.

1. **Object discovery.** *This stage occurs during the initial analysis of a program.* Objects may be discovered by looking for external factors and boundaries, duplication of elements in the system, and the smallest conceptual units. Some objects are obvious if you already have a set of class libraries. Commonality between classes suggesting base classes and inheritance may appear right away, or later in the design process.

2. **Object assembly.** *As you're building an object you'll discover the need for new members that didn't appear during discovery.* The internal needs of the object may require other classes to support it.

3. **System construction.** *Once again, more requirements for an object may appear at this later stage.* As you learn, you evolve your objects. The need for communication and interconnection with other objects in the system may change the needs of your classes or require new classes. For example, you may discover the need for facilitator or helper classes, such as a linked list, that contain little or no state information and simply help other classes function.

4. **System extension.** *As you add new features to a system you may discover that your previous design doesn't support easy system extension.* With this new information, you can restructure parts of the system, possibly adding new classes or class hierarchies.

5. **Object reuse.** *This is the real stress test for a class.* If someone tries to reuse it in an entirely new situation, they'll probably discover some shortcomings. As you change a class to adapt to more new programs, the general principles of the class will become clearer, until you have a *truly reusable type.* However, don't expect most objects from a system design to be reusable; it is perfectly acceptable for the bulk of your objects to be system-specific. Reusable types tend to be less common, and they must solve more general problems in order to be reusable.

Guidelines for Object Development

These stages suggest some guidelines when thinking about developing your classes.

1. **Let a specific problem generate a class**, then let the class grow and mature during the solution of other problems.

2. **Remember, discovering the classes you need (and their interfaces)** is the majority of the system design. If you already had those classes, this would be an easy project.

3. **Don't force yourself to know everything at the beginning**; learn as you go. This will happen anyway.

4. **Start programming; get something working so you can prove or disprove your design.** Don't fear that you'll end up with procedural-style spaghetti code— classes partition the problem and help control anarchy and entropy. Bad classes do not break good classes.

5. **Always keep it simple.** Little clean objects with obvious utility are better than big complicated interfaces. When decision points come up, consider the choices and select the one that is simplest, because simple classes are almost always best. Start small and simple, and you can expand the class interface when you understand it better, but as time goes on, it's difficult to remove elements from a class.

Phase 3: Build the Core

This is the initial conversion from the rough design into a compiling and executing body of code that can be tested, and especially that will prove or disprove your architecture. This is not a one-pass process, but rather the beginning of a series of steps that will iteratively build the system, as you'll see in Phase 4.

Your goal is to find the core of your system architecture that needs to be implemented in order to generate a running system, no matter how incomplete that system is in this initial pass. You're creating a framework that you can build upon with further iterations. You're also performing the first of many system integrations and tests, and giving the stakeholders feedback about what their system will look like and how it is progressing. Ideally, you are also exposing some of the critical risks. You'll probably also discover changes and improvements that can be made to your original architecture—things you would not have learned without implementing the system.

Part of building the system is the reality check that you get from testing against your requirements analysis and system specification (in whatever form they exist). Make sure that your tests verify the requirements and use cases. When the core of the system is stable, you're ready to move on and add more functionality.

Phase 4: Iterate the Use Cases

Once the core framework is running, each feature set you add is a small project in itself. You add a feature set during an *iteration,* a reasonably short period of development.

How big is an iteration? Ideally, each iteration lasts one to three weeks (*this can vary based on the implementation language*). At the end of that period, you have an integrated, tested system with more functionality than it had before. But what's particularly interesting is the basis for the iteration: a single use case. Each use case is a package of related functionality that you build into the system all at once, *during one iteration.* Not only does this give you a better idea of what the scope of a use case should be, but it also gives more validation to the idea of a use case, since the concept isn't discarded after analysis and design, but instead it is a fundamental unit of development throughout the software-building process.

You stop iterating when you achieve target functionality or an external deadline arrives and the customer can be satisfied with the current version. (*Remember, software is a subscription business.*) Because the process is iterative, you have many opportunities to ship a product instead of a single endpoint; open-source projects work exclusively in an iterative, high-feedback environment, which is precisely what makes them successful.

An iterative development process is valuable for many reasons. You can reveal and resolve critical risks early, the customers have ample opportunity to change their minds, programmer satisfaction is higher, and the project can be steered with more precision. But an additional important benefit is the feedback to the stakeholders, who can see by the current state of the product exactly where everything lies. This may reduce or eliminate the need for mind-numbing status meetings and increase the confidence and support from the stakeholders.

Phase 5: Evolution

This is the point in the development cycle that has traditionally been called *maintenance,* a catch-all term that can mean everything from "getting it to work the way it was really supposed to in the first place" to "adding features that the customer forgot to mention" to the more traditional "fixing the bugs that show up" and "adding new features as the need arises." So many misconceptions have been applied to the term "maintenance" that it has taken on a slightly deceiving quality, partly because it suggests that you've actually built a pristine program and all you need to do is change parts, oil it, and keep it from rusting. Perhaps there's a better term to describe what's going on.

Let's use the term *evolution*. In other words, *you won't get it right the first time, so give yourself the latitude to learn and to go back and make changes.* You might need to make a lot of changes as you learn and understand the problem more deeply. The elegance you'll produce if you evolve until you get it right will pay off, both in the short and the long term. *Evolution is where your program goes from good to great,* and where those issues that you didn't really understand in the first pass become clear. It's also where your classes can evolve from single-project usage to reusable resources.

What it means to "get it right" isn't just that the program works according to the requirements and the use cases. It also means that the internal structure of the code makes sense to you, and feels like it fits together well, with no awkward syntax, oversized objects, or ungainly exposed bits of code. In addition, you must have some sense that the program structure will survive the changes that it will inevitably go through during its lifetime, and that those changes can be made easily and cleanly. This is no small feat. You must not only understand what you're building, but also how the program will evolve. Fortunately, object-oriented programming languages are particularly adept at supporting this kind of continuing modification—the boundaries created by the objects are what tend to keep the structure from breaking down. They also allow you to make changes—ones that would seem drastic in a procedural program—without causing earthquakes throughout your code. In fact, support for evolution might be the most important benefit of OOP.

With evolution, you create something that at least approximates what you think you're building, and then you kick the tires, compare it to your requirements, and see where it falls short. Then you can go back and fix it by redesigning and reimplementing the portions of the program that didn't work right. You might actually need to solve the problem, or an aspect of the problem, several times before you hit on the right solution.

Evolution also occurs when you build a system, see that it matches your requirements, and then discover it wasn't actually what you wanted. When you see the system in operation, you find that you really wanted to solve a different problem. If you think this kind of evolution is going to happen, then you owe it to yourself to build your first version as quickly as possible so you can find out if it is indeed what you want.

Perhaps the most important thing to remember is that by default—by definition, really—*if you modify a class, then its super- and subclasses will still function.* You need not fear modification (*especially if you have a built-in set of unit tests to verify the correctness of your modifications*). Modification won't necessarily break the program, and any change in the outcome will be limited to subclasses and/or specific collaborators of the class you change.

Plans Pay Off

You wouldn't build a house without a lot of carefully-drawn plans. If you build a deck or a dog house, your plans won't be so elaborate but you'll probably still start with some kind of sketch to guide you on your way.

Software development has gone to extremes. For a long time, people didn't have much structure in their development, but then big projects began failing. In reaction, we ended up with methodologies that had an intimidating amount of structure and detail, primarily intended for those big projects. These methodologies were too scary to use—it looked like you'd spend all your time writing documents and no time programming.

But by following a plan (preferably one that is simple and brief) and coming up with design structure before coding, you'll discover that things fall together far more easily than if you dive in and start hacking, and you'll also realize a great deal of satisfaction. It's my experience that coming up with an elegant solution is deeply satisfying at an entirely different level; it feels closer to art than technology. And elegance always pays off; it's not a frivolous pursuit. Not only does it give you a program that's easier to build and debug, but it's also easier to understand and maintain, and that's where the financial value lies.

Extreme Programming

Of all the analysis and design techniques, the concept of *Extreme Programming* (*XP*) is the most radical, and delightful. XP is both a philosophy about programming work and a set of guidelines to do it. Some of these guidelines are reflected in other recent methodologies, but the two most important and distinct contributions, are *write tests first* and *pair programming*.

Write Tests First

Testing has traditionally been relegated to the last part of a project, after you've "gotten everything working, but just to be sure." It's implicitly had a low priority, and people who specialize in it have not been given a lot of status and have often even been cordoned off in a basement, away from the "real programmers." Test teams have responded in kind, going so far as to wear black clothing and cackling with glee whenever they broke something.

XP completely revolutionizes the concept of testing by giving it equal (or even greater) priority than the code. In fact, you write the tests *before* you write the code that's being tested, and the tests stay with the code forever. The tests must be executed successfully every time you do an integration of the project (which is often—sometimes more than once a day).

Writing tests first has two extremely important effects. *First, it forces a clear definition of the interface of a class.* The XP testing strategy goes further than that—it specifies *exactly* what the class must look like to the consumer of that class, and exactly how the class must behave in no uncertain terms. You can write all the prose or create all the diagrams you want describing how a class should behave and what it looks like, but nothing is as real as a set of tests. The former is a wish list, but the tests are a contract that is enforced by the compiler and the running program. It's hard to imagine a more concrete description of a class than the tests.

While creating the tests, you are forced to completely think out the class and will often discover needed functionality that might be missed during the thought experiments of UML diagrams, CRC cards, use cases, etc.

The second important effect of writing the tests first comes from running the tests every time you do a build of your software. This activity gives you the other half of the testing that's performed by the compiler. If you look at the evolution of programming languages from this perspective, you'll see that the real improvements in the technology have actually revolved around testing. Assembly language checked only for syntax, but C imposed some semantic restrictions, and these prevented you from making certain types of mistakes. OOP languages impose even more semantic restrictions, which if you think about it are actually forms of testing. "Is this data type being used properly? Is this function being called properly?" are the kinds of tests that are being performed by the compiler or runtime system.

We've seen the results of having these tests built into the language: people have been able to write more complex systems, and get them to work, with much less time and effort. But the built-in testing afforded by the design of the language can only go so far. At some point, *you* must step in and add the rest of the tests that produce a full suite (in cooperation with the compiler and runtime system) that verifies your entire program. And, just like having a compiler watching over your shoulder, wouldn't you want these tests helping you right from the beginning? That's why you write them first, and run them automatically with every build of your system. Your tests become an extension of the safety net provided by the language.

Using more and more powerful programming languages emboldens and allows you to try more brazen experiments because the language will keep you away from wasting time chasing bugs. The XP test scheme does the same thing for your entire project. Because you know your tests will always catch any problems that you introduce (and you regularly add any new tests as you think of them), you can make big changes when you need to without worrying that you'll throw the whole project into complete disarray. This is incredibly powerful.

Pair Programming

Pair programming goes against the rugged individualism that we've been indoctrinated into from the beginning. Programmers, too, are considered paragons of individuality. And yet XP, which is itself battling against conventional thinking, says *that code should be written with two people per workstation.* And that this should be done in an area with a group of workstations, without the barriers that the facilities design people are so fond of.

The value of pair programming is that one person is actually doing the coding while the other is thinking about it. The thinker keeps the big picture in mind, not only the picture of the problem at hand, but the guidelines of XP. If two people are working, it's less likely that one of them will get away with saying, "I don't want to write the tests first," for example. And if the coder gets stuck, they can swap places. If both of them get stuck, their musings may be overheard by someone else in the work area who can contribute. Working in pairs keeps things flowing and on track. Probably more important, it makes programming a lot more social and fun.

Why C++ Succeeds

Part of the reason C++ has been so successful is that the goal was not just to turn C into an OOP language (although it started that way), but also to solve many other problems facing developers today, especially those who have large investments in C. Traditionally, OOP languages have suffered from the attitude that you should abandon everything you know and start from scratch with a new set of concepts and a new syntax, arguing that it's better in the long run to lose all the old baggage that comes with procedural languages. This may be true, in the long run. But in the short run, a lot of that baggage was valuable. The most valuable elements may not be the existing code base (which, given adequate tools, could be translated), but instead the existing *mind base*. If you're a functioning C programmer and must drop everything you know about C in order to adopt a new language, you immediately become much less productive for many months, until your mind fits around the new paradigm. Whereas if you can leverage off of your existing C knowledge and expand on it, you can continue to be productive with what you already know while moving into the world of object-oriented programming. As everyone has his or her own mental model of programming, this move is messy enough as it is without the added expense of starting with a new language model from square one. So the reason for the success of C++, in a nutshell, is economic: it still costs to move to OOP, but C++ may cost less.

The goal of C++ is improved productivity. This productivity comes in many ways, but the language is designed to aid you as much as possible, while hindering you as little as possible with arbitrary rules or any requirement that you use a particular set of features. C++ is designed to be practical; C++ language design decisions were based on providing the maximum benefits to the programmer (at least, from the world view of C).

A Better C

You get an instant win even if you continue to write C code because C++ has closed many holes in the C language and provides better type checking and compile-time analysis. You're forced to declare functions so that the compiler can check their use. The need for the preprocessor has virtually been eliminated for value substitution and macros, which removes a set of difficult-to-find bugs. C++ has a feature called *references* that allows more convenient handling of addresses for function arguments and return values. The handling of names is improved through a feature called *function overloading*, which allows you to use the same name for different functions. A feature called *namespaces* also improves the control of names. There are numerous smaller features that improve the safety of C.

You're Already on the Learning Curve

The problem with learning a new language is productivity. No company can afford to suddenly lose a productive software engineer because he or she is learning a new language. C++ is an extension to C, not a complete new syntax and programming model. It allows you to continue creating useful code, applying the features gradually as you learn and understand them. This may be one of the most important reasons for the success of C++.

In addition, all of your existing C code is still viable in C++, but because the C++ compiler is pickier, you'll often find hidden C errors when recompiling the code in C++.

Efficiency

Sometimes it is appropriate to trade execution speed for programmer productivity. A financial model, for example, may be useful for only a short period of time, so it's more important to create the model rapidly than to execute it rapidly. *However, most applications require some degree of efficiency, so C++ always errs on the side of greater efficiency.* Because C programmers tend to be very efficiency-conscious, this is also a way to ensure that they won't be able to argue that the language is too fat and slow. A number of features in C++ are intended to allow you to tune for performance when the generated code isn't efficient enough.

Not only do you have the same low-level control as in C (and the ability to directly write assembly language within a C++ program), but anecdotal evidence suggests that the program speed for an object-oriented C++ program tends to be within ±10% of a program written in C, and often much closer. The design produced for an OOP program may actually be more efficient than the C counterpart.

Systems Are Easier to Express and Understand

Classes designed to fit the problem tend to express it better. This means that when you write the code, you're describing your solution in the terms of the problem space rather than the terms of the computer, which is the solution space. You deal with higher-level concepts and can do much more with a single line of code.

The other benefit of this ease of expression is maintenance, which takes a huge portion of the cost over a program's lifetime. If a program is easier to understand, then it's easier to maintain. This can also reduce the cost of creating and maintaining the documentation.

Maximal Leverage with Libraries

The fastest way to create a program is to use code that's already written: a library. A major goal in C++ is to make library use easier. This is accomplished by casting libraries into new data types (classes), so that bringing in a library means adding new types to the language. Because the C++ compiler takes care of how the library is used—guaranteeing proper initialization and cleanup, and ensuring that functions are called properly—you can focus on what you want the library to do, not how you have to do it.

Because names can be sequestered to portions of your program via C++ namespaces, you can use as many libraries as you want without the kinds of name clashes you'd run into with C.

Source-Code Reuse with Templates

There is a significant class of types that require source code modification in order to reuse them effectively. *The template feature in C++ performs the source code modification automatically, making it an especially powerful tool for reusing library code.* A type that you design using templates will work effortlessly with many other types. Templates are especially nice because they hide the complexity of this kind of code reuse from the client programmer.

Error Handling

Error handling in C is a notorious problem, and one that is often ignored; finger-crossing is usually involved. If you're building a large, complex program, there's nothing worse than having an error buried somewhere with no clue as to where it came from. *C++ exception handling* (introduced in this chapter, and fully covered later on in Chapter 17 as already mentioned) *is a way to guarantee that an error is noticed and that something happens as a result.*

Programming in the Large

Many traditional languages have built-in limitations to program size and complexity. BASIC, for example, can be great for pulling together quick solutions for certain classes of problems, but if the program gets more than a few pages long or ventures out of the normal problem domain of that language, it's like trying to swim through an ever-more viscous fluid. C, too, has these limitations. For example, when a program gets beyond perhaps 50,000 lines of code, name collisions start to become a problem—effectively, you run out of function and variable names. Another particularly bad problem is the little holes in the C language—errors buried in a large program can be extremely difficult to find.

There's no clear line that tells you when your language is failing you, and even if there were, you'd ignore it. You don't say, "My BASIC program just got too big; I'll have to rewrite it in C!" Instead, you try to shoehorn a few more lines in to add that one new feature. So the extra costs come creeping up on you.

C++ is designed to *aid* programming in the large—that is, to erase those creeping-complexity boundaries between a small program and a large one. You certainly don't need to use OOP, templates, namespaces, and exception handling when you're writing a Hello, World type of utility program, but those features are there when you need them. And the compiler is aggressive about ferreting out bug-producing errors for small and large programs alike.

Strategies for Transition

If you buy into OOP, your next question is probably, "How can I get my manager/colleagues/department/peers to start using objects?" Think about how you—one independent programmer—would go about learning to use a new language and a new programming paradigm. You've done it before. First comes education and examples; then comes a trial project to give you a feel for the basics without doing anything too confusing. Then, a real world project comes that actually does something useful. Throughout your first projects you continue your education by reading, asking questions of experts, and trading hints with friends. This is the approach many experienced programmers suggest for the switch from C to C++. Switching an entire company will of course introduce certain group dynamics, but it will help at each step to remember how one person would do it.

Guidelines

Here are some guidelines to consider when making the transition to OOP and C++.

Training

The first step is some form of education. Remember the company's investment in plain C code, and try not to throw everything into disarray for six to nine months while everyone puzzles over how multiple inheritance works. Pick a small group for indoctrination, preferably one composed of people who are curious, work well together, and can function as their own support network while they're learning C++.

An alternative approach that is sometimes suggested is the education of all company levels at once, including overview courses for strategic managers as well as design and programming courses for project builders. This is especially good for smaller companies making fundamental shifts in the way they do things, or at the division level of larger companies. Because the cost is higher, however, some may choose to start with project-level training, do a pilot project (possibly with an outside mentor), and let the project team become the teachers for the rest of the company.

Low-Risk Project

Try a low-risk project first and allow for mistakes. Once you've gained some experience, you can either seed other projects from members of this first team or use the team members as an OOP technical support staff. This first project may not work right the first time, so it should not be mission-critical for the company. It should be simple, self-contained, and instructive; this means that it should involve creating classes that will be meaningful to the other programmers in the company when they get their turn to learn C++.

Model from Success

Seek out examples of good object-oriented design before starting from scratch. There's a good probability that someone has solved your problem already, and if they haven't solved it exactly, you can probably apply what you've learned about abstraction to modify an existing design to fit your needs.

Use Existing Class Libraries

The primary economic motivation for switching to OOP is the easy use of existing code in the form of class libraries, in particular, the Standard C++ libraries. The shortest application development cycle will result when you don't have to write anything but `main( )`, creating and using objects from off-the-shelf libraries. However, some new programmers don't understand this, are unaware of existing class libraries, or, through fascination with the language, desire to write classes that may already exist. Your success with OOP and C++ will be optimized if you make an effort to seek out and reuse other people's code early in the transition process.

Don't Rewrite Existing Code in C++

Although *compiling* your *C* code with a C++ compiler usually produces (*sometimes tremendous*) benefits by finding problems in the old code, it is not usually the best use of your time to take existing, functional code and rewrite it in C++. (If you must turn it into objects, you can "wrap" the C code in C++ classes.) There are incremental benefits, especially if the code is slated for reuse. But chances are you aren't going to see the dramatic increases in productivity that you hope for in your first few projects unless that project is a new one. C++ and OOP shine best when taking a project from concept to reality.

Management Obstacles

If you're a manager, your job is to acquire resources for your team, to overcome barriers to your team's success, and in general to try to provide the most productive and enjoyable environment so your team is most likely to perform those miracles that are always being asked of you. Moving to C++ falls in all three of these categories, and it would be wonderful if it didn't cost you anything as well. Although moving to C++ may be cheaper (depending on your constraints) than the OOP alternatives for a team of C programmers (and probably for programmers in other procedural languages), *it isn't free,* and there are obstacles you should be aware of before trying to sell the move to C++ within your company and embarking on the move itself.

Startup Costs

The cost of moving to C++ is more than just the acquisition of C++ compilers (the GNU C++ compiler, one of the very best, is free).*Your medium- and long-term costs will be minimized if you invest in training (and possibly mentoring for your first project) and also if you identify and purchase class libraries that solve your problem rather than trying to build those libraries yourself.* These are hard-money costs that must be factored into a realistic proposal. In addition, there are the hidden costs in loss of productivity while learning a new language and possibly a new programming environment. Training and mentoring can certainly minimize these, but team members must overcome their own struggles to understand the new technology. During this process they will make more mistakes (*this is a feature, because acknowledged mistakes are the fastest path to learning*) and be less productive. Even then, with some types of programming problems, the right classes, and the right development environment, it's possible to be more productive while you're learning C++ (even considering that you're making more mistakes and writing fewer lines of code per day) than if you'd stayed with C.

Performance Issues

A common question is, "Doesn't OOP automatically make my programs a lot bigger and slower?" The answer is, "It depends." Most traditional OOP languages were designed with experimentation and rapid prototyping in mind rather than lean-and-mean operation. Thus, they virtually guaranteed a significant increase in size and decrease in speed. C++, however, is designed with production programming in mind. When your focus is on rapid prototyping, you can throw together components as fast as possible while ignoring efficiency issues. If you're using any third party libraries, these are usually already optimized by their vendors; in any case it's not an issue while you're in rapid-development mode. When you have a system that you like, if it's small and fast enough, then you're done.
If not, you begin tuning with a profiling tool, looking first for speedups that can be done with simple applications of built-in C++ features. If that doesn't help, you look for modifications that can be made in the underlying implementation so no code that uses a particular class needs to be changed. Only if nothing else solves the problem do you need to change the design. The fact that performance is so critical in that portion of the design is an indicator that it must be part of the primary design criteria. *You have the benefit of finding this out early using rapid development.*

Almost universally, programmers who have moved from C (or some other procedural language) to C++ (or some other OOP language) have had the personal experience of a great acceleration in their programming productivity, and that's the most compelling argument you can find.

Common Design Errors

When starting your team into OOP and C++, programmers will typically go through a series of common design errors. This often happens because of too little feedback from experts during the design and implementation of early projects, because no experts have been developed within the company, and there may be resistance to retaining consultants. It's easy to feel that you understand OOP too early in the cycle and go off on a bad tangent. Something that's obvious to someone experienced with the language may be a subject of great internal debate for a novice. Much of this trauma can be skipped by using an experienced outside expert for training and mentoring.

On the other hand, the fact that it is easy to make these design errors points to C++'s main drawback: *its backward compatibility with C* (of course, that's also its main strength). To accomplish the feat of being able to compile C code, the language had to make some compromises, which have resulted in a number of "dark corners." These are a reality, and comprise much of the learning curve for the language.

Review Session

1. This chapter attempts to give you a feel for the broad issues of object-oriented programming and C++, including why OOP is different, and why C++ in particular is different, concepts of OOP methodologies, and finally the kinds of issues you will encounter when moving your own company to OOP and C++.

2. *OOP and C++ may not be for everyone.* It's important to evaluate your own needs and decide whether C++ will optimally satisfy those needs, or if you might be better off with another programming system (including the one you're currently using). If you know that your needs will be very specialized for the foreseeable future and if you have specific constraints that may not be satisfied by C++, then you owe it to yourself to investigate the alternatives. *Even if you eventually choose C++ as your language, you'll at least understand what the options were and have a clear vision of why you took that direction.*

3. You know what a procedural program looks like: data definitions and function calls. To find the meaning of such a program you have to work a little, looking through the function calls and low-level concepts to create a model in your mind. This is the reason we need intermediate representations when designing procedural programs—by themselves, these programs tend to be confusing because the terms of expression are oriented more toward the computer than to the problem you're solving.

4. Because C++ adds many new concepts to the C language, your natural assumption may be that the main( ) in a C++ program will be far more complicated than for the equivalent C program. Here, you'll be pleasantly surprised: a well-written C++ program is generally far simpler and much easier to understand than the equivalent C program. What you'll see are the definitions of the objects that represent concepts in your problem space (rather than the issues of the computer representation) and messages sent to those objects to represent the activities in that space. *One of the delights of object-oriented programming is that, with a well-designed program, it's easy to understand the code by reading it.* Usually there's a lot less code, as well, because many of your problems will be solved by reusing existing library code.

■ ■ ■

CHAPTER 2

Making and Using Objects

This chapter will introduce enough C++ syntax and program construction concepts to allow you to write and run some simple object-oriented programs. In the next chapter, I will cover the basic syntax of "the *C* in C++" in detail.

By reading this chapter first, you'll get the basic flavor of what it is like to program with objects in C++, and you'll also discover some of the reasons for the enthusiasm surrounding this language. This should be enough to carry you through *Chapter 3*, which may be a bit exhausting since it contains most of the details of the C language, which are usable in C++ as well.

The user-defined data type, or class, is what distinguishes C++ from traditional procedural languages. A class is a new data type that you or someone else creates to solve a particular kind of problem. Once a class is created, anyone can use it without knowing the specifics of how it works, or even how classes are built. This chapter treats classes as if they are just another built-in data type available for use in programs.

Classes that someone else has created are typically packaged into a library. This chapter uses several of the class libraries that come with all C++ implementations. An especially important standard library is iostream, which (*among other things*) allows you to read from files and the keyboard, and to write to files and the display. You'll also see the very handy string class and the vector container from the *Standard C++ Library*. By the end of the chapter, you'll see how easy it is to use a predefined library of classes.

In order to create your first program, you must understand the tools used to build applications.

The Process of Language Translation

All computer languages are translated from something that tends to be easy for a human to understand (*source code*) into something that is executed on a computer (*machine instructions*). Traditionally, translators fall into two classes: *interpreters* and *compilers*.

Interpreters

An interpreter translates source code into activities (which may comprise groups of machine instructions) and immediately executes those activities. BASIC, for example, has been a popular interpreted language. Traditional BASIC interpreters translate and execute one line at a time, and then forget that the line has been translated. This makes them slow, since they must retranslate any repeated code. BASIC has also been compiled, for speed. More modern interpreters, such as those for the Python language, translate the entire program into an intermediate language that is then executed by a much faster interpreter.

Interpreters have many advantages. The transition from writing code to executing code is almost immediate, and the source code is always available so the interpreter can be much more specific when an error occurs. The benefits often cited for interpreters are ease of interaction and rapid development (*but not necessarily execution*) of programs.

Interpreted languages often have severe limitations when building large projects (Python seems to be an exception to this). The interpreter (*or a reduced version*) must always be in memory to execute the code, and even the fastest interpreter may introduce unacceptable speed restrictions. Most interpreters require that the complete source code be brought into the interpreter all at once. Not only does this introduce a space limitation, it can also cause more difficult bugs if the language doesn't provide facilities to localize the effect of different pieces of code.

Compilers

A compiler translates source code directly into assembly language or machine instructions. The eventual end product is a file or files containing machine code. This is an involved process, and it usually takes several steps. The transition from writing code to executing code is significantly longer with a compiler.

Depending on the acumen of the compiled program writer, *programs generated by a compiler tend to require much less space to run, and they run much more quickly*. Although size and speed are probably the most often cited reasons for using a compiler, in many situations they aren't the most important reasons. Some languages (such as *C*) are designed to allow pieces of a program to be compiled independently. These pieces are eventually combined into a final *executable* program by a tool called the *linker*. This process is called *separate compilation*.

Separate compilation has many benefits. A program that, taken all at once, would exceed the limits of the compiler or the compiling environment can be compiled in pieces. Programs can be built and tested one piece at a time. Once a piece is working, it can be saved and treated as a building block. Collections of tested and working pieces can be combined into *libraries* for use by other programmers. As each piece is created, the complexity of the other pieces is hidden. All these features support the creation of large programs.

Compiler debugging features have improved significantly over time. Early compilers only generated machine code, and the programmer inserted print statements to see what was going on. This is not always effective. Modern compilers can insert information about the source code into the executable program. This information is used by powerful *source-level debuggers* to show exactly what is happening in a program by tracing its progress through the source code.

Some compilers tackle the compilation-speed problem by performing *in-memory compilation*. Most compilers work with files, reading and writing them in each step of the compilation process. In-memory compilers keep the compiler program in RAM. For small programs, this can seem as responsive as an interpreter.

The Compilation Process

To program in *C* and C++, you need to understand the steps and tools in the compilation process. Some languages (*C* and C++, in particular) start compilation by running a *preprocessor* on the source code. The preprocessor is a simple program that replaces patterns in the source code with other patterns the programmer has defined (using *preprocessor directives*). Preprocessor directives are used to save typing and to increase the readability of the code. The preprocessed code is often written to an intermediate file.

Compilers usually do their work in two passes. The first pass parses the preprocessed code. The compiler breaks the source code into small units and organizes it into a structure called a *tree*. In the expression "A + B" the elements "A," "+," and "B" are leaves on the parse tree.

A *global optimizer* is sometimes used between the first and second passes to produce smaller, faster code. *In the second pass, the code generator walks through the parse tree and generates either assembly language code or machine code for the nodes of the tree*. If the code generator creates assembly code, the assembler must then be run. The end result in both cases is an object module (a file that typically has an extension of `.o or .obj`).

The use of the word "object" to describe chunks of machine code is an unfortunate artifact. The word came into use before object-oriented programming was in general use. "Object" is used in the same sense as "goal" when discussing compilation, while in object-oriented programming it means "a thing with boundaries."

The linker combines a list of object modules into an executable program that can be loaded and run by the operating system. When a function in one object module makes a reference to a function or variable in another object module, the linker resolves these references; it makes sure that all the external functions and data you claimed existed during compilation do exist. The linker also adds a special object module to perform startup activities.

The linker can search through special files called libraries in order to resolve all its references. A library contains a collection of object modules in a single file. A library is created and maintained by a program called a *librarian*.

Static Type Checking

The compiler performs type checking during the first pass. Type checking tests for the proper use of arguments in functions and prevents many kinds of programming errors. Since type checking occurs during compilation instead of when the program is running, it is called *static type checking*.

Some object-oriented languages (notably Java) perform some type checking at runtime (*dynamic type checking*). If combined with static type checking, dynamic type checking is more powerful than static type checking alone. However, it also adds overhead to program execution.

C++ *uses static type checking* because the language cannot assume any particular runtime support for bad operations. Static type checking notifies the programmer about misuses of types during compilation, and thus maximizes execution speed. As you learn C++, you will see that most of the language design decisions favor the same kind of high-speed, production-oriented programming the *C* language is famous for.

You can disable static type checking in C++. You can also do your own dynamic type checking; you just need to write the code.

Tools for Separate Compilation

Separate compilation is particularly important when building large projects. In *C* and C++, a program can be created in small, manageable, independently tested pieces. The most fundamental tool for breaking a program up into pieces is the ability to create named subroutines or subprograms. In *C* and C++, a subprogram is called a *function*, and functions are the pieces of code that can be placed in different files, enabling separate compilation. Put another way, the function is the atomic unit of code, since you cannot have part of a function in one file and another part in a different file; the entire function must be placed in a single file (although *files can and do contain more than one function*).

When you call a function, you typically pass it some *arguments*, which are values you'd like the function to work with during its execution. When the function is finished, you typically get back a *return value*, a value that the function hands back to you as a result. It's also possible to write functions that take no arguments and return no values.

To create a program with multiple files, functions in one file must access functions and data in other files. When compiling a file, the *C* or C++ compiler must know about the functions and data in the other files, in particular their names and proper usage. The compiler ensures that functions and data are used correctly. This process of telling the compiler the names of external functions and data and what they should look like is called *declaration*. Once you declare a function or variable, the compiler knows how to check to make sure it is used properly.

Declarations vs. Definitions

It's important to understand the *difference between declarations and definitions* because these terms will be used precisely throughout the book. Essentially all *C* and C++ programs require declarations. Before you can write your first program, you need to understand the proper way to write a declaration.

A declaration introduces a name—an identifier—to the compiler. It tells the compiler "This function or this variable exists somewhere, and here is what it should look like." *A definition,* on the other hand, says "Make this variable here" or "Make this function here." *It allocates storage for the name.* This meaning works whether you're talking about a variable or a function; in either case, at the point of definition the compiler allocates storage. For a variable, the compiler determines how big that variable is and causes space to be generated in memory to hold the data for that variable. For a function, the compiler generates code, which ends up occupying storage in memory.

You can declare a variable or a function in many different places, but there must be only one definition in *C* and C++ (*this is sometimes called the ODR, the One Definition Rule*). When the linker is uniting all the object modules, it will usually complain if it finds more than one definition for the same function or variable.

    A definition can also be a declaration. If the compiler hasn't seen the name x before and you define int x, the compiler sees the name as a declaration and allocates storage for it all at once.

Function Declaration Syntax

A function declaration in *C* and C++ gives the function name, the argument types passed to the function, and the return value of the function. For example, here is a declaration for a function called func1( ) that takes two integer arguments (integers are denoted in *C*/C++ with the keyword int) and returns an integer:

```
int func1(int,int);
```

    The first keyword you see is the return value all by itself: int. The arguments are enclosed in parentheses after the function name in the order they are used. The semicolon indicates the end of a statement; in this case, it tells the compiler "that's all—there is no function definition here!"

    C and C++ declarations attempt to mimic the form of the item's use. For example, if a is another integer, the above function might be used this way:

```
a = func1(2,3);
```

    Since func1( ) returns an integer, the *C* or C++ compiler will check the use of func1( ) to make sure that a can accept the return value and that the arguments are appropriate.

    Arguments in function declarations may have names. The compiler ignores the names but they can be helpful as mnemonic devices for the user. For example, you can declare func1( ) in a different fashion that has the same meaning, like:

```
int func1(int length, int width);
```

    There is a significant difference between *C* and C++ for functions with empty argument lists. In *C*, the declaration

```
int func2();
```

means "a function with any number and type of argument." This prevents type-checking, so in C++ it means "a function with no arguments."

Function Definitions

Function definitions look like function declarations except that they have bodies. A body is a collection of statements enclosed in braces. Braces denote the beginning and ending of a block of code. To give func1( ) a definition that is an *empty body* (a body containing no code), write

```
int func1(int length, int width) { }
```

    Notice that in the function definition, the braces replace the semicolon. Since braces surround a statement or group of statements, you don't need a semicolon. Notice also that the arguments in the function definition must have names if you want to use the arguments in the function body (since they are never used here, they are optional).

Variable Declaration Syntax

The meaning attributed to the phrase *"variable declaration"* has historically been confusing and contradictory, and it's important that you understand the correct definition so you can read code properly. *A variable declaration tells the compiler what a variable looks like.* It says, "I know you haven't seen this name before, but I promise it exists someplace, and it's a variable of X type."

In a function declaration, you give a type (the return value), the function name, the argument list, and a semicolon. That's enough for the compiler to figure out that it's a declaration and what the function should look like. By inference, a variable declaration might be a type followed by a name. For example,

```
int a;
```

could declare the variable a as an integer, using the logic above. Here's the conflict: there is enough information in the code above for the compiler to create space for an integer called a, and that's what happens. To resolve this dilemma, a keyword was necessary for *C* and C++ to say "This is only a declaration; it's defined elsewhere." The *keyword is* extern. It can mean the definition is external to the file, or that the definition occurs later in the file.

Declaring a variable without defining it means using the extern keyword before a description of the variable, like this:

```
extern int a;
```

extern can also apply to function declarations. For func1( ), it looks like this:

```
extern int func1(int length, int width);
```

This statement is equivalent to the previous func1( ) declarations. Since there is no function body, the compiler must treat it as a function declaration rather than a function definition. The extern keyword is thus superfluous and optional for function declarations. It is probably unfortunate that the designers of *C* did not require the use of extern for function declarations; it would have been more consistent and less confusing (*but would have required more typing, which probably explains the decision*). Listing 2-1 shows more examples of declarations and definitions.

Listing 2-1. More Examples of Declarations and Definitions

```cpp
//: C02:Declare.cpp
// Demonstrates more Declarations & Definitions extern inti; // Declaration without definition
extern float f(float); // Function declaration

float b;  // Declaration & definition
float f(float a) {      // Definition
  return a + 1.0;
}
int i;     // Definition
int h(int x) {          // Declaration & definition
  return x + 1;
}
int main() {
  b = 1.0;
  i = 2;
  f(b);
  h(i);
} ///:~
```

In the function declarations, the argument identifiers are optional. In the definitions, they are required (*the identifiers are required only in C, not C++*).

Including Headers

Most libraries contain significant numbers of functions and variables. To save work and ensure consistency when making the external declarations for these items, *C* and C++ use a device called the *header file*. A header file is a file containing the external declarations for a library; it conventionally has a file name extension of .h, such as headerfile.h.

■ **Note**   You may also see some older code using different extensions, such as .hxx or .hpp, but this is becoming rare.

The programmer who creates the library provides the header file. To declare the functions and external variables in the library, the user simply includes the header file. To include a header file, use the #include preprocessor directive. This tells the preprocessor to open the named header file and insert its contents where the #include statement appears. A #include may name a file in two ways: in angle brackets (<>) or in double quotes (" ").

File names in angle brackets, such as

```
#include <header>
```

cause the preprocessor to search for the file in a way that is particular to your implementation, but typically there's some kind of "include search path" that you specify in your environment or on the compiler command line. The mechanism for setting the search path varies between machines, operating systems, and C++ implementations, and may require some investigation on your part.

File names in double quotes, such as

```
#include "local.h"
```

tell the preprocessor to search for the file in (*according to the specification*) an "implementation-defined way." What this typically means is to search for the file relative to the current directory. If the file is not found, then the include directive is reprocessed as if it had angle brackets instead of quotes.

To include the iostream header file, you write

```
#include<iostream>
```

The preprocessor will find the iostream header file (often in a subdirectory called include) and insert it.

Standard C++ include Format

As C++ evolved, different compiler vendors chose different extensions for file names. In addition, various operating systems have different restrictions on file names, in particular on name length. These issues caused source code portability problems. To smooth over these rough edges, the standard uses a format that allows file names longer than the notorious eight characters and eliminates the extension. For example, instead of the old style of including iostream.h, which looks like

```
#include <iostream.h>
```

you can now write

```
#include <iostream>
```

The translator can implement the include statements in a way that suits the needs of that particular compiler and operating system, if necessary truncating the name and adding an extension. Of course, you can also copy the headers given to you by your compiler vendor to ones without extensions if you want to use this style before a vendor has provided support for it.

The libraries that have been inherited from *C* are still available with the traditional .h extension. However, you can also use them with the more modern C++ include style by prepending a "c" before the name. Thus,

```
#include <stdio.h>
#include <stdlib.h>
```

becomes

```
#include <cstdio>
#include <cstdlib>
```

and so on, for all the Standard *C* headers. This provides a nice distinction to the reader indicating when you're using *C* versus C++ libraries.

The effect of the new include format is not identical to the old: using the .h gives you the older, non-template version, and omitting the .h gives you the new templatized version. You'll usually have problems if you try to intermix the two forms in a single program.

Linking

The linker collects object modules (which often use file name extensions like .o or .obj), generated by the compiler into an executable program the operating system can load and run. It is the last phase of the compilation process.

Linker characteristics vary from system to system. In general, you just tell the linker the names of the object modules and libraries you want linked together and the name of the executable, and it goes to work. Some systems require you to invoke the linker yourself. With most C++ packages you invoke the linker through the C++ compiler. In many situations, the linker is invoked for you invisibly.

Some older linkers won't search object files and libraries more than once, and they search through the list you give them from left to right. This means that the order of object files and libraries can be important. If you have a mysterious problem that doesn't show up until link time, one possibility is the order in which the files are given to the linker.

Using Libraries

Now that you know the basic terminology, you can understand how to use a library. To use a library, follow these steps.

1. Include the library's header file.

2. Use the functions and variables in the library.

3. Link the library into the executable program.

These steps also apply when the object modules aren't combined into a library. Including a header file and linking the object modules are the basic steps for separate compilation in both *C* and C++.

How the Linker Searches a Library

When you make an external reference to a function or variable in C or C++, the linker, upon encountering this reference, can do one of two things. If it has not already encountered the definition for the function or variable, it adds the identifier to its list of "unresolved references." If the linker has already encountered the definition, the reference is resolved.

If the linker cannot find the definition in the list of object modules, it searches the libraries. Libraries have some sort of indexing so the linker doesn't need to look through all the object modules in the library—it just looks in the index. When the linker finds a definition in a library, the entire object module (not just the function definition) is linked into the executable program. Note that the whole library isn't linked, just the object module in the library that contains the definition you want (otherwise programs would be unnecessarily large). If you want to minimize executable program size, you might consider putting a single function in each source code file when you build your own libraries. This requires more editing, but it can be helpful to the user.

Because the linker searches files in the order you give them, you can preempt the use of a library function by inserting a file with your own function, using the same function name, into the list before the library name appears. Since the linker will resolve any references to this function by using your function before it searches the library, your function is used instead of the library function. Note that this can also be a bug, and the kind of thing C++ namespaces prevent.

Secret Additions

When a C or C++ executable program is created, certain items are secretly linked in. One of these is the startup module, which contains initialization routines that must be run any time a C or C++ program begins to execute. These routines set up the stack and initialize certain variables in the program.

The linker always searches the standard library for the compiled versions of any "standard" functions called in the program. Because the standard library is always searched, you can use anything in that library by simply including the appropriate header file in your program; you don't have to tell it to search the standard library. The iostream functions, for example, are in the Standard C++ Library. To use them, you just include the <iostream> header file. If you are using an add-on library, you must explicitly add the library name to the list of files handed to the linker.

Using Plain C Libraries

Just because you are writing code in C++, you are not prevented from using C library functions. In fact, the entire C library is included by default into Standard C++. There has been a tremendous amount of work done for you in these functions, so they can save you a lot of time.

This book will use Standard C++ (and thus also Standard C) library functions when convenient, but only *standard* library functions will be used, to ensure the portability of programs. In the few cases in which library functions must be used that are not in the C++ standard, all attempts will be made to use POSIX-compliant functions. POSIX is a standard based on a Unix standardization effort that includes functions that go beyond the scope of the C++ library. You can generally expect to find POSIX functions on Unix (in particular, Linux) platforms, and often under DOS/Windows. For example, if you're using multithreading, you are better off using the POSIX thread library because your code will then be easier to understand, port, and maintain (*and the POSIX thread library will usually just use the underlying thread facilities of the operating system, if these are provided*).

Your First C++ Program

You now know almost enough of the basics to create and compile a program. The program will use the Standard C++ iostream classes. These read from and write to files and "standard" input and output (*which normally come from and go to the console, but may be redirected to files or devices*). In this simple program, a stream object will be used to print a message on the screen.

Using the iostream Class

To declare the functions and external data in the `iostream` class, include the header file with the statement, like:

```
#include <iostream>
```

The first program uses *the concept of standard output*, which means "a general-purpose place to send output." You will see other examples using standard output in different ways, but here it will just go to the console. The `iostream` package automatically defines a variable (*an object*) called `cout` that accepts all data bound for standard output.

To send data to standard output, you use the operator `<<`. C programmers know this operator as the "bitwise left shift," which will be described in the next chapter. Suffice it to say that a bitwise left shift has nothing to do with output. However, C++ allows operators to be *overloaded*. When you overload an operator, you give it a new meaning when that operator is used with an object of a particular type. With `iostream` objects, the operator `<<` means "send to." For example,

```
cout << "rowdy!";
```

sends the string "rowdy!" to the object called `cout` (which is short for "console output").

That's enough operator overloading to get you started. *Chapter 12* covers operator overloading in detail.

Namespaces

As mentioned in *Chapter 1*, one of the problems encountered in the C language is that you *"run out of names"* for functions and identifiers when your programs reach a certain size. Of course, you don't really run out of names; it does, however, become harder to think of new ones after awhile. More importantly, when a program reaches a certain size, it's typically broken up into pieces, each of which is built and maintained by a different person or group. Since C effectively has a single arena where all the identifier and function names live, this means that all the developers must be careful not to accidentally use the same names in situations where they can conflict. This rapidly becomes tedious, time-wasting, and, ultimately, expensive.

Standard C++ has a mechanism to prevent this collision: the `namespace` keyword. Each set of C++ definitions in a library or program is *"wrapped"* in a namespace; if some other definition has an identical name, but is in a different namespace, there is no collision.

Namespaces are a convenient and helpful tool, but their presence means that you must be aware of them before you can write any programs. If you simply include a header file and use some functions or objects from that header, you'll probably get strange-sounding errors when you try to compile the program, to the effect that the compiler cannot find any of the declarations for the items that you just included in the header file! After you see this message a few times you'll become familiar with its meaning (which is *"You included the header file but all the declarations are within a namespace and you didn't tell the compiler that you wanted to use the declarations in that namespace."*).

There's a keyword that allows you to say *"I want to use the declarations and/or definitions in this namespace."* This keyword, appropriately enough, is `using`. All of the Standard C++ libraries are wrapped in a single namespace, which is `std` (for "standard"). As this book uses the standard libraries almost exclusively, you'll see the following *using directive* in almost every program:

```
using namespace std;
```

This means that you want to expose all the elements from the namespace called `std`. After this statement, you don't have to worry that your particular library component is inside a namespace, since the `using` directive makes that namespace available throughout the file where the `using` directive was written.

Exposing all the elements from a namespace after someone has gone to the trouble to hide them may seem a bit counterproductive, and in fact you should be careful about thoughtlessly doing this (as you'll learn later in the book). However, the using directive exposes only those names for the current file, so it is not quite as drastic as it first sounds. (*But think twice about doing it in a header file—that is reckless.*)

There's a relationship between namespaces and the way header files are included. Before the modern header file inclusion was standardized (without the trailing .h, as in<iostream>), the typical way to include a header file was with the .h, such as <iostream.h>. At that time, namespaces were not part of the language, either. So to provide backward compatibility with existing code, if you say

```
#include <iostream.h>
```

it means

```
#include <iostream>
using namespace std;
```

However, in this book the standard include format will be used (without the .h) and so the using directive must be explicit.

For now, that's all you need to know about namespaces, but in *Chapter 10* the subject is covered much more thoroughly.

Fundamentals of Program Structure

A *C* or C++ program is a collection of variables, function definitions, and function calls. When the program starts, it executes initialization code and calls a special function, main( ). You put the primary code for the program here.

As mentioned earlier, a function definition consists of a return type (which must be specified in C++), a function name, an argument list in parentheses, and the function code contained in braces. Here is a sample function definition:

```
int function() {
  // Function code here (this is a comment)
}
```

This function has an empty argument list and a body that contains only a comment.

There can be many sets of braces within a function definition, but there must always be at least one set surrounding the function body. Since main( ) is a function, it must follow these rules. In C++, main( ) always has return type of int.

C and C++ are free-form languages. With few exceptions, the compiler ignores newlines and white space, so it must have some way to determine the end of a statement. Statements are delimited by semicolons.

C comments start with /* and end with */. They can include newlines. C++ uses C-style comments and has an additional type of comment: //. The // starts a comment that terminates with a newline. It is more convenient than /* */ for one-line comments and is used extensively in this book.

"Hello, World!"

And now, finally, the first program. See Listing 2-2!

Listing 2-2. Hello, World!

```
//: C02:Hello.cpp
// Saying Hello with C++
#include <iostream> // Stream declarations
using namespace std;

int main() {
  cout << "Hello, World! I am "
       << 8 << " Today!" << endl;
} ///:~
```

The cout object is handed a series of arguments via the << operators. It prints out these arguments in left-to-right order. The special iostream function endl outputs the line and a newline. With iostream, you can string together a series of arguments like this, which makes the class easy to use.

In *C*, text inside double quotes is traditionally called a *string*. However, the Standard C++ library has a powerful class called string for manipulating text, and so I shall use the more precise term of "*character array*" for text inside double quotes.

The compiler creates storage for character arrays and stores the ASCII equivalent for each character in this storage. The compiler automatically terminates this array of characters with an extra piece of storage containing the value 0 to indicate the end of the character array.

Inside a character array, you can insert special characters by using *escape sequences*. These consist of a backslash (\) followed by a special code. For example \n means newline. Your compiler manual or local *C* guide gives a complete set of escape sequences; others include \t (tab), \\ (backslash), and \b (backspace).

Notice that the statement can continue over multiple lines, and that the entire statement terminates with a semicolon.

Character array arguments and constant numbers are mixed together in the above cout statement. Because the operator << is overloaded with a variety of meanings when used with cout, you can send cout a variety of different arguments and it will figure out what to do with the message.

Throughout this book you'll notice that the first line of each file will be a comment that starts with the characters that start a comment (typically //), followed by a colon, and the last line of the listing will end with a comment followed by /:~. This is a technique we use to allow easy extraction of information from code files. The first line also has the name and location of the file, so it can be referred to in text and in other files.

Running the Compiler

After downloading and unpacking the book's source code, find the program in the subdirectory C02. Invoke the compiler with Hello.cpp as the argument. For simple, one-file programs like this one, most compilers will take you all the way through the process. For example, to use the GNU C++ compiler (which is freely available on the Internet), you write

```
g++ Hello.cpp
```

Other compilers will have a similar syntax; consult your compiler's documentation for details.

More About iostream

So far you have seen only the most rudimentary aspect of the iostream class. (A detailed discussion of iostream has been deferred till *Chapter 19*). The output formatting available with iostream also includes features such as number formatting in decimal, octal, and hexadecimal. Listing 2-3 shows another example of the use of iostream.

Listing 2-3. Another Use of iostream

```
//: C02:Stream2.cpp
// Demonstrates more streams features
#include <iostream>
using namespace std;

int main() {
  // Specifying formats with manipulators:
  cout << "a number in decimal: "
       << dec << 15 << endl;
  cout << "in octal: " << oct << 15 << endl;
  cout << "in hex: " << hex << 15 << endl;
  cout << "a floating-point number: "
       << 3.14159 << endl;
  cout << "non-printing char (escape): "
       << char(27) << endl;
} ///:~
```

■ **Note** *the documentation comment ///:~*   - This is *repeated* throughout the book indicating *end of code*. You'll find more information about it in *Chapter 18* (in the "A String Application" section).

This example shows the iostream class printing numbers in decimal, octal, and hexadecimal using iostream *manipulators* (*which don't print anything, but change the state of the output stream*). The formatting of floating-point numbers is determined automatically by the compiler. In addition, any character can be sent to a stream object using a *cast* to a char (a char *is a data type that holds single characters*). This *cast* looks like a function call char( ), along with the character's ASCII value. In the program in Listing 2-3, the char(27) sends an "escape" to cout.

Character Array Concatenation

An important feature of the *C* preprocessor is *character array concatenation*. This feature is used in some of the examples in this book. If two quoted character arrays are adjacent, and no punctuation is between them, the compiler will paste the character arrays together into a single character array. This is particularly useful when code listings have width restrictions, as in Listing 2-4.

Listing 2-4. Character Array Concatenation

```
//: C02:Concat.cpp
// Demonstrates special use of Character array Concatenation
// in case of coding with width restrictions
#include <iostream>
using namespace std;

int main() {
  cout << "This is far too long to put on a "
    "single line but it can be broken up with "
    "no ill effects\as long as there is no "
```

```
    "punctuation separating adjacent character "
    "arrays.\n";
} ///:~
```

At first, the code in Listing 2-4 can look like an error because there's no familiar semicolon at the end of each line. Remember that *C* and C++ are free-form languages; although you'll usually see a semicolon at the end of each line, the actual requirement is for a semicolon at the end of each statement, and it's possible for a statement to continue over several lines.

Reading Input

The `iostream` classes provide the ability to read input. The object used for standard input is `cin` (*for* "console input"). `cin` normally expects input from the console, but this input can be redirected from other sources. An example of redirection is shown later in this chapter.

The iostreams operator used with `cin` is `>>`. This operator waits for the same kind of input as its argument. For example, if you give it an integer argument, it waits for an integer from the console. Listing 2-5 shows an example.

Listing 2-5. Reading Input

```
//: C02:Numconv.cpp
// Converts decimal to octal and hex
// Demonstrates use of cin operator
#include <iostream>
using namespace std;

int main() {
  int number;
  cout << "Enter a decimal number: ";
  cin >> number;
  cout << "value in octal = 0"
       << oct << number << endl;
  cout << "value in hex = 0x"
       << hex << number << endl;
} ///:~
```

This program converts a number typed in by the user into octal and hexadecimal representations.

Calling Other Programs

While the typical way to use a program that reads from standard input and writes to standard output is within a Unix shell script or DOS batch file, any program can be called from inside a *C* or C++ program using the Standard *C* `system( )` function, which is declared in the header file `<cstdlib>`, as shown in Listing 2-6.

Listing 2-6. Calling Other Programs

```
//: C02:CallHello.cpp
// Call another program
#include <cstdlib> // Declare "system()"
using namespace std;
```

```
int main() {
  system("Hello");
} ///:~
```

To use the `system( )` function, you give it a character array that you would normally type at the operating system command prompt. This can also include command-line arguments, and the character array can be one that you fabricate at runtime (instead of just using a static character array as shown in Listing 2-6). The command executes and control returns to the program.

This program shows how easy it is to use plain *C* library functions in C++: just include the header file and call the function. This upward compatibility from *C* to C++ is a big advantage if you are learning the language starting from a background in *C*.

Introducing Strings

While a character array can be fairly useful, it is quite limited. It's simply a group of characters in memory, but if you want to do anything with it you must manage all the little details. For example, the size of a quoted character array is fixed at compile time. If you have a character array and you want to add some more characters to it, you'll need to understand quite a lot (including dynamic memory management, character array copying, and concatenation) before you can get your wish. This is exactly the kind of thing we'd like to have an object do for us.

The Standard C++ `string` class is designed to take care of (and hide) all the low-level manipulations of character arrays that were previously required of the *C* programmer. These manipulations have been a constant source of time wasting and errors since the inception of the *C* language. So, although an entire chapter is devoted to the `string` class later on in this book, the `string` is so important and it makes life so much easier that it will be introduced here and used in much of the early part of the book.

To use `strings`, you include the C++ header file `<string>`. The `string` class is in the namespace `std` so a `using` directive is necessary. Because of operator overloading, the syntax for using `strings` is quite intuitive, as you can see in Listing 2-7.

Listing 2-7. Using Strings

```
//: C02:HelloStrings.cpp
//  Demonstrates the basics of the C++ string class
#include <string>
#include <iostream>
using namespace std;

int main() {
  string s1, s2;             // Empty strings
  string s3 = "Hello, World."; // Initialized
  string s4("I am");         // Also initialized
  s2 = "Today";              // Assigning to a string
  s1 = s3 + " " + s4;        // Combining strings
  s1 += " 8 ";               // Appending to a string
  cout << s1 + s2 + "!" << endl;
} ///:~
```

The first two `strings`, `s1` and `s2`, start out empty, while `s3` and `s4` show two equivalent ways to initialize `string` objects from character arrays (you can just as easily initialize `string` objects from other `string` objects).

You can assign to any `string` object using =. This replaces the previous contents of the string with whatever is on the right-hand side, and you don't have to worry about what happens to the previous contents—that's handled automatically for you. To combine `strings` you simply use the + operator, which also allows you to combine character arrays with `strings`. If you want to append either a `string` or a character array to another `string`, you can use the operator +=. Finally, note that `iostream` already knows what to do with `strings`, so you can just send a `string` (or an expression that produces a `string`, which happens with s1 + s2 + "!") directly to `cout` in order to print it.

Reading and Writing Files

In *C*, the process of opening and manipulating files requires a lot of language background to prepare you for the complexity of the operations. However, the C++ `iostream` library provides a simple way to manipulate files, and so this functionality can be introduced much earlier than it would be in *C*.

To open files for reading and writing, you must include `<fstream>`. Although this will automatically include `<iostream>`, it's generally prudent to explicitly include `<iostream>` if you're planning to use `cin`, `cout`, etc.

To open a file for reading, you create an `ifstream` object, which then behaves like `cin`. To open a file for writing, you create an `ofstream` object, which then behaves like `cout`. Once you've opened the file, you can read from it or write to it just as you would with any other `iostream` object. It's that simple (which is, of course, the whole point).

One of the most useful functions in the `iostream` library is `getline( )`, which allows you to read one line (terminated by a newline) into a `string` object. The first argument is the `ifstream` object you're reading from and the second argument is the `string` object. When the function call is finished, the `string` object will contain the line. Listing 2-8 contains a simple example, which copies the contents of one file into another.

Listing 2-8. Copy One file to another, a Line at a time

```
//: C02:Scopy.cpp
// Demonstrates use of the getline() function
#include <string>
#include <fstream>
using namespace std;

int main() {
  ifstream in("Scopy.cpp");    // Open for reading
  ofstream out("Scopy2.cpp"); // Open for writing
  string s;
  while(getline(in, s))        // Discards newline char
    cout << s << "\n";         // ... must add it back
} ///:~
```

To open the files, you just hand the `ifstream` and `ofstream` objects the file names you want to create, as seen in Listing 2-8.

There is a new concept introduced here, which is the `while` loop. Although this will be explained in detail in the next chapter, the basic idea is that the expression in parentheses following the `while` controls the execution of the subsequent statement (which can also be multiple statements, wrapped inside curly braces). As long as the expression in parentheses (in this case, getline(in, s)) produces a "true" result, then the statement controlled by the `while` will continue to execute. It turns out that getline( ) will return a value that can be interpreted as "true" if another line has been read successfully, and "false" upon reaching the end of the input. Thus, the above `while` loop reads every line in the input file and sends each line to the output file.

getline( ) reads in the characters of each line until it discovers a newline (the termination character can be changed, but that won't be an issue until *Chapter 19* on iostreams). However, it discards the newline and doesn't store it in the resulting `string` object. Thus, if you want the copied file to look just like the source file, you must add the newline back in, as shown.

Another interesting example is to copy the entire file into a single `string` object, as shown in Listing 2-9.

Listing 2-9. Reading an Entire File into a Single String

```
//: C02:FillString.cpp
//   Demonstrates use of fstream
#include <string>
#include <iostream>
#include <fstream>
using namespace std;

int main() {
  ifstream in("FillString.cpp");
  string s, line;
  while(getline(in, line))
    s += line + "\n";
  cout << s;
} ///:~
```

Because of the dynamic nature of strings, you don't have to worry about how much storage to allocate for a string; you can just keep adding things and the string will keep expanding to hold whatever you put into it.

One of the nice things about putting an entire file into a string is that the string class has many functions for searching and manipulation that would then allow you to modify the file as a single string. However, this has its limitations. For one thing, it is often convenient to treat a file as a collection of lines instead of just a big blob of text. For example, if you want to add line numbering it's much easier if you have each line as a separate string object. To accomplish this, you'll need another approach.

Introducing Vector

With strings, you can fill up a string object without knowing how much storage you're going to need. The problem with reading lines from a file into individual string objects is that you don't know up front how many strings you're going to need; you only know after you've read the entire file. To solve this problem, you need some sort of holder that will automatically expand to contain as many string objects as you care to put into it.

In fact, why limit yourself to holding string objects? It turns out that this kind of problem—not knowing how many of something you have while you're writing a program—happens a lot. And this "container" object sounds like it would be more useful if it would hold *any kind of object at all!* Fortunately, the Standard C++ Library has a ready-made solution: the standard container classes. The container classes are one of the real powerhouses of Standard C++.

There is often a bit of confusion between the containers and algorithms in the Standard C++ Library, and the entity known as the STL. The STL diverges from the Standard C++ Library on many subtle points. So, although it's a popular misconception, the C++ Standard does not "include" the STL. It can be a bit confusing since the containers and algorithms in the Standard C++ Library have the same root (and usually the same names) as the SGI STL. In this book, I shall say "The Standard C++ Library" or "The Standard Library containers" or something similar, and I will avoid the term "STL."

The Standard Library is so useful that the most basic of the standard containers, the vector, is introduced in this early chapter and used throughout the book. You'll find that you can do a tremendous amount just by using the basics of vector and not worrying about the underlying implementation (*again, an important goal of OOP*). You'll find that in most cases, the usage shown here is adequate.

The vector *class is a template*, which means that it can be efficiently applied to different types. That is, you can create a vector of shapes, a vector of cats, a vector of strings, etc. Basically, with a template you can create a "class of anything." To tell the compiler what it is that the class will work with (in this case, what the vector will hold), you put the name of the desired type in angle brackets, which means < and >. So a vector of string would be denoted vector<string>. When you do this, you end up with a customized vector that will hold only string objects, and you'll get an error message from the compiler if you try to put anything else into it.

Since vector expresses the concept of a container, there must be a way to put things into the container and get things back out of the container. To add a brand-new element on the end of a vector, you use the member function push_back( ). (*Remember that, since it's a member function, you use a '.' to call it for a particular object.*) The reason the name of this member function might seem a bit verbose (as in push_back( ) instead of something simpler like "put") is because there are other containers and other member functions for putting new elements into containers. For example, there is an insert( ) member function to put something in the middle of a container. vector supports this but its use is much more complicated and we shall not explore it any further here. There's also a push_front( ) (not part of vector) to put things at the beginning. There are many more member functions in vector and many more containers in the Standard C++ Library, but you'll be surprised at how much you can do just knowing about a few simple features.

So you can put new elements into a vector with push_back( ), but how do you get these elements back out again? This solution is more clever and elegant. Operator overloading is used to make the vector look like an *array*. The array (which will be described more fully in the next chapter) is a data type that is available in virtually every programming language, so you should already be somewhat familiar with it. Arrays are *aggregates*, which mean they consist of a number of elements clumped together. The distinguishing characteristic of an array is that these elements are the same size and are arranged to be one right after the other. Most importantly, these elements can be selected by *indexing*, which means you can say *"I want element number n"* and that element will be produced, usually quickly. Although there are exceptions in programming languages, the indexing is normally achieved using square brackets, so if you have an array a and you want to produce element five, you say a[4] (note that *indexing always starts at zero*).

This very compact and powerful indexing notation is incorporated into the vector using operator overloading, just like << and >> were incorporated into iostream. Again, you don't need to know how the overloading was implemented (that's saved for a later chapter) but it's helpful if you're aware that there's some magic going on under the covers in order to make the [ ] work with vector.

With that in mind, you can now see a program that uses vector. To use a vector, you include the header file <vector>, as shown in Listing 2-10.

Listing 2-10. Using a Vector//: C02:Fillvector.cpp

```
// Demonstrates copying an entire file into a vector of string #include <string>
#include <iostream>
#include <fstream>
#include <vector>
using namespace std;

int main() {
  vector <string> v;
  ifstream in("Fillvector.cpp");
  string line;
  while(getline(in, line))
    v.push_back(line); // Add the line to the end
  // Add line numbers:
  for(int i = 0; i < v.size(); i++)
    cout << i << ": " << v[i] << endl;
} ///:~
```

Much of this program is similar to the previous one; a file is opened and lines are read into string objects one at a time. However, these string objects are pushed onto the back of the vector v. Once the while loop completes, the entire file is resident in memory, inside v.

The next statement in the program is called a for loop. It is similar to a while loop except that it adds some extra control. After the for, there is a "control expression" inside of parentheses, just like the while loop. However, this control expression is in three parts: a part that initializes, one that tests to see if you should exit the loop, and one that changes something, typically to step through a sequence of items. This program shows the for loop in the way you'll see it most commonly used: the initialization part int i = 0 creates an integer i to use as a loop counter and gives it an initial value of zero. The testing portion says that to stay in the loop, i should be less than the number of elements in the vector v. (This is produced using the member function size( ), which was just sort of slipped in here, but you must admit it has a fairly obvious meaning.) The final portion uses a shorthand for C and C++, the "auto-increment" operator, to add 1 to the value of i. Effectively, i++ says "get the value of i, add 1 to it, and put the result back into i. Thus, the total effect of the for loop is to take a variable i and march it through the values from zero to one less than the size of the vector. For each value of i, the cout statement is executed and this builds a line that consists of the value of i (magically converted to a character array by cout), a colon and a space, the line from the file, and a newline provided by endl. When you compile and run it, you'll see the effect is to add line numbers to the file.

Because of the way that the >> operator works with iostream, you can easily modify the program in Listing 2-10 so that it breaks up the input into whitespace-separated words instead of lines, as shown in Listing 2-11.

Listing 2-11. Breaking a File into Whitespace-separated Words

```
//: C02:GetWords.cpp
// Modifies program in Listing 2-10
#include <string>
#include <iostream>
#include <fstream>
#include <vector>
using namespace std;

int main() {
  vector<string> words;
  ifstream in("GetWords.cpp");
  string word;
  while(in >> word)
    words.push_back(word);
  for(int i = 0; i < words.size(); i++)
    cout << words[i] << endl;
} ///:~
```

The expression

```
while(in >> word)
```

is what gets the input one "word" at a time, and when this expression evaluates to "false" it means the end of the file has been reached. Of course, delimiting words by whitespace is quite crude, but it makes for a simple example. Later in the book you'll see more sophisticated examples that let you break up input just about any way you'd like.

To demonstrate how easy it is to use a vector with any type, Listing 2-12 shows an example that creates a vector<int>.

Listing 2-12. Using a Vector with Any Type

```
//: C02:Intvector.cpp
// Demonstrates creation of a vector that holds integers
#include <iostream>
#include <vector>
using namespace std;
```

```
int main() {
  vector<int> v;
  for(int i = 0; i < 10; i++)
    v.push_back(i);
  for(int i = 0; i < v.size(); i++)
    cout << v[i] << ", ";
  cout << endl;
  for(int i = 0; i < v.size(); i++)
    v[i] = v[i] * 10; // Assignment
  for(int i = 0; i < v.size(); i++)
    cout << v[i] << ", ";
  cout << endl;
} ///:~
```

To create a vector that holds a different type, you just put that type in as the template argument (*the argument in angle brackets*). Templates and well-designed template libraries are intended to be exactly this easy to use.

This example goes on to demonstrate another essential feature of vector. In the expression

```
v[i] = v[i] * 10;
```

you can see that the vector is not limited to only putting things in and getting things out. You also have the ability to *assign* (and thus to change) to any element of a vector, also through the use of the square-brackets indexing operator. This means that vector is a general-purpose, flexible scratchpad for working with collections of objects. You will definitely make use of it in the coming chapters.

Review Session

1. The intent of this chapter is to show you how easy object-oriented programming can be—if someone else has gone to the work of defining the objects for you. In that case, you include a header file, create the objects, and send messages to them. If the types you are using are powerful and well-designed, then you won't have to do much work and your resulting program will also be powerful.

2. In the process of showing the ease of OOP when using library classes, this chapter also introduced some of the most basic and useful types in the *Standard C++ Library*: the family of iostream (*in particular, those that read from and write to the console and files*), the string class, and the vector template. You've seen how straightforward it is to use these types and can now probably imagine many things you can accomplish with them, but there's actually a lot more they can do.

3. Even though you'll only be using a limited subset of the functionality of these tools in the early part of the book, they nonetheless provide a large step up from the primitiveness of learning a low-level language like C. While learning the low-level aspects of C is educational, it's also time consuming. In the end, you'll be much more productive if you've got objects to manage the low-level issues. After all, the whole *point* of OOP is to hide the details so you can "paint with a bigger brush!"

4. However, as high-level as OOP tries to be, there are some *fundamental aspects of C* that you can't avoid knowing, and these will be covered in the next chapter.

CHAPTER 3

■ ■ ■

The C in C++

Since C++ is based on C, you must be familiar with the syntax of C in order to program in C++, just as you must be reasonably fluent in algebra in order to tackle calculus.

If you've never seen C before, this chapter will give you a decent background in the style of C used in C++. If you are familiar with the style of C described in Kernighan and Ritchie (often called K&R C), you will find some new and different features in C++ as well as in Standard C. If you are familiar with Standard C, you should skim through this chapter looking for features that are particular to C++. Note that there are some fundamental C++ features introduced here, which are basic ideas that are akin to the features in C or often modifications to the way that C does things. The more sophisticated C++ features will not be introduced until later chapters.

This chapter is a fairly fast coverage of C constructs and an introduction to some basic C++ constructs, with the understanding that you've had some experience programming in another language. This chapter basically covers features of C++, which identify C similarities.

Creating Functions

In old (pre-Standard) C, you could call a function with any number or type of arguments and the compiler wouldn't complain. Everything seemed fine until you ran the program. You got mysterious results (*or worse, the program crashed*) with no hints as to why. The lack of help with argument passing and the enigmatic bugs that resulted is probably one reason why C was dubbed a "high-level assembly language." Pre-Standard C programmers just adapted to it.

Standard C and C++ use a feature called *function prototyping*. With function prototyping, you must use a description of the types of arguments when declaring and defining a function. This description is the "prototype." When the function is called, the compiler uses the prototype to ensure that the proper arguments are passed in and that the return value is treated correctly. If the programmer makes a mistake when calling the function, the compiler catches the mistake.

Essentially, you learned about function prototyping (without naming it as such) in the previous chapter, since the form of function declaration in C++ requires proper prototyping. In a function prototype, the argument list contains the types of arguments that must be passed to the function and (optionally for the declaration) identifiers for the arguments. The order and type of the arguments must match in the declaration, definition, and function call. Here's an example of a function prototype in a declaration:

```
int translate(float x, float y, float z);
```

You do not use the same form when declaring variables in function prototypes as you do in ordinary variable definitions. That is, you cannot say float x, y, z. You must indicate the type of *each* argument. In a function declaration, the following form is also acceptable:

```
int translate(float, float, float);
```

Since the compiler doesn't do anything but check for types when the function is called, the identifiers are only included for clarity when someone is reading the code.

In the function definition, names are required because the arguments are referenced inside the function, like so:

```
int translate(float x, float y, float z) {
  x = y = z;
  // ...
}
```

It turns out this rule applies only to C. In C++, an argument may be unnamed in the argument list of the function definition. Since it is unnamed, you cannot use it in the function body, of course. Unnamed arguments are allowed in order to give the programmer a way to reserve space in the argument list. Whoever uses the function must still call the function with the proper arguments. However, the person creating the function can then use the argument in the future without forcing modification of code that calls the function. This option of ignoring an argument in the list is also possible if you leave the name in, but you will get an annoying warning message about the value being unused every time you compile the function. The warning is eliminated if you remove the name.

C and C++ have two other ways to declare an argument list. If you have an empty argument list, you can declare it as func( ) in C++, which tells the compiler there are exactly zero arguments. You should be aware that this only means an empty argument list in C++. In C, it means an indeterminate number of arguments (which is a "hole" in C since it disables type checking in that case). In both C and C++, the declaration func(void); means an empty argument list. The void keyword means "nothing" in this case (*it can also mean* "no type" *in the case of pointers*, as you'll see later in this chapter).

The other option for argument lists occurs when you don't know how many arguments or what type of arguments you will have; this is called a *variable argument list*. This uncertain argument list is represented by ellipses (. . .). Defining a function with a variable argument list is significantly more complicated than defining a regular function. You can use a variable argument list for a function that has a fixed set of arguments if (for some reason) you want to disable the error checks of function prototyping. Because of this, you should restrict your use of variable argument lists to C and avoid them in C++ (where, as you'll learn, there are much better alternatives).

Function Return Values

A C++ function prototype must specify the return value type of the function (in C, if you leave off the return value type it defaults to int). The return type specification precedes the function name. To specify that no value is returned, use the void keyword. This will generate an error if you try to return a value from the function. Here are some complete function prototypes:

```
int f1(void);                         // Returns an int, takes no arguments
int f2();                             // Like f1() in C++ but not in Standard C!
float f3(float, int, char, double);   // Returns a float
void f4(void);                        // Takes no arguments, returns nothing
```

To return a value from a function, you use the return statement. return exits the function back to the point right after the function call. If return has an argument, that argument becomes the return value of the function. If a function says that it will return a particular type, then each return statement must return that type. You can have more than one return statement in a function definition, as shown in Listing 3-1.

Listing 3-1. Several return Statements

```
//: C03:Return.cpp
// Use of "return"
#include <iostream>
```

```
using namespace std;

char cfunc(int i) {
  if(i == 0)
    return 'a';
  if(i == 1)
    return 'g';
  if(i == 5)
    return 'z';
  return 'c';
}

int main() {
  cout << "type an integer: ";
  int val;
  cin >> val;
  cout << cfunc(val) << endl;
} ///:~
```

In cfunc( ), the first if that evaluates to true exits the function via the return statement. Notice that a function declaration is not necessary because the function definition appears before it is used in main( ), so the compiler knows about it from that function definition.

Using the C Function Library

All the functions in your local C function library are available while you are programming in C++. You should look hard at the function library before defining your own function; there's a good chance that someone has already solved your problem for you, and probably given it a lot more thought and debugging.

A word of caution, though: many compilers include a lot of extra functions that make life even easier and are tempting to use, but are not part of the Standard C Library. If you are certain you will never want to move the application to another platform (*and who is certain of that?*), go ahead—use those functions and make your life easier. If you want your application to be portable, you should restrict yourself to Standard Library functions. If you must perform platform-specific activities, try to isolate that code in one spot so it can be changed easily when porting to another platform. In C++, platform-specific activities are often encapsulated in a class, which is the ideal solution.

The formula for using a library function is as follows: first, find the function in your programming reference (many programming references will index the function by category as well as alphabetically). The description of the function should include a section that demonstrates the syntax of the code. The top of this section usually has at least one #include line/directive, showing you the header file containing the function prototype. Duplicate this #include line/directive in your file so the function is properly declared. Now you can call the function in the same way it appears in the syntax section. If you make a mistake, the compiler will discover it by comparing your function call to the function prototype in the header and tell you about your error. The linker searches the Standard Library by default, so that's all you need to do: include the header file and call the function.

Creating Your Own Libraries with the Librarian

You can collect your own functions together into a library. Most programming packages come with a librarian that manages groups of object modules. Each librarian has its own commands, but the general idea is this: if you want to create a library, make a header file containing the function prototypes for all the functions in your library. Put this header file somewhere in the preprocessor's search path, either in the local directory (so it can be found by include "header") or in the include directory (so it can be found by #include <header>). Now take all the object modules and hand them to the librarian along with a name for the finished library (most librarians require a common extension, such as .lib or .a). Place the finished library where the other libraries reside so the linker can find it. When you use your library, you will have to add something to the command line so the linker knows to search the library for the functions you call. You must find all the details in your local manual, since they vary from system to system.

Controlling Execution

This section covers the execution control statements in C++. You must be familiar with these statements before you can read and write C or C++ code.

C++ uses all of C's execution control statements. These include if-else, while, do-while, for, and a selection statement called switch. C++ also allows the infamous goto, which will be avoided in this book.

True and False

All conditional statements use the truth or falsehood of a conditional expression to determine the execution path. An example of a conditional expression is A == B. This uses the conditional operator == to see if the variable A is equivalent to the variable B. The expression produces a Boolean true or false (these are keywords only in C++; in C, an expression is "true" if it evaluates to a nonzero value). Other conditional operators are >, <, >=, etc. Conditional statements are covered more fully later in this chapter.

Using if-else

The if-else statement can exist in two forms: with or without the else. The two forms are

```
if(expression)
    statement
```

or

```
if(expression)
    statement
else
    statement
```

The "expression" evaluates to true or false. The "statement" means either a simple statement terminated by a semicolon or a compound statement, which is a group of simple statements enclosed in braces. Any time the word "statement" is used, it always implies that the statement is simple or compound. Note that this statement can also be another if, so they can be strung together; see Listing 3-2.

Listing 3-2. Using if and if-else

```
//: C03:Ifthen.cpp
// Demonstration of if and if-else conditionals
#include <iostream>
using namespace std;

int main() {
  int i;
  cout << "type a number and 'Enter'" << endl;
  cin >> i;
```

```
  if(i > 5)
    cout << "It's greater than 5" << endl;
  else
    if(i < 5)
      cout << "It's less than 5 " << endl;
    else
      cout << "It's equal to 5 " << endl;

  cout << "type a number and 'Enter'" << endl;
  cin >> i;
  if(i < 10)
    if(i > 5)  // "if" is just another statement
      cout << "5 < i < 10" << endl;
    else
      cout << "i <= 5" << endl;
  else          // Matches "if(i < 10)"
    cout << "i >= 10" << endl;
} ///:~
```

It is conventional to indent the body of a control flow statement so the reader may easily determine where it begins and ends.

Using while

You can while, do-while, and for control looping. A statement repeats until the controlling expression evaluates to false. The form of a while loop is

```
while(expression)
    statement
```

The expression is evaluated once at the beginning of the loop and again before each further iteration of the statement. The code in Listing 3-3 stays in the body of the while loop until you type the secret number or press Control-C.

Listing 3-3. Using while

```
//: C03:Guess.cpp
// Guess a number (demonstrates "while")
#include <iostream>
using namespace std;

int main() {
  int secret = 15;
  int guess = 0;
  // "!=" is the "not-equal" conditional:
  while(guess != secret) { // Compound statement
    cout << "guess the number: ";
    cin >> guess;
  }
  cout << "You guessed it!" << endl;
} ///:~
```

The while's conditional expression is not restricted to a simple test, as in Listing 3-3; it can be as complicated as you like as long as it produces a true or false result. You will even see code where the loop has no body, just a bare semicolon, like so:

```
while(/* Do a lot here */)
  ;
```

In these cases, the programmer has written the conditional expression not only to perform the test but also to do the work.

Using do-while

The form of do-while is

```
do
    statement
while(expression);
```

The do-while is different from while because the statement always executes at least once, even if the expression evaluates to false the first time. In a regular while, if the conditional is false the first time, the statement never executes.

If a do-while is used in Guess.cpp, as shown in Listing 3-4, the variable guess does not need an initial dummy value, since it is initialized by the cin statement before it is tested.

Listing 3-4. Using do-while

```
//: C03:Guess2.cpp
// The guess program using do-while
#include <iostream>
using namespace std;

int main() {
  int secret = 15;
  int guess;        // No initialization needed here
  do {
    cout << "guess the number: ";
    cin >> guess; // Initialization happens
  }   while(guess != secret);
  cout << "You got it!" << endl;
} ///:~
```

For some reason, most programmers tend to avoid do-while and just work with while.

Using for

A for loop performs initialization before the first iteration. Then it performs conditional testing and, at the end of each iteration, some form of *stepping*. The form of the for loop is

```
for(initialization; conditional; step)
  statement
```

Any of the expressions *initialization, conditional,* or *step* may be empty. The *initialization* code executes once at the very beginning. The *conditional* is tested before each iteration (if it evaluates to false at the beginning, the statement never executes). At the end of each loop, the step executes.

As you can see in Listing 3-5, for loops are usually used for counting tasks.

Listing 3-5. Using for

```
//: C03:Charlist.cpp
// Display all the ASCII characters
// Demonstrates "for"

#include <iostream>

using namespace std;

int main() {
  for(int i = 0; i < 128; i = i + 1)
    if (i != 26)       // ANSI Terminal Clear screen
      cout << " value: " << i
           << " character: "
           << char(i) // Type conversion
           << endl;
} ///:~
```

You may notice that the variable i is defined at the point where it is used, instead of at the beginning of the block denoted by the open curly brace, {. This is in contrast to traditional procedural languages (including C), which require that all variables be defined at the beginning of the block. This will be discussed later in this chapter.

The break and continue Keywords

Inside the body of any of the looping constructs while, do-while, or for, you can control the flow of the loop using break and continue. break quits the loop without executing the rest of the statements in the loop. continue stops the execution of the current iteration and goes back to the beginning of the loop to begin a new iteration.

As an example of break and continue, Listing 3-6 contains a very simple menu system.

Listing 3-6. Using the break and continue Keywords

```
//: C03:Menu.cpp
// Simple menu program demonstrating
// the use of "break" and "continue"
#include <iostream>
using namespace std;

int main() {
  char c; // To hold response
  while(true) {
    cout << "MAIN MENU:" << endl;
    cout << "l: left, r: right, q: quit -> ";
    cin >> c;
    if(c == 'q')
      break; // Out of "while(1)"
```

```
    if(c == 'l') {
      cout << "LEFT MENU:" << endl;
      cout << "select a or b: ";
      cin >> c;
      if(c == 'a') {
        cout << "you chose 'a'" << endl;
        continue; // Back to main menu
      }
      if(c == 'b') {
        cout << "you chose 'b'" << endl;
        continue; // Back to main menu
      }
      else {
        cout << "you didn't choose a or b!"
             << endl;
        continue; // Back to main menu
      }
    }
    if(c == 'r') {
      cout << "RIGHT MENU:" << endl;
      cout << "select c or d: ";
      cin >> c;
      if(c == 'c') {
        cout << "you chose 'c'" << endl;
        continue; // Back to main menu
      }
      if(c == 'd') {
        cout << "you chose 'd'" << endl;
        continue; // Back to main menu
      }
      else {
        cout << "you didn't choose c or d!"
             << endl;
        continue; // Back to main menu
      }
    }
    cout << "you must type l or r or q!" << endl;
  }
  cout << "quitting menu..." << endl;
} ///:~
```

If the user selects "q" in the main menu, the break keyword is used to quit; otherwise the program just continues to execute indefinitely. After each of the submenu selections, the continue keyword is used to pop back up to the beginning of the while loop.

The while(true) statement is the equivalent of saying "do this loop forever." The break statement allows you to break out of this infinite while loop when the user types a "q."

Using switch

A `switch` statement selects from among pieces of code based on the value of an integral expression. Its form is

```
switch(selector) {
    case integral-value1 : statement; break;
    case integral-value2 : statement; break;
    case integral-value3 : statement; break;
    case integral-value4 : statement; break;
    case integral-value5 : statement; break;
    (...)
    default: statement;
}
```

Selector is an expression that produces an integral value. The `switch` compares the result of selector to each *integral value*. If it finds a match, the corresponding statement (simple or compound) executes. If no match occurs, the `default` statement executes.

You will notice in the definition above that each `case` ends with a `break`, which causes execution to jump to the end of the `switch` body (the closing brace that completes the `switch`). This is the conventional way to build a `switch` statement, but the `break` is optional. If it is missing, your `case` drops through to the one after it; that is, the code for the following `case` statements execute until a `break` is encountered. Although you don't usually want this kind of behavior, it can be useful to an experienced programmer.

The `switch` statement is a clean way to implement multi-way selection (i.e., selecting from among a number of different execution paths), but it requires a selector that evaluates to an integral value at compile time. If you want to use, for example, a `string` object as a selector, it won't work in a `switch` statement. For a `string` selector, you must instead use a series of `if` statements and compare the `string` inside the conditional.

The menu example in Listing 3-7 provides a particularly nice example of a `switch`.

Listing 3-7. Using switch

```cpp
//: C03:Menu2.cpp
// A menu using a switch statement
#include <iostream>

using namespace std;

int main() {
  bool quit = false;  // Flag for quitting
  while(quit == false) {
    cout << "Select a, b, c or q to quit: ";
    char response;
    cin >> response;
    switch(response) {
      case 'a' : cout << "you chose 'a'" << endl;
                 break;
      case 'b' : cout << "you chose 'b'" << endl;
                 break;
      case 'c' : cout << "you chose 'c'" << endl;
                 break;
```

```
        case 'q' : cout << "quitting menu" << endl;
                   quit = true;
                   break;
        default  : cout << "Please use a,b,c or q!"
                        << endl;
    }
  }
} ///:~
```

The quit flag is a bool, short for "Boolean," which is a type you'll find only in C++. It can have only the keyword values true or false. Selecting "q" sets the quit flag to true. The next time the selector is evaluated, quit == false returns false so the body of the while does not execute.

Using and Misusing goto

The goto keyword is supported in C++, since it exists in C. Using goto is often dismissed as poor programming style, and most of the time it is. Anytime you use goto, look at your code and see if there's another way to do it. On rare occasions, you may discover goto can solve a problem that can't be solved otherwise, but still, consider it carefully. Listing 3-8 is an example that might make a plausible candidate.

Listing 3-8. Using goto

```
//: C03:gotoKeyword.cpp
// The infamous goto is supported in C++
#include <iostream>
using namespace std;

int main() {
  long val = 0;
  for(int i = 1; i < 1000; i++) {
    for(int j = 1; j < 100; j += 10) {
      val = i * j;
      if(val > 47000)
        goto DOWN;
        // Break would only go to the outer 'for'
    }
  }
  DOWN: // A label
  cout << val << endl;
} ///:~
```

The alternative would be to set a Boolean that is tested in the outer for loop, and then do a break from the inner for loop. However, if you have several levels of for or while, this could get awkward.

Recursion

Recursion is an interesting and sometimes useful programming technique whereby you call the function that you're in. Of course, if this is all you do, you'll keep calling the function you're in until you run out of memory, so there must be some way to bottom out the recursive call. In Listing 3-9, this bottoming out is accomplished by simply saying that the recursion will go only until the cat exceeds "Z."

Listing 3-9. Using Recursion

```cpp
//: C03:CatsInHats.cpp
// Simple demonstration of recursion
#include <iostream>
using namespace std;

void removeHat(char cat) {
  for(char c = 'A'; c < cat; c++)
    cout << "  ";
  if(cat <= 'Z') {
    cout << "cat " << cat << endl;
    removeHat(cat + 1); // Recursive call
  } else
    cout << "VOOM!!!" << endl;
}

int main() {
  removeHat('A');
} ///:~
```

In removeHat( ), you can see that as long as cat is less than "Z," removeHat( ) will be called from *within* removeHat( ), thus effecting the recursion. Each time removeHat( ) is called, its argument is one greater than the current cat so the argument keeps increasing.

Recursion is often used when evaluating some sort of arbitrarily complex problem, since you aren't restricted to a particular "size" for the solution; the function can just keep recursing until it's reached the end of the problem.

Introduction to Operators

You can think of operators as a special type of function (you'll learn that C++ operator overloading treats operators precisely that way). An operator takes one or more arguments and produces a new value. The arguments are in a different form than ordinary function calls, but the effect is the same.

From your previous programming experience, you should be reasonably comfortable with the operators that have been used so far. The concepts of addition (+), subtraction and unary minus (-), multiplication (*), division (/), and assignment (=) all have essentially the same meaning in any programming language. The full set of operators is enumerated later in this chapter.

Precedence

Operator precedence defines the order in which an expression evaluates when several different operators are present. C and C++ have specific rules to determine the order of evaluation. The easiest to remember is that multiplication and division happen before addition and subtraction. After that, if an expression isn't transparent to you, it probably won't be for anyone reading the code, so you should use parentheses to make the order of evaluation explicit. For example,

```cpp
A = X + Y - 2/2 + Z;
```

has a very different meaning from the same statement with a particular grouping of parentheses, like

```cpp
A = X + (Y - 2)/(2 + Z);
```

(Try evaluating the result with X = 1, Y = 2, and Z = 3.)

Auto-Increment and Auto-Decrement

C, and therefore C++, is full of shortcuts. Shortcuts can make code much easier to type, and sometimes much harder to read. Perhaps the C language designers thought it would be easier to understand a tricky piece of code if your eyes didn't have to scan as large an area of print.

Two of the nicer shortcuts are the auto-increment and auto-decrement operators. You often use these to change loop variables, which control the number of times a loop executes.

The auto-decrement operator is - - and means "decrease by one unit." The auto-increment operator is ++ and means "increase by one unit." If A is an int, for example, the expression ++A is equivalent to (A = A + 1). Auto-increment and auto-decrement operators produce the value of the variable as a result. If the operator appears before the variable, (i.e., ++A), the operation is first performed and the resulting value is produced. If the operator appears after the variable (i.e., A++), the current value is produced, and then the operation is performed; see Listing 3-10.

Listing 3-10. Auto-Increment and Auto-Decrement

```
//: C03:AutoIncrement.cpp
// Shows use of auto-increment
// and auto-decrement operators.
#include <iostream>
using namespace std;

int main() {
  int i = 0;
  int j = 0;
  cout << ++i << endl; // Pre-increment
  cout << j++ << endl; // Post-increment
  cout << --i << endl; // Pre-decrement
  cout << j-- << endl; // Post decrement
} ///:~
```

If you've been wondering about the name "C++," now you understand. It implies "one step beyond C."

Introduction to Data Types

Data types define the way you use storage (*memory*) in the programs you write. By specifying a data type, you tell the compiler how to create a particular piece of storage, and also how to manipulate that storage.

Data types can be built-in or abstract. A built-in data type is one that the compiler intrinsically understands, one that is wired directly into the compiler. The types of built-in data are almost identical in C and C++. In contrast, a user-defined data type is one that you or another programmer creates as a class. These are commonly referred to as abstract data types. The compiler knows how to handle built-in types when it starts up; it "learns" how to handle abstract data types by reading header files containing class declarations (you'll learn about this in later chapters).

Basic Built-in Types

The Standard C specification for built-in types (which C++ inherits) doesn't say how many bits each of the built-in types must contain. Instead, it stipulates the minimum and maximum values that the built-in type must be able to hold. When a machine is based on binary, this maximum value can be directly translated into a minimum number of bits necessary to hold that value. However, if a machine uses, for example, binary-coded decimal (BCD) to represent numbers, then the amount of space in the machine required to hold the maximum numbers for each data type will be different. The minimum and maximum values that can be stored in the various data types are defined in the system header files limits.h and float.h (in C++ you will generally #include <climits> and <cfloat> instead).

C and C++ have four basic built-in data types, described here for binary-based machines. A char is for character storage and uses a minimum of 8 bits (1 byte) of storage, although it may be larger. An int stores an integral number and uses a minimum of 2 bytes of storage. The float and double types store floating-point numbers, usually in IEEE floating-point format. float is for single-precision floating point and double is for double-precision floating point.

As mentioned, you can define variables anywhere in a scope, and you can define and initialize them at the same time. Listing 3-11 shows how to define variables using the four basic data types.

Listing 3-11. Basic Data Types

```
//: C03:Basic.cpp
// Defining the four basic data
// types in C and C++

int main() {
  // Definition without initialization:
  char protein;
  int carbohydrates;
  float fiber;
  double fat;
  // Simultaneous definition & initialization:
  char pizza = 'A', pop = 'Z';
  int dongdings = 100, twinkles = 150,
    heehos = 200;
  float chocolate = 3.14159;
  // Exponential notation:
  double fudge_ripple = 6e-4;
} ///:~
```

The first part of the program defines variables of the four basic data types without initializing them. If you don't initialize a variable, the Standard says that its contents are undefined (usually, this means they contain garbage). The second part of the program defines and initializes variables at the same time (it's always best, if possible, to provide an initialization value at the point of definition). Notice the use of exponential notation in the constant 6e-4, meaning "6 times 10 to the minus fourth power."

Using bool, true, and false

Before bool became part of Standard C++, everyone tended to use different techniques in order to produce Boolean-like behavior. These produced portability problems and could introduce subtle errors.

The Standard C++ bool type can have two states expressed by the built-in constants true (which converts to an integral one) and false (which converts to an integral zero).

All three names are keywords. In addition, some language elements have been adapted, as shown in Table 3-1.

Table 3-1. C++ *(Additional) Language Elements*

Element	Usage with bool
&& || !	Take bool arguments and produce bool results.
<><= >= == !=	Produce bool results.
if, for, while, do	Conditional expressions convert to bool values.
? :	First operand converts to bool value.

Because there's a lot of existing code that uses an int to represent a flag, the compiler will implicitly convert from an int to a bool (nonzero values will produce true while zero values produce false). Ideally, the compiler will give you a warning as a suggestion to correct the situation.

An idiom that falls under poor programming style is the use of ++ to set a flag to true. This is still allowed, but *deprecated*, which means that at some time in the future it will be made illegal. The problem is that you're making an implicit type conversion from bool to int, incrementing the value (perhaps beyond the range of the normal bool values of zero and one), and then implicitly converting it back again.

Pointers (which will be introduced later in this chapter) will also be automatically converted to bool when necessary.

Using Specifiers

Specifiers modify the meanings of the basic built-in types and expand them to a much larger set. There are four specifiers: long, short, signed, and unsigned.

long and short modify the maximum and minimum values that a data type will hold. A plain int must be at least the size of a short. The size hierarchy for integral types is shortint, int, longint. All the sizes could conceivably be the same, as long as they satisfy the minimum/maximum value requirements. On a machine with a 64-bit word, for instance, all the data types might be 64 bits.

The size hierarchy for floating point numbers is float, double, and longdouble. "long float" is not a legal type. There are no short floating-point numbers.

The signed and unsigned specifiers tell the compiler how to use the sign bit with integral types and characters (floating point numbers always contain a sign). An unsigned number does not keep track of the sign and thus has an extra bit available, so it can store positive numbers twice as large as the positive numbers that can be stored in a signed number. signed is the default and is only necessary with char; char may or may not default to signed. By specifying signed char, you force the sign bit to be used.

Listing 3-12 shows the size of the data types in bytes by using the sizeof operator, introduced later in this chapter.

Listing 3-12. Using Specifiers

```
//: C03:Specify.cpp
// Demonstrates the use of specifiers
#include <iostream>
using namespace std;

int main() {
  char c;
  unsigned char cu;
  int i;
  unsigned int iu;
  short int is;
  short iis; // Same as short int
  unsigned short int isu;
  unsigned short iisu;
  long int il;
  long iil;   // Same as long int
  unsigned long int ilu;
  unsigned long iilu;
  float f;
  double d;
  long double ld;
  cout
```

```
      << "\n char = " << sizeof(c)
      << "\n unsigned char = " << sizeof(cu)
      << "\n int = " << sizeof(i)
      << "\n unsigned int = " << sizeof(iu)
      << "\n short = " << sizeof(is)
      << "\n unsigned short = " << sizeof(isu)
      << "\n long = " << sizeof(il)
      << "\n unsigned long = " << sizeof(ilu)
      << "\n float = " << sizeof(f)
      << "\n double = " << sizeof(d)
      << "\n long double = " << sizeof(ld)
      << endl;
} ///:~
```

Be aware that the results you get by running this program will probably be different from one machine/operating system/compiler to the next, since (as mentioned) the only thing that must be consistent is that each different type hold the minimum and maximum values specified in the standard.

When you are modifying an int with short or long, the keyword int is optional, as shown above.

Introduction to Pointers

Whenever you run a program, it is first loaded (typically from disk) into the computer's memory. Thus, all elements of your program are located somewhere in memory. Memory is typically laid out as a sequential series of memory locations; we usually refer to these locations as 8-bit *bytes* but actually the size of each space depends on the architecture of the particular machine and is usually called that machine's *word size*. Each space can be uniquely distinguished from all other spaces by its *address*. For the purposes of this discussion, let's just say that all machines use bytes that have sequential addresses starting at zero and going up to however much memory you have in your computer.

Since your program lives in memory while it's being run, every element of your program has an address. Listing 3-13 is a simple program.

Listing 3-13. A Simple Program

```
//: C03:YourPets1.cpp
#include <iostream>
using namespace std;

int dog, cat, bird, fish;

void f(int pet) {
  cout << "pet id number: " << pet << endl;
}

int main() {
  int i, j, k;
} ///:~
```

Each of the elements in this program has a location in storage when the program is running. Even the function occupies storage. As you'll see, it turns out that what an element is and the way you define it usually determines the area of memory where that element is placed.

There is an operator in C and C++ that will tell you the address of an element. This is the & operator. All you do is precede the identifier name with & and it will produce the address of that identifier. YourPets1.cpp can be modified to print out the addresses of all its elements, as shown in Listing 3-14.

Listing 3-14. Modifying the Program

```
//: C03:YourPets2.cpp
#include <iostream>
using namespace std;

int dog, cat, bird, fish;

void f(int pet) {
  cout << "pet id number: " << pet << endl;
}

int main() {
  int i, j, k;
  cout << "f(): " << (long)&f << endl;
  cout << "dog: " << (long)&dog << endl;
  cout << "cat: " << (long)&cat << endl;
  cout << "bird: " << (long)&bird << endl;
  cout << "fish: " << (long)&fish << endl;
  cout << "i: " << (long)&i << endl;
  cout << "j: " << (long)&j << endl;
  cout << "k: " << (long)&k << endl;
} ///:~
```

The (long) is a *cast*. It says, "Don't treat this as if it's normal type; instead treat it as a long." The cast isn't essential, but if it wasn't there, the addresses would have been printed out in hexadecimal instead, so casting to a long makes things a little more readable.

The results of this program will vary depending on your computer, OS, and all sorts of other factors, but it will always give you some interesting insights. For a single run on my computer, the results looked like this:

```
f(): 4198736
dog: 4323632
cat: 4323636
bird: 4323640
fish: 4323644
i: 6684160
j: 6684156
k: 6684152
```

You can see how the variables that are defined inside main( ) are in a different area than the variables defined outside of main( ); you'll understand why as you learn more about the language. Also, f( ) appears to be in its own area; code is typically separated from data in memory.

Another interesting thing to note is that variables defined one right after the other appear to be placed contiguously in memory. They are separated by the number of bytes that are required by their data type. Here, the only data type used is int, and cat is 4 bytes away from dog, bird is 4 bytes away from cat, etc. So it would appear that, on this machine, an int is 4 bytes long.

Other than this interesting experiment showing how memory is mapped out, what can you do with an address? The most important thing you can do is store it inside another variable for later use. C and C++ have a special type of variable that holds an address. This variable is called a *pointer*.

The operator that defines a pointer is the same as the one used for multiplication: *. The compiler knows that it isn't multiplication because of the context in which it is used, as you will see.

When you define a pointer, you must specify the type of variable it points to. You start out by giving the type name, then instead of immediately giving an identifier for the variable, you say, "Wait, it's a pointer" by inserting a star between the type and the identifier. So a pointer to an int looks like this:

```
int* ip; // ip points to an int variable
```

The association of the * with the type looks sensible and reads easily, but it can actually be a bit deceiving. Your inclination might be to say "intpointer" as if it is a single discrete type. However, with an int or other basic data type, it's possible to say

```
int a, b, c;
```

whereas with a pointer, you'd *like* to say

```
int* ipa, ipb, ipc;
```

C syntax (and by inheritance, C++ syntax) does not allow such sensible expressions. In the definitions above, only ipa is a pointer, but ipb and ipc are ordinary ints (you can say that "* *binds more tightly to the identifier*"). Consequently, the best results can be achieved by using only one definition per line; you still get the sensible syntax without the confusion, like so:

```
int* ipa;
int* ipb;
int* ipc;
```

Since a general guideline for C++ programming is that you should always initialize a variable at the point of definition, this form actually works better. For example, the variables above are not initialized to any particular value; they hold garbage. It's much better to say something like

```
int a = 47;
int* ipa = &a;
```

Now both a and ipa have been initialized, and ipa holds the address of a.

Once you have an initialized pointer, the most basic thing you can do with it is to use it to modify the value it points to. To access a variable through a pointer, you *dereference* the pointer using the same operator that you used to define it, like this:

```
*ipa = 100;
```

Now a contains the value 100 instead of 47.

These are the basics of pointers: you can hold an address, and you can use that address to modify the original variable. But the question still remains: why do you want to modify one variable using another variable as a proxy?

For this introductory view of pointers, I can put the answer into two broad categories:

1. To change "outside objects" from within a function. This is perhaps the most basic use of pointers, and it will be examined here.

2. To achieve many other clever programming techniques, which you'll learn about in portions of the rest of the book.

Modifying the Outside Object

Ordinarily, when you pass an argument to a function, a copy of that argument is made inside the function. This is referred to as *pass-by-value*. You can see the effect of pass-by-value in Listing 3-15.

Listing 3-15. Pass-by-value

```
//: C03:PassByValue.cpp
#include <iostream>

using namespace std;

void f(int a) {
  cout << "a = " << a << endl;
  a = 5;
  cout << "a = " << a << endl;
}

int main() {
  int x = 47;
  cout << "x = " << x << endl;
  f(x);
  cout << "x = " << x << endl;
} ///:~
```

In f( ), a is a *local variable*, so it exists only for the duration of the function call to f( ). Because it's a function argument, the value of a is initialized by the arguments that are passed when the function is called; in main( ) the argument is x, which has a value of 47, so this value is copied into a when f( ) is called.

When you run this program you'll see

```
x = 47
a = 47
a = 5
x = 47
```

Initially, of course, x is 47. When f( ) is called, temporary space is created to hold the variable a for the duration of the function call, and a is initialized by copying the value of x, which is verified by printing it out. Of course, you can change the value of a and show that it is changed. But when f( ) is completed, the temporary space that was created for a disappears, and you see that the only connection that ever existed between a and x happened when the value of x was copied into a.

When you're inside f( ), x is the *outside object* (as per my terminology), and changing the local variable does not affect the outside object, naturally enough, since they are two separate locations in storage. But what if you *do* want to modify the outside object? This is where pointers come in handy. In a sense, a pointer is an alias for another variable. So if you pass a *pointer* into a function instead of an ordinary value, you are actually passing an alias to the outside object, enabling the function to modify that outside object, as shown in Listing 3-16.

Listing 3-16. Illustrating Pass of an Alias

```
//: C03:PassAddress.cpp
#include <iostream>
using namespace std;
```

```
void f(int* p) {
  cout << "p = " << p << endl;
  cout << "*p = " << *p << endl;

  *p = 5;
  cout << "p = " << p << endl;
}

int main() {
  int x = 47;
  cout << "x = " << x << endl;

  cout << "&x = " << &x << endl;
  f(&x);
  cout << "x = " << x << endl;
} ///:~
```

Now f( ) takes a pointer as an argument and dereferences the pointer during assignment, and this causes the outside object x to be modified. The output is

```
x = 47
&x = 0065FE00
p = 0065FE00
*p = 47
p = 0065FE00
x = 5
```

Notice that the value contained in p is the same as the address of x; the pointer p does indeed point to x. If that isn't convincing enough, when p is dereferenced to assign the value 5, you see that the value of x is now changed to 5 as well.

Thus, passing a pointer into a function will allow that function to modify the outside object. You'll see plenty of other uses for pointers later, but this is arguably the most basic and possibly the most common use.

Introduction to C++ References

Pointers work roughly the same in C and in C++, but C++ adds an additional way to pass an address into a function. This is *pass-by-reference* and it exists in several other programming languages, so it was not a C++ invention.

Your initial perception of references may be that they are unnecessary, that you could write all your programs without references. In general, this is true, with the exception of a few important places that you'll learn about later in the book. You'll also learn more about references later, but the basic idea is the same as the demonstration of pointer use above: you can pass the address of an argument using a reference. The difference between references and pointers is that *calling* a function that takes references is cleaner, syntactically, than calling a function that takes pointers (and it is exactly this syntactic difference that makes references essential in certain situations). If PassAddress.cpp is modified to use references, you can see the difference in the function call in main( ) in Listing 3-17.

Listing 3-17. Illustrating Pass-by-reference

```
//: C03:PassReference.cpp
#include <iostream>
using namespace std;
```

```
    void f(int& r) {
    cout << "r = " << r << endl;
    cout << "&r = " <<&r << endl;

    r = 5;
    cout << "r = " << r << endl;
}

int main() {
  int x = 47;
  cout << "x = " << x << endl;

  cout << "&x = " << &x << endl;
  f(x); // Looks like pass-by-value,
        // is actually pass by reference
  cout << "x = " << x << endl;
} ///:~
```

In f( )'s argument list, instead of saying int* to pass a pointer, you say int& to pass a reference. Inside f( ), if you just say r (which would produce the address if r were a pointer) you get *the value in the variable that r references.* If you assign to r, you actually assign to the variable that r references. In fact, the only way to get the address that's held inside r is with the & operator.

In main( ), you can see the key effect of references in the syntax of the call to f( ), which is just f(x). Even though this looks like an ordinary pass-by-value, the effect of the reference is that it actually takes the address and passes it in, rather than making a copy of the value. The output is

```
x = 47
&x = 0065FE00
r = 47
&r = 0065FE00
r = 5
x = 5
```

So you can see that pass-by-reference allows a function to modify the outside object, just like passing a pointer does (you can also observe that the reference obscures the fact that an address is being passed; this will be examined later in the book). Thus, for this simple introduction you can assume that references are just a syntactically different way (sometimes referred to as *syntactic sugar*) to accomplish the same thing that pointers do: allow functions to change outside objects.

Pointers and References as Modifiers

So far, you've seen the basic data types char, int, float, and double, along with the specifiers signed, unsigned, short, and long, which can be used with the basic data types in almost any combination. Now you've added pointers and references that are orthogonal to the basic data types and specifiers, so the possible combinations have just tripled; see Listing 3-18.

Listing 3-18. All Possible Combinations

```
//: C03:AllDefinitions.cpp
// All possible combinations of basic data types,
// specifiers, pointers and references
#include <iostream>
using namespace std;

void f1(char c, int i, float f, double d);
void f2(short int si, long int li, long double ld);
void f3(unsigned char uc, unsigned int ui,
  unsigned short int usi, unsigned long int uli);
void f4(char* cp, int* ip, float* fp, double* dp);
void f5(short int* sip, long int* lip,
  long double* ldp);
void f6(unsigned char* ucp, unsigned int* uip,
  unsigned short int* usip,
  unsigned long int* ulip);
void f7(char& cr, int& ir, float& fr, double& dr);
void f8(short int& sir, long int& lir,
  long double& ldr);
void f9(unsigned char& ucr, unsigned int& uir,
  unsigned short int& usir,
  unsigned long int& ulir);

int main() {} ///:~
```

Pointers and references also work when passing objects into and out of functions; you'll learn about this in a later chapter.

There's one other type that works with pointers: void. If you state that a pointer is a void*, it means that any type of address at all can be assigned to that pointer (whereas if you have an int*, you can assign only the address of an int variable to that pointer). For an example, see Listing 3-19.

Listing 3-19. void Pointer

```
//: C03:VoidPointer.cpp

int main() {
  void* vp;
  char c;
  int i;
  float f;
  double d;
  // The address of ANY type can be
  // assigned to a void pointer:
  vp = &c;
  vp = &i;
  vp = &f;
  vp = &d;
} ///:~
```

Once you assign to a void* you lose any information about what type it is. This means that before you can use the pointer, you must cast it to the correct type, as shown in Listing 3-20.

Listing 3-20. Cast from void Pointer

```
//: C03:CastFromVoidPointer.cpp
int main() {
  int i = 99;
  void* vp = &i;
  // Can't dereference a void pointer:
  // *vp = 3; // Compile time error
  // Must cast back to int before dereferencing:
  *((int*)vp) = 3;
} ///:~
```

The cast (int*)vp takes the void* and tells the compiler to treat it as an int*, and thus it can be successfully dereferenced. You might observe that this syntax is ugly, and it is, but it's worse than that—the void* introduces a hole in the language's type system. That is, it allows, or even promotes, the treatment of one type as another type. In Listing 3-19, an int is treated as an int by casting vp to an int*, but there's nothing that says it can't be cast to a char* or double*, which would modify a different amount of storage that had been allocated for the int, possibly crashing the program. In general, void pointers should be avoided, and used only in rare special cases, the likes of which you won't be ready to consider until significantly later in the book.

You cannot have a void reference, for reasons that will be explained in Chapter 11.

Understanding Scoping

Scoping rules tell you where a variable is valid, where it is created, and where it gets destroyed (i.e., goes out of scope). The scope of a variable extends from the point where it is defined to the first closing brace that matches the closest opening brace before the variable was defined. That is, a scope is defined by its "nearest" set of braces. Listing 3-21 illustrates this point.

Listing 3-21. Scoping

```
//: C03:Scope.cpp
// How variables are scoped
int main() {
  int scp1;
  // scp1 visible here
  {
    // scp1 still visible here
    //.....
    int scp2;
    // scp2 visible here
    //.....
    {
      // scp1 & scp2 still visible here
      //..
      int scp3;
      // scp1, scp2 & scp3 visible here
      // ...
    } // <-- scp3 destroyed here
    // scp3 not available here
```

```
  // scp1 & scp2 still visible here
  // ...
  } // <-- scp2 destroyed here
  // scp3 & scp2 not available here
  // scp1 still visible here
  //..
} // <-- scp1 destroyed here
///:~
```

The code shows when variables are visible and when they are unavailable (that is, when they *go out of scope*). A variable can be used only when inside its scope. Scopes can be nested, indicated by matched pairs of braces inside other matched pairs of braces. Nesting means that you can access a variable in a scope that encloses the scope you are in. In Listing 3-21, the variable scp1 is available inside all of the other scopes, while scp3 is available only in the innermost scope.

Defining Variables on the Fly

As noted earlier in this chapter, there is a significant difference between C and C++ when defining variables. Both languages require that variables be defined before they are used, but C (and many other traditional procedural languages) forces you to define all the variables at the beginning of a scope, so that when the compiler creates a block it can allocate space for those variables.

While reading C code, a block of variable definitions is usually the first thing you see when entering a scope. Declaring all variables at the beginning of the block requires the programmer to write in a particular way because of the implementation details of the language. Most people don't know all the variables they are going to use before they write the code, so they must keep jumping back to the beginning of the block to insert new variables, which is awkward and causes errors. These variable definitions don't usually mean much to the reader, and they actually tend to be confusing because they appear apart from the context in which they are used.

C++ (but *not* C) allows you to define variables anywhere in a scope, so you can define a variable right before you use it. In addition, you can initialize the variable at the point you define it, which prevents a certain class of errors. Defining variables this way makes the code much easier to write and reduces the errors you get from being forced to jump back and forth within a scope. It makes the code easier to understand because you see a variable defined in the context of its use. This is especially important when you are defining and initializing a variable at the same time—you can see the meaning of the initialization value by the way the variable is used.

You can also define variables inside the control expressions of for loops and while loops, inside the conditional of an if statement, and inside the selector statement of a switch. Listing 3-22 shows on-the-fly variable definitions.

Listing 3-22. On-the-fly Variable Definitions

```
//: C03:OnTheFly.cpp
// On-the-fly variable definitions
#include <iostream>
using namespace std;

int main() {
  //..
  { // Begin a new scope
    int q = 0; // C requires definitions here
    //..
    // Define at point of use:
    for(int i = 0; i < 100; i++) {
      q++;      // q comes from a larger scope
```

```
        // Definition at the end of the scope:
        int p = 12;
      }
      int p = 1;   // A different p
  } // End scope containing q & outer p
  cout << "Type characters:" << endl;
  while(char c = cin.get() != 'q') {
    cout << c << " wasn't it" << endl;
    if(char x = c == 'a' || c == 'b')
      cout << "You typed a or b" << endl;
    else
      cout << "You typed " << x << endl;
  }
  cout << "Type A, B, or C" << endl;
  switch(int i = cin.get()) {
    case 'A': cout << "Snap" << endl; break;
    case 'B': cout << "Crackle" << endl; break;
    case 'C': cout << "Pop" << endl; break;
    default: cout << "Not A, B or C!" << endl;
  }
} ///:~
```

In the innermost scope, p is defined right before the scope ends, so it is really a useless gesture (*but it shows you can define a variable anywhere*). The p in the outer scope is in the same situation.

The definition of i in the control expression of the for loop is an example of being able to define a variable *exactly* at the point you need it (*you can do this only in* C++). The scope of i is the scope of the expression controlled by the for loop, so you can turn around and reuse i in the next for loop. This is a convenient and commonly-used idiom in C++; i is the classic name for a loop counter and you don't have to keep inventing new names.

Although the example also shows variables defined within while, if, and switch statements, this kind of definition is much less common than those in for expressions, possibly because the syntax is so constrained. For example, you cannot have any parentheses. That is, you cannot say

```
while((char c = cin.get()) != 'q')
```

The addition of the extra parentheses would seem like an innocent and useful thing to do, and because you cannot use them, the results are not what you might like. The problem occurs because != has a higher precedence than =, so the charc ends up containing a bool converted to char. When that's printed, on many terminals you'll see a smiley-face character.

In general, you can consider the ability to define variables within while, if, and switch statements as being there for completeness, but the only place you're likely to use this kind of variable definition is in a for loop (where you'll use it quite often).

Specifying Storage Allocation

When creating a variable, you have a number of options to specify the lifetime of the variable, how the storage is allocated for that variable, and how the variable is treated by the compiler.

Global Variables

Global variables are defined outside all function bodies and are available to all parts of the program (even code in other files). Global variables are unaffected by scopes and are always available (i.e., the lifetime of a global variable lasts until the program ends). If the existence of a global variable in one file is declared using the extern keyword in another file, the data is available for use by the second file. Listing 3-23 is an example of the use of global variables.

Listing 3-23. Using Global Variables

```
//: C03:Global.cpp
//{L} Global2
// Demonstration of global variables
#include <iostream>
using namespace std;

int globe;
void func();
int main() {
  globe = 12;
  cout << globe << endl;
  func(); // Modifies globe
  cout << globe << endl;
} ///:~
```

Listing 3-24 accesses globe as an extern.

Listing 3-24. Accessing Global Variables

```
//: C03:Global2.cpp {0}
// Accessing external global variables
extern int globe;
// (The linker resolves the reference)
void func() {
  globe = 47;
} ///:~
```

Storage for the variable globe is created by the definition in Global.cpp (Listing 3-23), and that same variable is accessed by the code in Global2.cpp (Listing 3-24). Since the code in Global2.cpp is compiled separately from the code in Global.cpp, the compiler must be informed that the variable exists elsewhere by the declaration

```
extern int globe;
```

When you run the program, you'll see that the call to func( ) does indeed affect the single global instance of globe.

In Global.cpp, you can see the special comment tag of

```
//{L} Global2
```

This says that to create the final program, the object file with the name Global2 must be linked in (there is no extension because the extension names of object files differ from one system to the next). In Global2.cpp, the first line has another special comment tag {0}, which says, "Don't try to create an executable out of this file; it's being compiled so that it can be linked into some other executable."

Local Variables

Local variables occur within a scope; they are "local" to a function. They are often called *automatic* variables because they automatically come into being when the scope is entered and automatically go away when the scope closes. The keyword auto makes this explicit, but local variables default to auto so it is never necessary to declare something as an auto.

Register Variables

A register variable is a type of local variable. The register keyword tells the compiler to make accesses to this variable as fast as possible. Increasing the access speed is implementation dependent, but, as the name suggests, it is often done by placing the variable in a register. There is no guarantee that the variable will be placed in a register or even that the access speed will increase. It is a hint to the compiler.

There are restrictions to the use of register variables. You cannot take or compute the address of a register variable. A register variable can be declared only within a block (you cannot have global or staticregister variables). You can, however, use a register variable as a formal argument in a function (i.e., in the argument list).

In general, you shouldn't try to second-guess the compiler's optimizer, since it will probably do a better job than you can. Thus, the register keyword is best avoided.

The static Keyword

The static keyword has several distinct meanings. Normally, variables defined as local to a function disappear at the end of the function scope. When you call the function again, storage for the variables is created anew and the values are reinitialized. If you want a value to be extant throughout the life of a program, you can define a function's local variable to be static and give it an initial value. The initialization is performed only the first time the function is called, and the data retains its value between function calls. This way, a function can "remember" some piece of information between function calls.

You may wonder why a global variable isn't used instead. The beauty of a static variable is that it is unavailable outside the scope of the function, so it can't be inadvertently changed. This localizes errors. Listing 3-25 shows the use of static variables.

Listing 3-25. Static Variables

```
//: C03:Static.cpp
// Using a static variable in a function
#include <iostream>
using namespace std;

void func() {
  static int i = 0;
  cout << "i = " << ++i << endl;
}

int main() {
  for(int x = 0; x < 10; x++)
    func();
} ///:~
```

Each time func( ) is called in the for loop, it prints a different value. If the keyword static is not used, the value printed will always be 1.

The second meaning of static is related to the first in the "unavailable outside a certain scope" sense. When static is applied to a function name or to a variable that is outside of all functions, it means, "This name is unavailable outside of this file." The function name or variable is local to the file; we say it has *file scope*. As a demonstration, compiling and linking Listings 3-26 and 3-27 will cause a linker error.

Listing 3-26. File Scope Demonstration

```
//: C03:FileStatic.cpp
// File scope demonstration. Compiling and
// linking this file with FileStatic2.cpp
// will cause a linker error

// File scope means only available in this file:
static int fs;

int main() {
  fs = 1;
} ///:~
```

Listing 3-27. More of the Demonstration

```
//: C03:FileStatic2.cpp {O}
// Trying to reference fs
extern int fs;
void func() {
  fs = 100;
} ///:~
```

Even though the variable fs is claimed to exist as an extern in Listing 3-27, the linker won't find it because it has been declared static in FileStatic.cpp (Listing 3-26).

The static specifier may also be used inside a class. This explanation will be delayed until you learn to create classes, which happens later in the book.

The extern Keyword

The extern keyword has already been briefly described and demonstrated. It tells the compiler that a variable or a function exists, even if the compiler hasn't yet seen it in the file currently being compiled. This variable or function may be defined in another file or further down in the current file. As an example of the latter, see Listing 3-28.

Listing 3-28. The extern Keyword

```
//: C03:Forward.cpp
// Forward function & data declarations
#include <iostream>
using namespace std;

// This is not actually external, but the
// compiler must be told it exists somewhere:
extern int i;
extern void func();
```

```
int main() {
  i = 0;
  func();
}
int i; // The data definition
void func() {
  i++;
  cout << i;
} ///:~
```

When the compiler encounters the declaration extern int i, it knows that the definition for i must exist somewhere as a global variable. When the compiler reaches the definition of i, no other declaration is visible, so it knows it has found the same i declared earlier in the file. If you were to define i as static, you would be telling the compiler that I is defined globally (via the extern), but it also has file scope (via the static), so the compiler will generate an error.

Linkage

To understand the behavior of C and C++ programs, you need to know about *linkage*. In an executing program, an identifier is represented by storage in memory that holds a variable or a compiled function body. Linkage describes this storage as it is seen by the linker. There are two types of linkage: internal linkage and external linkage.

Internal linkage means that storage is created to represent the identifier only for the file being compiled. Other files may use the same identifier name with internal linkage, or for a global variable, and no conflicts will be found by the linker—separate storage is created for each identifier. Internal linkage is specified by the keyword static in C and C++.

External linkage means that a single piece of storage is created to represent the identifier for all files being compiled. The storage is created once, and the linker must resolve all other references to that storage. Global variables and function names have external linkage. These are accessed from other files by declaring them with the keyword extern. Variables defined outside all functions (with the exception of const in C++) and function definitions default to external linkage. You can specifically force them to have internal linkage using the static keyword. You can explicitly state that an identifier has external linkage by defining it with the extern keyword. Defining a variable or function with extern is not necessary in C, but it is sometimes necessary for const in C++.

Automatic (local) variables exist only temporarily, on the stack, while a function is being called. The linker doesn't know about automatic variables, and so these have *no linkage*.

Constants

In old (pre-Standard) C, if you wanted to make a constant, you had to use the preprocessor, like so:

```
#define PI 3.14159
```

Everywhere you used PI, the value 3.14159 was substituted by the preprocessor (you can still use this method in C and C++).

When you use the preprocessor to create constants, you place control of those constants outside the scope of the compiler. No type checking is performed on the name PI and you can't take the address of PI (so you can't pass a pointer or a reference to PI). PI cannot be a variable of a user-defined type. The meaning of PI lasts from the point it is defined to the end of the file; the preprocessor doesn't recognize scoping.

C++ introduces the concept of a named constant that is just like a variable, except that its value cannot be changed. The modifier const tells the compiler that a name represents a constant. Any data type, built-in or user-defined, may be defined as const. If you define something as const and then attempt to modify it, the compiler will generate an error.

You must specify the type of a const, like this:

```
const int x = 10;
```

In Standard C and C++, you can use a named constant in an argument list, even if the argument it fills is a pointer or a reference (i.e., you can take the address of a const). A const has a scope, just like a regular variable, so you can "hide" a const inside a function and be sure that the name will not affect the rest of the program.

The const was taken from C++ and incorporated into Standard C, albeit quite differently. In C, the compiler treats a const just like a variable that has a special tag attached that says, "Don't change me." When you define a const in C, the compiler creates storage for it, so if you define more than one const with the same name in two different files (or put the definition in a header file), the linker will generate error messages about conflicts. The intended use of const in C is quite different from its intended use in C++ (in short, *it's nicer in C++*).

Constant Values

In C++, a const must always have an initialization value (in C, this is not true). Constant values for built-in types are expressed as decimal, octal, hexadecimal, or floating-point numbers (sadly, binary numbers were not considered important), or as characters.

In the absence of any other clues, the compiler assumes a constant value is a decimal number. The numbers 47, 0, and 1101 are all treated as decimal numbers.

A constant value with a leading 0 is treated as an octal number (base 8). Base 8 numbers can contain only digits 0–7; the compiler flags other digits as an error. A legitimate octal number is 017 (15 in base 10).

A constant value with a leading 0x is treated as a hexadecimal number (base 16). Base 16 numbers contain the digits 0–9 and a–f or A–F. A legitimate hexadecimal number is 0x1fe (510 in base 10).

Floating point numbers can contain decimal points and exponential powers (represented by e, which means "10 to the power of"). Both the decimal point and the e are optional. If you assign a constant to a floating-point variable, the compiler will take the constant value and convert it to a floating-point number (this process is one form of what's called *implicit type conversion*). However, it is a good idea to use either a decimal point or an e to remind the reader that you are using a floating-point number; some older compilers also need the hint.

Legitimate floating-point constant values are 1e4, 1.0001, 47.0, 0.0, and -1.159e-77. You can add suffixes to force the type of floating-point number: f or F forces a float and L or l forces a longdouble; otherwise the number will be a double.

Character constants are characters surrounded by single quotes, as: 'A', '0', ' '. Notice there is a big difference between the character '0' (ASCII 96) and the value 0. Special characters are represented with the backslash escape: '\n' (newline), '\t' (tab), '\\' (backslash), '\r' (carriage return), '\"' (double quotes), '\'' (single quote), etc. You can also express char constants in octal: '\17' or hexadecimal: '\xff'.

The volatile Qualifier

Whereas the qualifier const tells the compiler "This never changes" (which allows the compiler to perform extra optimizations), the qualifier volatile tells the compiler "You never know when this will change" and prevents the compiler from performing any optimizations based on the stability of that variable. Use this keyword when you read some value outside the control of your code, such as a register in a piece of communication hardware. A volatile variable is always read whenever its value is required, even if it was just read the line before.

A special case of some storage being "outside the control of your code" is in a multithreaded program. If you're watching a particular flag that is modified by another thread or process, that flag should be volatile so the compiler doesn't make the assumption that it can optimize away multiple reads of the flag.

Note that volatile may have no effect when a compiler is not optimizing, but may prevent critical bugs when you start optimizing the code (which is when the compiler will begin looking for redundant reads).

The const and volatile keywords will be further illuminated in a later chapter.

Operators and Their Use

This section covers all the operators in C and C++. All operators produce a value from their operands. This value is produced without modifying the operands, except with the assignment, increment, and decrement operators. Modifying an operand is called a *side effect*. The most common use for operators that modify their operands is to generate the side effect, but you should keep in mind that the value produced is available for your use just as in operators without side effects.

Assignment

Assignment is performed with the operator =. It means "Take the right-hand side (often called the rvalue) and copy it into the left-hand side (often called the lvalue)." An rvalue is any constant, variable, or expression that can produce a value, but an lvalue must be a distinct, named variable (that is, there must be a physical space in which to store data). For instance, you can assign a constant value to a variable (A = 4;), but you cannot assign anything to constant value—it cannot be an lvalue (you can't say 4 = A;).

Mathematical Operators

The basic mathematical operators are the same as the ones available in most programming languages: addition (+), subtraction (-), division (/), multiplication (*), and modulus (%; this produces the remainder from integer division). Integer division truncates the result (it doesn't round). The modulus operator cannot be used with floating point numbers.

C and C++ also use a shorthand notation to perform an operation and an assignment at the same time. This is denoted by an operator followed by an equal sign, and is consistent with all the operators in the language (whenever it makes sense). For example, to add 4 to the variable x and assign x to the result, you say: x += 4;.

Listing 3-29 shows the use of the mathematical operators.

Listing 3-29. Using Mathematical Operators

```
//: C03:Mathops.cpp
// Mathematical operators
#include <iostream>
using namespace std;

// A macro to display a string and a value.
#define PRINT(STR, VAR) \
  cout << STR " = " << VAR << endl

int main() {
  int i, j, k;
  float u, v, w;   // Applies to doubles, too
  cout << "enter an integer: ";
  cin >> j;
  cout << "enter another integer: ";
  cin >> k;
  PRINT("j",j);  PRINT("k",k);
  i = j + k; PRINT("j + k",i);
  i = j - k; PRINT("j - k",i);
  i = k / j; PRINT("k / j",i);
  i = k * j; PRINT("k * j",i);
  i = k % j; PRINT("k % j",i);
  // The following only works with integers:
  j %= k; PRINT("j %= k", j);
```

```
cout << "Enter a floating-point number: ";
cin >> v;
cout << "Enter another floating-point number:";
cin >> w;
PRINT("v",v); PRINT("w",w);
u = v + w; PRINT("v + w", u);
u = v - w; PRINT("v - w", u);
u = v * w; PRINT("v * w", u);
u = v / w; PRINT("v / w", u);
// The following works for ints, chars,
// and doubles too:
PRINT("u", u); PRINT("v", v);
u += v; PRINT("u += v", u);
u -= v; PRINT("u -= v", u);
u *= v; PRINT("u *= v", u);
u /= v; PRINT("u /= v", u);
} ///:~
```

The values of all the assignments can, of course, be much more complex.

Introduction to Preprocessor Macros

Notice the use of the macro PRINT( ) to save typing (*and typing errors!*). Preprocessor macros are traditionally named with all uppercase letters so they stand out. You'll learn later that macros can quickly become dangerous (and they can also be very useful).

The arguments in the parenthesized list following the macro name are substituted in all the code following the closing parenthesis. The preprocessor removes the name PRINT and substitutes the code wherever the macro is called, so the compiler cannot generate any error messages using the macro name, and it doesn't do any type checking on the arguments.

▓ Note   The latter can be beneficial, as shown in the debugging macros at the end of the chapter.

Relational Operators

Relational operators establish a relationship between the values of the operands. They produce a Boolean (specified with the bool keyword in C++) true if the relationship is true, and false if the relationship is false. The relational operators are less than (<), greater than (>), less than or equal to (<=), greater than or equal to (>=), equivalent (==), and not equivalent (!=). They may be used with all built-in data types in C and C++. They may be given special definitions for user-defined data types in C++.

▓ **Note**   You'll learn about this in Chapter 12, which covers operator overloading.

Logical Operators

The logical operators *and* (&&) and *or* (||) produce a true or false based on the logical relationship of its arguments. Remember that in C and C++, a statement is true if it has a non-zero value, and false if it has a value of zero. If you print a bool, you'll typically see a 1 for true and 0 for false.

Listing 3-30 uses the relational and logical operators.

Listing 3-30. Using Relational and Logical Operators

```
//: C03:Boolean.cpp
// Relational and logical operators.
#include <iostream>
using namespace std;

int main() {
  int i,j;
  cout << "Enter an integer: ";
  cin >> i;
  cout << "Enter another integer: ";
  cin >> j;
  cout << "i > j is " << (i > j) << endl;
  cout << "i < j is " << (i < j) << endl;

  cout << "i >= j is " << (i >= j) << endl;
  cout << "i <= j is " << (i <= j) << endl;
  cout << "i == j is " << (i == j) << endl;

  cout << "i != j is " << (i != j) << endl;
  cout << "i && j is " << (i && j) << endl;
  cout << "i || j is " << (i || j) << endl;

  cout << " (i < 10) && (j < 10) is "
  << ((i < 10) && (j < 10))  << endl;

} ///:~
```

You can replace the definition for int with float or double in Listing 3-30. Be aware, however, that the comparison of a floating point number with the value of zero is strict; a number that is the tiniest fraction different from another number is still "not equal." A floating point number that is the tiniest bit above zero is still true.

Bitwise Operators

The bitwise operators allow you to manipulate individual bits in a number (since floating point values use a special internal format, the bitwise operators work only with integral types: char, int and long). Bitwise operators perform Boolean algebra on the corresponding bits in the arguments to produce the result.

The bitwise *and* operator (&) produces a one in the output bit if both input bits are one; otherwise it produces a zero. The bitwise *or* operator (|) produces a one in the output bit if either input bit is a one and produces a zero only if both input bits are zero. The bitwise *exclusive or*, or *xor* (^) produces a one in the output bit if one or the other input bit is a one, but not both. The bitwise *not* (~, also called the *ones complement* operator) is a unary operator; it only takes one argument (all other bitwise operators are binary operators). Bitwise *not* produces the opposite of the input bit—a one if the input bit is zero, a zero if the input bit is one.

Bitwise operators can be combined with the = sign to unite the operation and assignment: &=, |=, and ^= are all legitimate operations (since ~ is a unary operator it cannot be combined with the= sign).

Shift Operators

The shift operators also manipulate bits. The left-shift operator (`<<`) produces the operand to the left of the operator shifted to the left by the number of bits specified after the operator. The right-shift operator (`>>`) produces the operand to the left of the operator shifted to the right by the number of bits specified after the operator. If the value after the shift operator is greater than the number of bits in the left-hand operand, the result is undefined. If the left-hand operand is unsigned, the right shift is a logical shift so the upper bits will be filled with zeros. If the left-hand operand is signed, the right shift may or may not be a logical shift (that is, the behavior is undefined).

Shifts can be combined with the equal sign (`<<=` and `>>=`). The lvalue is replaced by the lvalue shifted by the rvalue.

Listing 3-31 is an example that demonstrates the use of all the operators involving bits. First, there's a general-purpose function that prints a byte in binary format, created separately so that it may be easily reused. The header file declares the function.

Listing 3-31. All of the Operators Involving Bits

```
//: C03:printBinary.h
// Display a byte in binary
void printBinary(const unsigned char val);
///:~
```

```
//Here's the implementation of the function:
```

```
//: C03:printBinary.cpp {O}
#include <iostream>
void printBinary(const unsigned char val) {
  for(int i = 7; i >= 0; i--)
    if(val & (1 << i))
      std::cout << "1";
    else
      std::cout << "0";
} ///:~
```

The `printBinary( )` function takes a single byte and displays it bit-by-bit. The expression

```
(1 << i)
```

produces a one in each successive bit position; in binary: 00000001, 00000010, etc. If this bit is bitwise *and*ed with `val` and the result is nonzero, it means there was a one in that position in `val`.

Finally, the function is used in Listing 3-32, which shows the bit-manipulation operators.

Listing 3-32. Bit-Manipulation Operators

```
//: C03:Bitwise.cpp
//{L} printBinary
// Demonstration of bit manipulation
#include "printBinary.h"
#include <iostream>
using namespace std;

// A macro to save typing:
#define PR(STR, EXPR) \
  cout << STR; printBinary(EXPR); cout << endl;
```

```
int main() {
  unsigned int getval;
  unsigned char a, b;
  cout << "Enter a number between 0 and 255: ";
  cin >> getval; a = getval;
  PR("a in binary: ", a);
  cout << "Enter a number between 0 and 255: ";
  cin >> getval; b = getval;
  PR("b in binary: ", b);
  PR("a | b = ", a | b);
  PR("a & b = ", a & b);
  PR("a ^ b = ", a ^ b);
  PR("~a = ", ~a);
  PR("~b = ", ~b);
  // An interesting bit pattern:
  unsigned char c = 0x5A;
  PR("c in binary: ", c);
  a |= c;
  PR("a |= c; a = ", a);
  b &= c;
  PR("b &= c; b = ", b);
  b ^= a;
  PR("b ^= a; b = ", b);
} ///:~
```

Once again, a preprocessor macro is used to save typing. It prints the string of your choice, then the binary representation of an expression, then a newline.

In main( ), the variables are unsigned. This is because, in general, you don't want signs when you are working with bytes. An int must be used instead of a char for getval because the cin >> statement will otherwise treat the first digit as a character. By assigning getval to a and b, the value is converted to a single byte (by truncating it).

The << and >> provide bit-shifting behavior, but when they shift bits off the end of the number, those bits are lost (it's commonly said that they fall into the mythical *bit bucket*, a place where discarded bits end up, presumably so they can be reused…). When manipulating bits you can also perform *rotation*, which means that the bits that fall off one end are inserted back at the other end, as if they're being rotated around a loop. Even though most computer processors provide a machine-level rotate command (so you'll see it in the assembly language for that processor), there is no direct support for "rotate" in C or C++. Presumably the designers of C felt justified in leaving "rotate" off (aiming, as they said, for a minimal language) because you can build your own rotate command.

For example, Listing 3-33 shows functions to perform left and right rotations.

Listing 3-33. Rotations

```
//: C03:Rotation.cpp {O}

// Perform left and right rotations

unsigned char rol(unsigned char val) {
  int highbit;

  if(val & 0x80) // 0x80 is the high bit only
    highbit = 1;
  else
    highbit = 0;
```

```
  // Left shift (bottom bit becomes 0):
  val <<= 1;

  // Rotate the high bit onto the bottom:
  val |= highbit;
  return val;
}

unsigned char ror(unsigned char val) {
  int lowbit;
  if(val & 1) // Check the low bit
    lowbit = 1;
  else
    lowbit = 0;
  val >>= 1;   // Right shift by one position

  // Rotate the low bit onto the top:
  val |= (lowbit << 7);
  return val;
} ///:~
```

Try using these functions in Bitwise.cpp. Notice the definitions (or at least declarations) of rol( ) and ror( ) must be seen by the compiler in Bitwise.cpp before the functions are used.

The bitwise functions are generally extremely efficient to use because they translate directly into assembly language statements. Sometimes a single C or C++ statement will generate a single line of assembly code.

Unary Operators

Bitwise *not* isn't the only operator that takes a single argument. Its companion, the *logical not* (!), will take a true value and produce a false value. The unary minus (-) and unary plus (+) are the same operators as binary minus and plus; the compiler figures out which usage is intended by the way you write the expression. For instance, the statement

```
x = -a;
```

has an obvious meaning. The compiler can figure out

```
x = a * -b;
```

but the reader might get confused, so it is safer to say

```
x = a * (-b);
```

The unary minus produces the negative of the value. Unary plus provides symmetry with unary minus, although it doesn't actually do anything.

The increment and decrement operators (++ and --) were introduced earlier in this chapter. These are the only operators other than those involving assignment that have side effects. These operators increase or decrease the variable by one unit, although "unit" can have different meanings according to the data type—this is especially true with pointers.

The last unary operators are the address-of (&), dereference (* and ->), and cast operators in C and C++, and new and delete in C++. Address-of and dereference are used with pointers, described in this chapter. Casting is described later in this chapter, and new and delete are introduced in Chapter 4.

The Ternary Operator

The ternary if-else is unusual because it has three operands. It is truly an operator because it produces a value, unlike the ordinary if-else statement. It consists of three expressions: if the first expression (followed by a ?) evaluates to true, the expression following the ? is evaluated and its result becomes the value produced by the operator. If the first expression is false, the third expression (following a :) is executed and its result becomes the value produced by the operator.

The conditional operator can be used for its side effects or for the value it produces. Here's a code fragment that demonstrates both:

```
a = --b ? b : (b = -99);
```

Here, the conditional produces the rvalue. a is assigned to the value of b if the result of decrementing b is nonzero. If b became zero, a and b are both assigned to -99. b is always decremented, but it is assigned to -99 only if the decrement causes b to become 0. A similar statement can be used without the a = just for its side effects:

```
--b ? b : (b = -99);
```

Here the second B is superfluous, since the value produced by the operator is unused. An expression is required between the ? and :. In this case, the expression could simply be a constant that might make the code run a bit faster.

The Comma Operator

The comma is not restricted to separating variable names in multiple definitions, such as

```
int i, j, k;
```

Of course, it's also used in function argument lists. However, it can also be used as an operator to separate expressions—in this case, it produces only the value of the last expression. All the rest of the expressions in the comma-separated list are evaluated only for their side effects.

Listing 3-34 increments a list of variables and uses the last one as the rvalue.

Listing 3-34. Using the Comma Operator

```
//: C03:CommaOperator.cpp
#include <iostream>
using namespace std;

int main() {
  int a = 0, b = 1, c = 2, d = 3, e = 4;
  a = (b++, c++, d++, e++);
  cout << "a = " << a << endl;
  // The parentheses are critical here. Without
  // then, the statement will evaluate to:
  (a = b++), c++, d++, e++;
  cout << "a = " << a << endl;
} ///:~
```

In general, it's best to avoid using the comma as anything other than a separator since people are not used to seeing it as an operator.

Common Pitfalls when Using Operators

As illustrated above, one of the pitfalls when using operators is trying to get away without parentheses when you are even the least bit uncertain about how an expression will evaluate (consult your local C manual for the order of expression evaluation). Listing 3-35 shows another extremely common error.

Listing 3-35. Common Pitfall

```
//: C03:Pitfall.cpp
// Operator mistakes

int main() {
  int a = 1, b = 1;
  while(a = b) {
    // ....
  }
} ///:~
```

The statement a = b will always evaluate to true when b is non-zero. The variable a is assigned to the value of b, and the value of b is also produced by the operator =. In general, you want to use the equivalence operator == inside a conditional statement, not assignment. This one bites a lot of programmers (however, some compilers will point out the problem to you, which is helpful).

A similar problem is using bitwise *and* and *or* instead of their logical counterparts. Bitwise *and* and *or* use one of the characters (& or |), while logical *and* and *or* use two (&& and ||). Just as with = and ==, it's easy to just type one character instead of two. A useful mnemonic device is to observe that bits are smaller, so they don't need as many characters in their operators.

Casting Operators

The word *cast* is used in the sense of "casting into a mold." The compiler will automatically change one type of data into another if it makes sense. For instance, if you assign an integral value to a floating-point variable, the compiler will secretly call a function (or more probably, insert code) to convert the int to a float. Casting allows you to make this type conversion explicit, or to force it when it wouldn't normally happen.

To perform a cast, put the desired data type (including all modifiers) inside parentheses to the left of the value. This value can be a variable, a constant, the value produced by an expression, or the return value of a function. Listing 3-36 is an example.

Listing 3-36. Simple Cast

```
//: C03:SimpleCast.cpp
int main() {
  int b = 200;
  unsigned long a = (unsigned long int)b;
} ///:~
```

Casting is powerful, but it can cause headaches because in some situations it forces the compiler to treat data as if it were (for instance) larger than it really is, so it will occupy more space in memory; this can trample over other data. This usually occurs when casting pointers, not when making simple casts like the one In Listing 3-36.

C++ has an additional casting syntax, which follows the function call syntax. This syntax puts the parentheses around the argument, like a function call, rather than around the data type; see Listing 3-37.

Listing 3-37. Function Call Cast

```
//: C03:FunctionCallCast.cpp
int main() {
  float a = float(200);
  // This is equivalent to:
  float b = (float)200;
} ///:~
```

Of course, in this case you wouldn't really need a cast; you could just say 200.f or 200.0f (in effect, that's typically what the compiler will do for the above expression). Casts are usually used with variables, rather than with constants.

C++ Explicit Casts

Casts should be used carefully because what you are actually doing is saying to the compiler "Forget type checking—treat it as this other type instead." That is, you're introducing a hole in the C++ type system and preventing the compiler from telling you that you're doing something wrong with a type. What's worse, the compiler believes you implicitly and doesn't perform any other checking to catch errors. Once you start casting, you open yourself up for all kinds of problems. In fact, any program that uses a lot of casts should be viewed with suspicion, no matter how much you are told it simply "must" be done that way. In general, casts should be few and isolated to the solution of very specific problems.

Once you understand this and are presented with a buggy program, your first inclination may be to look for casts as culprits. But how do you locate C-style casts? They are simply type names inside of parentheses, and if you start hunting for such things you'll discover that it's often hard to distinguish them from the rest of your code.

Standard C++ includes an explicit cast syntax that can be used to completely replace the old C-style casts (of course, C-style casts cannot be outlawed without breaking code, but compiler writers could easily flag old-style casts for you). The explicit cast syntax is such that you can easily find them, as you can see by their names in Table 3-2.

Table 3-2. *C++ Explicit Cast Syntax*

static_cast	For "well-behaved" and "reasonably well-behaved" casts, including things you might now do without a cast (such as an automatic type conversion).
const_cast	To cast away const and/or volatile.
reinterpret_cast	To cast to a completely different meaning. The key is that you'll need to cast back to the original type to use it safely. The type you cast to is typically used only for bit twiddling or some other mysterious purpose. This is the most dangerous of all the casts.
dynamic_cast	For type-safe downcasting.

The first three explicit casts will be described more completely in the following sections, while the last one can be demonstrated only after you've learned a bit more, such as in Chapter 15.

Using static_cast

A static_cast is used for all conversions that are well-defined. These include "safe" conversions that the compiler would allow you to do without a cast and less-safe conversions that are nonetheless well-defined. The types of conversions covered by static_cast include typical castless conversions, narrowing (information-losing) conversions, forcing a conversion from a void*, implicit type conversions, and static navigation of class hierarchies. See Listing 3-38 for an example.

Listing 3-38. Using static_cast

```
//: C03:static_cast.cpp
void func(int) {}

int main() {
  int i = 0x7fff;            // Max pos value = 32767
  long l;
  float f;
  // (1) Typical castless conversions:
  l = i;
  f = i;
  // Also works:
  l = static_cast<long>(i);
  f = static_cast<float>(i);

  // (2) Narrowing conversions:
  i = l;                      // May lose digits
  i = f;                      // May lose info
  // Says "I know," eliminates warnings:
  i = static_cast<int>(l);
  i = static_cast<int>(f);
  char c = static_cast<char>(i);

  // (3) Forcing a conversion from void* :
  void* vp = &i;
  // Old way produces a dangerous conversion:
  float* fp = (float*)vp;
  // The new way is equally dangerous:
  fp = static_cast<float*>(vp);

  // (4) Implicit type conversions, normally
  // performed by the compiler:
  double d = 0.0;
  int x = d;                 // Automatic type conversion
  x = static_cast<int>(d);   // More explicit
  func(d);                   // Automatic type conversion
  func(static_cast<int>(d)); // More explicit
} ///:~
```

In Section (1), you see the kinds of conversions you're used to doing in C, with or without a cast. Promoting from an int to a long or float is not a problem because the latter can always hold every value that an int can contain. Although it's unnecessary, you can use static_cast to highlight these promotions.

Converting back the other way is shown in (2). Here, you can lose data because an int is not as "wide" as a long or a float; it won't hold numbers of the same size. Thus these are called *narrowing conversions*. The compiler will still perform these, but will often give you a warning. You can eliminate this warning and indicate that you really did mean to use a cast.

Assigning from a void* is not allowed without a cast in C++ (unlike C), as seen in (3). This is dangerous and requires that programmers know what they're doing. The static_cast, at least, is easier to locate than the old standard cast when you're hunting for bugs.

Section (4) of the program shows the kinds of implicit type conversions that are normally performed automatically by the compiler. These are automatic and require no casting, but again static_cast highlights the action in case you want to make it clear what's happening or hunt for it later.

Using const_cast

If you want to convert from a const to a non-const or from a volatile to a non-volatile, you use const_cast. This is the *only* conversion allowed with const_cast; if any other conversion is involved, it must be done using a separate expression or you'll get a compile time error; see Listing 3-39.

Listing 3-39. Using const_cast

```
//: C03:const_cast.cpp
int main() {
  const int i = 0;
  int* j = (int*)&i;              // Deprecated form
  j = const_cast<int*>(&i);       // Preferred
  // Can't do simultaneous additional casting:
//! long* l = const_cast<long*>(&i); // Error
  volatile int k = 0;
  int* u = const_cast<int*>(&k);
} ///:~
```

If you take the address of a const object, you produce a pointer to a const, and this cannot be assigned to a non-const pointer without a cast. The old-style cast will accomplish this, but the const_cast is the appropriate one to use. The same holds true for volatile.

Using reinterpret_cast

This is the least safe of the casting mechanisms, and the one most likely to produce bugs. A reinterpret_cast pretends that an object is just a bit pattern that can be treated (for some dark purpose) as if it were an entirely different type of object. This is the low-level bit twiddling that C is notorious for. You'll virtually always need to reinterpret_cast back to the original type (or otherwise treat the variable as its original type) before doing anything else with it; see Listing 3-40.

Listing 3-40. Using reinterpret_cast

```
//: C03:reinterpret_cast.cpp
#include <iostream>
using namespace std;
const int sz = 100;

struct X { int a[sz]; };
```

```
void print(X* x) {
  for(int i = 0; i < sz; i++)
    cout << x->a[i] << ' ';
  cout << endl << "--------------------" << endl;
}

int main() {
  X x;
  print(&x);
  int* xp = reinterpret_cast<int*>(&x);
  for(int* i = xp; i < xp + sz; i++)
    *i = 0;
  // Can't use xp as an X* at this point
  // unless you cast it back:
  print(reinterpret_cast<X*>(xp));
  // In this example, you can also just use
  // the original identifier:
  print(&x);
} ///:~
```

In this simple example, struct X just contains an array of int, but when you create one on the stack as in X x, the values of each of the ints are garbage (this is shown using ( ) function to display the contents of the struct). To initialize them, the address of the X is taken and cast to an int pointer, which is then walked through the array to set each int to zero. Notice how the upper bound for i is calculated by "adding" sz to xp; the compiler knows that you actually want sz pointer locations greater than xp and it does the correct pointer arithmetic for you.

The idea of reinterpret_cast is that when you use it, what you get is so foreign that it cannot be used for the type's original purpose unless you cast it back. Here, you see the cast back to an X* in the call to print, but of course since you still have the original identifier you can also use that. But the xp is only useful as an int*, which is truly a "reinterpretation" of the original X.

A reinterpret_cast often indicates inadvisable and/or nonportable programming, but it's available when you decide you have to use it.

sizeof—An Operator by Itself

The sizeof operator stands alone because it satisfies an unusual need. sizeof gives you information about the amount of memory allocated for data items. As described earlier in this chapter, sizeof tells you the number of bytes used by any particular variable. It can also give the size of a data type (with no variable name); see Listing 3-41.

Listing 3-41. Using sizeof

```
//: C03:sizeof.cpp
#include <iostream>
using namespace std;
int main() {
  cout << "sizeof(double) = " << sizeof(double);
  cout << ", sizeof(char) = " << sizeof(char);
} ///:~
```

By definition, the sizeof any type of char (signed, unsigned, or *plain*) is always 1, regardless of whether the underlying storage for a char is actually 1 byte. For all other types, the result is the size in bytes.

Note that sizeof is an operator, not a function. If you apply it to a type, it must be used with the parenthesized form shown above, but if you apply it to a variable, you can use it without parentheses; see Listing 3-42.

Listing 3-42. Using sizeof with a Variable

```
//: C03:sizeofOperator.cpp
int main() {
  int x;
  int i = sizeof x;
} ///:~
```

sizeof can also give you the sizes of user-defined data types. This is used later in the book.

The asm Keyword

The asm keyword is an escape mechanism that allows you to write assembly code for your hardware within a C++ program. Often you're able to reference C++ variables within the assembly code, which means you can easily communicate with your C++ code and limit the assembly code to that necessary for efficiency tuning or to use special processor instructions. The exact syntax that you must use when writing the assembly language is compiler-dependent and can be found in your compiler's documentation.

Explicit Operators

Explicit operators are keywords for bitwise and logical operators. Programmers without keyboard characters like &, |, ^, and so on, were forced to use C's horrible *trigraphs*, which were not only annoying to type, but obscure when reading. This is repaired in C++ with additional keywords shown in Table 3-3.

Table 3-3. *C++ (Additional) Keywords*

Keyword	Meaning
and	&& (logical *and*)
or	|| (logical *or*)
not	! (logical NOT)
not_eq	!= (logical not-equivalent)
bitand	& (bitwise *and*)
and_eq	&= (bitwise *and*-assignment)
bitor	| (bitwise *or*)
or_eq	|= (bitwise or-assignment)
xor	^ (bitwise exclusive-or)
xor_eq	^= (bitwise exclusive-or-assignment)
compl	~ (ones complement)

If your compiler complies with Standard C++, it will support these keywords.

Composite Type Creation

The fundamental data types and their variations are essential, but rather primitive. C and C++ provide tools that allow you to compose more sophisticated data types from the fundamental data types. As you'll see, the most important of these is `struct`, which is the foundation for `class` in C++. However, the simplest way to create more sophisticated types is simply to alias a name to another name via `typedef`.

Aliasing Names with typedef

This keyword promises more than it delivers: `typedef` suggests "type definition" when "alias" would probably have been a more accurate description, since that's what it really does. Here's the syntax:

```
typedef existing-type-description alias-name
```

People often use `typedef` when data types get slightly complicated, just to prevent extra keystrokes. Here is a commonly-used `typedef`:

```
typedef unsigned long ulong;
```

Now if you say `ulong` the compiler knows that you mean `unsigned long`. You might think that this could as easily be accomplished using preprocessor substitution, but there are key situations in which the compiler must be aware that you're treating a name as if it were a type, so `typedef` is essential.

One place where `typedef` comes in handy is for pointer types. As previously mentioned, if you say

```
int* x, y;
```

this actually produces an `int*`, which is `x`, and an `int` (*not an* `int*`), which is `y`. That is, the `*` binds to the right, not the left. However, if you use a `typedef`

```
typedef int* IntPtr;
IntPtr x, y;
```

then both `x` and `y` are of type `int*`.

You can argue that it's more explicit and therefore more readable to avoid `typedef`s for primitive types, and indeed programs rapidly become difficult to read when many `typedef`s are used. However, `typedef`s become especially important in C when used with `struct`.

Combining Variables with struct

A `struct` is a way to collect a group of variables into a structure. Once you create a `struct`, then you can make many instances of this "new" type of variable you've invented. For an example, see Listing 3-43.

Listing 3-43. A Simple struct

```
//: C03:SimpleStruct.cpp
struct Structure1 {
  char c;
  int i;
  float f;
  double d;
};
```

```
int main() {
  struct Structure1 s1, s2;
  s1.c = 'a'; // Select an element using a '.'
  s1.i = 1;
  s1.f = 3.14;
  s1.d = 0.00093;
  s2.c = 'a';
  s2.i = 1;
  s2.f = 3.14;
  s2.d = 0.00093;
} ///:~
```

The struct declaration must end with a semicolon. In main( ), two instances of Structure1 are created: s1 and s2. Each of these has their own separate versions of c, i, f, and d. So s1 and s2 represent clumps of completely independent variables. To select one of the elements within s1 or s2, you use a ., syntax you've seen in the previous chapter when using C++ class objects; since classes evolved from structs, this is where that syntax arose from.

One thing you'll notice is the awkwardness of the use of Structure1 (as it turns out, this is only required by C, not C++). In C, you can't just say Structure1 when you're defining variables, you must say struct Structure1. This is where typedef becomes especially handy in C; see Listing 3-44.

Listing 3-44. Another Simple struct

```
//: C03:SimpleStruct2.cpp
// Using typedef with struct
typedef struct {
  char c;
  int i;
  float f;
  double d;
} Structure2;

int main() {
  Structure2 s1, s2;
  s1.c = 'a';
  s1.i = 1;
  s1.f = 3.14;
  s1.d = 0.00093;
  s2.c = 'a';
  s2.i = 1;
  s2.f = 3.14;
  s2.d = 0.00093;
} ///:~
```

By using typedef in this way, you can pretend (in C; try removing the typedef for C++) that Structure2 is a built-in type, like into float, when you define s1 and s2 (but notice it only has data—characteristics—and does not include behavior, which is what we get with real objects in C++). You'll notice that the struct identifier has been left off at the beginning because the goal is to create the typedef. However, there are times when you might need to refer to the struct during its definition. In those cases, you can actually repeat the name of the struct as the struct name and as the typedef.

Listing 3-45. Allowing a struct to Refer to Itself

```
//: C03:SelfReferential.cpp
// Allowing a struct to refer to itself

typedef struct SelfReferential {
  int i;
  SelfReferential* sr; // Head spinning yet?
} SelfReferential;

int main() {
  SelfReferential sr1, sr2;
  sr1.sr = &sr2;
  sr2.sr = &sr1;
  sr1.i = 47;
  sr2.i = 1024;
} ///:~
```

If you look at this for a while, you'll see that sr1 and sr2 point to each other, as well as each holding a piece of data.

Actually, the struct name does not have to be the same as the typedef name, but it is usually done this way as it tends to keep things simpler.

Pointers and structs

In the examples above, all the structs are manipulated as objects. However, like any piece of storage, you can take the address of a struct object (as seen in SelfReferential.cpp). To select the elements of a particular struct object, you use a ., as seen above. However, if you have a pointer to a struct object, you must select an element of that object using a different operator, the ->, as shown in Listing 3-46.

Listing 3-46. Using Pointers to structs

```
//: C03:SimpleStruct3.cpp
// Using pointers to structs
typedef struct Structure3 {
  char c;
  int i;
  float f;
  double d;
} Structure3;

int main() {
  Structure3 s1, s2;
  Structure3* sp = &s1;
  sp->c = 'a';
  sp->i = 1;
  sp->f = 3.14;
  sp->d = 0.00093;
  sp = &s2; // Point to a different struct object
  sp->c = 'a';
  sp->i = 1;
  sp->f = 3.14;
  sp->d = 0.00093;
} ///:~
```

In main( ), the struct pointer sp is initially pointing to s1, and the members of s1 are initialized by selecting them with the -> (and you use this same operator in order to read those members). But then sp is pointed to s2, and those variables are initialized the same way. So you can see that another benefit of pointers is that they can be dynamically redirected to point to different objects; this provides more flexibility in your programming, as you will learn.

For now, that's all you need to know about structs, but you'll become much more comfortable with them (and especially their more potent successors, classes) as the book progresses.

Clarifying Programs with enum

An enumerated data type is a way of attaching names to numbers, thereby giving more meaning to anyone reading the code. The enum keyword (from C) automatically enumerates any list of identifiers you give it by assigning them values of 0, 1, 2, etc. You can declare enum variables (which are always represented as integral values). The declaration of an enum looks similar to a struct declaration. An enumerated data type is useful when you want to keep track of some sort of feature, as shown in Listing 3-47.

Listing 3-47. Using enum

```
//: C03:Enum.cpp
// Keeping track of shapes

enum ShapeType {
  circle,
  square,
  rectangle
};  // Must end with a semicolon like a struct

int main() {
  ShapeType shape = circle;
  // Activities here....
  // Now do something based on what the shape is:
  switch(shape) {
    case circle:     /* circle stuff    */ break;
    case square:     /* square stuff    */ break;
    case rectangle:  /* rectangle stuff */ break;
  }
} ///:~
```

shape is a variable of the ShapeType enumerated data type, and its value is compared with the value in the enumeration. Since shape is really just an int, however, it can be any value an int can hold (including a negative number). You can also compare an int variable with a value in the enumeration.

You should be aware that the example in Listing 3-47 of switching on type turns out to be a problematic way to program. C++ has a much better way to code this sort of thing, the explanation of which must be delayed until much later in the book.

If you don't like the way the compiler assigns values, you can do it yourself, like this:

```
enum ShapeType {
  circle = 10, square = 20, rectangle = 50
};
```

If you give values to some names and not to others, the compiler will use the next integral value. For example, with

```
enum snap { crackle = 25, pop };
```

the compiler gives pop the value 26.

You can see how much more readable the code is when you use enumerated data types. However, to some degree this is still an attempt (in C) to accomplish the things that you can do with a class in C++, so you'll see enum used less in C++.

Type Checking for Enumerations

C's enumerations are fairly primitive, simply associating integral values with names, but they provide no type checking. In C++, as you may have come to expect by now, the concept of type is fundamental, and this is true with enumerations. When you create a named enumeration, you effectively create a new type, just as you do with a class; the name of your enumeration becomes a reserved word for the duration of that translation unit.

In addition, there's stricter type checking for enumerations in C++ than in C. You'll notice this in particular if you have an instance of an enumeration color called a. In C, you can say a++, but in C++, you can't. This is because incrementing an enumeration is performing two type conversions, one of them legal in C++ and one of them illegal. First, the value of the enumeration is implicitly cast from a color to an int, then the value is incremented, then the int is cast back into a color. In C++, this isn't allowed because color is a distinct type and not equivalent to an int. This makes sense because how do you know the increment of blue will even be in the list of colors? If you want to increment a color, then it should be a class (with an increment operation) and not an enum, because the class can be made to be much safer. Any time you write code that assumes an implicit conversion to an enum type, the compiler will flag this inherently dangerous activity.

Unions (described next) have similar additional type checking in C++.

Saving Memory with union

Sometimes a program will handle different types of data using the same variable. In this situation, you have two choices: you can create a struct containing all the possible different types you might need to store, or you can use a union. A union piles all the data into a single space; it figures out the amount of space necessary for the largest item you've put in the union, and makes that the size of the union. Use a union to save memory.

Anytime you place a value in a union, the value always starts in the same place at the beginning of the union, but only uses as much space as is necessary. Thus, you create a "super-variable" capable of holding any of the union variables. All the addresses of the union variables are the same (in a class or struct, the addresses are different).

Listing 3-48 is a simple use of a union. Try removing various elements and see what effect it has on the size of the union. Notice that it makes no sense to declare more than one instance of a single data type in a union (unless you're just doing it to use a different name).

Listing 3-48. The Size and Simple Use of a union

```
//: C03:Union.cpp
// The size and simple use of a union
#include <iostream>
using namespace std;

union Packed { // Declaration similar to a class
  char i;
  short j;
  int k;
  long l;
```

```
    float f;
    double d;
    // The union will be the size of a
    // double, since that's the largest element
};  // Semicolon ends a union, like a struct

int main() {
  cout << "sizeof(Packed) = "
       << sizeof(Packed) << endl;
  Packed x;
  x.i = 'c';
  cout << x.i << endl;
  x.d = 3.14159;
  cout << x.d << endl;
} ///:~
```

The compiler performs the proper assignment according to the union member you select.

Once you perform an assignment, the compiler doesn't care what you do with the union. In the example above, you could assign a floating-point value to x, like

```
x.f = 2.222;
```

and then send it to the output as if it were an int, like

```
cout << x.i;
```

This would produce garbage.

Using Arrays

Arrays are a kind of composite type because they allow you to clump a lot of variables together, one right after the other, under a single identifier name. If you say

```
int a[10];
```

you create storage for 10 int variables stacked on top of each other, but without unique identifier names for each variable. Instead, they are all lumped under the name a.

To access one of these *array elements*, you use the same square-bracket syntax that you use to define an array, like so:

```
a[5] = 47;
```

However, you must remember that even though the size of a is 10, you select array elements starting at zero (this is sometimes called *zero indexing*), so you can select only the array elements 0–9, as shown in Listing 3-49.

Listing 3-49. Arrays

```
//: C03:Arrays.cpp
#include <iostream>
using namespace std;
```

```
int main() {
  int a[10];
  for(int i = 0; i < 10; i++) {
    a[i] = i * 10;
    cout << "a[" << i << "] = " << a[i] << endl;
  }
} ///:~
```

Array access is extremely fast. However, if you index past the end of the array, there is no safety net—you'll step on other variables. The other drawback is that you must define the size of the array at compile time; if you want to change the size at runtime you can't do it with the syntax above (C does have a way to create an array dynamically, but it's significantly messier). The C++ vector, introduced in the previous chapter, provides an array-like object that automatically resizes itself, so it is usually a much better solution if your array size cannot be known at compile time.

You can make an array of any type, even of structs, as shown in Listing 3-50.

Listing 3-50. An Array of structs

```
//: C03:StructArray.cpp
// An array of struct

typedef struct {

  int i, j, k;
}
ThreeDpoint;

int main() {

  ThreeDpoint p[10];

  for(int i = 0; i < 10; i++) {

      p[i].i = i + 1;
      p[i].j = i + 2;
      p[i].k = i + 3;
  }
} ///:~
```

Notice how the struct identifier i is independent of the for loop's i.

To see that each element of an array is contiguous with the next, you can print out the addresses, as shown in Listing 3-51.

Listing 3-51. Array Addresses

```
//: C03:ArrayAddresses.cpp
#include <iostream>
using namespace std;

int main() {
  int a[10];
  cout << "sizeof(int) = " << sizeof(int) << endl;
```

```
  for(int i = 0; i < 10; i++)
    cout << "&a[" << i << "] = "
         << (long)&a[i] << endl;
} ///:~
```

When you run this program, you'll see that each element is one int size away from the previous one. That is, they are stacked one on top of the other.

Pointers and Arrays

The identifier of an array is unlike the identifiers for ordinary variables. For one thing, an array identifier is not an lvalue; you cannot assign to it. It's really just a hook into the square-bracket syntax, and when you give the name of an array, without square brackets, what you get is the starting address of the array; see Listing 3-52.

Listing 3-52. Array Identifier

```
//: C03:ArrayIdentifier.cpp

#include <iostream>

using namespace std;

int main() {

  int a[10];
  cout << "a = " << a << endl;
  cout << "&a[0] =" <<&a[0] << endl;
} ///:~
```

When you run this program you'll see that the two addresses (which will be printed in hexadecimal, since there is no cast to long) are the same.

So one way to look at the array identifier is as a read-only pointer to the beginning of an array; and, although you can't change the array identifier to point somewhere else, you *can* create another pointer and use that to move around in the array.

In fact, the square-bracket syntax works with regular pointers as well, as you can see in Listing 3-53.

Listing 3-53. Square-Bracket Syntax

```
//: C03:PointersAndBrackets.cpp
int main() {
  int a[10];
  int* ip = a;
  for(int i = 0; i < 10; i++)
    ip[i] = i * 10;
} ///:~
```

The fact that naming an array produces its starting address turns out to be quite important when you want to pass an array to a function. If you declare an array as a function argument, what you're really declaring is a pointer. So in Listing 3-54, func1( )*and* func2( ) effectively have the same argument lists.

Listing 3-54. Array Arguments

```
//: C03:ArrayArguments.cpp
#include <iostream>
#include <string>
using namespace std;

void func1(int a[], int size) {
  for(int i = 0; i < size; i++)
    a[i] = i * i - i;
}

void func2(int* a, int size) {
  for(int i = 0; i < size; i++)
    a[i] = i * i + i;
}

void print(int a[], string name, int size) {
  for(int i = 0; i < size; i++)
    cout << name << "[" << i << "] = "
         << a[i] << endl;
}

int main() {
  int a[5], b[5];
  // Probably garbage values:
  print(a, "a", 5);
  print(b, "b", 5);
  // Initialize the arrays:
  func1(a, 5);
  func1(b, 5);
  print(a, "a", 5);
  print(b, "b", 5);
  // Notice the arrays are always modified:
  func2(a, 5);
  func2(b, 5);
  print(a, "a", 5);
  print(b, "b", 5);
} ///:~
```

Even though func1( ) and func2( ) declare their arguments differently, the usage is the same inside the function. There are some other issues that this example reveals: arrays cannot be passed by value; that is, you never automatically get a local copy of the array that you pass into a function. Thus, when you modify an array, you're always modifying the outside object. This can be a bit confusing at first, if you're expecting the pass-by-value provided with ordinary arguments.

You'll notice that print( ) uses the square-bracket syntax for array arguments. Even though the pointer syntax and the square-bracket syntax are effectively the same when passing arrays as arguments, the square-bracket syntax makes it clearer to the reader that you mean for this argument to be an array.

Also note that the size argument is passed in each case. Just passing the address of an array isn't enough information; you must always be able to know how big the array is inside your function, so you don't run off the end of that array.

Arrays can be of any type, including arrays of pointers. In fact, when you want to pass command-line arguments into your program, C and C++ have a special argument list for main( ), which looks like this:

```
int main(int argc, char* argv[]) { // ...
```

The first argument is the number of elements in the array, which is the second argument. The second argument is always an array of char* because the arguments are passed from the command line as character arrays (and remember, an array can be passed only as a pointer). Each whitespace-delimited cluster of characters on the command line is turned into a separate array argument.

Listing 3-55 prints out all its command-line arguments by stepping through the array.

Listing 3-55. Command-Line Arguments

```
//: C03:CommandLineArgs.cpp
#include <iostream>
using namespace std;

int main(int argc, char* argv[]) {
  cout << "argc = " << argc << endl;
  for(int i = 0; i < argc; i++)
    cout << "argv[" << i << "] = "
<< argv[i] << endl;
} ///:~
```

You'll notice that argv[0] is the path and name of the program itself. This allows the program to discover information about itself. It also adds one more to the array of program arguments, so a common error when fetching command-line arguments is to grab argv[0] when you want argv[1].

You are not forced to use argc and argv as identifiers in main( ); those identifiers are only conventions (but it will confuse people if you don't use them). Also, there is an alternate way to declare argv:

```
int main(int argc, char** argv) { // ...
```

Both forms are equivalent, but I find the version used in this book to be the most intuitive when reading the code, since it says, directly, "This is an array of character pointers."

All you get from the command-line is character arrays; if you want to treat an argument as some other type, you are responsible for converting it inside your program. To facilitate the conversion to numbers, there are some helper functions in the Standard C Library, declared in <cstdlib>. The simplest ones to use are atoi( ), atol( ), and atof( ) to convert an ASCII character array to an int, long, and double floating-point value, respectively. Listing 3-56 uses atoi( ); the other two functions are called the same way.

Listing 3-56. Using atoi( )

```
//: C03:ArgsToInts.cpp
// Converting command-line arguments to ints
#include <iostream>
#include <cstdlib>
using namespace std;

int main(int argc, char* argv[]) {
  for(int i = 1; i < argc; i++)
    cout << atoi(argv[i]) << endl;
} ///:~
```

In this program, you can put any number of arguments on the command line. You'll notice that the for loop starts at the value 1 to skip over the program name at argv[0]. Also, if you put a floating-point number containing a decimal point on the command line, atoi( ) takes only the digits up to the decimal point. If you put non-numbers on the command line, these come back from atoi( ) as zero.

Exploring Floating-Point Format

The printBinary( ) function introduced earlier in this chapter is handy for delving into the internal structure of various data types. The most interesting of these is the floating-point format that allows C and C++ to store numbers representing very large and very small values in a limited amount of space. Although the details can't be completely exposed here, the bits inside of floats and doubles are divided into three regions: the exponent, the mantissa, and the sign bit; thus it stores the values using scientific notation. Listing 3-57 allows you to play around by printing out the binary patterns of various floating point numbers so you can deduce for yourself the scheme used in your compiler's floating point format (usually this is the IEEE standard for floating point numbers, but your compiler may not follow that).

Listing 3-57. Floating As Binary

```
//: C03:FloatingAsBinary.cpp

//{L} printBinary

//{T} 3.14159

#include "printBinary.h"
#include <cstdlib>
#include <iostream>

using namespace std;

int main(int argc, char* argv[]) {
  if(argc != 2) {
    cout << "Must provide a number" << endl;
    exit(1);
  }
  double d = atof(argv[1]);
  unsigned char* cp =
    reinterpret_cast<unsigned char*> (&d);
  for(int i = sizeof(double)-1; i >= 0 ; i -= 2) {
    printBinary(cp[i-1]);
    printBinary(cp[i]);
  }
} ///:~
```

First, the program guarantees that you've given it an argument by checking the value of argc, which is two if there's a single argument (it's one if there are no arguments, since the program name is always the first element of argv). If this fails, a message is printed and the Standard C Library function exit( ) is called to terminate the program.

The program grabs the argument from the command line and converts the characters to a double using atof( ). Then the double is treated as an array of bytes by taking the address and casting it to an unsigned char*. Each of these bytes is passed to printBinary( ) for display.

This example has been set up to print the bytes in an order such that the sign bit appears first—on my machine; yours may be different, so you might want to rearrange the way things are printed. You should also be aware that floating point formats are not trivial to understand; for example, the exponent and mantissa are not generally arranged on byte boundaries, but instead a number of bits are reserved for each one and they are packed into the memory as tightly as possible. To truly see what's going on, you'd need to find out the size of each part of the number (sign bits are always one bit, but exponents and mantissas are of differing sizes) and print out the bits in each part separately.

Pointer Arithmetic

If all you could do with a pointer that points at an array is treat it as if it were an alias for that array, pointers into arrays wouldn't be very interesting. However, pointers are more flexible than this, since they can be modified to point somewhere else (but remember, *the array identifier cannot be modified to point somewhere else*).

Pointer arithmetic refers to the application of some of the arithmetic operators to pointers. The reason pointer arithmetic is a separate subject from ordinary arithmetic is that pointers must conform to special constraints in order to make them behave properly. For example, a common operator to use with pointers is ++, which adds one to the pointer. What this actually means is that the pointer is changed to move to "the next value," whatever that means. See Listing 3-58 for an example.

Listing 3-58. Pointer Increment

```
//: C03:PointerIncrement.cpp
#include <iostream>
using namespace std;

int main() {
  int i[10];
  double d[10];
  int* ip = i;
  double* dp = d;
  cout << "ip = " << (long)ip << endl;
  ip++;
  cout << "ip = " << (long)ip << endl;
  cout << "dp = " << (long)dp << endl;
  dp++;
  cout << "dp = " << (long)dp << endl;
} ///:~
```

For one run on a computer, the output is

```
ip = 6684124
ip = 6684128
dp = 6684044
dp = 6684052
```

What's interesting here is that even though the operation ++ appears to be the same operation for both the int* and the double*, you can see that the pointer has been changed only 4 bytes for the int* but 8 bytes for the double*. Not coincidentally, these are the sizes of int and double on my machine. And that's the trick of pointer arithmetic: the compiler figures out the right amount to change the pointer so that it's pointing to the next element in the array (*pointer arithmetic is only meaningful within arrays*). This even works with arrays of structs, as you can see in Listing 3-59.

Listing 3-59. Pointer Increment and an Array of structs

```
//: C03:PointerIncrement2.cpp
#include <iostream>
using namespace std;

typedef struct {
  char c;
  short s;
  int i;
  long l;
  float f;
  double d;
  long double ld;
} Primitives;

int main() {
  Primitives p[10];
  Primitives* pp = p;
  cout << "sizeof(Primitives) = "
       << sizeof(Primitives) << endl;
  cout << "pp = " << (long)pp << endl;
  pp++;
  cout << "pp = " << (long)pp << endl;
} ///:~
```

The output for one run on a computer is

```
sizeof(Primitives) = 40
pp = 6683764
pp = 6683804
```

So you can see the compiler also does the right thing for pointers to structs (and classes and unions).

Pointer arithmetic also works with the operators --, +, and -, but the latter two operators are limited: you cannot add two pointers, and if you subtract pointers, the result is the number of elements between the two pointers. However, you can add or subtract an integral value and a pointer.

Listing 3-60 demonstrates the use of pointer arithmetic.

Listing 3-60. Pointer Arithmetic

```
//: C03:PointerArithmetic.cpp
#include <iostream>
using namespace std;

#define P(EX) cout << #EX << ": " << EX << endl;

int main() {
  int a[10];
  for(int i = 0; i < 10; i++)
    a[i] = i; // Give it index values
  int* ip = a;
  P(*ip);
```

```
  P(*++ip);
  P(*(ip + 5));
  int* ip2 = ip + 5;
  P(*ip2);
  P(*(ip2 - 4));
  P(*--ip2);
  P(ip2 - ip); // Yields number of elements
} ///:~
```

It begins with another macro, but this one uses a preprocessor feature called *stringizing* (implemented with the # sign before an expression) that takes any expression and turns it into a character array. This is quite convenient, since it allows the expression to be printed, followed by a colon, followed by the value of the expression. In main( ), you can see the useful shorthand that is produced.

Although pre- and postfix versions of ++ and -- are valid with pointers, only the prefix versions are used in this example because they are applied before the pointers are dereferenced in the expressions above, so they allow us to see the effects of the operations. Note that only integral values are being added and subtracted; if two pointers were combined this way the compiler would not allow it.

Here is the output of the program:

```
*ip: 0
*++ip: 1
*(ip + 5): 6
*ip2: 6
*(ip2 - 4): 2
*--ip2: 5
```

In all cases, the pointer arithmetic results in the pointer being adjusted to point to the "right place," based on the size of the elements being pointed to.

If pointer arithmetic seems a bit overwhelming at first, don't worry. Most of the time you'll only need to create arrays and index into them with [ ], and the most sophisticated pointer arithmetic you'll usually need is ++ and --. Pointer arithmetic is generally reserved for more clever and complex programs, and many of the containers in the Standard C++ Library hide most of these clever details so you don't have to worry about them.

Debugging Hints

In an ideal environment, you have an excellent debugger available that easily makes the behavior of your program transparent so you can quickly discover errors. However, most debuggers have blind spots, and these will require you to embed code snippets in your program to help you understand what's going on. In addition, you may be developing in an environment (such as an embedded system, which is where I spent my formative years) that has no debugger available, and perhaps very limited feedback (such as a one-line LED display). In these cases you become creative in the ways you discover and display information about the execution of your program. This section suggests some techniques for doing this.

Debugging Flags

If you hard-wire debugging code into a program, you can run into problems. You start to get too much information, which makes the bugs difficult to isolate. When you think you've found the bug, you start tearing out debugging code, only to find you need to put it back in again. You can solve these problems with two types of flags: preprocessor debugging flags and runtime debugging flags.

Preprocessor Debugging Flags

By using the preprocessor to #define one or more debugging flags (preferably in a header file), you can test a flag using an #ifdef statement and conditionally include debugging code. When you think your debugging is finished, you can simply #undef the flag(s) and the code will automatically be removed (and you'll reduce the size and runtime overhead of your executable file).

It is best to decide on names for debugging flags before you begin building your project so the names will be consistent. Preprocessor flags are traditionally distinguished from variables by writing them in all upper case. A common flag name is simply DEBUG (but be careful you don't use NDEBUG, which is reserved in C). The sequence of statements might be

```
#define DEBUG // Probably in a header file
//...
#ifdef DEBUG  // Check to see if flag is defined
/* debugging code here */
#endif        // DEBUG
```

Most C and C++ implementations will also let you #define and #undef flags from the compiler command line, so you can recompile code and insert debugging information with a single command (preferably via the makefile, a tool that will be described shortly). Check your local documentation for details.

Runtime Debugging Flags

In some situations it is more convenient to turn debugging flags on and off during program execution, especially by setting them when the program starts up using the command line. Large programs are tedious to recompile just to insert debugging code.

To turn debugging code on and off dynamically, create bool flags, as shown in Listing 3-61.

Listing 3-61. Dynamic Debugging Flags

```cpp
//: C03:DynamicDebugFlags.cpp
#include <iostream>
#include <string>
using namespace std;
// Debug flags aren't necessarily global:
bool debug = false;

int main(int argc, char* argv[]) {
  for(int i = 0; i < argc; i++)
    if(string(argv[i]) == "--debug=on")
      debug = true;
  bool go = true;
  while(go) {
    if(debug) {
      // Debugging code here
      cout << "Debugger is now on!" << endl;
    } else {
      cout << "Debugger is now off." << endl;
    }
```

```
    cout << "Turn debugger [on/off/quit]: ";
    string reply;
    cin >> reply;
    if(reply == "on") debug = true;    // Turn it on
    if(reply == "off") debug = false; // Off
    if(reply == "quit") break;         // Out of 'while'
  }
} ///:~
```

This program continues to allow you to turn the debugging flag on and off until you type "quit" to tell it you want to exit. Notice it requires that full words are typed in, not just letters (you can shorten it to letter if you wish). Also, a command-line argument can optionally be used to turn debugging on at startup; this argument can appear any place in the command line, since the startup code in main( ) looks at all the arguments. The testing is quite simple because of the expression

```
string(argv[i])
```

This takes the argv[i] character array and creates a string, which then can be easily compared to the right-hand side of the ==. The program in Listing 3-61 searches for the entire string --debug=on. You can also look for --debug= and then see what's after that, to provide more options. Although a debugging flag is one of the relatively few areas where it makes a lot of sense to use a global variable, there's nothing that says it must be that way. Notice that the variable is in lower case letters to remind the reader it isn't a preprocessor flag.

Turning Variables and Expressions into Strings

When writing debugging code, it is tedious to write print expressions consisting of a character array containing the variable name, followed by the variable. Fortunately, Standard C includes the *stringize* operator, #, which was used earlier in this chapter. When you put a # before an argument in a preprocessor macro, the preprocessor turns that argument into a character array. This, combined with the fact that character arrays with no intervening punctuation are concatenated into a single character array, allows you to make a very convenient macro for printing the values of variables during debugging, such as:

```
#define PR(x) cout << #x " = " << x << "\n";
```

If you print the variable a by calling the macro PR(a), it will have the same effect as the code

```
cout << "a = " << a << "\n";
```

This same process works with entire expressions. Listing 3-62 uses a macro to create a shorthand that prints the stringized expression and then evaluates the expression and prints the result.

Listing 3-62. Stringized Expressions

```
//: C03:StringizingExpressions.cpp
#include <iostream>
using namespace std;

#define P(A) cout << #A << ": " << (A) << endl;
```

```
int main() {
  int a = 1, b = 2, c = 3;
  P(a); P(b); P(c);
  P(a + b);
  P((c - a)/b);
} ///:~
```

You can see how a technique like this can quickly become indispensable, especially if you have no debugger (or must use multiple development environments). You can also insert an #ifdef to cause P(A) to be defined as "nothing" when you want to strip out debugging.

The C assert( ) Macro

In the standard header file <cassert> you'll find assert( ), which is a convenient debugging macro. When you use assert( ), you give it an argument that is an expression you are "asserting to be true." The preprocessor generates code that will test the assertion. If the assertion isn't true, the program will stop after issuing an error message telling you what the assertion was and that it failed. See Listing 3-63 for a trivial example.

Listing 3-63. Using Assert

```
//: C03:Assert.cpp
// Use of the assert() debugging macro
#include <cassert>  // Contains the macro
using namespace std;

int main() {
  int i = 100;
  assert(i != 100); // Fails
} ///:~
```

The macro originated in Standard C, so it's also available in the header file assert.h.

When you are finished debugging, you can remove the code generated by the macro by placing the line

```
#define NDEBUG
```

in the program before the inclusion of <cassert>, or by defining NDEBUG on the compiler command line. NDEBUG is a flag used in <cassert> to change the way code is generated by the macros.

Later in this book you'll see some more sophisticated alternatives to assert( ).

Function Addresses

Once a function is compiled and loaded into the computer to be executed, it occupies a chunk of memory. That memory, and thus the function, has an address.

C has never been a language to bar entry where others fear to tread. You can use function addresses with pointers just as you can use variable addresses. The declaration and use of function pointers looks a bit opaque at first, but it follows the format of the rest of the language.

Defining a Function Pointer

To define a pointer to a function that has no arguments and no return value, you say

```
void (*funcPtr)();
```

When you are looking at a complex definition like this, the best way to attack it is to start in the middle and work your way out. "Starting in the middle" means starting at the variable name, which is funcPtr. "Working your way out" means looking to the right for the nearest item (nothing in this case; the right parenthesis stops you short), then looking to the left (a pointer denoted by the asterisk), then looking to the right (an empty argument list indicating a function that takes no arguments), then looking to the left (void, which indicates the function has no return value). This right-left-right motion works with most declarations.

To review, start in the middle (funcPtr *is a* ...), go to the right (nothing there—you're stopped by the right parenthesis), go to the left and find the * (... pointer to a ...), go to the right and find the empty argument list (... function that takes no arguments ...), go to the left and find the void (funcPtr is a pointer to a function that takes no arguments and returns void).

You may wonder why *funcPtr requires parentheses. If you didn't use them, the compiler would see

```
void *funcPtr();
```

You would be declaring a function (that returns avoid*) rather than defining a variable. You can think of the compiler as going through the same process you do when it figures out what a declaration or definition is supposed to be. It needs those parentheses to bump up against so it goes back to the left and finds the *, instead of continuing to the right and finding the empty argument list.

Complicated Declarations and Definitions

As an aside, once you figure out how the C and C++ declaration syntax works, you can create much more complicated items. For instance, consider Listing 3-64.

Listing 3-64. Complicated Definitions

```
//: C03:ComplicatedDefinitions.cpp

/* 1. */     void * (*(*fp1)(int))[10];

/* 2. */     float (*(*fp2)(int,int,float))(int);

/* 3. */     typedef double (*(*(*fp3)())[10])();
             fp3 a;

/* 4. */     int (*(*f4())[10])();

int main() {} ///:~
```

Walk through each one and use the right-left guideline to figure it out. Number 1 says, "fp1is a pointer to a function that takes an integer argument and returns a pointer to an array of 10 void pointers."

Number 2 says, "fp2 is a pointer to a function that takes three arguments (int, int, and float) and returns a pointer to a function that takes an integer argument and returns a float."

If you are creating a lot of complicated definitions, you might want to use a typedef. Number 3 shows how a typedef saves typing the complicated description every time. It says, "An fp3 is a pointer to a function that takes no arguments and returns a pointer to an array of 10 pointers to functions that take no arguments and return doubles." Then it says, "a is one of these fp3 types." typedef is generally useful for building complicated descriptions from simple ones.

Number 4 is a function declaration instead of a variable definition. It says, "f4 is a function that returns a pointer to an array of 10 pointers to functions that return integers."

You will rarely, if ever, need such complicated declarations and definitions as these. However, if you go through the exercise of figuring them out, you will not even be mildly disturbed with the slightly complicated ones you may encounter in real life.

Using a Function Pointer

Once you define a pointer to a function, you must assign it to a function address before you can use it. Just as the address of an array arr[10] is produced by the array name without the brackets (arr), the address of a function func() is produced by the function name without the argument list (func). You can also use the more explicit syntax &func(). To call the function, you dereference the pointer in the same way that you declared it (remember that C and C++ always try to make definitions look the same as the way they are used). Listing 3-65 shows how a pointer to a function is defined and used.

Listing 3-65. Pointer to Function

```
//: C03:PointerToFunction.cpp
// Defining and using a pointer to a function
#include <iostream>
using namespace std;

void func() {
  cout << "func() called..." << endl;
}

int main() {
  void (*fp)();            // Define a function pointer
  fp = func;               // Initialize it
  (*fp)();                 // Dereferencing calls the function
  void (*fp2)() = func;    // Define and initialize
  (*fp2)();
} ///:~
```

After the pointer to function fp is defined, it is assigned to the address of a function func() using fp = func (notice *the argument list is missing on the function name*). The second case shows simultaneous definition and initialization.

Arrays of Pointers to Functions

One of the more interesting constructs you can create is an array of pointers to functions. To select a function, you just index into the array and dereference the pointer. This supports the concept of *table-driven code*; instead of using conditionals or case statements, you select functions to execute based on a state variable (or a combination of state variables). This kind of design can be useful if you often add or delete functions from the table (or if you want to create or change such a table dynamically).

107

Listing 3-66 creates some dummy functions using a preprocessor macro, then creates an array of pointers to those functions using automatic aggregate initialization. As you can see, it is easy to add or remove functions from the table (and thus, functionality from the program) by changing a small amount of code.

Listing 3-66. Using an Array of Pointers to Functions

```
//: C03:FunctionTable.cpp
// Using an array of pointers to functions
#include <iostream>
using namespace std;

// A macro to define dummy functions:
#define DF(N) void N() { \
   cout << "function " #N " called..." << endl; }

DF(a); DF(b); DF(c); DF(d); DF(e); DF(f); DF(g);

void (*func_table[])() = { a, b, c, d, e, f, g };

int main() {
  while(1) {
    cout << "press a key from 'a' to 'g' "
      "or q to quit" << endl;
    char c, cr;
    cin.get(c); cin.get(cr); // second one for CR
    if ( c == 'q' )
      break;                      // ... out of while(1)
    if ( c < 'a' || c > 'g' )
      continue;
    (*func_table[c - 'a'])();
  }
} ///:~
```

At this point, you might be able to imagine how this technique could be useful when creating some sort of interpreter or list processing program.

make: Managing Separate Compilation

When using separate compilation (breaking code into a number of translation units), you need some way to automatically compile each file and to tell the linker to build all the pieces—along with the appropriate libraries and startup code—into an executable file. Most compilers allow you to do this with a single command-line statement. For the GNU C++ compiler, for example, you might say

```
g++ SourceFile1.cpp SourceFile2.cpp
```

The problem with this approach is that the compiler will first compile each individual file, regardless of whether that file *needs* to be rebuilt or not. With many files in a project, it can become prohibitive to recompile everything if you've changed only a single file.

The solution to this problem, developed on Unix but available everywhere in some form, is a program called make. The make utility manages all the individual files in a project by following the instructions in a text file called a makefile. When you edit some of the files in a project and type make, the make program follows the guidelines in the makefile to compare the dates on the source code files to the dates on the corresponding target files, and if a source code file date is more recent than its target file, make invokes the compiler on the source code file. make only recompiles the source code files that were changed and any other source-code files that are affected by the modified files. By using make, you don't have to recompile all the files in your project every time you make a change, nor do you have to check to see that everything was built properly. The makefile contains all the commands to put your project together. Learning to use make will save you a lot of time and frustration. You'll also discover that make is the typical way that you install new software on a Linux/Unix platform (although those makefiles tend to be far more complicated than the ones presented in this book, and you'll often automatically generate a makefile for your particular machine as part of the installation process).

Because make is available in some form for virtually all C++ compilers (and even if it isn't, you can use freely-available makes with any compiler), it will be the tool used throughout this book. However, compiler vendors have also created their own project-building tools. These tools ask you which files are in your project and determine all the relationships themselves. These tools use something similar to a makefile, generally called a *project file*, but the programming environment maintains this file so you don't have to worry about it. The configuration and use of project files varies from one development environment to another, so you must find the appropriate documentation on how to use them (although project file tools provided by compiler vendors are usually so simple to use that you can learn them by playing around—the best form of education).

The makefiles used within this book should work even if you are also using a specific vendor's project-building tool.

Make Activities

When you type make (or whatever the name of your "make" program happens to be), the make program looks in the current directory for a file named makefile, which you've created if it's your project. This file lists dependencies between source code files. make looks at the dates on files. If a dependent file has an older date than a file it depends on, make executes the rule given after the dependency.

All comments in makefiles start with a # and continue to the end of the line. As a simple example, the makefile for a program called "hello" might contain

```
# A comment
hello.exe: hello.cpp
        mycompiler hello.cpp
```

This says that hello.exe (the target) depends on hello.cpp. When hello.cpp has a newer date than hello.exe, make executes the "rule" mycompiler hello.cpp. There may be multiple dependencies and multiple rules. Many make programs require that all the rules begin with a tab. Other than that, whitespace is generally ignored so you can format for readability.

The rules are not restricted to being calls to the compiler; you can call any program you want from within make. By creating groups of interdependent dependency-rule sets, you can modify your source code files, type make, and be certain that all the affected files will be rebuilt correctly.

Macros

A makefile may contain *macros* (note that *these are completely different from C/C++ preprocessor macros*). Macros allow convenient string replacement.

The makefiles in this book use a macro to invoke the C++ compiler. For example,

```
CPP = mycompiler
hello.exe: hello.cpp
        $(CPP) hello.cpp
```

The = is used to identify CPP as a macro, and the $ and parentheses expand the macro. In this case, the expansion means that the macro call $(CPP) will be replaced with the string mycompiler. With the macro above, if you want to change to a different compiler called cpp, you just change the macro to

```
CPP = cpp
```

You can also add compiler flags, etc., to the macro, or use separate macros to add compiler flags.

Suffix Rules

It becomes tedious to tell make how to invoke the compiler for every single cpp file in your project when you know it's the same basic process each time. Since make is designed to be a time-saver, it also has a way to abbreviate actions, as long as they depend on file name suffixes. These abbreviations are called *suffix rules*. A suffix rule is the way to teach make how to convert a file with one type of extension (.cpp, for example) into a file with another type of extension (.obj or .exe). Once you teach make the rules for producing one kind of file from another, all you have to do is tell make which files depend on which other files. When make finds a file with a date earlier than the file it depends on, it uses the rule to create a new file.

The suffix rule tells make that it doesn't need explicit rules to build everything, but instead it can figure out how to build things based on their file extension. In this case, it says, "To build a file that ends in exe from one that ends in cpp, invoke the following command." Here's what it looks like for the example above:

```
CPP = mycompiler
.SUFFIXES: .exe .cpp
.cpp.exe:
        $(CPP) $<
```

The .SUFFIXES directive tells make that it should watch out for any of the following file-name extensions because they have special meaning for this particular makefile. Next you see the suffix rule .cpp.exe, which says, "Here's how to convert any file with an extension of cpp to one with an extension of exe" (when the cpp file is more recent than the exe file). As before, the $(CPP) macro is used, but then you see something new: $<. Because this begins with a $ it's a macro, but this is one of make's special built-in macros. The $< can be used only in suffix rules, and it means "whatever prerequisite triggered the rule" (sometimes called the *dependent*), which in this case translates to "the cpp file that needs to be compiled."

Once the suffix rules have been set up, you can simply say, for example, "make Union.exe," and the suffix rule will kick in, even though there's no mention of "Union" anywhere in the makefile.

Default Targets

After the macros and suffix rules, make looks for the first "target" in a file, and builds that, unless you specify differently. So for the following makefile

```
CPP = mycompiler
.SUFFIXES: .exe .cpp
.cpp.exe:
        $(CPP) $<
target1.exe:
target2.exe:
```

if you just type 'make', then target1.exe will be built (using the default suffix rule) because that's the first target that make encounters. To build target2.exe you'd have to explicitly say 'make target2.exe'. This becomes tedious, so you normally create a default dummy target that depends on all the rest of the targets, like this:

```
CPP = mycompiler
.SUFFIXES: .exe .cpp
.cpp.exe:
        $(CPP) $<
all: target1.exe target2.exe
```

Here, all does not exist and there's no file called all, so every time you type 'make', the program sees all as the first target in the list (and thus the default target), then it sees that all does not exist so it had better make it by checking all the dependencies. So it looks at target1.exe and (using the suffix rule) sees whether (1) target1.exe exists and (2) whether target1.cpp is more recent than target1.exe, and if so runs the suffix rule (if you provide an explicit rule for a particular target, that rule is used instead). Then it moves on to the next file in the default target list. Thus, by creating a default target list (typically called 'all' *by convention*, but you can call it anything) you can cause every executable in your project to be made simply by typing 'make'. In addition, you can have other non-default target lists that do other things; for example, you could set it up so that typing 'make debug' rebuilds all your files with debugging wired in.

An Example makefile

The example makefile follows in Listing 3-67. You'll find more than one makefile in each subdirectory (they have different names; you invoke a specific one with 'make -f'). This one is for GNU C++.

Listing 3-67. Example makefile

```
CPP = g++
OFLAG = -o
.SUFFIXES : .o .cpp .c
.cpp.o :
  $(CPP) $(CPPFLAGS) -c $<
.c.o :
  $(CPP) $(CPPFLAGS) -c $<

all: \
  Return \
  Declare \
  Ifthen \
  Guess \
  Guess2
# Rest of the files for this chapter not shown

Return: Return.o
  $(CPP) $(OFLAG)Return Return.o

Declare: Declare.o
  $(CPP) $(OFLAG)Declare Declare.o
```

```
Ifthen: Ifthen.o
  $(CPP) $(OFLAG)Ifthen Ifthen.o

Guess: Guess.o
  $(CPP) $(OFLAG)Guess Guess.o

Guess2: Guess2.o
  $(CPP) $(OFLAG)Guess2 Guess2.o

Return.o: Return.cpp
Declare.o: Declare.cpp
Ifthen.o: Ifthen.cpp
Guess.o: Guess.cpp
Guess2.o: Guess2.cpp
```

The macro CPP is set to the name of the compiler. To use a different compiler, you can either edit the makefile or change the value of the macro on the command line, like this:

```
make CPP=cpp
```

Note, however, that ExtractCode.cpp has an automatic scheme to automatically build makefiles for additional compilers.

The second macro OFLAG is the flag that's used to indicate the name of the output file. Although many compilers automatically assume the output file has the same base name as the input file, others don't (such as Linux/Unix compilers, which default to creating a file called a.out).

You can see that there are two suffix rules here, one for cpp files and one for .c files (in case any C source code needs to be compiled). The default target is all, and each line for this target is "continued" by using the backslash, up until Guess2, which is the last one in the list and thus has no backslash. There are many more files in this chapter, but only these are shown here for the sake of brevity.

The suffix rules take care of creating object files (with a .o *extension*) from cpp files, but in general you need to explicitly state rules for creating the executable, because normally an executable is created by linking many different object files and make cannot guess what those are. Also, in this case (Linux/Unix) there is no standard extension for executables so a suffix rule won't work for these simple situations. Thus, you see all the rules for building the final executables explicitly stated.

This makefile takes the absolute safest route of using as few make features as possible; it only uses the basic make concepts of targets and dependencies, as well as macros. This way it is virtually assured of working with as many make programs as possible. It tends to produce a larger makefile, but that's not so bad since it's automatically generated by ExtractCode.cpp.

There are lots of other make features that this book will not use, as well as newer and cleverer versions and variations of make with advanced shortcuts that can save a lot of time. Your local documentation may describe the further features of your particular make. Also, if your compiler vendor does not supply a make or it uses a non-standard make, you can find GNU make for virtually any platform in existence by searching the Internet for GNU archives (of which there are many).

The I/O System

C++ supports two complete I/O systems: the one inherited from C (which uses functions like printf() and scanf()) and the object-oriented I/O system defined by C++ (which uses iostreams like cout and cin). Since the I/O system inherited from C is extremely rich, flexible, and powerful, you might wonder as to why C++ defines yet another system. The answer lies in the fact that C's I/O system knows nothing about objects.

Therefore, for C++ to provide complete support for object-oriented programming, it is but imperative that C++ creates an I/O system, which could operate on user-defined objects. In addition to support for objects, there are several benefits to using C++'s I/O system as you will see in Chapter 19.

The Header File <require.h>

The header file in Listing 3-68 contains the code that is required to build some of the examples in the chapters to follow.

Listing 3-68. The Header File <require.h>

```
//: :require.h
// Test for error conditions in programs
// Local "using namespace std" for old compilers
#ifndef REQUIRE_H
#define REQUIRE_H
#include <cstdio>
#include <cstdlib>
#include <fstream>
#include <string>

inline void require(bool requirement,
const std::string &msg = "Requirement failed"){
using namespace std;
if (!requirement) {
fputs(msg.c_str(), stderr);
fputs("\n", stderr);
exit(1);
  }
}

inline void requireArgs(int argc, int args,
const std::string&msg =
    "Must use %d arguments") {
using namespace std;
if (argc != args + 1) {
fprintf(stderr, msg.c_str(), args);
fputs("\n", stderr);
exit(1);
  }
}

inline void requireMinArgs(int argc, int minArgs,
const std::string&msg =
    "Must use at least %d arguments") {
using namespace std;
if(argc < minArgs + 1) {
fprintf(stderr, msg.c_str(), minArgs);
fputs("\n", stderr);
exit(1);
  }
}
```

```
inline void assure(std::ifstream& in,
const std::string& filename = "") {
using namespace std;
if(!in) {
fprintf(stderr, "Could not open file %s\n",
filename.c_str());
exit(1);
  }
}

inline void assure(std::ofstream& out,
const std::string& filename = "") {
using namespace std;
if(!out) {
fprintf(stderr, "Could not open file %s\n",
filename.c_str());
exit(1);
  }
}
#endif // REQUIRE_H ///:~
```

Review Session

1. This chapter was a fairly *intense tour* through all the fundamental features of C++ syntax, most of which are inherited from and in common with C (and result in C++'s vaunted *backward compatibility with C*).

2. Although some C++ features were introduced here, this tour is primarily intended for people who are conversant in programming and simply need to be given an introduction to the *syntax basics* of C and C++.

3. If you're already a C programmer, you may have even seen one or two things about C here that were unfamiliar, aside from the C++ features that were most likely new to you.

4. C++ allows use of both its own I/O system based on objects as well as the I/O system inherited from C, which, in turn, allows for backward compatibility.

5. Note the header file require.h at the end of the chapter. Some of the features in this file, such as inline functions, may not be comprehensible to you at this juncture. I suggest you use this file as it is until Chapter 7 before you move on to the concept of *inlines* in Chapter 9, where this file has been repeated in the section on "Improved Error Checking" and all its *nuances have been duly elaborated and explained in detail*.

CHAPTER 4

■ ■ ■

Data Abstraction

C++ is a productivity enhancement tool. Why else would you make the effort (*and it is an effort, regardless of how easy we attempt to make the transition*) to switch from some language that you already know and are productive with to a new language in which you're going to be *less* productive for a while, until you get the hang of it? It's because you've become convinced that you're going to get big gains by using this new tool.

Productivity, in computer programming terms, means that fewer people can make much more complex and impressive programs in less time. There are certainly other issues when it comes to choosing a language, such as efficiency (does the nature of the language cause slowdown and code bloat?), safety (does the language help you ensure that your program will always do what you plan, and does it handle errors gracefully?), and maintenance (does the language help you create code that is easy to understand, modify, and extend?). These are certainly important factors that will be examined in this book.

But raw productivity means a program that formerly took three of you a week to write now takes one of you a day or two. This touches several levels of economics. You're happy because you get the rush of power that comes from building something, your client (or *boss*) is happy because products are produced faster and with fewer people, and the customers are happy because they get products more cheaply. The only way to get massive increases in productivity is to leverage off other people's code. In other words, to use libraries.

A library is simply a bunch of code that someone else has written and packaged together. Often, the most minimal package is a file with an extension like .lib and one or more header files to tell your compiler what's in the library. The linker knows how to search through the library file and extract the appropriate compiled code. But that's only one way to deliver a library. On platforms that span many architectures, such as Linux/Unix, often the only sensible way to deliver a library is with source code, so it can be reconfigured and recompiled on the new target.

Thus, libraries are probably the most important way to improve productivity, and one of the primary design goals of C++ is to make library use easier. This implies that there's something hard about using libraries in C. Understanding this factor will give you a first insight into the design of C++, and thus an insight into how to use it.

A Tiny *C*-like Library

A library usually starts out as a collection of functions, but if you have used third-party *C* libraries you know there's usually more to it than that because there's more to life than behavior, actions, and functions. There are also characteristics (*blue, pounds, texture, luminance*), which are represented by data. And when you start to deal with a set of characteristics in *C*, it is very convenient to clump them together into a struct, especially if you want to represent more than one similar thing in your problem space. Then you can make a variable of this struct for each thing.

Thus, most *C* libraries have a set of structs and a set of functions that act on those structs. As an example of what such a system looks like, consider a programming tool that acts like an array, but whose size can be established at runtime, when it is created. Let's call it a CStash. Although it's written in C++, it has the style of what you'd write in *C*, as you can see in Listing 4-1.

Listing 4-1. CStash

```
//: C04:CLib.h
// Header file for a C-like library
// An array-like entity created at runtime

typedef struct CStashTag {
  int size;        // Size of each space
  int quantity;    // Number of storage spaces
  int next;        // Next empty space
  // Dynamically allocated array of bytes:
  unsigned char* storage;
} CStash;

void initialize(CStash* s, int size);
void cleanup(CStash* s);
int add(CStash* s, const void* element);
void* fetch(CStash* s, int index);
int count(CStash* s);
void inflate(CStash* s, int increase);
///:~
```

A tag name like CStashTag is generally used for a struct in case you need to reference the struct inside itself. For example, when creating a *linked list* (*each element in your list contains a pointer to the next element*), you need a pointer to the next struct variable, so you need a way to identify the type of that pointer within the struct body. Also, you'll almost universally see the typedef shown in Listing 4-1 for every struct in a *C* library. This is done so you can treat the struct as if it were a new type and define variables of that struct like this:

```
CStash A, B, C;
```

The storage pointer is an unsigned char*. An unsigned char is the smallest piece of storage a *C* compiler supports, although on some machines it can be the same size as the largest. It's implementation-dependent, but is often one byte long. You might think that because the CStash is designed to hold any type of variable, a void* would be more appropriate here. However, the purpose is not to treat this storage as a block of some unknown type, but rather as a block of contiguous bytes.

The source code for the implementation file (*which you may not get if you buy a library commercially; you might get only a compiled* obj *or* lib *or* dll, *etc.*) is shown in Listing 4-2.

Listing 4-2. Source Code for the Implementation File

```
//: C04:CLib.cpp {O}
// Implementation of example C-like library
// Declare structure and functions:
#include "CLib.h"
#include <iostream>
#include <cassert>
using namespace std;
// Quantity of elements to add
// when increasing storage:
Const int increment = 100;
```

```
void initialize(CStash* s, int sz) {
  s->size = sz;
  s->quantity = 0;
  s->storage = 0;
  s->next = 0;
}

int add(CStash* s, const void* element) {
  if(s->next >= s->quantity) //Enough space left?
    inflate(s, increment);
  // Copy element into storage,
  // starting at next empty space:
  int startBytes = s->next * s->size;
  unsigned char* e = (unsigned char*)element;
  for(int i = 0; i < s->size; i++)

  s->next++;
  return(s->next - 1);        // Index number
}

void* fetch(CStash* s, int index) {
  // Check index boundaries:
  assert(0 <= index);
  if(index >= s->next)
    return 0;                 // To indicate the end
  // Produce pointer to desired element:
  return &(s->storage[index * s->size]);
}

int count(CStash* s) {
  return s->next;             // Elements in CStash
}

void inflate(CStash* s, int increase) {
  assert(increase > 0);
  int newQuantity = s->quantity + increase;
  int newBytes = newQuantity * s->size;
  int oldBytes = s->quantity * s->size;
  unsigned char* b = new unsigned char[newBytes];
  for(int i = 0; i < oldBytes; i++)
    b[i] = s->storage[i];    // Copy old to new
  delete [](s->storage);     // Old storage
  s->storage = b;            // Point to new memory
  s->quantity = newQuantity;
}

void cleanup(CStash* s) {
  if(s->storage != 0) {
  cout << "freeing storage" << endl;
  delete []s->storage;
  }
} ///:~
```

117

initialize( ) performs the necessary setup for structCStash by setting the internal variables to appropriate values. Initially, the storage pointer is set to zero—no initial storage is allocated.

The add( ) function inserts an element into the CStash at the next available location. First, it checks to see if there is any available space left. If not, it expands the storage using the inflate( ) function, described later.

Because the compiler doesn't know the specific type of the variable being stored (all the function gets is a void*), you can't just do an assignment, which would certainly be the convenient thing. Instead, you must copy the variable byte by byte. The most straightforward way to perform the copying is with array indexing. Typically, there are already data bytes in storage, and this is indicated by the value of next. To start with the right byte offset, next is multiplied by the size of each element (*in bytes*) to produce startBytes. Then the argument element is cast to an unsigned char* so that it can be addressed byte by byte and copied into the available storage space. next is incremented so that it indicates the next available piece of storage, and the "index number" where the value was stored so that value can be retrieved using this index number with fetch( ).

fetch( ) checks to see that the index isn't out of bounds and then returns the address of the desired variable, calculated using the index argument. Since index indicates the number of elements to offset into the CStash, it must be multiplied by the number of bytes occupied by each piece to produce the numerical offset in bytes. When this offset is used to index into storage using array indexing, you don't get the address, but instead the byte at the address. To produce the address, you must use the address-of operator &.

count( ) may look a bit strange at first to a seasoned C programmer. It seems like a lot of trouble to go through to do something that would probably be a lot easier to do by hand. If you have a structCStash called intStash, for example, it would seem much more straightforward to find out how many elements it has by saying intStash.next instead of making a function call (which has overhead), such as count(&intStash). However, if you wanted to change the internal representation of CStash and thus the way the count was calculated, the function call interface allows the necessary flexibility. But alas, most programmers won't bother to find out about your "better" design for the library. They'll look at the struct and grab the next value directly, and possibly even change next without your permission. If only there were some way for the library designer to have better control over things like this!

Dynamic Storage Allocation

You never know the maximum amount of storage you might need for a CStash, so the memory pointed to by storage is allocated from the *heap*. The heap is a big block of memory used for allocating smaller pieces at runtime. You use the heap when you don't know the size of the memory you'll need while you're writing a program. That is, only at runtime will you find out that you need space to hold 200 Airplane variables instead of 20. In Standard C, dynamic-memory allocation functions include malloc( ), calloc( ), realloc( ), *and* free( ). Instead of library calls, however, C++ has a more sophisticated (albeit simpler to use) approach to dynamic memory that is integrated into the language via the keywords new and delete.

The inflate( ) function uses new to get a bigger chunk of space for the CStash. In this situation, you will only expand memory and not shrink it, and the assert( ) will guarantee that a negative number is not passed to inflate( ) as the increase value. The new number of elements that can be held (*after* inflate( ) completes) is calculated as newQuantity, and this is multiplied by the number of bytes per element to produce newBytes, which will be the number of bytes in the allocation. So that you know how many bytes to copy over from the old location, oldBytes is calculated using the old quantity.

The actual storage allocation occurs in the *new-expression*, which is the expression involving the new keyword, such as:

```
new unsigned char[newBytes];
```

The general form of the new-expression is

```
new Type;
```

in which

Type describes the type of variable you want allocated on the heap. In this case, you want an array of unsigned char that is newBytes long, so that is what appears as the Type. You can also allocate something as simple as an int by saying

```
new int;
```

and although this is rarely done, you can see that the form is consistent.

A new-expression returns a *pointer* to an object of the exact type that you asked for. So, if you say new Type, you get back a pointer to a Type. If you say new int, you get back a pointer to an int. If you want a new unsigned char array, you get back a pointer to the first element of that array. The compiler will ensure that you assign the return value of the new-expression to a pointer of the correct type.

Of course, any time you request memory it's possible for the request to fail if there is no more memory. As you will learn, C++ has mechanisms that come into play if the memory-allocation operation is unsuccessful.

Once the new storage is allocated, the data in the old storage must be copied to the new storage; this is again accomplished with array indexing, copying one byte at a time in a loop. After the data is copied, the old storage must be released so that it can be used by other parts of the program if they need new storage. The delete keyword is the complement of new, and it must be applied to release any storage that is allocated with new (if you forget to use delete, that storage remains unavailable, and if this so-called *memory leak* happens enough, *you'll run out of memory*). In addition, there's a special syntax when you're deleting an array. It's as if you must remind the compiler that this pointer is not just pointing to one object, but to an array of objects: you put a set of empty square brackets in front of the pointer to be deleted, such as:

```
delete []myArray;
```

Once the old storage has been deleted, the pointer to the new storage can be assigned to the storage pointer, the quantity is adjusted, and inflate( ) has completed its job.

Note that the heap manager is fairly primitive. It gives you chunks of memory and takes them back when you delete them. There's no inherent facility for *heap compaction*, which compresses the heap to provide bigger free chunks. If a program allocates and frees heap storage for a while, you can end up with a *fragmented* heap that has lots of memory free, but without any pieces that are big enough to allocate the size you're looking for at the moment. A heap compactor complicates a program because it moves memory chunks around, so your pointers won't retain their proper values. Some operating environments have heap compaction built in, but they require you to use special memory *handles* (*which can be temporarily converted to pointers, after locking the memory so the heap compactor can't move it*) instead of pointers. You can also build your own heap-compaction scheme, but this is not a task to be undertaken lightly.

When you create a variable on the stack at compile time, the storage for that variable is automatically created and freed by the compiler. The compiler knows exactly how much storage is needed, and it knows the lifetime of the variables because of scoping. With dynamic memory allocation, however, the compiler doesn't know how much storage you're going to need, *and* it doesn't know the lifetime of that storage. That is, the storage doesn't get cleaned up automatically. Therefore, you're responsible for releasing the storage using delete, which tells the heap manager that storage can be used by the next call to new. The logical place for this to happen in the library is in the cleanup( ) function because that is where all the closing-up housekeeping is done.

To test the library, two CStashes are created. The first holds ints and the second holds arrays of 80 chars; see Listing 4-3.

Listing 4-3. Testing the C-like library with Two CStashes

```
//: C04:CLibTest.cpp
//{L} CLib


#include "CLib.h"         // To be INCLUDED from Header FILE above
#include <fstream>
#include <iostream>
```

```
#include <string>
#include <cassert>
using namespace std;

int main() {
  // Define variables at the beginning
  // of the block, as in C:
  CStashintStash, stringStash;
  int i;
  char* cp;
  ifstream in;
  string line;
  const int bufsize = 80;
  // Now remember to initialize the variables:
  initialize(&intStash, sizeof(int));
  for(i = 0; i < 100; i++)
    add(&intStash, &i);
  for(i = 0; i < count(&intStash); i++)
    cout << "fetch(&intStash, " << i << ") = "
         << *(int*)fetch(&intStash, i)
         << endl;
  // Holds 80-character strings:
  initialize(&stringStash, sizeof(char)*bufsize);
  in.open("CLibTest.cpp");
  assert(in);
  while(getline(in, line))
    add(&stringStash, line.c_str());
  i = 0;
  while((cp = (char*)fetch(&stringStash, i++))!=0)
    cout << "fetch(&stringStash, " << i << ") = "
         << cp << endl;
  cleanup(&intStash);
  cleanup(&stringStash);
} ///:~
```

Following the form required by C, all the variables are created at the beginning of the scope of main( ). Of course, you must remember to initialize the CStash variables later in the block by calling initialize( ). One of the problems with C libraries is that you must carefully convey to the user the importance of the initialization and cleanup functions. If these functions aren't called, there will be a lot of trouble. Unfortunately, the user doesn't always wonder if initialization and cleanup are mandatory. They know what *they* want to accomplish, and they're not as concerned about you jumping up and down saying, "Hey, wait, you have to do *this* first!" Some users have even been known to initialize the elements of a structure themselves. There's certainly no mechanism in C to prevent it (more foreshadowing).

The intStash is filled up with integers, and the stringStash is filled with character arrays. These character arrays are produced by opening the source code file, CLibTest.cpp, and reading the lines from it into a string called line, and then producing a pointer to the character representation of line using the member function c_str( ).

After each Stash is loaded, it is displayed. The intStash is printed using a for loop, which uses count( ) to establish its limit. The stringStash is printed with a while, which breaks out when fetch( ) returns zero to indicate it is out of bounds.

You'll also notice an additional cast in

```
cp = (char*)fetch(&stringStash,i++)
```

This is due to the stricter type checking in C++, which does not allow you to simply assign a void* to any other type (*C* allows this).

Bad Guesses

There is one more important issue you should understand before we look at the general problems in creating a *C* library. Note that the CLib.h header file *must* be included in any file that refers to CStash because the compiler can't even guess at what that structure looks like. However, it *can* guess at what a function looks like; this sounds like a feature but it turns out to be a major *C* pitfall.

Although you should always declare functions by including a header file, function declarations aren't essential in *C*. It's possible in *C* (but *not* in C++) to call a function that you haven't declared. A good compiler will warn you that you probably ought to declare a function first, but it isn't enforced by the *C* language standard. This is a dangerous practice, because the *C* compiler can assume that a function that you call with an int argument has an argument list containing int, even if it may actually contain a float. This can produce bugs that are very difficult to find, as you will see.

Each separate *C* implementation file (with an extension of .c) is a *translation unit*. That is, the compiler is run separately on each translation unit, and when it is running, it is aware of only that unit. Thus, any information you provide by including header files is quite important because it determines the *compiler's understanding of the rest of your program*. Declarations in header files are particularly important because everywhere the header is included, the compiler will know exactly what to do. If, for example, you have a declaration in a header file that says void func(float), the compiler knows that if you call that function with an integer argument, it should convert the int to a float as it passes the argument (this is called *promotion*). Without the declaration, the *C* compiler would simply assume that a function func(int) existed, it wouldn't do the promotion, and the wrong data would quietly be passed into func().

For each translation unit, the compiler creates an object file with an extension of .o or .obj or something similar. These object files, along with the necessary startup code, must be collected by the linker into the executable program. During linking, all the external references must be resolved. For example, in CLibTest.cpp, functions such as initialize() and fetch() are declared (that is, the compiler is told what they look like) and used, but not defined. They are defined elsewhere, in CLib.cpp. Thus, the calls in CLib.cpp are external references. The linker must, when it puts all the object files together, take the unresolved external references and find the addresses they actually refer to. Those addresses are put into the executable program to replace the external references.

It's important to realize that in *C*, the external references that the linker searches for are simply function names, generally with an underscore in front of them. So all the linker has to do is match up the function name where it is called and the function body in the object file, and it's done. If you accidentally made a call that the compiler interpreted as func(int) and there's a function body for func(float) in some other object file, the linker will see _func in one place and _func in another, and it will think everything's okay. The func() at the calling location will push an int onto the stack, and the func() function body will expect a float to be on the stack. If the function only reads the value and doesn't write to it, it won't blow up the stack. In fact, the float value it reads off the stack might even make some kind of sense. That's worse because it's harder to find the bug.

What's wrong?

We are remarkably adaptable, even in situations in which perhaps we *shouldn't* adapt. The style of the CStash library has been a staple for *C* programmers, but if you look at it for a while, you might notice that it's rather . . . *awkward*. When you use it, you have to pass the address of the structure to every single function in the library. When reading the code, the mechanism of the library gets mixed with the meaning of the function calls, which is confusing when you're trying to understand what's going on.

One of the biggest obstacles, however, to using libraries in *C* is the problem of *name clashes*. *C* has a single namespace for functions; that is, when the linker looks for a function name, it looks in a single master list. In addition, when the compiler is working on a translation unit, it can work only with a single function with a given name.

Now suppose you decide to buy two libraries from two different vendors, and each library has a structure that must be initialized and cleaned up. Both vendors decided that initialize() and cleanup() are good names. If you include both their header files in a single translation unit, what does the *C* compiler do? Fortunately, *C* gives you an error, telling you there's a type mismatch in the two different argument lists of the declared functions. But even if you don't include them in the same translation unit, the linker will still have problems. A good linker will detect that there's a name clash, but some linkers take the first function name they find, by searching through the list of object files in the order you give them in the link list.

■ **Note**   This can even be thought of as a feature because it allows you to replace a library function with your own version.

In either event, you can't use two *C* libraries that contain a function with the identical name. To solve this problem, *C* library vendors will often prepend a sequence of unique characters to the beginning of all their function names. So initialize( ) and cleanup( ) might become CStash_initialize( ) and CStash_cleanup( ). This is a logical thing to do because it "decorates" the name of the struct the function works on with the name of the function.

Now it's time to take the first step toward creating classes in C++. Variable names inside a struct do not clash with global variable names. So why not take advantage of this for function names, when those functions operate on a particular struct? That is, why not make functions members of structs?

The Basic Object

Step one is exactly that. C++ functions can be placed inside structs as "member functions." Listing 4-4 shows what it looks like after converting the *C* version of CStash to the C++ Stash.

Listing 4-4. Converting C-like library to C++

```
//: C04:CppLib.h

struct Stash {
  int size;      // Size of each space
  int quantity;  // Number of storage spaces
  int next;      // Next empty space
   // Dynamically allocated array of bytes:
  unsigned char* storage;
  // Functions!
  void initialize(int size);
  void cleanup();
  int add(const void* element);
  void* fetch(int index);
  int count();
  void inflate(int increase);
}; ///:~
```

First, notice there is no typedef. Instead of requiring you to create a typedef, the C++ compiler turns the name of the structure into a new type name for the program (just as int, char, float, and double *are type names*).

All the data members are exactly the same as before, but now the functions are inside the body of the struct. In addition, notice that the first argument from the *C* version of the library has been removed. In C++, instead of forcing you to pass the address of the structure as the first argument to all the functions that operate on that structure, the compiler secretly does this for you. Now the only arguments for the functions are concerned with what the function *does*, not the mechanism of the function's operation.

It's important to realize that the function code is effectively the same as it was with the *C* version of the library. The number of arguments is the same (*even though you don't see the structure address being passed in, it's still there*), and there's only one function body for each function. That is, just because you say

```
Stash A, B, C;
```

doesn't mean you get a different add( ) function for each variable.

So the code that's generated is almost identical to what you would have written for the *C* version of the library. Interestingly enough, this includes the "name decoration" you probably would have done to produce `Stash_ initialize( )`, `Stash_cleanup( )`, and so on. When the function name is inside the `struct`, the compiler effectively does the same thing. Therefore, `initialize( )` inside the structure `Stash` will not collide with a function named `initialize( )` inside any other structure, or even a global function named `initialize( )`. Most of the time you don't have to worry about the function name decoration—you use the undecorated name. But sometimes you do need to be able to specify that this `initialize( )` belongs to the `structStash`, and not to any other `struct`. In particular, when you're defining the function, you need to fully specify which one it is. To accomplish this full specification, C++ has an operator (`::`) called the *scope resolution operator* (named so because names can now be in different scopes—*at global scope or within the scope of a* `struct`). For example, if you want to specify `initialize( )`, which belongs to `Stash`, you say `Stash::initialize(int size)`. You can see how the scope resolution operator is used in the function definitions in Listing 4-5.

Listing 4-5. Using the Scope Resolution Operator in Function Definitions

```cpp
//: C04:CppLib.cpp {O}
// C library converted to C++
// Declare structure and functions:
#include "CppLib.h"      // To be INCLUDED from Header FILE above
#include <iostream>
#include <cassert>
using namespace std;
// Quantity of elements to add
// when increasing storage:
const int increment = 100;

void Stash::initialize(int sz) {
  size = sz;
  quantity = 0;
  storage = 0;
  next = 0;
}

int Stash::add(const void* element) {
  if(next >= quantity)  // Enough space left?
    inflate(increment);
  // Copy element into storage,
  // starting at next empty space:
  int startBytes = next * size;
  unsigned char* e = (unsigned char*)element;
  for(int i = 0; i < size; i++)
    storage[startBytes + i] = e[i];
  next++;
  return(next - 1);       // Index number
}

void* Stash::fetch(int index) {
  // Check index boundaries:
  assert(0 <= index);
```

```
      if(index >= next)
        return 0;           // To indicate the end
      // Produce pointer to desired element:
      return &(storage[index * size]);
}

int Stash::count() {
  return next;            // Number of elements in CStash
}

void Stash::inflate(int increase) {
  assert(increase > 0);
  int newQuantity = quantity + increase;
  int newBytes = newQuantity * size;
  int oldBytes = quantity * size;
  unsigned char* b = new unsigned char[newBytes];
  for(int i = 0; i < oldBytes; i++)
    b[i] = storage[i];   // Copy old to new
  delete []storage;      // Old storage
  storage = b;           // Point to new memory
  quantity = newQuantity;
}

void Stash::cleanup() {
  if(storage != 0) {
    cout << "freeing storage" << endl;
    delete []storage;
  }
} ///:~
```

There are several other things that are different between *C* and C++. First, the declarations in the header files are *required* by the compiler. In C++, you cannot call a function without declaring it first. The compiler will issue an error message otherwise. This is an important way to ensure that function calls are consistent between the point where they are called and the point where they are defined. By forcing you to declare the function before you call it, the C++ compiler virtually ensures that you will perform this declaration by including the header file. If you also include the same header file in the place where the functions are defined, the compiler checks to make sure that the declaration in the header and the function definition match up. This means that the header file becomes a validated repository for function declarations and ensures that functions are used consistently throughout all translation units in the project.

Of course, global functions can still be declared by hand every place where they are defined and used. However, structures must always be declared before they are defined or used, and the most convenient place to put a structure definition is in a header file, except for those you intentionally hide in a file.

■ **Note** This is so tedious that it becomes very unlikely.

You can see that all the member functions look almost the same as when they were *C* functions, except for the scope resolution and the fact that the first argument from the *C* version of the library is no longer explicit. It's still there, of course, because the function has to be able to work on a particular struct variable. But notice, inside the member function, that the member selection is also gone! Thus, instead of saying s->size = sz; you say size = sz; and eliminate the tedious s->, which didn't really add anything to the meaning of what you were doing anyway.

The C++ compiler is apparently doing this for you. Indeed, it is taking the "secret" first argument (*the address of the structure that you were previously passing in by hand*) and applying the member selector whenever you refer to one of the data members of a struct. This means that whenever you are inside the member function of another struct, you can refer to any member (*including another member function*) by simply giving its name. The compiler will search through the local structure's names before looking for a global version of that name. You'll find that this feature means that not only is your code easier to write, it's a lot easier to read.

But what if, for some reason, you *want* to be able to get your hands on the *address of the structure*? In the C version of the library it was easy because each function's first argument was a CStash* called s. In C++, things are even more consistent. There's a special keyword, called this, which produces the address of the struct. It's the equivalent of the "s" in the C version of the library. So you can revert to the C style of things by saying

```
this->size = Size;
```

The code generated by the compiler is exactly the same, so you don't need to use this in such a fashion; occasionally, you'll see code where people explicitly use this-> everywhere but it doesn't add anything to the meaning of the code and often indicates an inexperienced programmer. Usually, you don't use this often, but when you need it, it's there (*some of the examples later in the book will use* this).

There's one last item to mention. In C, you could assign a void* to any other pointer like this

```
int i = 10;
void* p = &i; // OK in both C and C++
int* ip = vp; // Only acceptable in C
```

and there would be no complaint from the compiler. But in C++, this statement is not allowed. Why? Because C is not so particular about type information, so it allows you to assign a pointer with an unspecified type to a pointer with a specified type. Not so with C++. Type is critical in C++, and the compiler stamps its foot when there are any violations of type information. This has always been important, but it is especially important in C++ because you have member functions in structs. If you could pass pointers to structs around with impunity in C++, then you could end up calling a member function for a struct that doesn't even logically exist for that struct! This is a real recipe for disaster. Therefore, while C++ allows the assignment of any type of pointer to a void* (this was the original intent of void*, *which is required to be large enough to hold a pointer to any type*), it will *not* allow you to assign a void pointer to any other type of pointer. A cast is always required to tell the reader and the compiler that you really do want to treat it as the destination type.

This brings up an interesting issue. One of the important goals for C++ is to compile as much existing C code as possible to allow for an easy transition to the new language. However, this doesn't mean any code that C allows will automatically be allowed in C++. There are a number of things the C compiler lets you get away with that are dangerous and error-prone.

■ **Note** We'll look at them as the book progresses.

The C++ compiler generates warnings and errors for these situations. This is often much more of an advantage than a hindrance. In fact, there are many situations in which you are trying to run down an error in C and just can't find it, but as soon as you recompile the program in C++, the compiler points out the problem! In C, you'll often find that you can get the program to compile, but then you have to get it to work. In C++, when the program compiles correctly, *it often works*, too! This is because the language is a lot stricter about type.

You can see a number of new things in the way the C++ version of Stash is used in the test program in Listing 4-6.

Listing 4-6. Using the C++ Version of CStash

```
//: C04:CppLibTest.cpp
//{L} CppLib
// Test of C++ library
#include "CppLib.h"
#include "../require.h" // To be INCLUDED from Header FILE in Chapter 3

#include <fstream>
#include <iostream>
#include <string>
using namespace std;

int main() {
  Stash intStash;
  intStash.initialize(sizeof(int));
  for(int i = 0; i < 100; i++)
    intStash.add(&i);
  for(int j = 0; j < intStash.count(); j++)
    cout << "intStash.fetch(" << j << ") = "
         << *(int*)intStash.fetch(j)
         << endl;
  // Holds 80-character strings:
  Stash stringStash;
  const int bufsize = 80;
  stringStash.initialize(sizeof(char) * bufsize);
  ifstream in("CppLibTest.cpp");
  assure(in, "CppLibTest.cpp");
  string line;
  while(getline(in, line))
    stringStash.add(line.c_str());
  int k = 0;
  char* cp;
  while((cp =(char*)stringStash.fetch(k++)) != 0)
    cout << "stringStash.fetch(" << k << ") = "
         << cp << endl;
  intStash.cleanup();
  stringStash.cleanup();
} ///:~
```

One thing you'll notice is that the variables are all defined "on the fly" (*as introduced in the previous chapter*). That is, they are defined at any point in the scope, rather than being restricted—as in *C*—to the beginning of the scope.

The code is quite similar to CLibTest.cpp, but when a member function is called, the call occurs using the member selection operator of . preceded by the name of the variable. This is a convenient syntax because it mimics the selection of a data member of the structure. The difference is that this is a function member, so it has an argument list.

Of course, the call that the compiler *actually* generates looks much more like the original *C* library function. Thus, considering name decoration and the passing of this, the C++ function call intStash.initialize(sizeof(int), 100) becomes something like Stash_initialize(&intStash, sizeof(int), 100). If you ever wonder what's going on underneath the covers, remember that the original C++ compiler cfront from AT&T produced *C* code as its output, which was then compiled by the underlying *C* compiler. This approach meant that cfront could be quickly ported to any machine that had a *C* compiler, and it helped to rapidly disseminate C++ compiler technology. But because the C++ compiler had to generate *C*, you know that there must be some way to represent C++ syntax in *C*.)

There's one other change from `ClibTest.cpp`, which is the introduction of the `require.h` header file. This is a header file that was created for this book to perform more sophisticated error checking than that provided by `assert( )`. It contains several functions, including the one used here called `assure( )`, which is used for files. This function checks to see if the file has successfully been opened, and if not, it reports to standard error that the file could not be opened (*thus it needs the name of the file as the second argument*) and exits the program. The `require.h` functions will be used throughout the book, in particular to ensure that there are the right number of command-line arguments and that files are opened properly. The `require.h` functions replace repetitive and distracting error-checking code, and yet they provide essentially useful error messages.

What's an object?

Now that you've seen an initial example, it's time to step back and take a look at some terminology. The act of bringing functions inside structures is the root of what C++ adds to *C*, and it introduces a new way of thinking about structures: as concepts. In *C*, a `struct` is an agglomeration of data, a way to package data so you can treat it in a clump. But it's hard to think about it as anything but a programming convenience. The functions that operate on those structures are elsewhere. However, with functions in the package, the structure becomes a new creature, capable of describing both characteristics (like a *C* `struct` does) *and* behaviors. The concept of an object—a free-standing, bounded entity that can remember *and* act—suggests itself.

In C++, an object is just a variable, and the purest definition is "a region of storage" (this is a more specific way of saying that *an object must have a unique identifier, which in the case of* C++ *is a unique memory address*). It's a place where you can store data, and it's implied that there are also operations that can be performed on this data.

Unfortunately, there's not complete consistency across languages when it comes to these terms, although they are fairly well accepted. You will also sometimes encounter disagreement about what an object-oriented language is, although that seems to be reasonably well sorted out by now. There are languages that are *object-based*, which means that they have objects like the C++ structures-with-functions that you've seen so far. This, however, is only part of the picture when it comes to an object-oriented language, and languages that stop at packaging functions inside data structures are object-based, not object-oriented.

Abstract Data Typing

The ability to package data with functions allows you to create a new data type. This is often called *encapsulation*. An existing data type may have several pieces of data packaged together. For example, a `float` has an exponent, a mantissa, and a sign bit. You can tell it to do things: add to another `float` or to an `int`, and so on. It has characteristics and behavior.

The definition of `Stash` creates a new data type. You can `add( )`, `fetch( )`, *and* `inflate( )`. You create one by saying `Stash s`, just as you create a `float` by saying `float f`. A `Stash` also has characteristics and behavior. Even though it acts like a real, built-in data type, we refer to it as an *abstract data type*, perhaps because it allows us to abstract a concept from the problem space into the solution space. In addition, the C++ compiler treats it like a new data type, and if you say a function expects a `Stash`, the compiler makes sure you pass a `Stash` to that function. So the same level of type checking happens with abstract data types (sometimes called *user-defined types*) as with built-in types.

You can immediately see a difference, however, in the way you perform operations on objects. You say `object.memberFunction(arglist)`. This is "calling a member function for an object." But in object-oriented parlance, this is also referred to as "sending a message to an object." So for a `Stash s`, the statement `s.add(&i)` sends a message to s saying "add( ) this to yourself." In fact, object-oriented programming can be summed up in a single phrase: *sending messages to objects*. Really, that's all you do—create a bunch of objects and send messages to them. The trick, of course, is figuring out what your objects and messages *are*, but once you accomplish this, the implementation in C++ is surprisingly straightforward.

Object Details

A question that often comes up in seminars is, "*How big is an object, and what does it look like?*" The answer is "*About what you expect from a C* struct." In fact, the code the *C* compiler produces for a *C* struct (with no C++ adornments) will usually look *exactly* the same as the code produced by a C++ compiler. This is reassuring to those *C* programmers who depend on the details of size and layout in their code, and for some reason directly access structure bytes instead of using identifiers (*relying on a particular size and layout for a structure is a nonportable activity*).

The *size of a* struct is the combined size of all of its members. Sometimes when the compiler lays out a struct, it adds extra bytes to make the boundaries come out neatly; this may increase execution efficiency. You can determine the size of a struct using the sizeof operator. Listing 4-7 contains a small example.

Listing 4-7. Finding the Sizes of structs Using the sizeof Operator

```
//: C04:Sizeof.cpp
// Sizes of structs
#include "CLib.h"
#include "CppLib.h"
#include <iostream>
using namespace std;

struct A {
  int i[100];
};

struct B {
  void f();
};

void B::f() {}

int main() {
  cout << "sizeof struct A = " << sizeof(A)
       << " bytes" << endl;
  cout << "sizeof struct B = " << sizeof(B)
       << " bytes" << endl;
  cout << "sizeof CStash in C = "
       << sizeof(CStash) << " bytes" << endl;
  cout << "sizeof Stash in C++ = "
       << sizeof(Stash) << " bytes" << endl;
} ///:~
```

The first print statement produces 200 because each int occupies two bytes.

■ **Note**   You may get a different result on your computer.

---

struct B is something of an anomaly because it is a struct with no data members. In *C*, this is illegal, but in C++ we need the option of creating a struct whose sole task is to scope function names, so it is allowed. Still, the result produced by the second print statement is a somewhat surprising nonzero value. In early versions of the language, the size was zero, but an awkward situation arises when you create such objects: they have the same address as the object created directly after them, and so are not distinct. One of the fundamental rules of objects is that each object must have a unique address, so structures with no data members will always have some minimum nonzero size.

The last two sizeof statements show you that the size of the structure in C++ is the same as the size of the equivalent version in *C*. C++ tries not to add any unnecessary overhead.

Header File Etiquette

When you create a struct containing member functions, you are creating a new data type. In general, you want this type to be easily accessible to yourself and others. In addition, you want to separate the interface (the declaration) from the implementation (the definition of the member functions) so the implementation can be changed without forcing a recompile of the entire system. You achieve this end by putting the declaration for your new type in a header file.

To most of the *C* beginners, header files are a mystery. Many *C* books don't emphasize it, and the compiler doesn't enforce function declarations, so it seems optional most of the time, except when structures are declared. In C++, the use of header files becomes crystal clear. They are virtually mandatory for easy program development, and you put very specific information in them: declarations. The header file tells the compiler what is available in your library. You can use the library even if you only possess the header file along with the object file or library file; you don't need the source code for the .cpp file. The header file is where the *interface specification is stored*.

Although it is not enforced by the compiler, the best approach to building large projects in *C* is to use libraries, collect associated functions into the same object module or library, and use a header file to hold all the declarations for the functions. You could throw any function into a *C* library, but the C++ abstract data type determines the functions that are associated by dint of their common access to the data in a struct. Any member function must be declared in the struct declaration; you cannot put it elsewhere. The use of function libraries was encouraged in *C* and institutionalized in C++.

Importance of Header Files

When using a function from a library, *C* allows you the option of ignoring the header file and simply declaring the function by hand. In the past, people would sometimes do this to speed up the compiler just a bit by avoiding the task of opening and including the file (this is usually not an issue with modern compilers). For example, here's an extremely lazy declaration of the *C* function printf( ) (from <stdio.h>):

```
printf(...)
```

The ellipses specify a *variable argument list*, which says printf( ) has some arguments, each of which has a type, but ignore that; just take whatever arguments you see and accept them. By using this kind of declaration, you suspend all error checking on the arguments.

This practice can cause subtle problems. If you declare functions by hand, in one file you may make a mistake. Since the compiler sees only your hand-declaration in that file, it may be able to adapt to your mistake. The program will then link correctly, but the use of the function in that one file will be faulty. This is a tough error to find and is easily avoided by using a header file.

If you place all your function declarations in a header file, and include that header everywhere you use the function and where you define the function, you ensure a consistent declaration across the whole system. You also ensure that the declaration and the definition match by including the header in the definition file.

If a struct is declared in a header file in C++, you *must* include the header file everywhere a struct is used and where struct member functions are defined. The C++ compiler will give an error message if you try to call a regular function, or to call or define a member function, without declaring it first. By enforcing the proper use of header files, the language ensures consistency in libraries and reduces bugs by forcing the same interface to be used everywhere.

The header is a contract between you and the user of your library. The contract describes your data structures, and it states the arguments and return values for the function calls. It says, "Here's what my library does." The user needs some of this information to develop the application, and the compiler needs all of it to generate proper code. The user of the struct simply includes the header file, creates objects (instances) of that struct, and links in the object module or library (*i.e., the compiled code*).

The compiler enforces the contract by requiring you to declare all structures and functions before they are used and, in the case of member functions, before they are defined. Thus, you're forced to put the declarations in the header and to include the header in the file where the member functions are defined and the *file(s)* where they are used. Because a single header file describing your library is included throughout the system, the compiler can ensure consistency and prevent errors.

There are certain issues that you must be aware of in order to organize your code properly and write effective header files. The first issue concerns what you can put into header files. The basic rule is "only declarations" (that is, only information to the compiler but nothing that allocates storage by generating code or creating variables). This is because the header file will typically be included in several translation units in a project, and if storage for one identifier is allocated in more than one place, the linker will come up with a multiple definition error.

■ **Note**   This is C++'s One Definition Rule: you can declare things as many times as you want, but there can be only one actual definition for each thing.

This rule isn't completely hard and fast. If you define a variable that is "file static" (*has visibility only within a file*) inside a header file, there will be multiple instances of that data across the project, but the linker won't have a collision. Basically, you don't want to do anything in the header file that will cause an ambiguity at link time.

The Multiple-Declaration Problem

The second header-file issue is this: when you put a struct declaration in a header file, it is possible for the file to be included more than once in a complicated program. Iostreams are a good example. Any time a struct does I/O it may include one of the iostream headers. If the cpp file you are working on uses more than one kind of struct (*typically including a header file for each one*), you run the risk of including the <iostream> header more than once and redeclaring iostream.

The compiler considers the redeclaration of a structure (this includes both structs and classes) to be an error, since it would otherwise allow you to use the same name for different types. To prevent this error when multiple header files are included, you need to build some intelligence into your header files using the preprocessor (*Standard C++ header files like* <iostream> already have this "intelligence").

Both C and C++ allow you to redeclare a function, as long as the two declarations match, but neither will allow the redeclaration of a structure. In C++, this rule is especially important because if the compiler allowed you to redeclare a structure and the two declarations differed, which one would it use?

The problem of redeclaration comes up quite a bit in C++ because each data type (*structure with functions*) generally has its own header file, and you have to include one header in another if you want to create another data type that uses the first one. In any .cpp file in your project, it's likely that you'll include several files that include the same header file. During a single compilation, the compiler can see the same header file several times. Unless you do something about it, the compiler will see the redeclaration of your structure and report a compile-time error. To solve the problem, you need to know a bit more about the preprocessor.

The Preprocessor Directives:#define, #ifdef, #endif

The preprocessor directive #define can be used to create compile-time flags. You have two choices: you can simply tell the preprocessor that the flag is defined, without specifying a value, like

```
#define FLAG
```

or you can give it a value (which is the typical C way to define a constant), like

```
#define PI 3.14159
```

In either case, the label can now be tested by the preprocessor to see if it has been defined.

```
#ifdef FLAG
```

This will yield a true result, and the code following the #ifdef will be included in the package sent to the compiler. This inclusion stops when the preprocessor encounters the statement

```
#endif
```

or

```
#endif // FLAG
```

Any non-comment after the #endif on the same line is illegal, even though some compilers may accept it. The #ifdef/#endif pairs may be nested within each other.

The complement of #define is #undef (short for "undefine"), which will make an #ifdef statement using the same variable yield a false result. #undef will also cause the preprocessor to stop using a macro. The complement of #ifdef is #ifndef, which will yield a true if the label has not been defined (this is the one we will use in header files).

There are other useful features in the *C* preprocessor. You should check your *local documentation* for the full set.

A Standard for Header Files

In each header file that contains a structure, you should first check to see if this header has already been included in this particular cpp file. You do this by testing a preprocessor flag. If the flag isn't set, the file wasn't included and you should set the flag (so the structure can't get redeclared) and declare the structure. If the flag was set, that type has already been declared so you should just ignore the code that declares it. Here's how the header file *should look*:

```
#ifndef HEADER_FLAG
#define HEADER_FLAG
// Type declaration here...
#endif // HEADER_FLAG
```

As you can see, the first time the header file is included, the contents of the header file (including your type declaration) will be included by the preprocessor. All the subsequent times it is included—in a single compilation unit—the type declaration will be ignored. The name HEADER_FLAG can be any unique name, but a reliable standard to follow is to capitalize the name of the header file and replace periods with underscores (*leading underscores, however, are reserved for system names*). Listing 4-8 shows an example.

Listing 4-8. Simple Header that Prevents Re-definition

```
//: C04:Simple.h
// Simple header that prevents redefinition

#ifndef SIMPLE_H
#define SIMPLE_H

struct Simple {

  int i,j,k;
  initialize() { i = j = k = 0; }
};
#endif // SIMPLE_H ///:~
```

Although the SIMPLE_H after the #endif is commented out and thus ignored by the preprocessor, it is useful for documentation.

These preprocessor statements that prevent multiple inclusion are often referred to as *include guards*.

Namespaces in Headers

You'll notice that *using directives* are present in nearly all the cpp files in this book, usually in the form of

```
using namespace std;
```

Since std is the namespace that surrounds the entire Standard C++ Library, this particular using directive allows the names in the Standard C++ Library to be used without qualification. However, you'll virtually never see a using directive in a header file (at least, not outside of a scope). The reason is that the using directive eliminates the protection of that particular namespace, and the effect lasts until the end of the current compilation unit. If you put a using directive (outside of a scope) in a header file, it means that this loss of *namespace protection* will occur with any file that includes this header, which often means other header files. Thus, if you start putting using directives in header files, it's very easy to end up "turning off" namespaces practically everywhere, and thereby neutralizing the beneficial effects of namespaces.

In short, don't put using directives in header files.

Using Headers in Projects

When building a project in C++, you'll usually create it by bringing together a lot of different types (*data structures with associated functions*). You'll usually put the declaration for each type or group of associated types in a separate header file, then define the functions for that type in a translation unit. When you use that type, you must include the header file to perform the declarations properly.

Sometimes that pattern will be followed in this book, but more often the examples will be very small, so everything—the structure declarations, function definitions, and the main( ) function—may appear in a single file. However, keep in mind that you'll want to use separate files and header files in practice.

Nested Structures

The convenience of taking data and function names out of the global namespace extends to structures. You can nest a structure within another structure and therefore keep associated elements together. The declaration syntax is what you would expect, as you can see in Listing 4-9, which implements a push-down stack as a simple linked list so it *"never"* runs out of memory.

Listing 4-9. Nested Structures

```
//: C04:Stack.h
// Nested struct in linked list
#ifndef STACK_H
#define STACK_H

struct Stack {
  struct Link {
    void* data;
    Link* next;
    void initialize(void* dat, Link* nxt);
  }* head;
  void initialize();
  void push(void* dat);
  void* peek();
  void* pop();
  void cleanup();
};
#endif // STACK_H ///:~
```

The nested struct is called Link, and it contains a pointer to the next Link in the list and a pointer to the data stored in the Link. If the next pointer is zero, it means you're at the end of the list.

Notice that the head pointer is defined right after the declaration for struct Link, instead of a separate definition Link* head. This is a syntax that came from C, but it emphasizes the importance of the semicolon after the structure declaration; the semicolon indicates the end of the comma-separated list of definitions of that structure type.

■ **Note**   Usually the list is empty.

The nested structure has its own initialize( ) function, like all the structures presented so far, to ensure proper initialization. Stack has both an initialize( ) and cleanup( ) function, as well as push( ), which takes a pointer to the data you wish to store (it assumes this has been allocated on the heap), and pop( ), which returns the data pointer from the top of the Stack and removes the top element. (*When you* pop( ) *an element, you are* responsible for destroying the object pointed to by the data.) The peek( ) function also returns the data pointer from the top element, but it leaves the top element on the Stack.

Listing 4-10 contains the definitions for the member functions.

Listing 4-10. Linked List with Nesting including Definitions of Member Functions

```
//: C04:Stack.cpp {0}

// Linked list with nesting
// Includes definitions of member functions
#include "Stack.h"      // To be INCLUDED from Header FILE above
#include "../require.h"
using namespace std;
```

```
void
Stack::Link::initialize(void* dat, Link* nxt) {
  data = dat;
  next = nxt;
}

void Stack::initialize() { head = 0; }

void Stack::push(void* dat) {
  Link* newLink = new Link;
  newLink->initialize(dat, head);
  head = newLink;
}

void* Stack::peek() {
  require(head != 0, "Stack empty");
  return head->data;
}

void* Stack::pop() {
  if(head == 0) return 0;
  void* result = head->data;
  Link* oldHead = head;
  head = head->next;
  delete oldHead;
  return result;
}

void Stack::cleanup() {
  require(head == 0, "Stack not empty");
} ///:~
```

The first definition is particularly interesting because it shows you how to define a member of a nested structure. You simply use an additional level of scope resolution to specify the name of the enclosing struct. Stack::Link::initialize( ) takes the arguments and assigns them to its members.

Stack::initialize( ) sets head to zero, so the object knows it has an empty list.

Stack::push( ) takes the argument, which is a pointer to the variable you want to keep track of, and pushes it on the Stack. First, it uses new to allocate storage for the Link it will insert at the top. Then it calls Link's initialize( ) function to assign the appropriate values to the members of the Link. Notice that the next pointer is assigned to the current head; then head is assigned to the new Link pointer. This effectively pushes the Link in at the top of the list.

Stack::pop( ) captures the data pointer at the current top of the Stack; then it moves the head pointer down and deletes the old top of the Stack, finally returning the captured pointer. When pop( ) removes the last element, then head again becomes zero, meaning the Stack is empty.

Stack::cleanup( ) doesn't actually do any cleanup. Instead, it establishes a firm policy that you (*the client programmer using this* Stack *object*) are responsible for popping all the elements off this Stack and deleting them. The require( ) is used to indicate that a programming error has occurred if the Stack is not empty.

Why couldn't the Stack destructor be responsible for all the objects that the client programmer didn't pop( )? The problem is that the Stack is holding void pointers, and you'll learn in *Chapter 13* that calling delete for a void* doesn't clean things up properly. The subject of who's responsible for the memory is not even *that* simple, as you'll see in *later chapters*.

Listing 4-11 contains an example to test the Stack.

Listing 4-11. Testing the Stack

```
//: C04:StackTest.cpp
//{L} Stack
//{T} StackTest.cpp
// Test of nested linked list
#include "Stack.h"
#include "../require.h"
#include<fstream>
#include<iostream>
#include<string>

using namespace std;

int main(int argc, char* argv[]) {
  requireArgs(argc, 1); // File name is argument
  ifstream in(argv[1]);
  assure(in, argv[1]);
  Stack textlines;
  textlines.initialize();
  string line;
  // Read file and store lines in the Stack:
  while(getline(in, line))
    textlines.push(new string(line));
  // Pop the lines from the Stack and print them:
  string* s;
  while((s = (string*)textlines.pop()) != 0) {
    cout << *s << endl;
    delete s;
  }
  textlines.cleanup();
} ///:~
```

This is similar to the earlier example, but it pushes lines from a file (*as* string *pointers*) on the Stack and then pops them off, which results in the file being printed out in reverse order. Note that the pop( ) member function returns a void*, and this must be cast back to a string* before it can be used. To print the string, the pointer is dereferenced.

As textlines is being filled, the contents of line is "cloned" for each push( ) by making a new string(line). The value returned from the new-expression is a pointer to the new string that was created and that copied the information from line. If you had simply passed the address of line to push( ), you would end up with a Stack filled with identical addresses, all pointing to line. The file name is taken from the command line. To guarantee that there are enough arguments on the command line, you see a second function used from the require.h header file: requireArgs( ), which compares argc to the desired number of arguments and prints an appropriate error message and exits the program if there aren't enough arguments.

Global Scope Resolution

The scope resolution operator gets you out of situations in which the name the compiler chooses by default (the "nearest" name) isn't what you want. For example, suppose you have a structure with a local identifier a, and you want to select a global identifier a from inside a member function. The compiler would default to choosing the local one, so you must tell it to do otherwise. When you want to specify a global name using scope resolution, you use the operator with nothing in front of it. Listing 4-12 shows global scope resolution for both a variable and a function.

Listing 4-12. Global Scope Resolution

```
//: C04:Scoperes.cpp

// Global scope resolution for a variable
// As well as a function

int a;
void f() {}

struct S {
  int a;
  void f();
};

void S::f() {
  ::f();   // Would be recursive otherwise!
  ::a++;   // Select the global a
  a--;     // The a at struct scope
}
int main() { S s; f(); } ///:~
```

Without scope resolution in S::f( ), the compiler would default to selecting the member versions of f( ) and a.

Review Session

1. In this chapter, you learned the fundamental "twist" of C++: that *you can place functions inside of structures.* This new type of structure is called an *abstract data type*, and variables you create using this structure are called *objects*, or *instances*, of that type.

2. Calling a member function for an object is called *sending a message* to that object. The primary action in *object-oriented programming* is sending messages to objects.

3. *Although packaging data and functions together is a significant benefit for code organization and makes library use easier because it prevents name clashes by hiding the names,* there's a lot more you can do to make programming safer in C++.

4. In the next chapter, you'll learn how to *protect* some members of a struct so that only you can *manipulate* them.

5. This establishes a clear boundary between what the *user of the structure can change* and what only the programmer may change.

■ ■ ■

CHAPTER 5

Hiding the Implementation

Although *C* is one of the most liked and widely used programming languages in the world, the invention of C++ was necessitated by one major programming factor: *increasing complexity*. Over the years, computer programs have become larger and more complex. Even though *C* is an excellent programming language, it has its limits. In *C*, once a program exceeds from 20,000 to 100,000 lines of code, it becomes unmanageable and difficult to grasp in its totality. The purpose of C++ is to break this barrier. The basic essence of C++ lies in allowing the programmer to understand, comprehend, and manage much more complex and larger programs.

C++ took the best ideas from *C* and combined them with several new concepts. The result was a different way of organizing your program. In *C*, a program is organized around its code (i.e., "What is happening?") while in C++, a program is organized around its data (i.e., "Who is being affected?"). A program written in *C* is defined by its functions, any of which may operate on any type of data used by the program. In C++, a program is organized around data, with the basic premise being that *data controls access to code*. Thus, you define the data and the routines that are allowed to act on that data and a *data type exactly and precisely defines what sort of operations are applicable to this data*.

To support this basic principle of object-oriented programming, C++ has the feature of *encapsulation* so that it can bind together code and the data it manipulates, keeping both safe from outside interference and misuse. By linking code and data in this manner, an *object* is created. Thus, an object is the device that supports encapsulation.

Within an object, code/data or both may be private/public to that object or protected, which comes into play only in case of *inherited objects*. We shall discuss this *access control* and more (such as classes) in this chapter; the topic *of inheritance* will be taken up in a later chapter.

We have previously discussed the need for using as much existing *C* code and libraries to enhance productivity through C++ in the previous chapter. A typical *C* library contains a struct and some associated functions to act on that struct. So far, you've seen how C++ takes functions that are *conceptually* associated and makes them *literally* associated by putting the function declarations inside the scope of the struct, changing the way functions are called for the struct, eliminating the passing of the structure address as the first argument, and adding a new type name to the program (*so you don't have to create a* type set *for the* struct *tag*).

This is all convenient; it helps you organize your code and makes it easier to write and read. However, there are other important issues when making libraries easier in C++, especially the issues of safety and control. This chapter looks at the subject of boundaries in structures.

Setting Limits

In any relationship it's important to have boundaries that are respected by all parties involved. When you create a library, you establish a relationship with the *client programmer* who uses that library to build an application or another library.

In a *C* struct, as with most things in *C*, there are no rules. Client programmers can do anything they want with that struct, and there's no way to force any particular behaviors. For example, even though you saw in the last chapter the importance of the functions named initialize( ) and cleanup( ), the client programmer has the option not to call those functions.

■ **Note**   We'll look at a better approach in the next chapter.

And even though you would really prefer that the client programmer not directly manipulate some of the members of your struct, in *C* there's no way to prevent it. '*Everything's naked to the world*.'

There are two reasons for controlling access to members. The first is to keep the client programmer's hands off tools they shouldn't touch—tools that are necessary for the internal machinations of the data type, but not part of the interface the client programmer needs to solve their particular problems. This is actually a service to client programmers because they can easily see what's important to them and what they can ignore.

The second reason for access control is to allow the library designer to change the internal workings of the structure without worrying about how it will affect the client programmer. In the Stack example in the last chapter, you might want to allocate the storage in big chunks for speed, rather than creating new storage each time an element is added. If the interface and implementation are clearly separated and protected, you can accomplish this and require only a relink by the client programmer.

C++ Access Control

C++ introduces three new keywords to set the boundaries in a structure: public, private, and protected. Their use and meaning are remarkably straightforward. These *access specifiers* are used only in a structure declaration, and they change the boundary for all the declarations that follow them. Whenever you use an access specifier, it must be followed by a colon.

Public means all member declarations that follow are available to everyone. public members are like struct members. For example, the struct declarations in Listing 5-1 are identical.

Listing 5-1. C++'s public is Just Like C's struct

```
//: C05:Public.cpp
// Uses identical struct declarations

struct A {
  int i;
  char j;
  float f;
  void func();
};

void A::func() {}

struct B {
public:
  int i;
  char j;
  float f;
  void func();
};

void B::func() {}

int main() {
  A a; B b;
  a.i = b.i = 1;
  a.j = b.j = 'c';
```

```
  a.f = b.f = 3.14159;
  a.func();
  b.func();
} ///:~
```

The private keyword, on the other hand, means that no one can access that member except you, the creator of the type, inside function members of that type. private is a brick wall between you and the client programmer; if someone tries to access a private member, they'll get a compile-time error. In struct B in Listing 5-1, you may want to make portions of the representation (*that is, the data members*) hidden, accessible only to you; you can see this in Listing 5-2.

Listing 5-2. The private Access Specifier

```
//: C05:Private.cpp
// Setting the Boundary
// and Hiding Portions of the Representation

struct B {
private:
  char j;
  float f;
public:
  int i;
  void func();
};

void B::func() {
  i = 0;
  j = '0';
  f = 0.0;
};

int main() {
  B b;
  b.i = 1;        // OK, public
//! b.j = '1';   // Illegal, private
//! b.f = 1.0;   // Illegal, private
} ///:~
```

Although func( ) can access any member of B (because func( ) is a member of B, thus automatically granting it permission), an ordinary global function like main( ) cannot. Of course, neither can member functions of other structures. Only the functions that are clearly stated in the structure declaration (the "contract") can have access to private members.

There is no required order for access specifiers, and they may appear more than once. They affect all the members declared after them and before the next access specifier.

Another Access Specifier: protected

The last access specifier is protected. protected acts just like private, with one exception that we can't really talk about right now: "inherited" structures (*which cannot access* private *members*) are granted access to protected members. This will become more clear in Chapter 14 when inheritance is introduced. For current purposes, consider protected to be just like private.

Friends

What if you want to explicitly grant access to a function that isn't a member of the current structure? This is accomplished by declaring that function a friend *inside* the structure declaration. It's important that the friend declaration occurs inside the structure declaration because you (and the compiler) must be able to read the structure declaration and see every rule about the size and behavior of that data type. And a very important rule in any relationship is *"Who can access my private implementation?"*

The class controls what code has access to its members. There's no magic way to "break in" from the outside if you aren't a friend; you can't declare a new class and say, "Hi, I'm a friend of Blah!" and expect to see the private and protected members of Blah.

You can declare a global function as a friend, and you can also declare a member function of another structure, or even an entire structure, as a friend. Listing 5-3 shows an example.

Listing 5-3. Declaring a Friend

```
//: C05:Friend.cpp
// Friend allows special access

// Declaration (incomplete type specification):
struct X;

struct Y {
  void f(X*);
};

struct X { // Definition
private:
  int i;
public:
  void initialize();
  friend void g(X*, int); // Global friend
  friend void Y::f(X*);   // Struct member friend
  friend struct Z;        // Entire struct is a friend
  friend void h();
};

void X::initialize() {
  i = 0;
}

void g(X* x, int i) {
  x->i = i;
}

void Y::f(X* x) {
  x->i = 47;
}

struct Z {
private:
  int j;
public:
```

```
  void initialize();
  void g(X* x);
};

void Z::initialize() {
  j = 99;
}

void Z::g(X* x) {
  x->i += j;
}

void h() {
  X x;
  x.i = 100; // Direct data manipulation
}

int main() {
  X x;
  Z z;
  z.g(&x);
} ///:~
```

struct Y has a member function f( ) that will modify an object of type X. This is a bit of a conundrum because the C++ compiler requires you to declare everything before you can refer to it, so struct Y must be declared before its member Y::f(X*) can be declared as a friend in struct X. But for Y::f(X*) to be declared, struct X must be declared first!

Here's the solution. Notice that Y::f(X*) takes the *address* of an X object. This is critical because the compiler always knows how to pass an address, which is of a fixed size regardless of the object being passed, even if it doesn't have full information about the size of the type. If you try to pass the whole object, however, the compiler must see the entire structure definition of X to know the size and how to pass it, before it allows you to declare a function such as Y::g(X).

By passing the address of an X, the compiler allows you to make an *incomplete type specification* of X prior to declaring Y::f(X*). This is accomplished in the declaration.

```
struct X;
```

This declaration simply tells the compiler there's a struct by that name, so it's okay to refer to it as long as you don't require any more knowledge than the name.

Now, in struct X, the function Y::f(X*) can be declared as a friend with no problem. If you tried to declare it before the compiler had seen the full specification for Y, it would have given you an error. This is a safety feature to ensure consistency and eliminate bugs.

Notice the two other friend functions. The first declares an ordinary global function g( ) as a friend. But g( ) has not been previously declared at the global scope! It turns out that friend can be used this way to simultaneously declare the function *and* give it friend status. This extends to entire structures, such as

```
friend struct Z;
```

is an incomplete type specification for Z, and it gives the entire structure friend status.

Nested Friends

Making a structure nested doesn't automatically give it access to private members. To accomplish this, you must follow a particular form: first, declare (*without defining*) the nested structure, then declare it as a friend, and finally define the structure. The structure definition must be separate from the friend declaration, otherwise it would be seen by the compiler as a non-member. Listing 5-4 shows an example.

Listing 5-4. Nested Friends

```
//: C05:NestFriend.cpp
// Demonstrates Nested friends
#include <iostream>
#include <cstring> // memset()
using namespace std;
const int sz = 20;

struct Holder {
private:
  int a[sz];
public:
  void initialize();
  struct Pointer;
  friend struct Pointer;
  struct Pointer {
  private:
    Holder* h;
    int* p;
  public:
    void initialize(Holder* h);
    // Move around in the array:
    void next();
    void previous();
    void top();
    void end();
    // Access values:
    int read();
    void set(int i);
  };
};

void Holder::initialize() {
  memset(a, 0, sz * sizeof(int));
}

void Holder::Pointer::initialize(Holder* rv) {
  h = rv;
  p = rv->a;
}

void Holder::Pointer::next() {
  if(p < &(h->a[sz - 1])) p++;
}
```

```
void Holder::Pointer::previous() {
  if(p > &(h->a[0])) p--;
}

void Holder::Pointer::top() {
  p = &(h->a[0]);
}

void Holder::Pointer::end() {
  p = &(h->a[sz - 1]);
}

int Holder::Pointer::read() {
  return *p;
}

void Holder::Pointer::set(int i) {
  *p = i;
}

int main() {
  Holder h;
  Holder::Pointer hp, hp2;
  int i;

  h.initialize();
  hp.initialize(&h);
  hp2.initialize(&h);
  for(i = 0; i < sz; i++) {
    hp.set(i);
    hp.next();
  }
  hp.top();
  hp2.end();
  for(i = 0; i < sz; i++) {
    cout << "hp = " << hp.read()
         << ", hp2 = " << hp2.read() << endl;
  hp.next();
  hp2.previous();
  }
} ///:~
```

Once Pointer is declared, it is granted access to the private members of Holder by saying

```
friend struct Pointer;
```

The struct Holder contains an array of ints and the Pointer allows you to access them. Because Pointer is strongly associated with Holder, it's sensible to make it a member structure of Holder. But because Pointer is a separate class from Holder, you can make more than one of them in main( ) and use them to select different parts of the array. Pointer is a structure instead of a raw C pointer, so you can guarantee that it will always safely point inside the Holder.

The Standard *C* Library function `memset( )` (in `<cstring>`) is used for convenience in the program in Listing 5-4. It sets all memory starting at a particular address (the first argument) to a particular value (the second argument) for n bytes past the starting address (n is the third argument). Of course, you could have simply used a loop to iterate through all the memory, but `memset( )` is available, well-tested (so it's less likely you'll introduce an error), and probably more efficient than if you coded it by hand.

Is it pure?

The class definition gives you an audit trail, so you can see from looking at the class which functions have permission to modify the private parts of the class. If a function is a `friend`, it means that it isn't a member, but you want to give permission to modify private data anyway, and it must be listed in the class definition so everyone can see that it's one of the privileged functions.

C++ is a hybrid object-oriented language, not a pure one, and `friend` was added to get around practical problems that crop up. It's fine to point out that this makes the language less "pure" because C++ is designed to be *pragmatic*, not to aspire to an abstract ideal.

Object Layout

Chapter 4 stated that a `struct` written for a *C* compiler and later compiled with C++ would be unchanged. This referred primarily to the object layout of the `struct`—that is, where the storage for the individual variables is positioned in the memory allocated for the object. If the C++ compiler changed the layout of *C* structs, then any *C* code you wrote that inadvisably took advantage of knowledge of the positions of variables in the `struct` would break.

When you start using access specifiers, however, you've moved completely into the C++ realm, and things change a bit. Within a particular *access block* (a group of declarations delimited by access specifiers), the variables are guaranteed to be laid out contiguously, as in *C*. However, the access blocks may not appear in the object in the order that you declare them. Although the compiler will *usually* lay the blocks out exactly as you see them, there is no rule about it because a particular machine architecture and/or operating environment may have explicit support for `private` and `protected` that might require those blocks to be placed in special memory locations. The language specification doesn't want to restrict this kind of advantage.

Access specifiers are part of the structure and don't affect the objects created from the structure. All of the access specification information disappears before the program is run; generally this happens during compilation. In a running program, objects become "regions of storage" and nothing more. If you really want to, you can break all the rules and access the memory directly, as you can in *C*. C++ is not designed to prevent you from doing unwise things; it just provides you with a much easier, highly desirable alternative.

In general, it's not a good idea to depend on anything that's implementation-specific when you're writing a program. When you must have implementation-specific dependencies, encapsulate them inside a structure so that any porting changes are focused in one place.

The Class

Access control is often referred to as *implementation hiding*. Including functions within structures (often referred to as *encapsulation*) produces a data type with characteristics and behaviors, but access control puts boundaries within that data type—for two important reasons. The first is to establish what the client programmers can and can't use. You can build your internal mechanisms into the structure without worrying that client programmers will think that these mechanisms are part of the interface they should be using.

This feeds directly into the second reason, which is to separate the interface from the implementation. If the structure is used in a set of programs, but the client programmers can't do anything but send messages to the `public` interface, then you can change anything that's `private` without requiring modifications to their code.

Encapsulation and access control, taken together, invent something more than a C struct. We're now in the world of object-oriented programming where a structure is describing a class of objects as you would describe a class of fishes or a class of birds: any object belonging to this class will share these characteristics and behaviors. That's what the structure declaration has become, a description of the way all objects of this type will look and act.

In the original OOP language, Simula-67, the keyword class was used to describe a new data type. This apparently inspired Stroustrup (the designer-in-chief of the C++ language) to choose the same keyword for C++ to emphasize that this was the focal point of the whole language: the creation of new data types that are more than just C structs with functions. This certainly seems like adequate justification for a new keyword.

However, the use of class in C++ comes close to being an unnecessary keyword. It's identical to the struct keyword in absolutely every way except one: class defaults to private, whereas struct defaults to public. Listing 5-5 shows two structures that produce the same result.

Listing 5-5. Comparing struct and class

```
//: C05:Class.cpp
// Similarity of struct and class

struct A {
private:
  int i, j, k;
public:
  int f();
  void g();
};

int A::f() {
  return(i + j + k);
}

void A::g() {
  i = j = k = 0;
}

// Identical results are produced with:

class B {
  int i, j, k;
public:
  int f();
  void g();
};

int B::f() {
  return(i + j + k);
}

void B::g() {
  i = j = k = 0;
}
```

```
int main() {
  A a;
  B b;
  a.f(); a.g();
  b.f(); b.g();
} ///:~
```

The class is the fundamental OOP concept in C++. It is one of the keywords that will *not* be set in bold in this book—it becomes annoying with a word repeated as often as "*class.*" The shift to classes is so important that preference of the C++ designers would have been to throw struct out altogether, but the need for backwards compatibility with C wouldn't allow that.

Many people prefer a style of creating classes that is more struct-*like* than *class*-like, because you override the default-to-private behavior of the class by starting out with public elements, such as:

```
class X {
public:
  void interface_function();
private:
  void private_function();
  int internal_representation;
};
```

The logic behind this is that it makes more sense for the reader to see the members of interest first, then they can ignore anything that says private. Indeed, the only reasons all the other members must be declared in the class at all are so the compiler knows how big the objects are and can allocate them properly, and so it can guarantee consistency.

The examples in this book, however, will put the private members first, like this:

```
class X {
  void private_function();
  int internal_representation;
public:
  void interface_function();
};
```

Some people even go to the trouble of decorating their own private names, like this:

```
class Y {
public:
  void f();
private:
  int mX;  // "Self-decorated" name
};
```

Because mX is already hidden in the scope of Y, the m (for "member") is unnecessary. However, in projects with many global variables (something you should strive to avoid, but which is sometimes inevitable in existing projects), it is helpful to be able to distinguish inside a member function definition which data is global and which is a member.

Modifying Stash to Use Access Control

It makes sense to take the examples from *Chapter 4* and modify them to use classes and access control. Notice how the client programmer portion of the interface is now clearly distinguished, so there's no possibility of client programmers accidentally manipulating a part of the class that they shouldn't. See Listing 5-6.

Listing 5-6. Updating Stash to Use Access Control

```
//: C05:Stash.h
// Converted to use access control
#ifndef STASH_H
#define STASH_H

class Stash {
  int size;       // Size of each space
  int quantity;   // Number of storage spaces
  int next;       // Next empty space
  // Dynamically allocated array of bytes:
  unsigned char* storage;
  void inflate(int increase);
public:
  void initialize(int size);
  void cleanup();
  int add(void* element);
  void* fetch(int index);
  int count();
};
#endif            // STASH_H ///:~
```

The inflate( ) function has been made private because it is used only by the add( ) function and is thus part of the underlying implementation, not the interface. This means that, sometime later, you can change the underlying implementation to use a different system for memory management.

Other than the name of the include file, the header is the only thing that's been changed for this example. The implementation file and test file are the same.

Modifying Stack to Use Access Control

As a second example, Listing 5-7 shows the Stack turned into a class. Now the nested data structure is private, which is nice because it ensures that the client programmer will neither have to look at it nor be able to depend on the internal representation of the Stack.

Listing 5-7. Turning Stack into a class

```
//: C05:Stack2.h
// Nested structs via linked list
#ifndef STACK2_H
#define STACK2_H

class Stack {
  struct Link {
    void* data;
```

```
    Link* next;
    void initialize(void* dat, Link* nxt);
  }* head;
public:
  void initialize();
  void push(void* dat);
  void* peek();
  void* pop();
  void cleanup();
};
#endif // STACK2_H ///:~
```

As before, the implementation doesn't change and so it is not repeated here. The test, too, is identical. The only thing that's been changed is the robustness of the class interface. The real value of access control is to prevent you from crossing boundaries during development. In fact, the compiler is the only thing that knows about the protection level of class members. There is no access control information mangled into the member name that carries through to the linker. All the protection checking is done by the compiler; it has vanished by runtime.

Notice that the interface presented to the client programmer is now truly that of a push-down stack. It happens to be implemented as a linked list, but you can change that without affecting what the client programmer interacts with, or (more importantly) a single line of client code.

Handle Classes

Access control in C++ allows you to separate interface from implementation, but the implementation hiding is only partial. The compiler must still see the declarations for all parts of an object in order to create and manipulate it properly. You could imagine a programming language that requires only the public interface of an object and allows the private implementation to be hidden, but C++ performs type checking statically (at compile time) as much as possible. This means that you'll learn as early as possible if there's an error. It also means that your program is more efficient. However, including the private implementation has two effects: the implementation is visible even if you can't easily access it, and it can cause needless recompilation.

Hiding the Implementation

Some projects cannot afford to have their implementation visible to the client programmer. It may show strategic information in a library header file that the company doesn't want available to competitors. For example, you may be working on a system where security is an issue—an encryption algorithm, for example—and you don't want to expose any clues in a header file that might help people to crack the code. Or you may be putting your library in a "hostile" environment where the programmers will directly access the private components anyway, using pointers and casting. In all these situations, it's valuable to have the actual structure compiled inside an implementation file rather than exposed in a header file.

Reducing Recompilation

The project manager in your programming environment will cause a recompilation of a file if that file is touched (that is, modified) *or* if another file it's dependent upon (that is, an included header file) is touched. This means that any time you make a change to a class, whether it's to the public interface or to the private member declarations, you'll force a recompilation of anything that includes that header file. For a large project in its early stages this can be very unwieldy because the underlying implementation may change often; if the project is very big, the time for compiles can prohibit rapid turnaround.

The technique to solve this is sometimes called *handle classes*—everything about the implementation disappears except for a single pointer, the *smile*. The pointer refers to a structure whose definition is in the implementation file along with all the member function definitions. Thus, as long as the interface is unchanged, the header file is untouched. The implementation can change at will, and only the implementation file needs to be recompiled and relinked with the project.

Listing 5-8 contains a simple example demonstrating the technique. The header file contains only the public interface and a single pointer of an incompletely specified class.

Listing 5-8. Handling Classes

```
//: C05:Handle.h
// Handle classes header file
#ifndef HANDLE_H
#define HANDLE_H

class Handle {
  struct Hire; // Class declaration only
  Hire* smile;
public:
  void initialize();
  void cleanup();
  int read();
  void change(int);
};
#endif          // HANDLE_H ///:~
```

This is all the client programmer is able to see. The line

```
struct Hire;
```

is an incomplete type specification or a class declaration (a class definition includes the body of the class). It tells the compiler that Hire is a structure name, but it doesn't give any details about the struct. This is only enough information to create a pointer to the struct; you can't create an object until the structure body has been provided. In this technique, that structure body is hidden away in the implementation file (see Listing 5-9).

Listing 5-9. Handling Implementation

```
//: C05:Handle.cpp {0}
// Handle implementation
#include "Handle.h"      // To be INCLUDED from Header FILE above
#include "../require.h" // To be INCLUDED from Header FILE in Chapter 3

// Define Handle's implementation:
struct Handle::Hire {
  int i;
};

void Handle::initialize() {
  smile = new Hire;
  smile->i = 0;
}
```

```
void Handle::cleanup() {
  delete smile;
}

int Handle::read() {
  return smile->i;
}

void Handle::change(int x) {
  smile->i = x;
} ///:~
```

Hire is a nested structure, so it must be defined with scope resolution, like:

```
struct Handle::Hire {
```

In Handle::initialize( ), storage is allocated for a Hire structure, and in Handle::cleanup( ) this storage is released. This storage is used in lieu of all the data elements you'd normally put into the private section of the class. When you compile Handle.cpp, this structure definition is hidden away in the object file where no one can see it. If you change the elements of Hire, the only file that must be recompiled is Handle.cpp because the header file is untouched.

The use of Handle is like the use of any class: include the header, create objects, and send messages (see Listing 5-10).

Listing 5-10. Using the Handle Class

```
//: C05:UseHandle.cpp
//{L} Handle
// Use the Handle class
#include "Handle.h"

int main() {
  Handle u;
  u.initialize();
  u.read();
  u.change(1);
  u.cleanup();
} ///:~
```

The only thing the client programmer can access is the public interface, so as long as the implementation is the only thing that changes, the file never needs recompilation. Thus, although this isn't perfect implementation hiding, it's a big improvement.

Review Session

1. Access control in C++ gives valuable control to the creator of a class. The users of the class can clearly see exactly what they can use and what to ignore. More important, though, is the ability to ensure that no client programmer becomes dependent on any part of the *underlying implementation* of a class. If you know this as the creator of the class, you can change the *underlying implementation* with the knowledge that no *client programmer* will be affected by the changes because they can't access that part of the class.

2. When you have the ability to change the *underlying implementation*, you can not only improve your design at some later time, but you also have the freedom to make mistakes. No matter how carefully you plan and design, you'll make mistakes. Knowing that it's relatively safe to make these mistakes means you'll be more experimental, you'll learn faster, and you'll finish your project sooner.

3. The *public interface* to a class is what the client programmer does see, so that is the most important part of the class to get "right" during analysis and design. But even that allows you some leeway for change. If you don't get the interface right the first time, you can *add* more functions, as long as you don't remove any that *client programmers* have already used in their code.

CHAPTER 6

■ ■ ■

Initialization and Cleanup

Chapter 4 made a significant improvement in library use by taking all the scattered components of a typical C library and encapsulating them into a structure (an abstract data type, called a *class* from now on).

This not only provides a single unified point of entry into a library component, but it also hides the names of the functions within the class name. In *Chapter 5*, access control (*implementation hiding*) was introduced. This gives the class designer a way to establish clear boundaries for determining what the client programmer is allowed to manipulate and what is off limits. It means the internal mechanisms of a data type's operation are under the control and discretion of the designer of the class, and it's clear to client programmers what members they can and should pay attention to.

Together, encapsulation and access control make a significant step in improving the ease of library use. The concept of "*new data type*" they provide is better in some ways than the existing built-in data types from C. The C++ compiler can now provide type-checking guarantees for that data type and thus ensure a level of safety when that data type is being used.

When it comes to safety, however, there's a lot more the compiler can do for us than C provides. In this and future chapters, you'll see additional features that have been engineered into C++ that make the bugs in your program almost leap out and grab you, sometimes before you even compile the program, but usually in the form of compiler warnings and errors. For this reason, you will soon get used to the unlikely-sounding scenario that a C++ program that compiles often runs right the first time.

Two of these safety issues are initialization and cleanup. A large segment of C bugs occur when the programmer forgets to initialize or clean up a variable. This is especially true with C libraries, when client programmers don't know how to initialize a struct, or even that they must.

■ Note Libraries often do not include an initialization function, so the client programmer is forced to initialize the struct by hand.

Cleanup is a special problem because C programmers are comfortable with forgetting about variables once they are finished, so any cleaning up that may be necessary for a library's struct is often missed.

In C++, the concept of initialization and cleanup is essential for easy library use and to eliminate the many subtle bugs that occur when the client programmer forgets to perform these activities. This chapter examines the features in C++ that help guarantee proper initialization and cleanup.

Guaranteed Initialization with the Constructor

Both the Stash and Stack classes defined previously have a function called initialize(), which hints by its name that it should be called before using the object in any other way. Unfortunately, this means the client programmer must ensure proper initialization. Client programmers are prone to miss details like initialization in their headlong rush to make your amazing library solve their problem. In C++, initialization is too important to leave to the client

153

programmer. The class designer can guarantee initialization of every object by providing a special function called the *constructor*. If a class has a constructor, the compiler automatically calls that constructor at the point an object is created, before client programmers can get their hands on the object. The constructor call isn't even an option for the client programmer; it is performed by the compiler at the point the object is defined.

The next challenge is what to name this function. There are two issues. The first is that any name you use is something that can potentially clash with a name you might like to use as a member in the class. The second is that because the compiler is responsible for calling the constructor, it must always know which function to call. The solution that the C++ designers chose seems the easiest and most logical: the name of the constructor is the same as the name of the class. It makes sense that such a function will be called automatically on initialization.

Here's a simple class with a constructor:

```cpp
class X {
  int i;
public:
  X();  // Constructor
};
```

Now, when an object is defined, such as:

```cpp
void f() {
  X a;
  // ...
}
```

the same thing happens as if a was an int; storage is allocated for the object. But when the program reaches the sequence point (*point of execution*) where a is defined, the constructor is called automatically. That is, the compiler quietly inserts the call to X::X() for the object a at the point of definition. Like any member function, the first ("*secret*") argument to the constructor is the this pointer—the address of the object for which it is being called. In the case of the constructor, however, this is pointing to an uninitialized block of memory, and it's the job of the constructor to initialize this memory properly.

Like any function, the constructor can have arguments to allow you to specify how an object is created, give it initialization values, and so on. Constructor arguments provide you with a way to guarantee that all parts of your object are initialized to appropriate values. For example, if a class called Tree has a constructor that takes a single integer argument denoting the height of the tree, then you must create a tree object like this:

```cpp
Tree t(12);  // 12-foot tree
```

If Tree(int) is your only constructor, the compiler won't let you create an object any other way.

■ **Note**   We'll look at multiple constructors and different ways to call constructors in the next chapter.

That's really all there is to a constructor; it's a specially named function that is called automatically by the compiler for every object at the point of that object's creation. Despite its simplicity, it is exceptionally valuable because it eliminates a large class of problems and makes the code easier to write and read. In the preceding code fragment, for example, you don't see an explicit function call to some initialize() function that is conceptually separate from definition. *In C++, definition and initialization are unified concepts*—you can't have one without the other.

Both the constructor and destructor are very unusual types of functions: they have no return value. This is distinctly different from a void return value, in which the function returns nothing but you still have the option to make it something else. Constructors and destructors return nothing and you don't have an option. The acts of bringing an object into and out of the program are special, like birth and death, and the compiler always makes the function calls itself, to make sure they happen. If there were a return value, and if you could select your own, the compiler would somehow have to know what to do with the return value, or the client programmer would have to explicitly call constructors and destructors, which would eliminate their safety.

Guaranteed Cleanup with the Destructor

As a C programmer, you often think about the importance of initialization, but it's rarer to think about cleanup. After all, what do you need to do to clean up an int? Just forget about it. However, with libraries, just "*letting go*" of an object once you're done with it is not so safe. What if it modifies some piece of hardware, or puts something on the screen, or allocates storage on the heap? If you just forget about it, your object never achieves closure upon its exit from this world. In C++, cleanup is as important as initialization and is therefore guaranteed with the destructor.

The syntax for the destructor is similar to that for the constructor: the class name is used for the name of the function. However, the destructor is distinguished from the constructor by a leading tilde (~). In addition, the destructor never has any arguments because destruction never needs any options. Here's the declaration for a destructor:

```
class Y {
public:
  ~Y();
};
```

The destructor is called automatically by the compiler when the object goes out of scope. You can see where the constructor gets called by the point of definition of the object, but the only evidence for a destructor call is the closing brace of the scope that surrounds the object. Yet the destructor is still called, even when you use goto to jump out of a scope. (goto still exists in C++ for backward compatibility with C and for the times when it comes in handy.) You should note that a *nonlocal goto*, implemented by the Standard C Library functions setjmp() and longjmp(), doesn't cause destructors to be called.

■ **Note** This is the specification, even if your compiler doesn't implement it that way. Relying on a feature that isn't in the specification means your code is non-portable.

Listing 6-1 demonstrates the features of constructors and destructors you've seen so far.

Listing 6-1. Constructors and Destructors

```
//: C06:Constructor1.cpp
// Demonstrates features of constructors & destructors
#include <iostream>
using namespace std;

class Tree {
  int height;
public:
  Tree(int initialHeight);  // Constructor
  ~Tree();                  // Destructor
  void grow(int years);
  void printsize();
};
```

```
Tree::Tree(int initialHeight) {
  height = initialHeight;
}

Tree::~Tree() {
  cout << "inside Tree destructor" << endl;
  printsize();
}

void Tree::grow(int years) {
  height += years;
}
void Tree::printsize() {
  cout << "Tree height is " << height << endl;
}

int main() {
  cout << "before opening brace" << endl;
  {
    Tree t(12);
    cout << "after Tree creation" << endl;
    t.printsize();
    t.grow(4);
    cout << "before closing brace" << endl;
  }
  cout << "after closing brace" << endl;
} ///:~
```

Here's the output of this program:

```
before opening brace
after Tree creation
Tree height is 12
before closing brace
inside Tree destructor
Tree height is 16
after closing brace
```

You can see that the destructor is automatically called at the closing brace of the scope that encloses it.

Elimination of the Definition Block

In *C*, you must always define all the variables at the beginning of a block, after the opening brace. This is not an uncommon requirement in programming languages, and the reason given has often been that it's *"good programming style."* At the same time, it seems inconvenient to pop back to the beginning of a block every time you need a new variable. Moreover, code is more readable when the variable definition is close to its point of use.

Perhaps these arguments are stylistic. In C++, however, there's a significant problem in being forced to define all objects at the beginning of a scope. If a constructor exists, it must be called when the object is created. However, if the constructor takes one or more initialization arguments, how do you know you will have that initialization information at the beginning of a scope? In the general programming situation, you won't. Because *C* has no concept of private, this separation of definition and initialization is no problem. However, C++ guarantees that when an object is created, it is simultaneously initialized. This ensures that you will have no uninitialized objects running around in your system. *C* doesn't care; in fact, *C encourages* this practice by requiring you to define variables at the beginning of a block before you necessarily have the initialization information.

In general, C++ will not allow you to create an object before you have the initialization information for the constructor. Because of this, the language wouldn't be feasible if you had to define variables at the beginning of a scope. In fact, the style of the language seems to encourage the definition of an object as close to its point of use as possible. In C++, any rule that applies to an "object" automatically refers to an object of a built-in type as well. This means that any class object or variable of a built-in type can also be defined at any point in a scope. It also means that you can wait until you have the information for a variable before defining it, so you can always define and initialize at the same time. See Listing 6-2 for an example.

Listing 6-2. Defining Variables Anywhere

```
//: C06:DefineInitialize.cpp
// Demonstrates that you can define variables anywhere
#include "../require.h"      // To be INCLUDED from Header FILE in Chapter 3
#include <iostream>
#include <string>
using namespace std;

class G {
  int i;
public:
  G(int ii);
};

G::G(int ii) { i = ii; }

int main() {
  cout << "initialization value? ";
  int retval = 0;
  cin >> retval;
  require(retval != 0);
  int y = retval + 3;
  G g(y);
} ///:~
```

You can see that some code is executed; then `retval` is defined, initialized, and used to capture user input; and then y and g are defined. *C*, on the other hand, does not allow a variable to be defined anywhere except at the beginning of the scope.

In general, you should define variables as close to their point of use as possible, and always initialize them when they are defined.

■ **Note**   This is a stylistic suggestion for built-in types, where initialization is optional.

This is a safety issue. By reducing the duration of the variable's availability within the scope, you are reducing the chance it will be misused in some other part of the scope. In addition, readability is improved because the reader doesn't have to jump back and forth to the beginning of the scope to know the type of a variable.

for loops

In C++, you will often see a for loop counter defined right inside the for expression, such as:

```
for(int j = 0; j < 100; j++) {
  cout << "j = " << j << endl;
}
for(int i = 0; i < 100; i++)
  cout << "i = " << i << endl;
```

The statements above are important special cases, which cause confusion to new C++ programmers.

The variables i and j are defined directly inside the for expression (*which you cannot do in C*). They are then available for use in the for loop. It's a very convenient syntax because the context removes all question about the purpose of i and j, so you don't need to use such ungainly names as i_loop_counter for clarity.

However, some confusion may result if you expect the lifetimes of the variables i and j to extend beyond the scope of the for loop—*they do not*.

Chapter 3 points out that while and switch statements also allow the definition of objects in their control expressions, although this usage seems far less important than with the for loop.

Watch out for local variables that hide variables from the enclosing scope. In general, using the same name for a nested variable and a variable that is global to that scope is confusing and error prone.

Smaller scopes are an indicator of good design, at least according to me. If you have several pages for a single function, perhaps you're trying to do too much with that function. More granular functions are not only more useful, but it's also easier to find bugs.

Storage Allocation

A variable can now be defined at any point in a scope, so it might seem that the storage for a variable may not be defined until its point of definition. It's actually more likely that the compiler will follow the practice in C of allocating all the storage for a scope at the opening brace of that scope. It doesn't matter because, as a programmer, you can't access the storage until it has been defined. Although the storage is allocated at the beginning of the block, the constructor call doesn't happen until the sequence point where the object is defined because the identifier isn't available until then. The compiler even checks to make sure that you don't put the object definition (*and thus the constructor call*) where the sequence point only conditionally passes through it, such as in a switch statement or somewhere a goto can jump past it. Uncommenting the statements in Listing 6-3 will generate a warning or an error.

Listing 6-3. Jumping Past Constructors is not Allowed in C++

```
//: C06:Nojump.cpp
// Demonstrates that you can't jump past constructors in C++

class X {
public:
  X();
};

X::X() {}

void f(int i) {
  if(i < 10) {
    //! goto jump1; // Error: goto bypasses init
  }
```

```
  X x1;  // Constructor called here
 jump1:
  switch(i) {
    case 1 :
      X x2;    // Constructor called here
      break;
  //! case 2 : // Error: case bypasses init
      X x3;    // Constructor called here
      break;
  }
}

int main() {
  f(9);
  f(11);
}///:~
```

In this code, both the goto and the switch can potentially jump past the sequence point where a constructor is called. That object will then be in scope even if the constructor hasn't been called, so the compiler gives an error message. This once again guarantees that an object cannot be created unless it is also initialized.

All the storage allocation discussed here happens, of course, on the stack. The storage is allocated by the compiler by moving the stack pointer down (*a relative term, which may indicate an increase or decrease of the actual stack pointer value, depending on your computer*). Objects can also be allocated on the heap using new, which is something you'll explore further in Chapter 13.

Stash with Constructors and Destructors

The examples from previous chapters have obvious functions that map to constructors and destructors: initialize() and cleanup(). Listing 6-4 shows the Stash header using constructors and destructors.

Listing 6-4. Stash Header Using Constructors and Destructors

```
//: C06:Stash2.h
// Demonstrates Stash header file with constructors & destructors
#ifndef STASH2_H
#define STASH2_H

class Stash {
  int size;       // Size of each space
  int quantity;   // Number of storage spaces
  int next;       // Next empty space
  // Dynamically allocated array of bytes:
  unsigned char* storage;
  void inflate(int increase);
public:
  Stash(int size);
  ~Stash();
  int add(void* element);
  void* fetch(int index);
  int count();
};
#endif            // STASH2_H ///:~
```

The only member function definitions that are changed are initialize() and cleanup(), which have been replaced with a constructor and destructor (see Listing 6-5).

Listing 6-5. Implementing Stash with Constructors & Destructors

```cpp
//: C06:Stash2.cpp {O}
// Demonstrates implementation of Stash
// with constructors & destructors
#include "Stash2.h"    // To be INCLUDED from Header FILE above
#include "../require.h"
#include <iostream>
#include <cassert>
using namespace std;
const int increment = 100;

Stash::Stash(int sz) {
  size = sz;
  quantity = 0;
  storage = 0;
  next = 0;
}

int Stash::add(void* element) {
  if(next >= quantity) // Enough space left?
    inflate(increment);
  // Copy element into storage,
  // starting at next empty space:
  int startBytes = (next * size);
  unsigned char* e = (unsigned char*)element;
  for(int i = 0; i < size; i++)
    storage[startBytes + i] = e[i];
  next++;
  return(next - 1);    // Index number
}

void* Stash::fetch(int index) {
  require(0 <= index, "Stash::fetch (-)index");
  if(index >= next)
    return 0; // To indicate the end
  // Produce pointer to desired element:
  return &(storage[index * size]);
}

int Stash::count() {
return next;            // Number of elements in CStash
}

void Stash::inflate(int increase) {
  require(increase > 0,
    "Stash::inflate zero or negative increase");
  int newQuantity = (quantity + increase);
  int newBytes = (newQuantity * size);
```

```
  int oldBytes = (quantity * size);
  unsigned char* b = new unsigned char[newBytes];
  for(int i = 0; i < oldBytes; i++)
    b[i] = storage[i]; // Copy old to new
  delete [](storage);  // Old storage
  storage = b; // Point to new memory
  quantity = newQuantity;
}

Stash::~Stash() {
  if(storage != 0) {
    cout << "freeing storage" << endl;
    delete []storage;
  }
} ///:~
```

You can see that the require.h functions are being used to watch for programmer errors, instead of assert(). The output of a failed assert() is not as useful as that of the require.h functions.

Because inflate() is private, the only way a require() could fail is if one of the other member functions accidentally passed an incorrect value to inflate(). If you are certain this can't happen, you could consider removing the require(), but you might keep in mind that until the class is stable, there's always the possibility that new code might be added to the class that could cause errors. The cost of the require() is low (and could be automatically removed using the preprocessor) and the value of code robustness is high).

Notice in Listing 6-6 how the definitions for Stash objects appear right before they are needed, and how the initialization appears as part of the definition in the constructor argument list.

Listing 6-6. Testing Stash (with Constructors & Destructors)

```
//: C06:Stash2Test.cpp

//{L} Stash2

// Demonstrates testing of Stash
// (with constructors & destructors)
#include "Stash2.h"
#include "../require.h"
#include <fstream>
#include <iostream>
#include <string>

using namespace std;

int main() {
  Stash intStash(sizeof(int));
  for(int i = 0; i < 100; i++)
    int Stash.add(&i);
  for(int j = 0; j < intStash.count(); j++)
    cout << "intStash.fetch(" << j << ") = "
         << *(int*) intStash.fetch(j)
         << endl;
  const int bufsize = 80;
  Stash stringStash(sizeof(char) * bufsize);
```

```
ifstream in("Stash2Test.cpp");
assure(in, " Stash2Test.cpp");
string line;
while(getline(in, line))
  stringStash.add((char*)line.c_str());
int k = 0;
char* cp;
while((cp = (char*)stringStash.fetch(k++))!=0)
  cout << "stringStash.fetch(" << k << ") = "
       << cp << endl;
} ///:~
```

Also notice how the cleanup() calls have been eliminated, but the destructors are still automatically called when intStash and stringStash go out of scope.

One thing to be aware of in the Stash examples: I am being very careful to use only built-in types; that is, those without destructors. If you were to try to copy class objects into the Stash, you'd run into all kinds of problems and it wouldn't work right. The Standard C++ Library can actually make correct copies of objects into its containers, but this is a rather messy and complicated process. In the following Stack example (Listing 6-7), you'll see that pointers are used to sidestep this issue.

Stack with Constructors and Destructors

Reimplementing the linked list (inside Stack) with constructors and destructors shows how neatly constructors and destructors work with new and delete. Listing 6-7 contains the modified header file.

Listing 6-7. Stack with Constructors/Destructors

```
//: C06:Stack3.h
// Demonstrates the modified header file


#ifndef STACK3_H
#define STACK3_H

class Stack {
  struct Link {
    void* data;
    Link* next;
    Link(void* dat, Link* nxt);
    ~Link();
  }* head;
public:
  Stack();
  ~Stack();
  void push(void* dat);
  void* peek();
  void* pop();
};
#endif // STACK3_H ///:~
```

Not only does Stack have a constructor and destructor, but so does the nested struct Link, as you can see in Listing 6-8.

Listing 6-8. Implementing Stack with Constructors/Destructors

```
//: C06:Stack3.cpp {O}
// Demonstrates implementation of Stack
// with constructors/destructors
#include "Stack3.h"    // To be INCLUDED from Header FILE above
#include "../require.h"
using namespace std;

Stack::Link::Link(void* dat, Link* nxt) {
  data = dat;
  next = nxt;
}

Stack::Link::~Link() { }

Stack::Stack() { head = 0; }

void Stack::push(void* dat) {
  head = new Link(dat, head);
}

void* Stack::peek() {
  require(head != 0, "Stack empty");
  return head->data;
}

void* Stack::pop() {
  if(head == 0) return 0;
  void* result = head->data;
  Link* oldHead = head;
  head = head->next;
  delete oldHead;
  return result;
}

Stack::~Stack() {
  require(head == 0, "Stack not empty");
} ///:~
```

The Link::Link() constructor simply initializes the data and next pointers, so in Stack::push() the line

```
head = new Link(dat, head);
```

not only allocates a new link (*using dynamic object creation with the keyword* new, introduced in Chapter 4), but it also neatly initializes the pointers for that link.

You may wonder why the destructor for Link doesn't do anything—in particular, why doesn't it delete the data pointer? There are two problems. In Chapter 4, where the Stack was introduced, it was pointed out that you cannot properly delete a void pointer if it points to an object (*an assertion* that will be proven in Chapter 13). But in addition, if the Link destructor deleted the data pointer, pop() would end up returning a pointer to a deleted object, which would definitely be a bug. This is sometimes referred to as the issue of *ownership*: the Link and thus the Stack only holds the pointers, but is not responsible for cleaning them up. This means that you must be very careful that you know who *is* responsible. For example, if you don't pop() and delete all the pointers on the Stack, they won't get cleaned up automatically by the Stack's destructor. This can be a sticky issue and leads to memory leaks, so knowing who is responsible for cleaning up an object can make the difference between a successful program and a buggy one; that's why Stack::~Stack() prints an error message if the Stack object isn't empty upon destruction.

Because the allocation and cleanup of the Link objects are hidden within Stack—it's part of the underlying implementation—you don't see it happening in the test program, although you *are* responsible for deleting the pointers that come back from pop(). See Listing 6-9.

Listing 6-9. Testing Stack (with Constructors/Destructors)

```
//: C06:Stack3Test.cpp

//{L} Stack3

//{T} Stack3Test.cpp

// Demonstrates testing of Stack
// (with constructors/destructors)

#include "Stack3.h"
#include "../require.h"
#include <fstream>
#include <iostream>
#include <string>

using namespace std;

int main(int argc, char* argv[]) {
  requireArgs(argc, 1); // File name is argument
  ifstream in(argv[1]);
  assure(in, argv[1]);
  Stack textlines;
  string line;
  // Read file and store lines in the stack:
  while(getline(in, line))
    textlines.push(new string(line));
  // Pop the lines from the stack and print them:
  string* s;
  while((s = (string*) textlines.pop()) != 0) {
    cout << *s << endl;
    delete s;
  }
} ///:~
```

In this case, all the lines in textlines are popped and deleted, but if they weren't, you'd get a require() message that would mean there was a memory leak.

Aggregate Initialization

An *aggregate* is just what it sounds like: *a bunch of things clumped together*. This definition includes aggregates of mixed types, like structs and classes. An array is an aggregate of a single type.

Initializing aggregates can be error-prone and tedious. In C++,something called *aggregate initialization* makes it much safer. When you create an object that's an aggregate, all you must do is make an assignment, and the initialization will be taken care of by the compiler. This assignment comes in several flavors, depending on the type of aggregate you're dealing with, but in all cases the elements in the assignment must be surrounded by curly braces. For an array of built-in types, this is quite simple.

```
int a[5] = { 1, 2, 3, 4, 5 };
```

If you try to give more initializers than there are array elements, the compiler gives an error message. But what happens if you give *fewer* initializers, such as:

```
int b[6] = {0};
```

Here, the compiler will use the first initializer for the first array element, and then use zero for all the elements without initializers. Notice this initialization behavior doesn't occur if you define an array without a list of initializers. So the expression above is a succinct way to initialize an array to zero, without using a for loop, and without any possibility of an off-by-one error.(*Depending on the compiler*, it may also be more efficient than the for loop.)

A second shorthand for arrays is *automatic counting*, in which you let the compiler determine the size of the array based on *the number of initializers,* such as:

```
int c[] = { 1, 2, 3, 4 };
```

Now if you decide to add another element to the array, you simply add another initializer. If you can set your code up so it needs to be changed in only one spot, you reduce the chance of errors during modification. But how do you determine the size of the array? The expression (sizeof () / sizeof (*c)) (*size of the entire array divided by the size of the first element*) does the trick in a way that doesn't need to be changed if the array size changes, such as:

```
for(int i = 0; i < (sizeof (c) / sizeof (*c)); i++)
  c[i]++;
```

Because structures are also aggregates, they can be initialized in a similar fashion. Because a C-style struct has all of its members public, they can be assigned directly such as:

```
struct X {
  int i;
  float f;
  char c;
};
```

```
X x1 = { 1, 2.2, 'c' };
```

If you have an array of such objects, you can initialize them by using a nested set of curly braces for each object, such as:

```
X x2[3] = { {1, 1.1, 'a'}, {2, 2.2, 'b'} };
```

Here, the third object is initialized to zero.

If any of the data members are private (*which is typically the case for a well-designed class in* C++), or even if everything's public but there's a constructor, things are different. In the examples above, the initializers are assigned directly to the elements of the aggregate, but constructors are a way of forcing initialization to occur through a formal interface. Here, the constructors must be called to perform the initialization. So if you have a struct that looks as:

```
struct Y {
  float f;
  int i;
  Y(int a);
};
```

You must indicate constructor calls. The best approach is the explicit one, as in:

```
Y y1[] = { Y(1), Y(2), Y(3) };
```

You get three objects and three constructor calls. Anytime you have a constructor, whether it's a struct with all members public or a class with private data members, all the initialization must go through the constructor, even if you're using aggregate initialization.

Listing 6-10 shows a second example showing multiple constructor arguments.

Listing 6-10. Using Multiple Constructor Arguments (with Aggregate Initialization)

```
//: C06:Multiarg.cpp
// Demonstrates use of multiple constructor arguments
// (with aggregate initialization)
#include <iostream>
using namespace std;

class Z {
  int i, j;
public:
  Z(int ii, int jj);
  void print();
};

Z::Z(int ii, int jj) {
  i = ii;
  j = jj;
}

void Z::print() {
  cout << "i = " << i << ", j = " << j << endl;
}

int main() {
  Z zz[] = { Z(1,2), Z(3,4), Z(5,6), Z(7,8) };
  for(int i = 0; i < (sizeof (zz) / sizeof (*zz)); i++)
    zz[i].print();
} ///:~
```

Notice that it looks like an explicit constructor is called for each object in the array.

Default Constructors

A *default constructor* is one that can be called with no arguments. A default constructor is used to create a "vanilla object," but it's also important *when the compiler is told to create an object but isn't given any details*. For example, if you take the struct Y defined previously and use it in a definition such as:

```
Y y2[2] = { Y(1) };
```

the compiler will complain that it cannot find a default constructor. The second object in the array wants to be created with no arguments, and that's where the compiler looks for a default constructor. In fact, if you simply define an array of Y objects such as:

```
Y y3[7];
```

the compiler will complain because it must have a default constructor to initialize every object in the array. The same problem occurs if you create an individual object like this:

```
Y y4;
```

Remember, if you have a constructor, the compiler ensures that construction *always* happens, regardless of the situation.

The default constructor is *so important* that if (and only if) there are no constructors for a structure (struct *or* class), the compiler will automatically create one for you. So the code in Listing 6-11 works.

Listing 6-11. Generating Automatic Default Constructor

```
//: C06:AutoDefaultConstructor.cpp

// Demonstrates automatically-generated default constructor

class V {
  int i;  // private
}; // No constructor

int main() {

  V v, v2[10];

}
///:~
```

If any constructors are defined, however, and there's no default constructor, the instances of V above will generate compile-time errors.

You might think that the compiler-synthesized constructor should do some intelligent initialization, like setting all the memory for the object to zero. But it doesn't—*that would add extra overhead but be out of the programmer's control.* If you want the memory to be initialized to zero, you must do it yourself by writing the default constructor explicitly.

Although the compiler will create a default constructor for you, the behavior of the compiler-synthesized constructor is rarely what you want. You should treat this feature as a safety net, but use it sparingly. In general, *you should define your constructors explicitly* and not allow the compiler to do it for you.

Review Session

1. The seemingly elaborate mechanisms provided by C++ should give you a strong hint about the critical importance placed on initialization and cleanup in the language.

2. One of the first observations the C++ designers made about productivity in *C* was that a significant portion of programming problems are caused by improper initialization of variables. These kinds of bugs are hard to find, and similar issues apply to improper cleanup.

3. Because constructors and destructors allow you to "guarantee" proper initialization and cleanup (*the compiler will not allow an object to be created and destroyed without the proper constructor and destructor calls*), you get complete control and safety.

4. *Aggregate initialization* is included in a similar vein—it prevents you from *making typical initialization mistakes* with aggregates of built-in types and makes your code more succinct.

5. Safety during coding is a big issue in C++. *Initialization and cleanup* are an important part of this, but you'll also see other safety issues as the book progresses.

CHAPTER 7

■ ■ ■

Function Overloading and Default Arguments

One of the important features in any programming language is the convenient use of names.

When you create an object (a *variable*), you give a name to a region of storage. A function is a name for an action. By making up names to describe the system at hand, you create a program that is easier for people to understand and change. It's a lot like writing prose—the goal is to communicate with your readers.

A problem arises when mapping the concept of nuance in human language onto a programming language.
Often, the same word expresses a number of different meanings, depending on context. That is, a single word has multiple meanings—it's "overloaded." This is very useful, especially when it comes to trivial differences. You say "*wash the shirt, wash the car.*" It would be silly to be forced to say, "*shirt_wash the shirt, car_wash the car*" just so the listener doesn't have to make any distinction about the action performed. Human languages have built-in redundancy, so even if you miss a few words, you can still determine the meaning. We don't need unique identifiers; we can deduce meaning from context.

Most programming languages, however, require that you have a unique identifier for each function. If you have three different types of data that you want to print: int, char, and float, you generally have to create three different function names, for example, print_int(), print_char(), and print_float(). This loads extra work on you as you write the program and on readers as they try to understand it.

In C++, another factor forces the overloading of function names: the constructor. Because the constructor's name is predetermined by the name of the class, it would seem that there can be only one constructor. But what if you want to create an object in more than one way? For example, suppose you build a class that can initialize itself in a standard way and also by reading information from a file. You need two constructors, one that takes no arguments (the *default constructor*) and one that takes a string as an argument, which is the name of the file to initialize the object. Both are constructors, so they must have the same name: the name of the class. Thus, function overloading is essential to allow the same function name—the constructor in this case—to be used with different argument types.

Although function overloading is a must for constructors, it's a general convenience and can be used with any function, not just class member functions. In addition, function overloading means that if you have two libraries that contain functions of the same name, they won't conflict as long as the argument lists are different. You'll look at all these factors in detail throughout this chapter.

The theme of this chapter is convenient use of function names. Function overloading allows you to use the same name for different functions, but there's a second way to make calling a function more convenient. What if you'd like to call the same function in different ways? When functions have long argument lists, it can become tedious to write (and confusing to read) the function calls when most of the arguments are the same for all the calls. A commonly used feature in C++ is called *default arguments*. A default argument is one the compiler inserts if it isn't specified in the function call. Thus, the calls f("hello"), f("hi", 1), and f("howdy", 2, 'c') can all be calls to the same function. They could also be calls to three overloaded functions, but when the argument lists are this similar, you'll usually want similar behavior, which calls for a single function.

Function overloading and default arguments really aren't very complicated. By the time you reach the end of this chapter, you'll understand when to use them and the underlying mechanisms that implement them during compiling and linking.

More Name Decoration

In Chapter 4, the concept of *name decoration* was introduced. In the code

```
void f();
class X { void f(); };
```

the function f() inside the scope of class X does not clash with the global version of f(). The compiler performs this scoping by manufacturing different internal names for the global version of f() and X::f(). In Chapter 4, it was suggested that the names are simply the class name "decorated" together with the function name, so the internal names the compiler uses might be _f and _X_f. However, it turns out that function name decoration involves more than the class name.

Here's why. Suppose you want to overload two function names,

```
void print(char);
void print(float);
```

It doesn't matter whether they are both inside a class or in the global scope. The compiler can't generate unique internal identifiers if it uses only the scope of the function names. You'd end up with _print in both cases. The idea of an overloaded function is that you use the same function name, but different argument lists. Thus, for overloading to work, the compiler must decorate the function name with the names of the argument types. The functions above, defined at global scope, produce internal names that might look something like _print_char and _print_float. It's worth noting there is no standard for the way names must be decorated by the compiler, so you will see very different results from one compiler to another.

■ **Note**   You can see what it looks like by telling the compiler to generate assembly-language output.

This, of course, causes problems if you want to buy compiled libraries for a particular compiler and linker—but even if name decoration were standardized, there would be other roadblocks because of the way different compilers generate code.

Here is an example of an *assembly language code fragment* in this context:

```
IF LCODE                             ;    if large code model
Extrn           _func1:far           ;    then far function
ELSE
Extrn           _func1:near          ;    else near function
ENDIF
```

```
Begcode func2                    ;      begin code for func2
Public  func2                    ;      make func2 global
IF LCODE                         ;      if large code model
      _func2  proc far           ;      then define func2 function
ELSE
      _func2  proc near          ;      else define func2 function
ENDIF
```

That's really all there is to function overloading: you can use the same function name for different functions as long as the argument lists are different. The compiler decorates the name, the scope, and the argument lists to produce internal names for it and the linker to use.

Overloading on Return Values

It's common to wonder, *"Why just scopes and argument lists? Why not return values?"* It seems at first that it would make sense to also decorate the return value with the internal function name. Then you could overload on return values as well, like so:

```
void f();
int f();
```

This works fine when the compiler can unequivocally determine the meaning from the context, as in int x = f();. However, in C you've always been able to call a function and ignore the return value (that is, you can call the function for its *side effects*). How can the compiler distinguish which call is meant in this case? Possibly worse is the difficulty the reader has in knowing which function call is meant. Overloading solely on return value is a bit too subtle, and thus isn't allowed in C++.

Type-Safe Linkage

There is an added benefit to all of this name decoration. A particularly sticky problem in C occurs when the client programmer *wrongly declares* a function, or, worse, a function is called without declaring it first, and the compiler infers the function declaration from the way it is called. Sometimes this function declaration is correct, but when it isn't, it can be a difficult bug to find.

Because all functions *must* be declared before they are used in C++, the opportunity for this problem to pop up is greatly diminished. The C++ compiler refuses to declare a function automatically for you, so it's likely that you will include the appropriate header file. However, if for some reason you still manage to wrongly declare a function, either by declaring by hand or including the wrong header file (perhaps one that is out of date), the name decoration provides a safety net that is often referred to as *type-safe linkage*.

Consider the following scenario. In one file is the definition for a function.

```
//: C07:Def.cpp {O}
// Function definition
void f(int) {}
///:~
```

In the second file, the function is WRONGLY declared and then called.

```
//: C07:Use.cpp
//{L} Def
// WRONG Function declaration
void f(char);

int main() {
//!  f(1); // Causes a linker error
} ///:~
```

Even though you can see that the function is actually f(int), the compiler doesn't know this because it was told—through an explicit declaration—that the function is f(char). Thus, the compilation is successful. In C, the linker would also be successful, but *not* in C++. Because the compiler decorates the names, the definition becomes something like f_int, whereas the use of the function is f_char. When the linker tries to resolve the reference to f_char, it can only find f_int, and it gives you an error message. This is type-safe linkage. Although the problem doesn't occur all that often, when it does it can be incredibly difficult to find, especially in a large project. This is one of the cases where you can easily find a difficult error in a C program simply by running it through the C++ compiler.

Overloading Example

Let's modify earlier examples to use function overloading. As stated before, an immediately useful place for overloading is in constructors. You can see this in the version of the Stash class in Listing 7-1.

Listing 7-1. Function Overloading

```
//: C07:Stash3.h
// Function overloading
#ifndef STASH3_H
#define STASH3_H

class Stash {
  int size;       // Size of each space
  int quantity;   // Number of storage spaces
  int next;       // Next empty space
  // Dynamically allocated array of bytes:
  unsigned char* storage;
  void inflate(int increase);
public:
  Stash(int size); // Zero quantity
  Stash(int size, int initQuantity);
  ~Stash();
  int add(void* element);
  void* fetch(int index);
  int count();
};
#endif // STASH3_H ///:~
```

The first Stash() constructor is the same as before, but the second one has a Quantity argument to indicate the initial number of storage places to be allocated. In the definition, you can see that the internal value of quantity is set to zero, along with the storage pointer. In the second constructor, the call to inflate(initQuantity) increases quantity to the allocated size (see Listing 7-2).

Listing 7-2. More Function Overloading

```cpp
//: C07:Stash3.cpp {0}
// Function overloading
#include "Stash3.h"            // To be INCLUDED from Header FILE above
#include "../require.h"        // To be INCLUDED from Header FILE in Chapter 3

#include <iostream>
#include <cassert>
using namespace std;
const int increment = 100;

Stash::Stash(int sz) {
  size = sz;
  quantity = 0;
  next = 0;
  storage = 0;
}

Stash::Stash(int sz, int initQuantity) {
  size = sz;
  quantity = 0;
  next = 0;
  storage = 0;
  inflate(initQuantity);
}

Stash::~Stash() {
  if(storage != 0) {
    cout << "freeing storage" << endl;
    delete []storage;
  }
}

int Stash::add(void* element) {
  if(next >= quantity) // Enough space left?
    inflate(increment);
  // Copy element into storage,
  // starting at next empty space:
  int startBytes = next * size;
  unsigned char* e = (unsigned char*)element;
  for(int i = 0; i < size; i++)
    storage[startBytes + i] = e[i];
  next++;
  return(next - 1); // Index number
}

void* Stash::fetch(int index) {
  require(0 <= index, "Stash::fetch (-)index");
  if(index >= next)
```

```
  return 0; // To indicate the end
  // Produce pointer to desired element:
  return &(storage[index * size]);
}

int Stash::count() {
return next;
        // Number of elements in CStash
}

void Stash::inflate(int increase) {
  assert(increase >= 0);
  if(increase == 0) return;
  int newQuantity = quantity + increase;
  int newBytes = newQuantity * size;
  int oldBytes = quantity * size;
  unsigned char* b = new unsigned char[newBytes];
  for(int i = 0; i < oldBytes; i++)
    b[i] = storage[i];
                // Copy old to new
  delete [](storage);
                // Release old storage
  storage = b; // Point to new memory
  quantity = newQuantity; // Adjust the size
} ///:~
```

When you use the first constructor, no memory is allocated for storage. The allocation happens the first time you try to add() an object and any time the current block of memory is exceeded inside add().

Both constructors are exercised in the test program in Listing 7-3.

Listing 7-3. The Test Program

```
//: C07:Stash3Test.cpp
//{L} Stash3
// Function overloading
#include "Stash3.h"
#include "../require.h"
#include <fstream>
#include <iostream>
#include <string>
using namespace std;

int main() {
  Stash intStash(sizeof(int));
  for(int i = 0; i < 100; i++)
    intStash.add(&i);
  for(int j = 0; j < intStash.count(); j++)
  cout << "intStash.fetch(" << j << ") = "
       << *(int*)intStash.fetch(j)
       << endl;
  const int bufsize = 80;
  Stash stringStash(sizeof(char) * bufsize, 100);
```

```
  ifstream in("Stash3Test.cpp");
  assure(in, "Stash3Test.cpp");
  string line;
  while(getline(in, line))
    stringStash.add((char*)line.c_str());
  int k = 0;
  char* cp;
  while((cp = (char*)stringStash.fetch(k++))!=0)
  cout << "stringStash.fetch(" << k << ") = "
       << cp << endl;
} ///:~
```

The constructor call for stringStash uses a second argument; presumably you know something special about the specific problem you're solving that allows you to choose an initial size for the Stash.

Unions

As you've seen, the only difference between struct and class in C++ is that struct defaults to public and class defaults to private. A struct can also have constructors and destructors, as you might expect. But it turns out that a union can also have a constructor, destructor, member functions, and even access control. You can again see the use and benefit of overloading in Listing 7-4.

Listing 7-4. Unions

```
//: C07:UnionClass.cpp
// Unions with constructors and member functions
#include <iostream>
using namespace std;

union U {
private: // Access control too!
  int i;
  float f;
public:
  U(int a);
  U(float b);
  ~U();
 int read_int();
  float read_float();
};

U::U(int a) { i = a; }

U::U(float b) { f = b;}

U::~U() { cout << "U::~U()\n"; }

int U::read_int() { return i; }

float U::read_float() { return f; }
```

```
int main() {
  U X(12), Y(1.9F);
  cout << X.read_int() << endl;
  cout << Y.read_float() << endl;
} ///:~
```

You might think from the code in Listing 7-4 that the only difference between a union and a class is the way the data is stored (*that is, the* int and float *are overlaid on the same piece of storage*). However, a union cannot be used as a base class during inheritance, which is quite limiting from an object-oriented design standpoint.

■ **Note**   You'll learn about inheritance in Chapter 14.

Although the member functions civilize access to the union somewhat, there is still no way to prevent the client programmer from selecting the wrong element type once the union is initialized. In Listing 7-4, you could say X.read_float() even though it is inappropriate. However, a "safe" union can be encapsulated in a class. In Listing 7-5, notice how the enum clarifies the code, and how overloading comes in handy with the constructors.

Listing 7-5. A Safe Union

```
//: C07:SuperVar.cpp
// A super-variable
#include <iostream>
using namespace std;

class SuperVar {
  enum {
    character,
    integer,
    floating_point
  } vartype;  // Define one
  union {       // Anonymous union
    char c;
    int i;
    float f;
  };
public:
  SuperVar(char ch);
  SuperVar(int ii);
  SuperVar(float ff);
  void print();
};

SuperVar::SuperVar(char ch) {
  vartype = character;
  c = ch;
}
```

```
SuperVar::SuperVar(int ii) {
  vartype = integer;
  i = ii;
}

SuperVar::SuperVar(float ff) {
 vartype = floating_point;
 f = ff;
}

voidSuperVar::print() {
  switch (vartype) {
    case character:
      cout << "character: " << c << endl;
      break;
    case integer:
      cout << "integer: " << i << endl;
      break;
    case floating_point:
      cout << "float: " << f << endl;
      break;
  }
}

int main() {
  SuperVarA('c'), B(12), C(1.44F);
  A.print();
  B.print();
  C.print();
} ///:~
```

In Listing 7-5, the enum has no type name (it is an untagged *enumeration*). This is acceptable if you are going to immediately define instances of the enum, as is done here. There is no need to refer to the enum's type name in the future, so the type name is optional.

The union has no type name and no variable name. This is called an *anonymous union,* and it creates space for the union but doesn't require accessing the union elements with a variable name and the dot operator. For instance, an example of an anonymous union is

```
//: C07:AnonymousUnion.cpp
int main() {
  union {
    int i;
    float f;
  };
  // Access members without using qualifiers:
  i = 12;
  f = 1.22;
} ///:~
```

Note that you access members of an anonymous union just as if they were ordinary variables. The only difference is that both variables occupy the same space. If the anonymous union is at file scope (outside all functions *and* classes) then it must be declared static so it has internal linkage.

Although SuperVar is now safe, its usefulness is a bit dubious; the reason for using a union in the first place is to save space, and the addition of vartype takes up quite a bit of space relative to the data in the union, so the savings are effectively eliminated. There are a couple of alternatives to make this scheme workable. If the vartype controlled more than one union instance—if they were all the same type—then you'd only need one for the group and it wouldn't take up more space. A more useful approach is to have #ifdefs around all the vartype code, which can then guarantee things are being used correctly during development and testing. For shipping code, the extra space and time overhead can be eliminated.

Default Arguments

In Stash3.h (Listing 7-1) examine the two constructors for Stash(). They don't seem all that different, do they? In fact, the first constructor seems to be a special case of the second one with the initial size set to zero. It's a bit of a waste of effort to create and maintain two different versions of a similar function.

C++ provides a remedy with *default arguments*. A default argument is a value given in the declaration that the compiler automatically inserts if you don't provide a value in the function call. In the Stash example, you can replace the two functions

```
Stash(int size); // Zero quantity
Stash(int size, int initQuantity);
```

with the single function

```
Stash(int size, int initQuantity = 0);
```

The Stash(int) definition is simply removed—all that is necessary is the single Stash(int, int) definition. Now, the two object definitions

```
Stash A(100), B(100, 0);
```

will produce exactly the same results. The identical constructor is called in both cases, but for A, the second argument is automatically substituted by the compiler when it sees the first argument is an int and that there is no second argument. The compiler has seen the default argument, so it knows it can still make the function call if it substitutes this second argument, which is what you've told it to do by making it a default.

Default arguments are a convenience, as function overloading is a convenience. Both features allow you to use a single function name in different situations. The difference is that with default arguments the compiler is substituting arguments when you don't want to put them in yourself. The preceding example is a good place to use default arguments instead of function overloading; otherwise you end up with two or more functions that have similar signatures and similar behaviors. If the functions have very different behaviors, it doesn't usually make sense to use default arguments (*for that matter, you might want to question whether two functions with very different behaviors should have the same name*).

There are two rules you must be aware of when using default arguments. First, only trailing arguments may be defaulted. That is, you can't have a default argument followed by a non-default argument. Second, once you start using default arguments in a particular function call, all the subsequent arguments in that function's argument list must be defaulted (this follows from the first rule).

Default arguments are only placed in the declaration of a function (typically placed in a header file). The compiler must see the default value before it can use it. Sometimes people will place the commented values of the default arguments in the function definition, for documentation purposes, such as:

```
Void fn(int x /* = 0 */) { // ...
```

Placeholder Arguments

Arguments in a function declaration can be declared without identifiers. When these are used with default arguments, it can look a bit funny. You can end up with

```
void f(int x, int = 0, float = 1.1);
```

In C++, you don't need identifiers in the function definition, either.

```
void f(int x, int, float flt) { /* ... */ }
```

In the function body, x and flt can be referenced, but not the middle argument, because it has no name. Function calls must still provide a value for the placeholder, though: f(1) or f(1,2,3.0). This syntax allows you to put the argument in as a placeholder without using it. The idea is that you might want to change the function definition to use the placeholder later, without changing all the code where the function is called. Of course, you can accomplish the same thing by using a named argument, but if you define the argument for the function body without using it, most compilers will give you a warning message, assuming you've made a logical error. By intentionally leaving the argument name out, you suppress this warning.

More important, if you start out using a function argument and later decide that you don't need it, you can effectively remove it without generating warnings, and yet not disturb any client code that was calling the previous version of the function.

Choosing Overloading vs. Default Arguments

Both function overloading and default arguments provide a convenience for calling function names. However, it can seem confusing at times to know which technique to use. For example, consider the following tool that is designed to automatically manage blocks of memory for you (Listing 7-6).

Listing 7-6. Managing Blocks of Memory (Header File)

```
//: C07:Mem.h
#ifndef MEM_H
#define MEM_H
typedef unsigned char byte;

classMem {
  byte* mem;
  int size;
  void ensureMinSize(int minSize);
public:
  Mem();
  Mem(int sz);
  ~Mem();
  int msize();
  byte* pointer();
  byte* pointer(int minSize);
};
#endif // MEM_H ///:~
```

A Mem object holds a block of bytes and makes sure that you have enough storage. The default constructor doesn't allocate any storage, and the second constructor ensures that there is sz storage in the Mem object. The destructor releases the storage, msize() tells you how many bytes there are currently in the Mem object, and pointer() produces a pointer to the starting address of the storage (Mem is a fairly low-level tool). There's an overloaded version of `pointer()` in which client programmers can say that they want a pointer to a block of bytes that is at least `minSize` large, and the member function ensures this.

Both the constructor and the `pointer()` member function use the `private ensureMinSize()` member function to increase the size of the memory block (notice that it's not safe to hold the result of `pointer()` if the memory is resized).

Listing 7-7 shows the implementation of the class.

Listing 7-7. Managing Blocks of Memory (Source Code Object cpp File)

```
//: C07:Mem.cpp {O}
#include "Mem.h"        // To be INCLUDED from Header FILE above
#include <cstring>
using namespace std;

Mem::Mem() { mem = 0; size = 0; }

Mem::Mem(int sz) {
  mem = 0;
  size = 0;
  ensureMinSize(sz);
}

Mem::~Mem() { delete []mem; }

int Mem::msize() { return size; }

void Mem::ensureMinSize(int minSize) {
  if(size < minSize) {
    byte* newmem = new byte[minSize];
    memset(newmem + size, 0, minSize - size);
    memcpy(newmem, mem, size);
    delete []mem;
    mem = newmem;
    size = minSize;
  }
}

byte* Mem::pointer() { return mem; }

byte* Mem::pointer(int minSize) {
  ensureMinSize(minSize);
  return mem;
} ///:~
```

You can see that `ensureMinSize()` is the only function responsible for allocating memory, and that it is used from the second constructor and the second overloaded form of `pointer()`. Inside `ensureMinSize()`, nothing needs to be done if the `size` is large enough. If new storage must be allocated in order to make the block bigger (which is also the case when the block is of size zero after default construction), the new "extra" portion is set to zero using the Standard C Library function `memset()`, which was introduced in Chapter 5. The subsequent function call is to the Standard C Library function `memcpy()`, which in this case copies the existing bytes from `mem` to `newmem` (typically in an efficient fashion). Finally, the old memory is deleted and the new memory and sizes are assigned to the appropriate members.

The Mem class is designed to be used as a tool within other classes to simplify their memory management (it could also be used to hide a more sophisticated memory-management system provided, for example, by the operating system). Appropriately, it is tested in Listing 7-8 by creating a simple *"string"* class.

Listing 7-8. Testing the Mem Class

```cpp
//: C07:MemTest.cpp
// Testing the Mem class
//{L} Mem
#include "Mem.h"
#include <cstring>
#include <iostream>
using namespace std;

classMyString {
  Mem* buf;
public:
  MyString();
  MyString(char* str);
  ~MyString();
  void concat(char* str);
  void print(ostream &os);
};

MyString::MyString() {  buf = 0; }

MyString::MyString(char* str) {
  buf = new Mem(strlen(str) + 1);
  strcpy((char*)buf->pointer(), str);
}

void MyString::concat(char* str) {
  if(!buf) buf = new Mem;
  strcat((char*)buf->pointer(
    buf->msize() + strlen(str) + 1), str);
}

void MyString::print(ostream &os) {
  if(!buf) return;
  os << buf->pointer() << endl;
}

MyString::~MyString() { delete buf; }

int main() {
  MyStrings("My test string");
  s.print(cout);
  s.concat(" some additional stuff");
  s.print(cout);
  MyString s2;
  s2.concat("Using default constructor");
  s2.print(cout);
} ///:~
```

All you can do with this class is create a MyString, concatenate text, and print to an ostream. The class only contains a pointer to a Mem, but note the distinction between the default constructor, which sets the pointer to zero, and the second constructor, which creates a Mem and copies data into it. The advantage of the default constructor is that you can create, for example, a large array of empty MyString objects very cheaply, since the size of each object is only one pointer and the only overhead of the default constructor is that of assigning to zero. The cost of a MyString only begins to accrue when you concatenate data; at that point the Mem object is created if it hasn't been already. However, if you use the default constructor and never concatenate any data, the destructor call is still safe because calling delete for zero is defined such that it does not try to release storage or otherwise cause problems.

If you look at these two constructors, it might at first seem like this is a prime candidate for default arguments. However, if you drop the default constructor and write the remaining constructor with a default argument, like

```
MyString(char* str = "");
```

everything will work correctly, but you'll lose the previous efficiency benefit since a Mem object will always be created. To get the efficiency back, you must modify the constructor in this way:

```
MyString::MyString(char* str) {
  if(!*str) { // Pointing at an empty string
    buf = 0;
    return;
  }
  buf = new Mem(strlen(str) + 1);
  strcpy((char*)buf->pointer(), str);
}
```

This means, in effect, that the default value becomes a flag that causes a separate piece of code to be executed than if a non-default value is used. Although it seems innocent enough with a small constructor like this one, in general this practice can cause problems.

If you have to *look* for the default rather than treating it as an ordinary value, that should be a clue that you will end up with effectively two different functions inside a single function body: one version for the normal case and one for the default. You might as well split it up into two distinct function bodies and let the compiler do the selection.

This results in a slight (*but usually invisible*) increase in efficiency because the extra argument isn't passed and the extra code for the conditional isn't executed. More importantly, you are keeping the code for two separate functions *in* two separate functions rather than combining them into one using default arguments, which will result in easier maintainability, especially if the functions are large.

On the other hand, consider the Mem class. If you look at the definitions of the two constructors and the two pointer() functions, you can see that using default arguments in both cases will not cause the member function definitions to change at all. Thus, the class could easily be the following:

Listing 7-9. Managing Blocks of Memory (Modified Header File)

```
//: C07:Mem2.h
#ifndef MEM2_H
#define MEM2_H
typedef unsigned char byte;

class Mem {
  byte* mem;
  int size;
  void ensureMinSize(int minSize);
```

```
public:
  Mem(int sz = 0);
  ~Mem();
  int msize();
  byte* pointer(int minSize = 0);
};
#endif // MEM2_H ///:~
```

Notice that a call to `ensureMinSize(0)` will always be quite efficient.

Although in both of these cases some of the decision-making processes were based on the issue of efficiency, you must be careful not to fall into the trap of thinking only about efficiency (*fascinating as it is!*).

The most important issue in class design is the interface of the class (its `public` members, *which are available to the client programmer*). If these produce a class that is easy to use and reuse, then you have a success; you can always tune for efficiency if necessary but the effect of a class that is designed badly because the programmer is over-focused on efficiency issues can be dire.

Your primary concern should be that the interface makes sense to those who use it and read the resulting code. Notice that in `MemTest.cpp` the usage of `MyString` does not change regardless of whether a default constructor is used or whether the efficiency is high or low.

Review Session

1. As a guideline, you shouldn't use a *default argument* as a flag upon which to conditionally execute code. You should *instead break the function into two or more overloaded functions* if you can.

2. A default argument should be a value you would ordinarily put in that position. It's a value that is more likely to occur than all the rest, so client programmers can generally ignore it or use it only if they want to change it from the default value.

3. The default argument is included *to make function calls easier*, especially when those functions have many arguments with typical values. *Not only is it much easier to write the calls, it's easier to read them, especially if the class creator can order the arguments such that the least-modified defaults appear latest in the list.*

4. *An especially important use of default arguments is when you start out with a function with a set of arguments*, and after it's been used for a while you discover you need to add arguments. By defaulting all the new arguments, *you ensure that all client code using the previous interface is not disturbed.*

CHAPTER 8

Constants

The concept of *constant* (expressed by the const keyword) was created to allow the programmer to draw a line between what changes and what doesn't. This provides safety and control in a C++ programming project.

Since its origin, const has taken on a number of different purposes. In the meantime, it trickled back into the C language where its meaning was changed. All this can seem a bit confusing at first, and in this chapter you'll learn when, why, and how to use the const keyword. At the end there's a discussion of volatile, which is a near cousin to const (because they both concern change) and has identical syntax.

The first motivation for const seems to have been to eliminate the use of preprocessor #defines for value substitution. It has since been put to use for pointers, function arguments, return types, class objects, and member functions. All of these have slightly different but conceptually compatible meanings and will be looked at in separate sections in this chapter.

Value Substitution

When programming in C, the preprocessor is liberally used to create macros and to substitute values. Because the preprocessor simply does text replacement and has neither concept nor facility for type checking, preprocessor value substitution introduces subtle problems that can be avoided in C++ by using const values.

The typical use of the preprocessor to substitute values for names in C looks like this:

```
#define BUFSIZE 100
```

BUFSIZE is a name that only exists during preprocessing, so it doesn't occupy storage and can be placed in a header file to provide a single value for all translation units that use it. It's very important for code maintenance to use value substitution instead of so-called "magic numbers." If you use magic numbers in your code, not only does the reader have no idea where the numbers come from or what they represent, but if you decide to change a value, you must perform hand editing, and you have no trail to follow to ensure you don't miss one of your values (or accidentally change one you shouldn't).

Most of the time, BUFSIZE will behave like an ordinary variable, but not all the time. In addition, there's no type information. This can hide bugs that are very difficult to find. C++ uses const to eliminate these problems by bringing value substitution into the domain of the compiler. Now you can say

```
const int bufsize = 100;
```

You can use bufsize any place where the compiler must know the value at compile time. The compiler can use bufsize to perform *constant folding*, which means the compiler will reduce a complicated constant expression to a simple one by performing the necessary calculations at compile time. This is especially important in array definitions, like

```
char buf[bufsize];
```

You can use const for all the built-in types (char, int, float, and double) and their variants (as well as class objects, as you'll see later in this chapter). Because of subtle bugs that the preprocessor might introduce, you should always use const instead of #define value substitution.

const in Header Files

To use const instead of #define, you must be able to place const definitions inside header files, as you can with #define. This way, you can place the definition for a const in a single place and distribute it to translation units by including the header file. A const in C++ defaults to "internal linkage;" that is, it is visible only within the file where it is defined and cannot be seen at link time by other translation units. You must always assign a value to a const when you define it, *except* when you make an explicit declaration using extern, such as:

```
extern const int bufsize;
```

Normally, the C++ compiler avoids creating storage for a const, but instead holds the definition in its symbol table. When you use extern with const, however, you force storage to be allocated (this is also true for certain other cases, such as taking the address of a const). Storage must be allocated because extern says "use external linkage," which means that several translation units must be able to refer to the item, which requires it to have storage.

In the ordinary case, when extern is not part of the definition, no storage is allocated. When the const is used, it is simply folded in at compile time.

The goal of never allocating storage for a const also fails with complicated structures. Whenever the compiler must allocate storage, constant folding is prevented (since there's no way for the compiler to know for sure what the value of that storage is; if it could know that, it wouldn't need to allocate the storage).

Because the compiler cannot always avoid allocating storage for a const, const definitions *must* default to internal linkage, that is, linkage only *within* that particular translation unit. Otherwise, linker errors would occur with complicated consts because they cause storage to be allocated in multiple cpp files. The linker would then see the same definition in multiple object files, and complain. Because a const defaults to internal linkage, the linker doesn't try to link those definitions across translation units, and there are no collisions. With built-in types, which are used in the majority of cases involving constant expressions, the compiler can always perform constant folding.

Safety consts

The use of const is not limited to replacing #defines in constant expressions. If you initialize a variable with a value that is produced at runtime and you know it will not change for the lifetime of that variable, it is good programming practice to make it a const so the compiler will give you an error message if you accidentally try to change it. See Listing 8-1 for an example.

Listing 8-1. Using const for Safety

```
//: C08:Safecons.cpp
// Using const for safety
#include <iostream>
using namespace std;

const int i = 100;
const int j = i + 10;
long address = (long)&j;  // Forces storage
char buf[j + 10];         // Still a const expression
```

```
int main() {
  cout << "type a character & CR:";
  const char c = cin.get(); // Can't change
  const char c2 = c + 'a';
  cout << c2;
  // ...
} ///:~
```

You can see that i is a compile-time const, but j is calculated from i. However, because i is a const, the calculated value for j still comes from a constant expression and is itself a compile-time constant. The very next line requires the address of j and therefore forces the compiler to allocate storage for j. Yet this doesn't prevent the use of j in the determination of the size of buf because the compiler knows j is const and that the value is valid even if storage was allocated to hold that value at some point in the program.

In main( ), you see a different kind of const in the identifier c because the value cannot be known at compile time. This means storage is required, and the compiler doesn't attempt to keep anything in its symbol table (the same behavior as in C). The initialization must still happen at the point of definition, and once the initialization occurs, the value cannot be changed. You can see that c2 is calculated from c and also that scoping works for consts as it does for any other type—yet another improvement over the use of #define.

As a matter of practice, if you think a value shouldn't change, you should make it a const. This not only provides insurance against inadvertent changes, it also allows the compiler to generate more efficient code by eliminating storage and memory reads.

Aggregates

It's possible to use const for aggregates, but you're virtually assured that the compiler will not be sophisticated enough to keep an aggregate in its symbol table, so storage will be allocated. In these situations, const means "*a piece of storage that cannot be changed.*" However, the value cannot be used at compile time because the compiler is not required to know the contents of the storage at compile time. In Listing 8-2, you can see the statements that are illegal.

Listing 8-2. Constants and Aggregates

```
//: C08:Constag.cpp
// Constants and aggregates
const int i[] = { 1, 2, 3, 4 };
//! float f[i[3]];     // Illegal
struct S { int i, j; };
const S s[] = { { 1, 2 }, { 3, 4 } };
//! double d[s[1].j]; // Illegal
int main() {} ///:~
```

In an array definition, the compiler must be able to generate code that moves the stack pointer to accommodate the array. In both of the illegal definitions in Listing 8-2, the compiler complains because it cannot find a constant expression in the array definition.

Differences with C

Constants were introduced in early versions of C++ while the Standard C specification was still being finished. Although the C committee then decided to include const in C, somehow it came to mean for them *"an ordinary variable that cannot be changed."* In C, a const always occupies storage and its name is global. The C compiler cannot treat a const as a compile-time constant. In C, if you say

```
const int bufsize = 100;
char buf[bufsize];
```

you will get an error, even though it seems like a rational thing to do. Because bufsize occupies storage somewhere, the C compiler cannot know the value at compile time. You can optionally say

```
const int bufsize;
```

in C, but not in C++, and the C compiler accepts it as a declaration indicating there is storage allocated elsewhere. Because C defaults to external linkage for consts, this makes sense. C++ defaults to internal linkage for consts so if you want to accomplish the same thing in C++, you must explicitly change the linkage to external using extern, such as:

```
extern const int bufsize; // Declaration only
```

This line also works in C.

In C++, a const doesn't necessarily create storage. In C, a const always creates storage. Whether or not storage is reserved for a const in C++ depends on how it is used. In general, if a const is used simply to replace a name with a value (*just as you would use a* #define), then storage doesn't have to be created for the const. If no storage is created (this depends on the complexity of the data type and the sophistication of the compiler), the values may be folded into the code for greater efficiency after type checking, not before, as with #define. If, however, you take an address of a const (*even unknowingly, by passing it to a function that takes a reference argument*) or you define it as extern, then storage is created for the const.

In C++, a const that is outside all functions has file scope (i.e., it is invisible outside the file). That is, it defaults to internal linkage. This is very different from all other identifiers in C++ (*and from* const *in C!*) that default to external linkage. Thus, if you declare a const of the same name in two different files and you don't take the address or define that name as extern, the ideal C++ compiler won't allocate storage for the const, but will simply fold it into the code. Because const has implied file scope, you can put it in C++ header files with no conflicts at link time.

Since a const in C++ defaults to internal linkage, you can't just define a const in one file and reference it as an extern in another file. To give a const external linkage so it can be referenced from another file, you must explicitly define it as extern, like this:

```
extern const int x = 1;
```

Notice that by giving it an initializer and saying it is extern, you force storage to be created for the const (*although the compiler still has the option of doing constant folding here*). The initialization establishes this as a definition, not a declaration. The declaration

```
extern const int x;
```

in C++ means that the definition exists elsewhere (*again, this is not necessarily true in C*). You can now see why C++ requires a const definition to have an initializer: the initializer distinguishes a declaration from a definition (in C it's always a definition, so no initializer is necessary). With an extern const declaration, the compiler cannot do constant folding because it doesn't know the value.

The C approach to const is not very useful, and if you want to use a named value inside a constant expression (*one that must be evaluated at compile time*), C almost *forces* you to use #define in the preprocessor.

Pointers

Pointers can be made const. The compiler will still endeavor to prevent storage allocation and do constant folding when dealing with const pointers, but these features seem less useful in this case. More importantly, the compiler will tell you if you attempt to change a const pointer, which adds a great deal of safety.

When using const with pointers, you have two options: const can be applied to what the pointer is pointing to, or the const can be applied to the address stored in the pointer itself. The syntax for these is a little confusing at first but becomes comfortable with practice.

Pointer to const

The trick with a pointer definition, as with any complicated definition, is to read it starting at the identifier and work your way out. The const specifier binds to the thing it is "closest to." So if you want to prevent any changes to the element you are pointing to, you write a definition like this:

```
const int* u;
```

Starting from the identifier, you read "u *is a pointer, which points to a* const int." Here, no initialization is required because you're saying that u can point to anything (that is, it is not const), but the thing it points to cannot be changed.

Here's the mildly confusing part. You might think that to make the pointer itself unchangeable, that is, to prevent any change to the address contained inside u, you would simply move the const to the other side of the int, like this:

```
const int* u;
```

It's not all that crazy to think that this should read "v is a const pointer to an int." However, the way it *actually* reads is "v is an ordinary pointer to an int that happens to be const." That is, the const has bound itself to the int again, and the effect is the same as the previous definition. The fact that these two definitions are the same is the confusing point; to prevent this confusion on the part of your reader, you should probably stick to the first form.

const Pointer

To make the pointer itself a const, you must place the const specifier to the right of the *, like this:

```
int d = 1;
int* const w = &d;
```

Now it reads: "w is a pointer, which is const, that points to an int." Because the pointer itself is now the const, the compiler requires that it be given an initial value that will be unchanged for the life of that pointer. It's OK, however, to change what that value points to by saying

```
*w = 2;
```

You can also make a const pointer to a const object using either of two legal forms:

```
int d = 1;
const int* const x = &d;   // (1)
int const* const x2 = &d; // (2)
```

Now neither the pointer nor the object can be changed.

Some people argue that the second form is more consistent because the const is always placed to the right of what it modifies. You'll have to decide which is clearer for your particular coding style.

Listing 8-3 shows the above lines in a compileable file.

Listing 8-3. Pointers

```
//: C08:ConstPointers.cpp
const int* u;
int const* v;
int d = 1;
int* const w = &d;
const int* const x = &d;  // (1)
int const* const x2 = &d; // (2)
int main() {} ///:~
```

Formatting

This book makes a point of only putting one pointer definition on a line, and initializing each pointer at the point of definition whenever possible. Because of this, the formatting style of "attaching" the '*' to the data type is possible and looks like

```
int* u = &i;
```

as if int* were a discrete type unto itself. This makes the code easier to understand, but unfortunately that's not actually the way things work. In fact, the '*' binds to the identifier, *not the type*. It can be placed anywhere between the type name and the identifier. So you could write

```
int *u = &i, v = 0;
```

which creates an int* u, as before, and a non-pointer int v. Because readers often find this confusing, it is best to follow the form shown in this book.

Assignment and Type Checking

C++ is very particular about type checking, and this extends to pointer assignments. You can assign the address of a non-const object to a const pointer because you're simply promising not to change something that is OK to change. However, you can't assign the address of a const object to a non-const pointer because then you're saying you might change the object via the pointer. Of course, you can always use a cast to force such an assignment, but this is bad programming practice because you are then breaking the const attribute of the object, along with any safety promised by the const. See Listing 8-4 for an example.

Listing 8-4. Pointer Assignment

```
//: C08:PointerAssignment.cpp
int d = 1;
const int e = 2;
int* u = &d;        // OK -- d not const
//! int* v = &e;    // Illegal -- e const
int* w = (int*)&e; // Legal but bad practice
int main() {} ///:~
```

Although C++ helps prevent errors, it does not protect you from yourself if you want to break the safety mechanisms.

Character Array Literals

The place where strict const attribute is not enforced is with character array literals. You can say

```
char* cp = "howdy";
```

and the compiler will accept it without complaint. This is technically an error because a character array literal ("howdy" in this case) is created by the compiler as a constant character array, and the result of the quoted character array is its starting address in memory. Modifying any of the characters in the array is a runtime error, although not all compilers enforce this correctly.

So character array literals are actually constant character arrays. Of course, the compiler lets you get away with treating them as non-const because there's so much existing C code that relies on this. However, if you try to change the values in a character array literal, the behavior is undefined, although it will probably work on many machines.

If you want to be able to modify the string, put it in an array, such as:

```
charcp[] = "howdy";
```

Since compilers often don't enforce the difference, you won't be reminded to use this latter form and so the point becomes rather subtle.

Function Arguments and Return Values

The use of const to specify function arguments and return values is another place where the concept of constants can be confusing. If you are passing objects *by value*, specifying const has no meaning to the client (it means that the passed argument cannot be modified inside the function). If you are returning an object of a user-defined type by value as a const, it means the returned value cannot be modified. If you are passing and returning *addresses*, const is a promise that the destination of the address will not be changed.

Passing by const Value

You can specify that function arguments are const when passing them by value, such as

```
void f1(const int i) {
  i++; // Illegal -- compile-time error
}
```

but what does this mean? You're making a promise that the original value of the variable will not be changed by the function f1( ). However, because the argument is passed by value, you immediately make a copy of the original variable, so the promise to the client is implicitly kept.

Inside the function, the const takes on meaning: the argument cannot be changed. So it's really a tool for the creator of the function, and not the caller.

To avoid confusion to the caller, you can make the argument a const *inside* the function, rather than in the argument list. You could do this with a pointer, but a nicer syntax is achieved with the *reference*, a subject that will be fully developed in Chapter 11. Briefly, a reference is like a constant pointer that is automatically dereferenced, so it has the effect of being an alias to an object. To create a reference, you use the & in the definition. So the non-confusing function definition looks like this:

```
void f2(int ic) {
  const int& i = ic;
  i++;  // Illegal -- compile-time error
}
```

Again, you'll get an error message, but this time the const attribute of the local object *is not part of the function signature*; it only has meaning to the implementation of the function and therefore it's hidden from the client.

Returning by const Value

A similar truth holds for the return value. If you say that a function's return value is const, like

```
const int g();
```

you are promising that the original variable (*inside the function frame*) will not be modified. And again, because you're returning it by value, it's copied so the original value could never be modified via the return value.

At first, this can make the specification of const seem meaningless. You can see the apparent lack of effect of returning consts by value in Listing 8-5.

Listing 8-5. Returning consts by Value

```
//: C08:Constval.cpp
// Returning consts by value
// has no meaning for built-in types

int f3() { return 1; }
const int f4() { return 1; }

int main() {
  const int j = f3(); // Works fine
  int k = f4();       // But this works fine too!
} ///:~
```

For built-in types, it doesn't matter whether you return by value as a const, so you should avoid confusing the client programmer and leave off the const when returning a built-in type by value.

Returning by value as a const becomes important when you're dealing with user-defined types. If a function returns a class object by value as a const, the return value of that function cannot be *an lvalue* (that is, it cannot be assigned to or otherwise modified). See Listing 8-6 for an example.

Listing 8-6. Constant Returned by Value

```
//: C08:ConstReturnValues.cpp
// Constant return by value
// Result cannot be used as an lvalue

class X {
  int i;
public:
  X(int ii = 0);
  void modify();
};

X::X(int ii) { i = ii; }

void X::modify() { i++; }
```

```
X f5() {
  return X();
}

const X f6() {
  return X();
}

void f7(X& x) {  // Pass by non-const reference
  x.modify();
}

int main() {
  f5() = X(1);    // OK -- non-const return value
  f5().modify(); // OK
//! f7(f5());    // Causes warning or error
// Causes compile-time errors:
//! f7(f5());
//! f6() = X(1);
//! f6().modify();
//! f7(f6());
} ///:~
```

f5() returns a non-constX object, while f6() returns a const X object. Only the non-const return value can be used as an lvalue. Thus, it's important to use const when returning an object by value if you want to prevent its use as an lvalue.

The reason const has no meaning when you're returning a built-in type by value is that the compiler already prevents it from being an lvalue (because it's always a value, and not a variable). Only when you're returning objects of user-defined types by value does it become an issue.

The function f7() takes its argument as a non-const *reference* (an additional way of handling addresses in C++ and the subject of Chapter 11). This is effectively the same as taking a non-const pointer; it's just that the syntax is different. The reason this won't compile in C++ is because of the creation of a temporary.

Temporaries

Sometimes, during the evaluation of an expression, the compiler must create *temporary objects*. These are objects like any other: they require storage and they must be constructed and destroyed. The difference is that you never see them—the compiler is responsible for deciding that they're needed and the details of their existence. But there is one thing about temporaries: they're automatically const. Because you usually won't be able to get your hands on a temporary object, telling it to do something that will change that temporary is almost certainly a mistake because you won't be able to use that information. By making all temporaries automatically const, the compiler informs you when you make that mistake.

In Listing 8-6, f5() returns a non-constX object. But in the expression

```
f7(f5());
```

the compiler must manufacture a temporary object to hold the return value of f5() so it can be passed to f7(). This would be fine if f7() took its argument by value; then the temporary would be copied into f7() and it wouldn't matter what happened to the temporary X. However, f7() takes its argument *by reference*, which means in this example that it takes the address of the temporary X. Since f7( ) doesn't take its argument by const reference, it has permission to modify the temporary object. But the compiler knows that the temporary will vanish as soon as the expression evaluation is complete, and thus any modifications you make to the temporary X will be lost. By making all temporary objects automatically const, *this situation causes a compile-time error message* so you don't get caught by what would be a very difficult bug to find.

However, notice the expressions that are legal:

```
f5() = X(1);
  f5().modify();
```

Although these pass muster for the compiler, they are actually problematic. f5( ) returns an X object, and for the compiler to satisfy the above expressions it must create a temporary to hold that return value. So in both expressions the temporary object is being modified, and as soon as the expression is over the temporary is cleaned up. As a result, the modifications are lost so this code is probably a bug—but the compiler doesn't tell you anything about it. Expressions like these are simple enough that you can detect the problem, but when things get more complex it's possible for a bug to slip through these cracks.

The way the const *attribute* of class objects is preserved is shown later in the chapter.

Passing and Returning Addresses

If you pass or return an address (*either a pointer or a reference*), it's possible for the client programmer to take it and modify the original value. If you make the pointer or reference a const, you prevent this from happening, which may save you some grief. In fact, whenever you're passing an address into a function, you should make it a const if at all possible. If you don't, you're excluding the possibility of using that function with anything that is a const.

The choice of whether to return a pointer or reference to a const depends on what you want to allow your client programmer to do with it. Listing 8-7 demonstrates the use of const pointers as function arguments and return values.

Listing 8-7. const Pointers as Function Arguments and Return Values

```
//: C08:ConstPointer.cpp
// Constant pointer arg/return

void t(int*) {}

void u(const int* cip) {
//!  *cip = 2;        // Illegal -- modifies value
  int i = *cip;       // OK -- copies value
//!  int* ip2 = cip; // Illegal: non-const
}

const char* v() {
  // Returns address of static character array:
  return "result of function v()";
}

const int* const w() {
  static int i;
  return &i;
}
```

```
int main() {
  int x = 0;
  int* ip = &;
  const int* cip = &x;
  t(ip);                          // OK
//! t(cip);                       // Not OK
  u(ip);                          // OK
  u(cip);                         // Also OK
//! char* cp = v();               // Not OK
  const char* ccp = v();          // OK
//! int* ip2 = w();               // Not OK
  const int* const ccip = w(); // OK
  const int* cip2 = w();          // OK
//! *w() = 1;                     // Not OK
} ///:~
```

The function t( ) takes an ordinary non-const pointer as an argument, and u( ) takes a const pointer. Inside u( ) you can see that attempting to modify the destination of the const pointer is illegal, but you can of course copy the information out into a non-const variable. The compiler also prevents you from creating a non-const pointer using the address stored inside a const pointer.

The functions v( ) and w( ) test return value semantics. v( ) returns a const char* that is created from a character array literal. This statement actually produces the address of the character array literal, after the compiler creates it and stores it in the static storage area. As mentioned earlier, this character array is technically a constant, which is properly expressed by the return value of v( ).

The return value of w( ) requires that both the pointer and what it points to must be const. As with v( ), the value returned by w( ) is valid after the function returns only because it is static. You never want to return pointers to local stack variables because they will be invalid after the function returns and the stack is cleaned up.

■ **Note** Another common pointer you might return is the address of storage allocated on the heap, which is still valid after the function returns.

In main( ), the functions are tested with various arguments. You can see that t( ) will accept a non-const pointer argument, but if you try to pass it a pointer to a const, there's no promise that t( ) will leave the pointer's destination alone, so the compiler gives you an error message. u( ) takes a const pointer, so it will accept both types of arguments. Thus, a function that takes a const pointer is more general than one that does not.

As expected, the return value of v( ) can be assigned only to a pointer to a const. You would also expect that the compiler refuses to assign the return value of w( ) to a non-const pointer and accepts a const int* const, but it might be a bit surprising to see that it also accepts a const int*, which is not an exact match to the return type. Once again, because the value (which is the address contained in the pointer) is being copied, the promise that the original variable is untouched is automatically kept. Thus, the second const in const int* const is only meaningful when you try to use it as an lvalue, in which case the compiler prevents you.

Standard Argument Passing

In C, it's very common to pass by value, and when you want to pass an address, your only choice is to use a pointer. However, neither of these approaches is preferred in C++. Instead, your first choice when passing an argument is to pass by reference, and by const reference at that. To the client programmer, the syntax is identical to that of passing by value, so there's no confusion about pointers—they don't even have to think about pointers. For the creator of the function, passing an address is virtually always more efficient than passing an entire class object, and if you pass by const reference, it means your function will not change the destination of that address, so the effect from the client programmer's point of view is exactly the same as pass-by-value (*only more efficient*).

Because of the syntax of references (it looks like *pass-by-value* to the caller) it's possible to pass a temporary object to a function that takes a const reference, whereas you can never pass a temporary object to a function that takes a pointer; with a pointer, the address must be explicitly taken. So passing by reference produces a new situation that never occurs in C: a temporary, which is always const, can have its *address* passed to a function. This is why, to allow temporaries to be passed to functions by reference, the argument must be a const reference. Listing 8-8 demonstrates this.

Listing 8-8. Temporaries

```
//: C08:ConstTemporary.cpp
// Temporaries are const

class X {};

X f() { return X(); } // Return by value

void g1(X&) {}        // Pass by non-const reference
void g2(const X&) {}  // Pass by const reference

int main() {
  // Error: const temporary created by f():
//!  g1(f());
  // OK: g2 takes a const reference:
  g2(f());
} ///:~
```

f( ) returns an object of class X *by value*. That means when you immediately take the return value of f( ) and pass it to another function, as in the calls to g1( ) and g2( ), a temporary is created and that temporary is const. Thus, the call in g1( ) is an error because g1( ) doesn't take a const reference, but the call to g2( ) is OK.

Classes

This section shows the ways you can use const with classes. You may want to create a local const in a class to use inside constant expressions that will be evaluated at compile time. However, the meaning of const is different inside classes, so you must understand the options in order to create const data members of a class.

You can also make an entire object const (and as you've just seen, the compiler always makes temporary objects const). But preserving the const attribute of an object is more complex. The compiler can ensure the const attribute of a built-in type but it cannot monitor the intricacies of a class. To guarantee the const attribute of a class object, the const member function is introduced: only a const member function may be called for a const object.

const in Classes

One of the places you'd like to use a const for constant expressions is inside classes. The typical example is when you're creating an array inside a class and you want to use a const instead of a #define to establish the array size and to use in calculations involving the array. The array size is something you'd like to keep hidden inside the class, so if you used a name like size, for example, you could use that name in another class without a clash. The preprocessor treats all #defines as global from the point they are defined, so this will not achieve the desired effect.

You might assume that the logical choice is to place a const inside the class. This doesn't produce the desired result. Inside a class, const partially reverts to its meaning in C. It allocates storage within each object and represents a value that is initialized once and then cannot change. The use of const inside a class means "This is *constant* for the *lifetime of the object.*" However, each different object may contain a different value for that constant.

Thus, when you create an ordinary (*non*-static) const inside a class, you cannot give it an initial value. This initialization must occur in the constructor, of course, but in a special place in the constructor. Because a const must be initialized at the point it is created, inside the main body of the constructor the const must *already* be initialized. Otherwise you're left with the choice of waiting until some point later in the constructor body, which means the const would be un-initialized for a while. Also, there would be nothing to keep you from changing the value of the const at various places in the constructor body.

The Constructor Initializer List

The special initialization point is called the *constructor initializer list,* and it was originally developed for use in inheritance (covered in Chapter 14). The constructor initializer list— which, as the name implies, occurs only in the definition of the constructor—is a list of "constructor calls" that occur after the function argument list and a colon, but before the opening brace of the constructor body. This is to remind you that the initialization in the list occurs before any of the main constructor code is executed. This is the place to put all const initializations. The proper form for const inside a class is shown in Listing 8-9.

Listing 8-9. Initializing const in Classes

```
//: C08:ConstInitialization.cpp
// Initializing const in classes
#include <iostream>
using namespace std;

class Fred {
  const int size;
public:
  Fred(int sz);
  void print();
};

Fred::Fred(int sz) : size(sz) {}
void Fred::print() { cout << size << endl; }

int main() {
  Fred a(1), b(2), c(3);
  a.print(), b.print(), c.print();
} ///:~
```

The form of the constructor initializer list shown in Listing 8-9 is confusing at first because you're not used to seeing a built-in type treated as if it has a constructor.

"Constructors" for Built-in Types

As the language developed and more effort was put into making user-defined types look like built-in types, it became apparent that there were times when it was helpful to make built-in types look like user-defined types. In the constructor initializer list, you can treat a built-in type as if it has a constructor, as in Listing 8-10.

Listing 8-10. Built-in Constructors

```cpp
//: C08:BuiltInTypeConstructors.cpp
#include <iostream>
using namespace std;

class B {
  int i;
public:
  B(int ii);
  void print();
};

B::B(int ii) : i(ii) {}
void B::print() { cout << I << endl; }

int main() {
  B a(1), b(2);
  float pi(3.14159);
  a.print(); b.print();
  cout << pi << endl;

} ///:~
```

This is especially critical when initializing const data members because they must be initialized before the function body is entered.

It made sense to extend this "constructor" for built-in types (which simply means *assignment*) to the general case, which is why the float pi(3.14159) definition works in Listing 8-10.

It's often useful to encapsulate a built-in type inside a class to guarantee initialization with the constructor. For example, Listing 8-11 shows an Integer class.

Listing 8-11. Encapsulating

```cpp
//: C08:EncapsulatingTypes.cpp
#include <iostream>
using namespace std;

class Integer {
  int i;
public:
  Integer(int ii = 0);
  void print();
};

Integer::Integer(int ii) : i(ii) {}
void Integer::print() { cout << I << ' '; }

int main() {
  Integer i[100];
  for(int j = 0; j < 100; j++)
    i[j].print();
} ///:~
```

The array of Integers in main( ) are all automatically initialized to zero. This initialization isn't necessarily more costly than a for loop or memset( ). Many compilers easily optimize this to a very fast process.

Compile-Time Constants in Classes

The above use of const is interesting and probably useful in cases, but it does not solve the original problem, which is how do you make a compile-time *constant inside a class*? The answer requires the use of an additional keyword (which will not be fully introduced until Chapter 10): static. The static keyword, in this situation, means "there's only one instance, *regardless* of how many objects of the class are created," which is precisely what we need here: a member of a class that is constant and cannot change from one object of the class to another. Thus, a static const of a built-in type can be treated as a compile-time constant.

There is one feature of static const when used inside classes that is a bit unusual: you must provide the initializer at the point of definition of the static const. This is something that only occurs with the static const; as much as you might like to use it in other situations, it won't work because all other data members must be initialized in the constructor or in other member functions.

Listing 8-12 shows the creation and use of a static const called size inside a class that represents a stack of string pointers.

Listing 8-12. Using a static const

```
//: C08:StringStack.cpp
// Using static const to create a
// compile-time constant inside a class
#include <string>
#include <iostream>
using namespace std;

class StringStack {
  static const int size = 100;
  const string* stack[size];
  int index;
public:
  StringStack();
  void push(const string* s);
  const string* pop();
};

StringStack::StringStack() : index(0) {
  memset(stack, 0, size * sizeof(string*));
}

void StringStack::push(const string* s) {
  if(index < size)
    stack[index++] = s;
}

const string* StringStack::pop() {
  if(index > 0) {
    const string* rv = stack[--index];
```

```
    stack[index] = 0;
    return rv;
  }
  return 0;
}

string iceCream[] = {
  "pralines& cream",
  "fudge ripple",
  "jamocha almond fudge",
  "wild mountain blackberry",
  "raspberry sorbet",
  "lemon swirl",
  "rocky road",
  "deep chocolate fudge"
};

const int iCsz =
  sizeof iceCream / sizeof *iceCream;

int main() {
  StringStack ss;
  for(int i = 0; i < iCsz; i++)
    ss.push(&iceCream[i]);
  const string* cp;
  while((cp = ss.pop()) != 0)
    cout << *cp << endl;
} ///:~
```

Since size is used to determine the size of the array stack, it is indeed a compile-time constant, but one that is hidden inside the class.

Notice that push( ) takes a const string* as an argument, pop( ) returns a const string*, and StringStack holds const string*. If this were not true, you couldn't use a StringStack to hold the pointers in iceCream. However, it also prevents you from doing anything that will change the objects contained by StringStack. Of course, not all containers are designed with this restriction.

The "enum hack" in Old Code

In older versions of C++, static const was not supported inside classes. This meant that const was useless for constant expressions inside classes. However, people still wanted to do this so a typical solution (usually referred to as the *"enum hack"*) was to use an untagged enum with no instances. An enumeration must have all its values established at compile time, it's local to the class, and its values are available for constant expressions. Thus, you will commonly see code like that in Listing 8-13.

Listing 8-13. enum Hack

```
//: C08:EnumHack.cpp
#include <iostream>
using namespace std;
```

```
class Bunch {
  enum { size = 1000 };
  int i[size];
};

int main() {
  cout << "sizeof(Bunch) = " << sizeof(Bunch)
       << ", sizeof(i[1000]) = "
       << sizeof(int[1000]) << endl;
} ///:~
```

The use of enum here is guaranteed to occupy no storage in the object, and the enumerators are all evaluated at compile time. You can also explicitly establish the values of the enumerators, such as:

```
enum { one = 1, two = 2, three };
```

With integral enum types, the compiler will continue counting from the last value, so the enumerator three will get the value 3.

In the StringStack.cpp example above, the line

```
Static const int size = 100;
```

would be instead

```
enum { size = 100 };
```

Although you'll often see the enum technique in legacy code, the static const feature was added to the language to solve just this problem. However, there is no overwhelming reason that you *must* choose static const over the enum hack, and in this book the enum hack is used because it is supported by more compilers at the time of writing.

const Objects and Member Functions

Class member functions can be made const. What does this mean? To understand, you must first grasp the concept of const objects.

A const object is defined the same for a user-defined type as a built-in type, such as

```
const int i = 1;
const blob b(2);
```

Here, b is a const object of type blob. Its constructor is called with an argument of two. For the compiler to enforce const attribute, it must ensure that no data members of the object are changed during the object's lifetime. It can easily ensure that no public data is modified, but how is it to know which member functions will change the data and which ones are "safe" for a const object?

If you declare a member function const, you tell the compiler the function can be called for a const object. A member function that is not specifically declared const is treated as one that will modify data members in an object, and the compiler will not allow you to call it for a const object.

It doesn't stop there, however. Just *claiming* a member function is const doesn't guarantee it will act that way, so the compiler forces you to reiterate the const specification when defining the function. (*The const becomes part of the function signature, so both the compiler and linker check for const attribute.*) Then it enforces const attribute during the function definition by issuing an error message if you try to change any members of the object *or* call a non-const member function. Thus, any member function you declare const is guaranteed to behave that way in the definition.

To understand the syntax for declaring const member functions, first notice that preceding the function declaration with const means the return value is const, so that doesn't produce the desired results. Instead, you must place the const specifier *after* the *argument list*. See Listing 8-14.

Listing 8-14. const Member Functions

```
//: C08:ConstMember.cpp
class X {
  int i;
public:
  X(int ii);
  int f() const;
};

X::X(int ii) : i(ii) {}
int X::f() const { return i; }

int main() {
  X x1(10);
  const X x2(20);
  x1.f();
  x2.f();
} ///:~
```

Note that the const keyword must be'repeated in the definition or the compiler sees it as a different function. Since f( ) is a const member function, if it attempts to change i in any way or to call another member function that is not const, the compiler flags it as an error.

You can see that a const member function is safe to call with both const and non-const objects. Thus, you could think of it as the most general form of a member function (and because of this, it is unfortunate that member functions do not automatically *default to* const). Any function that doesn't modify member data should be declared as const, so it can be used with const objects.

Listing 8-15 contrasts a const and a non-const member function.

Listing 8-15. Contrasting a const and a non-const Member Function

```
//: C08:Quoter.cpp
// Random quote selection
#include <iostream>
#include <cstdlib> // Random number generator
#include <ctime>   // To seed random generator
using namespace std;

class Quoter {
  int lastquote;
public:
  Quoter();
  int lastQuote() const;
  const char* quote();
};
```

```
Quoter::Quoter(){
  lastquote = -1;
  srand(time(0)); // Seed random number generator
}

int Quoter::lastQuote() const {
  return lastquote;
}

const char* Quoter::quote() {
  static const char* quotes[] = {
    "Are we having fun yet?",
    "Doctors always know best",
    "Is it ... Atomic?",
    "Fear is obscene",
    "There is no scientific evidence "
    "to support the idea "
    "that life is serious",
    "Things that make us happy, make us wise",
  };
  const int qsize = sizeof quotes/sizeof *quotes;
  int qnum = rand() % qsize;
  while(lastquote >= 0 && qnum == lastquote)
    qnum = rand() % qsize;
  return quotes[lastquote = qnum];
}

int main() {
  Quoter q;
  const Quoter cq;
  cq.lastQuote(); // OK
//! cq.quote();   // Not OK; non const function
  for(int i = 0; i < 20; i++)
    cout << q.quote() << endl;
} ///:~
```

Neither constructors nor destructors can be const member functions because they virtually always perform some modification on the object during initialization and cleanup. The quote( ) member function also cannot be const because it modifies the data member lastquote (see the return statement). However, lastQuote( ) makes no modifications, and so it can be const and can be safely called for the const object cq.

Mutable: Bitwise vs. Logical const

What if you want to create a const member function, but you'd still like to change some of the data in the object? This is sometimes referred to as the difference between *bitwise* const and *logical* const (also sometimes called *member-wise* const). Bitwise const means that every bit in the object is permanent, so a bit image of the object will never change. Logical const means that, although the entire object is conceptually constant, there may be changes on a member-by-member basis. However, if the compiler is told that an object is const, it will jealously guard that object to ensure bitwise const attribute. To affect the logical const attribute, there are two ways to change a data member from within a const member function.

The first approach is the historical one and is called *casting away* const attribute. It is performed in a rather odd fashion. You take this (the keyword that produces the address of the current object) and cast it to a pointer to an object of the current type. It would seem that this is *already* such a pointer. However, inside a const member function it's actually a const pointer, so by casting it to an ordinary pointer, you remove the const attribute for that operation. Listing 8-16 shows an example.

Listing 8-16. Casting Away const Attribute

```cpp
//: C08:Castaway.cpp
// "Casting away" const attribute

class Y {
  int i;
public:
  Y();
  void f() const;
};

Y::Y() { i = 0; }

void Y::f() const {
//!  i++;             // Error -- const member function
  ((Y*)this)->i++; // OK: cast away const-ness
  // Better: use C++ explicit cast syntax:
  (const_cast<Y*>(this))->i++;
}

int main() {
  const Y yy;
  yy.f();            // Actually changes it!
} ///:~
```

This approach works and you'll see it used in legacy code, but it is not the preferred technique. The problem is that this lack of const attribute is hidden away in a member function definition, and you have no clue from the class interface that the data of the object is actually being modified unless you have access to the source code (and you must suspect that const attribute is being castaway, *and look for the cast*). To put everything out in the open, you should use the mutable keyword in the class declaration to specify that a particular data member may be changed inside a const object, as in Listing 8-17.

Listing 8-17. The mutable Keyword

```cpp
//: C08:Mutable.cpp
// The "mutable" keyword

class Z {
  int i;
  mutable int j;
public:
  Z();
  void f() const;
};
```

```
Z::Z() : i(0), j(0) {}

void Z::f() const {
//! i++;   // Error -- const member function
  j++;     // OK: mutable
}

int main() {
  const Z zz;
  zz.f(); // Actually changes it!
} ///:~
```

This way, the user of the class can see from the declaration which members are likely to be modified in a const member function.

ROMability

If an object is defined as const, it is a candidate to be placed in read-only memory (ROM), which is often an important consideration in embedded systems programming. Simply making an object const, however, is not enough; the requirements for *ROMability* are much stricter. Of course, the object must be *bitwise*-const, rather than *logical*-const. This is easy to see if logical const attribute is implemented only through the mutable keyword, but probably not detectable by the compiler if const attribute is cast away inside a const member function. There are two additional rules.

1. The class or struct must have no user-defined constructors or destructor.

2. There can be no base classes (covered in Chapter 14) or member objects with user-defined constructors or destructors.

The effect of a write operation on any part of a const object of a ROMable type is undefined. Although a suitably formed object may be placed in ROM, no objects are ever *required* to be placed in ROM.

The volatile Keyword

The syntax of volatile is identical to that for const, but volatile means "This data may change outside the knowledge of the compiler." Somehow, the environment is changing the data (possibly through multitasking, multithreading, or interrupts), and volatile tells the compiler not to make any assumptions about that data, especially during optimization.

If the compiler says, "I read this data into a register earlier, and I haven't touched that register," normally it wouldn't need to read the data again. But if the data is volatile, the compiler cannot make such an assumption because the data may have been changed by another process, and it must reread that data rather than optimizing the code to remove what would normally be a redundant read.

You create volatile objects using the same syntax that you use to create const objects. You can also create const volatile objects, which can't be changed by the client programmer but instead change through some outside agency. Listing 8-18 contains an example that might represent a class associated with some piece of communication hardware.

Listing 8-18. The volatile Keyword

```
//: C08:Volatile.cpp
// The volatile keyword

classComm {
  const volatile unsigned char byte;
  volatile unsigned char flag;
  enum { bufsize = 100 };
  unsigned char buf[bufsize];
  int index;

public:
  Comm();
  void isr() volatile;
  char read(int index) const;
};

Comm::Comm() : index(0), byte(0), flag(0) {}

// Only a demo; won't actually work

// as an interrupt service routine:

void Comm::isr() volatile {
  flag = 0;
  buf[index++] = byte;
  // Wrap to beginning of buffer:
  if(index >= bufsize) index = 0;
}

charComm::read(int index) const {
  if(index < 0 || index >= bufsize)
    return 0;
  return buf[index];

}

int main() {
  volatile Comm Port;
  Port.isr();      // OK
//! Port.read(0); // Error, read() not volatile
} ///:~
```

As with const, you can use volatile for data members, member functions, and objects themselves. You can only call volatile member functions for volatile objects.

The reason that isr( ) can't actually be used as an interrupt service routine is that in a member function, the address of the current object (this) must be secretly passed, and an ISR generally wants no arguments at all. To solve this problem, you can make isr( ) a static member function, a subject covered in Chapter 10.

The syntax of volatile *is identical to* const, so discussions of the two are often treated together. The two are referred to in combination as *the c-v qualifier.*

Review Session

1. The const keyword gives you the ability to define objects, function arguments, return values, and member functions as constants, *and to eliminate the preprocessor for value substitution without losing any preprocessor benefits.*

2. All this provides a significant additional form of type checking and safety in your programming. The use of so-called "const correctness" (*the use of const anywhere you possibly can*) can be a lifesaver for projects.

3. Although you can ignore const and continue to use old C coding practices, it's there to help you. Chapter 11 and onward begin using references heavily, and there you'll see even more about how critical it is to use const with function arguments.

CHAPTER 9

■ ■ ■

Inline Functions

One of the important features C++ inherits from C is efficiency. If the efficiency of C++ were dramatically less than C, there would be a significant contingent of programmers who couldn't justify its use.

In C, one of the ways to preserve efficiency is through the use of *macros*, which allow you to make what *appears* to be, at a first glance, a function call without the normal function call overhead. The macro is implemented with the preprocessor instead of the compiler proper, and the preprocessor replaces all macro calls directly with the macro code, so there's no cost involved from pushing arguments, making an assembly-language CALL, returning arguments, and performing an assembly-language RETURN. All the work is performed by the preprocessor, so you have the convenience and readability of a function call but it doesn't cost you anything (in terms of function call overhead such as memory space or time consumed).

There are two problems with the use of preprocessor macros in C++. The first is also true with C: a macro seems to behave like a function call, but doesn't always act like one. This can result in *hiding* difficult-to-find bugs. The second problem is specific to C++: the preprocessor has no permission to access class member data. This means preprocessor macros cannot be used as class member functions.

To retain the efficiency of the preprocessor macro, but to add the safety and class scoping of true functions, C++ has the *inline function*. In this chapter, you'll look at the problems of preprocessor macros in C++, how these problems are solved with inline functions, and guidelines and insights on the way inlines work.

Preprocessor Pitfalls

The key to the problems of preprocessor macros is that you can be fooled into thinking that the behavior of the preprocessor is the same as the behavior of the compiler. Of course, it was intended that a macro look and act like a function call, so it's quite easy to fall into this fiction. The difficulties begin when the subtle differences appear.

As a simple example, consider the following:

```
#define F (x) (x + 1)
```

Now, if a call is made to F, like

```
F(1)
```

the preprocessor expands it, somewhat unexpectedly, to

```
(x) (x + 1)(1)
```

The problem occurs because of the gap between F and its opening parenthesis in the macro definition. When this gap is removed, you can actually *call* the macro with the gap

```
F (1)
```

and it will still expand properly to

```
(1 + 1)
```

The example above is fairly trivial, and the problem will make itself evident right away. The real difficulties occur when using expressions as arguments in macro calls.

There are two problems. The first is that expressions may expand inside the macro so that their evaluation precedence is different from what you expect. For example,

```
#define FLOOR(x,b) x>=b?0:1
```

Now, if expressions are used for the arguments, like

```
if(FLOOR(a&0x0f,0x07)) // ...
```

the macro will expand to

```
if(a&0x0f>=0x07?0:1)
```

The precedence of & is lower than that of >=, so the macro evaluation will surprise you. Once you discover the problem, you can solve it by putting parentheses around everything in the macro definition. (This is a good practice to use when creating preprocessor macros.) Thus,

```
#define FLOOR(x,b) ((x)>=(b)?0:1)
```

Discovering the problem may be difficult, however, and you may not find it until after you've taken the proper macro behavior for granted. In the unparenthesized version of the preceding macro, *most* expressions will work correctly because the precedence of >= is lower than most of the operators like +, /, - -, and even the bitwise shift operators. So you can easily begin to think that it works with all expressions, including those using bitwise logical operators.

The preceding problem can be solved with careful programming practice: parenthesize everything in a macro. However, the second difficulty is subtler. Unlike a normal function, every time you use an argument in a macro, that argument is evaluated. As long as the macro is called only with ordinary variables, this evaluation is benign, but if the evaluation of an argument has side effects, then the results can be surprising and will definitely not mimic function behavior.

For example, this macro determines whether its argument falls within a certain range:

```
#define BAND(x) (((x)>5 && (x)<10) ? (x) : 0)
```

As long as you use an "ordinary" argument, the macro works very much like a real function. But as soon as you relax and start believing it *is* a real function, the problems start, as you can see in Listing 9-1.

210

Listing 9-1. Macro Side Effects

```
//: C09:MacroSideEffects.cpp
#include "../require.h"          // To be INCLUDED from Header FILE
                                 // ahead (Section: Improved error
                                 // checking) Or Chapter 3

#include <fstream>
using namespace std;

#define BAND(x) (((x)>5 && (x)<10) ? (x) : 0)

int main() {
  ofstream out("macro.out");
  assure(out, "macro.out");
  for(int i = 4; i < 11; i++) {
    int a = i;
    out << "a = " << a << endl << '\t';
    out << "BAND(++a)=" << BAND(++a) << endl;
    out << "\t a = " << a << endl;
  }
} ///:~
```

Notice the use of all upper-case characters in the name of the macro. This is a helpful practice because it tells the reader this is a macro and not a function, so if there are problems, it acts as a little reminder.

Here's the output produced by the program, which is not at all what you would have expected from a true function:

```
a = 4
  BAND(++a)=0
   a = 5
a = 5
  BAND(++a)=8
   a = 8
a = 6
  BAND(++a)=9
   a = 9
a = 7
  BAND(++a)=10
   a = 10
a = 8
  BAND(++a)=0
   a = 10
a = 9
  BAND(++a)=0
   a = 11
a = 10
  BAND(++a)=0
   a = 12
```

When a is 4, only the first part of the conditional occurs, so the expression is evaluated only once, and the side effect of the macro call is that a becomes 5, which is what you would expect from a normal function call in the same situation. However, when the number is within the band, both conditionals are tested, which results in two increments. The result is produced by evaluating the argument again, which results in a third increment. Once the number gets out of the band, both conditionals are still tested so you get two increments. The side effects are different, depending on the argument.

This is clearly not the kind of behavior you want from a macro that looks like a function call. In this case, the obvious solution is to make it a true function, which of course adds the extra overhead and may reduce efficiency if you call that function a lot. Unfortunately, the problem may not always be so obvious, and you can unknowingly get a library that contains functions and macros mixed together, so a problem like this can hide some very difficult-to-find bugs. For example, the putc() macro in cstdio may evaluate its second argument twice. This is specified in Standard C. Also, careless implementations of toupper() as a macro may evaluate the argument more than once, which will give you unexpected results with toupper(*p++).

Macros and Access

Of course, careful coding and use of preprocessor macros is required with C, and you could certainly get away with the same thing in C++ if it weren't for one problem: a macro has no concept of the scoping required with member functions. The preprocessor simply performs text substitution, so you cannot say something like

```
class X {
  int i;
public:
#define VAL(X::i) // Error
```

or anything even close. In addition, there would be no indication of which object you were referring to. There is simply no way to express class scope in a macro. Without some alternative to preprocessor macros, programmers will be tempted to make some data members public for the sake of efficiency, thus exposing the underlying implementation and preventing changes in that implementation, as well as eliminating the guarding that private provides.

Inline Functions

In solving the C++ problem of a macro with access to private class members, *all* the problems associated with preprocessor macros were eliminated. This was done by bringing the concept of macros under the control of the compiler where they belong. C++ implements the macro as inline function, which is a true function in every sense. Any behavior you expect from an ordinary function, you get from an inline function. The only difference is that an inline function is expanded in place, like a preprocessor macro, so the overhead of the function call is eliminated. Thus, you should (*almost*) never use macros, only inline functions.

Any function defined within a class body is automatically inline, but you can also make a non-class function inline by preceding it with the inline keyword. However, for it to have any effect, you must include the function body with the declaration, otherwise the compiler will treat it as an ordinary function declaration. Thus,

```
Inline int plusOne(int x);
```

has no effect at all other than declaring the function (which may or may not get an inline definition sometime later). The successful approach provides the function body,:

```
inline int plusOne(int x) { return ++x; }
```

Notice that the compiler will check (as it always does) for the proper use of the function argument list and return value (performing any necessary conversions), something the preprocessor is incapable of. Also, if you try to write the above as a preprocessor macro, you will get an unwanted side effect.

You'll almost always want to put inline definitions in a header file. When the compiler sees such a definition, it puts the function type (the signature combined with the return value) *and* the function body in its symbol table. When you use the function, the compiler checks to ensure the call is correct and the return value is being used correctly, and then substitutes the function body for the function call, thus eliminating the overhead. The inline code does occupy space, but if the function is small, this can actually take less space than the code generated to do an ordinary function call (pushing arguments on the stack and doing the CALL).

An inline function in a header file has a special status, since you must include the header file containing the function *and* its definition in every file where the function is used, but you don't end up with multiple definition errors (*however, the definition must be identical in all places where the inline function is included*).

Inlines Inside Classes

To define an inline function, you must ordinarily precede the function definition with the `inline` keyword. However, this is not necessary inside a class definition. Any function you define inside a class definition is automatically an inline, as you can see in Listing 9-2.

Listing 9-2. Inlines Inside Classes

```
//: C09:Inline.cpp
// Inlines inside classes
#include <iostream>
#include <string>
using namespace std;

class Point {
  int i, j, k;
public:
  Point(): i(0), j(0), k(0) {}
  Point(int ii, int jj, int kk)

    : i(ii), j(jj), k(kk) {}
  void print(const string& msg = "") const {
  if(msg.size() != 0) cout << msg << endl;
  cout << "i = " << I << ", "
      << "j = " << j << ", "
      << "k = " << k << endl;
  }
};

int main() {
  Point p, q(1,2,3);
  p.print("value of p");
  q.print("value of q");
} ///:~
```

Here, the two constructors and the `print( )` function are all inlines by default. Notice in `main( )` that the fact you are using inline functions is transparent, as it should be. The logical behavior of a function must be identical regardless of whether it's an inline (*otherwise your compiler is broken*). The only difference you'll see is in performance.

Of course, the temptation is to use inlines everywhere inside class declarations because they save you the extra step of making the external member function definition. Keep in mind, however, that the idea of an inline is to

213

provide improved opportunities for optimization by the compiler. But inlining a big function will cause that code to be duplicated everywhere the function is called, producing code bloat that may mitigate the speed benefit.

▪ **Note** The only reliable course of action is to experiment to discover the effects of inlining on your program with your compiler.

Access Functions

One of the most important uses of inlines inside classes is the *access function*. This is a small function that allows you to read or change part of the state of an object—that is, an internal variable or variables. The reason inlines are so important for access functions can be seen in Listing 9-3.

Listing 9-3. Inline Access Functions

```
//: C09:Access.cpp
// Inline access functions

class Access {
  int i;
public:
  int read() const { return i; }
  void set(int ii) { i = ii; }
};

int main() {
  Access A;
  A.set(100);
  int x = A.read();
} ///:~
```

Here, the class user never has direct contact with the state variables inside the class, and they can be kept private, under the control of the class designer. All the access to the private data members can be controlled through the member function interface. In addition, access is remarkably efficient. Consider read(), for example. Without inlines, the code generated for the call to read() would typically include pushing this on the stack and making an assembly language CALL. With most machines, the size of this code would be larger than the code created by the inline, and the execution time would certainly be longer.

Without inline functions, an efficiency-conscious class designer will be tempted to simply make i a public member, eliminating the overhead by allowing the user to directly access i. From a design standpoint, this is disastrous because i then becomes part of the public interface, which means the class designer can never change it. You're stuck with an int called i. This is a problem because you may learn sometime later that it would be much more useful to represent the state information as a float rather than an int, but because inti is part of the public interface, you can't change it. Or you may want to perform some additional calculation as part of reading or setting i, which you can't do if it's public. If, on the other hand, you've always used member functions to read and change the state information of an object, you can modify the underlying representation of the object to your heart's content.

In addition, the use of member functions to control data members allows you to add code to the member function to detect when that data is being changed, which can be very useful during debugging. If a data member is public, anyone can change it anytime without you knowing about it.

Accessors and Mutators

Some people further divide the concept of access functions into *accessors* (to read state information from an object) and *mutators* (to change the state of an object). In addition, function overloading may be used to provide the same function name for *both* the accessor and mutator; how you call the function determines whether you're reading or modifying state information (see Listing 9-4).

Listing 9-4. Accessors and Mutators

```
//: C09:Rectangle.cpp
// Accessors & mutators

class Rectangle {
  int wide, high;
public:
  Rectangle(int w = 0, int h = 0)
    : wide(w), high(h) {}
  int width() const { return wide; }   // Read
  void width(int w) { wide = w; }       // Set
  int height() const { return high; }  // Read
  void height(int h) { high = h; }      // Set
};

int main() {
  Rectangle r(19, 47);
  // Change width & height:
  r.height(2 * r.width());
  r.width(2 * r.height());
} ///:~
```

The constructor uses the constructor initializer list (briefly introduced in Chapter 8 and covered fully in Chapter 14) to initialize the values of wide and high (using the *pseudo constructor* form for built-in types).

You cannot have member function names using the same identifiers as data members, so you might be tempted to distinguish the data members with a leading underscore. However, identifiers with leading underscores are reserved so you should not use them.

You may choose instead to use "*get*" and "*set*" to indicate accessors and mutators, as shown in Listing 9-5.

Listing 9-5. Using get and set

```
//: C09:Rectangle2.cpp
// Accessors & mutators with "get" and "set"

class Rectangle {
  int width, height;
public:
  Rectangle(int w = 0, int h = 0)
    : width(w), height(h) {}
  int getWidth() const { return width; }
  void setWidth(int w) { width = w; }
  int getHeight() const { return height; }
  void setHeight(int h) { height = h; }
};
```

```
int main() {
  Rectangle r(19, 47);
  // Change width & height:
  r.setHeight(2 * r.getWidth());
  r.setWidth(2 * r.getHeight());
} ///:~
```

Of course, accessors and mutators don't have to be simple pipelines to an internal variable. Sometimes they can perform more sophisticated calculations. Listing 9-6 uses the Standard C Library time functions to produce a simple Time class.

Listing 9-6. Using Time Functions

```
//: C09:Cpptime.h
// A simple time class
#ifndef CPPTIME_H
#define CPPTIME_H
#include <ctime>
#include <cstring>

class Time {
  std::time_t t;
  std::tm local;
  char asciiRep[26];
  unsigned char lflag, aflag;
  void updateLocal() {
    if(!lflag) {
      local = *std::localtime(&t);
      lflag++;
    }
  }
  void updateAscii() {
    if(!aflag) {
      updateLocal();
      std::strcpy(asciiRep,std::asctime(&local));
      aflag++;
    }
  }
public:
  Time() { mark(); }
  void mark() {
    lflag = aflag = 0;
    std::time(&t);
  }
  const char* ascii() {
    updateAscii();
    return asciiRep;
  }
  // Difference in seconds:
  int delta(Time* dt) const {
    return int(std::difftime(t, dt->t));
  }
```

216

```
  int daylightSavings() {
    updateLocal();
    return local.tm_isdst;
  }
  int dayOfYear() { // Since January 1
    updateLocal();
    return local.tm_yday;
  }
  int dayOfWeek() { // Since Sunday
    updateLocal();
    return local.tm_wday;
  }
  int since1900() { // Years since 1900
    updateLocal();
    return local.tm_year;
  }
  int month() {      // Since January
    updateLocal();
    return local.tm_mon;
  }
  int dayOfMonth() {
    updateLocal();
    return local.tm_mday;
  }
  int hour() {       // Since midnight, 24-hour clock
    updateLocal();
    return local.tm_hour;
  }
  int minute() {
    updateLocal();
    return local.tm_min;
  }
  int second() {
    updateLocal();
    return local.tm_sec;
  }
};
#endif            // CPPTIME_H ///:~
```

The Standard C Library functions have multiple representations for time, and these are all part of the Time class. However, it isn't necessary to update all of them, so instead the time_t t is used as the base representation, and the tm local and ASCII character representation asciiRep each have flags to indicate if they've been updated to the current time_t. The two private functions updateLocal() and updateAscii() check the flags and conditionally perform the update.

The constructor calls the mark() function (*which the user can also call to force the object to represent the current time*), and this clears the two flags to indicate that the local time and ASCII representation are now invalid. The ascii() function calls updateAscii(), which copies the result of the Standard C Library function asctime() into a local buffer because asctime() uses a static data area that is overwritten if the function is called elsewhere. The ascii() function return value is the address of this local buffer.

All the functions starting with daylightSavings() use the updateLocal() function, which causes the resulting composite inlines to be fairly large. This doesn't seem worthwhile, especially considering you probably won't call the functions very much. However, this doesn't mean all the functions should be made non-inline. If you make

CHAPTER 9 ■ INLINE FUNCTIONS

other functions non-inline, at least keep updateLocal() inline so that its code will be duplicated in the non-inline functions, eliminating extra function-call overhead.

Listing 9-7 is a small test program.

Listing 9-7. Testing a Simple Time Class

```
//: C09:Cpptime.cpp
// Testing a simple time class
#include "Cpptime.h"     // To be INCLUDED from Header FILE above
#include <iostream>
using namespace std;

int main() {
  Time start;
  for(int i = 1; i < 1000; i++) {
    cout << i << ' ';
    if(i%10 == 0) cout << endl;
  }

  Time end;
  cout << endl;
  cout << "start = " << start.ascii();
  cout << "end = " << end.ascii();
  cout << "delta = " << end.delta(&start);
} ///:~
```

A Time object is created, then some time-consuming activity is performed, then a second Time object is created to mark the ending time. They show starting, ending, and elapsed times.

Stash and Stack with Inlines

Armed with inlines, you can now convert the Stash and Stack classes to be more efficient; see Listing 9-8.

Listing 9-8. Stash Header File (with Inline Functions)

```
//: C09:Stash4.h
// Inline functions
#ifndef STASH4_H
#define STASH4_H
#include "../require.h"

class Stash {
  int size;       // Size of each space
  int quantity;   // Number of storage spaces
  int next;       // Next empty space
  // Dynamically allocated array of bytes:
  unsigned char* storage;
  void inflate(int increase);
public:
  Stash(int sz) : size(sz), quantity(0),
    next(0), storage(0) {}
```

```
  Stash(int sz, int initQuantity) : size(sz),
    quantity(0), next(0), storage(0) {
    inflate(initQuantity);
  }
  Stash::~Stash() {
    if(storage != 0)
      delete []storage;
  }
  int add(void* element);
  void* fetch(int index) const {
    require(0 <= index, "Stash::fetch (-)index");
    if(index >= next)
      return 0; // To indicate the end
    // Produce pointer to desired element:
    return &(storage[index * size]);
  }
  int count() const { return next; }
};
#endif            // STASH4_H ///:~
```

The small functions obviously work well as inlines, but notice that the two largest functions are still left as non-inlines, since inlining them probably wouldn't cause any performance gains; see Listing 9-9.

Listing 9-9. Stash Source Code cpp File (with Inline Functions)

```
//: C09:Stash4.cpp {O}
#include "Stash4.h"        // To be INCLUDED from Header FILE above
#include <iostream>
#include <cassert>
using namespace std;
const int increment = 100;

int Stash::add(void* element) {
  if(next >= quantity)      // Enough space left?
    inflate(increment);
  // Copy element into storage,
  // starting at next empty space:
  int startBytes = next * size;
  unsigned char* e = (unsigned char*) element;
  for(int i = 0; i < size; i++)
    storage[startBytes + i] = e[i];
  next++;
  return(next - 1);         // Index number
}

void Stash::inflate(int increase) {
  assert(increase >= 0);
  if(increase == 0) return;
  int newQuantity = quantity + increase;
  int newBytes = newQuantity * size;
  int oldBytes = quantity * size;
```

```
  unsigned char* b = new unsigned char[newBytes];
  for(int i = 0; i < oldBytes; i++)
    b[i] = storage[i];    // Copy old to new
  delete [](storage);     // Release old storage
  storage = b;            // Point to new memory
  quantity = newQuantity; // Adjust the size
} ///:~
```

Once again, the test program in Listing 9-10 verifies that everything is working correctly.

Listing 9-10. Testing the Stash (with Inline Functions)

```
//: C09:Stash4Test.cpp
//{L} Stash4
#include "Stash4.h"
#include "../require.h"
#include <fstream>
#include <iostream>
#include <string>
using namespace std;

int main() {
  Stash intStash(sizeof(int));
  for(int i = 0; i < 100; i++)
    intStash.add(&i);
  for(int j = 0; j <intStash.count(); j++)
    cout << "intStash.fetch(" << j << ") = "
         << *(int*)intStash.fetch(j)
         << endl;
  const int bufsize = 80;
  Stash stringStash(sizeof(char) * bufsize, 100);
  ifstream in("Stash4Test.cpp");
  assure(in, "Stash4Test.cpp");
  string line;
  while(getline(in, line))
    stringStash.add((char*)line.c_str());
  int k = 0;
  char* cp;
  while((cp = (char*)stringStash.fetch(k++))!=0)
    cout << "stringStash.fetch(" << k << ") = "
         << cp << endl;
} ///:~
```

This is the same test program that was used before, so the output should be basically the same. The Stack class makes even better use of inlines, as you can see in Listing 9-11.

Listing 9-11. Stack Header File (with Inline Functions)

```
//: C09:Stack4.h
// With inlines
#ifndef STACK4_H
#define STACK4_H
#include "../require.h"
```

```
class Stack {
  struct Link {
    void* data;
    Link* next;
    Link(void* dat, Link* nxt):
      data(dat), next(nxt) {}
  }* head;
public:
  Stack() : head(0) {}
  ~Stack() {
    require(head == 0, "Stack not empty");
  }
  void push(void* dat) {
    head = new Link(dat, head);
  }
  void* peek() const {
    return head ? head->data : 0;
  }
  void* pop() {
    if(head == 0) return 0;
    void* result = head->data;
    Link* oldHead = head;
    head = head->next;
    delete oldHead;
    return result;
  }
};
#endif // STACK4_H ///:~
```

Notice that the Link destructor that was present but empty in the previous version of Stack has been removed. In pop(), the expression delete oldHead simply releases the memory used by that Link (it does not destroy the data object pointed to by the Link).

Most of the functions inline work nicely and quite obviously, especially for Link. Even pop() seems legitimate, although anytime you have conditionals or local variables, it's not clear that inlines will be that beneficial. Here, the function is small enough that it probably won't hurt anything.

If all your functions are inlined, using the library becomes quite simple because there's no linking necessary, as you can see in the test example in Listing 9-12 (notice that there's no Stack4.cpp).

Listing 9-12. Testing the Stack (with Inline Functions)

```
//: C09:Stack4Test.cpp
//{T} Stack4Test.cpp
#include "Stack4.h"      // To be INCLUDED from Header FILE above
#include "../require.h"
#include <fstream>
#include <iostream>
#include <string>
using namespace std;

int main(int argc, char* argv[]) {
  requireArgs(argc, 1); // File name is argument
  ifstream in(argv[1]);
```

```
  assure(in, argv[1]);
  Stack textlines;
  string line;
  // Read file and store lines in the stack:
  while(getline(in, line))
    textlines.push(new string(line));
  // Pop the lines from the stack and print them:
  string* s;
  while((s = (string*)textlines.pop()) != 0) {
    cout << *s << endl;
    delete s;
  }
} ///:~
```

People will sometimes write classes with all inline functions so that the whole class will be in the header file. During program development, this is probably harmless, although sometimes it can make for longer compilations. Once the program stabilizes a bit, you'll probably want to go back and make functions non-inline where appropriate.

Inlines and the Compiler

To understand when inlining is effective, it's helpful to know what the compiler does when it encounters an inline. As with any function, the compiler holds the function *type* (that is, the function prototype including the name and argument types, in combination with the function return value) in its symbol table. In addition, when the compiler sees that the inline's function type and the function body parses without error, *the code for the function body is also brought into the symbol table*. Whether the code is stored in source form, compiled assembly instructions, or some other representation is up to the compiler.

When you make a call to an inline function, the compiler first ensures that the call can be correctly made. That is, all the argument types must either be the exact types in the function's argument list, or the compiler must be able to make a type conversion to the proper types and the return value must be the correct type (or convertible to the correct type) in the destination expression. This, of course, is exactly what the compiler does for any function and is markedly different from what the preprocessor does because the preprocessor cannot check types or make conversions.

If all the function type information fits the context of the call, then the inline code is substituted directly for the function call, eliminating the call overhead and allowing for further optimizations by the compiler. Also, if the inline is a member function, the address of the object (this) is put in the appropriate place(s), which of course is another action the preprocessor is unable to perform.

Limitations

There are two situations in which the compiler cannot perform inlining. In these cases, it simply reverts to the ordinary form of a function by taking the inline definition and creating storage for the function just as it does for a non-inline. If it must do this in multiple translation units (which would normally cause a multiple definition error), the linker is told to ignore the multiple definitions.

The compiler cannot perform inlining if the function is too complicated. This depends upon the particular compiler, but at the point most compilers give up, the inline probably wouldn't gain you any efficiency. In general, any sort of looping is considered too complicated to expand as an inline, and if you think about it, looping probably entails much more time inside the function than what is required for the function call overhead. If the function is just a collection of simple statements, the compiler probably won't have any trouble inlining it, but if there are a lot of statements, the overhead of the function call will be much less than the cost of executing the body. And remember, every time you call a big inline function, the entire function body is inserted in place of each call, so you can easily get code bloat without any noticeable performance improvement.

The compiler also cannot perform inlining if the address of the function is taken implicitly or explicitly. If the compiler must produce an address, then it will allocate storage for the function code and use the resulting address. However, where an address is not required, the compiler will probably still inline the code.

It is important to understand that an inline is just a suggestion to the compiler; the compiler is not forced to inline anything at all. A good compiler will inline small, simple functions while intelligently ignoring inlines that are too complicated. This will give you the results you want—the true semantics of a function call with the efficiency of a macro.

Forward References

If you're imagining what the compiler is doing to implement inlines, you can confuse yourself into thinking there are more limitations than actually exist. In particular, if an inline makes a forward reference to a function that hasn't yet been declared in the class (*whether that function is inline or not*), it can seem like the compiler won't be able to handle it, as in Listing 9-13.

Listing 9-13. Inline Evaluation Order

```
//: C09:EvaluationOrder.cpp

class Forward {
  int i;
public:
  Forward() : i(0) {}
  // Call to undeclared function:
  int f() const { return g() + 1; }
  int g() const { return i; }
};

int main() {
  Forward frwd;
  frwd.f();
} ///:~
```

In f(), a call is made to g(), although g() has not yet been declared. This works because the language definition states that no inline functions in a class shall be evaluated until the closing brace of the class declaration.

Of course, if g() in turn called f(), you'd end up with a set of recursive calls, which are too complicated for the compiler to inline. (Also, you'd have to perform some test in f() or g() to force one of them to "bottom out," or the recursion would be infinite.)

Hidden Activities in Constructors and Destructors

Constructors and destructors are two places where you can be fooled into thinking that an inline is more efficient than it actually is. Constructors and destructors may have hidden activities, because the class can contain *subobjects* whose constructors and destructors must be called. These subobjects may be member objects, or they may exist because of inheritance (covered in Chapter 14). As an example of a class with member objects, see Listing 9-14.

Listing 9-14. Illustrating Hidden Activities in Inlines (for a Class with Member Objects)

```
//: C09:Hidden.cpp
// Hidden activities in inlines
#include <iostream>
using namespace std;
```

```
class Member {
  int i, j, k;
public:
  Member(int x = 0) : i(x), j(x), k(x) {}
  ~Member() { cout << "~Member" << endl; }
};

classWithMembers {
  Member q, r, s;                    // Have constructors
  int i;
public:
  WithMembers(int ii) : i(ii) {} // Trivial?
  ~WithMembers() {
    cout << "~WithMembers" << endl;
  }
};

int main() {
  WithMembers wm(1);
} ///:~
```

The constructor for Member is simple enough to inline, since there's nothing special going on—no inheritance or member objects are causing extra hidden activities. But in class WithMembers there's more going on than meets the eye. The constructors and destructors for the member objects q, r, and s are being called automatically, and *those* constructors and destructors are also inline, so the difference is significant from normal member functions. This doesn't necessarily mean that you should always make constructor and destructor definitions non-inline; there are cases in which it makes sense. Also, when you're making an initial "sketch" of a program by quickly writing code, it's often more convenient to use inlines. But if you're concerned about efficiency, it's a place to look.

Reducing Clutter

If you want to optimize and reduce clutter, use the inline keyword. Using this approach, the earlier Rectangle.cpp example is shown in Listing 9-15.

Listing 9-15. Using the inline Keyword

```
//: C09:Noinsitu.cpp
// Removing in situ functions

class Rectangle {
  int width, height;
public:
  Rectangle(int w = 0, int h = 0);
  int getWidth() const;
  void setWidth(int w);
  int getHeight() const;
  void setHeight(int h);
};

inline Rectangle::Rectangle(int w, int h)
  : width(w), height(h) {}
```

```
inline int Rectangle::getWidth() const {
  return width;
}

inline void Rectangle::setWidth(int w) {
  width = w;
}

inline int Rectangle::getHeight() const {
  return height;
}

inline void Rectangle::setHeight(int h) {
  height = h;
}

int main() {
  Rectangle r(19, 47);
  // Transpose width & height:
  int iHeight = r.getHeight();
  r.setHeight(r.getWidth());
  r.setWidth(iHeight);
} ///:~
```

Now if you want to compare the effect of inline functions to non-inline functions, you can simply remove the inline keyword. (Inline functions should normally be put in header files, however, while non-inline functions must reside in their own translation unit.) If you want to put the functions into documentation, it's a simple cut-and-paste operation.

More Preprocessor Features

Earlier, I said that you *almost* always want to use inline functions instead of preprocessor macros. The exceptions are when you need to use three special features in the C preprocessor (which is also the C++ preprocessor): stringizing, string concatenation, and token pasting. *Stringizing*, introduced earlier in the book, is performed with the # directive, and it allows you to take an identifier and turn it into a character array. String concatenation takes place when two adjacent character arrays have no intervening punctuation, in which case they are combined. These two features are especially useful when writing debug code. Thus,

```
#define DEBUG(x) cout << #x " = " << x << endl
```

prints the value of any variable. You can also get a trace that prints out the statements as they execute, such as

```
#define TRACE(s) cerr << #s << endl; s
```

The #s stringizes the statement for output, and the second s reiterates the statement so it is such as:

```
for(int i = 0; I < 100; i++)
  TRACE(f(i));
```

Because there are actually two statements in the TRACE() macro, the one-line for loop executes only the first one. The solution is to replace the semicolon with a comma in the macro.

Token Pasting

Token pasting, implemented with the ## directive, is very useful when you are manufacturing code. It allows you to take two identifiers and paste them together to automatically create a new identifier. For example,

```
#define FIELD(a) char* a##_string; int a##_size
class Record {
  FIELD(one);
  FIELD(two);
  FIELD(three);
  // ...
};
```

Each call to the FIELD() macro creates an identifier to hold a character array and another to hold the length of that array. Not only is it easier to read, it can eliminate coding errors and make maintenance easier.

Improved Error Checking

The require.h functions have been used up to this point without defining them (although assert()*has also been used to help detect programmer errors where it's appropriate*). Now it's time to define this header file. Inline functions are convenient here because they allow everything to be placed in a header file, which simplifies the process of using the package. You just include the header file and you don't need to worry about linking an implementation file.

You should note that exceptions provide a much more effective way of handling many kinds of errors—especially those that you'd like to recover from—instead of just halting the program. The conditions that require.h handles, however, are ones that prevent the continuation of the program, such as if the user doesn't provide enough command-line arguments or if a file cannot be opened. Thus, it's acceptable that they call the Standard C Library function exit().

Listing 9-16 is this header file (which you saw in Chapter 3 as well since it is used to build some of the examples in the previous chapters. Left to myself, this is the most appropriate place for it since it makes use of inlines).

Listing 9-16. The require.h Header File

```
//: :require.h
// Test for error conditions in programs
// Local "using namespace std" for old compilers
#ifndef REQUIRE_H
#define REQUIRE_H
#include <cstdio>
#include <cstdlib>
#include <fstream>
#include <string>

inline void require(bool requirement,
  const std::string& msg = "Requirement failed"){
  using namespace std;
  if (!requirement) {
    fputs(msg.c_str(), stderr);
    fputs("\n", stderr);
    exit(1);
  }
}
```

```cpp
inline void requireArgs(int argc, int args,
  const std::string& msg =
    "Must use %d arguments") {
  using namespace std;
  if (argc != args + 1) {
    fprintf(stderr, msg.c_str(), args);
    fputs("\n", stderr);
    exit(1);
  }
}

inline void requireMinArgs(intargc, intminArgs,
  const std::string& msg =
    "Must use at least %d arguments") {
  using namespace std;
  if(argc < minArgs + 1) {
    fprintf(stderr, msg.c_str(), minArgs);
    fputs("\n", stderr);
    exit(1);
  }
}

inline void assure(std::ifstream& in,
  const std::string& filename = "") {
  using namespace std;
  if(!in) {
    fprintf(stderr, "Could not open file %s\n",
      filename.c_str());
    exit(1);
  }
}

inline void assure(std::ofstream& out,
  const std::string& filename = "") {
  using namespace std;
  if(!out) {
  fprintf(stderr, "Could not open file %s\n",
    filename.c_str());
  exit(1);
  }
}
#endif // REQUIRE_H ///:~
```

The default values provide reasonable messages that can be changed, if necessary.

You'll notice that instead of using char* arguments, const string& arguments are used. This allows both char* and strings as arguments to these functions, and thus is more generally useful (you may want to follow this form in your own coding).

In the definitions for requireArgs()and requireMinArgs(), one is added to the number of arguments you need on the command line because argc always includes the name of the program being executed as argument zero, and so always has a value that is one more than the number of actual arguments on the command line.

Note the use of local using namespace std declarations within each function. This is because some compilers at the time of this writing incorrectly did not include the Standard C Library functions in namespace std, so explicit qualification would cause a compile-time error. The local declaration allows require.h to work with both correct and incorrect libraries without opening up the namespace std for anyone who includes this header file.

Listing 9-17 is a simple program to test require.h.

Listing 9-17. Testing require.h

```
//: C09:ErrTest.cpp
//{T} ErrTest.cpp
// Testing require.h
#include "../require.h"
#include <fstream>
using namespace std;

int main(int argc, char* argv[]) {

  int i = 1;
  require(i, "value must be nonzero");
  requireArgs(argc, 1);
  requireMinArgs(argc, 1);
  ifstream in(argv[1]);
  assure(in, argv[1]);
                // Use the file name
  ifstream nofile("nofile.xxx");
                // Fails:
                //! assure(nofile);
                // The default argument
  ofstream out("tmp.txt");
  assure(out);
} ///:~
```

You might be tempted to go one step further for opening files and add a macro to require.h, such as:

```
#define IFOPEN(VAR, NAME) \
  ifstream VAR(NAME); \
  assure(VAR, NAME);
```

which could then be used like this:

```
IFOPEN(in, argv[1])
```

At first, this might seem appealing since it means there's less to type. It's not terribly unsafe, but it's a road best avoided. Note that, once again, a macro looks like a function but behaves differently; it's actually creating an object (in) whose scope persists beyond the macro. You may understand this, but for new programmers and code maintainers it's just one more thing they have to puzzle out. C++ is complicated enough without adding to the confusion, so try to talk yourself out of using preprocessor macros whenever you can.

Review Session

1. It's critical that you be able to hide the underlying implementation of a class because you may want to change that implementation sometime later.

2. You'll make these changes for *efficiency*, or because you get a better understanding of the problem, or because some *new class* becomes available that you want to use in the implementation.

3. Anything that jeopardizes the privacy of the underlying implementation reduces the flexibility of the language. Thus, the *inline* function is very important because it virtually eliminates the need for preprocessor macros and their attendant problems.

4. With `inlines`, member functions can be as *efficient* as preprocessor macros.

5. The `inline` function can be *overused* in class definitions, of course. The programmer is tempted to do so because it's easier, so it will happen. However, it's not that big of an issue because later, when looking for size reductions, you can always change the functions to non-`inlines` with no effect on their functionality.

6. The development guideline should be "First make the code work, then optimize it."

7. From this point onwards, I shall only mention the header file `require.h` as given in this chapter.

CHAPTER 10

Name Control

Creating names is a fundamental activity in programming, and when a project gets large, the number of names can easily be overwhelming.

C++ allows you a great deal of control over the creation and visibility of names, where storage for those names is placed, and linkage for names.

The static keyword was overloaded in C before people knew what the term "overload" meant, and C++ has added yet another meaning. The underlying concept with all uses of static seems to be "something that holds its position" (like static electricity), whether that means a physical location in memory or visibility within a file.

In this chapter, you'll learn how static controls storage and visibility, and an improved way to control access to names via C++'s namespace feature. You'll also find out how to use functions that were written and compiled in C.

Static Elements from C

In both C and C++, the keyword static has two basic meanings, which unfortunately often step on each other's toes.

1. Allocated once at a fixed address; that is, the object is created in a special static data area rather than on the stack each time a function is called. This is the concept of static storage.

2. Local to a particular translation unit (and local to a class scope in C++, as you will see later). Here, static controls the visibility of a name, so that name cannot be seen outside the translation unit or class. This also describes the concept of linkage, which determines what names the linker will see.

This section will look at the meanings of static as they were inherited from C.

Static Variables Inside Functions

When you create a local variable inside a function, the compiler allocates storage for that variable each time the function is called by moving the stack pointer down an appropriate amount. If there is an *initializer* for the variable, the initialization is performed each time that sequence point is passed.

Sometimes, however, you want to retain a value between function calls. You could accomplish this by making a global variable, but then that variable would not be under the sole control of the function. C and C++ allow you to create a static object inside a function; the storage for this object is not on the stack but instead in the program's static data area. This object is initialized only once, the first time the function is called, and then retains its value between function invocations. For example, in Listing 10-1, the function returns the next character in the array each time the function is called.

Listing 10-1. Static Variables in Functions

```cpp
//: C10:StaticVariablesInfunctions.cpp
#include "../require.h"        // To be INCLUDED from Header FILE in Chapter 9
#include <iostream>
using namespace std;

char oneChar(const char* charArray = 0) {
  static const char* s;
  if(charArray) {
    s = charArray;
    return *s;
  }
else
  require(s, "un-initialized s");
  if(*s == '\0')
    return 0;
  return *s++;
}

char* a = "abcdefghijklmnopqrstuvwxyz";

int main() {
  // oneChar(); // require() fails
  oneChar(a); // Initializes s to a
  char c;
  while((c = oneChar()) != 0)
    cout << c << endl;
} ///:~
```

The static char* s holds its value between calls of oneChar() because its storage is not part of the stack frame of the function, but is in the static storage area of the program. When you call oneChar() with a char* argument, s is assigned to that argument, and the first character of the array is returned. Each subsequent call to oneChar() without an argument produces the default value of zero for charArray, which indicates to the function that you are still extracting characters from the previously initialized value of s. The function will continue to produce characters until it reaches the null terminator of the character array, at which point it stops incrementing the pointer so it doesn't overrun the end of the array.

But what happens if you call oneChar() with no arguments and without previously initializing the value of s? In the definition for s, you could have provided an initializer, like

```cpp
static char* s = 0;
```

but if you do not provide an initializer for a static variable of a built-in type, the compiler guarantees that variable will be initialized to zero (converted to the proper type) at program startup. So in oneChar(), the first time the function is called, s is zero. In this case, the if(!s) conditional will catch it.

The initialization above for s is very simple, but initialization for static objects (like all other objects) can be arbitrary expressions involving constants and previously declared variables and functions.

You should be aware that the function above is very vulnerable to multithreading problems; whenever you design functions containing static variables you should keep multithreading issues in mind.

Static Class Objects Inside Functions

The rules are the same for static objects of user-defined types, including the fact that some initialization is required for the object. However, assignment to zero has meaning only for built-in types; user-defined types must be initialized with constructor calls. Thus, if you don't specify constructor arguments when you define the static object, the class must have a default constructor, as you can see in Listing 10-2.

Listing 10-2. Static Class Objects Inside Functions

```
//: C10:StaticObjectsInFunctions.cpp
#include <iostream>
using namespace std;

class X {
  int i;
public:
  X(int ii = 0) : i(ii) {} // Default
  ~X() { cout << "X::~X()" << endl; }
};

void f() {
  static X x1(47);
  static X x2; // Default constructor required
}

int main() {
  f();
} ///:~
```

The static objects of type X inside f() can be initialized either with the constructor argument list or with the default constructor. This construction occurs the first time control passes through the definition, and only the first time.

Static Object Destructors

Destructors for static objects (*that is, all objects with static storage, not just local static objects as in the example above*) are called when main() exits or when the Standard C Library function exit() is explicitly called. In most implementations, main() just calls exit() when it terminates. This means that it can be dangerous to call exit() inside a destructor because you can end up with infinite recursion. Static object destructors are *not* called if you exit the program using the Standard C Library function abort().

You can specify actions to take place when leaving main() (or calling exit()) by using the Standard C Library function atexit(). In this case, the functions registered by atexit() may be called before the destructors for any objects constructed before leaving main() (or calling exit()).

Like ordinary destruction, destruction of static objects occurs in the reverse order of initialization. However, only objects that have been constructed are destroyed. Fortunately, the C++ development tools keep track of initialization order and the objects that have been constructed. Global objects are always constructed before main() is entered and destroyed as main() exits, but if a function containing a local static object is never called, the constructor for that object is never executed, so the destructor is also not executed (see Listing 10-3).

Listing 10-3. Static Object Destructors

```cpp
//: C10:StaticDestructors.cpp
// Static object destructors
#include <fstream>
using namespace std;
ofstream out("statdest.out"); // Trace file

classObj {
  char c;                      // Identifier
public:
  Obj(char cc) : c(cc) {
    out << "Obj::Obj() for " << c << endl;
  }
  ~Obj() {
    out << "Obj::~Obj() for " << c << endl;
  }
};

Obj a('a');                    // Global (static storage)
// Constructor & destructor always called

void f() {
  static Obj b('b');
}

void g() {
  static Obj c('c');
}

int main() {
  out << "inside main()" << endl;
  f();                         // Calls static constructor for b
  // g() not called
  out << "leaving main()" << endl;
} ///:~
```

In Obj, the char c acts as an identifier so the constructor and destructor can print out information about the object they're working on. The Obj a is a global object, so the constructor is always called for it before main() is entered, but the constructors for the static Obj b inside f() and the static Obj c inside g() are called only if those functions are called.

To demonstrate which constructors and destructors are called, only f() is called. The output of the program is

```
Obj::Obj() for a
inside main()
Obj::Obj() for b
leaving main()
Obj::~Obj() for b
Obj::~Obj() for a
```

The constructor for a is called before main() is entered, and the constructor for b is called only because f() is called. When main() exits, the destructors for the objects that have been constructed are called in reverse order of their construction. This means that if g() *is* called, the order in which the destructors for b and c are called depends on whether f() or g() is called first.

Notice that the trace file ofstream object out is also a static object—since it is defined outside of all functions, it lives in the static storage area. It is important that its definition (as opposed to an extern declaration) appear at the beginning of the file, before there is any possible use of out. Otherwise, you'll be using an object before it is properly initialized.

In C++, the constructor for a global static object is called before main() is entered, so you now have a simple and portable way to execute code before entering main() and to execute code with the destructor after exiting main(). In C, this was always a trial that required you to root around in the compiler vendor's assembly-language startup code.

Controlling Linkage

Ordinarily, any name at file scope (that is, not nested inside a class or function) is visible throughout all translation units in a program. This is often called *external linkage* because at link time the name is visible to the linker everywhere, external to that translation unit. Global variables and ordinary functions have external linkage.

There are times when you'd like to limit the visibility of a name. You might like to have a variable at file scope so all the functions in that file can use it, but you don't want functions outside that file to see or access that variable, or to inadvertently cause name clashes with identifiers outside the file.

An object or function name at file scope that is explicitly declared static is local to its translation unit (in the terms of this book, the cpp file where the declaration occurs). That name has internal linkage. This means that you can use the same name in other translation units without a name clash.

One advantage to internal linkage is that the name can be placed in a header file without worrying that there will be a clash at link time. Names that are commonly placed in header files, such as const definitions and inline functions, default to internal linkage. (However, const defaults to internal linkage only in C++; in C, it defaults to external linkage.) Note that linkage refers only to elements that have addresses at link/load time; thus, class declarations and local variables have no linkage.

Confusion

Here's an example of how the two meanings of static can cross over each other. All global objects implicitly have static storage class, so if you say (at file scope),

```
int a = 0;
```

then storage for a will be in the program's static data area, and the initialization for a will occur once, before main() is entered. In addition, the visibility of a is global across all translation units. In terms of visibility, the opposite of static (*visible only in this translation unit*) is extern, which explicitly states that the visibility of the name is across all translation units. So the definition above is equivalent to saying.

```
extern int a = 0;
```

But if you say instead,

```
static int a = 0;
```

all you've done is change the visibility, so a has internal linkage. The storage class is unchanged—the object resides in the static data area whether the visibility is static or extern.

Once you get into local variables, static stops altering the visibility and instead alters the storage class.

If you declare what appears to be a local variable as extern, it means that the storage exists elsewhere (so the variable is actually global to the function). For examples, see Listings 10-4 and 10-5.

Listing 10-4. Local extern

```
//: C10:LocalExtern.cpp
//{L} LocalExtern2
#include<iostream>

int main() {
 extern int i;
 std::cout << i;
} ///:~
```

Listing 10-5. Another Local extern

```
//: C10:LocalExtern2.cpp {O}
int i = 5;
///:~
```

With function names (for non-member functions), static and extern can only alter visibility, so if you say

```
extern void f();
```

it's the same as the unadorned declaration of

```
void f();
```

and if you say,

```
static void f();
```

it means f() is visible only within this translation unit. This is sometimes called *file static*.

Other Storage Class Specifiers

You will see static and extern used commonly. There are two other storage class *specifiers* that occur less often. The auto specifier is almost never used because it tells the compiler that this is a local variable. auto is short for "automatic" and it refers to the way the compiler automatically allocates storage for the variable. The compiler can always determine this fact from the context in which the variable is defined, so auto is redundant.

A register variable is a local (auto) variable, along with a hint to the compiler that this particular variable will be heavily used so the compiler ought to keep it in a register if it can. Thus, it is an *optimization aid*. Various compilers respond differently to this hint; they have the option to ignore it. If you take the address of the variable, the register specifier will almost certainly be ignored. You should avoid using register because the compiler can usually do a better job of optimization than you.

Namespaces

Although names can be nested inside classes, the names of global functions, global variables, and classes are still in a single global namespace. The static keyword gives you some control over this by allowing you to give variables and functions internal linkage (that is, to make them file static). But in a large project, lack of control over the global name space can cause problems. To solve these problems for classes, vendors often create long complicated names that are unlikely to clash, but then you're stuck typing those names. (A typedef is often used to simplify this.) It's not an elegant, language-supported solution.

You can subdivide the global namespace into more manageable pieces using the namespace feature of C++. The namespace keyword, similar to class, struct, enum, and union, puts the names of its members in a distinct space. While the other keywords have additional purposes, the creation of a new name space is the only purpose for namespace.

Creating a namespace

The creation of a namespace is notably similar to the creation of a class; see Listing 10-6.

Listing 10-6. Creating a Namespace

```
//: C10:MyLib.cpp

namespace MyLib {

  // Declarations
}

int main() {} ///:~
```

This produces a new namespace containing the enclosed declarations. There are significant differences from class, struct, union and enum, however:

- A namespace definition can appear only at global scope, or nested within another namespace.

- No terminating semicolon is necessary after the closing brace of a namespace definition.

- A namespace definition can be "continued" over multiple header files using a syntax that, for a class, would appear to be a redefinition (see Listing 10-7).

Listing 10-7. Illustrating Continuation of a Namespace Definition

```
//: C10:Header1.h
#ifndef HEADER1_H
#define HEADER1_H
namespace MyLib {
  extern int x;
  void f();
  // ...
}
#endif              // HEADER1_H ///:~

//: C10:Header2.h
#ifndef HEADER2_H
#define HEADER2_H
#include "Header1.h"  // To be INCLUDED from Header FILE above
// Add more names to MyLib
namespace MyLib {     // NOT a redefinition!
  extern int y;
  void g();
  // ...
}
#endif              // HEADER2_H ///:~
```

```
//: C10:Continuation.cpp
#include "Header2.h"  // To be INCLUDED from Header FILE above
int main() {} ///:~
```

- A namespace name can be *aliased* to another name, so you don't have to type an unwieldy name created by a library vendor, as shown in Listing 10-8.

Listing 10-8. Illustrating Continuation of a Namespace Definition (over Multiple Header Files)

```
//: C10:BobsSuperDuperLibrary.cpp
namespace BobsSuperDuperLibrary {
  class Widget { /* ... */ };
  classPoppit { /* ... */ };
  // ...
}
// Too much to type! I'll alias it:
namespace Bob = BobsSuperDuperLibrary;
int main() {} ///:~
```

- You cannot create an instance of a namespace as you can with a class.

Unnamed Namespaces

Each translation unit contains an unnamed namespace that you can add to by saying "namespace" without an identifier, as shown in Listing 10-9.

Listing 10-9. Unnamed Namespaces

```
//: C10:UnnamedNamespaces.cpp
namespace {
  class Arm  { /* ... */ };
  class Leg  { /* ... */ };
  class Head { /* ... */ };
  class Robot {
    Arm arm[4];
    Leg leg[16];
    Head head[3];
    // ...
  } xanthan;
  int i, j, k;
}
int main() {} ///:~
```

The names in this space are automatically available in that translation unit without qualification. It is guaranteed that an unnamed space is unique for each translation unit. If you put local names in an unnamed namespace, you don't need to give them internal linkage by making them static.

C++ deprecates the use of file statics in favor of the unnamed namespace.

Friends

You can *inject* a friend declaration into a namespace by declaring it within an enclosed class, as shown in Listing 10-10.

Listing 10-10. Injecting a friend into a Namespace

```
//: C10:FriendInjection.cpp
namespace Me {
class Us {
    //...
friend void you();
  };
}
int main() {} ///:~
```

Now the function you() is a member of the namespace Me.

If you introduce a friend within a class in the global namespace, the friend is injected globally.

Using a Namespace

You can refer to a name within a namespace in three ways: by specifying the name using the scope resolution operator, with a using directive to introduce all names in the namespace, or with a using declaration to introduce names one at a time.

Scope Resolution

Any name in a namespace can be explicitly specified using the scope resolution operator in the same way that you can refer to the names within a class, as shown in Listing 10-11.

Listing 10-11. Explicitly Specifying a Name in a Namespace (using the Scope Resolution Operator)

```
//: C10:ScopeResolution.cpp
namespace X {
  class Y {
    static int i;
public:
  void f();
  };
  class Z;
  voidfunc();
}
int X::Y::i = 9;
class X::Z {
  int u, v, w;
public:
  Z(int i);
  int g();
};
X::Z::Z(int i) { u = v = w = i; }
int X::Z::g() { return u = v = w = 0; }
void X::func() {
  X::Z a(1);
  a.g();
}
int main(){} ///:~
```

Notice that the definition X::Y::i could just as easily be referring to a data member of a class Y nested in a class X instead of a namespace X.

So far, namespaces look very much like classes.

The using Directive

Because it can rapidly get tedious to type the full qualification for an identifier in a namespace, the using keyword allows you to import an entire namespace at once. When used in conjunction with the namespace keyword, this is called a *using directive*. The using directive makes names appear as if they belong to the nearest enclosing namespace scope, so you can conveniently use the unqualified names. Consider a simple namespace, shown in Listing 10-12.

Listing 10-12. Illustrating A Simple Namespace

```
//: C10:NamespaceInt.h
#ifndef NAMESPACEINT_H
#define NAMESPACEINT_H
namespace Int {
  enum sign { positive, negative };
  class Integer {
    int i;
    sign s;
public:
  Integer(int ii = 0)
    : i(ii),
      s(i>= 0 ? positive : negative)
    {}
    sign getSign() const { return s; }
    void setSign(sign sgn) { s = sgn; }
    // ...
  };
}
#endif // NAMESPACEINT_H ///:~
```

One use of the using directive is to bring all of the names in Int into another namespace, leaving those names nested within the namespace, as shown in Listing 10-13.

Listing 10-13. Illustrating the using Directive

```
//: C10:NamespaceMath.h
#ifndef NAMESPACEMATH_H
#define NAMESPACEMATH_H
#include "NamespaceInt.h"  // To be INCLUDED from Header FILE above
namespace Math {
  using namespace Int;
  Integer a, b;
  Integer divide(Integer, Integer);
  // ...
}
#endif // NAMESPACEMATH_H ///:~
```

You can also declare all of the names in Int inside a function, but leave those names nested within the function, as shown in Listing 10-14.

Listing 10-14. Illustrating the using Directive (albeit in a different way)

```
//: C10:Arithmetic.cpp
#include "NamespaceInt.h"
void arithmetic() {
  using namespace Int;
  Integer x;
  x.setSign(positive);
}
int main(){} ///:~
```

Without the using directive, all the names in the namespace would need to be fully qualified.

One aspect of the using directive may seem slightly counterintuitive at first. The visibility of the names introduced with a using directive is the scope in which the directive is made. But you can override the names from the using directive as if they've been declared globally to that scope! See Listing 10-15 for an example.

Listing 10-15. Illustrating Namespace Overriding

```
//: C10:NamespaceOverriding1.cpp
#include "NamespaceMath.h"     // To be INCLUDED from Header FILE
                               // above

int main() {

  using namespace Math;

  Integer a;
      // Hides Math::a;
  a.setSign(negative);
      // Now scope resolution is necessary
      // to select Math::a :

  Math::a.setSign(positive);
} ///:~
```

Suppose you have a second namespace that contains some of the names in namespace Math (see Listing 10-16).

Listing 10-16. Illustrating Namespace Overriding (again, albeit in a different way)

```
//: C10:NamespaceOverriding2.h
#ifndef NAMESPACEOVERRIDING2_H
#define NAMESPACEOVERRIDING2_H
#include "NamespaceInt.h"
namespace Calculation {
  using namespace Int;
  Integer divide(Integer, Integer);
  // ...
}
#endif // NAMESPACEOVERRIDING2_H ///:~
```

Since this namespace is also introduced with a using directive, you have the possibility of a collision. However, the ambiguity appears at the point of *use* of the name, not at the using directive, as you can see in Listing 10-17.

Listing 10-17. Illustrating Overriding Ambiguity

```
//: C10:OverridingAmbiguity.cpp
#include "NamespaceMath.h"
#include "NamespaceOverriding2.h"    // To be INCLUDED from Header
                                     // FILE above
void s() {
  using namespace Math;
  using namespace Calculation;
  // Everything's ok until:
  //! divide(1, 2); // Ambiguity
}
int main() {} ///:~
```

Thus, it's possible to write using directives to introduce a number of namespaces with conflicting names without ever producing an ambiguity.

The using Declaration

You can inject names one at a time into the current scope with a using *declaration*. Unlike the using directive, which treats names as if they were declared globally to the scope, a using declaration is a declaration within the current scope. This means it can override names from a using directive (see Listing 10-18).

Listing 10-18. Illustrating a using Declaration

```
//: C10:UsingDeclaration.h
#ifndef USINGDECLARATION_H
#define USINGDECLARATION_H
namespace U {
  inline void f() {}
  inline void g() {}
}
namespace V {
  inline void f() {}
  inline void g() {}
}
#endif                              // USINGDECLARATION_H ///:~

//: C10:UsingDeclaration1.cpp
#include "UsingDeclaration.h"      // To be INCLUDED from Header
                                   // FILE above
void h() {
  using namespace U;               // Using directive
  using V::f;                      // Using declaration
  f(); // Calls V::f();
  U::f();                          // Must fully qualify to call
}
int main() {} ///:~
```

The using declaration just gives the fully specified name of the identifier, but no type information. This means that if the namespace contains a set of overloaded functions with the same name, the using declaration declares all the functions in the overloaded set.

You can put a using declaration anywhere a normal declaration can occur. A using declaration works like a normal declaration in all ways but one: because you don't give an argument list, it's possible for a using declaration to cause the overload of a function with the same argument types (*which isn't allowed with normal overloading*). This ambiguity, however, doesn't show up until the point of use, rather than the point of declaration.

A using declaration can also appear within a namespace, and it has the same effect as anywhere else—that name is declared within the space (see Listing 10-19).

Listing 10-19. Illustrating a using Declaration within a Namespace

```
//: C10:UsingDeclaration2.cpp
#include "UsingDeclaration.h"
namespace Q {
  using U::f;
  using V::g;
  // ...
}
void m() {
  using namespace Q;
  f(); // Calls U::f();
  g(); // Calls V::g();
}
int main() {} ///:~
```

A using declaration is an alias, and it allows you to declare the same function in separate namespaces. If you end up redeclaring the same function by importing different namespaces, it's OK; there won't be any ambiguities or duplications.

The Use of Namespaces

Some of these rules may seem a bit daunting at first, especially if you get the impression that you'll be using them all the time. In general, however, you can get away with very simple usage of namespaces as long as you understand how they work. The key thing to remember is that when you introduce a global using directive (via a using namespace outside of any scope) you have thrown open the namespace for that file. This is usually fine for an implementation file (a cpp file) because the using directive is only in effect until the end of the compilation of that file. That is, it doesn't affect any other files, so you can adjust the control of the namespaces one implementation file at a time. For example, if you discover a name clash because of too many using directives in a particular implementation file, it is a simple matter to change that file so that it uses explicit qualifications or using declarations to eliminate the clash, without modifying other implementation files.

Header files are a different issue. You virtually never want to introduce a global using directive into a header file, because that would mean that any other file that included your header would also have the namespace thrown open (and header files can include other header files).

So, in header files you should either use explicit qualification or scoped using directives and using declarations. This is the practice that you will find in this book, and by following it you will not "pollute" the global namespace and throw yourself back into the pre-namespace world of C++.

Static Members in C++

There are times when you need a single storage space to be used by all objects of a class. In C, you would use a global variable, but this is not very safe. Global data can be modified by anyone, and its name can clash with other identical names in a large project. It would be ideal if the data could be stored as if it were global, but be hidden inside a class, and clearly associated with that class.

This is accomplished with `static` data members inside a class. There is a single piece of storage for a `static` data member, regardless of how many objects of that class you create. All objects share the same `static` storage space for that data member, so it is a way for them to "communicate" with each other. But the `static` data belongs to the class; its name is scoped inside the class and it can be `public`, `private`, or `protected`.

Defining Storage for Static Data Members

Because `static` data has a single piece of storage regardless of how many objects are created, that storage must be defined in a single place. The compiler will not allocate storage for you. The linker will report an error if a `static` data member is declared but not defined.

The definition must occur outside the class (*no inlining is allowed*), and only one definition is allowed. Thus, it is common to put it in the implementation file for the class. The syntax sometimes gives people trouble, but it is actually quite logical. For example, if you create a static data member inside a class, such as:

```
class A {
  static int i;
public:
  //...
};
```

then you must define storage for that static data member in the definition file, as in:

```
int A::i = 1;
```

If you were to define an ordinary global variable, you would say

```
int i = 1;
```

but here the scope resolution operator and the class name are used to specify `A::i`.

Some people have trouble with the idea that `A::i` is `private`, and yet here's something that seems to be manipulating it right out in the open. Doesn't this break the protection mechanism? It's a completely safe practice for two reasons. First, the only place this initialization is legal is in the definition. Indeed, if the `static` data were an object with a constructor, you would call the constructor instead of using the = operator. Second, once the definition has been made, the end user cannot make a second definition; the linker will report an error. And the class creator is forced to create the definition or the code won't link during testing. This ensures that the definition happens only once and that it's in the hands of the class creator.

The entire initialization expression for a static member is in the scope of the class. For example, see Listing 10-20.

Listing 10-20. Illustrating the Scope of Static Initializer

```
//: C10:Statinit.cpp
// Scope of static initializer
#include <iostream>
using namespace std;

int x = 100;
```

```
class WithStatic {
  static int x;
  static int y;
public:
  void print() const {
    cout << "WithStatic::x = " << x << endl;
    cout << "WithStatic::y = " << y << endl;
  }
};

int WithStatic::x = 1;
int WithStatic::y = x + 1;
// WithStatic::x NOT ::x

int main() {
  WithStatic ws;
  ws.print();
} ///:~
```

Here, the qualification WithStatic:: extends the scope of WithStatic to the entire definition.

static Array Initialization

Chapter 8 introduced the static const variable that allows you to define a constant value inside a class body. It's also possible to create arrays of static objects, both const and non-const. The syntax is reasonably consistent, as you can see in Listing 10-21.

Listing 10-21. Syntax of Static Arrays

```
//: C10:StaticArray.cpp
// Initializing static arrays in classes
class Values {
  // static consts are initialized in-place:
  static const int scSize = 100;
  static const long scLong = 100;
  // Automatic counting works with static arrays.
  // Arrays, Non-integral and non-const statics
  // must be initialized externally:
  static const int scInts[];
  static const long scLongs[];
  static const float scTable[];
  static const char scLetters[];
  static int size;
  static const float scFloat;
  static float table[];
  static char letters[];
};
```

```
int Values::size = 100;
const float Values::scFloat = 1.1;

const int Values::scInts[] = {
  99, 47, 33, 11, 7
};

const long Values::scLongs[] = {
  99, 47, 33, 11, 7
};

const float Values::scTable[] = {
  1.1, 2.2, 3.3, 4.4
};

const char Values::scLetters[] = {
  'a', 'b', 'c', 'd', 'e',
  'f', 'g', 'h', 'i', 'j'
};

float Values::table[4] = {
  1.1, 2.2, 3.3, 4.4
};

char Values::letters[10] = {
  'a', 'b', 'c', 'd', 'e',
  'f', 'g', 'h', 'i', 'j'
};

int main() { Values v; } ///:~
```

With static consts of integral types you can provide the definitions inside the class, but for everything else (including arrays of integral types, even if they are static const) you must provide a single external definition for the member. These definitions have internal linkage, so they can be placed in header files. The syntax for initializing static arrays is the same as for any aggregate, including automatic counting.

You can also create static const objects of class types and arrays of such objects. However, you cannot initialize them using the "inline syntax" allowed for static consts of integral built-in types (see Listing 10-22).

Listing 10-22. Illustrating Static Arrays of Class Objects

```
//: C10:StaticObjectArrays.cpp
// Static arrays of class objects
class X {
  int i;
public:
  X(int ii) : i(ii) {}
};
```

```
class Stat {
  // This doesn't work, although
  // you might want it to:
//!  static const X x(100);
  // Both const and non-const static class
  // objects must be initialized externally:
  static X x2;
  static X xTable2[];
  static const X x3;
  static const X xTable3[];
};

X Stat::x2(100);

X Stat::xTable2[] = {
  X(1), X(2), X(3), X(4)
};

const X Stat::x3(100);

const X Stat::xTable3[] = {
  X(1), X(2), X(3), X(4)
};

int main() { Stat v; } ///:~
```

The initialization of both const and non-const static arrays of class objects must be performed the same way, following the typical static definition syntax.

Nested and Local Classes

You can easily put static data members in classes that are nested inside other classes. The definition of such members is an intuitive and obvious extension—you simply use another level of scope resolution. However, you cannot have static data members inside local classes (a local class is a class defined inside a function). For example, refer to the code in Listing 10-23.

Listing 10-23. Illustrating Static Members and Local Classes

```
//: C10:Local.cpp
// Static members & local classes
#include <iostream>
using namespace std;

// Nested class CAN have static data members:
class Outer {
  class Inner {
    static int i; // OK
  };
};

int Outer::Inner::i = 47;
```

```
// Local class cannot have static data members:
void f() {
  class Local {
  public:
//! Static int i;   // Error
    // (How would you define i?)
  } x;
}

int main() { Outer x; f(); } ///:~
```

You can see the immediate problem with a static member in a local class: how do you describe the data member at file scope in order to define it? In practice, local classes are used very rarely.

static Member Functions

You can also create static member functions that, like static data members, work for the class as a whole rather than for a particular object of a class. Instead of making a global function that lives in and "pollutes" the global or local namespace, you bring the function inside the class. When you create a static member function, you are expressing an association with a particular class.

You can call a static member function in the ordinary way, with the dot or the arrow, in association with an object. However, it's more typical to call a static member function by itself, without any specific object, using the scope-resolution operator, as shown in Listing 10-24.

Listing 10-24. Illustrating a Simple static Member Function

```
//: C10:SimpleStaticMemberFunction.cpp
class X {
public:
  static void f(){};
};

int main() {
  X::f();
} ///:~
```

When you see static member functions in a class, remember that the designer intended that function to be conceptually associated with the class as a whole.

A static member function cannot access ordinary data members, only static data members. It can call only other static member functions. Normally, the address of the current object (this) is quietly passed in when any member function is called, but a static member has no this, which is the reason it cannot access ordinary members. Thus, you get the tiny increase in speed afforded by a global function because a static member function doesn't have the extra overhead of passing this. At the same time you get the benefits of having the function inside the class.

For data members, static indicates that only one piece of storage for member data exists for all objects of a class. This parallels the use of static to define objects "inside" a function to mean that only one copy of a local variable is used for all calls of that function.

Listing 10-25 is an example showing static data members and static member functions used together.

Listing 10-25. Illustrating static Data Members and static Member Functions (used in Combination)

```cpp
//: C10:StaticMemberFunctions.cpp
class X {
  int i;
  static int j;
public:
  X(int ii = 0) : i(ii) {
      // Non-static member function can access
      // static member function or data:
  j = i;
  }
  intval() const { return i; }
  static int incr() {
    //! i++;      // Error: static member function
    // cannot access non-static member data
    return ++j;
  }
  static int f() {
    //! val();    // Error: static member function
    // cannot access non-static member function
    returnincr(); // OK -- calls static
  }
};

int X::j = 0;

int main() {
  X x;
  X* xp = &x;
  x.f();
  xp->f();
  X::f();            // Only works with static members
} ///:~
```

Because they have no this pointer, static member functions can neither access non-static data members nor call non-static member functions.

Notice in main() that a static member can be selected using the usual dot or arrow syntax, associating that function with an object, but also with no object (*because a* static *member is associated with a class, not a particular object*), using the class name and scope resolution operator.

Here's an interesting feature: because of the way initialization happens for static member objects, you can put a static data member of the same class "inside" that class. Listing 10-26 is an example that allows only a single object of type E to exist by making the constructor private. You can access that object, but you can't create any new E objects.

■ **Note**   This is what is also referred to as the *"Singleton" pattern*!

Listing 10-26. Illustrating the "Singleton" Pattern

```cpp
//: C10:Singleton.cpp
// Static member of same type, ensures that
// only one object of this type exists.
// Also referred to as the "singleton" pattern.
#include <iostream>
using namespace std;

class E {
  static E e;
  int i;
  E(int ii) : i(ii) {}
  E(const E&); // Prevent copy-construction
public:
  static E* instance() { return &e; }
  int val() const { return i; }
};

E E::e(47);

int main() {
//! E x(1);   // Error -- can't create an E
  // You can access the single instance:
  cout << E::instance()->val() << endl;
} ///:~
```

The initialization for e happens after the class declaration is complete, so the compiler has all the information it needs to allocate storage and make the constructor call.

To completely prevent the creation of any other objects, something else has been added: a second private constructor called the *copy constructor*. At this point in the book, you cannot know why this is necessary since the copy constructor will not be introduced until the next chapter. However, as a sneak preview, if you were to remove the copy constructor defined in Listing 10-26, you'd be able to create an E object like this:

```cpp
E e = *Egg::instance();
E e2(*Egg::instance());
```

Both of these use the copy constructor, so to seal off that possibility the copy constructor is declared as private.

■ **Note** No definition is necessary because it never gets called.

A large portion of the next chapter is a discussion of the copy constructor so it should become clear to you then.

Static Initialization Dependency

Within a specific translation unit, the order of initialization of static objects is guaranteed to be the order in which the object definitions appear in that translation unit. The order of destruction is guaranteed to be the reverse of the order of initialization.

However, there is no guarantee concerning the order of initialization of static objects *across* translation units, and the language provides no way to specify this order. This can cause significant problems. As an example of an instant disaster (which will halt primitive operating systems and kill the process on sophisticated ones), if one file contains

```
//: C10:Out.cpp {O}
// First file
#include <fstream>
std::ofstream out("out.txt"); ///:~
```

and another file uses the out object in one of its *initializers*

```
//: C10:Oof.cpp
// Second file
//{L} Out
#include <fstream>
Extern std::ofstream out;
classOof {
public:
  Oof() { std::out << "ouch"; }
} oof;
int main() {} ///:~
```

the program may work, and it may not. If the programming environment builds the program so that the first file is initialized before the second file, then there will be no problem. However, if the second file is initialized before the first, the constructor for Oof relies upon the existence of out, which hasn't been constructed yet, and this causes chaos.

This problem only occurs with static object initializers *that depend on each other*. The statics in a translation unit are initialized before the first invocation of a function in that unit—but it could be after main(). You can't be sure about the order of initialization of static objects if they're in different files.

A subtler example can be found in the ARM. In one file you have at the global scope,

```
extern int y;
int x = y + 1;
```

and in a second file you have at the global scope

```
extern int x;
int y = x + 1;
```

For all static objects, the linking-loading mechanism guarantees a static initialization to zero before the dynamic initialization specified by the programmer takes place. In the previous example, zeroing of the storage occupied by the fstream out object has no special meaning, so it is truly undefined until the constructor is called. However, with built-in types, initialization to zero *does* have meaning, and if the files are initialized in the order they are shown above, y begins as statically initialized to zero, so x becomes one, and y is dynamically initialized to two. However, if the files are initialized in the opposite order, x is statically initialized to zero, y is dynamically initialized to one, and x then becomes two.

Programmers must be aware of this because they can create a program with static initialization dependencies and get it working on one platform, but move it to another compiling environment where it suddenly, mysteriously, doesn't work.

Solving the Problem

There are three approaches to dealing with this problem.

1. Don't do it. Avoiding static initialization dependencies is the best solution.

2. If you must do it, put the critical static object definitions in a single file, so you can portably control their initialization by putting them in the correct order.

3. If you're convinced it's unavoidable to scatter static objects across translation units—as in the case of a library, where you can't control the programmer who uses it—there are two programmatic techniques to solve the problem.

Technique One

This technique was pioneered by Jerry Schwarz while creating the iostream library (because the definitions for cin, cout, and cerr are static and live in a separate file). It's actually inferior to the second technique but it's been around a long time and so you may come across code that uses it; thus it's important that you understand how it works.

This technique requires an additional class in your library header file. This class is responsible for the dynamic initialization of your library's static objects. Listing 10-27 shows a simple example.

Listing 10-27. Illustrating "Technique One"

```
//: C10:Initializer.h
// Static initialization technique
#ifndef INITIALIZER_H
#define INITIALIZER_H
#include <iostream>
extern int x; // Declarations, not definitions
extern int y;

class Initializer {
  static int initCount;
public:
  Initializer() {
    std::cout << "Initializer()" << std::endl;
    // Initialize first time only
    if(initCount++ == 0) {
      std::cout << "performing initialization"
                << std::endl;
      x = 100;
      y = 200;
    }
  }
  ~Initializer() {
    std::cout << "~Initializer()" << std::endl;
    // Clean up last time only
    if(--initCount == 0) {
      std::cout << "performing cleanup"
                << std::endl;
      // Any necessary cleanup here
    }
  }
};
```

```
// The following creates one object in each
// file where Initializer.h is included, but that
// object is only visible within that file:
static Initializer init;
#endif          // INITIALIZER_H ///:~
```

The declarations for x and y announce only that these objects exist, but they don't allocate storage for the objects. However, the definition for the Initializer init allocates storage for that object in every file where the header is included. But because the name is static (controlling visibility this time, not the way storage is allocated; storage is at file scope by default), it is visible only within that translation unit, so the linker will not complain about multiple definition errors.

Listing 10-28 contains the definitions for x, y, and initCount.

Listing 10-28. Illustrating Definitions for the Header File in Listing 10-27

```
//: C10:InitializerDefs.cpp {O}
// Definitions for Initializer.h
#include "Initializer.h"       // To be INCLUDED from Header FILE
                               // above
// Static initialization will force
// all these values to zero:
int x;
int y;
int Initializer::initCount;
///:~
```

■ **Comment**   Of course, a file static instance of init is also placed in this file when the header is included.

Suppose that two other files are created by the library user (see Listings 10-29 and 10-30).

Listing 10-29. Illustrating Static Initialization (For First File)

```
//: C10:Initializer.cpp {O}
// Static initialization
#include "Initializer.h"
///:~
```

Listing 10-30. Illustrating More Static Initialization (for Second File)

```
//: C10:Initializer2.cpp
//{L} InitializerDefs Initializer
// Static initialization
#include "Initializer.h"
using namespace std;

int main() {
  cout << "inside main()" << endl;
  cout << "leaving main()" << endl;
} ///:~
```

Now it doesn't matter which translation unit is initialized first. The first time a translation unit containing Initializer.h is initialized, initCount will be zero so the initialization will be performed.

■ **Note** This depends heavily on the fact that the static storage area is set to zero before any dynamic initialization takes place.

For all the rest of the translation units, initCount will be nonzero and the initialization will be skipped. Cleanup happens in the reverse order, and ~Initializer() ensures that it will happen only once.

This example used built-in types as the global static objects. The technique also works with classes, but those objects must then be dynamically initialized by the Initializer class. One way to do this is to create the classes without constructors and destructors, but instead with initialization and cleanup member functions using different names. A more common approach, however, is to have pointers to objects and to create them using new inside Initializer().

Technique Two

Long after technique one was in use, someone (I don't know who) came up with the technique explained in this section, which is much simpler and cleaner than technique one. The fact that it took so long to discover is a tribute to the complexity of C++.

This technique relies on the fact that static objects inside functions are initialized the first time (only) that the function is called. Keep in mind that the problem we're really trying to solve here is not *when* the static objects are initialized (that can be controlled separately) but rather making sure that the initialization happens in the *proper order*.

This technique is very neat and clever. For any initialization dependency, you place a static object inside a function that returns a reference to that object. This way, the only way you can access the static object is by calling the function, and if that object needs to access other static objects on which it is dependent, it must call their functions. And the first time a function is called, it forces the initialization to take place. The order of static initialization is guaranteed to be correct because of the design of the code, not because of an arbitrary order established by the linker.

To set up an example, Listings 10-31 and 10-32 contain two classes that depend on each other. The first one contains a bolo that is initialized only by the constructor, so you can tell if the constructor has been called for a static instance of the class (the static storage area is initialized to zero at program startup, which produces a false value for the bolo if the constructor has not been called).

Listing 10-31. Illustrating the First Dependency Class

```
//: C10:Dependency1.h
#ifndef DEPENDENCY1_H
#define DEPENDENCY1_H
#include <iostream>

class Dependency1 {
  bool init;
public:
  Dependency1() : init(true) {
    std::cout << "Dependency1 construction"
              < <std::endl;
  }
void print() const {
  std::cout << "Dependency1 init: "
            << init << std::endl;
  }
};
#endif // DEPENDENCY1_H ///:~
```

Listing 10-32. Illustrating the Second Dependency Class

```
//: C10:Dependency2.h
#ifndef DEPENDENCY2_H
#define DEPENDENCY2_H
#include "Dependency1.h"      // To be INCLUDED from Header FILE
                              // above

class Dependency2 {
  Dependency1 d1;
public:
  Dependency2(const Dependency1& dep1): d1(dep1){
    std::cout << "Dependency2 construction ";
    print();
  }
  void print() const { d1.print(); }
};
#endif // DEPENDENCY2_H ///:~
```

The constructor also announces when it is being called, and you can print() the state of the object to find out if it has been initialized.

The second class is initialized from an object of the first class, which is what will cause the dependency (Listing 10-32).

The constructor announces itself and prints the state of the d1 object so you can see if it has been initialized by the time the constructor is called.

To demonstrate what can go wrong, the code in Listing 10-33 first puts the static object definitions in the wrong order, as they would occur if the linker happened to initialize the Dependency2 object before the Dependency1 object. Then the order is reversed to show how it works correctly if the order happens to be "right." Lastly, technique two is demonstrated.

Listing 10-33. Illustrating Technique Two

```
//: C10:Technique2.cpp
#include "Dependency2.h"      // To be INCLUDED from Header FILE
                              // above

using namespace std;

// Returns a value so it can be called as
// a global initializer:
int separator() {
  cout << "--------------------" << endl;
  return 1;
}

// Simulate the dependency problem:
extern Dependency1 dep1;
Dependency2 dep2(dep1);
Dependency1 dep1;
int x1 = separator();
```

```
// But if it happens in this order it works OK:
Dependency1 dep1b;
Dependency2 dep2b(dep1b);
int x2 = separator();

// Wrapping static objects in functions succeeds
Dependency1&d1() {
  static Dependency1 dep1;
  return dep1;
}

Dependency2&d2() {
  static Dependency2 dep2(d1());
  return dep2;
}

int main() {
  Dependency2& dep2 = d2();
} ///:~
```

To provide more readable output, the function separator() is created. The trick is that you can't call a function globally unless that function is being used to perform the initialization of a variable, so separator() returns a dummy value that is used to initialize a couple of global variables.

The functions d1() and d2() wrap static instances of Dependency1 and Dependency2 objects. Now the only way you can get to the static objects is by calling the functions and that forces static initialization on the first function call. This means that initialization is guaranteed to be correct, which you'll see when you run the program and look at the output.

Here's how you would actually organize the code to use the technique. Ordinarily, the static objects would be defined in separate files (because you're forced to for some reason; remember that defining the static objects in separate files is what causes the problem), so instead you define the wrapping functions in separate files. But they'll need to be declared in header files see Listings 10-34 and 10-35).

Listing 10-34. Illustrating the First Header File

```
//: C10:Dependency1StatFun.h
#ifndef DEPENDENCY1STATFUN_H
#define DEPENDENCY1STATFUN_H
#include "Dependency1.h"
extern Dependency1& d1();
#endif // DEPENDENCY1STATFUN_H ///:~
```

Actually, the "extern" is redundant for the function declaration. Here's the second header file (Listing 10-35).

Listing 10-35. Illustrating the Second Header File

```
//: C10:Dependency2StatFun.h
#ifndef DEPENDENCY2STATFUN_H
#define DEPENDENCY2STATFUN_H
#include "Dependency2.h"
extern Dependency2& d2();
#endif // DEPENDENCY2STATFUN_H ///:~
```

Now, in the implementation files where you would previously have placed the static object definitions, you instead place the wrapping function definitions, as shown in Listings 10-36 and 10-37.

Listing 10-36. Illustrating the first Implementation File

```
//: C10:Dependency1StatFun.cpp {O}
#include "Dependency1StatFun.h" // To be INCLUDED from Header FILE
                                 // above

Dependency1&d1() {
  static Dependency1 dep1;
  return dep1;
} ///:~
```

Presumably, other code might also be placed in these files. Here's the other file (Listing 10-37).

Listing 10-37. Illustrating the Second Implementation File

```
//: C10:Dependency2StatFun.cpp {O}
#include "Dependency1StatFun.h"
#include "Dependency2StatFun.h"  // To be INCLUDED from Header FILE
                                 // above

Dependency2&d2() {
  static Dependency2 dep2(d1());
  return dep2;
} ///:~
```

So now there are two files that could be linked in any order and if they contained ordinary static objects could produce any order of initialization. But since they contain the wrapping functions, there's no threat of incorrect initialization (see Listing 10-38).

Listing 10-38. Illustrating that Initialization is Not affected by the Order of Linking

```
//: C10:Technique2b.cpp

//{L} Dependency1StatFun Dependency2StatFun

#include "Dependency2StatFun.h"

int main() { d2(); } ///:~
```

When you run this program you'll see that the initialization of the Dependency1 static object always happens before the initialization of the Dependency2 static object. You can also see that this is a much simpler approach than technique one.

You might be tempted to write d1() and d2() as inline functions inside their respective header files, but this is something you must definitely not do. *An inline function can be duplicated in every file in which it appears—and this duplication includes the static object definition.* Because inline functions automatically default to internal linkage, this would result in having multiple static objects across the various translation units, which would certainly cause problems. So you must ensure that there is only one definition of each wrapping function, and this means not making the wrapping functions inline.

Alternate Linkage Specifications

What happens if you're writing a program in C++ and you want to use a C library? If you make the C function declaration,

```
float f(int a, char b);
```

the C++ compiler will decorate this name to something like _f_int_char to support function overloading (and type-safe linkage). However, the C compiler that compiled your C library has most definitely *not* decorated the name, so its internal name will be _f. Thus, the linker will not be able to resolve your C++ calls to f().

The escape mechanism provided in C++ is the *alternate linkage specification*, which was produced in the language by overloading the extern keyword. The extern is followed by a string that specifies the linkage you want for the declaration, followed by the declaration, such as:

```
extern "C" float f(int a, char b);
```

This tells the compiler to give C linkage to f() so that the compiler doesn't decorate the name. The only two types of linkage specifications supported by the standard are "C" and "C++," but compiler vendors have the option of supporting other languages in the same way.

If you have a group of declarations with alternate linkage, put them inside braces, like this:

```
extern "C" {

  float f(int a, char b);
  double d(int a, char b);

}
```

Or, for a header file,

```
extern "C" {
#include "Myheader.h"
}
```

Most C++ compiler vendors handle the alternate linkage specifications inside their header files that work with both C and C++, so you don't have to worry about it.

Review Session

1. The static keyword can be confusing because in some situations it controls the *location* of storage, and in others it controls *visibility* and *linkage of a name*.

2. With the introduction of C++ namespaces, you have an *improved* and more *flexible* alternative to control the proliferation of names in large projects.

3. The use of *static inside classes* is one more way to control names in a program. The names do not clash with global names, and the visibility and access is kept within the program, giving you *greater control* in the maintenance of your code.

CHAPTER 11

References and the Copy Constructor

References are like constant pointers that are automatically dereferenced by the compiler.

Although references also exist in Pascal, the C++ version was taken from the Algol language. They are essential in C++ to support the syntax of operator overloading (see Chapter 12), but they are also a general convenience to control the way arguments are passed into and out of functions.

This chapter will first look briefly at the differences between pointers in C and C++, then it will introduce references. But the bulk of the chapter will delve into a rather confusing issue for the new C++ programmer: the *copy-constructor*, a special constructor (*requiring references*) that makes a new object from an existing object of the same type. The copy-constructor is used by the compiler to pass and return objects *by value* into and out of functions. Finally, the somewhat obscure C++ pointer-to-member feature is illuminated.

Pointers in C++

The most important difference between pointers in C and those in C++ is that C++ is a more strongly typed language. This stands out where void* is concerned. C doesn't let you casually assign a pointer of one type to another, but *it does* allow you to accomplish this through a void*. Thus,

```
bird *b;
rock *r;
void *v;
v = r;
b = v;
```

Because this "feature" of C allows you to quietly treat any type like any other type, it leaves a big hole in the type system. C++ doesn't allow this; the compiler gives you an error message, and if you really want to treat one type as another, you must make it explicit, both to the compiler and to the reader, using a cast.

■ **Note**   Chapter 3 introduced C++'s improved "explicit" casting syntax.

References in C++

A reference(&) is like a constant pointer that is automatically *dereferenced*. It is usually used for function argument lists and function return values. But you can also make a freestanding reference. For an example, see Listing 11-1.

Listing 11-1. Illustrating A Freestanding Reference

```
//: C11:FreeStandingReferences.cpp
#include <iostream>
using namespace std;

// Ordinary free-standing reference:
int y;
int& r = y;
// When a reference is created, it must
// be initialized to a live object.
// However, you can also say:
    const int& q = 12;   // (1)
// References are tied to someone else's storage:
int x = 0;              // (2)
int& a = x;             // (3)
int main() {
  cout << "x = " << x << ", a = " << a << endl;
  a++;
  cout << "x = " << x << ", a = " << a << endl;
} ///:~
```

In line (1), the compiler allocates a piece of storage, initializes it with the value 12, and ties the reference to that piece of storage. The point is that any reference must be tied to someone *else's* piece of storage. When you access a reference, you're accessing that storage. Thus, if you write lines like (2) and (3), then incrementing a is actually incrementing x, as is shown in main( ). Again, the easiest way to think about a reference is as a fancy pointer. One advantage of this "pointer" is that you never have to wonder whether it's been initialized (*the compiler enforces it*) and how to dereference it (*the compiler does it*).

There are certain rules when using references.

1. A reference must be initialized when it is created. (Pointers can be initialized at any time.)

2. Once a reference is initialized to an object, it cannot be changed to refer to another object. (Pointers can be pointed to another object at any time.)

3. You cannot have NULL references. You must always be able to assume that a reference is connected to a legitimate piece of storage.

References in Functions

The most common place you'll see references are as function arguments and return values. When a reference is used as a function argument, any modification to the reference inside the function will cause changes to the argument outside the function. Of course, you could do the same thing by passing a pointer, but a reference has much cleaner syntax.

■ **Note**   You can think of a reference as nothing more than a syntax convenience, if you want.

If you return a reference from a function, you must take the same care as if you return a pointer from a function. Whatever the reference is connected to shouldn't go away when the function *returns*; otherwise you'll be referring to unknown memory. See Listing 11-2 for an example.

Listing 11-2. Illustrating Simple C++ References

```
//: C11:Reference.cpp

// Simple C++ references

int *f(int* x) {
  (*x)++;
  return x;     // Safe, x is outside this scope
}

int& g(int& x) {
  x++;          // Same effect as in f()
  return x;     // Safe, outside this scope
}

int& h() {
  int q;
//! return q;   // Error
  static int x;
  return x;     // Safe, x lives outside this scope
}

int main() {
  int a = 0;
  f(&a);        // Ugly (but explicit)
  g(a);         // Clean (but hidden)
} ///:~
```

The call to f( ) doesn't have the convenience and cleanliness of using references, but it's clear that an address is being passed. In the call to g( ), an address is being passed (via a reference), but you don't see it.

const References

The reference argument in Reference.cpp works only when the argument is a non-const object. If it is a const object, the function g( ) will not accept the argument, which is actually a good thing, because the function *does* modify the outside argument. If you know the function will respect the const attribute of an object, making the argument a const reference will allow the function to be used in all situations. This means that, for built-in types, the function will not modify the argument, and for user-defined types, the function will call only const member functions, and won't modify any public data members.

The use of const references in function arguments is especially important because your function may receive a temporary object. This might have been created as a return value of another function or explicitly by the user of your function. Temporary objects are always const, so if you don't use a const reference, that argument won't be accepted by the compiler. Listing 11-3 is a very simple example.

Listing 11-3. Illustrating Passing of References as const

```
//: C11:ConstReferenceArguments.cpp

// Passing references as const

void f(int&) {}
void g(const int&) {}

int main() {
//!  f(1); // Error
  g(1);
} ///:~
```

The call to f(1) causes a compile-time error because the compiler must first create a reference. It does so by allocating storage for an int, initializing it to one and producing the address to bind to the reference. The storage *must* be a const because changing it would make no sense—you can never get your hands on it again. With all temporary objects you must make the same assumption: that they're inaccessible. It's valuable for the compiler to tell you when you're changing such data because the result would be lost information.

Pointer References

In C, if you want to modify the *contents* of the pointer rather than what it points to, your function declaration looks like

```
void f(int**);
```

and you'd have to take the address of the pointer when passing it in, as:

```
int i = 47;
int* ip = &i;
f(&ip);
```

With *references* in C++, the syntax is cleaner. The function argument becomes a reference to a pointer, and you no longer have to take the address of that pointer, thus the code in Listing 11-4.

Listing 11-4. Illustrating Reference to A Pointer

```
//: C11:ReferenceToPointer.cpp
#include <iostream>
using namespace std;

void increment(int*& i) { i++; }

int main() {
int* i = 0;
cout << "i = " << i << endl;
increment(i);
cout << "i = " << i << endl;
} ///:~
```

By running this program, you'll prove to yourself that the pointer is *incremented,* not what it points to.

Argument-Passing Guidelines

Your normal habit when passing an argument to a function should be to pass by const reference. Although at first this may seem like only an efficiency concern (and you normally don't want to concern yourself with efficiency tuning while you're designing and assembling your program), there's more at stake: as you'll see in the remainder of the chapter, a copy-constructor is required to pass an object by value, and this isn't always available.

The efficiency savings can be substantial for such a simple habit: to pass an argument by value requires a constructor and destructor call, but if you're not going to modify the argument then passing by const reference only needs an address pushed on the stack.

In fact, virtually the only time passing an address *isn't* preferable is when you're going to do such damage to an object that passing by value is the only safe approach (*rather than modifying the outside object, something the caller doesn't usually expect*). This is the subject of the next section.

The Copy-Constructor

Now that you understand the basics of the reference in C++, you're ready to tackle one of the more confusing concepts in the language: the copy-constructor, often called X(X&) ("*X of X ref*"). This constructor is essential to control passing and returning of user-defined types by value during function calls. It's so important, in fact, that the compiler will automatically synthesize a copy-constructor if you don't provide one yourself, as you will see.

Passing and Returning by Value

To understand the need for the copy-constructor, consider the way C handles passing and returning variables by value during function calls. If you declare a function and make a function call, as in:

```
int f(int x, char c);
int g = f(a, b);
```

how does the compiler know how to pass and return those variables? It just knows! The range of the types it must deal with is so small (char, int, float, double, and their variations) that this information is built into the compiler.

If you figure out how to generate assembly code with your compiler and determine the statements generated by the function call to f( ), you'll get the equivalent of

```
push  b
push  a
call  f()
add   sp, 4
mov   g, register a
```

This code has been cleaned up significantly to make it generic; the expressions for b and a will be different depending on whether the variables are global (in which case they will be _b and _a) or local (the compiler will index them off the stack pointer). This is also true for the expression for g. The appearance of the call to f( ) will depend on your name-decoration scheme, and register a depends on how the CPU registers are named within your assembler. The logic behind the code, however, will remain the same.

In C and C++, arguments are first pushed on the stack from right to left, then the function call is made. The calling code is responsible for cleaning the arguments off the stack (which accounts for the add sp, 4). *But notice that to pass the arguments by value, the compiler simply pushes copies on the stack*. It knows how big they are and that pushing those arguments makes accurate copies of them.

The return value of f( ) is placed in a register. Again, the compiler knows everything there is to know about the return value type because that type is built into the language, so the compiler can return it by placing it in a register. With the primitive data types in C, the simple act of copying the bits of the value is equivalent to copying the object.

Passing and Returning Large Objects

Now let's consider user-defined types. If you create a class and you want to pass an object of that class by value, how is the compiler supposed to know what to do? This is not a type built into the compiler; it's a type you have created. To investigate this, you can start with a simple structure that is clearly too large to return in registers, as in Listing 11-5.

Listing 11-5. Illustrating Passing of Big Structures

```
//: C11:PassingBigStructures.cpp

struct Big {
  char buf[100];
  int i;
  long d;
} B, B2;

Big bigfun(Big b) {
  b.i = 100; // Do something to the argument
  return b;
}

int main() {
  B2 = bigfun(B);
} ///:~
```

Decoding the assembly output is a little more complicated here because most compilers use "helper" functions instead of putting all functionality inline. In main( ), the call to bigfun( ) starts as you might guess: the entire contents of B are pushed on the stack.

■ **Note**   Here you might see some compilers load registers with the address of the Big and its size, then call a helper function to push the Big onto the stack.

In the previous code fragment, pushing the arguments onto the stack was all that was required before making the function call. In PassingBigStructures.cpp (Listing 11-5), however, you'll see an additional action: the address of B2 is pushed before making the call, even though it's obviously not an argument. To comprehend what's going on here, you need to understand the constraints on the compiler when it's making a function call.

Function-Call Stack Frame

When the compiler generates code for a function call, it first pushes all the arguments on the stack, *then* it makes the call. Inside the function, code is generated to move the stack pointer down even farther to provide storage for the function's local variables. (*"Down" is relative here; your machine may increment or decrement the stack pointer during a push.*) But during the assembly-language CALL, the CPU pushes the address in the program code where the function call *came from*, so the assembly-language RETURN can use that address to return to the calling point. This address is, of course, sacred because without it your program will get completely lost. Figure 11-1 shows what the stack frame looks like after the CALL and the allocation of local variable storage in the function.

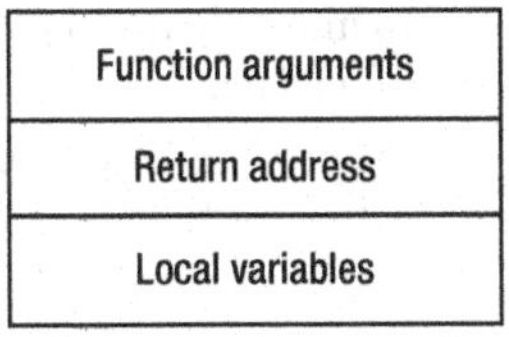

| Function arguments |
| Return address |
| Local variables |

Figure 11-1. *Stack frame*

The code generated for the rest of the function expects the memory to be laid out exactly this way, so that it can carefully pick from the function arguments and local variables without touching the return address. I shall call this block of memory, which is everything used by a function in the process of the function call, the *function frame*.

You might think it reasonable to try to return values on the stack. The compiler could simply push it, and the function could return an offset to indicate how far down in the stack the return value begins.

Reentrancy

The problem occurs because functions in C and C++ support interrupts; that is, the languages are reentrant. They also support recursive function calls. This means that at any point in the execution of a program, an *interrupt* can occur without breaking the program. Of course, the person who writes the interrupt service routine (ISR) is responsible for saving and restoring all the registers that are used in the ISR, but if the ISR needs to use any memory further down on the *stack*, this must be a safe thing to do.

■ **Note**   You can think of an ISR as an ordinary function with no arguments and void return value that saves and restores the CPU state. An ISR function call is triggered by some hardware event instead of an explicit call from within a program.

Now imagine what would happen if an ordinary function tried to return values on the stack. You can't touch any part of the stack that's above the return address, so the function would have to push the values below the return address. But when the assembly-language RETURN is executed, the stack pointer must be pointing to the return address (or right below it, depending on your computer), so right before the RETURN, the function must move the stack pointer up, thus clearing off all its local variables. If you're trying to return values on the stack below the return address, you become vulnerable at that moment because an interrupt could come along. The ISR would move the stack pointer down to hold its return address and its local variables and overwrite your return value.

To solve this problem, the caller *could* be responsible for allocating the extra storage on the stack for the return values before calling the function. However, C was not designed this way, and C++ must be compatible. As you'll see shortly, the C++ compiler uses a more efficient scheme.

Your next idea might be to return the value in some global data area, but this doesn't work either. Reentrancy means that any function can be an interrupt routine for any other function, including the same function you're currently inside. Thus, if you put the return value in a global area, you might return into the same function, which would overwrite that return value. The same logic applies to recursion.

The only safe place to return values is in the registers, so you're back to the problem of what to do when the registers aren't large enough to hold the return value. The answer is to push the address of the return value's destination on the stack as one of the function arguments, and let the function copy the return information directly into the destination. This not only solves all the problems, it's more efficient. It's also the reason that, in PassingBigStructures.cpp (Listing 11-5), the compiler pushes the address of B2 before the call to bigfun( ) in main( ). If you look at the assembly output for bigfun( ), you can see it expects this hidden argument and performs the copy to the destination *inside* the function.

A discussion of the assembly language code in context with such reentrant functions follows. To input characters from the keyboard, you use a system service to read a string (*syscall* 8). The specific set of assembly language instructions that may be used is

```
li  $v0, 8           # system call code to Read a String
la  $a0, buffer      # load address of input buffer into $a0
li  $a1, 60          # Length of buffer
syscall
```

This is obviously a non-reentrant function to read values in hexadecimal representation. There are two rules for writing reentrant code.

- All local variables must be dynamically allocated on the stack.

- No read/write data should exist in the global data segment.

Thus, to make such functions reentrant, allocation of space for character buffers must be removed from the global data segment and code must be inserted into the functions to dynamically allocate space on the stack for character buffers.

Suppose you want to allocate space on the stack for an input buffer of 32 characters, initialize a pointer in $a0 to point to the first character in this buffer, and then read in a string of characters from the keyboard. This can be accomplished with the following assembly language code:

```
addiu  $sp, $sp, -32    # Allocate Space on top of stack
move   $a0, $sp         # Initialize $a0 as a pointer to the buffer
li     $a1, 32          # Specify length of buffer
li     $v              # System call code to Read String
syscall
```

Bit-Copy vs. Initialization

So far, so good! There's a workable process for passing and returning large simple structures. But notice that all you have is a way to copy the bits from one place to another, which certainly works fine for the primitive way that C looks at variables. But in C++, objects can be much more sophisticated than a patch of bits; they have meaning. This meaning may not respond well to having its bits copied.

Consider a simple example: a class that knows how many objects of its type *exist at* any one time (see Listing 11-6). From Chapter 10, you know the way to do this is by including a static data member.

Listing 11-6. Illustrating a Class that Counts its Objects (by Including a Static Data Member)

```
//: C11:HowMany.cpp
// A class that counts its objects
#include <fstream>
#include <string>
using namespace std;
ofstream out("HowMany.out");

classHowMany {
  static int objectCount;
public:
  HowMany() { objectCount++; }
```

```
  static void print(const string&msg = "") {
    if(msg.size() != 0) out << msg << ": ";
    out << "objectCount = "
        << objectCount << endl;
  }
  ~HowMany() {
    objectCount--;
    print("~HowMany()");
  }
};

int HowMany::objectCount = 0;

// Pass and return BY VALUE:
HowManyf(HowMany x) {
  x.print("x argument inside f()");
  return x;
}

int main() {
  HowMany h;
  HowMany::print("after construction of h");
  HowMany h2 = f(h);
  HowMany::print("after call to f()");
} ///:~
```

The class HowMany contains a static int objectCount and a static member function print( ) to report the value of that objectCount, along with an optional message argument. The constructor increments the count each time an object is created, and the destructor decrements it.

The output, however, is not what you would expect.

```
after construction of h: objectCount = 1
x argument inside f(): objectCount = 1
~HowMany(): objectCount = 0
after call to f(): objectCount = 0
~HowMany(): objectCount = -1
~HowMany(): objectCount = -2
```

After h is created, the object count is 1, which is fine. But after the call to f( ) you would expect to have an object count of 2, because h2 is now in scope as well. Instead, the count is 0, which indicates something has gone horribly wrong. This is confirmed by the fact that the two destructors at the end make the object count go negative, something that should never happen.

Look at the point inside f( ), which occurs after the argument is passed by value. This means the original object h exists outside the function frame, and there's an additional object *inside* the function frame, which is the copy that has been passed by value. However, the argument has been passed using C's primitive notion of bit-copying, whereas the C++ HowMany class requires true initialization to maintain its integrity, so the default bitcopy fails to produce the desired effect.

When the local object goes out of scope at the end of the call to f( ), the destructor is called, which decrements objectCount, so outside the function objectCount is zero. The creation of h2 is also performed using a bit-copy, so the constructor isn't called there either, and when h and h2 go out of scope, their destructors cause the negative values of objectCount.

Copy-Construction

The problem occurs because the compiler makes an assumption about how to create a new object from an existing object. When you pass an object by value, you create a new object (the passed object inside the function frame) from an existing object (the original object outside the function frame). This is also often true when returning an object from a function. In the expression

```
HowMany h2 = f(h);
```

h2, a previously unconstructed object, is created from the return value of f( ), so again a new object is created from an existing one.

The compiler's assumption is that you want to perform this creation using a bitcopy, and in many cases this may work alright, but in HowMany it doesn't fly because the meaning of initialization goes beyond simply copying. Another common example occurs if the class contains pointers: what do they point to, and should you copy them or should they be connected to some new piece of memory?

Fortunately, you can intervene in this process and prevent the compiler from doing a bitcopy. You do this by defining your own function to be used whenever the compiler needs to make a new object from an existing object. Logically enough, you're making a new object, so this function is a constructor, and also logically enough, the single argument to this constructor has to do with the object you're constructing from. But that object can't be passed into the constructor by value because you're trying to *define* the function that handles passing by value, and syntactically it doesn't make sense to pass a pointer because, after all, you're creating the new object from an existing object. Here, references come to the rescue, so you take the reference of the source object. This function is called the *copy-constructor* and is often referred to as X(X&), which is its appearance for a class called X.

If you create a copy-constructor, the compiler will not perform a bitcopy when creating a new object from an existing one. It will always call your copy-constructor. So, if you don't create a copy-constructor, the compiler will do something sensible, but you have the choice of taking over complete control of the process.

Now it's possible to fix the problem in HowMany.cpp; see Listing 11-7.

Listing 11-7. Illustrating How to Fix the Problem

```
//: C11:HowMany2.cpp

// The copy-constructor
#include <fstream>
#include <string>
using namespace std;
ofstream out("HowMany2.out");

class HowMany2 {
  string name; // Object identifier
  static int objectCount;
public:
  HowMany2(const string &id = "") : name(id) {
    ++objectCount;
    print("HowMany2()");
  }
  ~HowMany2() {
    --objectCount;
  print("~HowMany2()");
  }
```

```
  // The copy-constructor:
  HowMany2(const HowMany2 &h) : name(h.name) {
    name += " copy";
    ++objectCount;
    print("HowMany2(const HowMany2&)");
  }
  void print(const string &msg = "") const {
    if(msg.size() != 0)
      out << msg << endl;
    out << '\t' << name << ": "
        << "objectCount = "
        << objectCount << endl;
  }
};

int HowMany2::objectCount = 0;

// Pass and return BY VALUE:
HowMany2 f(HowMany2 x) {
  x.print("x argument inside f()");
  out << "Returning from f()" << endl;
  return x;
}

int main() {
  HowMany2 h("h");
  out << "Entering f()" << endl;
  HowMany2 h2 = f(h);
  h2.print("h2 after call to f()");
  out << "Call f(), no return value" << endl;
  f(h);
  out << "After call to f()" << endl;
} ///:~
```

There are a number of new twists thrown in here so you can get a better idea of what's happening. First, the stringname acts as an object identifier when information about that object is printed. In the constructor, you can put an identifier string (usually the name of the object) that is copied to name using the string constructor. The default = "" creates an empty string. *The constructor increments the objectCount as before, and the destructor decrements it.*

Next is the copy-constructor, HowMany2(const HowMany2&). The copy-constructor can create a new object only from an existing one, so the existing object's name is copied to name, followed by the word "copy" so you can see where it came from. If you look closely, you'll see that the call name(h.name) in the constructor *initializer list* is actually calling the string copy-constructor.

Inside the copy-constructor, the object count is incremented just as it is inside the normal constructor. This means you'll now get an accurate object count when passing and returning by value.

The print( ) function has been modified to print out a message, the object identifier, and the object count. It must now access the name data of a particular object, so it can no longer be a static member function.

Inside main( ), you can see that a second call to f( ) has been added. However, this call uses the common C approach of ignoring the return value. But now that you know how the value is returned (that is, code *inside* the function handles the return process, putting the result in a destination whose address is passed as a hidden argument), you might wonder what happens when the return value is ignored. The output of the program will throw some illumination on this.

Before showing the output, Listing 11-8 is a little program that uses iostream to add line numbers to any file.

Listing 11-8. Illustrating Addition of Line Numbers to Any File (using iostream)

```
//: C11:Linenum.cpp
//{T} Linenum.cpp
// Add line numbers
#include "../require.h" // To be INCLUDED from Header FILE in Chapter 9
#include <vector>
#include <string>
#include <fstream>
#include <iostream>
#include <cmath>
using namespace std;

int main(int argc, char* argv[]) {
requireArgs(argc, 1, "Usage: linenum file\n"
    "Adds line numbers to file");
ifstream in(argv[1]);
assure(in, argv[1]);
string line;
vector<string> lines;
while(getline(in, line)) // Read in entire file
  lines.push_back(line);
if(lines.size() == 0) return 0;
int num = 0;
  // Number of lines in file determines width:
const int width =
  int(log10((double)lines.size())) + 1;
for(int i = 0; i < lines.size(); i++) {
  cout.setf(ios::right, ios::adjustfield);
  cout.width(width);
  cout << ++num << ") " << lines[i] << endl;
  }
} ///:~
```

The entire file is read into a vector<string> using the same code that you saw earlier in the book. When printing the line numbers, you'd like all the lines to be aligned with each other, and this requires adjusting for the number of lines in the file so that the width allowed for the line numbers is consistent. You can easily determine the number of lines using vector::size( ), but what you really need to know is whether there are more than 10 lines, 100 lines, 1,000 lines, etc. If you take the logarithm, base 10, of the number of lines in the file, truncate it to an int and add one to the value, you'll find out the maximum width that your line count will be.

You'll notice a couple of strange calls inside the for loop: setf( ) and width( ). These are iostream calls that allow you to control, in this case, the justification and width of the output. However, they must be called each time a line is output and that is why they are *inside* the for loop.

When Linenum.cpp is applied to HowMany2.out, the result is

```
1) HowMany2()
2)   h: objectCount = 1
3) Entering f()
4) HowMany2(const HowMany2&)
5)   h copy: objectCount = 2
6) x argument inside f()
```

```
7)    h copy: objectCount = 2
8) Returning from f()
9) HowMany2(const HowMany2&)
10)    h copy copy: objectCount = 3
11) ~HowMany2()
12)    h copy: objectCount = 2
13) h2 after call to f()
14)    h copy copy: objectCount = 2
15) Call f(), no return value
16) HowMany2(const HowMany2&)
17)    h copy: objectCount = 3
18) x argument inside f()
19)    h copy: objectCount = 3
20) Returning from f()
21) HowMany2(const HowMany2&)
22)    h copy copy: objectCount = 4
23) ~HowMany2()
24)    h copy: objectCount = 3
25) ~HowMany2()
26)    h copy copy: objectCount = 2
27) After call to f()
28) ~HowMany2()
29)    h copy copy: objectCount = 1
30) ~HowMany2()
31)    h: objectCount = 0
```

As you would expect, the first thing that happens is that the normal constructor is called for h, which increments the object count to one. But then, as f( ) is entered, the copy-constructor is quietly called by the compiler to perform the pass-by-value. A new object is created, which is the copy of h (thus the name h copy) inside the function frame of f( ), so the object count becomes 2, courtesy of the copy-constructor.

Line eight indicates the beginning of the return from f( ). But before the local variable h copy can be destroyed (it goes out of scope at the end of the function), it must be copied into the return value, which happens to be h2. A previously unconstructed object (h2) is created from an existing object (the local variable inside f( )), so of course the copy-constructor is used again in line nine. Now the name becomes h copy copy for h2's identifier because it's being copied from the copy that is the local object inside f( ). After the object is returned, but before the function ends, the object count becomes temporarily 3, but then the local object hcopy is destroyed. After the call to f( ) completes in line 13, there are only two objects, h and h2, and you can see that h2 did indeed end up as h copy copy.

Temporary Objects

Line 15 begins the call to f(h), this time ignoring the return value. You can see in line 16 that the copy-constructor is called just as before to pass the argument in. And also, as before, line 21 shows the copy-constructor is called for the return value. But the copy-constructor must have an address to work on as its destination (a this pointer). Where does this address come from?

It turns out the compiler can create a temporary object whenever it needs one to properly evaluate an expression. In this case, it creates one you don't even see to act as the destination for the ignored return value of f( ). The lifetime of this temporary object is as short as possible so the landscape doesn't get cluttered up with temporaries waiting to be destroyed and taking up valuable resources. In some cases, the temporary might immediately be passed to another function, but in this case it isn't needed after the function call, so as soon as the function call ends by calling the destructor for the local object (lines 23 and 24), the temporary object is destroyed (lines 25 and 26).

Finally, in lines 28-31, the h2 object is destroyed, followed by h, and the object count goes correctly back to zero.

271

Default Copy-Constructor

Because the copy-constructor implements pass and return by value, it's important that the compiler creates one for you in the case of simple structures—effectively the same thing it does in C. However, all you've seen so far is the default primitive behavior: a bit-copy.

When more complex types are involved, the C++ compiler will still automatically create a copy-constructor if you don't make one. Again, however, a bit-copy doesn't make sense, because it doesn't necessarily implement the proper meaning.

Here's an example to show the more intelligent approach the compiler takes. Suppose you create a new class composed of objects of several existing classes. This is called, appropriately enough, *composition*, and it's one of the ways you can make new classes from existing classes. Now take the role of a naive user who's trying to solve a problem quickly by creating a new class this way. You don't know about copy-constructors, so you don't create one. Listing 11-9 demonstrates what the compiler does while creating the default copy-constructor for your new class.

Listing 11-9. Illustrating Creation of The Default Copy-Constructor

```
//: C11:DefaultCopyConstructor.cpp
// Automatic creation of the copy-constructor
#include <iostream>
#include <string>
using namespace std;

class WithCC {    // With copy-constructor
public:
  // Explicit default constructor required:
  WithCC() {}
  WithCC(const WithCC&) {
    cout << "WithCC(WithCC&)" << endl;
  }
};

classWoCC {       // Without copy-constructor
  string id;
public:
  WoCC(const string &ident = "") : id(ident) {}
  void print(const string &msg = "") const {
    if(msg.size() != 0) cout << msg << ": ";
    cout << id << endl;
  }
};

class Composite {
  WithCC withcc; // Embedded objects
  WoCC wocc;
public:
  Composite() : wocc("Composite()") {}
  void print(const string &msg = "") const {
    wocc.print(msg);
  }
};
```

```
int main() {
  Composite c;
  c.print("Contents of c");
  cout << "Calling Composite copy-constructor"
       << endl;
  Composite c2 = c;  // Calls copy-constructor
  c2.print("Contents of c2");
} ///:~
```

The class WithCC contains a copy-constructor, which simply announces that it has been called, and this brings up an interesting issue. In the class Composite, an object of WithCC is created using a default constructor. If there were no constructors at all in WithCC, the compiler would automatically create a default constructor, which would do nothing in this case. However, if you add a copy-constructor, you've told the compiler you're going to handle constructor creation, so it no longer creates a default constructor for you and will complain unless you explicitly create a default constructor as was done for WithCC.

The class WoCC has no copy-constructor, but its constructor will store a message in an internal string that can be printed out using print( ). This constructor is explicitly called in Composite's constructor *initializer list* (briefly introduced in Chapter 8 and covered fully in Chapter 14). The reason for this becomes apparent later.

The class Composite has member objects of both WithCC and WoCC, and no explicitly defined copy-constructor

---

■ **Note**   The embedded object wocc is initialized in the constructor-initializer list, as it must be.

However, in main( ) an object is created using the copy-constructor in the definition:

```
Composite c2 = c;
```

The copy-constructor for Composite is created automatically by the compiler, and the output of the program reveals the way that it is created.

```
Contents of c: Composite()
Calling Composite copy-constructor
WithCC(WithCC&)
Contents of c2: Composite()
```

To create a copy-constructor for a class that uses composition (and inheritance, which is introduced in Chapter 14), the compiler recursively calls the copy-constructors for all the member objects and base classes. That is, if the member object also contains another object, its copy-constructor is also called. So in this case, the compiler calls the copy-constructor for WithCC. The output shows this constructor being called. Because WoCC has no copy-constructor, the compiler creates one for it that just performs a bitcopy, and calls that inside the Composite copy-constructor. The call to Composite::print( ) in main() shows that this happens because the contents of c2.wocc are identical to the contents of c.wocc. The process the compiler goes through to synthesize a copy-constructor is called *member-wise initialization*.

It's always best to create your own copy-constructor instead of letting the compiler do it for you. This guarantees that it will be under your control.

Alternatives to Copy-Construction

At this point your head may be swimming, and you might be wondering how you could have possibly written a working class without knowing about the copy-constructor. But remember: you need a copy-constructor only if you're going to pass an object of your class *by value*. If that never happens, you don't need a copy-constructor.

Preventing Pass-by-value

"But," *you say,* "if I don't make a copy-constructor, the compiler will create one for me. So how do I know that an object will never be passed by value?"

There's a simple technique for preventing pass-by-value: declare a private copy-constructor. You don't even need to create a definition, unless one of your member functions or a friend function needs to perform a pass-by-value. If the user tries to pass or return the object by value, the compiler will produce an error message because the copy-constructor is private. It can no longer create a default copy-constructor because you've explicitly stated that you're taking over that job. Listing 11-10 is an example.

Listing 11-10. Illustrating Prevention of Copy-Construction

```
//: C11:NoCopyConstruction.cpp
// Preventing copy-construction

Class NoCC {
  int i;
  NoCC(const NoCC&); // No definition
public:
  NoCC(int ii = 0) : i(ii) {}
};

void f(NoCC);

int main() {
  NoCC n;
//! f(n);              // Error: copy-constructor called
//! NoCC n2 = n;       // Error: c-c called
//! NoCCn3(n);         // Error: c-c called
} ///:~
```

Notice the use of the more general form

```
NoCC(const NoCC&);
```

using the const.

Functions That Modify Outside Objects

Reference syntax is nicer to use than pointer syntax, yet it clouds the meaning for the reader. For example, in the iostreams library one overloaded version of the get( ) function takes a char& as an argument, and the whole point of the function is to modify its argument by inserting the result of the get( ). However, when you read code using this function it's not immediately obvious to you that the outside object is being modified:

```
char c;
cin.get(c);
```

Instead, the function call looks like a pass-by-value, which suggests the outside object is *not* modified.

Because of this, it's probably safer from a code maintenance standpoint to use pointers when you're passing the address of an argument to modify. If you *always* pass addresses as const references *except* when you intend to modify the outside object via the address, where you pass by non-const pointer, then your code is far easier for the reader to follow.

Pointers-to-Members

A pointer is a variable that holds the address of some location. You can change what a pointer selects at runtime, and the destination of the pointer can be either data or a function. The C++ pointer-to-member follows this same concept, except that what it selects is a location inside a class. The dilemma here is that a pointer needs an address, but there is no "address" inside a class; selecting a member of a class means offsetting into that class. You can't produce an actual address until you combine that offset with the starting address of a particular object. The syntax of pointers to members requires that you select an object at the same time you're dereferencing the pointer to member.

To understand this syntax, consider a simple structure, with a pointer sp and an object so for this structure. You can select members with the syntax shown in Listing 11-11.

Listing 11-11. Illustrating Syntax for Selection of Members in a Simple Structure

```
//: C11:SimpleStructure.cpp
struct Simple { int a; };
int main() {
  Simple so, *sp = &so;
  sp->a;
  so.a;
} ///:~
```

Now suppose you have an ordinary pointer to an integer, ip. To access what ip is pointing to, you dereference the pointer with a '*', as in:

```
*ip = 4;
```

Finally, consider what happens if you have a pointer that happens to point to something inside a class object, even if it does in fact represent an offset into the object. To access what it's pointing at, you must dereference it with *. But it's an offset into an object, so you must also refer to that particular object. Thus, the * is combined with the object dereference. So the new syntax becomes->* for a pointer to an object, and .* for the object or a reference, like this:

```
objectPointer->*pointerToMember = 47;
object.*pointerToMember = 47;
```

Now, what is the syntax for defining pointerToMember? Like any pointer, you have to say what type it's pointing at, and you use a * in the definition. The only difference is that you must say what class of objects this pointer-to-member is used with. Of course, this is accomplished with the name of the class and the scope resolution operator. Thus,

```
int ObjectClass::*pointerToMember;
```

defines a pointer-to-member variable called pointerToMember that points to any int inside ObjectClass. You can also initialize the pointer-to-member when you define it (or at any other time), as in:

```
int ObjectClass::*pointerToMember = &ObjectClass::a;
```

There is actually no "address" of ObjectClass::a because you're just referring to t he class and not an object of that class. Thus, &ObjectClass::a can be used only as pointer-to-member syntax.

Listing 11-12 shows how to create and use pointers-to-members.

Listing 11-12. Illustrating Pointer-to-Member Syntax for Data Members (also, demonstrates creation & use of pointers-to-members)

```
//: C11:PointerToMemberData.cpp
#include <iostream>
using namespace std;

class Data {
public:
  int a, b, c;
  void print() const {
    cout << "a = " << a << ", b = " << b
         << ", c = " << c << endl;
  }
};

int main() {
  Data d, *dp = &d;
  int Data::*pmInt = &Data::a;
  dp->*pmInt = 47;
  pmInt = &Data::b;
  d.*pmInt = 48;
  pmInt = &Data::c;
  dp->*pmInt = 49;
  dp->print();
} ///:~
```

Obviously, these are too awkward to use anywhere except for special cases (*which is exactly what they were intended for*).

Also, pointers-to-members are quite limited: they can be assigned only to a specific location inside a class. You could not, for example, increment or compare them as you can with ordinary pointers.

Functions

A similar exercise produces the pointer-to-member syntax for member functions (see Listing 11-13). A pointer to a function (introduced at the end of Chapter 3) is defined like this:

```
int (*fp)(float);
```

The parentheses around (*fp) are necessary to force the compiler to evaluate the definition properly. Without them this would appear to be a function that returns an int*.

Parentheses also play an important role when defining and using pointers to member functions. If you have a function inside a class, you define a pointer to that member function by inserting the class name and scope resolution operator into an ordinary function pointer definition.

Listing 11-13. Illustrating Pointer-to-Member syntax for Member Functions

```
//: C11:PmemFunDefinition.cpp
class Simple2 {
public:
  int f(float) const { return 1; }
};
```

```
int (Simple2::*fp)(float) const;
int (Simple2::*fp2)(float) const = &Simple2::f;
int main() {
  fp = &Simple2::f;
} ///:~
```

In the definition for fp2 you can see that a pointer to member function can also be initialized when it is created, or at any other time. Unlike non-member functions, the &is *not* optional when taking the address of a member function. However, you can give the function identifier without an argument list because overload resolution can be determined by the type of the pointer to member.

An Example

The value of a pointer is that you can change what it points to at runtime, which provides an important flexibility in your programming because through a pointer you can select or change *behavior* at runtime. A pointer-to-member is no different; it allows you to choose a member at runtime. Typically, your classes will only have member functions publicly visible (*data members are usually considered part of the underlying implementation*), so that Listing 11-14 selects member functions at runtime.

Listing 11-14. Illustrating Selection of Member Functions at Runtime

```
//: C11:PointerToMemberFunction.cpp
#include <iostream>
using namespace std;

class Widget {
public:
  void f(int) const { cout << "Widget::f()\n"; }
  void g(int) const { cout << "Widget::g()\n"; }
  void h(int) const { cout << "Widget::h()\n"; }
  void i(int) const { cout << "Widget::i()\n"; }
};

int main() {
  Widget w;
  Widget* wp = &w;
void (Widget::*pmem)(int) const = &Widget::h;
  (w.*pmem)(1);
  (wp->*pmem)(2);
} ///:~
```

Of course, it isn't particularly reasonable to expect the casual user to create such complicated expressions. If the user must directly manipulate a pointer-to-member, then a typedef is in order. To really clean things up, you can use the pointer-to-member as part of the internal implementation mechanism. Listing 11-15 is a modification of Listing 11-14 using a pointer-to-member *inside* the class. All the user needs to do is pass a number in to select a function.

Listing 11-15. Illustrating Use of a Pointer-to-Member Inside the Class

```
//: C11:PointerToMemberFunction2.cpp
#include <iostream>
using namespace std;

class Widget {
  void f(int) const { cout<< "Widget::f()\n"; }
  void g(int) const { cout<< "Widget::g()\n"; }
  void h(int) const { cout<< "Widget::h()\n"; }
  void i(int) const { cout<< "Widget::i()\n"; }
  enum { cnt = 4 };
  void (Widget::*fptr[cnt])(int) const;
public:
  Widget() {
    fptr[0] = &Widget::f; // Full spec required
    fptr[1] = &Widget::g;
    fptr[2] = &Widget::h;
    fptr[3] = &Widget::i;
  }
  void select(int i, int j) {
    if(i < 0 || i >= cnt) return;
    (this->*fptr[i])(j);
  }
  int count() { return cnt; }
};

int main() {
  Widget w;
  for(int i = 0; i < w.count(); i++)
    w.select(i, 47);
} ///:~
```

In the class interface and in main( ), you can see that the entire implementation, including the functions, has been hidden away. The code must even ask for the count( ) of functions. This way, the class implementer can change the quantity of functions in the underlying implementation without affecting the code where the class is used.

The initialization of the pointers-to-members in the constructor may seem over-specified. Shouldn't you be able to say

```
fptr[1] = &g;
```

because the name g occurs in the member function, which is automatically in the scope of the class? The problem is this doesn't conform to the pointer-to-member syntax, which is required so everyone, especially the compiler, can figure out what's going on. Similarly, when the pointer-to-member is dereferenced, it seems like

```
(this->*fptr[i])(j);
```

is also over-specified; this looks redundant. Again, the syntax requires that a pointer-to-member always be bound to an object when it is dereferenced.

Review Session

1. Pointers in C++ are almost identical to pointers in C, which is good. Otherwise, a lot of C code wouldn't compile properly under C++. The only compile-time errors you will produce occur with dangerous assignments. If these are in fact what are intended, the compile-time errors can be removed with a simple (and explicit!) cast.

2. C++ also adds the *reference* from Algol and Pascal, which is like a constant pointer that is automatically dereferenced by the compiler. A reference holds an address, but you treat it like an object. References are essential for clean syntax with *operator overloading* (the subject of the next chapter), but they also add syntactic convenience for passing and returning objects for ordinary functions.

3. The *copy-constructor* takes a reference to an existing object of the same type as its argument, and it is used to create a new object from an existing one. The compiler automatically calls the copy-constructor when you pass or return an object by value. Although the compiler will automatically create a copy-constructor for you, if you think one will be needed for your class, you should always define it yourself to ensure that the proper behavior occurs. If you don't want the object passed or returned by value, you should create a private copy-constructor.

4. Pointers-to-members have the same functionality as ordinary pointers: you can choose a particular region of storage (data or function) at runtime. Pointers-to-members just happen to work with class members instead of with global data or functions. You get the programming flexibility that allows you to change behavior at *runtime*.

CHAPTER 12

Operator Overloading

Operator overloading is just "syntactic sugar," which means it is simply another way for you to make a function call.

The difference is that the arguments for this function don't appear inside parentheses, but instead they surround or are next to characters you've always thought of as immutable operators.

There are two differences between the use of an operator and an ordinary function call. The syntax is different; an operator is often "called" by placing it between or sometimes after the arguments. The second difference is that the compiler determines which "function" to call. For instance, if you are using the operator + with floating-point arguments, the compiler "calls" the function to perform floating-point addition (*this "call" is typically the act of inserting inline code, or a floating-point-processor instruction*). If you use operator + with a floating-point number and an integer, the compiler "calls" a special function to turn the int into a float, and then "calls" the floating-point addition code.

But in C++, it's possible to define new operators that work with classes. This definition is just like an ordinary function definition except that the name of the function consists of the keyword operator followed by the operator. That's the only difference, and it becomes a function like any other function, which the compiler calls when it sees the appropriate pattern.

Warning and Reassurance

It's tempting to become overenthusiastic with operator overloading. It's a fun toy, at first. But remember its *only* syntactic sugar, another way of calling a function. Looking at it this way, you have no reason to overload an operator except if it will make the code involving your class easier to write and especially easier to *read*. (Remember, code is read much more than it is written.) If this isn't the case, don't bother.

Another common response to operator overloading is panic; suddenly, C operators have no familiar meaning anymore. "Everything's changed and all my C code will do different things!" This isn't true. All the operators used in expressions that contain only built-in data types cannot be changed. You can never overload operators such that

```
1 << 4;
```

behaves differently, or

```
1.414 << 2;
```

has meaning. Only an expression containing a user-defined type can have an overloaded operator.

Syntax

Defining an overloaded operator is like defining a function, but the name of that function is operator@, in which @ represents the operator that's being overloaded. The number of arguments in the overloaded operator's argument list depends on two factors:

- Whether it's a unary operator (one argument) or a binary operator (two arguments).

- Whether the operator is defined as a global function (one argument for unary, two for binary) or a member function (zero arguments for unary, one for binary – the object becomes the left-hand argument).

Listing 12-1 contains a small class that shows the syntax for operator overloading.

Listing 12-1. Illustrating the Syntax for Operator Overloading

```
//: C12:OperatorOverloadingSyntax.cpp
#include <iostream>
using namespace std;

class Integer {
  int i;
public:
  Integer(int ii) : i(ii) {}
  const Integer
  operator+(const Integer& rv) const {
    cout << "operator+" << endl;
    return Integer(i + rv.i);
  }
  Integer&
  operator+=(const Integer& rv) {
    cout << "operator+=" << endl;
    i += rv.i;
    return *this;
  }
};

int main() {
  cout << "built-in types:" << endl;
  int i = 1, j = 2, k = 3;
  k += i + j;
  cout << "user-defined types:" << endl;
  Integer ii(1), jj(2), kk(3);
  kk += ii + jj;
} ///:~
```

The two overloaded operators are defined as inline member functions that announce when they are called. The single argument is what appears on the right-hand side of the operator for binary operators. Unary operators have no arguments when defined as member functions. The member function is called for the object on the left-hand side of the operator.

For non-conditional operators (conditionals usually return a Boolean value), you'll almost always want to return an object or reference of the same type you're operating on if the two arguments are the same type.

This way, complicated expressions can be built up, as in:

```
kk += ii + jj;
```

The operator+ produces a new Integer (a temporary) that is used as the rv argument for the operator+=. This temporary is destroyed as soon as it is no longer needed.

Overloadable Operators

Although you can overload almost all the operators available in C, the use of operator overloading is fairly restrictive. In particular, you cannot combine operators that currently have no meaning in C (such as ** to represent exponentiation), you cannot change the evaluation precedence of operators, and you cannot change the number of arguments required by an operator. This makes sense—all of these actions would produce operators that confuse meaning rather than clarify it.

The next two subsections give examples of all the "regular" operators, overloaded in the form that you'll most likely use.

Unary Operators

Listing 12-2 shows the syntax to overload all the unary operators, in the form of both global functions (non-member friend functions) and as member functions. These will expand upon the Integer class shown previously and add a new byte class. The meaning of your particular operators will depend on the way you want to use them, but consider the client programmer before doing something unexpected.

Listing 12-2. Illustrating the Syntax for Overloading Unary Operators

```
//: C12:OverloadingUnaryOperators.cpp
#include <iostream>
using namespace std;

// Non-member functions:
class Integer {
  long i;
  Integer* This() { return this; }
public:
  Integer(long ll = 0) : i(ll) {}
  // No side effects takes const& argument:
  friend const Integer&
    operator+(const Integer& a);
  friend const Integer
    operator-(const Integer& a);
  friend const Integer
    operator~(const Integer& a);
  friend Integer*
    operator&(Integer& a);
```

```
    friend int
      operator!(const Integer& a);
    // Side effects have non-const& argument:
    // Prefix:
    friend const Integer&
      operator++(Integer& a);
    // Postfix:
    friend const Integer
      operator++(Integer& a, int);
    // Prefix:
    friend const Integer&
      operator--(Integer& a);
    // Postfix:
    friend const Integer
      operator--(Integer& a, int);
};

// Global operators:
const Integer& operator+(const Integer& a) {
  cout << "+Integer\n";
  return a;            // Unary + has no effect
}
const Integer operator-(const Integer& a) {
  cout << "-Integer\n";
  return Integer(-a.i);
}
const Integer operator~(const Integer& a) {
  cout << "~Integer\n";
  return Integer(~a.i);
}
Integer* operator&(Integer& a) {
  cout << "&Integer\n";
  return a.This(); // &a is recursive!
}
int operator!(const Integer& a) {
  cout << "!Integer\n";
  return !a.i;
}
// Prefix; return incremented value
const Integer& operator++(Integer& a) {
  cout << "++Integer\n";
  a.i++;
  return a;
}
// Postfix; return the value before increment:
const Integer operator++(Integer& a, int) {
  cout << "Integer++\n";
  Integer before(a.i);
  a.i++;
  return before;
}
```

```
// Prefix; return decremented value
const Integer& operator--(Integer& a) {
  cout << "--Integer\n";
  a.i--;
  return a;
}
// Postfix; return the value before decrement:
const Integer operator--(Integer& a, int) {
  cout << "Integer--\n";
  Integer before(a.i);
  a.i--;
  return before;
}

// Show that the overloaded operators work:
void f(Integer a) {
  +a;
  -a;
  ~a;
  Integer* ip = &a;
  !a;
  ++a;
  a++;
  --a;
  a--;
}

// Member functions (implicit "this"):
class Byte {
  unsigned char b;
public:
  Byte(unsigned char bb = 0) : b(bb) {}
  // No side effects: const member function:
  const Byte& operator+() const {
    cout << "+Byte\n";
    return *this;
  }
  const Byte operator-() const {
    cout << "-Byte\n";
    return Byte(-b);
  }
  const Byte operator~() const {
    cout << "~Byte\n";
    return Byte(~b);
  }
  Byte operator!() const {
    cout << "!Byte\n";
    return Byte(!b);
  }
```

```
  Byte* operator&() {
    cout << "&Byte\n";
    return this;
  }
  // Side effects: non-const member function:
  const Byte& operator++() {    // Prefix
    cout << "++Byte\n";
    b++;
    return *this;
  }
  const Byte operator++(int) { // Postfix
    cout << "Byte++\n";
    Byte before(b);
    b++;
    return before;
  }
  const Byte& operator--() {    // Prefix
    cout << "--Byte\n";
    --b;
    return *this;
  }
  const Byte operator--(int) { // Postfix
    cout << "Byte--\n";
    Byte before(b);
    --b;
    return before;
  }
};

void g(Byte b) {
  +b;
  -b;
  ~b;
  Byte bp = &b;
  !b;
  ++b;
  b++;
  --b;
  b--;
}

int main() {
  Integer a;
  f(a);
  Byte b;
  g(b);
} ///:~
```

The functions are grouped according to the way their arguments are passed. Guidelines for how to pass and return arguments are given later. The forms above (*and* the ones that follow in the next section) are typically what you'll use, so start with them as a pattern when overloading your own operators.

Increment and Decrement

The overloaded ++ and – – operators present a dilemma because you want to be able to call different functions depending on whether they appear before (prefix) or after (postfix) the object they're acting upon. The solution is simple, but people sometimes find it a bit confusing at first. When the compiler sees, for example, ++a (a pre-increment), it generates a call to operator++(a); but when it sees a++, it generates a call to operator++(a, int). That is, the compiler differentiates between the two forms by making calls to different overloaded functions. In OverloadingUnaryOperators.cpp (Listing 12-2), for the member function versions, if the compiler sees ++b, it generates a call to B::operator++( ); if it sees b++ it calls B::operator++(int).

All the user sees is that a different function gets called for the prefix and postfix versions. Underneath, however, the two functions calls have different signatures, so they link to two different function bodies. The compiler passes a dummy constant value for the int argument (which is never given an identifier because the value is never used) to generate the different signature for the postfix version.

Binary Operators

Listings 12-3 & 12-4 repeat the example of OverloadingUnaryOperators.cpp for binary operators so you have an example of all the operators you might want to overload. Again, both global versions (see Listing 12-3) and member function versions (see Listing 12-4) are shown.

Listing 12-3. Illustrating the Syntax for Overloading Binary Operators (for Non-member Overloaded Operators)

```
//: C12:Integer.h
// Non-member overloaded operators
#ifndef INTEGER_H
#define INTEGER_H
#include <iostream>

// Non-member functions:
class Integer {
  long i;
public:
  Integer(long ll = 0) : i(ll) {}
  // Operators that create new, modified value:
  friend const Integer
    operator+(const Integer& left,
            const Integer& right);
  friend const Integer
    operator-(const Integer& left,
            const Integer& right);
  friend const Integer
    operator*(const Integer& left,
            const Integer& right);
  friend const Integer
    operator/(const Integer& left,
            const Integer& right);
  friend const Integer
    operator%(const Integer& left,
            const Integer& right);
```

```
  friend const Integer
    operator^(const Integer& left,
              const Integer& right);
  friend const Integer
    operator&(const Integer& left,
              const Integer& right);
  friend const Integer
    operator|(const Integer& left,
              const Integer& right);
  friend const Integer
    operator<<(const Integer& left,
              const Integer& right);
  friend const Integer
    operator>>(const Integer& left,
              const Integer& right);
  // Assignments modify & return lvalue:
  friend Integer&
    operator+=(Integer& left,
              const Integer& right);
  friend Integer&
    operator-=(Integer& left,
              const Integer& right);
  friend Integer&
    operator*=(Integer& left,
              const Integer& right);
  friend Integer&
    operator/=(Integer& left,
              const Integer& right);
  friend Integer&
    operator%=(Integer& left,
              const Integer& right);
  friend Integer&
    operator^=(Integer& left,
              const Integer& right);
  friend Integer&
    operator&=(Integer& left,
              const Integer& right);
  friend Integer&
    operator|=(Integer& left,
              const Integer& right);
  friend Integer&
    operator>>=(Integer& left,
               const Integer& right);
  friend Integer&
    operator<<=(Integer& left,
               const Integer& right);
  // Conditional operators return true/false:
  friend int
    operator==(const Integer& left,
              const Integer& right);
```

```
  friend int
    operator!=(const Integer& left,
               const Integer& right);
  friend int
    operator<(const Integer& left,
              const Integer& right);
  friend int
    operator>(const Integer& left,
              const Integer& right);
  friend int
    operator<=(const Integer& left,
               const Integer& right);
  friend int
    operator>=(const Integer& left,
               const Integer& right);
  friend int
    operator&&(const Integer& left,
               const Integer& right);
  friend int
    operator||(const Integer& left,
               const Integer& right);
  // Write the contents to an ostream:
  void print(std::ostream& os) const { os << i; }
};
#endif // INTEGER_H ///:~

//: C12:Integer.cpp {O}
// Implementation of overloaded operators
#include "Integer.h"        // TO be INCLUDED from Header FILE above
#include "../require.h"      // TO be INCLUDED From Header FILE in Chapter 9

const Integer
  operator+(const Integer& left,
            const Integer& right) {
  return Integer(left.i + right.i);
}
const Integer
  operator-(const Integer& left,
            const Integer& right) {
  return Integer(left.i - right.i);
}
const Integer
  operator*(const Integer& left,
            const Integer& right) {
  return Integer(left.i * right.i);
}
const Integer
  operator/(const Integer& left,
            const Integer& right) {
  require(right.i != 0, "divide by zero");
  return Integer(left.i / right.i);
}
```

```
const Integer
  operator%(const Integer& left,
            const Integer& right) {
  require(right.i != 0, "modulo by zero");
  return Integer(left.i % right.i);
}
const Integer
  operator^(const Integer& left,
            const Integer& right) {
  return Integer(left.i ^ right.i);
}
const Integer
  operator&(const Integer& left,
            const Integer& right) {
  return Integer(left.i & right.i);
}
const Integer
  operator|(const Integer& left,
            const Integer& right) {
  return Integer(left.i | right.i);
}
const Integer
  operator<<(const Integer& left,
             const Integer& right) {
  return Integer(left.i << right.i);
}
const Integer
  operator>>(const Integer& left,
             const Integer& right) {
  return Integer(left.i >> right.i);
}
// Assignments modify & return lvalue:
Integer& operator+=(Integer& left,
                    const Integer& right) {
  if(&left == &right) {/* self-assignment */}
  left.i += right.i;
  return left;
}
Integer& operator-=(Integer& left,
                    const Integer& right) {
  if(&left == &right) {/* self-assignment */}
  left.i -= right.i;
  return left;
}
Integer& operator*=(Integer& left,
                    const Integer& right) {
  if(&left == &right) {/* self-assignment */}
  left.i *= right.i;
  return left;
}
```

```
Integer& operator/=(Integer& left,
                    const Integer& right) {
   require(right.i != 0, "divide by zero");
   if(&left == &right) {/* self-assignment */}
   left.i /= right.i;
   return left;
}
Integer& operator%=(Integer& left,
                    const Integer& right) {
   require(right.i != 0, "modulo by zero");
   if(&left == &right) {/* self-assignment */}
   left.i %= right.i;
   return left;
}
Integer& operator^=(Integer& left,
                    const Integer& right) {
   if(&left == &right) {/* self-assignment */}
   left.i ^= right.i;
   return left;
}
Integer& operator&=(Integer& left,
                    const Integer& right) {
   if(&left == &right) {/* self-assignment */}
   left.i &= right.i;
   return left;
}
Integer& operator|=(Integer& left,
                    const Integer& right) {
   if(&left == &right) {/* self-assignment */}
   left.i |= right.i;
   return left;
}
Integer& operator>>=(Integer& left,
                     const Integer& right) {
   if(&left == &right) {/* self-assignment */}
   left.i >>= right.i;
   return left;
}
Integer& operator<<=(Integer& left,
                     const Integer& right) {
   if(&left == &right) {/* self-assignment */}
   left.i <<= right.i;
   return left;
}
// Conditional operators return true/false:
int operator==(const Integer& left,
               const Integer& right) {
    return left.i == right.i;
}
```

```
int operator!=(const Integer& left,
               const Integer& right) {
    return left.i != right.i;
}
int operator<(const Integer& left,
               const Integer& right) {
    return left.i < right.i;
}
int operator>(const Integer& left,
               const Integer& right) {
    return left.i > right.i;
}
int operator<=(const Integer& left,
               const Integer& right) {
    return left.i <= right.i;
}
int operator>=(const Integer& left,
               const Integer& right) {
    return left.i >= right.i;
}
int operator&&(const Integer& left,
               const Integer& right) {
    return left.i && right.i;
}
int operator||(const Integer& left,
               const Integer& right) {
    return left.i || right.i;
} ///:~

//: C12:IntegerTest.cpp
//{L} Integer
#include "Integer.h"
#include <fstream>
using namespace std;
ofstream out("IntegerTest.out");

void h(Integer& c1, Integer& c2) {
  // A complex expression:
  c1 += c1 * c2 + c2 % c1;
  #define TRY(OP) \
    out << "c1 = "; c1.print(out); \
    out << ", c2 = "; c2.print(out); \
    out << ";   c1 " #OP " c2 produces "; \
    (c1 OP c2).print(out); \
    out << endl;
  TRY(+) TRY(-) TRY(*) TRY(/)
  TRY(%) TRY(^) TRY(&) TRY(|)
  TRY(<<) TRY(>>) TRY(+=) TRY(-=)
  TRY(*=) TRY(/=) TRY(%=) TRY(^=)
  TRY(&=) TRY(|=) TRY(>>=) TRY(<<=)
```

```
  // Conditionals:
  #define TRYC(OP) \
    out << "c1 = "; c1.print(out); \
    out << ", c2 = "; c2.print(out); \
    out << ";  c1 " #OP " c2 produces "; \
    out << (c1 OP c2); \
    out << endl;
  TRYC(<) TRYC(>) TRYC(==) TRYC(!=) TRYC(<=)
  TRYC(>=) TRYC(&&) TRYC(||)
}

int main() {
  cout << "friend functions" << endl;
  Integer c1(47), c2(9);
  h(c1, c2);
} ///:~
```

Listing 12-4. Illustrating the Syntax for Overloading Binary Operators (for Member Overloaded Operators)

```
//: C12:Byte.h
// Member overloaded operators
#ifndef BYTE_H
#define BYTE_H
#include "../require.h"
#include <iostream>
// Member functions (implicit "this"):
class Byte {
  unsigned char b;
public:
  Byte(unsigned char bb = 0) : b(bb) {}
  // No side effects: const member function:
  const Byte
    operator+(const Byte& right) const {
    return Byte(b + right.b);
  }
  const Byte
    operator-(const Byte& right) const {
    return Byte(b - right.b);
  }
  const Byte
    operator*(const Byte& right) const {
    return Byte(b * right.b);
  }
  const Byte
    operator/(const Byte& right) const {
    require(right.b != 0, "divide by zero");
    return Byte(b / right.b);
  }
  const Byte
    operator%(const Byte& right) const {
    require(right.b != 0, "modulo by zero");
    return Byte(b % right.b);
  }
```

```
const Byte
  operator^(const Byte& right) const {
  return Byte(b ^ right.b);
}
const Byte
  operator&(const Byte& right) const {
  return Byte(b & right.b);
}
const Byte
  operator|(const Byte& right) const {
  return Byte(b | right.b);
}
const Byte
  operator<<(const Byte& right) const {
  return Byte(b << right.b);
}
const Byte
  operator>>(const Byte& right) const {
  return Byte(b >> right.b);
}
// Assignments modify & return lvalue.
// operator= can only be a member function:
Byte& operator=(const Byte& right) {
  // Handle self-assignment:
  if(this == &right) return *this;
  b = right.b;
  return *this;
}
Byte& operator+=(const Byte& right) {
  if(this == &right) {/* self-assignment */}
  b += right.b;
  return *this;
}
Byte& operator-=(const Byte& right) {
  if(this == &right) {/* self-assignment */}
  b -= right.b;
  return *this;
}
Byte& operator*=(const Byte& right) {
  if(this == &right) {/* self-assignment */}
  b *= right.b;
  return *this;
}
Byte& operator/=(const Byte& right) {
  require(right.b != 0, "divide by zero");
  if(this == &right) {/* self-assignment */}
  b /= right.b;
  return *this;
}
```

```
Byte& operator%=(const Byte& right) {
  require(right.b != 0, "modulo by zero");
  if(this == &right) {/* self-assignment */}
  b %= right.b;
  return *this;
}
Byte& operator^=(const Byte& right) {
  if(this == &right) {/* self-assignment */}
  b ^= right.b;
  return *this;
}
Byte& operator&=(const Byte& right) {
  if(this == &right) {/* self-assignment */}
  b &= right.b;
  return *this;
}
Byte& operator|=(const Byte& right) {
  if(this == &right) {/* self-assignment */}
  b |= right.b;
  return *this;
}
Byte& operator>>=(const Byte& right) {
  if(this == &right) {/* self-assignment */}
  b >>= right.b;
  return *this;
}
Byte& operator<<=(const Byte& right) {
  if(this == &right) {/* self-assignment */}
  b <<= right.b;
  return *this;
}
// Conditional operators return true/false:
int operator==(const Byte& right) const {
    return b == right.b;
}
int operator!=(const Byte& right) const {
    return b != right.b;
}
int operator<(const Byte& right) const {
    return b < right.b;
}
int operator>(const Byte& right) const {
    return b > right.b;
}
int operator<=(const Byte& right) const {
    return b <= right.b;
}
int operator>=(const Byte& right) const {
    return b >= right.b;
}
```

```
    int operator&&(const Byte& right) const {
        return b && right.b;
    }
    int operator||(const Byte& right) const {
        return b || right.b;
    }
    // Write the contents to an ostream:
    void print(std::ostream& os) const {
      os << "0x" << std::hex << int(b) << std::dec;
    }
};
#endif // BYTE_H ///:~

//: C12:ByteTest.cpp
#include "Byte.h"     // To be INCLUDED from Header FILE above
#include <fstream>
using namespace std;
ofstream out("ByteTest.out");

void k(Byte& b1, Byte& b2) {
  b1 = b1 * b2 + b2 % b1;

  #define TRY2(OP) \
    out << "b1 = "; b1.print(out); \
    out << ", b2 = "; b2.print(out); \
    out << ";  b1 " #OP " b2 produces "; \
    (b1 OP b2).print(out); \
    out << endl;

  b1 = 9; b2 = 47;
  TRY2(+) TRY2(-) TRY2(*) TRY2(/)
  TRY2(%) TRY2(^) TRY2(&) TRY2(|)
  TRY2(<<) TRY2(>>) TRY2(+=) TRY2(-=)
  TRY2(*=) TRY2(/=) TRY2(%=) TRY2(^=)
  TRY2(&=) TRY2(|=) TRY2(>>=) TRY2(<<=)
  TRY2(=) // Assignment operator

  // Conditionals:
  #define TRYC2(OP) \
    out << "b1 = "; b1.print(out); \
    out << ", b2 = "; b2.print(out); \
    out << ";  b1 " #OP " b2 produces "; \
    out << (b1 OP b2); \
    out << endl;

  b1 = 9; b2 = 47;
  TRYC2(<) TRYC2(>) TRYC2(==) TRYC2(!=) TRYC2(<=)
  TRYC2(>=) TRYC2(&&) TRYC2(||)

  // Chained assignment:
  Byte b3 = 92;
  b1 = b2 = b3;
}
```

296

```
int main() {
  out << "member functions:" << endl;
  Byte b1(47), b2(9);
  k(b1, b2);
} ///:~
```

You can see that operator= is only allowed to be a member function. This is explained later.

Notice that all of the assignment operators have code to check for self-assignment; this is a general guideline. In some cases this is not necessary; for example, with operator+= you often *want* to say A+=A and have it add A to itself. The most important place to check for self-assignment is operator= because with complicated objects disastrous results may occur. (In some cases it's OK, but you should always keep it in mind when writing operator=.)

All of the operators shown in the previous three listings (i.e., Listings 12-2, 12-3 and 12-4) are overloaded to handle a single type. It's also possible to overload operators to handle mixed types, so you can add apples to oranges, for example. Before you start on an exhaustive overloading of operators, however, you should look at the section on automatic type conversion later in this chapter. Often, a type conversion in the right place can save you a lot of overloaded operators.

Arguments and Return Values

It may seem a little confusing at first when you look at OverloadingUnaryOperators.cpp, Integer.h, and Byte.h and see all the different ways that arguments are passed and returned. Although you *can* pass and return arguments any way you want to, the choices in these examples were not selected at random. They follow a logical pattern, the same one you'll want to use in most of your choices.

1. As with any function argument, if you only need to read from the argument and not change it, default to passing it as a const reference. Ordinary arithmetic operations (like + and -, etc.) and Booleans will not change their arguments, so pass by const reference is predominantly what you'll use. When the function is a class member, this translates to making it a const member function. Only with the operator-assignments (like +=) and the operator=, which change the left-hand argument, is the left argument *not* a constant, but it's still passed in as an address because it will be changed.

2. The type of return value you should select depends on the expected meaning of the operator. (*Again, you can do anything you want with the arguments and return values.*) If the effect of the operator is to produce a new value, you will need to generate a new object as the return value. For example, Integer::operator+ must produce an Integer object that is the sum of the operands. This object is returned by value as a const, so the result cannot be modified as an lvalue.

3. All the assignment operators modify the lvalue. To allow the result of the assignment to be used in chained expressions, like a=b=c, it's expected that you will return a reference to that same lvalue that was just modified. But should this reference be a const or nonconst? Although you read a=b=c from left to right, the compiler parses it from right to left, so you're not forced to return a nonconst to support assignment chaining. However, people do sometimes expect to be able to perform an operation on the thing that was just assigned to, such as (a=b).func( ); to call func( ) on a after assigning b to it. Thus, the return value for all of the assignment operators should be a nonconst reference to the lvalue.

4. For the logical operators, everyone expects to get at worst an int back, and at best a bool. (Libraries developed before most compilers supported C++'s built-in bool will use int or an equivalent typedef.)

The increment and decrement operators present a dilemma because of the prefix and postfix versions. Both versions change the object and so cannot treat the object as a const. The prefix version returns the value of the object after it was changed, so you expect to get back the object that was changed. Thus, with prefix you can just return *this as a reference. The postfix version is supposed to return the value *before* the value is changed, so you're forced to create a separate object to represent that value and return it. So, it follows that with postfix you must return by value if you want to preserve the expected meaning. (Note that you'll sometimes find the increment and decrement operators returning an int or bool to indicate, for example, whether an object designed to move through a list is at the end of that list.) Now the question is: Should these be returned as const or nonconst? If you allow the object to be modified and someone writes (++a).func( ), func( ) will be operating on a itself, but with (a++).func( ), func( ) operates on the temporary object returned by the postfix operator++. Temporary objects are automatically const, so this would be flagged by the compiler, but for consistency's sake it may make more sense to make them both const, as was done here. Or you may choose to make the prefix version nonconst and the postfix const. Because of the variety of meanings you may want to give the increment and decrement operators, they will need to be considered on a case-by-case basis.

Return by Value as a const

Returning by value as a const can seem a bit subtle at first, so it deserves a bit more explanation. Consider the binary operator+. If you use it in an expression such as f(a+b), the result of a+b becomes a temporary object that is used in the call to f( ). Because it's a temporary, it's automatically const, so whether you explicitly make the return value const or not has no effect.

However, it's also possible for you to send a message to the return value of a+b, rather than just passing it to a function. For example, you can say (a+b).g( ), in which g( ) is some member function of Integer, in this case. By making the return value const, you state that only a const member function can be called for that return value. This is const-correct, because it prevents you from storing potentially valuable information in an object that will most likely be lost.

The Return Optimization

When new objects are created to return by value, notice the form used. In operator+, for example, the form is

```
return Integer(left.i + right.i);
```

This may look at first like a function call to a constructor, but it's not. The syntax is that of a temporary object; the statement says "make a temporary Integer object and return it." Because of this, you might think that the result is the same as creating a named local object and returning that. However, it's quite different. If you were to say instead

```
Integer tmp(left.i + right.i);
return tmp;
```

three things will happen. First, the tmp object is created including its constructor call. Second, the copy-constructor copies the tmp to the location of the outside return value. Third, the destructor is called for tmp at the end of the scope.

In contrast, the "returning a temporary" approach works quite differently. When the compiler sees you do this, it knows that you have no other need for the object it's creating than to return it. The compiler takes advantage of this by building the object *directly* into the location of the outside return value. This requires only a single ordinary constructor call (no copy-constructor is necessary) and there's no destructor call because you never actually create a local object. Thus, while it doesn't cost anything but programmer awareness, it's significantly more efficient. This is often called the *return value optimization*.

Unusual Operators

Several additional operators have a slightly different syntax for overloading.

The subscript, operator[ ], must be a member function and it requires a single argument. Because operator[ ] implies that the object it's being called for acts like an array, you will often return a reference from this operator, so it can be conveniently used on the left-hand side of an equal sign. This operator is commonly overloaded; you'll see examples in the rest of the book.

The operators new and delete control dynamic storage allocation and can be overloaded in a number of different ways. This topic is covered in Chapter 13.

Operator Comma

The comma operator is called when it appears next to an object of the type the comma is defined for. However, operator is *not* called for function argument lists, only for objects that are out in the open, separated by commas. There doesn't seem to be a lot of practical uses for this operator; it's in the language for consistency. Listing 12-5 shows an example showing how the comma function can be called when the comma appears *before* an object, as well as after.

Listing 12-5. Overloading the Comma Operator

```
//: C12:OverloadingOperatorComma.cpp
#include <iostream>
using namespace std;

class After {
public:
  const After& operator,(const After&) const {
    cout << "After::operator,()" << endl;
    return *this;
  }
};

class Before {};

Before& operator,(int, Before& b) {
  cout << "Before::operator,()" << endl;
  return b;
}

int main() {
  After a, b;
  a, b;  // Operator comma called

  Before c;
  1, c;  // Operator comma called
} ///:~
```

The global function allows the comma to be placed before the object in question. The usage shown is fairly obscure and questionable. Although you would probably use a comma-separated list as part of a more complex expression, it's too subtle to use in most situations.

Operator->

The operator-> is generally used when you want to make an object appear to be a pointer. Since such an object has more "smarts" built into it than exist for a typical pointer, an object like this is often called a *smart pointer*. These are especially useful if you want to "wrap" a class around a pointer to make that pointer safe, or in the common usage of an *iterator*, which is an object that moves through a *collection/container* of other objects and selects them one at a time, without providing direct access to the implementation of the container.

A pointer dereference operator must be a member function. It has additional, atypical constraints: it must return an object (or a reference to an object) that also has a pointer dereference operator, or it must return a pointer that can be used to select what the pointer dereference operator arrow is pointing at. See Listing 12-6 for a simple example.

Listing 12-6. A Smart Pointer Example

```cpp
//: C12:SmartPointer.cpp
#include <iostream>
#include <vector>
#include "../require.h"
using namespace std;

class Obj {
  static int i, j;
public:
  void f() const { cout << i++ << endl; }
  void g() const { cout << j++ << endl; }
};

// Static member definitions:
int Obj::i = 47;
int Obj::j = 11;

// Container:
class ObjContainer {
  vector<Obj*> a;
public:
  void add(Obj* obj) { a.push_back(obj); }
  friend class SmartPointer;
};

class SmartPointer {
  ObjContainer& oc;
  int index;
public:
  SmartPointer(ObjContainer& objc) : oc(objc) {
    index = 0;
  }
  // Return value indicates end of list:
  bool operator++() { // Prefix
    if(index >= oc.a.size()) return false;
    if(oc.a[++index] == 0) return false;
    return true;
  }
```

```
  bool operator++(int) { // Postfix
    return operator++(); // Use prefix version
  }
  Obj* operator->() const {
    require(oc.a[index] != 0, "Zero value "
      "returned by SmartPointer::operator->()");
    return oc.a[index];
  }
};

int main() {
const int sz = 10;
  Obj o[sz];
  ObjContainer oc;
for(int i = 0; i < sz; i++)
    oc.add(&o[i]);        // Fill it up
  SmartPointer sp(oc);    // Create an iterator
  do {
    sp->f();              // Pointer dereference operator call
    sp->g();
  } while(sp++);
} ///:~
```

The class Obj defines the objects that are manipulated in this program. The functions f( ) and g( ) simply print out interesting values using static data members. Pointers to these objects are stored inside containers of type ObjContainer using the add( ) function. ObjContainer looks like an array of pointers, but you'll notice there's no way to get the pointers back out again. However, SmartPointer is declared as a friend class, so it has permission to look inside the container. The SmartPointer class looks very much like an intelligent pointer; you can move it forward using operator++ (you can also define an operator- -), it won't go past the end of the container it's pointing to, and it produces (via the pointer dereference operator) the value it's pointing to. Notice that the SmartPointer is a custom fit for the container it's created for; unlike an ordinary pointer, there isn't a "general purpose" smart pointer. In main( ), once the container oc is filled with Obj objects, a SmartPointer sp is created. The smart pointer calls happen in the expressions, as in:

```
sp->f();  // Smart pointer calls
sp->g();
```

Here, even though sp doesn't actually have f( ) and g( ) member functions, the pointer dereference operator automatically calls those functions for the Obj* that is returned by SmartPointer::operator->. The compiler performs all the checking to make sure the function call works properly.

Although the underlying mechanics of the pointer dereference operator are more complex than the other operators, the goal is exactly the same: to provide a more convenient syntax for the users of your classes.

A Nested Iterator

It's more common to see a smart pointer or iterator class nested within the class that it services. In Listing 12-7, the code from Listing 12-6 is rewritten to nest SmartPointer inside ObjContainer.

Listing 12-7. A Nested Smart Pointer/Iterator

```cpp
//: C12:NestedSmartPointer.cpp
#include <iostream>
#include <vector>
#include "../require.h"
using namespace std;

class Obj {
  static int i, j;
public:
  void f() { cout << i++ << endl; }
  void g() { cout << j++ << endl; }
};

// Static member definitions:
int Obj::i = 47;
int Obj::j = 11;

// Container:
class ObjContainer {
  vector<Obj*> a;
public:
  void add(Obj* obj) { a.push_back(obj); }
  class SmartPointer;
  friend class SmartPointer;
  class SmartPointer {
    ObjContainer& oc;
    unsigned int index;
  public:
    SmartPointer(ObjContainer& objc) : oc(objc) {
      index = 0;
    }
    // Return value indicates end of list:
    bool operator++() {     // Prefix
      if(index >= oc.a.size()) return false;
      if(oc.a[++index] == 0) return false;
      return true;
    }
    bool operator++(int) { // Postfix
      return operator++(); // Use prefix version
    }
    Obj* operator->() const {
      require(oc.a[index] != 0, "Zero value "
        "returned by SmartPointer::operator->()");
      return oc.a[index];
    }
  };
};
```

```
  // Function to produce a smart pointer that
  // points to the beginning of the ObjContainer:
  SmartPointer begin() {
    return SmartPointer(*this);
  }
};

int main() {
  const int sz = 10;
  Obj o[sz];
  ObjContainer oc;
  for(int i = 0; i < sz; i++)
    oc.add(&o[i]); // Fill it up
  ObjContainer::SmartPointer sp = oc.begin();
  do {
    sp->f();          // Pointer dereference operator call
    sp->g();
  } while(++sp);
} ///:~
```

Besides the actual nesting of the class, there are only two differences here. The first is in the declaration of the class so that it can be a friend, as in:

```
class SmartPointer;
friend SmartPointer;
```

The compiler must first know that the class exists before it can be told that it's a friend.

The second difference is in the ObjContainer member function begin( ), which produces a SmartPointer that points to the beginning of the ObjContainer sequence. Although it's really only a convenience, it's valuable because it follows part of the form used in the Standard C++ Library.

Operator->*

The operator->* is a binary operator that behaves like all the other binary operators. It is provided for those situations when you want to mimic the behavior provided by the built-in *pointer-to-member* syntax, described in the previous chapter.

Just like operator->, the pointer-to-member dereference operator is generally used with some kind of object that represents a smart pointer, although the example shown here will be simpler so it's understandable. The trick when defining operator->* is that it must return an object for which the operator( ) can be called with the arguments for the member function you're calling.

The function call operator( ) must be a member function, and it is unique in that it allows any number of arguments. It makes your object look like it's actually a function. Although you could define several overloaded operator( ) functions with different arguments, it's often used for types that only have a single operation, or at least an especially prominent one.

To create an operator->* you must first create a class with an operator( ) that is the type of object that operator->* will return. This class must somehow capture the necessary information so that when the operator( ) is called (which happens automatically), the pointer-to-member will be dereferenced for the object. In Listing 12-8, the FunctionObject constructor captures and stores both the pointer to the object and the pointer to the member function, and then the operator( ) uses those to make the actual pointer-to-member call.

Listing 12-8. The Pointer-to-Member Operator

```
//: C12:PointerToMemberOperator.cpp
#include <iostream>
using namespace std;

class Dog {
public:
  int run(int i) const {
    cout << "run\n";
    return i;
  }
  int eat(int i) const {
    cout << "eat\n";
    return i;
  }
  int sleep(int i) const {
    cout << "ZZZ\n";
    return i;
  }
  typedef int (Dog::*PMF)(int) const;
  // operator->* must return an object
  // that has an operator():
  class FunctionObject {
    Dog* ptr;
    PMF pmem;
  public:
    // Save the object pointer and member pointer
    FunctionObject(Dog* wp, PMF pmf)
      : ptr(wp), pmem(pmf) {
      cout << "FunctionObject constructor\n";
    }
    // Make the call using the object pointer
    // and member pointer
    int operator()(int i) const {
      cout << "FunctionObject::operator()\n";
      return (ptr->*pmem)(i); // Make the call
    }
  };
  FunctionObject operator->*(PMF pmf) {
    cout << "operator->*" << endl;
    return FunctionObject(this, pmf);
  }
};

int main() {
  Dog w;
  Dog::PMF pmf = &Dog::run;
  cout << (w->*pmf)(1) << endl;
  pmf = &Dog::sleep;
```

```
  cout << (w->*pmf)(2) << endl;
  pmf = &Dog::eat;
  cout << (w->*pmf)(3) << endl;
} ///:~
```

Dog has three member functions, all of which take an int argument and return an int. PMF is a typedef to simplify defining a pointer-to-member to Dog's member functions.

A FunctionObject is created and returned by operator->*. Notice that operator->* knows both the object that the pointer-to-member is being called for (this) and the pointer-to-member, and it passes those to the FunctionObject constructor that stores the values. When operator->* is called, the compiler immediately turns around and calls operator( ) for the return value of operator->*, passing in the arguments that were given to operator->*. The FunctionObject::operator( ) takes the arguments and then dereferences the "real" pointer-to-member using its stored object pointer and pointer-to-member.

Notice that what you are doing here, just as with operator->, is inserting yourself in the middle of the call to operator->*. This allows you to perform some extra operations if necessary.

The operator->* mechanism implemented here only works for member functions that take an int argument and return an int. This is limiting, but if you try to create overloaded mechanisms for each different possibility, it seems like a prohibitive task. Fortunately, C++'s template mechanism (discussed in Chapter 16) is designed to handle just such a problem.

Operators You Can't Overload

There are certain operators in the available set that cannot be overloaded. The general reason for the restriction is safety. If these operators were overloadable, it would somehow jeopardize or break safety mechanisms, make things harder, or confuse existing practice.

- The member selection operator.. Currently, the dot has a meaning for any member in a class, but if you allow it to be overloaded, then you couldn't access members in the normal way; instead you'd have to use a pointer and the arrow operator->.

- The pointer to member dereference operator.*, for the same reason as operator..

- There's no exponentiation operator. The most popular choice for this was operator** from Fortran, but this raised difficult parsing questions. Also, C has no exponentiation operator, so C++ didn't seem to need one either because you can always perform a function call. An exponentiation operator would add a convenient notation, but no new language functionality to account for the added complexity of the compiler.

- There are no user-defined operators. That is, you can't make up new operators that aren't currently in the set. Part of the problem is how to determine precedence, and part of the problem is an insufficient need to account for the necessary trouble.

- You can't change the precedence rules. They're hard enough to remember as it is without letting people play with them.

Non-Member Operators

In some of the previous examples, the operators may be members or non-members, and it doesn't seem to make much difference. This usually raises the question of which to choose. In general, if it doesn't make any difference; they should be members, to emphasize the association between the operator and its class. When the left-hand operand is always an object of the current class, this works fine.

However, sometimes you want the left-hand operand to be an object of some other class. A common place you'll see this is when the operators << and >> are overloaded for iostream. Since iostream is a fundamental C++ library, you'll probably want to overload these operators for most of your classes, so the process is worth memorizing; see Listing 12-9.

Listing 12-9. Iostream Operator Overloading

```
//: C12:IostreamOperatorOverloading.cpp

// Example of non-member overloaded operators

#include "../require.h"

#include <iostream>

#include <sstream>
        // "String streams"

#include <cstring>

using namespace std;

class IntArray {
  enum { sz = 5 };
  int i[sz];
public:
  IntArray() { memset(i, 0, sz* sizeof(*i)); }
  int& operator[](int x) {
    require(x >= 0 && x < sz,
      "IntArray::operator[] out of range");
    return i[x];
  }
  friend ostream&
    operator<<(ostream& os, const IntArray& ia);
  friend istream&
    operator>>(istream& is, IntArray& ia);
};

ostream&
operator<<(ostream& os, const IntArray& ia) {
  for(int j = 0; j < ia.sz; j++) {
    os << ia.i[j];
    if(j != ia.sz -1)
      os << ", ";
  }
  os << endl;
  return os;
}

istream& operator>>(istream& is, IntArray& ia){
  for(int j = 0; j < ia.sz; j++)
    is >> ia.i[j];
  return is;
}
```

```
int main() {
  stringstream input("47 34 56 92 103");
  IntArray I;
  input >> I;
  I[4] = -1; // Use overloaded operator[]
  cout << I;
} ///:~
```

This class also contains an overloaded operator [ ], which returns a reference to a legitimate value in the array. Because a reference is returned, the expression

```
I[4] = -1;
```

not only looks much more civilized than if pointers were used, it also accomplishes the desired effect.

It's important that the overloaded shift operators pass and return *by reference*, so the actions will affect the external objects. In the function definitions, expressions like

```
os << ia.i[j];
```

cause the *existing* overloaded operator functions to be called (that is, those defined in <iostream>). In this case, the function called is ostream& operator<<(ostream&, int) because ia.i[j] resolves to an int.

Once all the actions are performed on the istream or ostream, it is returned so it can be used in a more complicated expression.

In main( ), a new type of iostream is used: the stringstream (declared in <sstream>). This is a class that takes a string (which it can create from a char array, as shown here) and turns it into an iostream. In the example in Listing 12-9, this means that the shift operators can be tested without opening a file or typing data onto the command line.

The form shown in this example (Listing 12-9) for the inserter and extractor is standard. If you want to create these operators for your own class, copy the function signatures and return types above and follow the form of the body.

Basic Guidelines

The guidelines in Table 12-1 are recommended for choosing between members and non-members.

Table 12-1. *Guidelines For Choosing Members*

Operator	Recommended Use
All Unary Operators	Member
= ( ) [ ] -> ->*	*Must* be member
+= -= /= *= ^= &= |= %= >>= <<=	Member
All Other Binary Operators	Non-member

Overloading Assignment

A common source of confusion with new C++ programmers is assignment. This is no doubt because the = sign is such a fundamental operation in programming, right down to copying a register at the machine level. In addition, the copy-constructor (described in Chapter 11) is also sometimes invoked when the = sign is used, as in:

```
MyType b;
MyType a = b;
a = b;
```

In the second line, the object a is being *defined*. A new object is being created where one didn't exist before. Because you know by now how defensive the C++ compiler is about object initialization, you know that a constructor must always be called at the point where an object is defined. *But which constructor?* a is being created from an existing MyType object (b, on *the right side* of the equal sign), so there's only one choice: the copy-constructor. Even though an equal sign is involved, the copy-constructor is called.

In the third line, things are different. On the left side of the equal sign is a previously initialized object. Clearly, you don't call a constructor for an object that's already been created. In this case MyType::operator= is called for a, taking as an argument whatever appears on the right-hand side.

■ **Note** You can have multiple operator= functions to take different types of right-hand arguments.

This behavior is not restricted to the copy-constructor. Any time you're initializing an object using an = instead of the ordinary function call form of the constructor, the compiler will look for a constructor that accepts whatever is on the right-hand side; see Listing 12-10.

Listing 12-10. Copying vs. Initialization

```
//: C12:CopyingVsInitialization.cpp
class Fi {
public:
  Fi() {}
};

class Fee {
public:
  Fee(int) {}
  Fee(const Fi&) {}
};

int main() {
  Fee fee = 1;  // Fee(int)
  Fi fi;
  Fee fum = fi; // Fee(Fi)
} ///:~
```

When dealing with the = sign, it's important to keep this distinction in mind: if the object hasn't been created yet, initialization is required; otherwise the assignment operator= is used.

It's even better to avoid writing code that uses the = for initialization; instead, always use the explicit constructor form. The two constructions with the equal sign then become

```
Fee fee(1);
Fee fum(fi);
```

Behavior of operator=

In Integer.h and Byte.h, you saw that operator= can be only a member function. It is intimately connected to the object on the left side of the =. If it was possible to define operator= globally, then you might attempt to redefine the built-in = sign as in:

```
int operator=(int, MyType); // Global = not allowed!
```

The compiler skirts this whole issue by forcing you to make operator= a member function.

When you create an operator=, you must copy all of the necessary information from the right-hand object into the current object (that is, the object that operator= is being called for) to perform whatever you consider "assignment" for your class. For simple objects, this is obvious, as you can see in Listing 12-11.

Listing 12-11. Simple Assignment

```
//: C12:SimpleAssignment.cpp
// Simple operator=()
#include <iostream>
using namespace std;

class Value {
  int a, b;
  float c;
public:
  Value(int aa = 0, int bb = 0, float cc = 0.0)
    : a(aa), b(bb), c(cc) {}
  Value& operator=(const Value& rv) {
    a = rv.a;
    b = rv.b;
    c = rv.c;
    return *this;
  }
  friend ostream&
  operator<<(ostream& os, const Value& rv) {
    return os << "a = " << rv.a << ", b = "
              << rv.b << ", c = " << rv.c;
  }
};

int main() {
  Value a, b(1, 2, 3.3);
  cout << "a: " << a << endl;
  cout << "b: " << b << endl;
  a = b;
  cout << "a after assignment: " << a << endl;
} ///:~
```

Here, the object on the left side of the = copies all the elements of the object on the right, *then* returns a reference to itself, which allows a more complex expression to be created.

This example includes a common mistake. When you're assigning two objects of the same type, you should always check first for self-assignment: is the object being assigned to itself? In some cases, such as this one, it's harmless if you perform the assignment operations anyway, but if changes are made to the implementation of the class, it can make a difference, and if you don't do it as a matter of habit, you may forget and cause hard-to-find bugs.

Pointers in Classes

What happens if the object is not so simple? For example, what if the object contains pointers to other objects? *Simply copying a pointer means that you'll end up with two objects pointing to the same storage location.* In situations like these, you need to do bookkeeping of your own.

There are two common approaches to this problem. The simplest technique is to copy whatever the pointer refers to when you do an assignment or a copy-construction. This is straightforward, as shown in Listing 12-12.

Listing 12-12. Copying with Pointers

```
//: C12:CopyingWithPointers.cpp
// Solving the pointer aliasing problem by
// duplicating what is pointed to during
// assignment and copy-construction.

#include "../require.h"
#include <string>
#include <iostream>

using namespace std;

class Dog {
  string nm;

public:
  Dog(const string& name) : nm(name) {
    cout << "Creating Dog: " << *this << endl;
  }
  // Synthesized copy-constructor & operator= are correct.

  // Create a Dog from a Dog pointer:
  Dog(const Dog* dp, const string& msg)
    : nm(dp->nm + msg) {
    cout << "Copied dog " << *this << " from "
         << *dp << endl;
  }
  ~Dog() {
    cout << "Deleting Dog: " << *this << endl;
  }
  void rename(const string& newName) {
    nm = newName;
    cout << "Dog renamed to: " << *this << endl;
  }
```

```
    friend ostream&
    operator<<(ostream& os, const Dog& d) {
      return os << "[" << d.nm << "]";
    }
};

class DogHouse {
  Dog* p;
  string houseName;
public:
  DogHouse(Dog* dog, const string& house)
    : p(dog), houseName(house) {}
  DogHouse(const DogHouse& dh)
    : p(new Dog(dh.p, " copy-constructed")),
      houseName(dh.houseName
        + " copy-constructed") {}
  DogHouse& operator=(const DogHouse& dh) {
    // Check for self-assignment:
    if(&dh != this) {
      p = new Dog(dh.p, " assigned");
      houseName = dh.houseName + " assigned";
    }
    return *this;
  }
void renameHouse(const string& newName) {
    houseName = newName;
  }

Dog* getDog() const { return p; }

  ~DogHouse() { delete p; }

  friend ostream&
  operator<<(ostream& os, const DogHouse& dh) {

    return os << "[" << dh.houseName
              << "] contains " << *dh.p;
  }
};

int main() {

  DogHouse fidos(new Dog("Fido"), "FidoHouse");
  cout << fidos << endl;

  DogHouse fidos2 = fidos; // Copy construction
  cout << fidos2 << endl;

  fidos2.getDog()->rename("Spot");
    fidos2.renameHouse("SpotHouse");
  cout << fidos2 << endl;
```

```
    fidos = fidos2; // Assignment
    cout << fidos << endl;

    fidos.getDog()->rename("Max");
    fidos2.renameHouse("MaxHouse");
} ///:~
```

Dog is a simple class that contains only a string that holds the name of the dog. However, you'll generally know when something happens to a Dog because the constructors and destructors print information when they are called. Notice that the second constructor is a bit like a copy-constructor except that it takes a pointer to a Dog instead of a reference, and it has a second argument that is a message that's concatenated to the argument Dog's name. This is used to help trace the behavior of the program.

You can see that whenever a member function prints information, it doesn't access that information directly but instead sends *this to cout. This in turn calls the ostreamoperator<<. It's valuable to do it this way because if you want to reformat the way that Dog information is displayed (as was done by adding the [and]) you only need to do it in one place.

A DogHouse contains a Dog* and demonstrates the four functions you will always need to define when your class contains pointers: all necessary ordinary constructors, the copy-constructor, operator= (*either define it or disallow it*), and a destructor. The operator= checks for self-assignment as a matter of course, even though it's not strictly necessary here. This virtually eliminates the possibility that you'll forget to check for self-assignment if you *do* change the code so that it matters.

Reference Counting

In Listing 12-12, the copy-constructor and operator= make a new copy of what the pointer points to, and the destructor deletes it. However, if your object requires a lot of memory or a high initialization overhead, you may want to avoid this copying. A common approach to this problem is called *reference counting*. You give intelligence to the object that's being pointed to so it knows how many objects are pointing to it. Then copy-construction or assignment means attaching another pointer to an existing object and incrementing the reference count. Destruction means reducing the reference count and destroying the object if the reference count goes to zero.

But what if you want to write to the object (the Dog in Listing 12-12)? More than one object may be using this Dog, so you'd be modifying someone else's Dog as well as yours, which doesn't seem very neighborly. To solve this "aliasing" problem, an additional technique called *copy-on-write* is used. Before writing to a block of memory, you make sure no one else is using it. If the reference count is greater than one, you must make yourself a personal copy of that block before writing it, so you don't disturb someone else's turf. See Listing 12-13 for a simple example of reference counting and copy-on-write.

Listing 12-13. Illustrating Reference Counting and Copy-on-Write

```
//: C12:ReferenceCounting.cpp
// Reference count, copy-on-write
#include "../require.h"
#include <string>
#include <iostream>
using namespace std;

class Dog {
  string nm;
  int refcount;
  Dog(const string& name)
    : nm(name), refcount(1) {
    cout << "Creating Dog: " << *this << endl;
  }
```

```
  // Prevent assignment:
  Dog& operator=(const Dog& rv);
public:
  // Dogs can only be created on the heap:
  static Dog* make(const string& name) {
    return new Dog(name);
  }
  Dog(const Dog& d)
    : nm(d.nm + " copy"), refcount(1) {
    cout << "Dog copy-constructor: "
         << *this << endl;
  }
  ~Dog() {
    cout << "Deleting Dog: " << *this << endl;
  }
  void attach() {
    ++refcount;
    cout << "Attached Dog: " << *this << endl;
  }
  void detach() {
    require(refcount != 0);
    cout << "Detaching Dog: " << *this << endl;
    // Destroy object if no one is using it:
    if(--refcount == 0) delete this;
  }
  // Conditionally copy this Dog.
  // Call before modifying the Dog, assign
  // resulting pointer to your Dog*.
  Dog* unalias() {
    cout << "Unaliasing Dog: " << *this << endl;
    // Don't duplicate if not aliased:
    if(refcount == 1) return this;
    --refcount;
    // Use copy-constructor to duplicate:
    return new Dog(*this);
  }
  void rename(const string& newName) {
    nm = newName;
    cout << "Dog renamed to: " << *this << endl;
  }
  friend ostream&
  operator<<(ostream& os, const Dog& d) {
    return os << "[" << d.nm << "], rc = "
              << d.refcount;
  }
};

class DogHouse {
  Dog* p;
  string houseName;
public:
  DogHouse(Dog* dog, const string& house)
```

```
    : p(dog), houseName(house) {
      cout << "Created DogHouse: "<< *this << endl;
  }
  DogHouse(const DogHouse& dh)
    : p(dh.p),
      houseName("copy-constructed " +
        dh.houseName) {
    p->attach();
    cout << "DogHouse copy-constructor: "
        << *this << endl;
  }
  DogHouse& operator=(const DogHouse& dh) {
    // Check for self-assignment:
    if(&dh != this) {
      houseName = dh.houseName + " assigned";
      // Clean up what you're using first:
      p->detach();
      p = dh.p; // Like copy-constructor
      p->attach();
    }
    cout << "DogHouse operator= : "
        << *this << endl;
    return *this;
  }
  // Decrement refcount, conditionally destroy
  ~DogHouse() {
    cout << "DogHouse destructor: "
        << *this << endl;
    p->detach();
  }

  void renameHouse(const string& newName) {
    houseName = newName;
  }

  void unalias() { p = p->unalias(); }
  // Copy-on-write. Anytime you modify the
  // contents of the pointer you must
  // first unalias it:

  void renameDog(const string& newName) {
    unalias();
    p->rename(newName);
  }
  // ... or when you allow someone else access:
  Dog* getDog() {
    unalias();
    return p;
  }
  friend ostream&
  operator<<(ostream& os, const DogHouse& dh) {
```

```
      return os << "[" << dh.houseName
                << "] contains " << *dh.p;
  }
};

int main() {
  DogHouse
    fidos(Dog::make("Fido"), "FidoHouse"),
    spots(Dog::make("Spot"), "SpotHouse");
  cout << "Entering copy-construction" << endl;

  DogHouse bobs(fidos);
  cout << "After copy-constructing bobs" << endl;
  cout << "fidos:" << fidos << endl;
  cout << "spots:" << spots << endl;
  cout << "bobs:" << bobs << endl;
  cout << "Entering spots = fidos" << endl;

  spots = fidos;
  cout << "After spots = fidos" << endl;
  cout << "spots:" << spots << endl;
  cout << "Entering self-assignment" << endl;

  bobs = bobs;
  cout << "After self-assignment" << endl;
  cout << "bobs:" << bobs << endl;
  // Comment out the following lines:
  cout << "Entering rename(\"Bob\")" << endl;

  bobs.getDog()->rename("Bob");
  cout << "After rename(\"Bob\")" << endl;
} ///:~
```

The class Dog is the object pointed to by a DogHouse. It contains a reference count and functions to control and read the reference count. There's a copy-constructor so you can make a new Dog from an existing one.

The attach( ) function increments the reference count of a Dog to indicate there's another object using it and detach( ) decrements the reference count. If the reference count goes to zero, then no one is using it anymore, so the member function destroys its own object by saying delete this.

Before you make any modifications (such as renaming a Dog), you should ensure that you aren't changing a Dog that some other object is using. You do this by calling DogHouse::unalias( ), which in turn calls Dog::unalias( ). The latter function will return the existing Dog pointer if the reference count is one (meaning no one else is pointing to that Dog), but will duplicate the Dog if the reference count is more than one.

The copy-constructor, instead of creating its own memory, assigns Dog to the Dog of the source object. Then, because there's now an additional object using that block of memory, it increments the reference count by calling Dog::attach( ).

The operator= deals with an object that has already been created on the left side of the =, so it must first clean that up by calling detach( ) for that Dog, which will destroy the old Dog if no one else is using it. Then operator= repeats the behavior of the copy-constructor. Notice that it first checks to detect whether you're assigning the same object to itself.

The destructor calls detach( ) to conditionally destroy the Dog.

To implement copy-on-write, you must control all the actions that write to your block of memory. For example, the renameDog( ) member function allows you to change the values in the block of memory. But first, it uses unalias( ) to prevent the modification of an aliased Dog (a Dog with more than one DogHouse object pointing to it). And if you need to produce a pointer to a Dog from within a DogHouse, you unalias( ) that pointer first.

main( ) tests the various functions that must work correctly to implement reference counting: the constructor, copy-constructor, operator=, and destructor. It also tests the copy-on-write by calling renameDog( ).

Here's the output (after a little reformatting):

```
Creating Dog: [Fido], rc = 1
Created DogHouse: [FidoHouse]
  contains [Fido], rc = 1
Creating Dog: [Spot], rc = 1
Created DogHouse: [SpotHouse]
  contains [Spot], rc = 1
Entering copy-construction
Attached Dog: [Fido], rc = 2
DogHouse copy-constructor:
  [copy-constructed FidoHouse]
    contains [Fido], rc = 2
After copy-constructing bobs
fidos:[FidoHouse] contains [Fido], rc = 2
spots:[SpotHouse] contains [Spot], rc = 1
bobs:[copy-constructed FidoHouse]
  contains [Fido], rc = 2
Entering spots = fidos
Detaching Dog: [Spot], rc = 1
Deleting Dog: [Spot], rc = 0
Attached Dog: [Fido], rc = 3
DogHouse operator= : [FidoHouse assigned]
  contains [Fido], rc = 3
After spots = fidos
spots:[FidoHouse assigned] contains [Fido],rc = 3
Entering self-assignment
DogHouse operator= : [copy-constructed FidoHouse]
  contains [Fido], rc = 3
After self-assignment
bobs:[copy-constructed FidoHouse]
  contains [Fido], rc = 3
Entering rename("Bob")
After rename("Bob")
DogHouse destructor: [copy-constructed FidoHouse]
  contains [Fido], rc = 3
Detaching Dog: [Fido], rc = 3
DogHouse destructor: [FidoHouse assigned]
  contains [Fido], rc = 2
Detaching Dog: [Fido], rc = 2
DogHouse destructor: [FidoHouse]
  contains [Fido], rc = 1
Detaching Dog: [Fido], rc = 1
Deleting Dog: [Fido], rc = 0
```

By studying the output, tracing through the source code, and experimenting with the program, you'll deepen your understanding of these techniques.

Automatic operator= Creation

Because assigning an object to another object *of the same type* is an activity most people expect to be possible, the compiler will automatically create a type::operator=(type) if you don't make one. The behavior of this operator mimics that of the automatically created copy-constructor; if the class contains objects (or is inherited from another class), the operator= for those objects is called recursively. This is called member-wise assignment. See Listing 12-14 for an example.

Listing 12-14. Illustrating Member-Wise Assignment

```
//: C12:AutomaticOperatorEquals.cpp
#include <iostream>
using namespace std;

class Cargo {
public:
  Cargo& operator=(const Cargo&) {
    cout << "inside Cargo::operator=()" << endl;
    return *this;
  }
};

class Truck {
  Cargo b;
};

int main() {
  Truck a, b;
  a = b; // Prints: "inside Cargo::operator=()"
} ///:~
```

The automatically generated operator= for Truck calls Cargo::operator=.

In general, you don't want to let the compiler do this for you. With classes of any sophistication (especially if they contain pointers!) you want to explicitly create an operator=. If you really don't want people to perform assignment, declare operator= as a private function.

■ **Note**   You don't need to define it unless you're using it inside the class.

Automatic Type Conversion

In C and C++, if the compiler sees an expression or function call using a type that isn't quite the one it needs, it can often perform an automatic type conversion from the type it has to the type it wants. In C++, you can achieve this same effect for user-defined types by defining automatic type conversion functions. These functions come in two flavors: a particular type of constructor and an overloaded operator.

Constructor Conversion

If you define a constructor that takes as its single argument an object (or reference) of another type, that constructor allows the compiler to perform an automatic type conversion. See Listing 12-15 for an example.

Listing 12-15. Illustrating Automatic Type Conversion

```
//: C12:AutomaticTypeConversion.cpp
// Type conversion constructor
class One {
public:
  One() {}
};

class Two {
public:
  Two(const One&) {}
};

void f(Two) {}

int main() {
  One one;
  f(one); // Wants a Two, has a One
} ///:~
```

When the compiler sees f( ) called with a One object, it looks at the declaration for f( ) and notices it wants a Two. Then it looks to see if there's any way to get a Two from a One, and it finds the constructor Two::Two(One), which it quietly calls. The resulting Two object is handed to f( ).

In this case, automatic type conversion has saved you from the trouble of defining two overloaded versions of f( ). However, the cost is the hidden constructor call to Two, which may matter if you're concerned about the efficiency of calls to f( ).

Preventing Constructor Conversion

There are times when automatic type conversion via the constructor can cause problems. To turn it off, you modify the constructor by prefacing with the keyword explicit (which only works with constructors). Listing 12-16 uses this keyword to modify the constructor of class Two from Listing 12-15.

Listing 12-16. Illustrating Use of the Explicit Keyword

```
//: C12:ExplicitKeyword.cpp
// Using the "explicit" keyword
class One {
public:
  One() {}
};

class Two {
public:
  explicit Two(const One&) {}
};

void f(Two) {}
```

```
int main() {

  One one;

//! f(one);   // No auto conversion allowed

  f(Two(one)); // OK -- user performs conversion

} ///:~
```

By making Two's constructor explicit, the compiler is told not to perform any automatic conversion using that particular constructor (other non-explicit constructors in that class can still perform automatic conversions). If the user wants to make the conversion happen, the code must be written out. In Listing 12-16, f(Two(one)) creates a temporary object of type Two from one, just like the compiler did in Listing 12-15.

Operator Conversion

The second way to produce automatic type conversion is through operator overloading. You can create a member function that takes the current type and converts it to the desired type using the operator keyword followed by the type you want to convert to. This form of operator overloading is unique because you don't appear to specify a return type—the return type is the *name* of the operator you're overloading. See Listing 12-17 for an example.

Listing 12-17. Illustrating Operator Overloading Conversion

```
//: C12:OperatorOverloadingConversion.cpp

class Three {
  int i;

public:
  Three(int ii = 0, int = 0) : i(ii) {}
};

class Four {
  int x;

public:
  Four(int xx) : x(xx) {}
  operator Three() const { return Three(x); }
};

void g(Three) {}

int main() {
  Four four(1);
  g(four);
  g(1);  // Calls Three(1,0)
} ///:~
```

With the constructor technique, the destination class is performing the conversion, but with operators, the source class performs the conversion. The value of the constructor technique is that you can add a new conversion path to an existing system as you're creating a new class. However, creating a single-argument constructor always defines an automatic type conversion (*even if it's got more than one argument, if the rest of the arguments are defaulted*), which may not be what you want (in which case you can turn it off using `explicit`). In addition, there's no way to use a constructor conversion from a user-defined type to a built-in type; this is possible only with operator overloading.

Reflexivity

One of the most convenient reasons to use global overloaded operators instead of member operators is that in the global versions, automatic type conversion may be applied to either operand, whereas with member objects, the left-hand operand must already be the proper type. If you want both operands to be converted, the global versions can save a lot of coding; see Listing 12-18.

Listing 12-18. Illustrating Reflexivity in Overloading

```
//: C12:ReflexivityInOverloading.cpp
class Number {
  int i;

public:
  Number(int ii = 0) : i(ii) {}
  const Number
  operator+(const Number& n) const {
    return Number(i + n.i);
  }
  friend const Number
    operator-(const Number&, const Number&);
};

const Number
  operator-(const Number& n1,
            const Number& n2) {
    return Number(n1.i - n2.i);
}

int main() {
  Number a(47), b(11);
  a + b;    // OK
  a + 1;    // 2nd arg converted to Number
//! 1 + a; // Wrong! 1st arg not of type Number
  a - b;    // OK
  a - 1;    // 2nd arg converted to Number
  1 - a;    // 1st arg converted to Number
} ///:~
```

Class Number has both a member `operator+` and a `friend operator-`. Because there's a constructor that takes a single `int` argument, an `int` can be automatically converted to a Number, but only under the right conditions. In main( ), you can see that adding a Number to another Number works fine because it's an exact match to the overloaded operator. Also, when the compiler sees a Number followed by a + and an `int`, it can match to the member function `Number::operator+` and convert the `int` argument to a Number using the constructor. But when it sees an `int`, a +, and a Number, it doesn't know what to do because all it has is `Number::operator+`, which requires that the left operand already be a Number object. Thus, the compiler issues an error.

With the friendoperator–, things are different. The compiler needs to fill in both its arguments however it can; it isn't restricted to having a Number as the left-hand argument. Thus, if it sees

```
1 - a
```

it can convert the first argument to a Number using the constructor.

Sometimes you want to be able to restrict the use of your operators by making them members. For example, when multiplying a matrix by a vector, the vector must go on the right. But if you want your operators to be able to convert either argument, make the operator a friend function.

Fortunately, the compiler will not take 1 – 1 and convert both arguments to Number objects and then call operator–. That would mean that existing C code might suddenly start to work differently. The compiler matches the "simplest" possibility first, which is the built-in operator for the expression 1 – 1.

Type Conversion Example

An example in which automatic type conversion is extremely helpful occurs with any class that encapsulates character strings (in this case, you will just implement the class using the Standard C++ string class because it's simple). Without automatic type conversion, if you want to use all the existing string functions from the Standard C Library, you have to create a member function for each one, as in Listing 12-19.

Listing 12-19. Using No Automatic Type Conversion

```cpp
//: C12:Strings1.cpp
// No auto type conversion

#include "../require.h"
#include <cstring>
#include <cstdlib>
#include <string>

using namespace std;

class Stringc {
  string s;

public:
  Stringc(const string& str = "") : s(str) {}
  int strcmp(const Stringc& S) const {
    return ::strcmp(s.c_str(), S.s.c_str());
  }
  // ... etc., for every function in string.h
};

int main() {
  Stringc s1("hello"), s2("there");
  s1.strcmp(s2);
} ///:~
```

Here, only the strcmp( ) function is created, but you'd have to create a corresponding function for everyone in <cstring> that might be needed. Fortunately, you can provide an automatic type conversion allowing access to all the functions in <cstring>, as shown in Listing 12-20.

Listing 12-20. Using Automatic Type Conversion

```
//: C12:Strings2.cpp
// With auto type conversion

#include "../require.h"
#include <cstring>
#include <cstdlib>
#include <string>

using namespace std;

class Stringc {
  string s;
public:
  Stringc(const string& str = "") : s(str) {}
  operator const char*() const {
    return s.c_str();
  }
};

int main() {
  Stringc s1("hello"), s2("there");
  strcmp(s1, s2); // Standard C function
  strspn(s1, s2); // Any string function!
} ///:~
```

Now any function that takes a char* argument can also take a Stringc argument because the compiler knows how to make a char* from a Stringc.

Pitfalls in Automatic Type Conversion

Because the compiler must choose how to quietly perform a type conversion, it can get into trouble if you don't design your conversions correctly. A simple and obvious situation occurs with a class X that can convert itself to an object of class Y with an operator Y( ). If class Y has a constructor that takes a single argument of type X, this represents the identical type conversion. The compiler now has two ways to go from X to Y, so it will generate an ambiguity error when that conversion occurs; see Listing 12-21.

Listing 12-21. Illustrating Ambiguity in Automatic Type Conversion

```
//: C12:TypeConversionAmbiguity.cpp
class Orange;              // Class declaration

class Apple {
public:
  operator Orange() const; // Convert Apple to Orange
};

class Orange {
public:
  Orange(Apple);            // Convert Apple to Orange
};
```

```
void f(Orange) {}

int main() {
  Apple a;
//! f(a);                    // Error: ambiguous conversion
} ///:~
```

The obvious solution to this problem is not to do it. Just provide a single path for automatic conversion from one type to another.

A more difficult problem to spot occurs when you provide automatic conversion to more than one type. This is sometimes called *fan-out*; see Listing 12-22.

Listing 12-22. Illustrating "Fan-out"

```
//: C12:TypeConversionFanout.cpp

class Orange {};

class Pear {};

class Apple {

public:
  operator Orange() const;
  operator Pear() const;
};

// Overloaded eat():

void eat(Orange);
void eat(Pear);

int main() {

  Apple c;

//! eat(c);
  // Error: Apple -> Orange or Apple -> Pear ???

} ///:~
```

Class Apple has automatic conversions to both Orange and Pear. The insidious thing about this is that there's no problem until someone innocently comes along and creates two overloaded versions of eat( ). (With only one version, the code in main( ) works fine.)

Again, the solution—and the general watchword with automatic type conversion—is to provide only a single automatic conversion from one type to another. You can have conversions to other types; they just shouldn't be automatic. You can create explicit function calls with names like makeA( ) and makeB( ).

Hidden Activities

Automatic type conversion can introduce more underlying activities than you may expect. As a little brain teaser, look at the following modification (Listing 12-23) of the CopyingVsInitialization.cpp program earlier.

Listing 12-23. Illustrating Hidden Activities in Automatic Type Conversion

```
//: C12:CopyingVsInitialization2.cpp
class Fi {};
class Fee {
public:
  Fee(int) {}
  Fee(const Fi&) {}
};

class Fo {
  int i;

public:
  Fo(int x = 0) : i(x) {}
  operator Fee() const { return Fee(i); }
};

int main() {
  Fo fo;
  Fee fee = fo;
} ///:~
```

There is no constructor to create the Fee fee from a Fo object. However, Fo has an automatic type conversion to a Fee. There's no copy-constructor to create a Fee from a Fee, but this is one of the special functions the compiler can create for you. (*The default constructor, copy-constructor,* operator=, *and destructor can be synthesized automatically by the compiler.*) So for the relatively innocuous statement

```
Fee fee = fo;
```

the automatic type conversion operator is called, and a copy-constructor is created.

Use automatic type conversion carefully. As with all operator overloading, it's excellent when it significantly reduces a coding task, but it's usually not worth using gratuitously.

Review Session

1. The whole reason for the existence of *operator overloading* is for those situations when it makes life easier. *There's nothing particularly magical about it;* the overloaded operators are just functions with funny names, and the function calls happen to be made for you by the compiler when it spots the right pattern.

2. But if operator overloading doesn't provide a *significant benefit* to you (the creator of the class) or the user of the class, *don't confuse the issue by adding it.*

CHAPTER 13

■ ■ ■

Dynamic Object Creation

Sometimes you know the exact quantity, type, and lifetime of the objects in your program, but not always. How many planes will an air-traffic system need to handle? How many shapes will a CAD system use? How many nodes will there be in a network?

To solve the general programming problem, it's essential that you be able to create and destroy objects at runtime. Of course, C has always provided the dynamic memory allocation functions malloc() and free() (along with variants of malloc()) that allocate storage from the *heap* (also called *the free store*) at runtime.

However, this simply won't work in C++. The constructor doesn't allow you to hand it the address of the memory to initialize, and for good reason. If you could do that, you might do one or more of the following:

1. Forget. Then guaranteed initialization of objects in C++ wouldn't be guaranteed.

2. Accidentally doing something to the object before you initialize it, expecting the right thing to happen (akin to moving the ignition key in a car the wrong way and getting stuck).

3. Hand it the wrong-sized object (akin to trying to start a car with the ignition key of a motorbike).

And of course, even if you did everything correctly, anyone who modifies your program is prone to the same errors. Improper initialization is responsible for a large portion of programming problems, so it's especially important to guarantee constructor calls for objects created on the heap.

So how does C++ guarantee proper initialization and cleanup, but also allow you to create objects dynamically on the heap?

The answer is by bringing dynamic object creation into the core of the language. malloc() and free() are library functions, and thus outside the control of the compiler. However, if you have an *operator* to perform the combined act of dynamic storage allocation and initialization, and *another* operator to perform the combined act of cleanup and releasing storage, the compiler can still guarantee that constructors and destructors will be called for all objects.

In this chapter, you'll learn how C++'s new and delete elegantly solve this problem by safely creating objects on the heap.

Object Creation

When a C++ object is created, two events occur.

1. Storage is allocated for the object.

2. The constructor is called to initialize that storage.

By now you should comprehend that step two *always* happens. C++ enforces it because uninitialized objects are a major source of program bugs. It doesn't matter where or how the object is created—the constructor is always called.

Step 1, however, can occur in several ways, or at alternate times.

1. Storage can be allocated before the program begins, in the static storage area. This storage exists for the life of the program.

2. Storage can be created on the stack whenever a particular execution point is reached (an opening brace). That storage is released automatically at the complementary execution point (the closing brace). These stack-allocation operations are built into the instruction set of the processor and are very efficient. However, you have to know exactly how many variables you need when you're writing the program so the compiler can generate the right code.

3. Storage can be allocated from a pool of memory called the heap (also known as the free store). This is called *dynamic memory allocation*. To allocate this memory, a function is called at runtime; this means you can decide at any time that you want some memory and how much you need. You are also responsible for determining when to release the memory, which means the lifetime of that memory can be as long as you choose; it isn't determined by scope.

Often these three regions are placed in a single contiguous piece of physical memory: the static area, the stack, and the heap (in an order determined by the compiler writer). However, there are no rules. The stack may be in a special place, and the heap may be implemented by making calls for chunks of memory from the operating system. As a programmer, these things are normally shielded from you, so all you need to think about is that the memory is there when you call for it.

C's Approach to the Heap

To allocate memory dynamically at runtime, C provides functions in its standard library: malloc() and its variants calloc() and realloc() to produce memory from the heap, and free() to release the memory back to the heap. These functions are pragmatic but primitive and require understanding and care on the part of the programmer. To create an instance of a class on the heap using C's dynamic memory functions, you'd have to do something like that in Listing 13-1.

Listing 13-1. malloc() with Class Objects

```
//: C13:MallocClass.cpp
// Malloc with class objects
// What you'd have to do if not for "new"
#include "../require.h"      // To be INCLUDED from Chapter 9
#include <cstdlib>           // malloc() & free()
#include <cstring>           // memset()
#include <iostream>
using namespace std;

classObj {
  int i, j, k;
  enum { sz = 100 };
  charbuf[sz];
public:
  void initialize() {        // Can't use constructor
    cout << "initializing Obj" << endl;
    i = j = k = 0;
    memset(buf, 0, sz);
  }
```

```
  void destroy() const { // Can't use destructor
    cout << "destroying Obj" << endl;
  }
};

int main() {
  Obj *obj = (Obj*)malloc(sizeof(Obj));
  require(obj != 0);
  obj->initialize();
  // ... sometime later:
  obj->destroy();
  free(obj);
} ///:~
```

You can see the use of malloc() to create storage for the object in the line:

```
Obj* obj = (Obj*)malloc(sizeof(Obj));
```

Here, the user must determine the size of the object (one place for an error). malloc() returns a void* because it just produces a patch of memory, not an object. C++ doesn't allow a void* to be assigned to any other pointer, so it must be cast.

Because malloc() may fail to find any memory (in which case it returns zero), you must check the returned pointer to make sure it was successful.

But the worst problem is this line:

```
Obj->initialize();
```

If users make it this far correctly, they must remember to initialize the object before it is used. Notice that a constructor was not used because the constructor cannot be called explicitly; it's called for you by the compiler when an object is created. The problem here is that the user now has the option to forget to perform the initialization before the object is used, thus reintroducing a major source of bugs.

It also turns out that many programmers seem to find C's dynamic memory functions too confusing and complicated; it's not uncommon to find C programmers who use virtual memory machines allocating huge arrays of variables in the static storage area to avoid thinking about dynamic memory allocation. Because C++ is attempting to make library use safe and effortless for the casual programmer, C's approach to dynamic memory is unacceptable.

Operator new

The solution in C++ is to combine all the actions necessary to create an object into a single operator called new. When you create an object with new (using a *new-expression*), it allocates enough storage on the heap to hold the object and calls the constructor for that storage. Thus, if you say

```
MyType *fp = new MyType(1,2);
```

at runtime, the equivalent of malloc(sizeof(MyType)) is called (often, it is literally a call to malloc()), and the constructor for MyType is called with the resulting address as the this pointer, using (1, 2) as the argument list. By the time the pointer is assigned to fp, it's a live, initialized object; you can't even get your hands on it before then. It's also automatically the proper MyType type so no cast is necessary.

The default new checks to make sure the memory allocation was successful before passing the address to the constructor, so you don't have to explicitly determine if the call was successful. Later in the chapter you'll find out what happens if there's no memory left.

You can create a new-expression using any constructor available for the class. If the constructor has no arguments, you write the new-expression without the constructor argument list, as in:

```
MyType *fp = new MyType;
```

Notice how simple the process of creating objects on the heap becomes—a single expression, with all the sizing, conversions, and safety checks built in. It's as easy to create an object on the heap as it is on the stack.

Operator delete

The complement to the new-expression is the *delete-expression*, which first calls the destructor and then releases the memory (often with a call to free()). Just as a new-expression returns a pointer to the object, a delete-expression requires the address of an object, as in:

```
delete fp;
```

This destructs and then releases the storage for the dynamically allocated MyType object created earlier.

delete can be called only for an object created by new. If you malloc() (or calloc() or realloc()) an object and then delete it, the behavior is undefined. Because most default implementations of new and delete use malloc() and free(), you'd probably end up releasing the memory without calling the destructor.

If the pointer you're deleting is zero, nothing will happen. For this reason, people often recommend setting a pointer to zero immediately after you delete it, to prevent deleting it twice. Deleting an object more than once is definitely a bad thing to do, and will cause problems. Listing 13-2 shows that initialization takes place.

Listing 13-2. Illustrating new and delete

```
//: C13:Tree.h
#ifndef TREE_H
#define TREE_H
#include <iostream>

class Tree {
  int height;
public:
  Tree(int treeHeight) : height(treeHeight) {}
  ~Tree() { std::cout << "*"; }
  Friend std::ostream&
  operator<<(std::ostream &os, const Tree* t) {
    return os << "Tree height is: "
            << t->height << std::endl;
  }
};
#endif              // TREE_H ///:~

//: C13:NewAndDelete.cpp
// Simple demo of new & delete
#include "Tree.h" // Header FILE to be INCLUDED from above
using namespace std;
```

```
int main() {
  Tree *t = new Tree(40);
  cout << t;
  delete t;
} ///:~
```

You can prove that the constructor is called by printing out the value of the Tree. Here, it's done by overloading the operator<< to use with an ostream and a Tree*. Note, however, that even though the function is declared as a friend, it is defined as an inline! This is a mere convenience; defining a friend function as an inline to a class doesn't change the friend status or the fact that it's a global function and not a class member function. Also notice that the return value is the result of the entire output expression, which is an ostream& (*which it must be in order to satisfy the return value type of the function*).

Memory Manager Overhead

When you create automatic objects on the stack, the size of the objects and their lifetime is built right into the generated code because the compiler knows the exact type, quantity, and scope. Creating objects on the heap involves additional overhead, both in time and in space. The following is a typical scenario.

■ **Note**   You can replace malloc() with calloc() or realloc().

You call malloc(), which requests a block of memory from the pool. (This code may actually be part of malloc().)

The pool is searched for a block of memory large enough to satisfy the request. This is done by checking a map or directory of some sort that shows which blocks are currently in use and which are available. It's a quick process, but it may take several tries so it might not be deterministic—that is, you can't necessarily count on malloc() always taking exactly the same amount of time.

Before a pointer to that block is returned, the size and location of the block must be recorded so further calls to malloc() won't use it, and so that when you call free(), the system knows how much memory to release.

The way all this is implemented can vary widely. For example, there's nothing to prevent primitives for memory allocation being implemented in the processor. If you're curious, you can write test programs to try to guess the way your malloc() is implemented. You can also read the library source code, if you have it (the GNU C sources are always available).

Early Examples Redesigned

Using new and delete, the Stash example introduced previously in this book can be rewritten using all the features discussed in the book so far. Examining the new code will also give you a useful review of the topics.

At this point in the book, neither the Stash nor Stack classes will "own" the objects they point to; that is, when the Stash or Stack object goes out of scope, it will not call delete for all the objects it points to. The reason this is not possible is because, in an attempt to be generic, they hold void pointers. If you delete a void pointer, the only thing that happens is the memory gets released, because there's no type information and no way for the compiler to know what destructor to call.

delete void* is Probably a Bug

It's worth making a point that if you call delete for a void*, it's almost certainly going to be a bug in your program unless the destination of that pointer is very simple; in particular, it should not have a destructor. Listing 13-3 shows what happens.

Listing 13-3. Illustrating a Case of Bad void Pointer Deletion

```cpp
//: C13:BadVoidPointerDeletion.cpp
// Deleting void pointers can cause memory leaks
#include <iostream>
using namespace std;

class Object {
  void *data;      // Some storage
  const int size;
  const char id;

public:

  Object(int sz, char c) : size(sz), id(c) {
    data = new char[size];
    cout << "Constructing object " << id
         << ", size = " << size << endl;
  }

  ~Object() {
    cout << "Destructing object " << id << endl;
    delete []data; // OK, just releases storage,
    // no destructor calls are necessary
  }
};

int main() {
  Object* a = new Object(40, 'a');
  delete a;
  void* b = new Object(40, 'b');
  delete b;
} ///:~
```

The class Object contains a void* that is initialized to "raw" data (*it doesn't point to objects that have destructors*). In the Object destructor, delete is called for this void* with no ill effects, since the only thing you need to happen is for the storage to be released.

However, in main() you can see that it's very necessary that delete know what type of object it's working with. Here's the output:

```
Constructing object a, size = 40
Destructing object a
Constructing object b, size = 40
```

Because delete a knows that a points to an Object, the destructor is called and thus the storage allocated for data is released. However, if you manipulate an object through a void* as in the case of delete b, the only thing that happens is that the storage for the Object is released—but the destructor is not called so there is no release of the memory that data points to. When this program compiles, you probably won't see any warning messages; the compiler assumes you know what you're doing. So you get a very quiet memory leak.

If you have a memory leak in your program, search through all the delete statements and check the type of pointer being deleted. If it's a void* then you've probably found one source of your memory leak.

■ **Note** C++ provides ample other opportunities for memory leaks, however.

Cleanup Responsibility with Pointers

To make the Stash and Stack containers flexible (able to hold any type of object), they will hold void pointers. This means that when a pointer is returned from the Stash or Stack object, you must cast it to the proper type before using it; as seen previously, you must also cast it to the proper type before deleting it or you'll get a memory leak.

The other memory leak issue has to do with making sure that delete is actually called for each object pointer held in the container. The container cannot "own" the pointer because it holds it as a void* and thus cannot perform the proper cleanup. The user must be responsible for cleaning up the objects. This produces a serious problem if you add pointers to objects created on the stack and objects created on the heap to the same container because a delete-expression is unsafe for a pointer that hasn't been allocated on the heap. (*And when you fetch a pointer back from the container, how will you know where its object has been allocated?*) Thus, you must be sure that objects stored in the following versions of Stash and Stack are made only on the heap, either through careful programming or by creating classes that can only be built on the heap.

It's also important to make sure that the client programmer takes responsibility for cleaning up all the pointers in the container. You've seen in previous examples how the Stack class checks in its destructor that all the Link objects have been popped. For a Stash of pointers, however, another approach is needed.

Stash for Pointers

This new version of the Stash class, called PStash, holds *pointers* to objects that exist by themselves on the heap, whereas the old Stash in earlier chapters copied the objects by value into the Stash container. Using new and delete, it's easy and safe to hold pointers to objects that have been created on the heap. Listing 13-4 contains the header file for the "pointer Stash."

Listing 13-4. Header File for "pointer Stash"

```
//: C13:PStash.h
// Holds pointers instead of objects
#ifndef PSTASH_H
#define PSTASH_H

class PStash {
  int quantity; // Number of storage spaces
  int next;     // Next empty space
  // Pointer storage:
  void** storage;
  void inflate(int increase);
```

```
public:
  PStash() : quantity(0), storage(0), next(0) {}
  ~PStash();
  int add(void* element);
  void* operator[](int index) const; // Fetch
  // Remove the reference from this PStash:
  void* remove(int index);
  // Number of elements in Stash:
  int count() const { return next; }
};
#endif                             // PSTASH_H ///:~
```

The underlying data elements are fairly similar, but now storage is an array of void pointers, and the allocation of storage for that array is performed with new instead of malloc(). In the expression

```
void** st = new void*[quantity + increase];
```

the type of object allocated is a void*, so the expression allocates an array of void pointers.

The destructor deletes the storage where the void pointers are held rather than attempting to delete what they point at (which, as previously noted, will release their storage and not call the destructors because a void pointer has no type information).

The other change is the replacement of the fetch() function with operator[ ], which makes more sense syntactically. Again, however, a void* is returned, so the user must remember what types are stored in the container and cast the pointers when fetching them out (a problem that will be taken care of in the chapters to follow).

Listing 13-5 shows the member function definitions.

Listing 13-5. Implementation of "pointer Stash"

```
//: C13:PStash.cpp {0}
// Pointer Stash definitions
#include "PStash.h"                 // To be INCLUDED from above
#include "../require.h"
#include <iostream>
#include <cstring>                  // 'mem' functions
using namespace std;

int PStash::add(void* element) {
  const int inflateSize = 10;
  if(next >= quantity)
    inflate(inflateSize);
  storage[next++] = element;
  return(next - 1);                 // Index number
}

// No ownership:
PStash::~PStash() {
  for(int i = 0; i < next; i++)
    require(storage[i] == 0,
      "PStash not cleaned up");
  delete []storage;
}
```

```
// Operator overloading replacement for fetch
void* PStash::operator[](int index) const {
  require(index >= 0,
    "PStash::operator[] index negative");
  if(index >= next)
  return 0;              // To indicate the end
  // Produce pointer to desired element:
  return storage[index];
}

void* PStash::remove(int index) {
void* v = operator[](index);
  // "Remove" the pointer:
  if(v != 0) storage[index] = 0;
  return v;
}

void PStash::inflate(int increase) {
  const int psz = sizeof(void*);
  void** st = new void*[quantity + increase];
  memset(st, 0, (quantity + increase) * psz);
  memcpy(st, storage, quantity * psz);
  quantity += increase;
  delete []storage; // Old storage
  storage = st;      // Point to new memory
} ///:~
```

The add() function is effectively the same as before, except that a pointer is stored instead of a copy of the whole object.

The inflate() code is modified to handle the allocation of an array of void* instead of the previous design, which was only working with raw bytes. Here, instead of using the prior approach of copying by array indexing, the Standard C Library function memset() is first used to set all the new memory to zero (*this is not strictly necessary, since the PStash is presumably managing all the memory correctly—but it usually doesn't hurt to throw in a bit of extra care*). Then memcpy() moves the existing data from the old location to the new. Often, functions like memset() and memcpy() have been optimized over time, so they may be faster than the loops shown previously. But with a function like inflate()that will probably not be used that often you may not see a performance difference. However, the fact that the function calls are more concise than the loops may help prevent coding errors.

To put the responsibility of object cleanup squarely on the shoulders of the client programmer, there are two ways to access the pointers in the PStash: the operator[], which simply returns the pointer but leaves it as a member of the container, and a second member function called remove(), which returns the pointer but also removes it from the container by assigning that position to zero. When the destructor for PStash is called, it checks to make sure that all object pointers have been removed; if not, you're notified so you can prevent a memory leak (more elegant solutions will be forthcoming in the chapters to follow).

A Test

Listing 13-6 is the old test program for Stash rewritten for the PStash.

Listing 13-6. Test Program for "pointer Stash"

```
//: C13:PStashTest.cpp
//{L} PStash
// Test of pointer Stash
#include "PStash.h"
#include "../require.h"
#include <iostream>
#include <fstream>
#include <string>
using namespace std;

int main() {
  PStash intStash;
  // 'new' works with built-in types, too. Note
  // the "pseudo-constructor" syntax:
  for(int i = 0; i < 25; i++)
    intStash.add(new int(i));
  for(int j = 0; j < intStash.count(); j++)
    cout << "intStash[" << j << "] = "
         << *(int*)intStash[j] << endl;
  // Clean up:
  for(int k = 0; k < intStash.count(); k++)
    delete intStash.remove(k);
  ifstream in ("PStashTest.cpp");
  assure(in, "PStashTest.cpp");
  PStash stringStash;
  string line;
  while(getline(in, line))
    stringStash.add(new string(line));
  // Print out the strings:
  for(int u = 0; stringStash[u]; u++)
    cout << "stringStash[" << u << "] = "
         << *(string*)stringStash[u] << endl;
  // Clean up:
  for(int v = 0; v < stringStash.count(); v++)
    delete (string*)stringStash.remove(v);
} ///:~
```

As before, Stashes are created and filled with information, but this time the information is the pointers resulting from new-expressions. In the first case, note the line.

```
intStash.add(new int(i));
```

The expression new int(i) uses the pseudo-constructor form, so storage for a new int object is created on the heap, and the int is initialized to the value i.

During printing, the value returned by PStash::operator[ ] must be cast to the proper type; this is repeated for the rest of the PStash objects in the program. It's an undesirable effect of using void pointers as the underlying representation and will be fixed in later chapters.

The second test opens the source code file and reads it one line at a time into another PStash. Each line is read into a string using getline(), then a newstring is created from line to make an independent copy of that line. If you just passed in the address of line each time, you'd get a whole bunch of pointers pointing to line, which would only contain the last line that was read from the file.

When fetching the pointers, you see the expression.

```
*(string*)stringStash[v]
```

The pointer returned from operator[ ] must be cast to a string* to give it the proper type. Then the string* is dereferenced so the expression evaluates to an object, at which point the compiler sees a string object to send to cout.

The objects created on the heap must be destroyed through the use of the remove() statement or you'll get a message at runtime telling you that you haven't completely cleaned up the objects in the PStash. Notice that in the case of the int pointers, no cast is necessary because there's no destructor for an int and all you need is memory release, as in:

```
delete intStash.remove(k);
```

However, for the string pointers, if you forget to do the cast you'll have another (quiet) memory leak, so the cast is essential.

```
delete (string*)stringStash.remove(k);
```

Some of these issues (but not all) can be removed using templates (which you'll learn about in Chapter 16).

Using new and delete for Arrays

In C++, you can create arrays of objects on the stack or on the heap with equal ease, and (of course) the constructor is called for each object in the array. There's one constraint, however: there must be a default constructor, except for aggregate initialization on the stack (refer to Chapter 6), because a constructor with no arguments must be called for every object.

When creating arrays of objects on the heap using new, there's something else you must do. An example of such an array is

```
MyType* fp = new MyType[100];
```

This allocates enough storage on the heap for 100 MyType objects and calls the constructor for each one. Now, however, you simply have a MyType*, which is exactly the same as you'd get if you said

```
MyType* fp2 = new MyType;
```

to create a single object. Because you wrote the code, you know that fp is actually the starting address of an array, so it makes sense to select array elements using an expression like fp[3]. But what happens when you destroy the array? The statements

```
delete fp2; // OK
delete fp;  // Not the desired effect
```

look exactly the same, and their effect will be the same. The destructor will be called for the MyType object pointed to by the given address, and then the storage will be released. For fp2 this is fine, but for fp this means that the other 99 destructor calls won't be made. The proper amount of storage will still be released, however, because it is allocated in one big chunk, and the size of the whole chunk is stashed somewhere by the allocation routine.

The solution requires you to give the compiler the information that this is actually the starting address of an array. This is accomplished with the following syntax:

```
delete []fp;
```

The empty brackets tell the compiler to generate code that fetches the number of objects in the array, stored somewhere when the array is created, and calls the destructor for that many array objects. This is actually an improved syntax from the earlier form (which you may still occasionally see in old code); for example,

```
delete [100]fp;
```

forced the programmer to include the number of objects in the array and introduced the possibility that the programmer would get it wrong. The additional overhead of letting the compiler handle it was very low, and it was considered better to specify the number of objects in one place instead of two.

Making a Pointer More Like an Array

As an aside, the fp defined above can be changed to point to anything, which doesn't make sense for the starting address of an array. It makes more sense to define it as a constant, so any attempt to modify the pointer will be flagged as an error. To get this effect, you might try

```
int const *q = new int[10];
```

or

```
const int *q = new int[10];
```

but in both cases the const will bind to the int—that is, what is being pointed *to*, rather than the quality of the pointer itself. Instead, you must say

```
int* const q = new int[10];
```

Now the array elements in q can be modified, but any change to q (like q++) is illegal, as it is with an ordinary array identifier.

Running Out of Storage

What happens when the operator new() cannot find a contiguous block of storage large enough to hold the desired object? A special function called the *new*-handler is called. Or rather, a pointer to a function is checked, and if the pointer is nonzero, then the function it points to is called.

The default behavior for the new-handler is to throw an exception, a subject covered in Chapter 17. However, if you're using heap allocation in your program, it's wise to at least replace the new-handler with a message that says you've run out of memory and then aborts the program. That way, during debugging, you'll have a clue about what happened. For the final program you'll want to use more robust recovery.

You replace the new-handler by including new.h and then calling set_new_handler() with the address of the function you want installed; see Listing 13-7.

Listing 13-7. Handling a Case of Running Out of Memory

```
//: C13:NewHandler.cpp
// Changing the new-handler
#include <iostream>
#include <cstdlib>
#include <new>
using namespace std;

int count = 0;

void out_of_memory() {
  cerr << "memory exhausted after " << count
       << " allocations!" << endl;
exit(1);
}

int main() {
  set_new_handler(out_of_memory);
  while(1) {
    count++;
    new int[1000];
      // Exhausts memory
  }
} ///:~
```

The new-handler function must take no arguments and have a void return value. The while loop will keep allocating int objects (and throwing away their return addresses) until the free store is exhausted. At the very next call to new, no storage can be allocated, so the new-handler will be called.

The behavior of the new-handler is tied to operator new(), so if you overload operator new() (covered in the next section) the new-handler will not be called by default. If you still want the new-handler to be called you'll have to write the code to do so inside your overloaded operator new().

Of course, you can write more sophisticated new-handlers, even one to try to reclaim memory (commonly known as a *garbage collector*). This is not a job for the novice programmer.

Overloading new and delete

When you create a new-expression, two things occur. First, storage is allocated using the operator new(), then the constructor is called. In a delete-expression, the destructor is called, then storage is deallocated using the operator delete(). The constructor and destructor calls are never under your control (*otherwise you might accidentally subvert them*), but you can change the storage allocation functions operator new() and operator delete().

The memory allocation system used by new and delete is designed for general-purpose use. In special situations, however, it doesn't serve your needs. The most common reason to change the allocator is efficiency: you might be creating and destroying so many objects of a particular class that it has become a speed bottleneck. C++ allows you to overload new and delete to implement your own storage allocation scheme, so you can handle problems like this.

Another issue is heap fragmentation. By allocating objects of different sizes it's possible to break up the heap so that you effectively run out of storage. That is, the storage might be available, but because of fragmentation no piece is big enough to satisfy your needs. By creating your own allocator for a particular class, you can ensure this never happens.

In embedded and real-time systems, a program may have to run for a very long time with restricted resources. Such a system may also require that memory allocation always take the same amount of time, and there's no allowance for heap exhaustion or fragmentation. A custom memory allocator is the solution; otherwise, programmers will avoid using new and delete altogether in such cases and miss out on a valuable C++ asset.

When you overload operator new() and operator delete(), it's important to remember that you're changing only the way raw storage is *allocated*. The compiler will simply call your new instead of the default version to allocate storage, *then* call the constructor for that storage. So, although the compiler allocates storage *and* calls the constructor when it sees new, all you can change when you overload new is the storage allocation portion. (delete *has a similar limitation.*)

When you overload operator new(), you also replace the behavior when it runs out of memory, so you must decide what to do in your operator new(): return zero, write a loop to call the new-handler and retry allocation, or (*typically*) throw a bad_alloc exception.

Overloading new and delete is like overloading any other operator. However, you have a choice of overloading the global allocator or using a different allocator for a particular class.

Overloading Global new and delete

This is the drastic approach, when the global versions of new and delete are unsatisfactory for the whole system. If you overload the global versions, you make the defaults completely inaccessible—you can't even call them from inside your redefinitions.

The overloaded new must take an argument of size_t (the Standard C standard type for sizes). This argument is generated and passed to you by the compiler and is the size of the object you're responsible for allocating. You must return a pointer either to an object of that size (or bigger, if you have some reason to do so), or to zero if you can't find the memory (in which case the constructor is *not* called!). However, if you can't find the memory, you should probably do something more informative than just returning zero, like calling the new-handler or throwing an exception, to signal that there's a problem.

The return value of operator new() is a void*, *not* a pointer to any particular type. All you've done is produce memory, not a finished object—that doesn't happen until the constructor is called, an act the compiler guarantees and which is out of your control.

The operator delete() takes a void* to memory that was allocated by operator new(). It's a void* because operator delete() only gets the pointer after the destructor is called, which removes the object-*ness* from the piece of storage. The return type is void.

See Listing 13-8 for a simple example showing how to overload the global new and delete.

Listing 13-8. Overloading the Global new and delete

```
//: C13:GlobalOperatorNew.cpp
// Overload global new/delete
#include <cstdio>
#include <cstdlib>
using namespace std;

void* operator new(size_t sz) {
  printf("operator new: %d Bytes\n", sz);
  void* m = malloc(sz);
 if(!m) puts("out of memory");
 return m;
}
```

```
void operator delete(void* m) {
  puts("operator delete");
  free(m);
}

class S {
  int i[100];
public:
  S() { puts("S::S()"); }
  ~S() { puts("S::~S()"); }
};

int main() {
  puts("creating & destroying an int");
  int* p = new int(47);
  delete p;
  puts("creating & destroying an s");
  S *s = new S;
  delete s;
  puts("creating & destroying S[3]");
  S *sa = new S[3];
  delete []sa;
} ///:~
```

Here you can see the general form for overloading new and delete. These use the Standard C Library functions malloc() and free() for the allocators (*which is probably what the default* new *and* delete *use as well!*). However, they also print messages about what they are doing. Notice that printf() and puts() are used rather than iostream. This is because when an iostream object is created (like the global cin, cout, and cerr), it calls new to allocate memory. With printf(), you don't get into a deadlock because it doesn't call new to initialize itself.

In main(), objects of built-in types are created to prove that the overloaded new and delete are also called in that case. Then a single object of type S is created, followed by an array of S. For the array, you'll see from the number of bytes requested that extra memory is allocated to store information (*inside the array*) about the number of objects it holds. In all cases, the global overloaded versions of new and delete are used.

Overloading new and delete for a Class

Although you don't have to explicitly say static, when you overload new and delete for a class, you're creating static member functions. As before, the syntax is the same as overloading any other operator. When the compiler sees you use new to create an object of your class, it chooses the member operator new() over the global version. However, the global versions of new and delete are used for all other types of objects (*unless* they have their own new and delete).

In Listing 13-9, a primitive storage allocation system is created for the class Framis. A chunk of memory is set aside in the static data area at program startup, and that memory is used to allocate space for objects of type Framis. To determine which blocks have been allocated, a simple array of bytes is used, one byte for each block.

Listing 13-9. Overloading the Local (for a Class) new and delete

```
//: C13:Framis.cpp
// Local overloaded new & delete
#include <cstddef>          // Size_t
#include <fstream>
#include <iostream>
#include <new>
using namespace std;
ofstream out("Framis.out");

class Framis {
  enum { sz = 10 };
  char c[sz];               // To take up space, not used
  static unsigned char pool[];
  static bool alloc_map[];
public:
  enum { psize = 100 };     // framis allowed
  Framis() { out << "Framis()\n"; }
  ~Framis() { out << "~Framis() ... "; }
  void* operator new(size_t) throw(bad_alloc);
  void operator delete(void*);
};
unsigned char Framis::pool[psize * sizeof(Framis)];
bool Framis::alloc_map[psize] = {false};

// Size is ignored -- assume a Framis object
void*
Framis::operator new(size_t) throw(bad_alloc) {
  for(int i = 0; i < psize; i++)
    if(!alloc_map[i]) {
      out << "using block " << i << " ... ";
      alloc_map[i] = true; // Mark it used
      return pool + (i * sizeof(Framis));
    }
  out << "out of memory" << endl;
  throw bad_alloc();
}

void Framis::operator delete(void* m) {
  if(!m) return;            // Check for null pointer
  // Assume it was created in the pool
  // Calculate which block number it is:
  unsigned long block = (unsigned long)m
    - (unsigned long)pool;
  block /= sizeof(Framis);
  out << "freeing block " << block << endl;
  // Mark it free:
  alloc_map[block] = false;
}
```

```
int main() {
  Framis *f[Framis::psize];
  try {
    for(int i = 0; i < Framis::psize; i++)
      f[i] = new Framis;
    new Framis;  // Out of memory
  } catch(bad_alloc) {
    cerr << "Out of memory!" << endl;
  }
  delete f[10];
  f[10] = 0;
  // Use released memory:
  Framis *x = new Framis;
  delete x;
  for(int j = 0; j < Framis::psize; j++)
    delete f[j]; // Delete f[10] OK
} ///:~
```

The pool of memory for the Framis heap is created by allocating an array of bytes large enough to hold psize Framis objects. The allocation map is psize elements long, so there's one bool for every block. All the values in the allocation map are initialized to false using the aggregate initialization trick of setting the first element so the compiler automatically initializes all the rest to their normal default value (which is false, in the case of bool).

The local operator new() has the same syntax as the global one. All it does is search through the allocation map looking for a false value, then sets that location to true to indicate it's been allocated and returns the address of the corresponding memory block. If it can't find any memory, it issues a message to the trace file and throws a bad_alloc exception.

This is the first example of exceptions that you've seen in this book. Since detailed discussion of exceptions is delayed until Chapter 17, this is a very simple use of them. In operator new() there are two artifacts of exception handling. First, the function argument list is followed by throw(bad_alloc), which tells the compiler and the reader that this function may throw an exception of type bad_alloc. Second, if there's no more memory, the function actually does throw the exception in the statement throw bad_alloc. When an exception is thrown, the function stops executing and control is passed to an exception handler, which is expressed as a catch clause.

In main(), you see the other part of the picture, which is the try-catch clause. The try block is surrounded by braces and contains all the code that may throw exceptions—in this case, any call to new that involves Framis objects. Immediately following the try block is one or more catch clauses, each one specifying the type of exception that they catch. In this case, catch(bad_alloc) says that that bad_alloc exceptions will be caught here. This particular catch clause is only executed when a bad_alloc exception is thrown, and execution continues after the end of the last catch clause in the group (*there's only one here, but there could be more*).

In this example, it's okay to use iostream because the global operator new() and delete() are untouched.

The operator delete() assumes the Framis address was created in the pool. This is a fair assumption, because the local operator new() will be called whenever you create a single Framis object on the heap—but not an array of them: global new is used for arrays. So the user might accidentally have called operator delete() without using the empty bracket syntax to indicate array destruction. This would cause a problem. Also, the user might be deleting a pointer to an object created on the stack. If you think these things could occur, you might want to add a line to make sure the address is within the pool and on a correct boundary.

■ **Note**   You may also begin to see the potential of overloaded new and delete for finding memory leaks.

---

operator delete() calculates the block in the pool that this pointer represents, and then sets the allocation map's flag for that block to false to indicate the block has been released.

In main(), enough Framis objects are dynamically allocated to run out of memory; this checks the out-of-memory behavior. Then one of the objects is freed, and another one is created to show that the released memory is reused.

Because this allocation scheme is specific to Framis objects, it's probably much faster than the general-purpose memory allocation scheme used for the default new and delete. However, you should note that it doesn't automatically work if *inheritance* is used (inheritance is covered in Chapter 14).

Overloading new and delete for Arrays

If you overload operators new() and delete() for a class, those operators are called whenever you create an object of that class. However, if you create an array of those class objects, the global operator new() is called to allocate enough storage for the array all at once, and the global operator delete() is called to release that storage. You can control the allocation of arrays of objects by overloading the special array versions of operator new[ ] and operator delete[ ] for the class. See Listing 13-10 for an example of two different versions being called.

Listing 13-10. Using operator new() for Arrays

```
//: C13:ArrayOperatorNew.cpp
// Operator new for arrays
#include <new> // Size_t definition
#include <fstream>
using namespace std;
ofstream trace("ArrayOperatorNew.out");

class Widget {
  enum { sz = 10 };
  int i[sz];
public:
  Widget() { trace << "*"; }
  ~Widget() { trace << "~"; }
  void* operator new(size_tsz) {
    trace << "Widget::new: "
          << sz << " bytes" << endl;
    return ::new char[sz];
  }
  void operator delete(void* p) {
    trace << "Widget::delete" << endl;
    ::delete []p;
  }
  void* operator new[](size_tsz) {
    trace << "Widget::new[]: "
          << sz << " bytes" << endl;
    return ::new char[sz];
  }
  void operator delete[](void* p) {
    trace << "Widget::delete[]" << endl;
    ::delete []p;
  }
};
```

```
int main() {
  trace << "new Widget" << endl;
  Widget *w = new Widget;
  trace << "\ndelete Widget" << endl;
  delete w;
  trace << "\n new Widget[25]" << endl;
  Widget *wa = new Widget[25];
  trace << "\n delete []Widget" << endl;
  delete []wa;
} ///:~
```

Here, the global versions of new and delete are called so the effect is the same as having no overloaded versions of new and delete except that trace information is added. Of course, you can use any memory allocation scheme you want in the overloaded new and delete.

You can see that the syntax of array new and delete is the same as for the individual object versions except for the addition of the brackets. In both cases, you're handed the size of the memory you must allocate. The size handed to the array version will be the size of the entire array. It's worth keeping in mind that the only thing the overloaded operator new() is required to do is hand back a pointer to a large enough memory block. Although you may perform initialization on that memory, normally that's the job of the constructor that will automatically be called for your memory by the compiler.

The constructor and destructor simply print out characters so you can see when they've been called. Here's what the trace file looks like for one compiler:

```
new Widget
Widget::new: 40 bytes
*
delete Widget
~Widget::delete

new Widget[25]
Widget::new[]: 1004 bytes
************************
delete []Widget
~~~~~~~~~~~~~~~~~~~~~~~~~Widget::delete[]
```

Creating an individual object requires 40 bytes, as you might expect.

■ **Note**   This computer uses four bytes for an int.

The operator new() is called, then the constructor (indicated by the*). In a complementary fashion, calling delete causes the destructor to be called, then the operator delete().

When an array of Widget objects is created, the array version of operator new() is used, as promised. But notice that the size requested is four more bytes than expected. This extra four bytes is where the system keeps information about the array, in particular, the number of objects in the array. That way, when you say

```
delete []Widget;
```

the brackets tell the compiler it's an array of objects, so the compiler generates code to look for the number of objects in the array and to call the destructor that many times. You can see that, even though the array `operator new()` and `operator delete()` are only called once for the entire array chunk, the default constructor and destructor are called for each object in the array.

Constructor Calls

Considering that

```
MyType *f = new MyType;
```

calls new to allocate a MyType-sized piece of storage, then invokes the MyType constructor on that storage, what happens if the storage allocation in new fails? The constructor is not called in that case, so although you still have an unsuccessfully created object, at least you haven't invoked the constructor and handed it a zero this pointer. Listing 13-11 proves it.

Listing 13-11. Illustrating that the Constructor Doesn't Come into Play in Case new Fails

```cpp
//: C13:NoMemory.cpp
// Constructor isn't called if new fails
#include <iostream>
#include <new>
        // bad_alloc definition
using namespace std;

class NoMemory {

public:
  NoMemory() {
    cout << "NoMemory::NoMemory()" << endl;
  }
void* operator new(size_tsz) throw(bad_alloc){
    cout << "NoMemory::operator new" << endl;
    throw bad_alloc(); // "Out of memory"
  }
};

int main() {
  NoMemory *nm = 0;
  try {
    nm = new NoMemory;
  } catch(bad_alloc) {
    cerr << "Out of memory exception" << endl;
  }
  cout << "nm = " << nm << endl;
} ///:~
```

When the program runs, it does not print the constructor message, only the message from operator new() and the message in the exception handler. Because new never returns, the constructor is never called so its message is not printed.

It's important that nm be initialized to zero because the new expression never completes, and the pointer should be zero to make sure you don't misuse it. However, you should actually do more in the exception handler than just print out a message and continue on as if the object had been successfully created. Ideally, you will do something that will cause the program to recover from the problem, or at the least exit after logging an error.

In earlier versions of C++, it was standard practice to return zero from new if storage allocation failed. That would prevent construction from occurring. However, if you try to return zero from new with a Standard-conforming compiler, it should tell you that you ought to throw bad_alloc instead.

Placing new and delete

There are two other, less common, uses for overloading operator new().

1. You may want to place an object in a specific location in memory. This is especially important with hardware-oriented embedded systems where an object may be synonymous with a particular piece of hardware.

2. You may want to be able to choose from different allocators when calling new.

Both of these situations are solved with the same mechanism: the overloaded operator new() can take more than one argument.

As you've seen before, the first argument is always the size of the object, which is secretly calculated and passed by the compiler. But the other arguments can be anything you want: the address you want the object placed at, a reference to a memory allocation function or object, or anything else that is convenient for you.

The way that you pass the extra arguments to operator new() during a call may seem slightly curious at first. You put the argument list (*without* the size_t argument, which is handled by the compiler) after the keyword new and before the class name of the object you're creating. For example,

```
X* xp = new(a) X;
```

will pass a as the second argument to operator new(). Of course, this can work only if such an operator new() has been declared.

See Listing 13-12 for an example showing how you can place an object at a particular location.

Listing 13-12. Illustrating a Case of Placement with operator new()

```
//: C13:PlacementOperatorNew.cpp
// Placement with operator new()
#include <cstddef> // Size_t
#include <iostream>
using namespace std;

class X {
  int i;
public:
  X(int ii = 0) : i(ii) {
    cout << "this = " << this << endl;
  }
```

```
  ~X() {
    cout << "X::~X(): " << this << endl;
  }
  void* operator new(size_t, void* loc) {
    return loc;
  }
};

int main() {
  int l[10];
  cout << "l = " << l << endl;
  X *xp = new(l) X(47); // X at location l
  xp->X::~X();          // Explicit destructor call
  // ONLY use with placement!
} ///:~
```

Notice that operator new() only returns the pointer that's passed to it. Thus, the caller decides where the object is going to sit, and the constructor is called for that memory as part of the new-expression.

Although this example shows only one additional argument, there's nothing to prevent you from adding more if you need them for other purposes.

A dilemma occurs when you want to destroy the object. There's only one version of operator delete(), so there's no way to say, "Use my special *deallocator* for this object." You want to call the destructor, but you don't want the memory to be released by the dynamic memory mechanism because it wasn't allocated on the heap.

The answer is a very special syntax. You can explicitly call the destructor, as in

```
xp->X::~X();              // Explicit destructor call
```

A stern warning is in order here. Some people see this as a way to destroy objects at some time before the end of the scope, rather than either adjusting the scope or (*more correctly*) using dynamic object creation if they want the object's lifetime to be determined at runtime.

You will have serious problems if you call the destructor this way for an ordinary object created on the stack because the destructor will be called again at the end of the scope. If you call the destructor this way for an object that was created on the heap, the destructor will execute, but the memory won't be released, which probably isn't what you want. The only reason that the destructor can be called explicitly this way is to support the placement syntax for operator new.

There's also a placement operator delete() that is only called if a constructor for a placement new expression throws an exception (*so that the memory is automatically cleaned up during the exception*). The placement operator delete() has an argument list that corresponds to the placement operator new() that is called before the constructor throws the exception.

This topic will be explored in Chapter 17 on exception handling.

Review Session

1. It's *convenient* and *optimally efficient* to create automatic objects on the stack, but to solve the general programming problem you must be able to create and destroy objects at *any time* during a program's execution, particularly to respond to information from outside the program.

2. Although C's dynamic memory allocation will get storage from the heap, it doesn't provide the ease of use and guaranteed construction necessary in C++. By bringing *dynamic object creation* into the core of the language with new and delete, you can create objects on the heap as easily as making them on the stack.

3. In addition, you get a great deal of *flexibility*. You can change the behavior of new and delete if they don't suit your needs, particularly if they aren't efficient enough.

4. Also, you can modify what happens when the heap runs out of storage.

CHAPTER 14

■ ■ ■

Inheritance and Composition

One of the most compelling features about C++ is code reuse. But to be revolutionary, you need to be able to do a lot more than copy code and change it.

As with most everything in C++, the solution revolves around the class. You reuse code by creating new classes, but instead of creating them from scratch, you use existing classes that someone else has built and debugged.

The trick is to use the classes without *modifying* the existing code. In this chapter, you'll see two ways to accomplish this. The first is quite straightforward: you simply create objects of your existing class inside the new class. This is called composition because the new class is composed of objects of existing classes.

The second approach is more subtle. You create a new class as a type of an existing class. You literally take the form of the existing class and add code to it, without modifying the existing class. This magical act is called *inheritance*, and most of the work is done by the compiler. Inheritance is one of the cornerstones of object-oriented programming and has additional implications that will be explored in the next chapter.

It turns out that much of the syntax and behavior are similar for both composition and inheritance (*which makes sense; they are both ways of making new types from existing types*). In this chapter, you'll learn about these code reuse mechanisms.

Composition Syntax

Actually, you've been using composition all along to create classes. You've just been composing classes primarily with built-in types (*and* sometimes `strings`). It turns out to be almost as easy to use composition with user-defined types. Consider Listing 14-1, which shows a class that is valuable for some reason.

Listing 14-1. A Valuable and Useful Reusable Class

```
//: C14:Useful.h
// A class to reuse
#ifndef USEFUL_H
#define USEFUL_H

class X {
  int i;
public:
  X() { i = 0; }
  void set(int ii) { i = ii; }
  int read() const { return i; }
  int permute() { return i = i * 47; }
};
#endif // USEFUL_H ///:~
```

The data members are private in this class, so it's completely safe to embed an object of type X as a public object in a new class, which makes the *interface* straightforward, as you can see in Listing 14-2.

Listing 14-2. Reusing Code with Composition

```
//: C14:Composition.cpp
// Reuse code with composition
#include "Useful.h" // To be INCLUDED from Header FILE above

class Y {
  int i;
public:
  X x;                // Embedded object
  Y() { i = 0; }
  void f(int ii) { i = ii; }
  int g() const { return i; }
};

int main() {
  Y y;
  y.f(47);
  y.x.set(37);        // Access the embedded object
} ///:~
```

Accessing the member functions of the embedded object (referred to as a *subobject*) simply requires another member selection.

It's more common to make the embedded objects private, so they become part of the underlying implementation (which means you can *change* the implementation if you want). The public interface functions for your new class then involve the use of the embedded object, but they don't necessarily mimic the object's interface; see Listing 14-3.

Listing 14-3. A Composition with Private Embedded Objects

```
//: C14:Composition2.cpp
// Private embedded objects
#include "Useful.h"

class Y {
  int i;
  X x;                // Embedded object
public:
  Y() { i = 0; }
  void f(int ii) { i = ii; x.set(ii); }
  int g() const { return i * x.read(); }
  void permute() { x.permute(); }
};

int main() {
  Y y;
  y.f(47);
  y.permute();
} ///:~
```

Here, the permute( ) function is carried through to the new class interface, but the other member functions of X are used within the members of Y.

Inheritance Syntax

The syntax for composition is obvious, but to perform inheritance there's a new and different form.

When you inherit, you are saying, "This new class is like that old class." You state this in code by giving the name of the class as usual, but before the opening brace of the class body, you put a colon and the name of the *base class* (or *base classes*, separated by commas, for multiple inheritance). When you do this, you automatically get all the data members and member functions in the *base class*. Listing 14-4 shows an example.

Listing 14-4. Illustrating Simple Inheritance

```
//: C14:Inheritance.cpp
// Simple inheritance
#include "Useful.h"
#include <iostream>
using namespace std;

class Y : public X {
  int i;            // Different from X's i
public:
  Y() { i = 0; }
  int change() {
    i = permute(); // Different name call
    return i;
  }
  void set(int ii) {
    i = ii;
    X::set(ii);     // Same-name function call
  }
};

int main() {
  cout << "sizeof(X) = " << sizeof(X) << endl;
  cout << "sizeof(Y) = "
       << sizeof(Y) << endl;
  Y D;
  D.change();
  // X function interface comes through:
  D.read();
  D.permute();
  // Redefined functions hide base versions:
  D.set(12);
} ///:~
```

You can see Y being inherited from X, which means that Y will contain all the data elements in X and all the member functions in X. In fact, Y contains a subobject of X just as if you had created a member object of X inside Y instead of inheriting from X. Both member objects and base class storage are referred to as subobjects.

All the private elements of X are still private in Y; that is, just because Y inherits from X doesn't mean Y can break the protection mechanism. The private elements of X are still there, they take up space—you just can't access them directly.

In main() you can see that Y's data elements are combined with X's because the sizeof(Y) is twice as big as sizeof(X).

You'll notice that the base class is preceded by public. During inheritance, everything defaults to private. If the base class were not preceded by public, it would mean that all of the public members of the base class would be private in the derived class. This is almost never what you want; the desired result is to keep all the public members of the base class public in the derived class. You do this by using the public keyword during inheritance.

In change(), the base class permute() function is called. The derived class has direct access to all the public base class functions.

The set() function in the derived class redefines the set() function in the base class. That is, if you call the functions read() and permute() for an object of type Y, you'll get the base class versions of those functions (you can see this happen inside main()). But if you call set() for a Y object, you get the redefined version. This means that if you don't like the version of a function you get during inheritance, you can change what it does.

■ **Note** You can also add completely new functions like change().

However, when you're redefining a function, you may still want to call the base class version. If, inside set(), you simply call set() you'll get the local version of the function—a recursive function call. To call the base class version, you must explicitly name the base class using the scope resolution operator.

The Constructor Initializer List

You've seen how important it is in C++ to guarantee proper initialization, and it's no different during composition and inheritance. When an object is created, the compiler guarantees that constructors for all of its subobjects are called. In the examples so far, all of the subobjects have default constructors, and that's what the compiler automatically calls. But what happens if your subobjects don't have default constructors, or if you want to change a default argument in a constructor? This is a problem because the new class constructor doesn't have permission to access the private data elements of the subobject, so it can't initialize them directly.

The solution is simple: call the constructor for the subobject. C++ provides a special syntax for this, *the constructor initializer list*. The form of the constructor initializer list echoes the act of inheritance. With inheritance, you put the base classes after a colon and before the opening brace of the class body. In the constructor initializer list, you put the calls to subobject constructors after the constructor argument list and a colon, but before the opening brace of the function body. For a class MyType, inherited from Bar, this might look like

```
MyType::MyType(inti) : Bar(i) { // ...
```

if Bar has a constructor that takes a single int argument.

Member Object Initialization

It turns out that you use this very same syntax for member object initialization when using composition. For composition, you give the names of the objects instead of the class names. If you have more than one constructor call in the initializer list, you separate the calls with commas, as in:

```
MyType2::MyType2(int i) : Bar(i), m(i+1) { // ...
```

This is the beginning of a constructor for class MyType2, which is inherited from Bar and contains a member object called m. Note that while you can see the type of the base class in the constructor initializer list, you only see the member object identifier.

Built-in Types in the Initializer List

The constructor initializer list allows you to explicitly call the constructors for member objects. In fact, there's no other way to call those constructors. The idea is that the constructors are all called before you get into the body of the new class's constructor. That way, any calls you make to member functions of subobjects will always go to initialized objects. There's no way to get to the opening brace of the constructor without some constructor being called for all the member objects and base-class objects, even if the compiler must make a hidden call to a default constructor. This is a further enforcement of the C++ guarantee that no object (*or* part of an object) can get out of the starting gate without its constructor being called.

This idea that all of the member objects are initialized by the time the opening brace of the constructor is reached is a convenient programming aid as well. Once you hit the opening brace, you can assume all subobjects are properly initialized and focus on specific tasks you want to accomplish in the constructor. However, there's a hitch: what about member objects of built-in types, which don't have constructors?

To make the syntax consistent, you are allowed to treat built-in types as if they have a single constructor, which takes a single argument: a variable of the same type as the variable you're initializing, as shown in Listing 14-5.

Listing 14-5. Demonstrating Pseudo-constructor

```
//: C14:PseudoConstructor.cpp
class X {
  int i;
  float f;
  char c;
  char *s;
public:
  X() : i(7), f(1.4), c('x'), s("howdy") {}
};
int main() {
  X x;
  int i(100);  // Applied to ordinary definition
  int* ip = new int(47);
} ///:~
```

The action of these "pseudo-constructor calls" is to perform a simple assignment. It's a convenient technique and a good coding style, so you'll see it used often.

It's even possible to use the pseudo-constructor syntax when creating a variable of a built-in type outside of a class, as in:

```
int i(100);
int* ip = new int(47);
```

This makes built-in types act a little bit more like objects. Remember, though, that these are not real constructors. In particular, if you don't explicitly make a pseudo-constructor call, no initialization is performed.

Combining Composition and Inheritance

Of course, you can use composition and inheritance together. Listing 14-6 shows the creation of a more complex class using both of them.

Listing 14-6. Illustrating Combined Composition and Inheritance

```
//: C14:Combined.cpp
// Inheritance & composition

class A {
  int i;
public:
  A(int ii) : i(ii) {}
  ~A() {}
  void f() const {}
};

class B {
  int i;
public:
  B(int ii) : i(ii) {}
  ~B() {}
  void f() const {}
};

class C : public B {
  A a;
public:
  C(int ii) : B(ii), a(ii) {}
  ~C() {} // Calls ~A() and ~B()
  void f() const {  // Redefinition
    a.f();
    B::f();
  }
};

int main() {
  C c(47);
} ///:~
```

C inherits from B and has a member object ("is composed of") of type A. You can see the constructor initializer list contains calls to both the base class constructor and the member-object constructor.

The function C::f() redefines B::f(), which it inherits, and also calls the base class version. In addition, it calls a.f(). Notice that the only time you can talk about redefinition of functions is during inheritance; with a member object you can only manipulate the public interface of the object, not redefine it. In addition, calling f() for an object of class C would not call a.f() if C::f() had not been defined, whereas it would call B::f().

Automatic Destructor Calls

Although you are often required to make explicit constructor calls in the initializer list, you never need to make explicit destructor calls because there's only one destructor for any class, and it doesn't take any arguments. However, the compiler still ensures that all destructors are called, and that means all of the destructors in the entire hierarchy, starting with the most-derived destructor and working back to the root.

It's worth emphasizing that constructors and destructors are quite unusual in that *everyone in the hierarchy* is called, whereas with a normal member function only that function is called, but not any of the base class versions. If you also want to call the base class version of a normal member function that you're overriding, you must do it explicitly.

Order of Constructor and Destructor Calls

It's interesting to know the order of constructor and destructor calls when an object has many subobjects. Listing 14-7 shows exactly how it works.

Listing 14-7. Demonstrating Order of Constructor/Destructor Calls

```
//: C14:Order.cpp
// Constructor/destructor order
#include <fstream>
using namespace std;
ofstream out("order.out");

#define CLASS(ID) class ID { \
public: \
  ID(int) { out << #ID " constructor\n"; } \
  ~ID() { out << #ID " destructor\n"; } \
};

CLASS(Base1);
CLASS(Member1);
CLASS(Member2);
CLASS(Member3);
CLASS(Member4);

class Derived1 : public Base1 {
  Member1 m1;
  Member2 m2;
public:
  Derived1(int) : m2(1), m1(2), Base1(3) {
    out << "Derived1 constructor\n";
  }
  ~Derived1() {
    out << "Derived1 destructor\n";
  }
};

class Derived2 : public Derived1 {
  Member3 m3;
  Member4 m4;
```

```
public:
  Derived2() : m3(1), Derived1(2), m4(3) {
    out << "Derived2 constructor\n";
  }
  ~Derived2() {
    out << "Derived2 destructor\n";
  }
};

int main() {
  Derived2 d2;
} ///:~
```

First, an ofstream object is created to send all the output to a file. Then, to save some typing and demonstrate a macro technique that will be replaced by a much improved technique in Chapter 16, a macro is created to build some of the classes, which are then used in inheritance and composition. Each of the constructors and destructors report themselves to the trace file. Note that the constructors are not default constructors; they each have an int argument. The argument itself has no identifier; the only reason for its existence is to force you to explicitly call the constructors in the initializer list.

■ **Note**   Eliminating the identifier prevents compiler warning messages.

The output of this program is

```
Base1 constructor
Member1 constructor
Member2 constructor
Derived1 constructor
Member3 constructor
Member4 constructor
Derived2 constructor
Derived2 destructor
Member4 destructor
Member3 destructor
Derived1 destructor
Member2 destructor
Member1 destructor
Base1 destructor
```

You can see that construction starts at the very root of the class hierarchy, and that at each level the base class constructor is called first, followed by the member object constructors. The destructors are called in exactly the reverse order of the constructors— this is important because of potential dependencies (in the derived-class constructor or destructor, you must be able to assume that the base-class subobject is still available for use, and has already been constructed—or not destroyed yet).

It's also interesting that the order of constructor calls for member objects is completely unaffected by the order of the calls in the constructor initializer list. The order is determined by the order that the member objects are declared in the class. If you could change the order of constructor calls via the constructor initializer list, you could have two different call sequences in two different constructors, but the poor destructor wouldn't know how to properly reverse the order of the calls for destruction, and you could end up with a dependency problem.

Name Hiding

If you inherit a class and provide a new definition for one of its member functions, there are two possibilities. The first is that you provide the exact signature and return type in the derived class definition as in the base class definition. This is called *redefining* for ordinary member functions and *overriding* when the base class member function is a virtual function (virtual functions are the normal case, and will be covered in detail in Chapter 15). But what happens if you change the member function argument list or return type in the derived class? See Listing 14-8.

Listing 14-8. Illustrating Hiding of Overloaded Names (during Inheritance)

```cpp
//: C14:NameHiding.cpp
// Hiding overloaded names during inheritance
#include <iostream>
#include <string>
using namespace std;

class Base {
public:
  int f() const {
    cout << "Base::f()\n";
    return 1;
  }
  int f(string) const { return 1; }
  void g() {}
};

class Derived1 : public Base {
public:
  void g() const {}
};

class Derived2 : public Base {
public:
  // Redefinition:
  int f() const {
    cout << "Derived2::f()\n";
    return 2;
  }
};

class Derived3 : public Base {
public:
  // Change return type:
  void f() const { cout << "Derived3::f()\n"; }
};
```

```cpp
class Derived4 : public Base {
public:
  // Change argument list:
  int f(int) const {
    cout << "Derived4::f()\n";
    return 4;
  }
};

int main() {
string s("hello");
  Derived1 d1;
  int x = d1.f();
  d1.f(s);
  Derived2 d2;
  x = d2.f();
//!  d2.f(s);     // string version hidden
  Derived3 d3;
//!  x = d3.f(); // return int version hidden
  x = d3.g();
  Derived4 d4;
//!  x = d4.f(); // f() version hidden
 x = d4.f(1);
} ///:~
```

In Base you see an overloaded function f(), and Derived1 doesn't make any changes to f() but it does redefine g(). In main(), you can see that both overloaded versions of f() are available in Derived1. However, Derived2 redefines one overloaded version of f() but not the other, and the result is that the second overloaded form is unavailable. In Derived3, changing the return type hides both the base class versions, and Derived4 shows that changing the argument list also hides both the base class versions. In general, anytime you redefine an overloaded function name from the base class, all the other versions are automatically hidden in the new class. In Chapter 15, you'll see that the addition of the virtual keyword affects function overloading a bit more.

If you change the interface of the base class by modifying the signature and/or return type of a member function from the base class, then you're using the class in a different way than inheritance is normally intended to support. It doesn't necessarily mean you're doing it wrong, it's just that the ultimate goal of inheritance is to support polymorphism, and if you change the function signature or return type, then you are actually changing the interface of the base class. If this is what you have intended to do, then you are using inheritance primarily to reuse code, and not to maintain the common interface of the base class (which is an essential aspect of *polymorphism*). In general, when you use inheritance this way it means you're taking a general-purpose class and specializing it for a particular need, which is usually, but not always, considered the realm of composition.

For example, consider the Stack class from Chapter 9. One of the problems with that class is that you had to perform a cast every time you fetched a pointer from the container. This is not only tedious, it's unsafe; you could cast the pointer to anything you want. An approach that seems better at first glance is to *specialize* the general Stack class using inheritance. See Listing 14-9 for an example that uses the class from Chapter 9.

Listing 14-9. Specializing the General Stack class Using Inheritance

```cpp
//: C14:InheritStack.cpp
// Specializing the Stack class
#include "../C09/Stack4.h"    // Refer Chapter 9
#include "../require.h"       // To be INCLUDED from Chapter 9
#include <iostream>
```

```
#include <fstream>
#include <string>
using namespace std;

class StringStack : public Stack {
public:
  void push(string* str) {
    Stack::push(str);
  }
  string* peek() const {
    return (string*)Stack::peek();
  }
  string* pop() {
    return (string*)Stack::pop();
  }
  ~StringStack() {
    string* top = pop();
    while(top) {
      delete top;
      top = pop();
    }
  }
};

int main() {
  ifstream in("InheritStack.cpp");
  assure(in, "InheritStack.cpp");
  string line;
  StringStack textlines;
  while(getline(in, line))
    textlines.push(new string(line));
  string* s;
  while((s = textlines.pop()) != 0) { // No cast!
    cout << *s << endl;
    delete s;
  }
} ///:~
```

Since all of the member functions in Stack4.h are inlines, nothing needs to be linked.

StringStack specializes Stack so that push() will accept only String pointers. Before, Stack would accept void pointers, so the user had no type checking to make sure the proper pointers were inserted. In addition, peek() and pop() now return String pointers instead of void pointers, so no cast is necessary to use the pointer.

Amazingly enough, this extra type-checking safety is free in push(), peek(), and pop()! The compiler is being given extra type information that it uses at compile-time, but the functions are inlined and no extra code is generated.

Name hiding comes into play here because, in particular, the push() function has a different signature: the argument list is different. If you had two versions of push() in the same class, that would be overloading, but in this case overloading is not what you want because that would still allow you to pass any kind of pointer into push() as a void*. Fortunately, C++ hides the push(void*) version in the base class in favor of the new version that's defined in the derived class, and therefore it only allows you to push()string pointers onto the StringStack.

Because you can now guarantee that you know exactly what kind of objects are in the container, the destructor works correctly and the ownership problem is solved—or at least, one approach to the ownership problem. Here, if you push() a string pointer onto the StringStack, then (according to the semantics of the StringStack) you're also passing ownership of that pointer to the StringStack. If you pop() the pointer, you not only get the pointer, but you also get ownership of that pointer. Any pointers that are left on the StringStack when its destructor is called are then deleted by that destructor. And since these are always string pointers and the delete statement is working on string pointers instead of void pointers, the proper destruction happens and everything works correctly.

There is a drawback: this class works *only* for string pointers. If you want a Stack that works with some other kind of object, you must write a new version of the class so that it works only with your new kind of object. This rapidly becomes tedious, and is finally solved using templates, as you will see in Chapter 16.

We can make an additional observation about this example: it changes the interface of the Stack in the process of inheritance. If the interface is different, then a StringStack really isn't a Stack, and you will never be able to correctly use a StringStack as a Stack. This makes the use of inheritance questionable here; if you're not creating a StringStack that is a type *of* Stack, then why are you inheriting? A more appropriate version of StringStack will be shown later in this chapter.

Functions That Don't Automatically Inherit

Not all functions are automatically inherited from the base class into the derived class. Constructors and destructors deal with the creation and destruction of an object, and they can know what to do with the aspects of the object only for their particular class, so all the constructors and destructors in the hierarchy below them must be called. Thus, constructors and destructors don't inherit and must be created especially for each derived class.

In addition, the operator= doesn't inherit because it performs a constructor-like activity. That is, just because you know how to assign all the members of an object on the left-hand side of the = from an object on the right-hand side doesn't mean that assignment will still have the same meaning after inheritance.

In lieu of inheritance, these functions are synthesized by the compiler if you don't create them yourself.

■ **Note**   With constructors, you can't create any constructors in order for the compiler to synthesize the default constructor and the copy-constructor.

This was briefly described in Chapter 6. The synthesized constructors use member-wise initialization and the synthesized operator= uses member-wise assignment. Listing 14-10 shows an example of the functions that are synthesized by the compiler.

Listing 14-10. Illustrating Synthesized Functions

```
//: C14:SynthesizedFunctions.cpp
// Functions that are synthesized by the compiler
#include <iostream>
using namespace std;

classGameBoard {
public:
  GameBoard() { cout << "GameBoard()\n"; }
  GameBoard(constGameBoard&) {
    cout << "GameBoard(constGameBoard&)\n";
  }
```

```cpp
  GameBoard& operator=(constGameBoard&) {
    cout << "GameBoard::operator=()\n";
    return *this;
  }
  ~GameBoard() { cout << "~GameBoard()\n"; }
};

class Game {
  GameBoard gb; // Composition
public:
  // Default GameBoard constructor called:
  Game() { cout << "Game()\n"; }
  // You must explicitly call the GameBoard
  // copy-constructor or the default constructor
  // is automatically called instead:
  Game(const Game& g) : gb(g.gb) {
    cout << "Game(const Game&)\n";
  }
  Game(int) { cout << "Game(int)\n"; }
  Game& operator=(const Game& g) {
    // You must explicitly call the GameBoard
    // assignment operator or no assignment at
    // all happens for gb!
    gb = g.gb;
    cout << "Game::operator=()\n";
    return *this;
  }
  class Other {}; // Nested class
  // Automatic type conversion:
  operator Other() const {
    cout << "Game::operator Other()\n";
    return Other();
  }
  ~Game() { cout<< "~Game()\n"; }
};

class Chess : public Game {};

void f(Game::Other) {}

class Checkers : public Game {
public:
  // Default base-class constructor called:
  Checkers() { cout << "Checkers()\n"; }
  // You must explicitly call the base-class
  // copy constructor or the default constructor
  // will be automatically called instead:
  Checkers(const Checkers& c) : Game(c) {
    cout << "Checkers(const Checkers& c)\n";
  }
```

```
  Checkers& operator=(const Checkers& c) {
    // You must explicitly call the base-class
    // version of operator=() or no base-class
    // assignment will happen:
    Game::operator=(c);
    cout << "Checkers::operator=()\n";
    return *this;
  }
};

int main() {
  Chess d1;        // Default constructor
  Chess d2(d1);    // Copy-constructor
//! Chess d3(1); // Error: no int constructor
  d1 = d2;         // Operator= synthesized
  f(d1);           // Type-conversion IS inherited
  Game::Other go; /* This declaration is only fordemonstrating to you the next line of
                     code which has been commented out for obvious reasons!(otherwise,
                     the program will not compile!!)*/
//!  d1 = go;      // Operator= not synthesized
                   // for differing types
  Checkers c1, c2(c1);
  c1 = c2;
} ///:~
```

The constructors and the operator= for GameBoard and Game announce themselves so you can see when they're used by the compiler. In addition, the operator Other() performs automatic type conversion from a Game object to an object of the nested class Other. The class Chess simply inherits from Game and creates no functions (to see how the compiler responds). The function f() takes an Other object to test the automatic type conversion function.

In main(), the synthesized default constructor and copy-constructor for the derived class Chess are called. The Game versions of these constructors are called as part of the constructor-call hierarchy. Even though it looks like inheritance, new constructors are actually synthesized by the compiler. As you might expect, no constructors with arguments are automatically created because that's too much for the compiler to intuit.

The operator= is also synthesized as a new function in Chess using member-wise assignment (thus the base class version is called) because that function was not explicitly written in the new class. And of course the destructor was automatically synthesized by the compiler.

Because of all these rules about rewriting functions that handle object creation, it may seem a little strange at first that the automatic type conversion operator *is* inherited. But it's not too unreasonable—if there are enough pieces in Game to make an Other object, those pieces are still there in anything derived from Game and the type conversion operator is still valid (even though you may in fact want to redefine it).

operator= is synthesized *only* for assigning objects of the same type. If you want to assign one type to another you must always write that operator= yourself.

If you look more closely at Game, you'll see that the copy-constructor and assignment operators have explicit calls to the member object copy-constructor and assignment operator. You will normally want to do this because otherwise, in the case of the copy-constructor, the default member object constructor will be used instead, and in the case of the assignment operator, *no* assignment at all will be done for the member objects!

Lastly, look at Checkers, which explicitly writes out the default constructor, copy-constructor, and assignment operators. In the case of the default constructor, the default base-class constructor is automatically called, and that's typically what you want. But, and this is an important point, as soon as you decide to write your own copy-constructor and assignment operator, the compiler assumes that you know what you're doing and does not automatically call the base-class versions, as it does in the synthesized functions. If you want the base class versions called (*and you typically do*) then you must explicitly call them yourself. In the Checkers copy-constructor, this call appears in the constructor initializer list:

```
Checkers(const Checkers& c) : Game(c) {
```

In the Checkers assignment operator, the base class call is the first line in the function body, as in:

```
Game::operator=(c);
```

These calls should be part of the canonical form that you use whenever you inherit a class.

Inheritance and Static Member Functions

static member functions act the same as non-static member functions.

1. They inherit into the derived class.

2. If you redefine a static member, all the other overloaded functions in the base class are hidden.

3. If you change the signature of a function in the base class, all the base class versions with that function name are hidden (*this is really a variation of the previous point*).

However, static member functions cannot be virtual (a topic covered thoroughly in Chapter 15).

Choosing Composition vs. Inheritance

Both composition and inheritance place subobjects inside your new class. Both use the constructor initializer list to construct these subobjects. You may now be wondering what the difference is between the two, and when to choose one over the other.

Composition is generally used when you want the features of an existing class inside your new class, but not its interface. That is, you embed an object to implement features of your new class, but the user of your new class sees the interface you've defined rather than the interface from the original class. To do this, you follow the typical path of embedding private objects of existing classes inside your new class.

Occasionally, however, it makes sense to allow the class user to directly access the composition of your new class, that is, to make the member objects public. The member objects use access control themselves, so this is a safe thing to do and when the user knows you're assembling a bunch of parts, it makes the interface easier to understand.

A Car class is a good example; see Listing 14-11.

Listing 14-11. Illustrating A Public Composition

```
//: C14:Car.cpp
// Public composition

class Engine {
public:
  void start() const {}
  void rev() const {}
  void stop() const {}
};
```

```
class Wheel {
public:
  void inflate(int psi) const {}
};

class Window {
public:
  void rollup() const {}
  void rolldown() const {}
};

class Door {
public:
  Window window;
  void open() const {}
  void close() const {}
};

class Car {
public:
  Engine engine;
  Wheel wheel[4];
  Door left, right; // 2-door
};

int main() {
  Car car;
  car.left.window.rollup();
  car.wheel[0].inflate(72);
} ///:~
```

Because the composition of a Car is part of the analysis of the problem (*and not simply part of the underlying design*), making the members public assists the client programmer's understanding of how to use the class and requires less code complexity for the creator of the class.

With a little thought, you'll also see that it would make no sense to compose a Car using a "vehicle" object—a car doesn't contain a vehicle, it *is* a vehicle. The *is-a* relationship is expressed with inheritance, and the *has-a* relationship is expressed with composition.

Subtyping

Now suppose you want to create a type of ifstream object that not only opens a file but also keeps track of the name of the file. You can use composition and embed both an ifstream and a string into the new class, as shown in Listing 14-12.

Listing 14-12. Embedding both an ifstream and a string (a File Name) using Composition

```
//: C14:FName1.cpp
// An ifstream with a file name
#include "../require.h"
#include <iostream>
#include <fstream>
```

```
#include <string>
using namespace std;

class FName1 {
 ifstream file;
  string fileName;
  bool named;
public:
  FName1() : named(false) {}
  FName1(const string &fname)
    : fileName(fname), file(fname.c_str()) {
    assure(file, fileName);
    named = true;
  }
  string name() const { return fileName; }
  void name(const string &newName) {
    if(named) return; // Don't overwrite
    fileName = newName;
    named = true;
  }
  operator ifstream&() { return file; }
};

int main() {
  FName1 file("FName1.cpp");
  cout << file.name() << endl;
  // Error: close() not a member:
//!  file.close();
} ///:~
```

There's a problem here, however. An attempt is made to allow the use of the FName1 object anywhere an ifstream object is used by including an automatic type conversion operator from FName1 to an ifstream&. But in main( ), the line

```
file.close();
```

will not compile because automatic type conversion happens only in function calls, not during member selection. So this approach won't work.

A second approach is to add the definition of close() to FName1, as in:

```
void close() { file.close(); }
```

This will work if there are only a few functions you want to bring through from the ifstream class. In that case, you're only using part of the class, and composition is appropriate.

But what if you want everything in the class to come through? This is called *subtyping* because you're making a new type from an existing type, and you want your new type to have exactly the same interface as the existing type (*plus any other member functions you want to add*), so you can use it everywhere you'd use the existing type. This is where inheritance is essential. In Listing 14-13, you can see that subtyping solves the problem in the preceding example (Listing 14-12) perfectly.

Listing 14-13. Illustrating that Subtyping Solves the Problem in Listing 14-12

```
//: C14:FName2.cpp
// Subtyping solves the problem
#include "../require.h"
#include <iostream>
#include <fstream>
#include <string>
using namespace std;

class FName2 : public ifstream {
  string fileName;
  bool named;
public:
  FName2() : named(false) {}
  FName2(const string &fname)
    : ifstream(fname.c_str()), fileName(fname) {
    assure(*this, fileName);
    named = true;
  }
  string name() const { return fileName; }
  void name(const string &newName) {
    if(named) return; // Don't overwrite
    fileName = newName;
    named = true;
  }
};

int main() {
  FName2 file("FName2.cpp");
  assure(file, "FName2.cpp");
  cout << "name: " << file.name() << endl;
  string s;
  getline(file, s); // These work too!
  file.seekg(-200, ios::end);
  file.close();
} ///:~
```

Now any member function available for an ifstream object is available for an FName2 object. You can also see that non-member functions like getline() that expect an ifstream can also work with an FName2. That's because an FName2 *is* a type of ifstream; it doesn't simply contain one. This is a very important issue that will be explored at the end of this chapter and in the next one.

private Inheritance

You can inherit a base class privately by leaving off the public in the base class list, or by explicitly saying private (probably a better policy because it is clear to the user that you mean it). When you inherit privately, you're "implementing in terms of;" that is, you're creating a new class that has all of the data and functionality of the base class, but that functionality is hidden, so it's only part of the underlying implementation. The class user has no access to the underlying functionality, and an object cannot be treated as an instance of the base class (as it was in FName2.cpp).

You may wonder what the purpose of private inheritance is, because the alternative of using composition to create a private object in the new class seems more appropriate. private inheritance is included in the language for completeness, but if for no other reason than to reduce confusion, you'll usually want to use composition rather than private inheritance. However, there may occasionally be situations where you want to produce part of the same interface as the base class and disallow the treatment of the object as if it were a base-class object. private inheritance provides this ability.

Publicizing Privately Inherited Members

When you inherit privately, all the public members of the base class become private. If you want any of them to be visible, just say their names (no arguments or return values) along with the using keyword in the public section of the derived class, as shown in Listing 14-14.

Listing 14-14. Demonstrating Private Inheritance

```
//: C14:PrivateInheritance.cpp

class Pet {

public:
  char eat() const { return 'a'; }
  int speak() const { return 2; }

  float sleep() const { return 3.0; }
  float sleep(int) const { return 4.0; }
};

class Goldfish : Pet { // Private inheritance

public:

  using Pet::eat;     // Name publicizes member
  using Pet::sleep;   // Both overloaded members exposed
};

int main() {
  Goldfish bob;
  bob.eat();
  bob.sleep();
  bob.sleep(1);
//! bob.speak();      // Error: private member function
} ///:~
```

Thus, private inheritance is useful if you want to hide part of the *functionality of the base class.*

Notice that giving/exposing the name of an overloaded function exposes all the versions of the overloaded function in the base class. You should think carefully before using private inheritance instead of composition; private inheritance has particular complications when combined with runtime type identification

Note   Runtime type identification is discussed in Chapter 20.

The protected Keyword

Now that you've been introduced to inheritance, the keyword protected finally has meaning. In an ideal world, private members would always be hard-and-fast private, but in real projects there are times when you want to make something hidden from the world at large and yet allow access for members of derived classes. The protected keyword is a nod to pragmatism; it says, "This *is* private *as far as the class user is concerned, but available to anyone who inherits from this class."*

The best approach is to leave the data members private—you should always preserve your right to change the underlying implementation. You can then allow controlled access to inheritors of your class through protected member functions; see Listing 14-15.

Listing 14.15. Illustrating Use of The protected Keyword

```
//: C14:Protected.cpp
// The protected keyword
#include <fstream>
using namespace std;

class Base {
  int i;
protected:
  int read() const { return i; }
  void set(int ii) { i = ii; }
public:
  Base(int ii = 0) : i(ii) {}
  int value(int m) const { return m*i; }
};

class Derived : public Base {
  int j;
public:
  Derived(int jj = 0) : j(jj) {}
  void change(int x) { set(x); }
};

int main() {
  Derived d;
  d.change(10);
} ///:~
```

You will find examples of the need for protected in examples later in this book.

protected Inheritance

When you're inheriting, the base class defaults to private, which means that all of the public member functions are private to the user of the new class. Normally, you'll make the inheritance public so the interface of the base class is also the interface of the derived class. However, you can also use the protected keyword during inheritance.

Protected derivation means "*implemented-in-terms-of*" to other classes but "*is-a*" for derived classes and friends. It's something you don't use very often, but it's in the language for completeness.

Operator Overloading and Inheritance

Except for the assignment operator, operators are automatically inherited into a derived class. This can be demonstrated by inheriting from C12:Byte.h, as shown in Listing 14-16.

Listing 14-16. Illustrating Inheritance of Overloaded Operators

```
//: C14:OperatorInheritance.cpp
// Inheriting overloaded operators
#include "../C12/Byte.h"        // Refer Chapter 12
#include <fstream>
using namespace std;
ofstream out("ByteTest.out");

class Byte2 : public Byte {
public:
  // Constructors don't inherit:
  Byte2(unsigned char bb = 0) : Byte(bb) {}
  // operator= does not inherit, but
  // is synthesized for memberwise assignment.
  // However, only the SameType = SameType
  // operator= is synthesized, so you have to
  // make the others explicitly:
  Byte2& operator=(const Byte& right) {
    Byte::operator=(right);
    return *this;
  }
  Byte2& operator=(inti) {
    Byte::operator=(i);
    return *this;
  }
};

// Similar test function as in C12:ByteTest.cpp:
void k(Byte2& b1, Byte2& b2) {
  b1 = b1 * b2 + b2 % b1;

  #define TRY2(OP) \
    out << "b1 = "; b1.print(out); \
    out << ", b2 = "; b2.print(out); \
    out << ";  b1 " #OP " b2 produces "; \
    (b1 OP b2).print(out); \
    out << endl;

  b1 = 9; b2 = 47;
  TRY2(+) TRY2(-) TRY2(*) TRY2(/)
  TRY2(%) TRY2(^) TRY2(&) TRY2(|)
  TRY2(<<) TRY2(>>) TRY2(+=) TRY2(-=)
  TRY2(*=) TRY2(/=) TRY2(%=) TRY2(^=)
  TRY2(&=) TRY2(|=) TRY2(>>=) TRY2(<<=)
  TRY2(=) // Assignment operator
```

```
  // Conditionals:
  #define TRYC2(OP) \
    out << "b1 = "; b1.print(out);
    out << ", b2 = "; b2.print(out); \
    out << ";   b1 " #OP " b2 produces "; \
    out << (b1 OP b2); \
    out << endl;

  b1 = 9; b2 = 47;
  TRYC2(<) TRYC2(>) TRYC2(==) TRYC2(!=) TRYC2(<=)
  TRYC2(>=) TRYC2(&&) TRYC2(||)

  // Chained assignment:
  Byte2 b3 = 92;
  b1 = b2 = b3;
}

int main() {
  out << "member functions:" << endl;
  Byte2 b1(47), b2(9);
  k(b1, b2);
} ///:~
```

The test code is identical to that in C12:ByteTest.cpp (refer Listing 12-4) except that Byte2 is used instead of Byte. This way all the operators are verified to work with Byte2 via inheritance.

When you examine the class Byte2, you'll see that the constructor must be explicitly defined, and that only the operator= that assigns a Byte2 to a Byte2 is synthesized; any other assignment operators that you need you'll have to synthesize on your own.

Multiple Inheritance

You can inherit from one class, so it would seem to make sense to inherit from more than one class at a time. Indeed you can, but whether it makes sense as part of a design is a subject of continuing debate. One thing is generally agreed upon: you shouldn't try this until you've been programming quite a while and understand the language thoroughly. By that time, you'll probably realize that no matter how much you think you absolutely must use *multiple inheritance*, you can almost always get away with single inheritance.

Initially, multiple inheritance seems simple enough: you add more classes in the base-class list during inheritance, separated by commas. However, multiple inheritance introduces a number of possibilities for ambiguity, which is why a later chapter (in fact, Chapter 21, the last of the book) is devoted to the subject.

Incremental Development

One of the advantages of inheritance and composition is that they support incremental development by allowing you to introduce new code without causing bugs in existing code. If bugs do appear, they are isolated within the new code. By inheriting from (*or composing with*) an existing, functional class and adding data members and member functions (*and redefining existing member functions during inheritance*) you leave the existing code—that someone else may still be using—untouched and unbugged. If a bug happens, you know it's in your new code, which is much shorter and easier to read than if you had modified the body of existing code.

It's rather amazing how cleanly the classes are separated. You don't even need the source code for the member functions in order to reuse the code, just the header file describing the class and the object file or library file with the compiled member functions.

■ **Note**   This is true for both inheritance and composition.

It's important to realize that program development is an incremental process, just like human learning. You can do as much analysis as you want, but you still won't know all the answers when you set out on a project. You'll have much more success—and more immediate feedback—if you start out to "grow" your project as an organic, evolutionary creature, rather than constructing it all at once, like a glass-box skyscraper.

Although inheritance for experimentation is a useful technique, at some point after things stabilize you need to take a new look at your class hierarchy with an eye to collapsing it into a sensible structure. Remember that underneath it all, inheritance is meant to express a relationship that says, "This *new class* is a type of that *old class*." Your program should not be concerned with pushing bits around, but instead with creating and manipulating objects of various types to express a model in the terms given you from the problem space.

Upcasting

Earlier in the chapter, you saw how an object of a class derived from ifstream has all the characteristics and behaviors of an ifstream object. In FName2.cpp, any ifstream member function could be called for an FName2 object.

The most important aspect of inheritance is not that it provides member functions for the new class, however. It's the relationship expressed between the new class and the base class. This relationship can be summarized by saying, "The *new class* is a type of the *existing class*."

This description is not just a fanciful way of explaining inheritance—it's supported directly by the compiler. As an example, consider a base class called Instrument that represents musical instruments and a derived class called Wind. Because inheritance means that all the functions in the base class are also available in the derived class, any message you can send to the base class can also be sent to the derived class. So if the Instrument class has a play() member function, so will Wind instruments. This means you can accurately say that a Wind object is also a type of Instrument. Listing 14-17 shows how the compiler supports this notion.

Listing 14-17. Illustrating Inheritance and Upcasting

```
//: C14:Instrument.cpp
// Inheritance & upcasting
enum note { middleC, Csharp, Cflat }; // Etc.

class Instrument {
public:
  void play(note) const {}
};

// Wind objects are Instruments
// because they have the same interface:
class Wind : public Instrument {};

void tune(Instrument &i) {
  // ...
  i.play(middleC);
}
```

```
int main() {
  Wind flute;
 tune(flute); // Upcasting
} ///:~
```

What's interesting in this example is the tune() function, which accepts an Instrument reference. However, in main() the tune() function is called by handing it a reference to a Wind object. Given that C++ is very particular about type checking, it seems strange that a function that accepts one type will readily accept another type, until you realize that a Wind object is also an Instrument object, and there's no function that tune() could call for an Instrument that isn't also in Wind (this is what inheritance guarantees). Inside tune(), the code works for Instrument and anything derived from Instrument, and the act of converting a Wind reference or pointer into an Instrument reference or pointer is called upcasting.

Why "upcasting?"

The reason for the term is historical and is based on the way class inheritance diagrams have traditionally been drawn: with the root at the top of the page, growing downward.

■ **Note**   Of course, you can draw your diagrams any way you find helpful.

The inheritance diagram for Instrument.cpp is shown in Figure 14-1.

Figure 14-1. *Inheritance diagram for Instruments*

Casting from derived to base moves up on the inheritance diagram, so it's commonly referred to as upcasting. Upcasting is always safe because you're going from a more specific type to a more general type—the only thing that can occur to the class interface is that it can lose member functions, not gain them. This is why the compiler allows upcasting without any explicit casts or other special notation.

Upcasting and the copy-constructor

If you allow the compiler to synthesize a copy-constructor for a derived class, it will automatically call the base-class copy-constructor, and then the copy-constructors for all the member objects (*or* perform a bit-copy on built-in types) so you'll get the right behavior, as shown Listing 14-18.

Listing 14-18. Demonstrating Correct Creation of the copy-constructor

```cpp
//: C14:CopyConstructor.cpp
// Correctly creating the copy-constructor
#include <iostream>
using namespace std;

class Parent {
  int i;
public:
  Parent(int ii) : i(ii) {
   cout << "Parent(int ii)\n";
  }
Parent(const Parent& b) : i(b.i) {
  cout<< "Parent(const Parent&)\n";
  }
  Parent() : i(0) { cout << "Parent()\n"; }
  friend ostream&
    operator <<(ostream& os, const Parent& b) {
    return os << "Parent: " << b.i << endl;
  }
};

class Member {
  int i;
public:
  Member(int ii) : i(ii) {
    cout << "Member(int ii)\n";
  }
  Member(const Member& m) : i(m.i) {
    cout << "Member(const Member&)\n";
  }
  friend ostream&
    operator<<(ostream& os, const Member& m) {
    return os << "Member: " << m.i<< endl;
  }
};

class Child : public Parent {
  int i;
  Member m;
public:
  Child(int ii) : Parent(ii), i(ii), m(ii) {
    cout << "Child(int ii)\n";
  }
friend ostream&
  operator<<(ostream& os, const Child& c){
  return os << (Parent&)c << c.m
            << "Child: " << c.i << endl;
  }
};
```

```
int main() {
  Child c(2);
  cout << "calling copy-constructor: " << endl;
  Child c2 = c; // Calls copy-constructor
  cout << "values in c2:\n" << c2;
} ///:~
```

The operator<< for Child is interesting because of the way that it calls the operator<< for the Parent part within it: by casting the Child object to a Parent& (if you cast to a base class object instead of a reference, you will usually get undesirable results):

```
return os << (Parent&)c << c.m
```

Since the compiler then sees it as a Parent, it calls the Parent version of operator<<.

You can see that Child has no explicitly-defined copy-constructor. The compiler then synthesizes the copy-constructor (since that is one of the four functions it will synthesize, along with the default constructor—if you don't create any constructors—the operator= and the destructor) by calling the Parent copy-constructor and the Member copy-constructor. This is shown in the output:

```
Parent(int ii)
Member(int ii)
Child(int ii)
calling copy-constructor:
Parent(const Parent&)
Member(const Member&)
values in c2:
Parent: 2
Member: 2
Child: 2
```

However, if you try to write your own copy-constructor for Child and you make an innocent mistake and do it badly, like

```
Child(const Child& c) : i(c.i), m(c.m) {}
```

then the default constructor will automatically be called for the base-class part of Child, since that's what the compiler falls back on when it has no other choice of constructor to call (remember that some constructor must always be called for every object, regardless of whether it's a subobject of another class). The output will then be

```
Parent(int ii)
Member(int ii)
Child(int ii)
calling copy-constructor:
Parent()
Member(const Member&)
values in c2:
Parent: 0
Member: 2
Child: 2
```

This is probably not what you expect, since generally you'll want the base-class portion to be copied from the existing object to the new object as part of copy-construction.

To repair the problem, you must remember to properly call the base-class copy-constructor (as the compiler does) whenever you write your own copy-constructor. This can seem a little strange-looking at first but it's another example of upcasting:

```
Child(const Child& c)
    : Parent(c), i(c.i), m(c.m) {
    cout << "Child(Child&)\n";
}
```

The strange part is where the Parent copy-constructor is called Parent(c). What does it mean to pass a Child object to a Parent constructor? But Child is inherited from Parent, so a Child reference *is* a Parent reference. The base-class copy-constructor call upcasts a reference to Child to a reference to Parent and uses it to perform the copy-construction. When you write your own copy constructors you'll almost always want to do the same thing.

Composition vs. Inheritance (Revisited)

One of the clearest ways to determine whether you should be using composition or inheritance is by asking whether you'll ever need to upcast from your new class. Earlier in this chapter, the Stack class was specialized using inheritance. However, chances are the StringStack objects will be used only as string containers and never upcast, so a more appropriate alternative is composition; see Listing 14-19.

Listing 14-19. Comparing Compositing with Inheritance

```
//: C14:InheritStack2.cpp
// Composition vs. inheritance
#include "../C09/Stack4.h"
#include "../require.h"
#include <iostream>
#include <fstream>
#include <string>
using namespace std;

class StringStack {
  Stack stack; // Embed instead of inherit
public:
  void push(string* str) {
    stack.push(str);
  }
  string* peek() const {
    return (string*)stack.peek();
  }
  string* pop() {
    return (string*)stack.pop();
  }
};

int main() {
  ifstream in("InheritStack2.cpp");
  assure(in, "InheritStack2.cpp");
  string line;
  StringStack textlines;
```

```
  while(getline(in, line))
    textlines.push(new string(line));
  string* s;
  while((s = textlines.pop()) != 0) // No cast!
    cout << *s << endl;
} ///:~
```

The file is identical to InheritStack.cpp (Listing 14-9), except that a Stack object is embedded in StringStack, and member functions are called for the embedded object. There's still no time or space overhead because the subobject takes up the same amount of space, and all the additional type checking happens at compile time.

Although it tends to be more confusing, you could also use private inheritance to express "implemented in terms of." This would also solve the problem adequately. One place it becomes important, however, is when multiple inheritance might be warranted. In that case, if you see a design in which composition can be used instead of inheritance, you may be able to eliminate the need for multiple inheritance.

Pointer and Reference Upcasting

In Instrument.cpp, the upcasting occurs during the function call—a Wind object outside the function has its reference taken and becomes an Instrument reference inside the function. Upcasting can also occur during a simple assignment to a pointer or reference:

```
Wind w;
Instrument* ip = &w; // Upcast
Instrument& ir = w;  // Upcast
```

Like the function call, neither of these cases requires an explicit cast.

A Crisis

Of course, any upcast loses type information about an object. If you say

```
Wind w;
Instrument* ip = &w;
```

the compiler can deal with ip only as an Instrument pointer and nothing else. That is, it cannot know that ip *actually* happens to point to a Wind object. So when you call the play() member function by saying

```
ip->play(middleC);
```

the compiler can know only that it's calling play() for an Instrument pointer, and call the base-class version of Instrument::play() instead of what it should do, which is call Wind::play(). So you won't get the correct behavior.

This is a significant problem; it is solved in Chapter 15 by introducing the third cornerstone of object-oriented programming: *polymorphism,* which is implemented in C++ with the help of virtual *functions.*

Review Session

1. Both inheritance and composition allow you to create a new type from existing types, and both embed *subobjects* of the existing types inside the new type.

2. Typically, however, you use composition to reuse existing types as part of the underlying implementation of the new type and inheritance when you want to force the new type to be the same type as the base class (by the way, type equivalence guarantees interface equivalence). Since the derived class has the base-class interface, it can be *upcast* to the base, which is critical for *polymorphism*, as you'll see in Chapter 15.

3. Although code reuse through composition and inheritance is very helpful for rapid project development, you'll generally want to redesign your class hierarchy before allowing other programmers to become dependent on it.

4. Your goal is a hierarchy in which each class has a specific use and is neither too big (that is to say, *encompassing so much functionality that it's unwieldy to reuse*) nor annoyingly small (that is to say, *you can't use it by itself or without adding functionality*).

CHAPTER 15

■ ■ ■

Polymorphism and Virtual Functions

Polymorphism (*implemented in C++ with virtual functions*) is the third essential feature of an object-oriented programming language, after data abstraction and inheritance.

It provides another dimension of separation of interface from implementation, to decouple *what* from *how*. *What* implies the interface details while *how* implies the implementation details. You have already learned about *hiding the implementation* in Chapter 5. The idea here is akin to simulating a system first (the *what* aspect) without worrying about getting a working system in place itself (the *how* aspect).

Polymorphism allows improved code organization and readability as well as the creation of *extensible* programs that can be "grown" not only during the original creation of the project, but also when new features are desired.

Encapsulation creates new data types by combining characteristics and behaviors. Access control separates the interface from the implementation by making the details private. This kind of mechanical organization makes ready sense to someone with a procedural programming background. But *virtual functions* deal with decoupling in terms of types. In Chapter 14, you saw how inheritance allows the treatment of an object as its own type *or* its base type. This ability is critical because it allows many types (*derived from* the same base type) to be treated as if they were one type, and a single piece of code to work on all those different types equally. The virtual function allows one type to express its distinction from another, similar type, as long as they're both derived from the same base type. This distinction is expressed through differences in behavior of the functions that you can call through the base class.

In this chapter, you'll learn about virtual functions, starting from the basics with simple examples that do away with everything *but the virtual part of the function*.

Evolution of C++ Programmers

C programmers seem to acquire C++ in three steps. First, as simply a "better C," because C++ forces you to declare all functions before using them and is much pickier about how variables are used. You can often find the errors in a C program simply by compiling it with a C++ compiler.

The second step is "object-based" C++. This means that you easily see the code organization benefits of grouping a data structure together with the functions that act upon it, the value of constructors and destructors, and perhaps some simple inheritance. Most programmers who have been working with C for a while quickly see the usefulness of this because, whenever they create a library, this is exactly what they try to do. With C++, you have the aid of the compiler.

You can get stuck at the object-based level because you can quickly get there and you get a lot of benefit without much mental effort. It's also easy to feel like you're creating data types—you make classes and objects, you send messages to those objects, and everything is nice and neat.

But don't be fooled. If you stop here, you're missing out on the greatest part of the language, which is the jump to true object-oriented programming. You can do this only with virtual functions.

Virtual functions enhance the concept of type, instead of just encapsulating code inside structures and behind walls, so they are without a doubt the most difficult concept for the new C++ programmer to fathom. However, they're also the turning point in the understanding of object-oriented programming. If you don't use virtual functions, you don't understand OOP yet.

Because the virtual function is intimately bound with the concept of type, and type is at the core of object-oriented programming, there is no analog to the virtual function in a traditional procedural language. As a procedural programmer, you have no referent with which to think about virtual functions, as you do with almost every other feature in the language. Features in a procedural language can be understood on an algorithmic level, but virtual functions can be understood only from a design viewpoint.

Upcasting

In Chapter 14, you saw how an object can be used as its own type or as an object of its base type. In addition, it can be manipulated through an address of the base type. Taking the address of an object (*either* a pointer or a reference) and treating it as the address of the base type is called *upcasting* because of the way inheritance trees are drawn with the base class at the top.

You also saw a problem arise, which is embodied in Listing 15-1.

Listing 15-1. Illustrating Inheritance and the Upcasting Problem

```
//: C15:Instrument2.cpp
// Inheritance & upcasting
#include <iostream>
using namespace std;
enum note { middleC, Csharp, Eflat }; // Etc.

class Instrument {
public:
  void play(note) const {
    cout << "Instrument::play" << endl;
  }
};

// Wind objects are Instruments
// because they have the same interface:
class Wind : public Instrument {
public:
  // Redefine interface function:
  void play(note) const {
    cout << "Wind::play" << endl;
  }
};

void tune(Instrument &i) {
  // ...
  i.play(middleC);
}

int main() {
  Wind flute;
  tune(flute);                       // Upcasting
} ///:~
```

The function tune( ) accepts (by reference) an Instrument, but also without complaint anything derived from Instrument. In main( ), you can see this happening as a Wind object is passed to tune( ), with no cast necessary. This is acceptable; the interface in Instrument must exist in Wind, because Wind is publicly inherited from Instrument. Upcasting from Wind to Instrument may "narrow" that interface, but never less than the full interface to Instrument.

The same arguments are true when dealing with pointers; the only difference is that the user must explicitly take the addresses of objects as they are passed into the function.

The Problem

The problem with Instrument2.cpp can be seen by running the program. The output is Instrument::play. This is clearly not the desired output, because you happen to know that the object is actually a Wind and not just an Instrument. The call should produce Wind::play. For that matter, any object of a class derived from Instrument should have its version of play( ) used, regardless of the situation.

The behavior of Instrument2.cpp is not surprising, given C's approach to functions. To understand the issues, you need to be aware of the concept of binding.

Function Call Binding

Connecting a function call to a function body is called *binding*. When binding is performed before the program is run (*by the compiler and linker*), it's called *early binding*. You may not have heard the term before because it's never been an option with procedural languages: C compilers have only one kind of function call, and that's early binding.

The problem in the program in Listing 15-1 is caused by early binding because the compiler cannot know the correct function to call when it has only an Instrument address. The solution is called *late* binding, which means the binding occurs at *runtime*, based on the type of the object. Late binding is also called *dynamic binding* or *runtime binding*. When a language implements late binding, there must be some mechanism to determine the type of the object at runtime and call the appropriate member function. In the case of a compiled language, the compiler still doesn't know the actual object type, but it inserts code that finds out and calls the correct function body. The late binding mechanism varies from language to language, but you can imagine that some sort of type information must be installed in the objects. You'll see how this works later.

Using Virtual Functions

To cause late binding to occur for a particular function, C++ requires that you use the virtual keyword when declaring the function in the base class. Late binding occurs only with virtual functions, and only when you're using an address of the base class where those virtual functions exist, although they may also be defined in an earlier base class.

To create a member function as virtual, you simply precede the declaration of the function with the keyword virtual. Only the declaration needs the virtual keyword, not the definition. If a function is declared as virtual in the base class, it is virtual in all the derived classes. The redefinition of a virtual function in a derived class is usually called *overriding*.

Notice that you are only required to declare a function virtual in the base class. All derived class functions that match the signature of the base class declaration will be called using the virtual mechanism. You can use the virtual keyword in the derived class declarations (*it does no harm to do so*), but it is redundant and can be confusing.

To get the desired behavior from Instrument2.cpp, simply add the virtual keyword in the base class before play( ), as shown in Listing 15-2.

Listing 15-2. Illustrating Late Binding with the virtual Keyword

```cpp
//: C15:Instrument3.cpp
// Late binding with the virtual keyword
#include <iostream>
using namespace std;
enum note { middleC, Csharp, Cflat }; // Etc.

class Instrument {
public:
  virtual void play(note) const {
    cout << "Instrument::play" << endl;
  }
};

// Wind objects are Instruments
// because they have the same interface:
class Wind : public Instrument {
public:

  // Override interface function:
  void play(note) const {
    cout << "Wind::play" << endl;
  }
};

void tune(Instrument &i) {
  // ...
  i.play(middleC);
}

int main() {
  Wind flute;
  tune(flute);
      // Upcasting
} ///:~
```

This file is identical to `Instrument2.cpp` except for the addition of the `virtual` keyword, and yet the behavior is significantly different: now the output is `Wind::play`.

Extensibility

With `play( )` defined as `virtual` in the base class, you can add as many new types as you want without changing the `tune( )` function. In a well-designed OOP program, most or all of your functions will follow the model of `tune( )` and communicate only with the base class interface. Such a program is extensible because you can add new functionality by inheriting new data types from the common base class. The functions that manipulate the base class interface will not need to be changed at all to accommodate the new classes.

Listing 15-3 shows the instrument example with more virtual functions and a number of new classes, all of which work correctly with the old, unchanged `tune( )` function.

Listing 15-3. Illustrating Extensibility in OOP

```cpp
//: C15:Instrument4.cpp
// Extensibility in OOP
#include <iostream>
using namespace std;
enum note { middleC, Csharp, Cflat }; // Etc.

class Instrument {
public:
  virtual void play(note) const {
    cout << "Instrument::play" << endl;
  }
  virtual char* what() const {
    return "Instrument";
  }
  // Assume this will modify the object:
  virtual void adjust(int) {}
};

class Wind : public Instrument {
public:
  void play(note) const {
    cout << "Wind::play" << endl;
  }
  char* what() const { return "Wind"; }
  void adjust(int) {}
};

class Percussion : public Instrument {
public:
  void play(note) const {
    cout << "Percussion::play" << endl;
  }
  char* what() const { return "Percussion"; }
  void adjust(int) {}
};

class Stringed : public Instrument {
public:
  void play(note) const {
    cout << "Stringed::play" << endl;
  }
  char* what() const { return "Stringed"; }
  void adjust(int) {}
};

class Brass : public Wind {
public:
  void play(note) const {
    cout << "Brass::play" << endl;
  }
  char* what() const { return "Brass"; }
};
```

```
class Woodwind : public Wind {
public:
  void play(note) const {
    cout << "Woodwind::play" << endl;
  }
  char* what() const { return "Woodwind"; }
};

// Identical function from before:
void tune(Instrument&i) {
  // ...
  i.play(middleC);
}

// New function:
void f(Instrument&i) { i.adjust(1); }

// Upcasting during array initialization:
Instrument* A[] = {
  new Wind,
  new Percussion,
  new Stringed,
  new Brass,
};

int main() {
  Wind flute;
  Percussion drum;
  Stringed violin;
  Brass flugelhorn;
  Woodwind recorder;
  tune(flute);
  tune(drum);
  tune(violin);
  tune(flugelhorn);
  tune(recorder);
  f(flugelhorn);
} ///:~
```

You can see that another inheritance level has been added beneath Wind, but the virtual mechanism works correctly no matter how many levels there are. The adjust() function *is not* overridden for Brass and Woodwind. When this happens, the "closest" definition in the inheritance hierarchy is automatically used; the compiler guarantees there's always *some* definition for a virtual function, so you'll never end up with a call that doesn't bind to a function body.

■ **Note**   That would be disastrous.

The array A[ ] contains pointers to the base class Instrument, so upcasting occurs during the process of array initialization. This array and the function f( ) will be used in later discussions.

In the call to tune( ), upcasting is performed on each different type of object, yet the desired behavior always takes place. This can be described as "sending a message to an object and letting the object worry about what to do with it." The virtual function is the lens to use when you're trying to analyze a project: Where should the base classes occur, and how might you want to extend the program? However, even if you don't discover the proper base class interfaces and virtual functions at the initial creation of the program, you'll often discover them later, even much later, when you set out to extend or otherwise maintain the program. This is not an analysis or design error; it simply means you didn't or couldn't know all the information the first time. Because of the tight class modularization in C++, it isn't a large problem when this occurs because changes you make in one part of a system tend not to propagate to other parts of the system as they do in C.

How C++ Implements Late Binding

How can late binding happen? All the work goes on behind the scenes by the compiler, which installs the necessary late binding mechanism when you ask it to (and you ask by creating virtual functions). Because programmers often benefit from understanding the mechanism of virtual functions in C++, this section will elaborate on the way the compiler implements this mechanism.

The keyword virtual tells the compiler it should not perform early binding. Instead, it should automatically install all the mechanisms necessary to perform late binding. This means that if you call play( ) for a Brass object through an address for the base class Instrument, you'll get the proper function.

To accomplish this, the typical compiler creates a single table (called the VTABLE) for each class that contains virtual functions. The compiler places the addresses of the virtual functions for that particular class in the VTABLE. In each class with virtual functions, it secretly places a pointer, called the vpointer (abbreviated as VPTR), which points to the VTABLE for that object. When you make a virtual function call through a base class pointer (that is, when you make a polymorphic call), the compiler quietly inserts code to fetch the VPTR and looks up the function address in the VTABLE, thus calling the correct function and causing late binding to take place.

All of this—setting up the VTABLE for each class, initializing the VPTR, inserting the code for the virtual function call—happens automatically, so you don't have to worry about it. With virtual functions, the proper function gets called for an object, even if the compiler cannot know the specific type of the object. The following sections go into this process in more detail.

Storing Type Information

You can see that there is no explicit type information stored in any of the classes. But the previous examples, and simple logic, tell you that there must be some sort of type information stored in the objects; otherwise the type could not be established at runtime. This is true, but the type information is hidden. See Listing 15-4 to examine the sizes of classes that use virtual functions compared with those that don't.

Listing 15-4. Illustrating Comparison of Object Sizes (with and without virtual functions)

```
//: C15:Sizes.cpp
// Object sizes with/without virtual functions
#include <iostream>
using namespace std;

classNoVirtual {
  int a;
```

```
public:

  void x() const {}
  int i() const { return 1; }
};

class OneVirtual {
  int a;

public:

  virtual void x() const {}
  int i() const { return 1; }
};

class TwoVirtuals {
  int a;

public:
  virtual void x() const {}
  virtual int i() const { return 1; }
};

int main() {
  cout << "int: " << sizeof(int) << endl;
  cout << "NoVirtual: "
       << sizeof(NoVirtual) << endl;
  cout << "void* : " << sizeof(void*) << endl;
  cout << "OneVirtual: "
       << sizeof(OneVirtual) << endl;
  cout << "TwoVirtuals: "
       << sizeof(TwoVirtuals) << endl;
} ///:~
```

With no virtual functions, the size of the object is exactly what you'd expect: the size of a single int. With a single virtual function in OneVirtual, the size of the object is the size of NoVirtual plus the size of a void pointer. It turns out that the compiler inserts a single pointer (the VPTR) into the structure if you have one or more virtual functions. There is no size difference between OneVirtual and TwoVirtuals. That's because the VPTR points to a table of function addresses. You need only one table because all the virtual function addresses are contained in that single table.

This example required at least one data member. If there had been no data members, the C++ compiler would have forced the objects to be a nonzero size because each object must have a distinct address. If you imagine indexing into an array of zero-sized objects, you'll understand. A "dummy" member is inserted into objects that would otherwise be zero-sized. When the type information is inserted because of the virtual keyword, this takes the place of the dummy member. Try commenting out the int a in all the classes in Listing 15-4 to see this.

Picturing Virtual Functions

To understand exactly what's going on when you use a virtual function, it's helpful to visualize the activities going on behind the curtain. Figure 15-1 is a drawing of the array of pointers A[ ] in Instrument4.cpp.

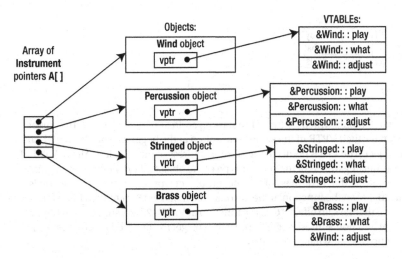

Figure 15-1. *Array of instrument pointers*

The array of Instrument pointers has no specific type information; they each point to an object of type Instrument. Wind, Percussion, Stringed, and Brass all fit into this category because they are derived from Instrument (and thus have the same interface as Instrument, and can respond to the same messages), so their addresses can also be placed into the array. However, the compiler doesn't know that they are anything more than Instrument objects, so left to its own devices it would normally call the base class versions of all the functions. But in this case, all those functions have been declared with the virtual keyword, so something different happens.

Each time you create a class that contains virtual functions, or you derive from a class that contains virtual functions, the compiler creates a unique VTABLE for that class, seen on the right of the diagram. In that table it places the addresses of all the functions that are declared virtual in this class or in the base class. If you don't override a function that was declared virtual in the base class, the compiler uses the address of the base class version in the derived class.

■ **Note**   You can see this in the adjust entry in the Brass VTABLE.

Then it places the VPTR (discovered in Listing 15-4 in Sizes.cpp) into the class. There is only one VPTR for each object when using simple inheritance like this. The VPTR must be initialized to point to the starting address of the appropriate VTABLE. (This happens in the constructor, which you'll see later in more detail.)

Once the VPTR is initialized to the proper VTABLE, the object in effect "knows" what type it is. But this self-knowledge is worthless unless it is used at the point a virtual function is called.

When you call a virtual function through a base class address (the situation when the compiler doesn't have all the information necessary to perform early binding), something special happens. Instead of performing a typical function call, which is simply an assembly language CALL to a particular address, the compiler generates different code to perform the function call. Figure 15-2 shows what a call to adjust( ) for a Brass object looks like, if made through an Instrument pointer. (An Instrument reference produces the same result.)

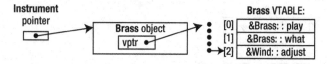

Figure 15-2. *Call to adjust for a Brass object*

The compiler begins with the `Instrument` pointer, which points to the starting address of the object. All `Instrument` objects or objects derived from `Instrument` have their VPTR in the same place (often at the beginning of the object), so the compiler can pick the VPTR out of the object. The VPTR points to the starting address of the VTABLE. All the VTABLE function addresses are laid out in the same order, regardless of the specific type of the object. `play()` is first, `what()` is second, and `adjust()` is third. The compiler knows that regardless of the specific object type, the `adjust()` function is at the location VPTR+2. Thus, instead of saying, "Call the function at the absolute location `Instrument::adjust`" (early binding—the wrong action), it generates code that says, in effect, "Call the function at VPTR+2." Because the fetching of the VPTR and the determination of the actual function address occur at runtime, you get the desired late binding. You send a message to the object, and the object figures out what to do with it.

Under the Hood

It can be helpful to see the assembly language code generated by a virtual function call, so you can see that late binding is indeed taking place. Here's the output from one compiler for the call

```
i.adjust(1);
```

inside the function f(Instrument &i):

```
push  1
pushsi
movbx, word ptr [si]
call  word ptr [bx+4]
addsp, 4
```

The arguments of a C++ function call, like a C function call, are pushed on the stack from right to left (this order is required to support C's variable argument lists), so the argument 1 is pushed on the stack first. At this point in the function, the register si (part of the Intel X86 processor architecture) contains the address of i. This is also pushed on the stack because it is the starting address of the object of interest. Remember that the starting address corresponds to the value of this, and this is quietly pushed on the stack as an argument before every member function call, so the member function knows which particular object it is working on. So you'll always see one more than the number of arguments pushed on the stack before a member function call (except for static member functions, which have no this).

Now the actual virtual function call must be performed. First, the VPTR must be produced, so the VTABLE can be found. For this compiler the VPTR is inserted at the beginning of the object, so the contents of this correspond to the VPTR. The line

```
mov bx, word ptr [si]
```

fetches the word that si (that is, this)points to, which is the VPTR. It places the VPTR into the register bx.

The VPTR contained in bx points to the starting address of the VTABLE, but the function pointer to call isn't at location zero of the VTABLE, but instead at location two (because it's the third function in the list). For this memory model, each function pointer is two bytes long, so the compiler adds four to the VPTR to calculate where the address of the proper function is. Note that this is a constant value, established at compile time, so the only thing that matters is that the function pointer at location number two is the one for adjust( ). Fortunately, the compiler takes care of all the bookkeeping for you and ensures that all the function pointers in all the VTABLEs of a particular class hierarchy occur in the same order, regardless of the order that you may override them in derived classes.

Once the address of the proper function pointer in the VTABLE is calculated, that function is called. So the address is fetched and called all at once in the statement

```
call word ptr [bx+4]
```

Finally, the stack pointer is moved back up to clean off the arguments that were pushed before the call. In C and C++ assembly code, you'll often see the caller clean off the arguments but this may vary depending on processors and compiler implementations.

Installing the Vpointer

Because the VPTR determines the virtual function behavior of the object, you can see how it's critical that the VPTR always be pointing to the proper VTABLE. You don't ever want to be able to make a call to a virtual function before the VPTR is properly initialized. Of course, the place where initialization can be guaranteed is in the constructor, but none of the Instrument examples has a constructor.

This is where creation of the default constructor is essential. In the Instrument examples, the compiler creates a default constructor that does nothing except initialize the VPTR. This constructor, of course, is automatically called for all Instrument objects before you can do anything with them, so you know that it's always safe to call virtual functions. The implications of the automatic initialization of the VPTR inside the constructor are discussed in a later section.

Objects Are Different

It's important to realize that upcasting deals only with addresses. If the compiler has an object, it knows the exact type and therefore (in C++) will not use late binding for any function calls—or at least, the compiler doesn't *need* to use late binding. For efficiency's sake, most compilers will perform early binding when they are making a call to a virtual function for an object because they know the exact type. See Listing 15-5 for an example.

Listing 15-5. Illustrating Early Binding and Virtual Functions

```
//: C15:Early.cpp
// Early binding & virtual functions
#include <iostream>
#include <string>
using namespace std;

class Pet {
public:
  virtual string speak() const { return ""; }
};

class Dog : public Pet {
public:
  string speak() const { return "Bark!"; }
};

int main() {
  Dog ralph;
  Pet* p1 = &ralph;
  Pet& p2 = ralph;
```

```
   Pet p3;
   // Late binding for both:
   cout << "p1->speak() = " << p1->speak() << endl;
   cout << "p2.speak() = " << p2.speak() << endl;
   // Early binding (probably):
   cout << "p3.speak() = " << p3.speak() << endl;
} ///:~
```

In p1->speak( ) and p2.speak( ), addresses are used, which means the information is incomplete: p1 and p2 can represent the address of a Pet *or* something derived from Pet, so the virtual mechanism must be used. When calling p3.speak( ) there's no ambiguity. The compiler knows the exact type and that it's an object, so it can't possibly be an object derived from Pet—it's exactly a Pet. Thus, early binding is probably used. However, if the compiler doesn't want to work so hard, it can still use late binding and the same behavior will occur.

Why virtual functions?

At this point you might be wondering, "If this technique is so important, and if it makes the 'right' function call all the time, why is it an option? Why do I even need to know about it?"

This is a good question, and the answer is part of the fundamental philosophy of C++: "*Because it's not quite as efficient.*" You can see from the previous assembly language output that instead of one simple CALL to an absolute address, there are two (more sophisticated) assembly instructions required to set up the virtual function call. This requires both code space and execution time.

Some object-oriented languages have taken the approach that late binding is so intrinsic to object-oriented programming that it should always take place, that it should not be an option, and the user shouldn't have to know about it. This is a design decision when creating a language, and that particular path is appropriate for many languages. However, C++ comes from the C heritage, where efficiency is critical. After all, C was created to replace assembly language for the implementation of an operating system (thereby rendering that operating system, Unix, far more portable than its predecessors). One of the main reasons for the invention of C++ was to make C programmers more efficient. And the first question asked when C programmers encounter C++ is, "What kind of size and speed impact will I get?" If the answer were, "Everything's great except for function calls when you'll always have a little extra overhead," many people would stick with C rather than make the change to C++. In addition, inline functions would not be possible, because virtual functions must have an address to put into the VTABLE. So the virtual function is an option, and the language defaults to *nonvirtual*, which is the fastest configuration.

Thus, the virtual keyword is provided for efficiency tuning. When designing your classes, however, you shouldn't be worrying about efficiency tuning. If you're going to use polymorphism, use virtual functions everywhere. You only need to look for functions that can be made non-virtual when searching for ways to speed up your code (*and there are usually much bigger gains to be had in other areas; a good profiler will do a better job of finding bottlenecks than you will by making guesses*).

Anecdotal evidence suggests that the size and speed impacts of going to C++ are within 10 percent of the size and speed of C, and often much closer to the same. The reason you might get better size and speed efficiency is because you may design a C++ program in a smaller, faster way than you would using C.

Abstract Base Classes and Pure Virtual Functions

Often in a design you want the base class to present only an interface for its derived classes. That is, you don't want anyone to actually create an object of the base class, only to upcast to it so that its interface can be used. This is accomplished by making that class abstract, which happens if you give it at least one pure virtual function. You can recognize a pure virtual function because it uses the virtual keyword and is followed by = 0. If anyone tries to make an object of an abstract class, the compiler prevents them. This is a tool that allows you to enforce a particular design.

When an abstract class is inherited, all pure virtual functions must be implemented, or the inherited class becomes abstract as well. Creating a pure virtual function allows you to put a member function in an interface without being forced to provide a possibly meaningless body of code for that member function. At the same time, a pure virtual function forces inherited classes to provide a definition for it.

In all of the instrument examples, the functions in the base class Instrument were always dummy functions. If these functions are ever called, something is wrong. That's because the intent of Instrument is to create a common interface for all of the classes derived from it.

The only reason to establish the common interface is so it can be expressed differently for each different subtype (see Figure 15-3). It creates a basic form that determines what's in common with all of the derived classes—nothing else. So Instrument is an appropriate candidate to be an abstract class. You create an abstract class when you only want to manipulate a set of classes through a common interface, but the common interface doesn't need to have an implementation (or at least a full implementation).

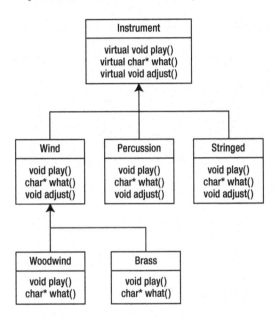

Figure 15-3. *Common interface for Instruments*

If you have a concept like Instrument that works as an abstract class, objects of that class almost always have no meaning. That is, Instrument is meant to express only the interface, and not a particular implementation, so creating an object that is only an Instrument makes no sense, and you'll probably want to prevent the user from doing it. This can be accomplished by making all the virtual functions in Instrument print error messages, but that delays the appearance of the error information until runtime and it requires reliable exhaustive testing on the part of the user. It is much better to catch the problem at compile time.

Here is the syntax used for a pure virtual declaration:

```
virtual void f() = 0;
```

By doing this, you tell the compiler to reserve a slot for a function in the VTABLE, but not to put an address in that particular slot. Even if only one function in a class is declared as pure virtual, the VTABLE is incomplete.

If the VTABLE for a class is incomplete, what is the compiler supposed to do when someone tries to make an object of that class? It cannot safely create an object of an abstract class, so you get an error message from the compiler. Thus, the compiler guarantees the purity of the abstract class. By making a class abstract, you ensure that the client programmer cannot misuse it.

Listing 15-6 shows `Instrument4.cpp` modified to use pure virtual functions. Because the class has nothing but pure virtual functions, it's called a *pure abstract class*.

Listing 15-6. Illustrating a Pure Abstract Class

```
//: C15:Instrument5.cpp
// Pure abstract base classes
#include <iostream>
using namespace std;
enum note { middleC, Csharp, Cflat }; // Etc.

class Instrument {
public:
  // Pure virtual functions:
  virtual void play(note) const = 0;
  virtual char* what() const = 0;
  // Assume this will modify the object:
  virtual void adjust(int) = 0;
};
// Rest of the file is the same ...

class Wind : public Instrument {
public:
  void play(note) const {
    cout << "Wind::play" << endl;
  }
  char* what() const { return "Wind"; }
  void adjust(int) {}
};

class Percussion : public Instrument {

public:
 void play(note) const {
   cout << "Percussion::play" << endl;
  }
  char* what() const { return "Percussion"; }
  void adjust(int) {}
};

class Stringed : public Instrument {

public:
  void play(note) const {
    cout << "Stringed::play" << endl;
  }
  char* what() const { return "Stringed"; }
  void adjust(int) {}
};
```

```
class Brass : public Wind {

public:
  void play(note) const {
    cout << "Brass::play" << endl;
  }
  char* what() const { return "Brass"; }
};

class Woodwind : public Wind {

public:
  void play(note) const {
      cout << "Woodwind::play" << endl;
  }
  char* what() const { return "Woodwind"; }
};

// Identical function from before:
void tune(Instrument&i) {
  // ...
  i.play(middleC);
}

// New function:
void f(Instrument&i) { i.adjust(1); }

int main() {
  Wind flute;
  Percussion drum;
  Stringed violin;
  Brass flugelhorn;
  Woodwind recorder;
  tune(flute);
  tune(drum);
  tune(violin);
  tune(flugelhorn);
  tune(recorder);
  f(flugelhorn);
} ///:~
```

Pure virtual functions are helpful because they make explicit the abstractness of a class and tell both the user and the compiler how it was intended to be used.

Note that pure virtual functions prevent an abstract class from being passed into a function by value. Thus, it is also a way to prevent object slicing (which will be described shortly). By making a class *abstract*, you can ensure that a pointer or reference is always used during upcasting to that class.

Just because one pure virtual function prevents the VTABLE from being completed doesn't mean that you don't want function bodies for some of the others. Often you will want to call a base class version of a function, even if it is virtual. It's always a good idea to put common code as close as possible to the root of your hierarchy. Not only does this save code space, it allows easy propagation of changes.

Pure Virtual Definitions

It's possible to provide a definition for a pure virtual function in the base class. You're still telling the compiler not to allow objects of that abstract base class, and the pure virtual functions must still be defined in derived classes in order to create objects. However, there may be a common piece of code that you want some or all of the derived class definitions to call rather than duplicating that code in every function. Listing 15-7 shows what a pure virtual definition looks like.

Listing 15-7. Illustrating Pure Virtual Definitions

```
//: C15:PureVirtualDefinitions.cpp
// Pure virtual base definitions
#include <iostream>
using namespace std;

class Pet {
public:
  virtual void speak() const = 0;
  virtual void eat() const = 0;
  // Inline pure virtual definitions illegal:
  //!  virtual void sleep() const = 0 {}
};

// OK, not defined inline
void Pet::eat() const {
  cout << "Pet::eat()" << endl;
}

void Pet::speak() const {
  cout << "Pet::speak()" << endl;
}

class Dog : public Pet {
public:
  // Use the common Pet code:
  void speak() const { Pet::speak(); }
  void eat() const { Pet::eat(); }
};

int main() {
  Dog simba;  // Richard's dog
  simba.speak();
  simba.eat();
} ///:~
```

The slot in the Pet VTABLE is still empty, but there happens to be a function by that name that you can call in the derived class.

The other benefit to this feature is that it allows you to change from an ordinary virtual to a pure virtual without disturbing the existing code.

■ **Note**   This is a way for you to locate classes that don't override that virtual function.

Inheritance and the VTABLE

You can imagine what happens when you perform inheritance and override some of the virtual functions. The compiler creates a new VTABLE for your new class, and it inserts your new function addresses using the base class function addresses for any virtual functions you don't override. One way or another, for every object that can be created (that is, its class has no pure virtuals) there's always a full set of function addresses in the VTABLE, so you'll never be able to make a call to an address that isn't there (*which would be disastrous*).

But what happens when you inherit and add new virtual functions in the derived class? See Listing 15-8.

Listing 15-8. Illustrating Addition of Virtual Functions in the Derived Class

```
//: C15:AddingVirtuals.cpp
// Adding virtuals in derivation
#include <iostream>
#include <string>
using namespace std;

class Pet {
  string pname;
public:
  Pet(const string &petName) : pname(petName) {}
  virtual string name() const { return pname; }
  virtual string speak() const { return ""; }
};

class Dog : public Pet {
  string name;
public:
  Dog(const string &petName) : Pet(petName) {}
  // New virtual function in the Dog class:
  virtual string sit() const {
    return Pet::name() + " sits";
  }
  string speak() const {        // Override
    return Pet::name() + " says 'Bark!'";
  }
};

int main() {
  Pet* p[] = {new Pet("generic"),new Dog("bob")};
  cout << "p[0]->speak() = "
       << p[0]->speak() << endl;
  cout << "p[1]->speak() = "
       << p[1]->speak() << endl;
//! cout << "p[1]->sit() = "
//!      << p[1]->sit() << endl; // Illegal
} ///:~
```

The class Pet contains two virtual functions, speak( ) and name( ). Dog adds a third virtual function called sit( ), as well as overriding the meaning of speak( ). Figure 15-4 will help you visualize what's happening. It depicts the VTABLEs created by the compiler for Pet and Dog.

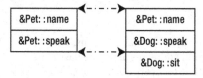

Figure 15-4. *Virtual tables for Pet and Dog*

Notice that the compiler maps the location of the speak( ) address into exactly the same spot in the Dog VTABLE as it is in the Pet VTABLE. Similarly, if a class Pug is inherited from Dog, its version of sit( ) would be placed in its VTABLE in exactly the same spot as it is in Dog. This is because (as you saw with the assembly language example) the compiler generates code that uses a simple numerical offset into the VTABLE to select the virtual function. Regardless of the specific subtype the object belongs to, its VTABLE is laid out the same way, so calls to the virtual functions will always be made the same way.

In this case, however, the compiler is working only with a pointer to a base class object. The base class has only the speak( ) and name( ) functions, so those are the only functions the compiler will allow you to call. How could it possibly know that you are working with a Dog object, if it has only a pointer to a base class object? That pointer might point to some other type, which doesn't have a sit( ) function. It may or may not have some other function address at that point in the VTABLE, but in either case, making a virtual call to that VTABLE address is not what you want to do. So the compiler is doing its job by protecting you from making virtual calls to functions that exist only in derived classes.

There are some less common cases in which you may know that the pointer actually points to an object of a specific subclass. If you want to call a function that only exists in that subclass, then you must cast the pointer. You can remove the error message produced by the previous program like this:

```
((Dog*)p[1])->sit()
```

Here, you happen to know that p[1] points to a Dog object, but in general you don't know that. If your problem is set up so that you must know the exact types of all objects, you should rethink it, because you're probably not using virtual functions properly. However, there are some situations in which the design works best (or you have no choice) if you know the exact type of all objects kept in a generic container. This is the problem of *run-time type identification* (RTTI).

RTTI is all about casting base class pointers down to derived class pointers ("up" and "down" are relative to a typical class diagram, with the base class at the top). Casting *up* happens automatically, with no coercion, because it's completely safe. Casting *down* is unsafe because there's no compile-time information about the actual types, so you must know exactly what type the object is. If you cast it into the wrong type, you'll be in trouble. (RTTI is described later in this chapter and Chapter 20 is fully devoted to the subject as well.)

Object Slicing

There is a distinct difference between passing the addresses of objects and passing objects by value when using polymorphism. All the examples you've seen here, and virtually all the examples you should see, pass addresses and not values. This is because addresses all have the same size, so passing the address of an object of a derived type (which is usually a bigger object) is the same as passing the address of an object of the base type (which is usually a smaller object). As explained before, this is the goal when using polymorphism: code that manipulates a base type can transparently manipulate derived type objects as well.

If you upcast to an object instead of a pointer or reference, something will happen that may surprise you: the object is "sliced" until all that remains is the subobject that corresponds to the destination type of your cast. In Listing 15-9, you can see what happens when an object is sliced.

Listing 15-9. Illustrating Object Slicing

```
//: C15:ObjectSlicing.cpp
#include <iostream>
#include <string>
using namespace std;

class Pet {
  string pname;
public:
  Pet(const string& name) : pname(name) {}
  virtual string name() const { return pname; }
  virtual string description() const {
    return "This is " + pname;
  }
};

class Dog : public Pet {
  string favoriteActivity;
public:
  Dog(const string& name, const string& activity)
    : Pet(name), favoriteActivity(activity) {}
  string description() const {
    return Pet::name() + " likes to " +
      favoriteActivity;
  }
};

void describe(Pet p) { // Slices the object
  cout << p.description() << endl;
}

int main() {
  Pet p("Bob");
  Dog d("Peter", "sleep");
  describe(p);
  describe(d);
} ///:~
```

The function describe( ) is passed an object of type Pet *by value*. It then calls the virtual function description( ) for the Pet object. In main( ), you might expect the first call to produce "This is Bob," and the second to produce "Peter likes to sleep." In fact, both calls use the base class version of description( ).

Two things are happening in this program. First, because describe( ) accepts a Pet object (rather than a pointer or reference), any calls to describe( ) will cause an object the size of Pet to be pushed on the stack and cleaned up after the call. This means that if an object of a class inherited from Pet is passed to describe( ), the compiler accepts it, but it copies only the Pet portion of the object. It *slices* the derived portion off of the object, as shown in Figure 15-5.

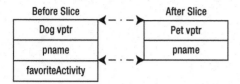

Figure 15-5. *Showing slicing of the derived part (Dog) from the basic Content (Pet)*

Now you may wonder about the virtual function call. Dog::description() makes use of portions of both Pet (which still exists) and Dog, which no longer exists because it was sliced off! So what happens when the virtual function is called?

You're saved from disaster because the object is being passed by value. Because of this, the compiler knows the precise type of the object because the derived object has been forced to become a base object. When passing by value, the copy-constructor for a Pet object is used, which initializes the VPTR to the Pet VTABLE and copies only the Pet parts of the object. There's no explicit copy-constructor here, so the compiler synthesizes one. Under all interpretations, the object truly becomes a Pet during slicing.

Object slicing actually removes part of the existing object as it copies it into the new object, rather than simply changing the meaning of an address as when using a pointer or reference. Because of this, upcasting into an object is not done often; in fact, it's usually something to watch out for and prevent. Note that, in this example, if description() were made into a pure virtual function in the base class (which is not unreasonable, since it doesn't really do anything in the base class), then the compiler would prevent object slicing because that wouldn't allow you to "create" an object of the base type (which is what happens when you upcast by value). This could be the most important value of pure virtual functions: to prevent object slicing by generating a compile-time error message if someone tries to do it.

Overloading and Overriding

In Chapter 14, you saw that redefining an overloaded function in the base class hides all of the other base class versions of that function. When virtual functions are involved, the behavior is a little different. Listing 15-10 shows a modified version of the NameHiding.cpp example from Chapter 14.

Listing 15-10. Demonstrating that Virtual Functions Restrict Overloading

```
//: C15:NameHiding2.cpp
// Virtual functions restrict overloading
#include <iostream>
#include <string>
using namespace std;

class Base {
public:
  virtual int f() const {
    cout << "Base::f()\n";
    return 1;
  }
  virtual void f(string) const {}
  virtual void g() const {}
};
```

```
class Derived1 : public Base {
public:
  void g() const {}
};

class Derived2 : public Base {
public:
  // Overriding a virtual function:
  int f() const {
    cout << "Derived2::f()\n";
    return 2;
  }
};

class Derived3 : public Base {
public:
  // Cannot change return type:
  //! void f() const{ cout<< "Derived3::f()\n";}
};

class Derived4 : public Base {
public:
  // Change argument list:
  int f(int) const {
    cout << "Derived4::f()\n";
    return 4;
  }
};

int main() {
  string s("hello");
  Derived1 d1;
  int x = d1.f();
  d1.f(s);
  Derived2 d2;
  x = d2.f();
//! d2.f(s);     // string version hidden
  Derived4 d4;
  x = d4.f(1);
//! x = d4.f(); // f() version hidden
//! d4.f(s);     // string version hidden
  Base &br = d4; // Upcast
//! br.f(1);     // Derived version unavailable
  br.f();         // Base version available
  br.f(s);        // Base version available
} ///:~
```

The first thing to notice is that in Derived3 the compiler will not allow you to change the return type of an overridden function (it will allow it if f( ) is not virtual). This is an important restriction because the compiler must guarantee that you can polymorphically call the function through the base class, and if the base class is expecting an int to be returned from f( ), then the derived-class version of f( ) must keep that contract or else things will break.

CHAPTER 15 ■ POLYMORPHISM AND VIRTUAL FUNCTIONS

The rule shown in Chapter 14 still works: if you override one of the overloaded member functions in the base class, the other overloaded versions become hidden in the derived class. In main( ), the code that tests Derived4 shows that this happens even if the new version of f( ) isn't actually overriding an existing virtual function interface—both of the base class versions of f( ) are hidden by f(int). However, if you upcast d4 to Base, then only the base class versions are available (because that's what the base class contract promises) and the derived-class version is not available (because it isn't specified in the base class).

Variant Return Type

The Derived3 class above suggests that you cannot modify the return type of a virtual function during overriding. This is generally true, but there is a special case in which you can slightly modify the return type. If you're returning a pointer or a reference to a base class, then the overridden version of the function may return a pointer or reference to a class derived from what the base returns. See Listing 15-11 for an example.

Listing 15-11. Illustrating Variant Return Type

```
//: C15:VariantReturn.cpp
// Returning a pointer or reference to a derived
// type during overriding
#include <iostream>
#include <string>
using namespace std;

class PetFood {
public:
  virtual string foodType() const = 0;
};

class Pet {
public:
  virtual string type() const = 0;
  virtual PetFood* eats() = 0;
};

class Bird : public Pet {
public:
  string type() const { return "Bird"; }
  class BirdFood : public PetFood {
  public:
  string foodType() const {
    return "Bird food";
    }
  };
  // Upcast to base type:
  PetFood* eats() { return &bf; }
private:
  BirdFood bf;
};
```

```
class Cat : public Pet {
public:
  string type() const { return "Cat"; }
  class CatFood : public PetFood {
  public:
    string foodType() const { return "Birds"; }
  };
  // Return exact type instead:
  CatFood* eats() { return &cf; }
private:
  CatFood cf;
};

int main() {
  Bird b;
  Cat c;
  Pet* p[] = { &b, &c, };
  for(int i = 0; i < sizeof p / sizeof *p; i++)
    cout << p[i]->type() << " eats "
         << p[i]->eats()->foodType() << endl;
  // Can return the exact type:
  Cat::CatFood* cf = c.eats();
  Bird::BirdFood* bf;
  // Cannot return the exact type:
  //!  bf = b.eats();
  // Must downcast:
  bf = dynamic_cast<Bird::BirdFood*>(b.eats());
} ///:~
```

The Pet::eats() member function returns a pointer to a PetFood. In Bird, this member function is overloaded exactly as in the base class, including the return type. That is, Bird::eats() upcasts the BirdFood to a PetFood.

But in Cat, the return type of eats() is a pointer to CatFood, a type derived from PetFood. The fact that the return type is inherited from the return type of the base class function is the only reason this compiles. That way, the contract is still fulfilled; eats() always returns a PetFood pointer.

If you think polymorphically, this doesn't seem necessary. Why not just upcast all the return types to PetFood*, just as Bird::eats() did? This is typically a good solution, but at the end of main(), you see the difference: Cat::eats() can return the exact type of PetFood, whereas the return value of Bird::eats() must be downcast to the exact type.

So being able to return the exact type is a little more general, and doesn't lose the specific type information by automatically upcasting. However, returning the base type will generally solve your problems so this is a rather specialized feature.

Virtual Functions and Constructors

When an object containing virtual functions is created, its VPTR must be initialized to point to the proper VTABLE. This must be done before there's any possibility of calling a virtual function. As you might guess, because the constructor has the job of bringing an object into existence, it is also the constructor's job to set up the VPTR. The compiler secretly inserts code into the beginning of the constructor that initializes the VPTR. And as described in Chapter 14, if you don't explicitly create a constructor for a class, the compiler will synthesize one for you. If the class has virtual functions, the synthesized constructor will include the proper VPTR initialization code. This has several implications.

The first concerns efficiency. The reason for inline functions is to reduce the calling overhead for small functions. If C++ didn't provide inline functions, the preprocessor might be used to create these "macros." However, the preprocessor has no concept of access or classes, and therefore couldn't be used to create member function macros. In addition, with constructors that must have hidden code inserted by the compiler, a preprocessor macro wouldn't work at all.

You must be aware when hunting for efficiency holes that the compiler is inserting hidden code into your constructor function. Not only must it initialize the VPTR, it must also check the value of this (in case the operator new( ) returns zero) and call base class constructors. Taken together, this code can impact what you thought was a tiny inline function call. In particular, the size of the constructor may overwhelm the savings you get from reduced function call overhead. If you make a lot of inline constructor calls, your code size can grow without any benefits in speed.

Of course, you probably won't make all tiny constructors non-inline right away, because they're much easier to write as inlines. But when you're tuning your code, remember to consider removing the inline constructors.

Order of Constructor Calls

The second interesting facet of constructors and virtual functions concerns the order of constructor calls and the way virtual calls are made within constructors.

Base class constructors are always called in the constructor for an inherited class. This makes sense because the constructor has a special job: to see that the object is built properly. A derived class has access only to its own members, and not those of the base class. Only the base class constructor can properly initialize its own elements. Therefore it's essential that all constructors get called; otherwise the entire object wouldn't be constructed properly. That's why the compiler enforces a constructor call for every portion of a derived class. It will call the default constructor if you don't explicitly call a base class constructor in the constructor initializer list. If there is no default constructor, the compiler will complain.

The order of the constructor calls is important. When you inherit, you know all about the base class and can access any public and protected members of the base class. This means you must be able to assume that all the members of the base class are valid when you're in the derived class. In a normal member function, construction has already taken place, so all the members of all parts of the object have been built. Inside the constructor, however, you must be able to assume that all members that you use have been built. The only way to guarantee this is for the base class constructor to be called first. Then when you're in the derived class constructor, all the members you can access in the base class have been initialized. Knowing all members are valid inside the constructor is also the reason that, whenever possible, you should initialize all member objects (that is, objects placed in the class using *composition*) in the constructor initializer list. If you follow this practice, you can assume that all base class members and member objects of the current object have been initialized.

Behavior of Virtual Functions Inside Constructors

The hierarchy of constructor calls brings up an interesting dilemma. What happens if you're inside a constructor and you call a virtual function? Inside an ordinary member function you can imagine what will happen—the virtual call is resolved at runtime because the object cannot know whether it belongs to the class the member function is in, or some class derived from it. For consistency, you might think this is what should happen inside constructors.

This is not the case. If you call a virtual function inside a constructor, only the local version of the function is used. That is, the virtual mechanism doesn't work within the constructor.

This behavior makes sense for two reasons. Conceptually, the constructor's job is to bring the object into existence (which is hardly an ordinary feat). Inside any constructor, the object may only be partially formed; you can only know that the base class objects have been initialized, but you cannot know which classes are inherited from you. A virtual function call, however, reaches "forward" or "outward" into the inheritance hierarchy. It calls a function in a derived class. If you could do this inside a constructor, you'd be calling a function that might manipulate members that hadn't been initialized yet, a sure recipe for disaster.

The second reason is a mechanical one. When a constructor is called, one of the first things it does is initialize its VPTR. However, it can only know that it is of the "current" type—the type the constructor was written for. The constructor code is completely ignorant of whether or not the object is in the base of another class. When the compiler generates code for that constructor, it generates code for a constructor of that class, not a base class and not a class derived from it (because a class can't know who inherits it). So the VPTR it uses must be for the VTABLE of *that* class. The VPTR remains initialized to that VTABLE for the rest of the object's lifetime *unless* this isn't the last constructor call. If a more-derived constructor is called afterwards, that constructor sets the VPTR *to* its VTABLE, and so on, until the last constructor finishes. The state of the VPTR is determined by the constructor that is called last. This is another reason why the constructors are called in order from base to most-derived.

But while all this series of constructor calls is taking place, each constructor has set the VPTR to its own VTABLE. If it uses the virtual mechanism for function calls, it will produce only a call through its own VTABLE, not the most-derived VTABLE (as would be the case after all the constructors were called). In addition, many compilers recognize that a virtual function call is being made inside a constructor, and perform early binding because they know that late binding will produce a call only to the local function. In either event, you won't get the results you might initially expect from a virtual function call inside a constructor.

Destructors and Virtual Destructors

You cannot use the `virtual` keyword with constructors, but destructors can and often must be virtual.

The constructor has the special job of putting an object together *piece by piece* first by calling the base constructor, then the more derived constructors in order of inheritance (it must also call member-object constructors along the way). Similarly, the destructor has a special job: it must disassemble an object that may belong to a hierarchy of classes. To do this, the compiler generates code that calls all the destructors, but in the *reverse* order that they are called by the constructor. That is, the destructor starts at the most-derived class and works its way down to the base class. This is the safe and desirable thing to do because the current destructor can always know that the base class members are alive and active. If you need to call a base class member function inside your destructor, it is safe to do so. Thus, the destructor can perform its own cleanup, *then* call the next-down destructor, which will perform *its* own cleanup, etc. Each destructor knows what its class is derived *from*, but not what is derived from it.

You should keep in mind that constructors and destructors are the only places where this hierarchy of calls must happen (and thus the proper hierarchy is automatically generated by the compiler). In all other functions, only *that* function will be called (*and not base class versions*), whether they're virtual or not. The only way for base class versions of the same function to be called in ordinary functions (*virtual or not*) is if you explicitly *call* that function.

Normally, the action of the destructor is quite adequate. But what happens if you want to manipulate an object through a pointer to its base class (that is, manipulate the object through its generic interface)? This activity is a major objective in object-oriented programming. The problem occurs when you want to `delete` a pointer of this type for an object that has been created on the heap with `new`. If the pointer is to the base class, the compiler can only know to call the base class version of the destructor during `delete`.

Sound familiar?

This is the same problem that virtual functions were created to solve for the general case. Fortunately, virtual functions work for destructors as they do for all other functions *except* constructors; see Listing 15-12.

Listing 15-12. Illustrating Behavior of Virtual vs. Non-Virtual Destructors

```
//: C15:VirtualDestructors.cpp
// Behavior of virtual vs. non-virtual destructor
#include <iostream>
using namespace std;

class Base1 {
public:
  ~Base1() { cout << "~Base1()\n"; }
};
```

```cpp
class Derived1 : public Base1 {
public:
  ~Derived1() { cout << "~Derived1()\n"; }
};

class Base2 {
public:
  virtual ~Base2() { cout << "~Base2()\n"; }
};

class Derived2 : public Base2 {
public:
  ~Derived2() { cout << "~Derived2()\n"; }
};

int main() {
  Base1* bp = new Derived1;  // Upcast
  delete bp;
  Base2* b2p = new Derived2; // Upcast
  delete b2p;
} ///:~
```

When you run the program, you'll see that delete bp only calls the base class destructor, while delete b2p calls the derived class destructor followed by the base class destructor, which is the behavior we desire. Forgetting to make a destructor virtual is an insidious bug because it often doesn't directly affect the behavior of your program, but it can quietly introduce a memory leak. Also, the fact that some destruction is occurring can further mask the problem.

Even though the destructor, like the constructor, is an "exceptional" function, it is possible for the destructor to be virtual because the object already knows what type it is (whereas it doesn't during construction). Once an object has been constructed, its VPTR is initialized, so virtual function calls can take place.

Pure Virtual Destructors

While pure virtual destructors are legal in Standard C++, there is an added constraint when using them: you must provide a function body for the pure virtual destructor. This seems counterintuitive; how can a virtual function be "pure" if it needs a function body? But if you keep in mind that constructors and destructors are special operations, it makes more sense, especially if you remember that all destructors in a class hierarchy are always called. If you *could* leave off the definition for a pure virtual destructor, what function body would be called during destruction? Thus, it's absolutely necessary that the compiler and linker enforce the existence of a function body for a pure virtual destructor.

If it's pure, but it has to have a function body, what's the value of it? The only difference you'll see between the pure and non-pure virtual destructor is that the pure virtual destructor does cause the base class to be abstract, so you cannot create an object of the base class (although this would also be true if any other member function of the base class were pure virtual).

Things are a bit confusing, however, when you inherit a class from one that contains a pure virtual destructor. Unlike every other pure virtual function, you are *not* required to provide a definition of a pure virtual destructor in the derived class. The fact that the code in Listing 15-13 compiles and links is the proof.

Listing 15-13. Illustrating Pure Virtual Destructors

```cpp
//: C15:UnAbstract.cpp
// Pure virtual destructors
// seem to behave strangely
```

```
classAbstractBase {
public:
  virtual ~AbstractBase() = 0;
};

AbstractBase::~AbstractBase() {}

class Derived : public AbstractBase {};
// No overriding of destructor necessary?

int main() { Derived d; } ///:~
```

Normally, a pure virtual function in a base class would cause the derived class to be abstract unless it (and all other pure virtual functions) is given a definition. But here this seems not to be the case. However, remember that the compiler automatically creates a destructor definition for every class if you don't create one. That's what's happening here—the base class destructor is being quietly overridden, and thus the definition is being provided by the compiler and Derived is not actually abstract.

This brings up an interesting question: What is the point of a pure virtual destructor? Unlike an ordinary pure virtual function, you must *give it* a function body. In a derived class, you aren't forced to provide a definition since the compiler synthesizes the destructor for you. So what's the difference between a regular virtual destructor and a pure virtual destructor?

The only distinction occurs when you have a class that only has a single pure virtual function: the destructor. In this case, the only effect of the purity of the destructor is to prevent the instantiation of the base class. If there were any other pure virtual functions, they would prevent the instantiation of the base class, but if there are no others, then the pure virtual destructor will do it. So, while the addition of a virtual destructor is essential, whether it's pure or not isn't so important.

When you run the code in Listing 15-14, you can see that the pure virtual function body is called after the derived class version, just as with any other destructor.

Listing 15-14. Illustrating that Pure Virtual Destructors Require a Function Body(also, shows that the Virtual Function Body is Called after the Derived Class Version)

```
//: C15:PureVirtualDestructors.cpp
// Pure virtual destructors
// require a function body
#include <iostream>
using namespace std;

class Pet {
public:
  virtual ~Pet() = 0;
};

Pet::~Pet() {
  cout << "~Pet()" << endl;
}

class Dog : public Pet {
public:
  ~Dog() {
    cout << "~Dog()" << endl;
  }
};
```

```
int main() {
  Pet* p = new Dog; // Upcast
  delete p;         // Virtual destructor call
} ///:~
```

As a guideline, any time you have a virtual function in a class, you should immediately add a virtual destructor (*even if it does nothing*). This way, you ensure against any surprises later.

Virtuals in Destructors

There's something that happens during destruction that you might not immediately expect. If you're inside an ordinary member function and you call a virtual function, that function is called using the late binding mechanism. This is not true with destructors, virtual or not. Inside a destructor, only the "local" version of the member function is called; the virtual mechanism is ignored, as you can see in Listing 15-15.

Listing 15-15. Illustrating Virtual Calls Inside Destructors

```
//: C15:VirtualsInDestructors.cpp
// Virtual calls inside destructors
#include <iostream>
using namespace std;

class Base {
public:
  virtual ~Base() {
    cout << "Base1()\n";
    f();
  }
  virtual void f() { cout << "Base::f()\n"; }
};

class Derived : public Base {

public:
  ~Derived() { cout << "~Derived()\n"; }
  void f() { cout << "Derived::f()\n"; }
};

int main() {
  Base* bp = new Derived; // Upcast
  delete bp;
} ///:~
```

During the destructor call, Derived::f( ) is *not* called, even though f( ) is virtual.

Why is this? Suppose the virtual mechanism *were* used inside the destructor. Then it would be possible for the virtual call to resolve to a function that was "farther out" (more derived) on the inheritance hierarchy than the current destructor. But destructors are called from the "outside in" (from the most-derived destructor down to the base destructor), so the actual function called would rely on portions of an object that have already been destroyed! Instead, the compiler resolves the calls at compile-time and calls only the "local" version of the function. Notice that the same is true for the constructor (as described earlier), but in the constructor's case the type information wasn't available, whereas in the destructor the information (that is, the VPTR) is there, but it *isn't* reliable.

Creating an Object-Based Hierarchy

An issue that has been recurring throughout this book during the demonstration of the container classes Stack and Stash is the "ownership problem." The "owner" refers to who or what is responsible for calling delete for objects that have been created dynamically (using new). The problem when using containers is that they need to be flexible enough to hold different types of objects. To do this, the containers have held void pointers and so they haven't known the type of object they've held. Deleting a void pointer doesn't call the destructor, so the container couldn't be responsible for cleaning up its objects.

One solution was presented in the example C14:InheritStack.cpp (Listing 14-9), in which the Stack was inherited into a new class that accepted and produced only string pointers. Since it knew that it could hold only pointers to string objects, it could properly delete them. This was a nice solution, but it requires you to inherit a new container class for each type that you want to hold in the container.

> ■ **Note** Although this seems tedious now, it will actually work quite well in Chapter 16, when templates are introduced.

The problem is that you want the container to hold more than one type, but you don't want to use void pointers. Another solution is to use polymorphism by forcing all the objects held in the container to be inherited from the same base class. That is, the container holds the objects of the base class, and then you can call virtual functions—in particular, you can call virtual destructors to solve the ownership problem.

This solution uses what is referred to as a *singly-rooted hierarchy* or an *object-based hierarchy* (because the root class of the hierarchy is usually named "Object"). It turns out that there are many other benefits to using a singly-rooted hierarchy; in fact, every other object-oriented language but C++ enforces the use of such a hierarchy. When you create a class, you are automatically inheriting it directly or indirectly from a common base class, a base class that was established by the creators of the language. In C++, it was thought that the enforced use of this common base class would cause too much overhead, so it was left out. However, you can choose to use a common base class in your own projects.

To solve the ownership problem, you can create an extremely simple Object for the base class, which contains only a virtual destructor. The Stack can then hold classes inherited from Object. See Listing 15-16.

Listing 15-16. Illustrating a Singly-Rooted Hierarchy (also, Known as an Object-based Hierarchy)

```
//: C15:OStack.h
// Using a singly-rooted hierarchy
#ifndef OSTACK_H
#define OSTACK_H

class Object {
public:
  virtual ~Object() = 0;
};

// Required definition:
inline Object::~Object() {}

class Stack {
  struct Link {
    Object* data;
    Link* next;
    Link(Object* dat, Link* nxt) :
      data(dat), next(nxt) {}
  }* head;
```

```
public:
  Stack() : head(0) {}
  ~Stack(){
    while(head)
      delete pop();
  }
  void push(Object* dat) {
    head = new Link(dat, head);
  }
  Object* peek() const {
    return head ? head->data : 0;
  }
  Object* pop() {
    if(head == 0) return 0;
    Object* result = head->data;
    Link* oldHead = head;
    head = head->next;
    delete oldHead;
    return result;
  }
};
#endif // OSTACK_H ///:~
```

To simplify things by keeping everything in the header file, the (required) definition for the pure virtual destructor *is* inlined into the header file, and pop( ) (which might be considered too large for inlining) is also inlined.

Link objects now hold pointers to Object rather than void pointers, and the Stack will only accept and return Object pointers. Now Stack is much more flexible, since it will hold lots of different types but will also destroy any objects that are left on the Stack. The new limitation (which will be finally removed when templates are applied to the problem in Chapter 16) is that anything that is placed on the Stack must be inherited from Object. That's fine if you are starting your class from scratch, but what if you already have a class such as string that you want to be able to put onto the Stack? In this case, the new class must be both a string and an Object, which means it must be inherited from both classes. This is called *multiple inheritance* and it is the subject of an entire chapter later on in this book. In Chapter 21, you'll see that multiple inheritance can be fraught with complexity, and is a feature you should use sparingly. In Listing 15-17, however, everything is simple enough that we don't trip across any multiple inheritance pitfalls.

Listing 15-17. Testing Out the OStack in Listing 15-16

```
//: C15:OStackTest.cpp
//{T} OStackTest.cpp
#include "OStack.h"          // To be INCLUDED from above
#include "../require.h"       // To be INCLUDED from Chapter 9
#include <fstream>
#include <iostream>
#include <string>
using namespace std;

// Use multiple inheritance. We want
// both a string and an Object:
class MyString: public string, public Object {
public:
  ~MyString() {
    cout << "deleting string: " << *this << endl;
  }
```

```
  MyString(string s) : string(s) {}
};

int main(int argc, char* argv[]) {
  requireArgs(argc, 1); // File name is argument
  ifstream in(argv[1]);
  assure(in, argv[1]);
  Stack textlines;
  string line;
  // Read file and store lines in the stack:
  while(getline(in, line))
    textlines.push(new MyString(line));
  // Pop some lines from the stack:
  MyString* s;
  for(int i = 0; i < 10; i++) {
    if((s=(MyString*)textlines.pop())==0) break;
    cout << *s << endl;
    delete s;
  }
  cout << "Letting the destructor do the rest:" << endl;
} ///:~
```

Although this is similar to the previous version of the test program for Stack, you'll notice that only 10 elements are popped from the stack, which means there are probably some objects remaining. Because the Stack knows that it holds Objects, the destructor can properly clean things up, and you'll see this in the output of the program, since the MyString objects print messages as they are destroyed.

Creating containers that hold Objects is not an unreasonable approach—*if* you have a singly-rooted hierarchy (enforced either by the language or by the requirement that every class inherit from Object). In that case, everything is guaranteed to be an Object and so it's not very complicated to use the containers. In C++, however, you cannot expect this from every class, so you're bound to trip over multiple inheritance if you take this approach. You'll see in Chapter 16 that templates solve the problem in a much simpler and more elegant fashion.

Operator Overloading

You can make operators virtual just like other member functions. Implementing virtual operators often becomes confusing, however, because you may be operating on two objects, both with unknown types. This is usually the case with mathematical components (for which you often overload operators). For example, consider a system that deals with matrices, vectors, and scalar values, all three of which are derived from class Math, as shown in Listing 15-18.

Listing 15-18. Illustrating Polymorphism with Overloaded Operators

```
//: C15:OperatorPolymorphism.cpp
// Polymorphism with overloaded operators
#include <iostream>
using namespace std;

class Matrix;
class Scalar;
class Vector;
```

```
class Math {
public:
  virtual Math& operator*(Math& rv) = 0;
  virtual Math& multiply(Matrix*) = 0;
  virtual Math& multiply(Scalar*) = 0;
  virtual Math& multiply(Vector*) = 0;
  virtual ~Math() {}
};

class Matrix : public Math {
public:
  Math& operator*(Math& rv) {
   return rv.multiply(this);  // 2nd dispatch
   }
  Math& multiply(Matrix*) {
    cout << "Matrix * Matrix" << endl;
    return *this;
}
  Math& multiply(Scalar*) {
    cout << "Scalar * Matrix" << endl;
    return *this;
  }
  Math& multiply(Vector*) {
    cout << "Vector * Matrix" << endl;
    return *this;
  }
};

class Scalar : public Math  {
public:
  Math& operator*(Math& rv) {
    return rv.multiply(this); // 2nd dispatch
  }
  Math& multiply(Matrix*) {
    cout << "Matrix * Scalar" << endl;
    return *this;
  }
  Math& multiply(Scalar*) {
   cout << "Scalar * Scalar" << endl;
   return *this;
  }
  Math& multiply(Vector*) {
   cout << "Vector * Scalar" << endl;
   return *this;
  }
};

class Vector : public Math  {
public:
  Math& operator*(Math& rv) {
   return rv.multiply(this);  // 2nd dispatch
  }
```

410

```
  Math& multiply(Matrix*) {
    cout << "Matrix * Vector" << endl;
    return *this;
  }
  Math& multiply(Scalar*) {
    cout << "Scalar * Vector" << endl;
    return *this;
  }
  Math& multiply(Vector*) {
    cout << "Vector * Vector" << endl;
    return *this;
  }
};

int main() {
  Matrix m; Vector v; Scalar s;
  Math* math[] = { &m, &v, &s };
  for(int i = 0; i < 3; i++)
     for(int j = 0; j < 3; j++) {
         Math& m1 = *math[i];
         Math& m2 = *math[j];
         m1 * m2;
     }
} ///:~
```

For simplicity, only the operator* has been overloaded. The goal is to be able to multiply any two Math objects and produce the desired result—and note that multiplying a matrix by a vector is a very different operation than multiplying a vector by a matrix.

The problem is that, in main( ), the expression m1 * m2 contains two upcast Math references, and thus two objects of unknown type. A virtual function is only capable of making a single dispatch—that is, determining the type of one unknown object. To determine both types a technique called *multiple dispatching* is used in this example, whereby what appears to be a single virtual function call results in a second virtual call. By the time this second call is made, you've determined both types of object, and can perform the proper activity. It's not transparent at first, but if you stare at the example for awhile it should begin to make sense.

Downcasting

As you might guess, since there's such a thing as upcasting (moving up an inheritance hierarchy) there should also be *downcasting* to move down a hierarchy. But upcasting is easy since as you move up an inheritance hierarchy the classes always converge to more general classes. That is, when you upcast you are always clearly derived from an ancestor class (typically only one, except in the case of multiple inheritance) but when you downcast there are usually several possibilities that you could cast to. More specifically, a Circle is a type of Shape (that's the upcast), but if you try to downcast a Shape it could be a Circle, Square, Triangle, etc. So the dilemma is figuring out a way to safely downcast.

■ **Note**   But an even more important issue is asking yourself why you're downcasting in the first place instead of just using polymorphism to automatically figure out the correct type.

C++ provides a special *explicit cast* (introduced in Chapter 3) called `dynamic_cast` that is a *type-safe* downcast operation. When you use `dynamic_cast` to try to cast down to a particular type, the return value will be a pointer to the desired type only if the cast is proper and successful; otherwise it will return zero to indicate that this was not the correct type. Listing 15-19 contains a minimal example.

Listing 15-19. Illustrating a dynamic_cast

```
//: C15:DynamicCast.cpp
#include <iostream>
using namespace std;

class Pet { public: virtual ~Pet(){}};
class Dog : public Pet {};
class Cat : public Pet {};

int main() {
  Pet* b = new Cat; // Upcast
  // Try to cast it to Dog*:
  Dog* d1 = dynamic_cast<Dog*>(b);
  // Try to cast it to Cat*:
  Cat* d2 = dynamic_cast<Cat*>(b);
  cout << "d1 = " << (long)d1 << endl;
  cout << "d2 = " << (long)d2 << endl;
} ///:~
```

When you use `dynamic_cast`, you must be working with a true polymorphic hierarchy (one with virtual functions) because `dynamic_cast` uses information stored in the VTABLE to determine the actual type. Here, the base class contains a virtual destructor and that suffices. In `main( )`, a Cat pointer is upcast to a Pet, and then a downcast is attempted to both a Dog pointer and a Cat pointer. Both pointers are printed, and you'll see when you run the program that the incorrect downcast produces a zero result. Of course, whenever you downcast you are responsible for checking to make sure that the result of the cast is nonzero. Also, you should not assume that the pointer will be exactly the same, because sometimes pointer adjustments take place during upcasting *and* downcasting (in particular, with multiple inheritance).

A `dynamic_cast` requires a little bit of extra overhead to run; not much, but if you're doing a lot of `dynamic_casting` (in which case you should be *seriously questioning* your program design) this may become a performance issue. In some cases you may know something special during downcasting that allows you to say for sure what type you're dealing with, in which case the extra overhead of the `dynamic_cast` becomes unnecessary, and you can use a `static_cast` instead. Listing 15-20 shows how it might work.

Listing 15-20. Illustrating Navigation of Class Hierarchies with static_cast

```
//: C15:StaticHierarchyNavigation.cpp
// Navigating class hierarchies with static_cast
#include <iostream>
#include <typeinfo>
using namespace std;

class Shape { public: virtual ~Shape() {}; };
class Circle : public Shape {};
class Square : public Shape {};
class Other {};
```

```
int main() {
  Circle c;

  Shape* s = &c;                    // Upcast: normal and OK
  // More explicit but unnecessary:
  s = static_cast<Shape*>(&c);
  // (Since upcasting is such a safe and common
  // operation, the cast becomes cluttering)

  Circle* cp = 0;
  Square* sp = 0;
  // Static Navigation of class hierarchies
  // requires extra type information:
  if(typeid(s) == typeid(cp)) // C++ RTTI
    cp = static_cast<Circle*>(s);
  if(typeid(s) == typeid(sp))
    sp = static_cast<Square*>(s);
  if(cp != 0)
    cout << "It's a circle!" << endl;
  if(sp != 0)
    cout << "It's a square!" << endl;
  // Static navigation is ONLY an efficiency hack;
  // dynamic_cast is always safer. However:
  // Other* op = static_cast<Other*>(s);
  // Conveniently gives an error message, while

  Other* op2 = (Other*)s;
  // does not
} ///:~
```

In this program, C++'s run-time type information (RTTI) mechanism (a new feature fully described in Chapter 20) is used. RTTI allows you to discover type information that has been lost by upcasting. The dynamic_cast is actually one form of RTTI. Here, the typeid keyword (declared in the header file <typeinfo>) is used to detect the types of the pointers. You can see that the type of the upcast Shape pointer is successively compared to a Circle pointer and a Square pointer to see if there's a match. There's more to RTTI than typeid, and you can also imagine that it would be fairly easy to implement your own type information system using a virtual function.

A Circle object is created and the address is upcast to a Shape pointer; the second version of the expression shows how you can use static_cast to be more explicit about the upcast. However, since an upcast is always safe and it's a common thing to do, an explicit cast for upcasting is just cluttering and unnecessary.

RTTI is used to determine the type, and then static_cast is used to perform the downcast. But notice that in this design the process is effectively the same as using dynamic_cast, and the client programmer must do some testing to discover the cast that was actually successful. You'll typically want a situation that's more deterministic than in Listing 15-20 before using static_cast rather than dynamic_cast (and, again, you want to carefully examine your design before using dynamic_cast).

If a class hierarchy has no virtual functions (*which is a questionable design*) or if you have other information that allows you to safely downcast, it's a tiny bit faster to do the downcast statically than with dynamic_cast. In addition, static_cast won't allow you to cast out of the hierarchy, as the traditional cast will, so it's safer. However, statically navigating class hierarchies is always risky, and you should use dynamic_cast unless you have a special situation.

Review Session

1. *Polymorphism*—implemented in C++ with *virtual functions*—means *"different forms."* In object-oriented programming, you have the same face (the common interface in the base class) and different forms using that face: the different versions of the virtual functions.

2. You've seen in this chapter that it's impossible to understand, or even create, an example of polymorphism without using data abstraction and inheritance. Polymorphism is a feature that cannot be viewed in isolation (like const or a switch statement, for example), but instead works only in concert, as part of the *"big picture"* of *class relationships*.

3. People are often confused by other, non-object-oriented features of C++, like *overloading* and *default arguments*, which are sometimes presented as *object-oriented*. Don't be fooled; if it isn't *late binding*, it isn't *polymorphism*.

4. To use polymorphism—and thus object-oriented techniques—effectively in your programs you must *expand your view of programming* to include not just members and messages of an individual class, but also the *commonality among classes* and their *relationships* with each other.

5. Although this requires significant effort, it's a *worthy struggle* because the results are faster program development, better code organization, extensible programs, and easier code maintenance.

6. Polymorphism completes the object-oriented features of the language, but there are two more major features in C++: templates (which are introduced in Chapter 16), and exception handling (which is covered in Chapter 17). These two features provide you as much increase in programming power as each of the object-oriented features: abstract data typing, inheritance, and polymorphism.

CHAPTER 16

■ ■ ■

Introduction to Templates

Inheritance and composition provide a way to reuse object code. The *template* feature in C++ provides a way to reuse *source* code.

Although C++ templates are a general-purpose programming tool, when they were introduced in the language, they seemed to discourage the use of object-based container class hierarchies (demonstrated at the end of Chapter 15).

This chapter not only demonstrates the basics of templates, it is also an introduction to containers, which are fundamental components of object-oriented programming and are almost completely realized through the containers in the Standard C++ Library. You'll see that this book has been using container examples—Stash and Stack—throughout, precisely to get you comfortable with containers; in this chapter the concept of the *iterator* will also be added. Although containers are ideal examples for use with templates, *there are* many other uses for templates as well.

Containers

Suppose you want to create a stack, as we have been doing throughout the book. The stack class in Listing 16-1 will hold ints, to keep it simple.

Listing 16-1. Illustrating a Simple Integer Stack

```cpp
//: C16:IntStack.cpp
// Simple integer stack
//{L} fibonacci
#include "fibonacci.h"     // SEE ahead in this Section
#include "../require.h"     // To be INCLUDED from Chapter 9
#include <iostream>
using namespace std;

class IntStack {
  enum { ssize = 100 };
  int stack[ssize];
  int top;
public:
  IntStack() : top(0) {}
  void push(int i) {
    require(top < ssize, "Too many push()es");
    stack[top++] = i;
  }
  int pop() {
```

```
    require(top > 0, "Too many pop()s");
    return stack[--top];
  }
};

int main() {
  IntStack is;
  // Add some Fibonacci numbers, for interest:
  for(int i = 0; i < 20; i++)
    is.push(fibonacci(i));
  // Pop & print them:
  for(int k = 0; k < 20; k++)
    cout << is.pop() << endl;
} ///:~
```

The class `IntStack` is a trivial example of a push-down stack. For simplicity it has been created here with a fixed size, but you can also modify it to automatically expand by allocating memory off the heap, as in the `Stack` class that has been examined throughout the book.

`main()` adds some integers to the stack, and pops them off again. To make the example more interesting, the integers are created with the `fibonacci()` function, which generates the traditional rabbit-reproduction numbers. Listing 16-2 is the header file that declares the function.

Listing 16-2. Header File for The Fibonacci Number Generator

```
//: C16:fibonacci.h
// Fibonacci number generator
int fibonacci(int n); ///:~
```

Listing 16-3 is the implementation.

Listing 16-3. The Implementation of The Fibonacci Number Generator

```
//: C16:fibonacci.cpp {O}
#include "../require.h"

int fibonacci(int n) {
  const int sz = 100;
  require(n < sz);
  static int f[sz]; // Initialized to zero
  f[0] = f[1] = 1;
  // Scan for unfilled array elements:
  int i;
  for(i = 0; i < sz; i++)
    if(f[i] == 0) break;
  while(i <= n) {
    f[i] = f[i-1] + f[i-2];
    i++;
  }
  return f[n];
} ///:~
```

This is a fairly efficient implementation, because it never generates the numbers more than once. It uses a `static` array of `int`, and relies on the fact that the compiler will initialize a `static` array to zero. The first `for` loop moves the index `i` to where the first array element is zero, then a `while` loop adds Fibonacci numbers to the array until the desired element is reached. But notice that if the Fibonacci numbers through element `n` are already initialized, it skips the `while` loop altogether.

The Need for Containers

Obviously, an integer stack isn't a crucial tool. The real need for containers comes when you start making objects on the heap using `new` and destroying them with `delete`. In the general programming problem, you don't know how many objects you're going to need while you're writing the program. For example, in an air traffic control system you don't want to limit the number of planes your system can handle. You don't want the program to abort just because you exceed some number. In a computer-aided design system, you're dealing with lots of shapes, but only the user determines (at runtime) exactly how many shapes you're going to need. Once you notice this tendency, you'll discover lots of examples in your own programming situations.

C programmers who rely on virtual memory to handle their "memory management" often find the idea of `new`, `delete`, and container classes disturbing. Apparently, one practice in C is to create a huge global array, larger than anything the program would appear to need. This may not require much thought (or awareness of `malloc()` and `free()`), but it does produce programs that don't port well and that hide subtle bugs.

In addition, if you create a huge global array of objects in C++, the constructor and destructor overhead can slow things down significantly. The C++ approach works *much better*: when you need an object, create it with `new`, and put its pointer in a container. Later on, fish it out and do something to it. This way, you create only the objects you absolutely need. And usually you don't have all the initialization conditions available at the startup of the program. `new` allows you to wait until something happens in the environment before you can actually create the object.

So in the most common situation, you'll make a container that holds pointers to some objects of interest. You will create those objects using `new` and put the resulting pointer in the container (*potentially* upcasting it in the process), pulling it out later when you want to do something with the object. This technique produces the most flexible, general sort of program.

Overview of Templates

Now a problem arises. You have an `IntStack`, which holds integers. But you want a stack that holds shapes or aircraft or plants or something else. Reinventing your source code every time doesn't seem like a very intelligent approach with a language that touts reusability. There must be a better way.

There are three techniques for source code reuse in this situation: the C way, presented here for contrast; the Smalltalk approach, which significantly affected C++; and the C++ approach of templates.

The C Solution

Of course you're trying to get away from the C approach because it's messy and error prone and completely inelegant. In this approach, you copy the source code for a `Stack` and make modifications by hand, introducing new errors in the process. This is certainly not a very productive technique.

The Smalltalk Solution

Smalltalk (and Java, following its example) took a simple and straightforward approach: you want to reuse code, so use inheritance. To implement this, each container class holds items of the generic base class `Object` (similar to the example at the end of Chapter 15). But because the library in Smalltalk is of such fundamental importance, you don't ever create a class from scratch. Instead, you must always inherit it from an existing class. You find a class as close as possible to the one you want, inherit from it, and make a few changes. Obviously, this is a benefit because it minimizes your effort (and explains why you spend a lot of time learning the class library before becoming an effective Smalltalk programmer).

But it also means that all classes in Smalltalk end up being part of a single inheritance tree. You must inherit from a branch of this tree when creating a new class. Most of the tree is already there (it's the Smalltalk class library), and at the root of the tree is a class called Object—the same class that each Smalltalk container holds.

This is a neat trick because it means that every class in the Smalltalk (and Java) class hierarchy is derived from Object, so every class can be held in every container (including that container itself). This type of single-tree hierarchy based on a fundamental generic type (often named Object, which is also the case in Java) is referred to as an *object-based hierarchy*. You may have heard this term and assumed it was some new fundamental concept in OOP, like polymorphism. It simply refers to a class hierarchy with Object (or, some similar name) at its root and container classes that hold Object.

Because the Smalltalk class library had a much longer history and experience behind it than did C++, and because the original C++ compilers had *no* container class libraries, it seemed like a good idea to duplicate the Smalltalk library in C++. This was done as an experiment with an early C++ implementation, and because it represented a significant body of code, many people began using it. In the process of trying to use the container classes, they discovered a problem.

The problem was that in Smalltalk (and most other OOP languages), all classes are automatically derived from a single hierarchy, but this isn't true in C++. You might have your nice object-based hierarchy with its container classes, but then you might buy a set of shape classes or aircraft classes from another vendor who didn't use that hierarchy. (For one thing, using that hierarchy imposes overhead, which C programmers eschew.) How do you insert a separate class tree into the container class in your object-based hierarchy? Figure 16-1 shows what the problem looks like.

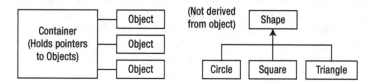

Figure 16-1. *How to insert a separate class tree (Shapes) into the container class in an object-based hierarchy?*

Because C++ supports multiple independent hierarchies, Smalltalk's object-based hierarchy does not work so well. The solution seemed obvious. If you can have many inheritance hierarchies, then you should be able to inherit from more than one class. *Multiple inheritance* will solve the problem. See Figure 16-2 for the solution (a similar example was given at the end of Chapter 15).

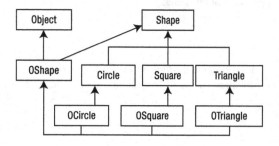

Figure 16-2. *Solution to the problem by way of multiple inheritance*

Now OShape has Shape's characteristics and behaviors, but because it is also derived from Object it can be placed in Container. The extra inheritance into OCircle, OSquare, etc. is necessary so that those classes can be upcast into OShape and thus retain the correct behavior. You can see that things are rapidly getting messy.

Compiler vendors invented and included their own object-based container class hierarchies, most of which have since been replaced by template versions. You can argue that multiple inheritance is needed for solving general programming problems, but you'll see in Chapter 21 that its complexity is best avoided except in special cases.

The Template Solution

Although an object-based hierarchy with multiple inheritance is conceptually straightforward, it turns out to be painful to use. In his original book, Stroustrup demonstrated what he considered a preferable alternative to the object-based hierarchy. Container classes were created as large preprocessor macros with arguments that could be substituted with your desired type. When you wanted to create a container to hold a particular type, you made a couple of macro calls.

Unfortunately, this approach was confused by all the existing Smalltalk literature and programming experience, and it was a bit unwieldy. Basically, nobody got it.

In the meantime, Stroustrup and the C++ team at Bell Labs had modified his original macro approach, simplifying it and moving it from the domain of the preprocessor into the compiler. This new code-substitution device is called a template, and it represents a completely different way to reuse code. Instead of reusing object code, as with inheritance and composition, a template reuses source code. The container no longer holds a generic base class called Object, but instead it holds an unspecified parameter. When you use a template, the parameter is substituted *by the compiler*, much like the old macro approach, but cleaner and easier to use.

Now, instead of worrying about inheritance or composition when you want to use a container class, you take the template version of the container and stamp out a specific version for your particular problem, as in Figure 16-3.

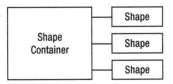

Figure 16-3. *Reuse of code through the source template*

The compiler does the work for you, and you end up with exactly the container you need to do your job, rather than an unwieldy inheritance hierarchy. In C++, the template implements the concept of a *parameterized type*. Another benefit of the template approach is that the novice programmer who may be unfamiliar or uncomfortable with inheritance can still use canned container classes right away (as we've been doing with vector throughout the book).

Template Syntax

The template keyword tells the compiler that the class definition that follows will manipulate one or more unspecified types. At the time the actual class code is generated from the template, those types must be specified so that the compiler can substitute them. To demonstrate the syntax, see Listing 16-4 for a small example that produces a bounds-checked array.

Listing 16-4. Illustrating The Template Syntax

```
//: C16:Array.cpp
#include "../require.h"
#include <iostream>
using namespace std;

template<class T>
class Array {
  enum { size = 100 };
  T A[size];
public:
  T& operator[](int index) {
    require(index >= 0 && index < size,
      "Index out of range");
    return A[index];
  }
};

int main() {
  Array<int> ia;
  Array<float> fa;
  for(int i = 0; i < 20; i++) {
    ia[i] = i * i;
    fa[i] = float(i) * 1.414;
  }
  for(int j = 0; j < 20; j++)
    cout << j << ": " << ia[j]
         << ", " << fa[j] << endl;
} ///:~
```

You can see that it looks like a normal class except for the line

```
template<class T>
```

which says that T is the substitution parameter, and that it represents a type name. Also, you see T used everywhere in the class where you would normally see the specific type the container holds.

In Array, elements are inserted *and* extracted with the same function: the overloaded operator [ ]. It returns a reference, so it can be used on both sides of an equal sign (that is, as both a lvalue and a rvalue). Notice that if the index is out of bounds, the require() function is used to print a message. Since operator[] is an inline, you could use this approach to guarantee that no array-bounds violations occur, then remove the require() for the shipping code.

In main(), you can see how easy it is to create Arrays that hold different types of objects. When you say

```
Array<int> ia;
Array<float> fa;
```

the compiler expands the Array template (this is called *instantiation*) twice, to create two new generated classes, which you can think of as Array_int and Array_float.

■ **Note**   Different compilers may decorate the names in different ways.

These are classes just like the ones you would have produced if you had performed the substitution by hand, except that the compiler creates them for you as you define the objects ia and fa. Also note that duplicate class definitions are either avoided by the compiler or merged by the linker.

Non-Inline Function Definitions

Of course, there are times when you'll want to have non-inline member function definitions. In this case, the compiler needs to see the template declaration before the member function definition. Listing 16-5 shows the code form Listing 16-4 modified to show the non-inline member definition.

Listing 16-5. Illustrating The Non-Inline Template/Function Definition

```
//: C16:Array2.cpp
// Non-inline template definition
#include "../require.h"

template<class T>
class Array {
  enum { size = 100 };
  T A[size];
public:
  T& operator[](int index);
};

template<class T>
T& Array<T>::operator[](int index) {
  require(index >= 0 && index < size,
    "Index out of range");
  return A[index];
}

int main() {
  Array<float> fa;
  fa[0] = 1.414;
} ///:~
```

Any reference to a template's class name must be accompanied by its template argument list, as in Array<T>::operator[]. You can imagine that internally the class name is being decorated with the arguments in the template argument list to produce a unique class name identifier for each template instantiation.

Header Files

Even if you create non-inline function definitions, you'll usually want to put all declarations *and* definitions for a template into a header file. This may seem to violate the normal header file rule of "don't put in anything that allocates storage," (which prevents multiple definition errors at link-time), but template definitions are special. Anything preceded by template<...> means the compiler won't allocate storage for it at that point, but will instead wait until it's told to (by a template instantiation), and that somewhere in the compiler and linker there's a mechanism for removing multiple definitions of an identical template. So you'll almost always put the entire template declaration *and* definition in the header file, for ease of use.

There are times when you may need to place the template definitions in a separate cpp file to satisfy special needs (for example, forcing template instantiations to exist in only a single Windows dll file). Most compilers have some mechanism to allow this; you'll have to investigate your particular compiler's documentation to use it.

Some people feel that putting all of the source code for your implementation in a header file makes it possible for people to steal and modify your code if they buy a library from you. This might be an issue, but it probably depends on the way you look at the problem. Are they buying a product or a service? If it's a product, then you have to do everything you can to protect it, and probably you don't want to give source code, just compiled code. But many people see software as a service, and even more than that, a subscription service. The customer wants your expertise; they want you to continue maintaining this piece of reusable code so that they don't have to and so they can focus on getting *their* job done. I personally think most customers will treat you as a valuable resource and will not want to jeopardize their relationship with you. As for the few who want to steal rather than buy or do original work, they probably can't keep up with you anyway.

IntStack as a Template

Listing 16-6 shows the container and iterator from IntStack.cpp, implemented as a generic container class using templates.

Listing 16-6. Illustrating A Simple Integer Stack Template

```
//: C16:StackTemplate.h
// Simple stack template
#ifndef STACKTEMPLATE_H
#define STACKTEMPLATE_H
#include "../require.h"

template<class T>
class StackTemplate {
  enum { ssize = 100 };
  T stack[ssize];
  int top;
public:
  StackTemplate() : top(0) {}
  void push(const T& i) {
    require(top < ssize, "Too many push()es");
    stack[top++] = i;
  }
  T pop() {
    require(top > 0, "Too many pop()s");
    return stack[--top];
  }
  int size() { return top; }
};
#endif // STACKTEMPLATE_H ///:~
```

Notice that a template makes certain assumptions about the objects it is holding. For example, StackTemplate assumes there is some sort of assignment operation for T inside the push() function. You could say that a template "implies an interface" for the types it is capable of holding.

Another way to say this is that templates provide a kind of *weak typing* mechanism for C++, which is ordinarily a strongly-typed language. Instead of insisting that an object be of some exact type in order to be acceptable, weak typing requires only that the member functions that it wants to call are *available* for a particular object. Thus, weakly-typed code can be applied to any object that can accept those member function calls, and is thus much more flexible.

Listing 16-7 contains the revised example to test the template.

Listing 16-7. Testing Out The Integer Stack Template in Listing 16-6

```
//: C16:StackTemplateTest.cpp
// Test simple stack template
//{L} fibonacci
#include "fibonacci.h"
#include "StackTemplate.h"    // To be INCLUDED from above
#include <iostream>
#include <fstream>
#include <string>
using namespace std;

int main() {
  StackTemplate<int> is;
  for(int i = 0; i < 20; i++)
    is.push(fibonacci(i));
  for(int k = 0; k < 20; k++)
    cout << is.pop() << endl;
  ifstream in("StackTemplateTest.cpp");
  assure(in, "StackTemplateTest.cpp");
  string line;
  StackTemplate<string> strings;
  while(getline(in, line))
    strings.push(line);
  while(strings.size() > 0)
    cout << strings.pop() << endl;
} ///:~
```

The only difference is in the creation of is. Inside the template argument list you specify the type of object the stack and iterator should hold. To demonstrate the *generic-ness* of the template, a StackTemplate is also created to hold string. This is tested by reading in lines from the source code file.

Constants in Templates

Template arguments are not restricted to class types; you can also use built-in types. The values of these arguments then become compile-time constants for that particular instantiation of the template. You can even use default values for these arguments. Listing 16-8 allows you to set the size of the Array class during instantiation, but also provides a default value.

Listing 16-8. Illustrating use of Built-in Types as Template Arguments

```
//: C16:Array3.cpp
// Built-in types as template arguments
#include "../require.h"
```

```cpp
#include <iostream>
using namespace std;
template<class T, int size = 100>
class Array {
  T array[size];

public:

  T& operator[](int index) {
    require(index >= 0 && index < size,
      "Index out of range");
    return array[index];
  }
  int length() const { return size; }
};

class Number {
  float f;

public:

  Number(float ff = 0.0f) : f(ff) {}
  Number& operator=(const Number& n) {
    f = n.f;
    return *this;
  }
  operator float() const { return f; }
  friend ostream&
    operator<<(ostream& os, const Number& x) {
      return os << x.f;
  }
};

template<class T, int size = 20>
class Holder {
  Array<T, size>* np;

public:

  Holder() : np(0) {}
  T& operator[](int i) {
    require(0 <= i && i < size);
    if(!np) np = new Array<T, size>;
    return np->operator[](i);
  }

  int length() const { return size; }
  ~Holder() { delete np; }
};
```

```
int main() {
  Holder<Number> h;
  for(int i = 0; i < 20; i++)
    h[i] = i;
  for(int j = 0; j < 20; j++)
    cout << h[j] << endl;
} ///:~
```

As before, Array is a checked array of objects and prevents you from indexing out of bounds. The class Holder is much like Array except that it has a pointer to an Array instead of an embedded object of type Array. This pointer is not initialized in the constructor; the initialization is delayed until the first access. This is called *lazy initialization*; you might use a technique like this if you are creating a lot of objects, but not accessing them all, and want to save storage.

You'll notice that the size value in both templates is never stored internally in the class, but it is used as if it were a data member inside the member functions.

Stack and Stash as Templates

The recurring "ownership" problems with the Stash and Stack container classes that have been revisited throughout this book come from the fact that these containers haven't been able to know exactly what types they hold. The nearest they've come is the Stack "container of Object" that was seen at the end of Chapter 15 in OStackTest.cpp (Listing 15-17).

If the client programmer doesn't explicitly remove all the pointers to objects that are held in the container, then the container should be able to correctly delete those pointers. That is to say, the container "*owns*" any objects that haven't been removed, and is thus responsible for cleaning them up. The snag has been that cleanup requires knowing the type of the object, and creating a generic container class requires *not* knowing the type of the object. With templates, however, you can write code that doesn't know the type of the object, and easily instantiate a new version of that container for every type that you want to contain. The individual instantiated containers *do* know the type of objects they hold and can thus call the correct destructor (assuming, in the typical case where polymorphism is involved, that a virtual destructor has been provided).

For the Stack this turns out to be quite simple since all of the member functions can be reasonably inlined; see Listing 16-9.

Listing 16-9. Illustrating Creation of The Stack as a Template

```
//: C16:TStack.h
// The Stack as a template
#ifndef TSTACK_H
#define TSTACK_H

template<class T>
class Stack {
  struct Link {
    T* data;
    Link* next;
    Link(T* dat, Link* nxt):
      data(dat), next(nxt) {}
  }* head;
public:
  Stack() : head(0) {}
  ~Stack(){
    while(head)
      delete pop();
  }
```

```
  void push(T* dat) {
    head = new Link(dat, head);
  }
  T* peek() const {
    return head ? head->data : 0;
  }
  T* pop(){
    if(head == 0) return 0;
    T* result = head->data;
    Link* oldHead = head;
    head = head->next;
    delete oldHead;
    return result;
  }
};
#endif // TSTACK_H ///:~
```

If you compare this to the OStack.h example at the end of Chapter 15, you will see that Stack is virtually identical, except that Object has been replaced with T. The test program is also nearly identical, except that the necessity for multiply-inheriting from string and Object (and even the need for Object *itself*) has been eliminated. Now there is no MyString class to announce its destruction, so a small new class is added in Listing 16-10 to show a Stack container cleaning up its objects.

Listing 16-10. Testing Out the Template Stack in Listing 16-9

```
//: C16:TStackTest.cpp
//{T} TStackTest.cpp
#include "TStack.h"    // To be INCLUDED from above
#include "../require.h"
#include <fstream>
#include <iostream>
#include <string>
using namespace std;

class X {
public:
  virtual ~X() { cout << "~X " << endl; }
};

int main(int argc, char* argv[]) {
  requireArgs(argc, 1); // File name is argument
  ifstream in(argv[1]);
  assure(in, argv[1]);
  Stack<string> textlines;
  string line;
  // Read file and store lines in the Stack:
  while(getline(in, line))
    textlines.push(new string(line));
  // Pop some lines from the stack:
  string* s;
  for(int i = 0; i < 10; i++) {
    if((s = (string*)textlines.pop())==0) break;
```

```
    cout << *s << endl;
    delete s;
  } // The destructor deletes the other strings.
  // Show that correct destruction happens:
  Stack<X> xx;
  for(int j = 0; j < 10; j++)
    xx.push(new X);
} ///:~
```

The destructor for X is *virtual*, not because it's necessary here, but because xx could later be used to hold objects derived from X.

Notice how easy it is to create different kinds of Stacks for string and for X. Because of the template, you get the best of both worlds: the ease of use of the Stack class along with proper cleanup.

Templatized pointer Stash

Reorganizing the PStash code into a template isn't quite so simple because there are a number of member functions that should not be inlined. However, as a template those function definitions still belong in the header file (the compiler and linker take care of any multiple definition problems). The code in Listing 16-11 looks quite similar to the ordinary PStash except that you'll notice the size of the increment (used by inflate()) has been templatized as a non-class parameter with a default value, so that the increment size can be modified at the point of instantiation (notice that this means that the increment size is fixed; you may also argue that the increment size should be changeable throughout the lifetime of the object).

Listing 16-11. Illustrating the Templatized Pointer Stash

```
//: C16:TPStash.h
#ifndef TPSTASH_H
#define TPSTASH_H

template<class T, int incr = 10>
class PStash {
  int quantity; // Number of storage spaces
  int next; // Next empty space
  T** storage;
  void inflate(int increase = incr);
public:
  PStash() : quantity(0), next(0), storage(0) {}
  ~PStash();
  int add(T* element);
  T* operator[](int index) const; // Fetch
  // Remove the reference from this PStash:
  T* remove(int index);
  // Number of elements in Stash:
  int count() const { return next; }
};

template<class T, int incr>
int PStash<T, incr>::add(T* element) {
  if(next >= quantity)
    inflate(incr);
```

```
    storage[next++] = element;
    return(next - 1); // Index number
}

// Ownership of remaining pointers:
template<class T, int incr>
PStash<T, incr>::~PStash() {
    for(int i = 0; i < next; i++) {
        delete storage[i]; // Null pointers OK
        storage[i] = 0; // Just to be safe
    }
    delete []storage;
}

template<class T, int incr>
T* PStash<T, incr>::operator[](int index) const {
    require(index >= 0,
        "PStash::operator[] index negative");
    if(index >= next)
        return 0; // To indicate the end
    require(storage[index] != 0,
        "PStash::operator[] returned null pointer");
    // Produce pointer to desired element:
    return storage[index];
}

template<class T, int incr>
T* PStash<T, incr>::remove(int index) {
    // operator[] performs validity checks:
    T* v = operator[](index);
    // "Remove" the pointer:
    if(v != 0) storage[index] = 0;
    return v;
}

template<class T, int incr>
void PStash<T, incr>::inflate(int increase) {
    const int psz = sizeof(T*);
    T** st = new T*[quantity + increase];
    memset(st, 0, (quantity + increase) * psz);
    memcpy(st, storage, quantity * psz);
    quantity += increase;
    delete []storage; // Old storage
    storage = st; // Point to new memory
}
#endif // TPSTASH_H ///:~
```

The default increment size used here is small to guarantee that calls to inflate() occur. This way you can make sure it works correctly.

To test the ownership control of the templatized PStash, the class in Listing 16-12 will report creations and destructions of itself, and also guarantee that all objects that have been created were also destroyed. AutoCounter will allow only objects of its type to be created on the stack.

Listing 16-12. Testing Out the Ownership Control (of the Templatized Pointer Stash)

```cpp
//: C16:AutoCounter.h
#ifndef AUTOCOUNTER_H
#define AUTOCOUNTER_H
#include "../require.h"
#include <iostream>
#include <set> // Standard C++ Library container
#include <string>

class AutoCounter {
  static int count;
  int id;
  class CleanupCheck {
    std::set<AutoCounter*> trace;
  public:
    void add(AutoCounter* ap) {
      trace.insert(ap);
    }
    void remove(AutoCounter* ap) {
      require(trace.erase(ap) == 1,
        "Attempt to delete AutoCounter twice");
    }
    ~CleanupCheck() {
      std::cout << "~CleanupCheck()"<< std::endl;
      require(trace.size() == 0,
        "All AutoCounter objects not cleaned up");
    }
  };
  static CleanupCheck verifier;
  AutoCounter() : id(count++) {
    verifier.add(this); // Register itself
    std::cout << "created[" << id << "]"
            << std::endl;
  }
  // Prevent assignment and copy-construction:
  AutoCounter(const AutoCounter&);
  void operator=(const AutoCounter&);
public:
  // You can only create objects with this:
  static AutoCounter* create() {
    return new AutoCounter();
  }
  ~AutoCounter() {
    std::cout << "destroying[" << id
            << "]" << std::endl;
    verifier.remove(this);
  }
```

```
  // Print both objects and pointers:
  friend std::ostream& operator<<(
    std::ostream& os, const AutoCounter& ac){
    return os << "AutoCounter " << ac.id;
  }
  friend std::ostream& operator<<(
    std::ostream& os, const AutoCounter* ac){
    return os << "AutoCounter " << ac->id;
  }
};
#endif // AUTOCOUNTER_H ///:~
```

The AutoCounter class does two things. First, it sequentially numbers each instance of AutoCounter: the value of this number is kept in id, and the number is generated using the static data member count.

Second, and more complex, a static instance (called verifier) of the nested class CleanupCheck keeps track of all of the AutoCounter objects that are created and destroyed, and reports back to you if you don't clean all of them up (i.e., if there is a memory leak). This behavior is accomplished using a set class from the Standard C++ Library, which is a wonderful example of how well-designed templates can make life easy.

The set class is templatized on the type that it holds; here it is instantiated to hold AutoCounter pointers. A set will allow only one instance of each distinct object to be added; in add() you can see this take place with the set::insert() function. insert() actually informs you with its return value if you're trying to add something that's already been added; however, since object addresses are being added you can rely on C++'s guarantee that all objects have unique addresses.

In remove(), set::erase() is used to remove an AutoCounter pointer from the set. The return value tells you how many instances of the element were removed; in our case we only expect zero or one. If the value is zero, however, it means this object was already deleted from the set and you're trying to delete it a second time, which is a programming error that will be reported through require().

The destructor for CleanupCheck does a final check by making sure that the size of the set is zero—this means that all of the objects have been properly cleaned up. If it's not zero, you have a memory leak, which is reported through require().

The constructor and destructor for AutoCounter register and unregister themselves with the verifier object. Notice that the constructor, copy-constructor, and assignment operator are private, so the only way for you to create an object is with the static create() member function. This is a simple example of a *factory*, and it guarantees that all objects are created on the heap, so verifier will not get confused over assignments and copy-constructions.

Since all of the member functions have been inlined, the only reason for the implementation file is to contain the static data member definitions; see Listing 16-13.

Listing 16-13. Implementing the AutoCounter in Listing 16-12

```
//: C16:AutoCounter.cpp {O}
// Definition of static class members
#include "AutoCounter.h" // To be INCLUDED from above
AutoCounter::CleanupCheck AutoCounter::verifier;
int AutoCounter::count = 0;
///:~
```

With AutoCounter in hand, you can now test the facilities of the PStash. Listing 16-14 not only shows that the PStash destructor cleans up all the objects that it currently owns, but it also demonstrates how the AutoCounter class detects objects that haven't been cleaned up.

Listing 16-14. Testing Out The Templatized Pointer Stash Using AutoCounter

```
//: C16:TPStashTest.cpp
//{L} AutoCounter
#include "AutoCounter.h"
#include "TPStash.h" // To be INCLUDED from above
#include <iostream>
#include <fstream>
using namespace std;

int main() {
  PStash<AutoCounter> acStash;
  for(int i = 0; i < 10; i++)
    acStash.add(AutoCounter::create());
  cout << "Removing 5 manually:" << endl;
  for(int j = 0; j < 5; j++)
    delete acStash.remove(j);
  cout << "Remove two without deleting them:"
       << endl;
  // ... to generate the cleanup error message.
  cout << acStash.remove(5) << endl;
  cout << acStash.remove(6) << endl;
  cout << "The destructor cleans up the rest:"
       << endl;
  // Repeat the test from earlier chapters:
  ifstream in("TPStashTest.cpp");
  assure(in, "TPStashTest.cpp");
  PStash<string> stringStash;
  string line;
  while(getline(in, line))
    stringStash.add(new string(line));
  // Print out the strings:
  for(int u = 0; stringStash[u]; u++)
    cout << "stringStash[" << u << "] = "
         << *stringStash[u] << endl;
} ///:~
```

When AutoCounter elements 5 and 6 are removed from the PStash, they become the responsibility of the caller, but since the caller never cleans them up they cause memory leaks, which are then detected by AutoCounter at runtime.

When you run the program, you'll see that the error message isn't as specific as it could be. If you use the scheme presented in AutoCounter to discover memory leaks in your own system, you will probably want to have it print out more detailed information about the objects that haven't been cleaned up. There are more sophisticated ways to do this, as you will see later on in this book.

Turning Ownership On and Off

Let's return to the ownership problem. Containers that hold objects by value don't usually worry about ownership because they clearly own the objects they contain. But if your container holds pointers (which is more common with C++, *especially with polymorphism*), then it's very likely those pointers may also be used somewhere else in the program, and you don't necessarily want to delete the object because then the other pointers in the program would be referencing a destroyed object. To prevent this from happening, you must consider ownership when designing and using a container.

Many programs are much simpler than this, and don't encounter the ownership problem; one container holds pointers to objects that are used only by that container. In this case ownership is very straightforward: The container owns its objects.

The best approach to handling the ownership problem is to give the client programmer a choice. This is often accomplished by a constructor argument that defaults to indicating ownership (the simplest case). In addition there may be "get" and "set" functions to view and modify the ownership of the container. If the container has functions to remove an object, the ownership state usually affects that removal, so you may also find options to control destruction in the removal function. You could conceivably add ownership data for every element in the container, so each position would know whether it needed to be destroyed; this is a variant of reference counting, except that the container and not the object knows the number of references pointing to an object (see Listing 16-15).

Listing 16-15. Demonstrating a Stack with Runtime Controllable Ownership

```cpp
//: C16:OwnerStack.h
// Stack with runtime controllable ownership
#ifndef OWNERSTACK_H
#define OWNERSTACK_H

template<class T> class Stack {
  struct Link {
    T* data;
    Link* next;
    Link(T* dat, Link* nxt)
      : data(dat), next(nxt) {}
  }* head;
  bool own;
public:
  Stack(bool own = true) : head(0), own(own) {}
  ~Stack();
  void push(T* dat) {
    head = new Link(dat,head);
  }
  T* peek() const {
    return head ? head->data : 0;
  }
  T* pop();
  bool owns() const { return own; }
  void owns(bool newownership) {
    own = newownership;
  }
  // Auto-type conversion: true if not empty:
  operator bool() const { return head != 0; }
};

template<class T> T* Stack<T>::pop() {
if(head == 0) return 0;
  T* result = head->data;
  Link* oldHead = head;
```

```
  head = head->next;
  delete oldHead;
  return result;
}

template<class T> Stack<T>::~Stack() {
  if(!own) return;
  while(head)
    delete pop();
}
#endif // OWNERSTACK_H ///:~
```

The default behavior is for the container to destroy its objects but you can change this by either modifying the constructor argument or using the owns() read/write member functions.

As with most templates you're likely to see, the entire implementation is contained in the header file. Listing 16-16 is a small test that exercises the ownership abilities.

Listing 16-16. Testing Out the Ownership of the Stack in Listing 16-15

```
//: C16:OwnerStackTest.cpp
//{L} AutoCounter
#include "AutoCounter.h"
#include "OwnerStack.h"    // To be INCLUDED from above
#include "../require.h"
#include <iostream>
#include <fstream>
#include <string>
using namespace std;

int main() {
  Stack<AutoCounter> ac; // Ownership on
  Stack<AutoCounter> ac2(false); // Turn it off
  AutoCounter* ap;
  for(int i = 0; i < 10; i++) {
    ap = AutoCounter::create();
    ac.push(ap);
    if(i % 2 == 0)
      ac2.push(ap);
  }
  while(ac2)
    cout << ac2.pop() << endl;
  // No destruction necessary since
  // ac "owns" all the objects
} ///:~
```

The ac2 object doesn't own the objects you put into it, thus ac is the "master" container that takes responsibility for ownership. If, partway through the lifetime of a container, you want to change whether a container owns its objects, you can do so using owns().

It would also be possible to change the granularity of the ownership so that it is on an object-by-object basis, but that will probably make the solution to the ownership problem more complex than the problem.

Holding Objects by Value

Actually creating a copy of the objects inside a generic container is a complex problem if you don't have templates. With templates, things are relatively simple; you just say that you are holding objects rather than pointers, as shown in Listing 16-17.

Listing 16-17. Illustrating Holding of Objects by Value Using Templates

```
//: C16:ValueStack.h
// Holding objects by value in a Stack
#ifndef VALUESTACK_H
#define VALUESTACK_H
#include "../require.h"

template<class T, int ssize = 100>
class Stack {
  // Default constructor performs object
  // initialization for each element in array:
  T stack[ssize];
  int top;
public:
  Stack() : top(0) {}
  // Copy-constructor copies object into array:
  void push(const T& x) {
    require(top < ssize, "Too many push()es");
    stack[top++] = x;
  }
  T peek() const { return stack[top]; }
  // Object still exists when you pop it;
  // it just isn't available anymore:
  T pop() {
    require(top > 0, "Too many pop()s");
    return stack[--top];
  }
};
#endif // VALUESTACK_H ///:~
```

The copy constructor for the contained objects does most of the work by passing and returning the objects by value. Inside push(), storage of the object onto the Stack array is accomplished with T::operator=. To guarantee that it works, a class called SelfCounter keeps track of object creations and copy-constructions; see Listing 16-18.

Listing 16-18. Making the ValueStack in Listing 16-17 Work Using SelfCounter

```
//: C16:SelfCounter.h
#ifndef SELFCOUNTER_H
#define SELFCOUNTER_H
#include "ValueStack.h"    // To be INCLUDED from above
#include <iostream>
```

```
class SelfCounter {
  static int counter;
  int id;
public:
  SelfCounter() : id(counter++) {
    std::cout << "Created: " << id << std::endl;
  }
  SelfCounter(const SelfCounter& rv) : id(rv.id){
    std::cout << "Copied: " << id << std::endl;
  }
  SelfCounter operator=(const SelfCounter& rv) {
    std::cout << "Assigned " << rv.id << " to "
              << id << std::endl;
    return *this;
  }
  ~SelfCounter() {
    std::cout << "Destroyed: "<< id << std::endl;
  }
  friend std::ostream& operator<<(
    std::ostream& os, const SelfCounter& sc){
    return os << "SelfCounter: " << sc.id;
  }
};
#endif // SELFCOUNTER_H ///:~

//: C16:SelfCounter.cpp {O}
#include "SelfCounter.h"    // To be INCLUDED from above
int SelfCounter::counter = 0; ///:~

//: C16:ValueStackTest.cpp
//{L} SelfCounter
#include "ValueStack.h"
#include "SelfCounter.h"
#include <iostream>
using namespace std;

int main() {
  Stack<SelfCounter> sc;
  for(int i = 0; i < 10; i++)
    sc.push(SelfCounter());
  // OK to peek(), result is a temporary:
  cout << sc.peek() << endl;
  for(int k = 0; k < 10; k++)
    cout << sc.pop() << endl;
} ///:~
```

When a Stack container is created, the default constructor of the contained object is called for each object in the array. You'll initially see 100 SelfCounter objects created for no apparent reason, but this is just the array initialization. This can be a bit expensive, but there's no way around it in a simple design like this. An even more complex situation arises if you make the Stack more general by allowing the size to grow dynamically, because in the implementation shown in Listing 16-18 this would involve creating a new (larger) array, copying the old array to the new, and destroying the old array (this is, in fact, what the Standard C++ Library vector class does).

Introducing Iterators

An *iterator* is an object that moves through a container of other objects and selects them one at a time, without providing direct access to the implementation of that container. Iterators provide a standard way to access elements, whether or not a container provides a way to access the elements directly. You will see iterators used most often in association with container classes; iterators are a fundamental concept in the design and use of the Standard C++ containers.

In many ways, an iterator is a smart pointer, and in fact you'll notice that iterators usually mimic most pointer operations. Unlike a pointer, however, the iterator is designed to be safe, so you're much less likely to do the equivalent of walking off the end of an array (*or if you do,* you find out about it more easily).

Consider the first example in this chapter. Listing 16-19 has a simple iterator added.

Listing 16-19. Illustrating A Simple Integer Stack with Iterators

```cpp
//: C16:IterIntStack.cpp
// Simple integer stack with iterators
//{L} fibonacci
#include "fibonacci.h"
#include "../require.h"
#include <iostream>
using namespace std;

class IntStack {
  enum { ssize = 100 };
  int stack[ssize];
  int top;
public:
  IntStack() : top(0) {}
  void push(int i) {
    require(top < ssize, "Too many push()es");
    stack[top++] = i;
  }
  int pop() {
    require(top > 0, "Too many pop()s");
    return stack[--top];
  }
  friend class IntStackIter;
};

// An iterator is like a "smart" pointer:
class IntStackIter {
  IntStack& s;
  int index;
public:
  IntStackIter(IntStack& is) : s(is), index(0) {}
  int operator++() { // Prefix
    require(index < s.top,
      "iterator moved out of range");
    return s.stack[++index];
  }
  int operator++(int) { // Postfix
    require(index < s.top,
```

```
      "iterator moved out of range");
    return s.stack[index++];
  }
};

int main() {
  IntStack is;
  for(int i = 0; i < 20; i++)
    is.push(fibonacci(i));
  // Traverse with an iterator:
  IntStackIter it(is);
  for(int j = 0; j < 20; j++)
    cout << it++ << endl;
} ///:~
```

The `IntStackIter` has been created to work only with an `IntStack`. Notice that `IntStackIter` is a friend of `IntStack`, which gives it access to all the `private` elements of `IntStack`.

Like a pointer, `IntStackIter`'s job is to move through an `IntStack` and retrieve values. In this simple example, the `IntStackIter` can move only forward (using both the prefix and postfix forms of the `operator++`). However, there is no boundary to the way an iterator can be defined, other than those imposed by the constraints of the container it works with. It is perfectly acceptable (within the limits of the underlying container) for an iterator to move around in any way within its associated container and to cause the contained values to be modified.

It is customary that an iterator is created with a constructor that attaches it to a single container object, and that the iterator is not attached to a different container during its lifetime.

■ **Note**   Iterators are usually small and cheap, so you can easily make another one.

With the iterator, you can traverse the elements of the stack without popping them, just as a pointer can move through the elements of an array. However, the iterator knows the underlying structure of the stack and how to traverse the elements, so even though you are moving through them by pretending to "increment a pointer," what's going on underneath is more involved. That's the key to the iterator: it is abstracting the complicated process of moving from one container element to the next into something that looks like a pointer. The goal is for *every iterator* in your program to have the same interface so that any code that uses the iterator doesn't care what it's pointing to; it just knows that it can reposition all iterators the same way, so the container that the iterator points to is unimportant. In this way you can write more generic code. All of the containers and algorithms in the Standard C++ Library are based on this principle of iterators.

To aid in making things more generic, it would be nice to be able to say "every container has an associated class called `iterator`," but this will typically cause naming problems. The solution is to add a nested `iterator` class to each container (notice that in this case, "`iterator`" begins with a lowercase letter so that it conforms to the style of the Standard C++ Library). Listing 16-20 shows `IterIntStack.cpp` with a nested `iterator`.

Listing 16-20. Illustrating Nesting of an Iterator Inside the Container

```
//: C16:NestedIterator.cpp
// Nesting an iterator inside the container
//{L} fibonacci
#include "fibonacci.h"
#include "../require.h"
#include <iostream>
#include <string>
using namespace std;
```

```cpp
class IntStack {
  enum { ssize = 100 };
  int stack[ssize];
  int top;
public:
  IntStack() : top(0) {}
  void push(int i) {
    require(top < ssize, "Too many push()es");
    stack[top++] = i;
  }
  int pop() {
    require(top > 0, "Too many pop()s");
    return stack[--top];
  }
  class iterator;
  friend class iterator;
  class iterator {
    IntStack& s;
    int index;
  public:
    iterator(IntStack& is) : s(is), index(0) {}
    // To create the "end sentinel" iterator:
    iterator(IntStack& is, bool)
      : s(is), index(s.top) {}
    int current() const { return s.stack[index]; }
    int operator++() { // Prefix
      require(index < s.top,
        "iterator moved out of range");
      return s.stack[++index];
    }
    int operator++(int) { // Postfix
      require(index < s.top,
        "iterator moved out of range");
      return s.stack[index++];
    }
    // Jump an iterator forward
    iterator& operator+=(int amount) {
      require(index + amount < s.top,
        "IntStack::iterator::operator+=() "
        "tried to move out of bounds");
      index += amount;
      return *this;
    }
    // To see if you're at the end:
    bool operator==(const iterator& rv) const {
      return index == rv.index;
    }
    bool operator!=(const iterator& rv) const {
      return index != rv.index;
    }
```

```
    friend ostream&
    operator <<(ostream& os, const iterator& it) {
      return os << it.current();
    }
  };
  iterator begin() { return iterator(*this); }
  // Create the "end sentinel":
  iterator end() { return iterator(*this, true);}
};

int main() {
  IntStack is;
  for(int i = 0; i < 20; i++)
    is.push(fibonacci(i));
  cout << "Traverse the whole IntStack\n";
  IntStack::iterator it = is.begin();
  while(it != is.end())
    cout << it++ << endl;
  cout << "Traverse a portion of the IntStack\n";
  IntStack::iterator
    start = is.begin(), end = is.begin();
  start += 5, end += 15;
  cout << "start = " << start << endl;
  cout << "end = " << end << endl;
  while(start != end)
    cout << start++ << endl;
} ///:~
```

When making a nested friend class, you must go through the process of first declaring the name of the class, then declaring it as a friend, then defining the class. Otherwise, the compiler will get confused.

Some new twists have been added to the iterator. The current() member function produces the element in the container that the iterator is currently selecting. You can "jump" an iterator forward by an arbitrary number of elements using operator+=. Also, you'll see two overloaded operators,== and !=, that will compare one iterator with another. These can compare any two IntStack::iterators, but they are primarily intended as a test to see if the iterator is at the end of a sequence in the same way that the "real" Standard C++ Library iterators do. The idea is that two iterators define a range, including the first element pointed to by the first iterator and up to but *not* including the last element pointed to by the second iterator. So if you want to move through the range defined by the two iterators, you say something like

```
while(start != end)
  cout << start++ << endl;
```

where start and end are the two iterators in the range. Note that the end iterator, which we often refer to as the *end sentinel*, is not dereferenced and is there only to tell you that you're at the end of the sequence. Thus it represents "one past the end."

Much of the time you'll want to move through the entire sequence in a container, so the container needs some way to produce the iterators indicating the beginning of the sequence and the end sentinel. Here, as in the Standard C++ Library, these iterators are produced by the container member functions begin() and end(). begin() uses the first iterator constructor that defaults to pointing at the beginning of the container (this is the first element pushed on the stack). However, a second constructor, used by end(), is necessary to create the end sentinel iterator. Being "at the end" means pointing to the top of the stack, because top always indicates the next available—but unused—space on the stack. This iterator constructor takes a second argument of type bool, which is a dummy to distinguish the two constructors.

The Fibonacci numbers are used again to fill the IntStack in main( ), and iterators are used to move through the whole IntStack and also within a narrowed range of the sequence.

The next step, of course, is to make the code general by *templatizing it* on the type that it holds, so that instead of being forced to hold only ints you can hold any type; see Listing 16-21.

Listing 16-21. Illustrating A Simple Stack Template with Nested Iterator

```
//: C16:IterStackTemplate.h
// Simple stack template with nested iterator
#ifndef ITERSTACKTEMPLATE_H
#define ITERSTACKTEMPLATE_H
#include "../require.h"
#include <iostream>

template<class T, int ssize = 100>
class StackTemplate {
  T stack[ssize];
  int top;
public:
  StackTemplate() : top(0) {}
  void push(const T& i) {
    require(top < ssize, "Too many push()es");
    stack[top++] = i;
  }
  T pop() {
    require(top > 0, "Too many pop()s");
    return stack[--top];
  }
  class iterator; // Declaration required
  friend class iterator; // Make it a friend
  class iterator { // Now define it
    StackTemplate& s;
    int index;
  public:
    iterator(StackTemplate& st): s(st),index(0){}
    // To create the "end sentinel" iterator:
    iterator(StackTemplate& st, bool)
      : s(st), index(s.top) {}
    T operator*() const { return s.stack[index];}
    T operator++() { // Prefix form
      require(index < s.top,
        "iterator moved out of range");
      return s.stack[++index];
    }
    T operator++(int) { // Postfix form
      require(index < s.top,
        "iterator moved out of range");
      return s.stack[index++];
    }
    // Jump an iterator forward
    iterator& operator+=(int amount) {
      require(index + amount < s.top,
```

440

```
        " StackTemplate::iterator::operator+=() "
        "tried to move out of bounds");
      index += amount;
      return *this;
    }
    // To see if you're at the end:
    bool operator==(const iterator& rv) const {
      return index == rv.index;
    }
    bool operator!=(const iterator& rv) const {
      return index != rv.index;
    }

    friend std::ostream& operator<<(
      std::ostream& os, const iterator& it) {
      return os << *it;
    }
  };

  iterator begin() { return iterator(*this); }
  // Create the "end sentinel":
  iterator end() { return iterator(*this, true);}
};
#endif // ITERSTACKTEMPLATE_H ///:~
```

You can see that the transformation from a regular class to a template is reasonably transparent. This approach of first creating and debugging an ordinary class, then making it into a template, is generally considered to be easier than creating the template from scratch.

Notice that instead of just saying

```
friend iterator; // Make it a friend
```

this code says

```
friend class iterator; // Make it a friend
```

This is important because the name *"iterator"* is already in scope, from an included file.

Instead of the current() member function, the iterator has an operator* to select the current element, which makes the iterator look more like a pointer and is a common practice.

Listing 16-22 shows the revised example to test the template.

Listing 16-22. Testing Out the Stack Template in Listing 16-21

```
//: C16:IterStackTemplateTest.cpp
//{L} fibonacci
#include "fibonacci.h"
#include "IterStackTemplate.h"    // To be INCLUDED from above
#include <iostream>
#include <fstream>
#include <string>
using namespace std;
```

```
int main() {
  StackTemplate<int> is;
  for(int i = 0; i < 20; i++)
    is.push(fibonacci(i));
  // Traverse with an iterator:
  cout << "Traverse the whole StackTemplate\n";
  StackTemplate<int>::iterator it = is.begin();
  while(it != is.end())
    cout << it++ << endl;
  cout << "Traverse a portion\n";
  StackTemplate<int>::iterator
    start = is.begin(), end = is.begin();
  start += 5, end += 15;
  cout << "start = " << start << endl;
  cout << "end = " << end << endl;
  while(start != end)
    cout << start++ << endl;
  ifstream in("IterStackTemplateTest.cpp");
  assure(in, "IterStackTemplateTest.cpp");
  string line;
  StackTemplate<string> strings;
  while(getline(in, line))
    strings.push(line);
  StackTemplate<string>::iterator
    sb = strings.begin(), se = strings.end();
  while(sb != se)
    cout << sb++ << endl;
} ///:~
```

The first use of the iterator just marches it from beginning to end (and shows that the end sentinel works properly). In the second usage, you can see how iterators allow you to easily specify a range of elements (the *containers* and *iterators* in the Standard C++ Library use this concept of *ranges* almost everywhere). The overloaded operator+= moves the start and end iterators to positions in the middle of the range of the elements in is, and these elements are printed out. Notice in the output that the end sentinel is *not* included in the range, thus it can be one past the end of the range to let you know you've passed the end—but you don't dereference the end sentinel, or else you can end up dereferencing a null pointer. Lastly, to verify that the StackTemplate works with class objects, one is instantiated for string and filled with the lines from the source code file, which are then printed out.

Stack with Iterators

You can repeat the process with the dynamically-sized Stack class that has been used as an example throughout the book. Listing 16-23 shows the Stack class with a nested iterator folded into the mix.

Listing 16-23. Illustrating A Templatized Stack with Nested Iterator

```
//: C16:TStack2.h
// Templatized Stack with nested iterator
#ifndef TSTACK2_H
#define TSTACK2_H
```

```
template<class T> class Stack {
  struct Link {
    T* data;
    Link* next;
    Link(T* dat, Link* nxt)
      : data(dat), next(nxt) {}
  }* head;
public:
  Stack() : head(0) {}
  ~Stack();
  void push(T* dat) {
    head = new Link(dat, head);
  }
  T* peek() const {
    return head ? head->data : 0;
  }
  T* pop();
  // Nested iterator class:
  class iterator; // Declaration required
  friend class iterator; // Make it a friend
  class iterator { // Now define it
    Stack::Link* p;
  public:
    iterator(const Stack<T>& tl) : p(tl.head) {}
    // Copy-constructor:
    iterator(const iterator& tl) : p(tl.p) {}
    // The end sentinel iterator:
    iterator() : p(0) {}
    // operator++ returns boolean indicating end:
    bool operator++() {
      if(p->next)
        p = p->next;
      else p = 0; // Indicates end of list
      return bool(p);
    }
    bool operator++(int) { return operator++(); }
    T* current() const {
      if(!p) return 0;
      return p->data;
    }
    // Pointer dereference operator:
    T* operator->() const {
      require(p != 0,
        "PStack::iterator::operator->returns 0");
      return current();
    }
    T* operator*() const { return current(); }
    // bool conversion for conditional test:
    operator bool() const { return bool(p); }
    // Comparison to test for end:
    bool operator==(const iterator&) const {
      return p == 0;
    }
```

```
    bool operator!=(const iterator&) const {
      return p != 0;
    }
  };
  iterator begin() const {
    return iterator(*this);
  }
  iterator end() const { return iterator(); }
};

template<class T> Stack<T>::~Stack() {
  while(head)
    delete pop();
}

template<class T> T* Stack<T>::pop() {
  if(head == 0) return 0;
  T* result = head->data;
  Link* oldHead = head;
  head = head->next;
  delete oldHead;
  return result;
}
#endif // TSTACK2_H ///:~
```

You'll also notice the class has been changed to support ownership, which works now because the class knows the exact type (or at least the base type, *which will work assuming virtual destructors are used*). The default is for the container to destroy its objects but you are responsible for any pointers that you pop().

The iterator is simple and physically very small—the size of a single pointer. When you create an iterator, it's initialized to the head of the linked list, and you can only increment it forward through the list. If you want to start over at the beginning, you create a new iterator, and if you want to remember a spot in the list, you create a new iterator from the existing iterator pointing at that spot (using the iterator's copy-constructor).

To call functions for the object referred to by the iterator, you can use the current() function, the operator*, or the pointer dereference operator-> (a common sight in iterators). The latter has an implementation that *looks* identical to current() because it returns a pointer to the current object, but is different because the pointer dereference operator performs the extra levels of dereferencing (refer Chapter 12).

The iterator class follows the form you saw in Listing 16-21. class iterator is nested inside the container class, it contains constructors to create both an iterator pointing at an element in the container and an "end sentinel" iterator, and the container class has the begin() and end() methods to produce these iterators. The entire implementation is contained in the header file, so there's no separate cpp file.

Listing 16-24 contains a small test that exercises the iterator.

Listing 16-24. Testing Out the Templatized Stack in Listing 16-23

```
//: C16:TStack2Test.cpp

#include "TStack2.h"    // To be INCLUDED from above
#include "../require.h"
#include <iostream>
#include <fstream>
#include <string>
```

```
using namespace std;

int main() {
  ifstream file("TStack2Test.cpp");

  assure(file, "TStack2Test.cpp");

  Stack<string> textlines;
  // Read file and store lines in the Stack:

  string line;

  while(getline(file, line))
    textlines.push(new string(line));

  int i = 0;
  // Use iterator to print lines from the list:
  Stack<string>::iterator it = textlines.begin();

  Stack<string>::iterator* it2 = 0;

  while(it != textlines.end()) {
    cout << it->c_str() << endl;
    it++;
    if(++i == 10) // Remember 10th line
      it2 = new Stack<string>::iterator(it);
  }
  cout << (*it2)->c_str() << endl;
  delete it2;
} ///:~
```

A Stack is instantiated to hold string objects and filled with lines from a file. Then an iterator is created and used to move through the sequence. The tenth line is remembered by copy-constructing a second iterator from the first; later this line is printed and the iterator—created dynamically—is destroyed. Here, dynamic object creation is used to control the lifetime of the object.

PStash with Iterators

For most container classes it makes sense to have an iterator. Listing 16-25 shows an iterator added to the PStash class.

Listing 16-25. Illustrating A Templatized PStash with Nested Iterator

```
//: C16:TPStash2.h
// Templatized PStash with nested iterator
#ifndef TPSTASH2_H
#define TPSTASH2_H
#include "../require.h"
#include <cstdlib>
```

```cpp
template<class T, int incr = 20>
class PStash {
  int quantity;
  int next;
  T** storage;
  void inflate(int increase = incr);
public:
  PStash() : quantity(0), storage(0), next(0) {}
  ~PStash();
  int add(T* element);
  T* operator[](int index) const;
  T* remove(int index);
  int count() const { return next; }
  // Nested iterator class:
  class iterator; // Declaration required
  friend class iterator; // Make it a friend
  class iterator { // Now define it
    PStash& ps;
    int index;
  public:
    iterator(PStash& pStash)
      : ps(pStash), index(0) {}
    // To create the end sentinel:
    iterator(PStash& pStash, bool)
      : ps(pStash), index(ps.next) {}
    // Copy-constructor:
    iterator(const iterator& rv)
      : ps(rv.ps), index(rv.index) {}
    iterator& operator=(const iterator& rv) {
      ps = rv.ps;
      index = rv.index;
      return *this;
    }
    iterator& operator++() {
      require(++index <= ps.next,
        "PStash::iterator::operator++ "
        "moves index out of bounds");
      return *this;
    }
    iterator& operator++(int) {
      return operator++();
    }
    iterator& operator--() {
      require(--index >= 0,
        "PStash::iterator::operator-- "
        "moves index out of bounds");
      return *this;
    }
    iterator& operator--(int) {
      return operator--();
    }
```

```
    // Jump interator forward or backward:
    iterator& operator+=(int amount) {
      require(index + amount < ps.next &&
        index + amount >= 0,
        "PStash::iterator::operator+= "
        "attempt to index out of bounds");
      index += amount;
      return *this;
    }
    iterator& operator-=(int amount) {
      require(index - amount < ps.next &&
        index - amount >= 0,
        "PStash::iterator::operator-= "
        "attempt to index out of bounds");
      index -= amount;
      return *this;
    }
    // Create a new iterator that's moved forward
    iterator operator+(int amount) const {
      iterator ret(*this);
      ret += amount; // op+= does bounds check
      return ret;
    }
    T* current() const {
      return ps.storage[index];
    }
    T* operator*() const { return current(); }
    T* operator->() const {
      require(ps.storage[index] != 0,
        "PStash::iterator::operator->returns 0");
      return current();
    }
    // Remove the current element:
    T* remove(){
      return ps.remove(index);
    }
    // Comparison tests for end:
    bool operator==(const iterator& rv) const {
      return index == rv.index;
    }
    bool operator!=(const iterator& rv) const {
      return index != rv.index;
    }
  };
  iterator begin() { return iterator(*this); }
  iterator end() { return iterator(*this, true);}
};

// Destruction of contained objects:
template<class T, int incr>
```

```
PStash<T, incr>::~PStash() {
  for(int i = 0; i < next; i++) {
    delete storage[i]; // Null pointers OK
    storage[i] = 0; // Just to be safe
  }
  delete []storage;
}

template<class T, int incr>
int PStash<T, incr>::add(T* element) {
if(next >= quantity)
    inflate();
  storage[next++] = element;
  return(next - 1); // Index number
}

template<class T, int incr> inline
T* PStash<T, incr>::operator[](int index) const {
  require(index >= 0,
    "PStash::operator[] index negative");
  if(index >= next)
    return 0; // To indicate the end
  require(storage[index] != 0,
    "PStash::operator[] returned null pointer");
  return storage[index];
}

template<class T, int incr>
T* PStash<T, incr>::remove(int index) {
  // operator[] performs validity checks:
  T* v = operator[](index);
  // "Remove" the pointer:
  storage[index] = 0;
  return v;
}

template<class T, int incr>
void PStash<T, incr>::inflate(int increase) {
  const int tsz = sizeof(T*);
  T** st = new T*[quantity + increase];
  memset(st, 0, (quantity + increase) * tsz);
  memcpy(st, storage, quantity * tsz);
  quantity += increase;
  delete []storage; // Old storage
  storage = st; // Point to new memory
}
#endif // TPSTASH2_H ///:~
```

Most of this file is a fairly straightforward translation of both the previous PStash and the nested iterator into a template. This time, however, the operators return references to the current iterator, which is the more typical and flexible approach to take.

448

The destructor calls delete for all contained pointers, and because the type is captured by the template, proper destruction will take place. You should be aware that if the container holds pointers to a base class type, that type should have a virtual destructor to ensure proper cleanup of derived objects whose addresses have been upcast when placing them in the container.

The PStash::iterator follows the iterator model of bonding to a single container object for its lifetime. In addition, the copy-constructor allows you to make a new iterator pointing at the same location as the existing iterator that you create it from, effectively making a bookmark into the container. The operator+= and operator-= member functions allow you to move an iterator by a number of spots, while respecting the boundaries of the container. The overloaded increment and decrement operators move the iterator by one place. The operator+ produces a new iterator that's moved forward by the amount of the addend. As in Listing 16-11, the pointer dereference operators are used to operate on the element the iterator is referring to, and remove() destroys the current object by calling the container's remove().

The same kind of code as in Listing 16-11 (just like the Standard C++ Library containers) is used for creating the end sentinel: a second constructor, the container's end() member function, and operator== and operator!= for comparison.

Listing 16-26 creates and tests two different kinds of Stash objects, one for a new class called Int that announces its construction and destruction and one that holds objects of the Standard library string class.

Listing 16-26. Creating and Testing Two Different Stash Objects

```
//: C16:TPStash2Test.cpp
#include "TPStash2.h"    // To be INCLUDED from above
#include "../require.h"
#include <iostream>
#include <vector>
#include <string>
using namespace std;

class Int {
  int i;
public:
  Int(int ii = 0) : i(ii) {
    cout << ">" << i << ' ';
  }
  ~Int() { cout << "~" << i << ' '; }
  operator int() const { return i; }
  friend ostream&
    operator <<(ostream& os, const Int& x) {
      return os << "Int: " << x.i;
  }
  friend ostream&
    operator <<(ostream& os, const Int* x) {
      return os << "Int: " << x->i;
  }
};

int main() {
  { // To force destructor call
    PStash<Int> ints;
    for(int i = 0; i < 30; i++)
      ints.add(new Int(i));
```

```
    cout << endl;
    PStash<Int>::iterator it = ints.begin();
    it += 5;
    PStash<Int>::iterator it2 = it + 10;
    for(; it != it2; it++)
      delete it.remove(); // Default removal
    cout << endl;
    for(it = ints.begin();it != ints.end();it++)
      if(*it) // Remove() causes "holes"
        cout << *it << endl;
  } // "ints" destructor called here
  cout << "\n-------------------\n";
  ifstream in("TPStash2Test.cpp");
  assure(in, "TPStash2Test.cpp");
  // Instantiate for String:
  PStash<string> strings;
  string line;
  while(getline(in, line))
    strings.add(new string(line));
  PStash<string>::iterator sit = strings.begin();
  for(; sit != strings.end(); sit++)
    cout << **sit << endl;
  sit = strings.begin();
  int n = 26;
  sit += n;
  for(; sit != strings.end(); sit++)
    cout << n++ << ": " << **sit << endl;
} ///:~
```

For convenience, Int has an associated ostream operator<< for both an Int& and an Int*.

The first block of code in main() is surrounded by braces to force the destruction of the PStash<Int> and thus the automatic cleanup by that destructor. A range of elements is removed and deleted by hand to show that the PStash cleans up the rest.

For both instances of PStash, an iterator is created and used to move through the container. Notice the elegance produced by using these constructs; you aren't assailed with the implementation details of using an array. You tell the container *and iterator* objects *what* to do, not how. This makes the solution easier to conceptualize, to build, and to modify.

Why iterators?

Up until now you've seen the *mechanics of iterators*, but understanding why they are so important takes a more complex example.

It's common to see polymorphism, dynamic object creation, and containers used together in a true object-oriented program. Containers and dynamic object creation solve the problem of not knowing how many or what type of objects you'll need. And if the container is configured to hold pointers to base-class objects, an upcast occurs every time you put a derived class pointer into the container (with the associated code organization and extensibility benefits). As the final code in this chapter, Listing 16-27 will also pull together various aspects of everything you've learned so far. If you can follow this example, *then* you're ready for the following chapters.

Listing 16-27. Putting It All Together

```
//: C16:Shape.h
#ifndef SHAPE_H
#define SHAPE_H
#include <iostream>
#include <string>

class Shape {
public:
  virtual void draw() = 0;
  virtual void erase() = 0;
  virtual ~Shape() {}
};

class Circle : public Shape {
public:
  Circle() {}
  ~Circle() { std::cout << "Circle::~Circle\n"; }
  void draw() { std::cout << "Circle::draw\n";}
  void erase() { std::cout << "Circle::erase\n";}
};

class Square : public Shape {
public:
  Square() {}
  ~Square() { std::cout << "Square::~Square\n"; }
  void draw() { std::cout << "Square::draw\n";}
  void erase() { std::cout << "Square::erase\n";}
};

class Line : public Shape {
public:
  Line() {}
  ~Line() { std::cout << "Line::~Line\n"; }
  void draw() { std::cout << "Line::draw\n";}
  void erase() { std::cout << "Line::erase\n";}
};
#endif // SHAPE_H ///:~
```

Suppose you are creating a program that allows the user to edit and produce different kinds of drawings. Each drawing is an object that contains a collection of Shape objects; see Listing 16-27.

This uses the classic structure of virtual functions in the base class that are overridden in the derived class. Notice that the Shape class includes a virtual destructor, something you should automatically add to any class with virtual functions. If a container holds pointers or references to Shape objects, then when the virtual destructors are called for those objects, everything will be properly cleaned up.

Each different type of drawing in Listing 16-28 makes use of a different kind of templatized container class: the PStash and Stack that have been defined in this chapter, and the vector class from the Standard C++ Library. The "use'" of the containers is extremely simple; in general, inheritance might not be the best approach (composition could make more sense), but in this case inheritance is a simple approach and it doesn't detract from the point made in the example.

Listing 16-28. Using the header file in Listing 16-27

```
//: C16:Drawing.cpp
#include <vector> // Uses Standard vector too!
#include "TPStash2.h"
#include "TStack2.h"
#include "Shape.h"    // To be INCLUDED from above
using namespace std;

// A Drawing is primarily a container of Shapes:
class Drawing : public PStash<Shape> {
public:
  ~Drawing() { cout << "~Drawing" << endl; }
};

// A Plan is a different container of Shapes:
class Plan : public Stack<Shape> {
public:
  ~Plan() { cout << "~Plan" << endl; }
};
// A Schematic is a different container of Shapes:
class Schematic : public vector<Shape*> {
public:
  ~Schematic() { cout << "~Schematic" << endl; }
};
// A function template:
template<class Iter>
void drawAll(Iter start, Iter end) {
  while(start != end) {
    (*start)->draw();
    start++;
  }
}

int main() {
  // Each type of container has
  // a different interface:
  Drawing d;
  d.add(new Circle);
  d.add(new Square);
  d.add(new Line);
  Plan p;
  p.push(new Line);
  p.push(new Square);
  p.push(new Circle);
  Schematic s;
  s.push_back(new Square);
  s.push_back(new Circle);
  s.push_back(new Line);
  Shape* sarray[] = {
    new Circle, new Square, new Line
  };
```

```
// The iterators and the template function
// allow them to be treated generically:
cout << "Drawing d:" << endl;
drawAll(d.begin(), d.end());
cout << "Plan p:" << endl;
drawAll(p.begin(), p.end());
cout << "Schematic s:" << endl;
drawAll(s.begin(), s.end());
cout << "Array sarray:" << endl;
// Even works with array pointers:
drawAll(sarray,
   sarray + sizeof(sarray)/sizeof(*sarray));
cout << "End of main" << endl;
} ///:~
```

The different types of containers all hold pointers to Shape and pointers to upcast objects of classes derived from Shape. However, because of polymorphism, the proper behavior still occurs when the virtual functions are called.

Note that sarray, the array of Shape*, can also be thought of as a container.

Function Templates

In drawAll() you see something new. So far in this chapter, we have been using only *class templates*, which instantiate new classes based on one or more type parameters. However, you can as easily create *function templates*, which create new functions based on type parameters.

The reason you create a function template is the same reason you use for a class template: you're trying to create generic code, and you do this by delaying the specification of one or more types. You just want to say that these type parameters support certain operations, not exactly what types they are.

The function template drawAll() can be thought of as an *algorithm* (and this is what most of the function templates in the Standard C++ Library are called). It just says how to do something given iterators describing a range of elements, as long as these iterators can be dereferenced, incremented, and compared. These are exactly the kind of iterators we have been developing in this chapter, and also—not coincidentally—the kind of iterators that are produced by the containers in the Standard C++ Library, evidenced by the use of vector in this example.

You'd also like drawAll() to be a *generic algorithm*, so that the containers can be any type at all and you don't have to write a new version of the algorithm for each different type of container. Here's where function templates are essential, because they automatically generate the specific code for each different type of container.

But without the extra indirection provided by the iterators, this genericity (the *generic attribute* or the *generic nature* of the programs) wouldn't be possible. That's why iterators are important; they allow you to write general-purpose code that involves containers without knowing the underlying structure of the container.

■ **Note**   In C++, iterators and generic algorithms require function templates in order to work.

You can see the proof of this in main(), since drawAll() works unchanged with each different type of container. And even more interesting, drawAll() also works with pointers to the beginning and end of the array sarray. This ability to treat arrays as containers is integral to the design of the Standard C++ Library, whose algorithms look much like drawAll().

Because container class templates are rarely subject to the inheritance and upcasting you see with "ordinary" classes, you'll almost never see virtual functions in container classes. Container class reuse is *implemented* with *templates*, not with inheritance.

Review Session

1. Container classes are an *essential* part of object-oriented programming. They are another way to simplify and hide the details of a program and to speed the process of *program development*.

2. In addition, they provide a great deal of *safety* and *flexibility* by replacing the primitive arrays and relatively crude data structure techniques found in C.

3. Because the client programmer needs containers, it's essential that they be easy to use. This is where the *template* comes in.

4. With templates the syntax for *source code reuse* (as opposed to object code reuse provided by *inheritance and* composition) becomes trivial enough for the novice user. In fact, *reusing code with templates* is notably *easier* than inheritance and composition.

5. The issues involved with container class design have been touched upon in this chapter, but you may have gathered that they can go *much further*.

6. In fact, a *complicated container class library* may cover all sorts of additional issues, including multithreading, persistence, and garbage collection.

CHAPTER 17

■ ■ ■

Exception Handling

Improving error recovery is one of the most powerful ways you can increase the robustness of your code.

Unfortunately, it's almost accepted practice to ignore error conditions, as if we're in a state of denial about errors. One reason, no doubt, is the tediousness and code bloat of checking for many errors. For example, printf() returns the number of characters that were successfully printed, but virtually no one checks this value. The proliferation of code alone would be disgusting, not to mention the difficulty it would add in reading the code.

The problem with C's approach to error handling could be thought of as coupling—the user of a function must tie the error-handling code so closely to that function that it becomes too ungainly and awkward to use.

One of the major features in C++ is exception handling, which is a better way of thinking about and handling errors. Exception handling provides several benefits.

1. Error-handling code is not nearly so tedious to write, and it doesn't become mixed up with your "normal" code. You write the code you *want* to happen; later in a separate section you write the code to cope with the problems. If you make multiple calls to a function, you handle the errors from that function once, in one place.

2. Errors cannot be ignored. If a function needs to send an error message to the caller of that function, it "throws" an object representing that error out of the function. If the caller doesn't "catch" the error and handle it, it goes to the next enclosing dynamic scope, and so on until the error is either caught or the program terminates because there was no handler to catch that type of exception.

This chapter examines C's approach to error handling (such as it is), discusses why it did not work well for C, and explains why it won't work at all for C++. This chapter also covers try, throw, and catch, the C++ keywords that support exception handling.

Traditional Error Handling

In most of the examples in this book, I use assert() as it was intended: for debugging during development with code that can be disabled with #define NDEBUG for the shipping product. Runtime error checking uses the require.h functions (assure() and require()) developed in Chapter 9. These functions are a convenient way to say, "There's a problem here you'll probably want to handle with some more sophisticated code, but you don't need to be distracted by it in this example." The require.h functions might be enough for small programs, but for complicated products you'll want to write more sophisticated error-handling code.

Error handling is quite straightforward when you know exactly what to do, because you have all the necessary information in that context. You can just handle the error at that point.

The problem occurs when *you* don't have enough information in that context, and you need to pass the error information into a different context where that information does exist. In C, you can handle this situation using three approaches.

1. Return error information from the function or, if the return value cannot be used this way, set a global error condition flag. (Standard C provides errno and perror() to support this.) As mentioned, the programmer is likely to ignore the error information because tedious and obfuscating error checking must occur with each function call. In addition, returning from a function that hits an exceptional condition might not make sense.

2. Use the little-known Standard C Library signal-handling system, implemented with the signal() function (to determine what happens when the event occurs) and raise() (to generate an event). Again, this approach involves high coupling because it requires the user of any library that generates signals to understand and install the appropriate signal-handling mechanism. In large projects, the signal numbers from different libraries might clash.

3. Use the nonlocal goto functions in the Standard C Library: setjmp() and longjmp(). With setjmp() you save a known good state in the program, and if you get into trouble, longjmp() will restore that state. Again, there is high coupling between the place where the state is stored and the place where the error occurs.

When considering error-handling schemes with C++, there's an additional critical problem: the C techniques of signals and setjmp()/longjmp() do not call destructors, so objects aren't properly cleaned up. (In fact, if longjmp() jumps past the end of a scope where destructors should be called, the behavior of the program is undefined.) This makes it virtually impossible to effectively recover from an exceptional condition because you'll always leave objects behind that haven't been cleaned up and that can no longer be accessed. Listing 17-1 demonstrates this with setjmp/longjmp.

Listing 17-1. Demonstrating Exception Handling (with C's setjmp() & longjmp())

```cpp
//: C17:Nonlocal.cpp
// setjmp() & longjmp().
#include <iostream>
#include <csetjmp>
using namespace std;
class Rainbow {
public:
  Rainbow() { cout << "Rainbow()" << endl; }
  ~Rainbow() { cout << "~Rainbow()" << endl; }
};
jmp_buf kansas;
void oz() {
  Rainbow rb;
  for(int i = 0; i< 3; i++)
    cout << "there's no place like home" << endl;
  longjmp(kansas, 47);
}
int main() {
  if(setjmp(kansas) == 0) {
    cout << "tornado, witch, munchkins..." << endl;
    oz();
  } else {
    cout << "Auntie Em! "
         << "I had the strangest dream..."
         << endl;
  }
} ///:~
```

The setjmp() function is odd because if you call it directly, it stores all the relevant information about the current processor state (such as the contents of the instruction pointer and runtime stack pointer) in the jmp_buf and returns zero. In this case, it behaves like an ordinary function. However, if you call longjmp() using the same jmp_buf, it's as if you're returning from setjmp() again—you pop right out the back end of the setjmp(). This time, the value returned is the second argument to longjmp(), so you can detect that you're actually coming back from a longjmp(). You can imagine that with many different jmp_bufs, you could pop around to many different places in the program. The difference between a local goto (with a label) and this nonlocal goto is that you can return to any predetermined location higher up in the runtime stack with setjmp()/longjmp() (wherever you've placed a call to setjmp()).

The problem in C++ is that longjmp() doesn't respect objects; in particular it doesn't call destructors when it jumps out of a scope. Destructor calls are essential, so this approach won't work with C++. In fact, the C++ Standard states that branching into a scope with goto (effectively bypassing constructor calls), or branching out of a scope with longjmp() where an object on the stack has a destructor, constitutes undefined behavior.

Throwing an Exception

If you encounter an exceptional situation in your code—that is, if you don't have enough information in the current context to decide what to do—you can send information about the error into a larger context by creating an object that contains that information and "throwing" it out of your current context. This is called throwing an exception. Listing 17-2 shows what it looks like.

Listing 17-2. Throwing an Exception

```
//: C17:MyError.cpp {RunByHand}
 classMyError {
 const char* const data;
public:
  MyError(const char* const msg = 0) : data(msg) {}
};
void f() {
  // Here we "throw" an exception object:
  throw MyError("something bad happened");
}
int main() {
  // As you'll see shortly, we'll want a "try block" here:
  f();
} ///:~
```

MyError is an ordinary class, which in this case takes a char* as a constructor argument. You can use any type when you throw (including built-in types), but usually you'll create special classes for throwing exceptions.

The keyword throw causes a number of relatively magical things to happen. First, it creates a copy of the object you're throwing and, in effect, "returns" it from the function containing the throw expression, even though that object type isn't normally what the function is designed to return. A naive way to think about exception handling is as an alternate return mechanism (although you'll find you can get into trouble if you take that analogy too far). You can also exit from ordinary scopes by throwing an exception. In any case, a value is returned, and the function or scope exits.

Any similarity to a return statement ends there because *where* you return is some place completely different from where a normal function call returns.

■ **Note**   You end up in an appropriate part of the code—called an exception handler—that might be far removed from where the exception was thrown.

In addition, any local objects created by the time the exception occurs are destroyed. This automatic cleanup of local objects is often called *stack unwinding*.

In addition, you can throw as many different types of objects as you want. Typically, you'll throw a different type for each category of error. The idea is to store the information in the object and in the *name* of its class so that someone in a calling context can figure out what to do with your exception.

Catching an Exception

As mentioned, one of the advantages of C++ exception handling is that you can concentrate on the problem you're trying to solve in one place and then deal with the errors from that code in another place.

The try Block

If you're inside a function and you throw an exception (or a called function throws an exception), the function exits because of the thrown exception. If you don't want a throw to leave a function, you can set up a special block within the function where you try to solve your actual programming problem (and potentially generate exceptions). This block is called the *try block* because you try your various function calls there. The try block is an ordinary scope, preceded by the keyword try, as in:

```
try {
  // Code that may generate exceptions
}
```

If you check for errors by carefully examining the return codes from the functions you use, you need to surround every function call with setup and test code, even if you call the same function several times. With exception handling, you put everything in a try block and handle exceptions after the try block. Thus, your code is a lot easier to write and to read because the goal of the code is not confused with the error handling.

Exception Handlers

Of course, the thrown exception must end up some place. This place is the *exception handler*, and you need one exception handler for every exception type you want to catch. However, polymorphism also works for exceptions, so one exception handler can work with an exception type and classes derived from that type.

Exception handlers immediately follow the try block and are denoted by the keyword catch, as in:

```
try {
  // Code that may generate exceptions
} catch(type1 id1) {
  // Handle exceptions of type1
} catch(type2 id2) {
  // Handle exceptions of type2
} catch(type3 id3)
  // Etc...
} catch(typeNidN)
  // Handle exceptions of typeN
}
// Normal execution resumes here...
```

The syntax of a catch clause resembles functions that take a single argument. The identifier (id1, id2, and so on) can be used inside the handler, just like a function argument, although you can omit the identifier if it's not needed in the handler. The exception type usually gives you enough information to deal with it.

The handlers must appear directly after the try block. If an exception is thrown, the exception-handling mechanism goes hunting for the first handler with an argument that matches the type of the exception. It then enters that catch clause, and the exception is considered handled. (The search for handlers stops once the catch clause is found.) Only the matching catch clause executes; control then resumes after the last handler associated with that try block.

Notice that, within the try block, a number of different function calls might generate the same type of exception, but you need only one handler.

To illustrate try and catch, the Listing 17-3 modifies Nonlocal.cpp (Listing 17-1) by replacing the call to setjmp() with a try block and replacing the call to longjmp() with a throw statement.

Listing 17-3. Illustrating Try & Catch Blocks

```
//: C17:Nonlocal2.cpp
// Illustrates exceptions.
#include <iostream>
using namespace std;
class Rainbow {
public:
  Rainbow() { cout << "Rainbow()" << endl; }
  ~Rainbow() { cout << "~Rainbow()" << endl; }
};
void oz() {
  Rainbow rb;
  for(int i = 0; i < 3; i++)
    cout << "there's no place like home" << endl;
  throw 47;
}
int main() {
  try {
    cout << "tornado, witch, munchkins..." << endl;
    oz();
  } catch(int) {
    cout << "Auntie Em! I had the strangest dream..."
         << endl;
  }
} ///:~
```

When the throw statement in oz() executes, program control backtracks until it finds the catch clause that takes an int parameter. Execution resumes with the body of that catch clause. The most important difference between this program and Nonlocal.cpp is that the destructor for the object rb is called when the throw statement causes execution to leave the function oz().

Termination and Resumption

There are two basic models in exception-handling theory: termination and resumption. In *termination* (which is what C++ supports), you assume the error is so critical that there's no way to automatically resume execution at the point where the exception occurred. In other words, whoever threw the exception decided there was no way to salvage the situation, and they don't *want* to come back.

The alternative error-handling model is called *resumption*, first introduced with the PL/I language in the 1960s. Using resumption semantics means that the exception handler is expected to do something to rectify the situation, and then the faulting code is automatically retried, presuming success the second time. If you want resumption in C++, you must explicitly transfer execution back to the code where the error occurred, usually by repeating the function call that sent you there in the first place. It is not unusual to place your try block inside a while loop that keeps reentering the try block until the result is satisfactory.

Historically, programmers using operating systems that supported resumptive exception handling eventually ended up using termination-like code and skipping resumption. Although resumption sounds attractive at first, it seems it isn't quite so useful in practice. One reason may be the distance that can occur between the exception and its handler. It is one thing to terminate to a handler that's far away, but to jump to that handler and then back again may be too conceptually difficult for large systems where the exception is generated from many points.

Exception Matching

When an exception is thrown, the exception-handling system looks through the "nearest" handlers in the order they appear in the source code. When it finds a match, the exception is considered handled and no further searching occurs.

Matching an exception doesn't require a perfect correlation between the exception and its handler. An object or reference to a derivedclass object will match a handler for the base class. (However, if the handler is for an object rather than a reference, the exception object is "sliced"—truncated to the base type—as it is passed to the handler. This does no damage, but loses all the derived-type information.) For this reason, as well as to avoid making yet another copy of the exception object, it is always better to catch an exception by *reference* instead of by value. If a pointer is thrown, the usual standard pointer conversions are used to match the exception. However, no automatic type conversions are used to convert from one exception type to another in the process of matching. For example, see Listing 17-4.

Listing 17-4. Illustrating Exception Matching

```
//: C17:Autoexcp.cpp
// No matching conversions.
#include <iostream>
using namespace std;
class Except1 {};
class Except2 {
public:
  Except2(const Except1&) {}
};
void f() { throw Except1(); }
int main() {
  try { f();
  } catch(Except2&) {
    cout << "inside catch(Except2)" << endl;
  } catch(Except1&) {
    cout << "inside catch(Except1)" << endl;
  }
} ///:~
```

Even though you might think the first handler could be matched by converting an Except1 object into an Except2 using the converting constructor, the system will not perform such a conversion during exception handling, and you'll end up at the Except1 handler.

Listing 17-5 shows how a baseclass handler can catch a derivedclass exception.

Listing 17-5. Illustrating Exception Hierarchies

```
//: C17:Basexcpt.cpp
// Exception hierarchies.
#include <iostream>
```

```
using namespace std;
class X {
public:
  class Trouble {};
  class Small : public Trouble {};
  class Big : public Trouble {};
  void f() { throw Big(); }
};
int main() {
  X x;
  try {
    x.f();
  } catch(X::Trouble&) {
    cout << "caught Trouble" << endl;
  // Hidden by previous handler:
  } catch(X::Small&) {
    cout << "caught Small Trouble" << endl;
  } catch(X::Big&) {
    cout << "caught Big Trouble" << endl;
  }
} ///:~
```

Here, the exception-handling mechanism will always match a Trouble object, *or anything that is a* Trouble (*through public inheritance*), to the first handler. That means the second and third handlers are never called because the first one captures them all. It makes more sense to catch the derived types first and put the base type at the end to catch anything less specific.

Notice that these examples catch exceptions by reference, although for these classes it isn't important because there are no additional members in the derived classes, and there are no argument identifiers in the handlers anyway. You'll usually want to use reference arguments rather than value arguments in your handlers to avoid slicing off information.

Catching Any Exception

Sometimes you want to create a handler that catches *any* type of exception. You do this using the ellipsis in the argument list, as in:

```
catch(...) {
  cout << "an exception was thrown" << endl;
}
```

Because an ellipsis catches any exception, you'll want to put it at the *end* of your list of handlers to avoid preempting any that follow it.

The ellipsis gives you no possibility to have an argument, so you can't know anything about the exception or its type. It's a catch all; it's often used to clean up some resources and then rethrow the exception.

Rethrowing an Exception

You usually want to rethrow an exception when you have some resource that needs to be released, such as a network connection or heap memory that needs to be deallocated.

■ **Note**   See the section "Resource Management" later in this chapter for more detail.

If an exception occurs, you don't necessarily care what error caused the exception—you just want to close the connection you opened previously. After that, you'll want to let some other context closer to the user (that is, higher up in the call chain) handle the exception. In this case, the ellipsis specification is just what you want. You want to catch *any* exception, clean up your resource, and then rethrow the exception for handling elsewhere. You rethrow an exception by using throw with no argument inside a handler, as in:

```
catch(...) {
cout << "an exception was thrown" << endl;
// Deallocate your resource here, and then rethrow
  throw;
}
```

Any further catch clauses for the same try block are still ignored—the throw causes the exception to go to the exception handlers in the next-higher context. In addition, everything about the exception object is preserved, so the handler at the higher context that catches the specific exception type can extract any information the object may contain.

Uncaught Exceptions

As I explained in the beginning of this chapter, exception handling is considered better than the traditional return-an-error-code technique because exceptions can't be ignored, and because the error handling logic is separated from the problem at hand. If none of the exception handlers following a particular try block matches an exception, that exception moves to the next-higher context, that is, the function or try block surrounding the try block that did not catch the exception. (The location of this try block is not always obvious at first glance, since it's higher up in the call chain.) This process continues until, at some level, a handler matches the exception. At that point, the exception is considered "caught," and no further searching occurs.

The terminate() Function

If no handler at any level catches the exception, the special library function terminate() (declared in the <exception> header) is automatically called. By default, terminate() calls the Standard C Library function abort(), which abruptly exits the program. On Unix systems, abort() also causes a core dump. When abort() is called, no calls to normal program termination functions occur, which means that destructors for global and static objects do not execute. The terminate() function also executes if a destructor for a local object throws an exception while the stack is unwinding (interrupting the exception *that was in progress*) or if a global or static object's constructor or destructor throws an exception. (In general, do not allow a destructor to throw an exception.)

The set_terminate() Function

You can install your own terminate() function using the standard set_terminate() function, which returns a pointer to the terminate() function you are replacing (which will be the default library version the first time you call it), so you can restore it later if you want. Your custom terminate() must take no arguments and have a void return value. In addition, any terminate() handler you install must not return or throw an exception, but instead must execute some sort of program-termination logic. If terminate() is called, the problem is unrecoverable.

Listing 17-6 shows the use of set_terminate(). Here, the return value is saved and restored so that the terminate() function can be used to help isolate the section of code where the uncaught exception occurs.

Listing 17-6. Using set_terminate(); also, Demonstrates Uncaught Exceptions

```
//: C17:Terminator.cpp
// Use of set_terminate(). Also shows uncaught exceptions.
#include <exception>
#include <iostream>
using namespace std;
void terminator() {
  cout << "I'll be back!" << endl;
  exit(0);
}
void (*old_terminate)() = set_terminate(terminator);
class Botch {
public:
  class Fruit {};
  void f() {
    cout << "Botch::f()" << endl;
    throw Fruit();
  }
  ~Botch() { throw 'c'; }
};
int main() {
  try {
    Botch b;
    b.f();
  } catch(...) {
    cout << "inside catch(...)" << endl;
  }
} ///:~
```

The definition of old_terminate looks a bit confusing at first: it not only creates a pointer to a function, but it initializes that pointer to the return value of set_terminate(). Even though you might be familiar with seeing a semicolon right after a pointer-to-function declaration, here it's just another kind of variable and can be initialized when it is defined.

The class Botch not only throws an exception inside f(), but also in its destructor. This causes a call to terminate(), as you can see in main(). Even though the exception handler says catch(...), which would seem to catch everything and leave no cause for terminate() to be called, terminate() is called anyway. In the process of cleaning up the objects on the stack to handle one exception, the Botch destructor is called, and that generates a second exception, forcing a call to terminate(). Thus, a destructor that throws an exception or causes one to be thrown is usually a sign of poor design or sloppy coding.

Cleaning Up

Part of the magic of exception handling is that you can pop from normal program flow into the appropriate exception handler. Doing so wouldn't be useful, however, if things weren't cleaned up properly as the exception was thrown. C++ exception handling guarantees that as you leave a scope, all objects in that scope *whose constructors have been completed* will have their destructors called.

Listing 17-7 demonstrates that constructors that aren't completed don't have the associated destructors called. It also shows what happens when an exception is thrown in the middle of the creation of an array of objects.

Listing 17-7. Demonstrates that Exceptions don't Clean up Incomplete Objects

```
//: C17:Cleanup.cpp
// Exceptions clean up complete objects only.
#include <iostream>
using namespace std;
class Trace {
  static int counter;
  int objid;
public:
  Trace() {
    objid = counter++;
    cout << "constructing Trace #" << objid << endl;
    if(objid == 3) throw 3;
  }
  ~Trace() {
    cout << "destructing Trace #" << objid << endl;
  }
};
int Trace::counter = 0;
int main() {
  try {
    Trace n1;
    // Throws exception:
    Trace array[5];
    Trace n2;  // Won't get here.
  } catch(int i) {
    cout << "caught " << i << endl;
  }
} ///:~
```

The class Trace keeps track of objects so that you can trace program progress. It keeps a count of the number of objects created with a static data member counter and tracks the number of the particular object with objid.

The main program creates a single object, n1 (objid 0), and then attempts to create an array of five Trace objects, but an exception is thrown before the fourth object (#3) is fully created. The object n2 is never created. You can see the results in the output of the program:

```
constructing Trace #0
constructing Trace #1
constructing Trace #2
constructing Trace #3
destructing Trace #2
destructing Trace #1
destructing Trace #0
caught 3
```

Three array elements are successfully created, but in the middle of the constructor for the fourth element, an exception is thrown. Because the fourth construction in main() for array[2]) never completes, only the destructors for objects array[1] and array[0] are called. Finally, object n1 is destroyed, but not object n2, because it was never created.

Resource Management

When writing code with exceptions, it's particularly important that you always ask, "If an exception occurs, will my resources be properly cleaned up?" Most of the time you're fairly safe, but in constructors there's a particular problem: if an exception is thrown before a constructor is completed, the associated destructor will not be called for that object. Thus, you must be especially diligent while writing your constructor.

The difficulty is in allocating resources in constructors. If an exception occurs in the constructor, the destructor doesn't get a chance to deallocate the resource. This problem occurs most often with "*naked*" pointers. I am calling them "*naked*" pointers for good reason. They behave like a person who has taken off his clothes and started bathing but after completing the bath has to come out in the open naked since someone has run away with his clothes. Thus, after taking off his clothes, an exception occurred in the form of his clothes being stolen, and now he has to come out naked since he wasn't prepared for this exceptional situation. For a code example, see Listing 17-8.

Listing 17-8. Demonstrates a Case of Naked Pointers

```
//: C17:Rawp.cpp
// Naked pointers.
#include <iostream>
#include <cstddef>
using namespace std;
class Cat {
public:
  Cat() { cout << "Cat()" << endl; }
  ~Cat() { cout << "~Cat()" << endl; }
};
class Dog {
public:
  void* operator new(size_tsz) {
    cout << "allocating a Dog" << endl;
    throw 47;
  }
  void operator delete(void* p) {
    cout << "deallocating a Dog" << endl;
    ::operator delete(p);
  }
};
class UseResources {
  Cat* bp;
  Dog* op;
public:
  UseResources(int count = 1) {
    cout << "UseResources()" << endl;
    bp = new Cat[count];
    op = new Dog;
  }
  ~UseResources() {
    cout << "~UseResources()" << endl;
    delete [] bp; // Array delete
    delete op;
  }
};
```

```
int main() {
  try {
    UseResources ur(3);
  } catch(int) {
    cout << "inside handler" << endl;
  }
} ///:~
```

The output is

```
UseResources()
Cat()
Cat()
Cat()
allocating a Dog
inside handler
```

The UseResources constructor is entered, and the Cat constructor is successfully completed for the three array objects. However, inside Dog::operator new(), an exception is thrown (to simulate an out-of-memory error). Suddenly, you end up inside the handler, *without* the UseResources destructor being called. This is correct because the UseResources constructor was unable to finish, but it also means the Cat objects that were successfully created on the heap were never destroyed.

Making Everything an Object

To prevent such resource leaks, you must guard against these "raw" resource allocations in one of two ways (I am calling them *raw resource allocations* for the same reason as above. They behave like a "raw" person who had the clothes (the *resources)* but was *not well prepared* for the exceptional situation arising out of somebody running away with his clothes (the *resources)* during the bath, and eventually has to come out in the open naked).

- You can catch exceptions inside the constructor and then release the resource.

- You can place the allocations inside an object's constructor, and you can place the deallocations inside an object's destructor.

Using the latter approach, each allocation becomes atomic by virtue of being part of the lifetime of a local object, and if it fails, the other resource allocation objects are properly cleaned up during stack unwinding. This technique is called Resource Acquisition Is Initialization (RAII, for short) because it equates resource control with object lifetime. Using templates is an excellent way to modify Listing 17-8 to achieve the code shown in Listing 17-9.

Listing 17-9. Illustrates Safe Atomic Pointers & Using RAII

```
//: C17:Wrapped.cpp
// Safe, atomic pointers.
#include <iostream>
#include <cstddef>
using namespace std;
// Simplified. Yours may have other arguments.
template<class T, int sz = 1> class PWrap {
  T* ptr;
public:
  class RangeError {}; // Exception class
  PWrap() {
```

```
    ptr = new T[sz];
    cout << "PWrap constructor" << endl;
  }
  ~PWrap() {
    delete[] ptr;
    cout << "PWrap destructor" << endl;
  }
  T& operator[](int i) throw(RangeError) {
    if(i >= 0 && i < sz) return ptr[i];
    throw RangeError();
  }
};
class Cat {
public:
  Cat() { cout << "Cat()" << endl; }
  ~Cat() { cout << "~Cat()" << endl; }
  void g() {}
};
class Dog {
public:
  void* operator new[](size_t) {
    cout << "Allocating a Dog" << endl;
    throw 47;
  }
  void operator delete[](void* p) {
    cout << "Deallocating a Dog" << endl;
    ::operator delete[](p);
  }
};
class UseResources {
  PWrap<Cat, 3> cats;
  PWrap<Dog> dog;
public:
  UseResources() { cout << "UseResources()" << endl; }
  ~UseResources() { cout << "~UseResources()" << endl; }
  void f() { cats[1].g(); }
};
int main() {
  try {
    UseResources ur;
  } catch(int) {
    cout << "inside handler" << endl;
  } catch(...) {
    cout << "inside catch(...)" << endl;
  }
} ///:~
```

The difference is the use of the template to wrap the pointers and make them into objects. The constructors for these objects are called *before* the body of the UseResources constructor, and any of these constructors that complete before an exception is thrown will have their associated destructors called during stack unwinding.

The PWrap template shows a more typical use of exceptions than you've seen so far: a nested class called RangeError is created to use in operator[ ] if its argument is out of range. Because operator[ ] returns a reference, it cannot return zero.

■ **Note**   There are no null references.

This is a true exceptional condition—you don't know what to do in the current context and you can't return an improbable value. In Listing 17-9, RangeError[5] is simple and assumes all the necessary information is in the class name, but you might also want to add a member that contains the value of the index, if that is useful.

Now the output is

```
Cat()
Cat()
Cat()
PWrap constructor
allocating a Dog
~Cat()
~Cat()
~Cat()
PWrap destructor
inside handler
```

Again, the storage allocation for Dog throws an exception, but this time the array of Cat objects is properly cleaned up, so there is no memory leak.

Using auto_ptr

Since dynamic memory is the most frequent resource used in a typical C++ program, the standard provides an RAII wrapper for pointers to heap memory that automatically frees the memory. The auto_ptr class template, defined in the <memory> header, has a constructor that takes a pointer to its generic type (whatever you use in your code). The auto_ptr class template also overloads the pointer operators * and -> to forward these operations to the original pointer the auto_ptr object is holding. So you can use the auto_ptr object as if it were a raw pointer. Listing 17-10 shows how it works.

Listing 17-10. Demonstrates The RAII Nature of auto_ptr

```
//: C17:Auto_ptr.cpp
// Illustrates the RAII nature of auto_ptr.
#include <memory>
#include <iostream>
#include <cstddef>
using namespace std;
class TraceHeap {
  int i;
public:
  static void* operator new(size_t siz) {
    void* p = ::operator new(siz);
    cout << "Allocating TraceHeap object on the heap "
```

```
         << "at address " << p << endl;
      return p;
   }
   static void operator delete(void* p) {
      cout << "Deleting TraceHeap object at address "
           << p << endl;
      ::operator delete(p);
   }
   TraceHeap(int i) : i(i) {}
   intgetVal() const { return i; }
};
int main() {
   auto_ptr<TraceHeap> pMyObject(new TraceHeap(5));
   cout << pMyObject->getVal() << endl;   // Prints 5
} ///:~
```

The TraceHeap class overloads the operator new and operator delete so you can see exactly what's happening. Notice that, like any other class template, you specify the type you're going to use in a template parameter. You don't say TraceHeap*, however—auto_ptr already knows that it will be storing a pointer to your type. The second line of main() verifies that auto_ptr's operator->() function applies the indirection to the original, underlying pointer. Most important, even though you didn't explicitly delete the original pointer, pMyObject's destructor deletes the original pointer during stack unwinding, as the following output verifies:

```
Allocating TraceHeap object on the heap at address 8930040
5
Deleting TraceHeap object at address 8930040
```

The auto_ptr class template is also handy for pointer data members. Since class objects contained by value are always destructed, auto_ptr members always delete the raw pointer they wrap when the containing object is destructed.

Function–Level try Blocks

Since constructors can routinely throw exceptions, you might want to handle exceptions that occur when an object's member or base subobjects are initialized. To do this, you can place the initialization of such subobjects in a *function-level try block*. In a departure from the usual syntax, the try block for constructor initializers is the constructor body, and the associated catch block follows the body of the constructor, as in Listing 17-11.

Listing 17-11. Illustrates Handling Exceptions from Subobjects

```
//: C17:InitExcept.cpp {-bor}
// Handles exceptions from subobjects.
#include <iostream>
using namespace std;
 class Base {
   int i;
public:
   classBaseExcept {};
   Base(int i) : i(i) { throw BaseExcept(); }
};
```

```
class Derived : public Base {
public:
  class DerivedExcept {
    const char* msg;
  public:
    DerivedExcept(const char* msg) : msg(msg) {}
    const char* what() const { return msg; }
  };
  Derived(int j) try : Base(j) {
    // Constructor body
    cout << "This won't print" << endl;
  } catch(BaseExcept&) {
    throw DerivedExcept("Base subobject threw");;
  }
};
int main() {
  try {
    Derived d(3);
  } catch(Derived::DerivedExcept& d) {
    cout << d.what() << endl;  // "Base subobject threw"
  }
} ///:~
```

Notice that the initializer list in the constructor for Derived goes after the try keyword but before the constructor body. If an exception does occur, the contained object is not constructed, so it makes no sense to return to the code that created it. For this reason, the only sensible thing to do is to throw an exception in the function-level catch clause.

Although it is not terribly useful, C++ also allows function-level try blocks for *any* function, as Listing 17-12 illustrates.

Listing 17-12. Demonstrates Function-Level try Blocks

```
//: C17:FunctionTryBlock.cpp {-bor}
// Function-level try blocks.
// {RunByHand} (Don't run automatically by the makefile)
#include <iostream>
using namespace std;

int main() try {
  throw "main";
} catch(const char* msg) {
cout << msg << endl;
return 1;
} ///:~
```

In this case, the catch block can return in the same manner that the function body normally returns. Using this type of function-level try block isn't much different from inserting a try-catch around the code inside of the function body.

Standard Exceptions

The exceptions used with the Standard C++ Library are also available for your use. Generally it's easier and faster to start with a standard exception class than to try to define your own. If the standard class doesn't do exactly what you need, you can derive from it.

All standard exception classes derive ultimately from the class exception, defined in the header <exception>. The two main derived classes are logic_error and runtime_error, which are found in <stdexcept> (which itself includes <exception>). The class logic_error represents errors in programming logic, such as passing an invalid argument. Runtime errors are those that occur as the result of unforeseen forces such as hardware failure or memory exhaustion. Both runtime_error and logic_error provide a constructor that takes a std::string argument so that you can store a message in the exception object and extract it later with exception::what(), as Listing 17-13 illustrates.

Listing 17-13. Demonstrates Deriving an Exception Class

```
//: C17:StdExcept.cpp
// Derives an exception class from std::runtime_error.
#include <stdexcept>
#include <iostream>
using namespace std;

class MyError : public runtime_error {
public:
  MyError(const string& msg = "") : runtime_error(msg) {}
};
int main() {
  try {
    throw MyError("my message");
  } catch(MyError& x) {
    cout << x.what() << endl;
  }
} ///:~
```

Although the runtime_error constructor inserts the message into its std::exception subobject, std::exception does not provide a constructor that takes a std::string argument. You'll usually want to derive your exception classes from either runtime_error or logic_error (or *one of their derivatives*), and not from std::exception.

Table 17-1 describes the standard exception classes.

Table 17-1. *Standard Exception Classes*

exception	The base class for all the exceptions thrown by the C++ Standard Library. You can ask what() and retrieve the optional string with which the exception was initialized.
logic_error	Derived from exception. Reports program logic errors, which could presumably be detected by inspection.
runtime_error	Derived from exception. Reports runtime errors, which can presumably be detected only when the program executes.

The iostream exception class ios::failure is also derived from exception, but it has no further subclasses.

You can use the classes in both of the following tables as they are, or you can use them as base classes from which to derive your own more specific types of exceptions. See Tables 17-2 and 17-3.

Table 17-2. *Exception Classes Derived from Standard Exception Classlogic_error*

Exception Classes Derived from `logic_error`	
domain_error	Reports violations of a precondition.
invalid_argument	Indicates an invalid argument to the function from which it is thrown.
length_error	Indicates an attempt to produce an object whose length is greater than or equal to npos (the largest representable value of context's size type, usually `std::size_t`).
out_of_range	Reports an out-of-range argument.
bad_cast	Thrown for executing an invalid `dynamic_cast` expression in runtime type identification (see Chapter 8).
bad_typeid	Reports a null pointer p in an expression `typeid(*p)`. (Again, a runtime type identification feature; see Chapter 20).

Table 17-3. *Exception Classes Derived from Standard Exception Class - runtime_error*

Exception Classes Derived from `runtime_error`	
range_error	Reports violation of a post condition.
overflow_error	Reports an arithmetic overflow.
bad_alloc	Reports a failure to allocate storage.

Exception Specifications

You're not required to inform the people using your function what exceptions you might throw. However, failure to do so can be considered uncivilized because it means that users cannot be sure what code to write to catch all potential exceptions. If they have your source code, they can hunt through and look for throw statements, but often a library doesn't come with sources. Good documentation can help alleviate this problem, but how many software projects are well documented? C++ provides syntax to tell the user the exceptions that are thrown by this function, so the user can handle them. This is the optional *exception specification*, which adorns a function's declaration, appearing after the argument list.

The exception specification reuses the keyword throw, followed by a parenthesized list of all the types of potential exceptions that the function can throw. Your function declaration might look like this:

```
void f() throw(toobig, toosmall, divzero);
```

As far as exceptions are concerned, the traditional function declaration

```
void f();
```

means that *any* type of exception can be thrown from the function. If you say

```
void f() throw();
```

no exceptions whatsoever will be thrown from the function (so you'd better be sure that no functions farther down in the call chain let any exceptions propagate up!).

For good coding policy, good documentation, and ease-of-use for the function caller, consider using exception specifications when you write functions that throw exceptions.

■ **Note** Variations on this guideline are discussed later in this chapter.

The unexpected() Function

If your exception specification claims you're going to throw a certain set of exceptions and then you throw something that isn't in that set, what's the penalty? The special function unexpected( ) is called when you throw something other than what appears in the exception specification. Should this unfortunate situation occur, the default unexpected( ) calls the terminate( ) function described earlier in this chapter.

The set_unexpected() Function

Like terminate( ), the unexpected( ) mechanism installs your own function to respond to unexpected exceptions. You do so with a function called set_unexpected( ), which, like set_terminate( ), takes the address of a function with no arguments and void return value. Also, because it returns the previous value of the unexpected( ) pointer, you can save it and restore it later. To use set_unexpected( ), include the header file <exception>. Listing 17-14 shows a simple use of the features discussed so far in this section.

Listing 17-14. Using Exception Specifications & the unexpected() Mechanism

```
//: C17:Unexpected.cpp
// Exception specifications & unexpected(),
//{-msc} (Doesn't terminate properly)
#include <exception>
#include <iostream>
using namespace std;
class Up {};
class Fit {};
void g();
void f(int i) throw(Up, Fit) {
  switch(i) {
    case 1: throw Up();
    case 2: throw Fit();
  }
  g();
}
// void g() {}                    // Version 1
void g() { throw 47; }           // Version 2
void my_unexpected() {
  cout << "unexpected exception thrown" << endl;
  exit(0);
}

int main() {
  set_unexpected(my_unexpected); // (Ignores return value)
  for(int i = 1; i <= 3; i++)
    try {
      f(i);
    } catch(Up) {
      cout << "Up caught" << endl;
```

```
  } catch(Fit) {
    cout << "Fit caught" << endl;
  }
} ///:~
```

The classes Up and Fit are created solely to throw as exceptions. Often exception classes will be small, but they can certainly hold additional information so that the handlers can query for it.

The f() function promises in its exception specification to throw only exceptions of type Up and Fit, and from looking at the function definition, this seems plausible. Version one of g(), called by f(), doesn't throw any exceptions, so this is true. But if someone changes g() so that it throws a different type of exception (like the second version in this example, which throws an int), the exception specification for f() is violated.

The my_unexpected() function has no arguments or return value, following the proper form for a custom unexpected() function. It simply displays a message so that you can see that it was called, and then exits the program (exit(0) is used here so that the book's make process is not aborted). Your new unexpected() function should not have a return statement.

In main(), the try block is within a for loop, so all the possibilities are exercised. In this way, you can achieve something like resumption. Nest the try block inside a for, while, do, or if and cause any exceptions to attempt to repair the problem; then attempt the try block again.

Only the Up and Fit exceptions are caught because those are the only exceptions that the programmer of f() said would be thrown. Version two of g() causes my_unexpected() to be called because f() then throws an int.

In the call to set_unexpected(), the return value is ignored, but it can also be saved in a pointer to function and be restored later, as in the set_terminate() example earlier (Listing 17-6) in this chapter.

A typical unexpected handler logs the error and terminates the program by calling exit(). It can, however, throw another exception (or, rethrow the same exception) or call abort(). If it throws an exception of a type allowed by the function whose specification was originally violated, the search resumes at the *call* of the function with this exception specification.

■ **Note** This behavior is unique to unexpected().

If the exception thrown from your unexpected handler is not allowed by the original function's specification, one of two events occurs.

1. If std::bad_exception (defined in <exception>) was in the function's exception specification, the exception thrown from the unexpected handler is replaced with a std::bad_exception object, and the search resumes from the function as before.

2. If the original function's specification did not include std::bad_exception, terminate() is called.

Listing 17-15 illustrates this behavior.

Listing 17-15. Ilustrating The Two Cases of Bad Exceptions

```
//: C17:BadException.cpp {-bor}
#include <exception>     // For std::bad_exception
#include <iostream>
#include <cstdio>
using namespace std;
// Exception classes:
class A {};
class B {};
```

```
// terminate() handler
void my_thandler() {
  cout << "terminate called" << endl;
  exit(0);
}
// unexpected() handlers
void my_uhandler1() { throw A(); }
void my_uhandler2() { throw; }
// If we embed this throw statement in f or g,
// the compiler detects the violation and reports
// an error, so we put it in its own function.
void t() { throw B(); }
void f() throw(A) { t(); }
void g() throw(A, bad_exception) { t(); }
int main() {
  set_terminate(my_thandler);
  set_unexpected(my_uhandler1);
  try {
    f();
  } catch(A&) {
    cout << "caught an A from f" << endl;
  }
  set_unexpected(my_uhandler2);
  try {
    g();
  } catch(bad_exception&) {
    cout << "caught a bad_exception from g" << endl;
  }
  try {
    f();
  } catch(...) {
    cout << "This will never print" << endl;
  }
} ///:~
```

The my_uhandler1() handler throws an acceptable exception (A), so execution resumes at the first catch, which succeeds. The my_uhandler2() handler does not throw a valid exception (B), but since g specifies bad_exception, the B exception is replaced by a bad_exception object, and the second catch also succeeds. Since f does not include bad_exception in its specification, my_thandler() is called as a terminate handler. Here's the output:

```
caught an A from f
caught a bad_exception from g
terminate called
```

Better Exception Specifications?

You may feel that the existing exception specification rules aren't very safe, and that

```
void f();
```

should mean that no exceptions are thrown from this function. If the programmer wants to throw any type of exception, you might think he or she *should* have to say

```
void f() throw(...); // Not in C++
```

This would surely be an improvement because function declarations would be more explicit. Unfortunately, you can't always know by looking at the code in a function whether an exception will be thrown—it could happen because of a memory allocation, for example. Worse, existing functions written before exception handling was introduced into the language may find themselves inadvertently throwing exceptions because of the functions they call (which might be linked into new, exception-throwing versions). Hence, the uninformative situation whereby

```
void f();
```

means, "Maybe I'll throw an exception; *maybe I won't.*" This ambiguity is necessary to avoid hindering code evolution. If you want to specify that f throws no exceptions, use the empty list, as in:

```
void f() throw();
```

Exception Specifications and Inheritance

Each public function in a class essentially forms a contract with the user; if you pass it certain arguments, it will perform certain operations and/or return a result. The same contract must hold true in derived classes; otherwise the expected *is-a* relationship between derived and base classes is violated. Since exception specifications are logically part of a function's declaration, they too must remain consistent across an inheritance hierarchy. For example, if a member function in a base class says it will only throw an exception of type A, an override of that function in a derived class must not add any other exception types to the specification list because that would break any programs that adhere to the base class interface. You can, however, specify *fewer* exceptions or *none at all*, since that doesn't require the user to do anything differently. You can also specify anything that *is-a* A in place of A in the derived function's specification. Listing 17-16 shows an example.

Listing 17-16. Illustrating Covariance (Exception Specifications & Inheritance)

```
//: C17:Covariance.cpp {-xo}
// Should cause compile error. {-mwcc}{-msc}
#include <iostream>
using namespace std;
class Base {
public:
  class BaseException {};
  class DerivedException : public BaseException {};
  virtual void f() throw(DerivedException) {
    throw DerivedException();
  }
  virtual void g() throw(BaseException) {
    throw BaseException();
  }
};
class Derived : public Base {
public:
  void f() throw(BaseException) {
    throw BaseException();
  }
```

```
  virtual void g() throw(DerivedException) {
    throw DerivedException();
  }
}; ///:~
```

A compiler should flag the override of Derived::f() with an error (*or at least a warning*) since it changes its exception specification in a way that violates the specification of Base::f(). The specification for Derived::g() is acceptable because DerivedException is-a BaseException (not the other way around). You can think of Base/Derived and BaseException/DerivedException as parallel class hierarchies; when you are in Derived, you can replace references to BaseException in exception specifications and return values with DerivedException. This behavior is called *covariance* (since both sets of classes vary down their respective hierarchies together).

When Not to Use Exception Specifications

If you peruse the function declarations throughout the Standard C++ Library, you'll find that not a single exception specification occurs anywhere! Although this might seem strange, there is a good reason for this seeming incongruity: the library consists mainly of templates, and you never know what a generic type or function might do. For example, suppose you are developing a generic stack template and attempt to affix an exception specification to your pop function, like this:

```
T pop() throw(logic_error);
```

Since the only error you anticipate is a stack underflow, you might think it's safe to specify a logic_error or some other appropriate exception type. But type T's copy constructor could throw an exception. Then unexpected() would be called, and your program would terminate. You can't make unsupportable guarantees. If you don't know what exceptions might occur, don't use exception specifications. That's why template classes, which constitute the majority of the Standard C++ Library, do not use exception specifications—they specify the *exceptions they know about* in *documentation* and leave the rest to you. Exception specifications are mainly for non-template classes.

Exception Safety

The Standard C++ Library includes the stack container. One thing you'll notice is that the declaration of the pop() member function looks like this:

```
void pop();
```

You might think it strange that pop() doesn't return a value. Instead, it just removes the element at the top of the stack. To retrieve the top value, call top() before you call pop(). There is an important reason for this behavior, and it has to do with *exception safety*, a crucial consideration in library design. There are different levels of exception safety, but most importantly—and just as the name implies—exception safety is about correct semantics in the face of exceptions.

Suppose you are implementing a stack with a dynamic array (let's call it data and the counter integer count), and you try to write pop() so that it returns a value. The code for such a pop() might look something like this:

```
template<class T> T stack<T>::pop() {
  if(count == 0)
    throw logic_error("stack underflow");

  else

  return data[--count];
}
```

What happens if the copy constructor that is called for the return value in the last line throws an exception when the value is returned? The popped element is not returned because of the exception, and yet count has already been decremented, so the top element you wanted is lost forever! The problem is that this function attempts to do two things at once: (1) return a value, and (2) change the state of the stack. It is better to separate these two actions into two separate member functions, which is exactly what the standard stack class does. (In other words, follow the design practice of *cohesion*—every function should do *one thing well*.) Exception-safe code leaves objects in a consistent state and does not leak resources.

You also need to be careful writing custom assignment operators. In Chapter 12, you saw that operator= should adhere to the following pattern.

1. Make sure you're not assigning to self. If you are, go to step 6. (*This is strictly an optimization.*)

2. Allocate new memory required by pointer data members.

3. Copy data from the old memory to the new.

4. Delete the old memory.

5. Update the object's state by assigning the new heap pointers to the pointer data members.

6. Return *this.

It's important to not change the state of your object until all the new pieces have been safely allocated and initialized. A good technique is to move steps 2 and 3 into a separate function, often called clone(). Listing 17-17 does this for a class that has two pointer members, theString and theInts.

Listing 17-17. Illustrating an Exception-Safe Operator (=)

```cpp
//: C17:SafeAssign.cpp
// An Exception-safe operator=.
#include <iostream>
#include <new>        // For std::bad_alloc
#include <cstring>
#include <cstddef>
using namespace std;
// A class that has two pointer members using the heap
class HasPointers {
  // A Handle class to hold the data
  struct MyData {
    const char* theString;
    const int* theInts;
    size_t numInts;
    MyData(const char* pString, const int* pInts,
      size_t nInts)
    : theString(pString), theInts(pInts), numInts(nInts) {}
  } *theData;        // The handle
  // Clone and cleanup functions:
  static MyData* clone(const char* otherString,
      const int* otherInts, size_t nInts) {
    char* newChars = new char[strlen(otherString)+1];
```

```
      int* newInts;
      try {
        newInts = new int[nInts];
      } catch(bad_alloc&) {
        delete [] newChars;
        throw;
      }
      try {
        // This example uses built-in types, so it won't
        // throw, but for class types it could throw, so we
        // use a try block for illustration. (This is the
        // point of the example!)
        strcpy(newChars, otherString);
        for(size_t i = 0; i < nInts; ++i)
          newInts[i] = otherInts[i];
      } catch(...) {
        delete [] newInts;
        delete [] newChars;
        throw;
      }
      return new MyData(newChars, newInts, nInts);
    }
    static MyData* clone(const MyData* otherData) {
      return clone(otherData->theString, otherData->theInts,
                   otherData->numInts);
    }
    static void cleanup(const MyData* theData) {
      delete [] theData->theString;
      delete [] theData->theInts;
      delete theData;
    }
public:
    HasPointers(const char* someString, constint* someInts,
                size_t numInts) {
      theData = clone(someString, someInts, numInts);
    }
    HasPointers(const HasPointers& source) {
      theData = clone(source.theData);
    }
    HasPointers& operator=(const HasPointers& rhs) {
      if(this != &rhs) {
        MyData* newData = clone(rhs.theData->theString,
          rhs.theData->theInts, rhs.theData->numInts);
        cleanup(theData);
        theData = newData;
      }
      return *this;
    }
    ~HasPointers() { cleanup(theData); }
    friend ostream&
    operator<<(ostream& os, const HasPointers& obj) {
      os << obj.theData->theString << ": ";
```

```
    for(size_t i = 0; i < obj.theData->numInts; ++i)
      os << obj.theData->theInts[i] << ' ';
    return os;
  }
};
int main() {
  int someNums[] = { 1, 2, 3, 4 };
  size_t someCount = sizeof someNums / sizeof someNums[0];
  int someMoreNums[] = { 5, 6, 7 };
  size_t someMoreCount =
  sizeof someMoreNums / sizeof someMoreNums[0];
  HasPointers h1("Hello", someNums, someCount);
  HasPointers h2("Goodbye", someMoreNums, someMoreCount);
  cout << h1 << endl;  // Hello: 1 2 3 4
  h1 = h2;
  cout << h1 << endl;  // Goodbye: 5 6 7
} ///:~
```

For convenience, HasPointers uses the MyData class as a handle to the two pointers. Whenever it's time to allocate more memory, whether during construction or assignment, the first clone function is ultimately called to do the job. If memory fails for the first call to the new operator, a bad_alloc exception is thrown automatically. If it happens on the second allocation (for theInts), you must clean up the memory for theString—hence the first try block that catches a bad_alloc exception. The second try block isn't crucial here because you're just copying ints and pointers (so no exceptions will occur), but whenever you copy objects, their assignment operators can possibly cause an exception, so everything needs to be cleaned up. In both exception handlers, notice that you *rethrow* the *exception*. That's because you're just managing resources here; the user still needs to know that something went wrong, so you let the exception propagate up the dynamic chain. Software libraries that don't silently swallow exceptions are called *exception neutral*. Always strive to write libraries that are both exception safe and exception neutral.

If you inspect the previous code closely, you'll notice that none of the delete operations will throw an exception. This code depends on that fact. Recall that when you call delete on an object, the object's destructor is called. It turns out to be practically impossible to design exception-safe code without assuming that destructors don't throw exceptions. Don't let destructors throw exceptions.

■ **Note**   We're going to remind you about this once more before this chapter is done.

Programming with Exceptions

For most programmers, especially C programmers, exceptions are not available in their existing language and require some adjustment. Here are guidelines for programming with exceptions.

When to Avoid Exceptions

Exceptions aren't the answer to all problems; overuse can cause trouble. The following sections point out situations where exceptions are *not* warranted. The best advice for deciding when to use exceptions is to throw exceptions only when a function fails to meet its specification.

Not for Asynchronous Events

The Standard C `signal()` system and any similar system handle asynchronous events—events that happen outside the flow of a program, and thus events the program cannot anticipate. You cannot use C++ exceptions to handle asynchronous events because the exception and its handler are on the same call stack. That is, exceptions rely on the dynamic chain of function calls on the program's runtime stack (they have *dynamic scope*), whereas asynchronous events must be handled by completely separate code that is not part of the normal program flow (typically, interrupt service routines or event loops). Don't throw exceptions from interrupt handlers.

This is not to say that asynchronous events cannot be *associated* with exceptions. But the interrupt handler should do its job as quickly as possible and then return. The typical way to handle this situation is to set a flag in the interrupt handler and check it synchronously in the mainline code.

Not for Benign Error Conditions

If you have enough information to handle an error, it's not an exception. Take care of it in the current context rather than throwing an exception to a larger context.

Also, C++ exceptions are not thrown for machine-level events such as divide-by-zero. It's assumed that some other mechanism, such as the operating system or hardware, deals with these events. In this way, C++ exceptions can be reasonably efficient, and their use is isolated to program-level exceptional conditions.

Not for Flow—of—Control

An exception looks somewhat like an alternate return mechanism and somewhat like a `switch` statement, so you might be tempted to use an exception instead of these ordinary language mechanisms. This is a bad idea, partly because the exception-handling system is significantly less efficient than normal program execution. Exceptions are a rare event, so the normal program shouldn't pay for them. Also, exceptions from anything other than error conditions are quite confusing to the user of your class or function.

You're Not Forced To Use Exceptions

Some programs are quite simple (small utilities, for example). You might only need to take input and perform some processing. In these programs, you might attempt to allocate memory and fail, try to open a file and fail, and so on. It is acceptable in these programs to display a message and exit the program, allowing the system to clean up the mess, rather than to work hard to catch all exceptions and recover all the resources yourself. Basically, if you don't need exceptions, you're not forced to use them.

New Exceptions, Old Code

Another situation that arises is the modification of an existing program that doesn't use exceptions. You might introduce a library that *does* use exceptions and wonder if you need to modify all your code throughout the program. Assuming you have an acceptable error-handling scheme already in place, the most straightforward thing to do is surround the largest block that uses the new library (this might be all the code in `main()` with a `try` block, *followed by a* `catch(...)` and basic error message). You can refine this to whatever degree necessary by adding more specific handlers, but, in any case, the code you must add can be minimal. It's even better to isolate your exception-generating code in a `try` block and write handlers to convert the exceptions into your existing error-handling scheme.

It's truly important to think about exceptions when you're creating a library for someone else to use, especially if you can't know how they need to respond to critical error conditions.

■ **Note**   Recall the earlier discussions on exception safety and why there are no exception specifications in the Standard C++ Library.

Typical Uses of Exceptions

Do use exceptions to do the following:

- Fix the problem and retry the function that caused the exception.

- Patch things up and continue without retrying the function.

- Do whatever you can in the current context and rethrow the *same* exception to a higher context.

- Do whatever you can in the current context and throw a *different* exception to a higher context.

- Terminate the program.

- Wrap functions (especially C Library functions) that use ordinary error schemes so they produce exceptions instead.

- Simplify. If your error-handling scheme makes things more complicated, it is painful and annoying to use. Exceptions can be used to make error handling simpler and more effective.

- Make your library and program safer. This is a short-term investment (for debugging) and a long-term investment (for application robustness).

When to Use Exception Specifications

The exception specification is like a function prototype: it tells the user to write exception-handling code and what exceptions to handle. It tells the compiler the exceptions that might come out of this function so that it can detect violations at runtime.

You can't always look at the code and anticipate which exceptions will arise from a particular function. Sometimes, the functions it calls produce an unexpected exception, and sometimes an old function that didn't throw an exception is replaced with a new one that does, and you get a call to unexpected(). Any time you use exception specifications or call functions that do, consider creating your own unexpected() function that logs a message and then either throws an exception or aborts the program.

As explained, you should avoid using exception specifications in template classes since you can't anticipate what types of exceptions the template parameter classes might throw.

Start with Standard Exceptions

Check out the Standard C++ Library exceptions before creating your own. If a standard exception does what you need, chances are it's a lot easier for your user to understand and handle.

If the exception type you want isn't part of the Standard C++ Library, try to inherit one from an existing standard exception. It's nice if your users can always write their code to expect the what() function defined in the exception() class interface.

Nest Your Own Exceptions

If you create exceptions for your particular class, it's a good idea to nest the exception classes either inside your class or inside a namespace containing your class to provide a clear message to the reader that this exception is only for your class. In addition, it prevents pollution of the global namespace. You can nest your exceptions even if you're deriving them from C++ Standard exceptions.

Use Exception Hierarchies

Using exception hierarchies is a valuable way to classify the types of critical errors that might be encountered with your class or library. This gives helpful information to users, assists them in organizing their code, and gives them the option of ignoring all the specific types of exceptions and just catching the base-class type. Also, any exceptions added later by inheriting from the same base class will not force all existing code to be rewritten—the baseclass handler will catch the new exception.

The Standard C++ exceptions are a good example of an exception hierarchy. Build your exceptions on top of it if you can.

Multiple Inheritance (MI)

As you'll read in Chapter 21, the only *essential* place for MI is if you need to upcast an object pointer to two different base classes—that is, if you need polymorphic behavior with both of those base classes. It turns out that exception hierarchies are useful places for multiple inheritance because a baseclass handler from any of the roots of the multiply inherited exception class can handle the exception.

Catch By Reference, Not By Value

As you saw in the section "Exception Matching," you should catch exceptions by reference for two reasons:

- To avoid making a needless copy of the exception object when it is passed to the handler.

- To avoid object slicing when catching a derived exception as a base class object.

Although you can also throw and catch pointers, by doing so you introduce more coupling—the thrower and the catcher must agree on how the exception object is allocated and cleaned up. This is a problem because the exception itself might have occurred from heap exhaustion. If you throw exception objects, the exception-handling system takes care of all storage.

Throw Exceptions in Constructors

Because a constructor has no return value, you've previously had two ways to report an error during construction:

- Set a nonlocal flag and hope the user checks it.

- Return an incompletely created object and hope the user checks it.

This problem is serious because C programmers expect that object creation is always successful, which is not unreasonable in C because the types are so primitive. But continuing execution after construction fails in a C++ program is a guaranteed disaster, so constructors are one of the most important places to throw exceptions—now you have a safe, effective way to handle constructor errors. However, you must also pay attention to pointers inside objects and the way cleanup occurs when an exception is thrown inside a constructor.

Don't Cause Exceptions in Destructors

Because destructors are called in the process of throwing other exceptions, you'll never want to throw an exception in a destructor or cause another exception to be thrown by some action you perform in the destructor. If this happens, a new exception can be thrown *before* the catch-clause for an existing exception is reached, which will cause a call to terminate().

If you call any functions inside a destructor that can throw exceptions, those calls should be within a try block in the destructor, and the destructor must handle all exceptions itself. None must escape from the destructor.

Avoid Naked Pointers

See Wrapped.cpp in Listing 17-9. A naked pointer usually means vulnerability in the constructor if resources are allocated for that pointer. A pointer doesn't have a destructor, so those resources aren't released if an exception is thrown in the constructor. Use auto_ptr or other smart pointer types for pointers that reference heap memory.

Overhead

When an exception is thrown, there's considerable runtime overhead (but it's *good* overhead, since objects are cleaned up automatically!). For this reason, you never want to use exceptions as part of your normal flow-of-control, no matter how tempting and clever it may seem.

Exceptions should occur only rarely, so the overhead is piled on the exception and not on the normally executing code. One of the important design goals for exception handling was that it could be implemented with no impact on execution speed when it *wasn't* used; that is, as long as you don't throw an exception, your code runs as fast as it would without exception handling. Whether this is true depends on the particular compiler implementation you're using.

■ **Note**   See the description of the "zero-cost model" later in this section.

You can think of a throw expression as a call to a special system function that takes the exception object as an argument and backtracks up the chain of execution. For this to work, extra information needs to be put on the stack by the compiler, to aid in stack unwinding. To understand this, you need to know about the runtime stack.

Whenever a function is called, information about that function is pushed onto the runtime stack in an *activation record instance* (*ARI*), also called a *stack frame*. A typical stack frame contains the address of the calling function (so execution can return to it), a pointer to the ARI of the function's static parent (the scope that lexically contains the called function, so variables global to the function can be accessed), and a pointer to the function that called it (its dynamic parent). The path that logically results from repetitively following the dynamic parent links is the *dynamic chain*, or *call chain*, mentioned previously in this chapter.

This is how execution can backtrack when an exception is thrown, and it is the mechanism that makes it possible for components developed without knowledge of one another to communicate errors at runtime.

To enable stack unwinding for exception handling, extra exception-related information about each function needs to be available for each stack frame. This information describes which destructors need to be called (so that local objects can be cleaned up), indicates whether the current function has a try block, and lists which exceptions the associated catch clauses can handle.

There is space penalty for this extra information, so programs that support exception handling can be somewhat larger than those that don't. Even the compile-time size of programs using exception handling is greater, since the logic of how to generate the expanded stack frames during runtime must be generated by the compiler.

To illustrate this, I compiled the program in Listing 17-18 both with and without exception-handling support in Borland C++ Builder and Microsoft Visual C++.

Listing 17-18. Illustrating A Program With/Without Exception-Handling Support

```
//: C17:HasDestructor.cpp {O}
/* shows that programs with exception-handling support are bigger than those without */
class HasDestructor {
public:
  ~HasDestructor() {}
};
void g(); // For all we know, g may throw.
void f() {
  HasDestructor h;
  g();
} ///:~
```

If exception handling is enabled, the compiler must keep information about ~HasDestructor() available at runtime in the *ARI* for f() (so it can destroy h properly should g() throw an exception).

Table 17-4 summarizes the result of the compilations in terms of the size of the compiled(.obj)files (in bytes).

Table 17-4. *Compiling Process Results (Summarized)*

Compiler\Mode	With Exception Support	Without Exception Support
Borland	616	234
Microsoft	1162	680

Don't take the percentage differences between the two modes too seriously.

Remember that exceptions (*should*) typically constitute a small part of a program, so the space overhead tends to be much smaller (usually between 5 and 15 percent).

This extra housekeeping slows down execution, but a clever compiler implementation avoids this. Since information about exception-handling code and the offsets of local objects can be computed once at compile time, such information can be kept in a single place associated with each function, but not in each ARI.

You essentially remove exception overhead from each ARI and thus avoid the extra time to push them onto the stack. This approach is called the *zero-cost model* of exception handling, and the optimized storage mentioned earlier is known as the *shadow stack*.

Review Session

1. *Error recovery* is a fundamental concern for every program you write. It's especially important in C++ when creating program components for others to use. To create a *robust system*, each component must be robust.

2. The goals for *exception handling* in C++ are to simplify the creation of large, reliable programs using less code than currently possible, with more confidence that your application doesn't have an unhandled error. This is accomplished with little or no performance penalty and with low impact on existing code.

3. Basic exceptions are *not terribly difficult to learn*; begin using them in your programs as soon as you can.

4. *Exceptions* are one of those features that *provide immediate and significant benefits* to your project.

CHAPTER 18

■ ■ ■

Strings in Depth

String processing with character arrays is one of the biggest time–wasters in C. Character arrays require the programmer to keep track of the difference between static quoted strings and arrays created on the stack and the heap, and the fact that sometimes you're passing around a char* and sometimes you must copy the whole array.

Especially because string manipulation is so common, character arrays are a great source of misunderstandings and bugs. Despite this, creating string classes remained a common exercise for beginning C++ programmers for many years. The Standard C++ Library string class solves the problem of character array manipulation once and for all, keeping track of memory even during assignments and copy-constructions. You simply don't need to think about it.

This chapter examines the Standard C++ string class, beginning with a look at what constitutes a C++ string and how the C++ version differs from a traditional C character array. You'll learn about operations and manipulations using string objects, and you'll see how C++ strings accommodate variation in character sets and string data conversion.

Handling text is one of the oldest programming applications, so it's not surprising that the C++ string draws heavily on the ideas and terminology that have long been used in C and other languages. As you begin to acquaint yourself with C++ strings, this fact should be reassuring. No matter which programming idiom you choose, there are three common things you may want to do with a string:

- Create or modify the sequence of characters stored in the string.

- Detect the presence or absence of elements within the string.

- Translate between various schemes for representing string characters.

You'll see how each of these jobs is accomplished using C++ string objects.

What's in a string?

In C, a string is simply an array of characters that always includes a binary zero (often called the *null terminator*) as its final array element. There are significant differences between C++ strings and their C progenitors. First, and most important, C++ strings hide the physical representation of the sequence of characters they contain. You don't need to be concerned about array dimensions or null terminators. A string also contains certain "housekeeping" information about the size and storage location of its data. Specifically, a C++ string object knows its starting location in memory, its content, its length in characters, and the length in characters to which it can grow before it must resize its internal data buffer. C++ strings thus greatly reduce the likelihood of making three of the most common and destructive C programming errors: overwriting array bounds, trying to access arrays through uninitialized or incorrectly valued pointers, and leaving pointers "dangling" after an array ceases to occupy the storage that was once allocated to it.

The exact implementation of memory layout for the string class is not defined by the C++ Standard. This ` is intended to be *flexible* enough to allow differing implementations by compiler vendors, yet *guarantee predictable behavior* for users. In particular, the exact conditions under which storage is allocated to hold data for a string object are not defined. String allocation rules were formulated to *allow but not require* a reference-counted implementation, but whether or not the implementation uses reference counting, the semantics must be the same. To put this a bit differently, in C, every char array occupies a unique physical region of memory. In C++, individual string objects may or may not occupy unique physical regions of memory, but if reference counting avoids storing duplicate copies of data, the individual objects must look and act as though they exclusively own unique regions of storage. For an example, see Listing 18-1.

Listing 18-1. Illustrating String Storage

```
//: C18:StringStorage.cpp
#include <string>
#include <iostream>
using namespace std;

int main() {

  string s1("12345");

  // Set the iterator indicate the first element
  string::iterator it = s1.begin();

  // This may copy the first to the second or
  // use reference counting to simulate a copy
  string s2 = s1;

  // Either way, this statement may ONLY modify first
  *it = '0';
  cout << "s1 = " << s1 << endl;
  cout << "s2 = " << s2 << endl;

} ///:~
```

Reference counting may serve to make an implementation more memory efficient, but it is transparent to users of the string class.

Creating and Initializing C++ Strings

Creating and initializing strings is a straightforward proposition and fairly flexible. In SmallString.cpp in Listing 18-2, the first string, imBlank, is declared but contains no initial value. Unlike a C char array, which would contain a random and meaningless bit pattern until initialization, imBlank does contain meaningful information. This string object is initialized to hold "no characters" and can properly report its zero length and absence of data elements using class member functions.

The next string, heyMom, is initialized by the literal argument "Where are my socks?" This form of initialization uses a quoted character array as a parameter to the string constructor. By contrast, standardReply is simply initialized with an assignment. The last string of the group, useThisOneAgain, is initialized using an existing C++ string object. Put another way, Listing 18-2 illustrates that string objects let you do the following:

- Create an empty string and defer initializing it with character data.

- Initialize a string by passing a literal, quoted character array as an argument to the constructor.

- Initialize a string using the equal sign (=).

- Use one string to initialize another.

Listing 18-2. Illustrating String Features

```
//: C18:SmallString.cpp
#include <string>
using namespace std;

int main() {
  string imBlank;
  string heyMom("Where are my socks?");
  string standardReply = "Beamed into deep "
    "space on wide angle dispersion?";
  string useThisOneAgain(standardReply);
} ///:~
```

These are the simplest forms of string initialization, but variations offer more flexibility and control. You can do the following:

- Use a portion of either a C char array or a C++ string.

- Combine different sources of initialization data using operator+.

- Use the string object's substr() member function to create a substring.

Listing 18-3 illustrates these features.

Listing 18-3. Illustrating More String Features

```
//: C18:SmallString2.cpp
#include<string>
#include<iostream>
using namespace std;

int main() {
  string s1("What is the sound of one clam napping?");
  string s2("Anything worth doing is worth overdoing.");
  string s3("I saw Elvis in a UFO");
  // Copy the first 8 chars:
  string s4(s1, 0, 8);
  cout << s4 << endl;
  // Copy 6 chars from the middle of the source:
  string s5(s2, 15, 6);
  cout << s5 << endl;
  // Copy from middle to end:
  string s6(s3, 6, 15);
  cout << s6 << endl;
```

```
  // Copy many different things:
  string quoteMe = s4 + "that" +
  // substr() copies 10 chars at element 20
  s1.substr(20, 10) + s5 +
  // substr() copies up to either 100 char
  // or eos starting at element 5
  "with" + s3.substr(5, 100) +
  // OK to copy a single char this way
  s1.substr(37, 1);
  cout << quoteMe << endl;
} ///:~
```

The `string` member function `substr()` takes a starting position as its first argument and the number of characters to select as the second argument. Both arguments have default values. If you say `substr()` with an empty argument list, you produce a copy of the entire `string`, so this is a convenient way to duplicate a `string`.

Here's the output from the program:

```
What is
doing
Elvis in a UFO
What is that one clam doing with Elvis in a UFO?
```

Notice the final line in Listing 18-3. C++ allows `string` initialization techniques to be mixed in a single statement, a flexible and convenient feature. Also notice that the last initializer copies *just one character* from the source `string`.

Another slightly more subtle initialization technique involves the use of the `string` iterators `string::begin()` and `string::end()`. This technique treats a `string` like a *container* object (which you've seen primarily in the form of vector), which uses *iterators* to indicate the start and end of a sequence of characters. In this way you can hand a string constructor two iterators, and it copies from one to the other into the new `string`, as shown in Listing 18-4.

Listing 18-4. Illustrating String Iterators

```
//: C18:StringIterators.cpp
#include <string>
#include <iostream>
#include <cassert>
using namespace std;

int main() {
  string source("xxx");
  string s(source.begin(), source.end());
  assert(s == source);
} ///:~
```

The iterators are not restricted to `begin()` and `end()`; you can increment, decrement, and add integer offsets to them, allowing you to extract a subset of characters from the source `string`.

C++ strings may *not* be initialized with single characters or with ASCII or other integer values. You can initialize a string with a number of copies of a single character, however; see Listing 18-5.

Listing 18-5. Illustrating Initialization of Strings

```
//: C18:UhOh.cpp
#include <string>
#include <cassert>
using namespace std;
```

```
int main() {
  // Error: no single char inits
  //! string nothingDoing1('a');
  // Error: no integer inits
  //! string nothingDoing2(0x37);
  // The following is legal:
  string okay(5, 'a');
  assert(okay == string("aaaaa"));
} ///:~
```

The first argument indicates the number of copies of the second argument to place in the string. The second argument can only be a single char, not a char array.

Operating on Strings

If you've programmed in C, you are accustomed to the family of functions that write, search, modify, and copy char arrays. There are two unfortunate aspects of the Standard C Library functions for handling char arrays. First, there are two loosely organized families of them: the "plain" group, and the ones that require you to supply a count of the number of characters to be considered in the operation at hand. The roster of functions in the C char array library shocks the unsuspecting user with a long list of cryptic, mostly unpronounceable names. Although the type and number of arguments to the functions are somewhat consistent, to use them properly you must be attentive to details of function naming and parameter passing.

The second inherent trap of the Standard C char array tools is that they all rely explicitly on the assumption that the character array includes a null terminator. If by oversight or error the null is omitted or overwritten, there's little to keep the C char array functions from manipulating the memory beyond the limits of the allocated space, sometimes with disastrous results.

C++ provides a vast improvement in the convenience and safety of string objects. For purposes of actual string-handling operations, there are about the same number of distinct member function names in the string class as there are functions in the C Library, but because of overloading, the functionality is much greater. Coupled with sensible naming practices and the judicious use of default arguments, these features combine to make the string class much easier to use than the C Library char array functions.

Appending, Inserting, and Concatenating Strings

One of the most valuable and convenient aspects of C++ strings is that they grow as needed, without intervention on the part of the programmer. Not only does this make string-handling code inherently more trustworthy, it also almost entirely eliminates a tedious housekeeping chore—keeping track of the bounds of the storage where your strings live. For example, if you create a string object and initialize it with a string of 50 copies of "X", and later store in it 50 copies of "Zowie," the object itself will reallocate sufficient storage to accommodate the growth of the data. Perhaps nowhere is this property more appreciated than when the strings manipulated in your code change size and you don't know how big the change is. The string member functions append() and insert() transparently reallocate storage when a string grows, as shown in Listing 18-6.

Listing 18-6. Illustrating Reallocation of Storage as per String Size

```
//: C18:StrSize.cpp
#include <string>
#include <iostream>
using namespace std;
```

```
int main() {
  string bigNews("I saw Elvis in a UFO. ");
  cout << bigNews << endl;
  // How much data have we actually got?
  cout << "Size = " << bigNews.size() << endl;
  // How much can we store without reallocating?
  cout << "Capacity = " << bigNews.capacity() << endl;
  // Insert this string in bigNews immediately
  // before bigNews[1]:
  bigNews.insert(1, " thought I");
  cout << bigNews << endl;
  cout << "Size = " << bigNews.size() << endl;
  cout << "Capacity = " << bigNews.capacity() << endl;
  // Make sure that there will be this much space
  bigNews.reserve(500);
  // Add this to the end of the string:
  bigNews.append("I've been working too hard.");
  cout << bigNews << endl;
  cout<< "Size = " << bigNews.size() << endl;
  cout << "Capacity = " << bigNews.capacity() << endl;
} ///:~
```

Here is the output from one particular compiler:

```
I saw Elvis in a UFO.
Size = 22
Capacity = 31
I thought I saw Elvis in a UFO.
Size = 32
Capacity = 47
I thought I saw Elvis in a UFO. I've been
working too hard.
Size = 59
Capacity = 511
```

Listing 18-6 demonstrates that even though you can safely relinquish much of the responsibility for allocating and managing the memory your strings occupy, C++ strings provide you with several tools to monitor and manage their size. Notice how easy it was to change the size of the storage allocated to the string. The size() function returns the number of characters currently stored in the string and is identical to the length() member function. The capacity() function returns the size of the current underlying allocation, meaning the number of characters the string can hold without requesting more storage. The reserve() function is an optimization mechanism that indicates your intention to specify a certain amount of storage for future use; capacity() always returns a value at least as large as the most recent call to reserve(). A resize() function appends spaces if the new size is greater than the current string size or truncates the string otherwise. (An overload of resize() can specify a different character to append.)

The exact fashion that the string member functions allocate space for your data depends on the implementation of the library. When testing one implementation of the code from Listing 18-6, it appeared that reallocations occurred on even word (that is, full-integer) boundaries, with 1 byte held back. The architects of the string class have endeavored to make it possible to mix the use of C char arrays and C++ string objects, so it is likely that figures reported by StrSize.cpp for capacity reflect that, in this particular implementation, a byte is set aside to easily accommodate the insertion of a null terminator.

Replacing String Characters

The insert() function is particularly nice because it absolves you from making sure the insertion of characters in a string won't overrun the storage space or overwrite the characters immediately following the insertion point. Space grows, and existing characters politely move over to accommodate the new elements. Sometimes this might not be what you want. If you want the size of the string to remain unchanged, use the replace() function to overwrite characters. There are a number of overloaded versions of replace(), but the simplest one takes three arguments: an integer indicating where to start in the string, an integer indicating how many characters to eliminate from the original string, and the replacement string (which can be a different number of characters than the eliminated quantity). See Listing 18-7 for a simple example.

Listing 18-7. Illustrating Replacement of String Characters

```
//: C18:StringReplace.cpp
// Simple find-and-replace in strings.
#include <cassert>
#include <string>
using namespace std;

int main() {
  string s("A piece of text");
  string tag("$tag$");
  s.insert(8, tag + ' ');
  assert(s == "A piece $tag$ of text");
  int start = s.find(tag);
  assert(start == 8);
  assert(tag.size() == 5);
  s.replace(start, tag.size(), "hello there");
  assert(s == "A piece hello there of text");
} ///:~
```

The tag is first inserted into s (notice that the insert happens *before* the value indicating the insert point and that an extra space was added after tag), and then it is found and replaced.

You should check to see if you've found anything before you perform a replace(). The previous example replaces with a char*, but there's an overloaded version that replaces with a string. Listing 18-8 provides a more complete demonstration of replace().

Listing 18-8. Illustrating A More Complete Demonstration of replace()

```
//: C18:Replace.cpp
#include <cassert>
#include <cstddef>  // For size_t
#include <string>
using namespace std;

void replaceChars(string& modifyMe,
  const string& findMe, const string& newChars) {
  // Look in modifyMe for the "find string"
  // starting at position 0:
  size_t i = modifyMe.find(findMe, 0);
  // Did we find the string to replace?
  if(i != string::npos)
```

```
    // Replace the find string with newChars:
    modifyMe.replace(i, findMe.size(), newChars);
}
int main() {
  string bigNews = "I thought I saw Elvis in a UFO. "
                    "I have been working too hard.";
  string replacement("wig");
  string findMe("UFO");
  // Find "UFO" in bigNews and overwrite it:
  replaceChars(bigNews, findMe, replacement);
  assert(bigNews == "I thought I saw Elvis in a "
        "wig. I have been working too hard.");
} ///:~
```

If replace doesn't find the search string, it returns string::npos. The npos data member is a static constant member of the string class that represents a nonexistent character position.

Unlike insert(), replace() won't grow the string's storage space if you copy new characters into the middle of an existing series of array elements. However, it *will* grow the storage space if needed, for example, when you make a "replacement" that would expand the original string beyond the end of the current allocation, as shown in Listing 18-9.

Listing 18-9. Illustrating String Replacement and Growth

```
//: C18:ReplaceAndGrow.cpp
#include<cassert>
#include<string>
using namespace std;

int main() {
  string bigNews("I have been working the grave.");
  string replacement("yard shift.");
  // The first argument says "replace chars
  // beyond the end of the existing string":
  bigNews.replace(bigNews.size() - 1,
    replacement.size(), replacement);
  assert(bigNews == "I have been working the "
        "graveyard shift.");
} ///:~
```

The call to replace() begins "replacing" beyond the end of the existing array, which is equivalent to an append operation. Notice that in Listing 18-9 replace() expands the array accordingly.

You may have been hunting through this chapter trying to do something relatively simple such as replace all the instances of one character with a different character. Upon finding the previous material on replacing, you thought you found the answer, but then you started seeing groups of characters and counts and other things that looked a bit too complex. Doesn't string have a way to just replace one character with another everywhere? You can easily write such a function using the find() and replace() member functions, as shown in Listing 18-10.

Listing 18-10. Illustrating ReplaceAll

```
//: C18:ReplaceAll.h
#ifndef REPLACEALL_H
#define REPLACEALL_H
#include <string>
```

```
std::string& replaceAll(std::string& context,
  const std::string& from, const std::string& to);
#endif // REPLACEALL_H ///:~
```

```
//: C18:ReplaceAll.cpp {O}
#include <cstddef>
#include "ReplaceAll.h"// To be INCLUDED from Header FILE above
using namespace std;

string& replaceAll(string& context, const string& from,
  const string& to) {
  size_t lookHere = 0;
  size_t foundHere;
  while((foundHere = context.find(from, lookHere))
    != string::npos) {
    context.replace(foundHere, from.size(), to);
    lookHere = foundHere + to.size();
  }
  return context;
} ///:~
```

The version of find() used here takes as a second argument the position to start looking in and returns string::npos if it doesn't find it. It is important to advance the position held in the variable lookHere past the replacement string, in this case from is a substring of to. Listing 18-11 tests the replaceAll function.

Listing 18-11. Illustrating Test of The ReplaceAll in Listing 18-10

```
//: C18:ReplaceAllTest.cpp
//{L} ../C18/ReplaceAll
#include <cassert>
#include <iostream>
#include <string>
#include "ReplaceAll.h"
using namespace std;

int main() {
  string text = "a man, a plan, a canal, Panama";
  replaceAll(text, "an", "XXX");
  assert(text == "a mXXX, a plXXX, a cXXXal, PXXXama");
} ///:~
```

As you can see, the string class by itself doesn't solve all possible problems. Many solutions have been left to the algorithms in the Standard C++ Library because the string class can look just like an STL sequence (*by virtue of the iterators discussed earlier*). All the generic algorithms work on a "range" of elements within a container. Usually that range is just "from the beginning of the container to the end." A string object looks like a container of characters: to get the beginning of the range, use string::begin(), and to get the end of the range, use string::end().

Simple Character Replacement Using the STL replace() Algorithm

Is there a simpler way to replace one character with another character everywhere? Yes, string has it; Listing 18-12 shows the use of the replace() algorithm to replace all instances of the single character 'X' with 'Y.'

Listing 18-12. Illustrating String Character Replacement

```
//: C18:StringCharReplace.cpp
#include <algorithm>
#include <cassert>
#include <string>
using namespace std;

int main() {
  string s("aaaXaaaXXaaXXXaXXXXaaa");
  replace(s.begin(), s.end(), 'X', 'Y');
  assert(s == "aaaYaaaYYaaYYYaYYYYaaa");

} ///:~
```

Notice that this replace() is *not* called as a member function of string. Also, unlike the string::replace() functions that only perform one replacement, the replace() algorithm replaces *all instances* of one character with another.

The replace() algorithm only works with single objects (in this case, char objects) and will not replace quoted char arrays or string objects. Since a string behaves like an STL sequence, a number of other algorithms can be applied to it, which might solve other problems that are not directly addressed by the string member functions.

Concatenation Using Nonmember Overloaded Operators

One of the most delightful discoveries awaiting a C programmer learning about C++ string handling is how simply strings can be combined and appended using operator+ and operator+=.These operators make combining strings syntactically similar to adding numeric data, as shown in Listing 18-13.

Listing 18-13. Illustrating Addition of Strings

```
//: C18:AddStrings.cpp
#include <string>
#include <cassert>
using namespace std;

int main() {
  string s1("This ");
  string s2("That ");
  string s3("The other ");
  // operator+ concatenates strings
  s1 = s1 + s2;
  assert(s1 == "This That ");
  // Another way to concatenates strings
  s1 += s3;
  assert(s1 == "This That The other ");
  // You can index the string on the right
  s1 += s3 + s3[4] + "ooh lama";
  assert(s1 == "This That The other The other oooh lala");
} ///:~
```

Using the operator+ and operator+= operators is a flexible and convenient way to combine string data. On the right side of the statement, you can use almost any type that evaluates to a group of one or more characters.

Searching in Strings

The find family of string member functions locates a character or group of characters within a given string. Table 18-1 shows the members of the find family and their general usage.

Table 18-1. *Searching by Means of the find Family of String Member Functions*

String find Member Function	What/How It Finds
find()	Searches a string for a specified character or group of characters and returns the starting position of the first occurrence found or npos if no match is found.
find_first_of()	Searches a target string and returns the position of the first match of *any* character in a specified group. If no match is found, it returns npos.
find_last_of()	Searches a target string and returns the position of the last match of *any* character in a specified group. If no match is found, it returns npos.
find_first_not_of()	Searches a target string and returns the position of the first element that *doesn't* match *any* character in a specified group. If no such element is found, it returns npos.
find_last_not_of()	Searches a target string and returns the position of the element with the largest subscript that *doesn't* match *any* character in a specified group. If no such element is found, it returns npos.
rfind()	Searches a string from end to beginning for a specified character or group of characters and returns the starting position of the match if one is found. If no match is found, it returns npos.

The simplest use of find() searches for one or more characters in a string. This overloaded version of find() takes a parameter that specifies the character(s) for which to search and optionally a parameter that tells it where in the string to begin searching for the occurrence of a substring. (The default position at which to begin searching is 0.) By setting the call to find inside a loop, you can easily move through a string, repeating a search to find all the occurrences of a given character or group of characters within the string.

Listing 18-14 uses the method of *The Sieve of Eratosthenes* to find prime numbers *less than 50*. This method starts with the number 2, marks all subsequent multiples of 2 as not prime, and repeats the process for the next prime candidate. The initial size of the character array sieveChars is set and the value 'P' is written to each of its members.

Listing 18-14. Illustrating The Sieve of Eratosthenes (to find prime numbers < 50)

```
//: C18:Sieve.cpp
#include <string>
#include <iostream>

using namespace std;

int main() {
// Create a 50 char string and set each
// element to 'P' for Prime
string sieveChars(50, 'P');
```

```
// By definition neither 0 nor 1 is prime.
// Change these elements to "N" for Not Prime
sieveChars.replace(0, 2, "NN");

// Walk through the array:
for(int i = 2;
i <= (sieveChars.size() / 2) - 1; i++)
// Find all the factors:
for(int factor = 2;
factor * i < sieveChars.size();factor++)
sieveChars[factor * i] = 'N';
cout << "Prime:" << endl;

// Return the index of the first 'P' element:
int j = sieveChars.find('P');

// While not at the end of the string:
while(j != sieveChars.npos) {

// If the element is P, the index is a prime
cout << j << " ";

// Move past the last prime
j++;

// Find the next prime
j = sieveChars.find('P', j);
}
cout << "\n Not prime:" << endl;

// Find the first element value not equal P:
j = sieveChars.find_first_not_of('P');
while(j != sieveChars.npos) {
cout << j << " ";
j++;
j = sieveChars.find_first_not_of('P', j);
}
} ///:~
```

The output from Sieve.cpp looks like this:

```
Prime:
2 3 5 7 11 13 17 19 23 29 31 37 41 43 47

Not prime:
0 1 4 6 8 9 10 12 14 15 16 18 20 21 22
24 25 26 27 28 30 32 33 34 35 36 38 39
40 42 44 45 46 48 49
```

find() allows you to walk forward through a string, detecting multiple occurrences of a character or group of characters, while find_first_not_of() allows you to test for the absence of a character or group.

The find() member is also useful for detecting the occurrence of a sequence of characters in a string, as shown in Listing 18-15.

Listing 18-15. Using find() to Detect a Sequence of Characters

```
//: C18:Find.cpp
// Find a group of characters in a string

#include <string>
#include <iostream>

using namespace std;

int main() {
string chooseOne("Eenie, meenie, miney, mo");
int i = chooseOne.find("een");
while(i != string::npos) {
cout << i << endl;
i++;
i = chooseOne.find("een", i);
}
} ///:~
```

Find.cpp produces a single line of output:

8

This tells us that the first "e" of the search group "een" was found in the word "meenie," and
it is the eighth element in the string. Notice that find passed over the "Een" group of characters in the word "Eenie". The find member function performs a *case-sensitive* search.

There are no functions in the string class to change the case of a string, but these functions can be easily created using the Standard C Library functions toupper() and tolower(), which change the case of one character at a time. A few small changes will make Find.cpp perform a case-insensitive search, as shown in Listing 18-16.

Listing 18-16. Using find() for A Case-Insensitive Search

```
//: C18:NewFind.cpp
#include <string>
#include <iostream>
using namespace std;
// Make an uppercase copy of s:
string upperCase(string& s) {
char* buf = new char[s.length()];
s.copy(buf, s.length());

for(int i = 0; i < s.length(); i++)
buf[i] = toupper(buf[i]);

string r(buf, s.length());
delete buf;
return r;
}
```

```cpp
// Make a lowercase copy of s:
string lowerCase(string& s) {
char* buf = new char[s.length()];

s.copy(buf, s.length());

for(int i = 0; i < s.length(); i++)
buf[i] = tolower(buf[i]);

string r(buf, s.length());
delete buf;
return r;
}

int main() {
string chooseOne("Eenie, meenie, miney, mo");
cout << chooseOne << endl;
cout << upperCase(chooseOne) << endl;
cout << lowerCase(chooseOne) << endl;

// Case sensitive search
int i = chooseOne.find("een");

while(i != string::npos) {
cout << i << endl;

i++;
i = chooseOne.find("een", i);
}

// Search lowercase:
string lcase = lowerCase(chooseOne);

cout << lcase << endl;
i = lcase.find("een");

while(i != lcase.npos) {
cout << i << endl;
i++;
i = lcase.find("een", i);
}

// Search uppercase:
string ucase = upperCase(chooseOne);
cout << ucase << endl;

i = ucase.find("EEN");

while(i != ucase.npos) {
cout << i << endl;
```

```
i++;
i = ucase.find("EEN", i);
}
} ///:~
```

Both the upperCase() and lowerCase() functions follow the same form: they allocate storage to hold the data in the argument string, copy the data, and change the case. Then they create a new string with the new data, release the buffer, and return the result string.

The c_str() function cannot be used to produce a pointer to directly manipulate the data in the string because c_str() returns a pointer to const. That is, you're not allowed to manipulate string data with a pointer, only with member functions. If you need to use the more primitive char array manipulation, you should use the technique shown above (refer to Listing 18-16).

The output looks like this:

```
Eenie, meenie, miney, mo
EENIE, MEENIE, MINEY, MO
eenie, meenie, miney, mo
8
eenie, meenie, miney, mo
0
8
EENIE, MEENIE, MINEY, MO
0
8
```

The case-insensitive searches found both occurrences in the "een" group.

Find.cpp and NewFind.cpp aren't the best solution to the case sensitivity problem, so we'll revisit it in the section on "*Strings and Character Traits.*"

Finding in Reverse

If you need to search through a string from end to beginning (to find the data in last in, first out (LIFO) order), you can use the string member function rfind(), as shown in Listing 18-17.

Listing 18-17. Finding in Reverse Using rfind()

```
//: C18:Rparse.cpp
// Reverse the order of words in a string
#include <string>
#include <iostream>
#include <vector>
using namespace std;

int main() {
// The ';' characters will be delimiters
string s("now.;sense;make;to;going;is;This");
cout << s << endl;
```

```
// To store the words:
vector<string> strings;

// The last element of the string:
int last = s.size();

// The beginning of the current word:
int current = s.rfind(';');

// Walk backward through the string:
while(current != string::npos){

// Push each word into the vector.
// Current is incremented before copying to
// avoid copying the delimiter.
strings.push_back(
s.substr(++current,last - current));

// Back over the delimiter we just found,
// and set last to the end of the next word
current -= 2;
last = current;

// Find the next delimiter
current = s.rfind(';', current);
}

// Pick up the first word - it's not
// preceded by a delimiter
strings.push_back(s.substr(0, last - current));

// Print them in the new order:
for(int j = 0; j < strings.size(); j++)
cout << strings[j] << " ";
} ///:~
```

Here's how the output from Rparse.cpp in Listing 18-17 looks:

```
now.;sense;make;to;going;is;This
This is going to make sense now.
```

rfind() backs through the string looking for tokens, reporting the array index of matching characters or string::npos if it is unsuccessful.

Finding First/Last of a Set of Characters

The find_first_of() and find_last_of() member functions can be conveniently put to work to *create a little utility that will strip whitespace characters from both ends of a string*. Noticethat it doesn't touch the original string, but instead returns a new string, as shown in Listing 18-18.

Listing 18-18. Stripping Whitespaces, that is, Trimming a String

```
//: C18:trim.h
#ifndef TRIM_H
#define TRIM_H
#include <string>

// General tool to strip spaces from both ends:
inline std::string trim(const std::string& s) {
if(s.length() == 0)
return s;

int b = s.find_first_not_of(" \t");
int e = s.find_last_not_of(" \t");

if(b == -1) // No non-spaces
return "";

return std::string(s, b, e - b + 1);
}
#endif // TRIM_H ///:~
```

The first test checks for an empty string; in that case no tests are made and a copy is returned.

Notice that once the end points are found, the string constructor is used to build a new string from the old one, giving the starting count and the length. The return value is also "optimized."

Testing such a general-purpose tool needs to be thorough, as you can see in Listing 18-19.

Listing 18-19. Testing Out "trim.h" in Listing 18-18

```
//: C18:TrimTest.cpp
#include "trim.h" // To be INCLUDED from Header FILE above
#include <iostream>
using namespace std;

string s[] = {
" \t abcdefghijklmnop \t ",

"abcdefghijklmnop \t ",

" \t abcdefghijklmnop",

"a", "ab", "abc", "a b c",

" \t a b c \t ", " \t a \t b \t c \t ",

"", // Must also test the empty string
};
```

```
void test(string s) {
cout << "[" << trim(s) << "]" << endl;
}

int main() {
for(int i = 0; i < sizeof s / sizeof *s; i++)
test(s[i]);
} ///:~
```

In the array of string s, you can see that the character arrays are automatically converted to string objects. This array provides cases to check the removal of spaces and tabs from both ends, as well as ensuring that spaces and tabs do not get removed from the middle of a string.

Removing Characters from Strings

Removing characters is easy and efficient with the erase() member function, which takes two arguments: where to start removing characters (which defaults to 0), and how many to remove (which defaults to string::npos). If you specify more characters than remain in the string, the remaining characters are all erased anyway (so calling erase()without any arguments removes all characters from a string). Sometimes it's useful to take an HTML file and strip its tags and special characters so that you have something approximating the text that would be displayed in the web browser, only as a plain text file. Listing 18-20 uses erase() to do the job.

Listing 18-20. Illustrating An HTML Stripper Using erase()

```
//: C18:HTMLStripper.cpp {RunByHand}
//{L} ../C18/ReplaceAll
// Filter to remove html tags and markers.
#include <cassert>
#include <cmath>
#include <cstddef>
#include <fstream>
#include <iostream>
#include <string>
#include "ReplaceAll.h" // SEE Above
#include "../require.h" // To be INCLUDED from Chapter 9
using namespace std;

string& stripHTMLTags(string& s) {
  static bool inTag = false;
  bool done = false;
  while(!done) {
    if(inTag) {
      // The previous line started an HTML tag
      // but didn't finish. Must search for '>'.
      size_t rightPos = s.find('>');
      if(rightPos != string::npos) {
        inTag = false;
        s.erase(0, rightPos + 1);
      }
```

```
      else {
        done = true;
        s.erase();
      }
    }
    else {
      // Look for start of tag:
      size_t leftPos = s.find('<');
      if(leftPos != string::npos) {
        // See if tag close is in this line:
        size_t rightPos = s.find('>');
        if(rightPos == string::npos) {
          inTag = done = true;
          s.erase(leftPos);
        }
        else
          s.erase(leftPos, rightPos - leftPos + 1);
      }
      else
        done = true;
    }
  }
  // Remove all special HTML characters
  replaceAll(s, "&lt;", "<");
  replaceAll(s, "&gt;", ">");
  replaceAll(s, "&amp;", "&");
  replaceAll(s, " ", " ");
  // Etc...
  return s;
}
int main(int argc, char* argv[]) {
  requireArgs(argc, 1,
    "usage: HTMLStripper InputFile");
  ifstream in(argv[1]);
  assure(in, argv[1]);
  string s;
  while(getline(in, s))
    if(!stripHTMLTags(s).empty())
      cout << s << endl;
} ///:~
```

This code will even strip HTML tags that span multiple lines. This is accomplished with the static flag, inTag, which is true whenever the start of a tag is found, but the accompanying tag end is not found in the same line. All forms of erase() appear in the stripHTMLTags() function. The version of getline()used here is a (global) function declared in the <string> header and is handy because it stores an arbitrarily long line in its string argument. You don't need to worry about the dimension of a character array as you do with istream::getline(). Notice that Listing 18-20 uses the replaceAll() function from earlier in this chapter. In the next chapter, you'll use string streams to create a more elegant solution.

Comparing Strings

Comparing strings is inherently different from comparing numbers. Numbers have constant, universally meaningful values. To evaluate the relationship between the magnitudes of two strings, you must make a *lexical comparison*. Lexical comparison means that when you test a character to see if it is "greater than" or "less than" another character, you are actually comparing the numeric representation of those characters as specified in the collating sequence of the character set being used. Most often this will be the ASCII collating sequence, which assigns the printable characters for the English language numbers in the range 32 through 127 decimal. In the ASCII collating sequence, the first "character" in the list is the space, followed by several common punctuation marks, and then uppercase and lowercase letters. With respect to the alphabet, this means that the letters nearer the front have lower ASCII values than those nearer the end. With these details in mind, it becomes easier to remember that when a lexical comparison that reports s1 is "greater than" s2, it simply means that when the two were compared, the first differing character in s1 came later in the alphabet than the character in that same position in s2.

C++ provides several ways to compare strings, and each has advantages. The simplest to use are the nonmember, overloaded operator functions: operator ==, operator != operator >, operator <, operator >=, and operator <=. See Listing 18-21 for an example.

Listing 18-21. Illustrating Comparison of Strings

```
//: C18:CompStr.cpp
#include <string>
#include <iostream>

using namespace std;
int main() {

// Strings to compare
string s1("This ");
string s2("That ");
for(int i = 0; i < s1.size() &&
i < s2.size(); i++)

// See if the string elements are the same:
if(s1[i] == s2[i])
cout << s1[i] << " " << i << endl;

// Use the string inequality operators
if(s1 != s2) {
cout << "Strings aren't the same:" << " ";
if(s1 > s2)
cout << "s1 is > s2" << endl;
else
cout << "s2 is > s1" << endl;
}
} ///:~
```

Here's the output from CompStr.cpp:

```
T 0
h 1
4
Strings aren't the same: s1 is > s2
```

The overloaded comparison operators are useful for comparing both full strings and individual string character elements.

Notice in Listing 18-22 the flexibility of argument types on both the left and right side of the comparison operators. For efficiency, the string class provides overloaded operators for the direct comparison of string objects, quoted literals, and pointers to C-style strings without having to create temporary string objects.

Listing 18-22. Illustrating Equivalence in String Comparison

```
//: C18:Equivalence.cpp
#include <iostream>
#include <string>
using namespace std;

int main() {
  string s2("That"), s1("This");
  // The lvalue is a quoted literal
  // and the rvalue is a string:
  if("That" == s2)
    cout << "A match" << endl;
  // The left operand is a string and the right is
  // a pointer to a C-style null terminated string:
  if(s1 != s2.c_str())
    cout << "No match" << endl;
} ///:~
```

The c_str() function returns a const char* that points to a *C-style, null-terminated string* equivalent to the contents of the string object. This comes in handy when you want to pass a string to a standard C function, such as atoi() or any of the functions defined in the <cstring> header. It is an error to use the value returned by c_str() as non-const argument to any function.

You won't find the logical not (!) or the logical comparison operators (&& and ||) among operators for a string. (Neither will you find overloaded versions of the bitwise C operators &, |, ^, or ~.) The overloaded nonmember comparison operators for the string class are limited to the subset that has clear, unambiguous application to single characters or groups of characters.

The compare() member function offers you a great deal more sophisticated and precise comparison than the nonmember operator set. It provides overloaded versions to compare

- Two complete strings

- Part of either string to a complete string

- Subsets of two strings

Listing 18-23 compares complete strings.

Listing 18-23. Comparing Complete Strings

```
//: C18:Compare.cpp
// Demonstrates compare() and swap().
#include <cassert>
#include <string>
using namespace std;
```

```
int main() {
  string first("This");
  string second("That");
  assert(first.compare(first) == 0);
  assert(second.compare(second) == 0);
  // Which is lexically greater?
  assert(first.compare(second) > 0);
  assert(second.compare(first) < 0);
  first.swap(second);
  assert(first.compare(second) < 0);
  assert(second.compare(first) > 0);
} ///:~
```

The swap() function in Listing 18-23 does what its name implies: it exchanges the contents of its object and argument. To compare a subset of the characters in one or both strings, you add arguments that define where to start the comparison and how many characters to consider. For example, you can use the following overloaded version of compare():

```
s1.compare(s1StartPos, s1NumberChars, s2, s2StartPos,s2NumberChars);
```

See Listing 18-24 for an example.

Listing 18-24. Comparing a Subset of Characters in One or Both Strings

```
//: C18:Compare2.cpp
// Illustrate overloaded compare().
#include <cassert>
#include <string>
using namespace std;

int main() {
  string first("This is a day that will live in infamy");
  string second("I don't believe that this is what "
                "I signed up for");
  // Compare "his is" in both strings:
  assert(first.compare(1, 7, second, 22, 7) == 0);
  // Compare "his is a" to "his is w":
  assert(first.compare(1, 9, second, 22, 9) < 0);
} ///:~
Indexing with [] vs. at()
```

In the examples so far, I have used the *C-style array indexing syntax* to refer to an individual character in a string. C++ strings provide an alternative to the s[n] notation: the at() member. These two indexing mechanisms produce the same result in C++ if all goes well; see Listing 18-25.

Listing 18-25. Demonstrating Similarity between String Indexing with [] and at()

```
//: C18:StringIndexing.cpp
#include <cassert>
#include <string>
using namespace std;
```

```
int main() {
  string s("1234");
  assert(s[1] == '2');
  assert(s.at(1) == '2');
} ///:~
```

There is one important difference, however, between [ ] and at(). When you try to reference an array element that is out of bounds, at() will do you the kindness of throwing an exception, while ordinary [ ] subscripting syntax will leave you to your own devices, as shown in Listing 18-26.

Listing 18-26. Demonstrating Difference between String Indexing with [] and at()

```
//: C18:BadStringIndexing.cpp
#include <exception>
#include <iostream>
#include <string>
using namespace std;

int main() {
  string s("1234");
  // at() saves you by throwing an exception:
  try {
    s.at(5);
  } catch(exception& e) {
    cerr << e.what() << endl;
  }
} ///:~
```

Responsible programmers will not use errant indexes, but should you want the benefits of automatic index checking, using at()in place of [ ] will give you a chance to gracefully recover from references to array elements that don't exist. The execution of Listing 18-26 on one of our test compilers gave the following output:

```
invalid string position
```

The at() member throws an object of class out_of_range, which derives (ultimately) from std::exception. By catching this object in an exception handler, you can take appropriate remedial actions such as recalculating the offending subscript or growing the array. Using string::operator[]() gives no such protection and is as dangerous as char array processing in C.

Strings and Character Traits

The programs Find.cpp and NewFind.cpp (Listings 18-15 and 18-16, respectively) earlier in this chapter lead me to ask the obvious question: Why isn't case-insensitive comparison part of the standard string class? The answer provides interesting background on the true nature of C++ string objects.

Consider what it means for a character to have "case." Written Hebrew, Farsi, and Kanji don't use the concept of uppercase and lowercase, so for those languages this idea has no meaning. It would seem that if there were a way to designate some languages as "all uppercase" or "all lowercase," we could design a generalized solution. However, some languages that employ the concept of "case" *also* change the meaning of particular characters with diacritical marks, such as the cedilla in Spanish, the circumflex in French, and the umlaut in German. For this reason, any case-sensitive collating scheme that attempts to be comprehensive will be nightmarishly complex to use.

Although we usually treat the C++ string as a class, this is really not the case. The string type is a specialization of a more general constituent, the basic_string< > template. Observe how string is declared in the Standard C++ header file:

```
typedef basic_string<char> string;
```

To understand the nature of the string class, look at the basic_string< > template:

```
template<class charT, class traits = char_traits<charT>,
  class allocator = allocator<charT>> class basic_string;
```

For now, just notice that the string type is created when the basic_string template is instantiated with char. Inside the basic_string< >template declaration, the line

```
class traits = char_traits<charT>,
```

tells you that the behavior of the class made from the basic_string< > template is specified by a class based on the template char_traits< >. Thus, the basic_string< > template produces string-oriented classes that manipulate types other than char (wide characters, for example). To do this, the char_traits< > template controls the content and collating behaviors of a variety of character sets using the character comparison functions eq() (equal), ne() (not equal), and lt() (less than). The basic_string< >string comparison functions rely on these.

This is why the string class doesn't include case-insensitive member functions: that's not in its job description. To change the way the string class treats character comparison, you must supply a different char_traits< > template because that defines the behavior of the individual character comparison member functions.

You can use this information to make a new type of string class that ignores case. First, you'll define a new case-insensitive char_traits< > template that inherits from the existing template. Next, you'll override only the members you need to change to make character-by-character comparison case insensitive. (In addition to the three lexical character comparison members mentioned earlier, you'll also supply a new implementation for the char_traits functions find() *and* compare()). Finally, you'll typedef a new class based on basic_string, but using the case-insensitive ichar_traits template for its second argument, as shown in Listing 18-27.

Listing 18-27. Developing ichar_traits

```
//: C18:ichar_traits.h
// Creating your own character traits.
#ifndef ICHAR_TRAITS_H
#define ICHAR_TRAITS_H
#include <cassert>
#include <cctype>
#include <cmath>
#include <cstddef>
#include <ostream>
#include <string>
using std::allocator;
using std::basic_string;
using std::char_traits;
using std::ostream;
using std::size_t;
using std::string;
using std::toupper;
using std::tolower;
```

```
struct ichar_traits : char_traits<char> {
  // We'll only change character-by-
  // character comparison functions
  static bool eq(char c1st, char c2nd) {
    return toupper(c1st) == toupper(c2nd);
  }
  static bool ne(char c1st, char c2nd) {
    return !eq(c1st, c2nd);
  }
  static bool lt(char c1st, char c2nd) {
    return toupper(c1st) < toupper(c2nd);
  }
  static int
  compare(const char* str1, const char* str2, size_t n) {
    for(size_t i = 0; i < n; ++i) {
      if(str1 == 0)
        return -1;
      else if(str2 == 0)
        return 1;
      else if(tolower(*str1) < tolower(*str2))
        return -1;
      else if(tolower(*str1) > tolower(*str2))
        return 1;
      assert(tolower(*str1) == tolower(*str2));
      ++str1; ++str2; // Compare the other chars
    }
    return 0;
  }
  static const char*
  find(const char* s1, size_t n, char c) {
    while(n-- > 0)
      if(toupper(*s1) == toupper(c))
        return s1;
      else
        ++s1;
    return 0;
  }
};
typedef basic_string<char, ichar_traits> istring;
inline ostream& operator<<(ostream& os, const istring& s) {
  return os << string(s.c_str(), s.length());
}
#endif                // ICHAR_TRAITS_H ///:~
```

You provide a typedef named istring so that your class will act like an ordinary string in every way, except that it will make all comparisons without respect to case. For convenience, you've also provided an overloaded operator<<() so that you can print istrings. See Listing 18-28 for an example.

Listing 18-28. Implementing the header file in Listing 18-27

```
//: C18:ICompare.cpp
#include <cassert>
#include <iostream>
#include "ichar_traits.h"    // To be INCLUDED from Header FILE
                             // above
using namespace std;

int main() {
  // The same letters except for case:
  istring first = "tHis";
  istring second = "ThIS";
  cout << first << endl;
  cout << second << endl;
  assert(first.compare(second) == 0);
  assert(first.find('h') == 1);
  assert(first.find('I') == 2);
  assert(first.find('x') == string::npos);
} ///:~
```

This is just a toy example. To make istring fully equivalent to string, you'd have to create the other functions necessary to support the new istring type.

The <string> header provides a wide string class via the following typedef:

```
typedef basic_string<wchar_t> wstring;
```

Wide string support also reveals itself in wide streams (wostream in place of ostream, also defined in <iostream>) and in the header <cwctype>, a wide-character version of <cctype>. This, along with the wchar_t specialization of char_traits in the Standard C++ Library, allows you to do a wide-character version of ichar_traits, as shown in Listing 18-29.

Listing 18-29. Developing Wide-Character Version of ichar_traits

```
//: C18:iwchar_traits.h {-g++}
// Creating your own wide-character traits.
#ifndef IWCHAR_TRAITS_H
#define IWCHAR_TRAITS_H
#include <cassert>
#include <cmath>
#include <cstddef>
#include <cwctype>
#include <ostream>
#include <string>
using std::allocator;
using std::basic_string;
using std::char_traits;
using std::size_t;
using std::towlower;
using std::towupper;
using std::wostream;
using std::wstring;
```

```
struct iwchar_traits : char_traits<wchar_t> {
  // We'll only change character-by-
  // character comparison functions
  static bool eq(wchar_t c1st, wchar_t c2nd) {
    return towupper(c1st) == towupper(c2nd);
  }
  static bool ne(wchar_t c1st, wchar_t c2nd) {
    return towupper(c1st) != towupper(c2nd);
  }
  static bool lt(wchar_t c1st, wchar_t c2nd) {
    return towupper(c1st) < towupper(c2nd);
  }
  static int compare(
    const wchar_t* str1, const wchar_t* str2, size_t n) {
    for(size_t i = 0; i < n; i++) {
      if(str1 == 0)
        return -1;
      else if(str2 == 0)
        return 1;
      else if(towlower(*str1) < towlower(*str2))
        return -1;
      else if(towlower(*str1) > towlower(*str2))
        return 1;
      assert(towlower(*str1) == towlower(*str2));
      ++str1; ++str2; // Compare the other wchar_ts
    }
    return 0;
  }
  static const wchar_t*
  find(const wchar_t* s1, size_t n, wchar_t c) {
    while(n-- > 0)
      if(towupper(*s1) == towupper(c))
        return s1;
      else
        ++s1;
    return 0;
  }
};
typedef basic_string<wchar_t, iwchar_traits> iwstring;
inline wostream& operator<<(wostream& os,
  const iwstring& s) {
  return os << wstring(s.c_str(), s.length());
}
#endif                    // IWCHAR_TRAITS_H  ///:~
```

As you can see, this is mostly an exercise in placing a "w" in the appropriate place in the source code. Listing 18-30 contains the test program.

Listing 18-30. Testing Out the header file Developed in Listing 18-29

```
//: C18:IWCompare.cpp {-g++}
#include <cassert>
#include <iostream>
#include "iwchar_traits.h"    // To be INCLUDED from Header FILE
                             // above
using namespace std;

int main() {
  // The same letters except for case:
  iwstring wfirst = L"tHis";
  iwstring wsecond = L"ThIS";
  wcout << wfirst << endl;
  wcout << wsecond << endl;
  assert(wfirst.compare(wsecond) == 0);
  assert(wfirst.find('h') == 1);
  assert(wfirst.find('I') == 2);
  assert(wfirst.find('x') == wstring::npos);
} ///:~
```

Unfortunately, some compilers still do not provide robust support for wide characters.

A String Application

If you've looked at the sample code in this book closely, you've noticed that certain tokens in the comments surround the code. These are used by a Python program that was written to extract the code into files and set up makefiles for building the code. For example, a double slash followed by a colon at the beginning of a line denotes the first line of a source file. The rest of the line contains information describing the file's name and location and whether it should be only compiled rather than fully built into an executable file. For example, the first line in Listing 18-30 contains the string C18:IWCompare.cpp, indicating that the file IWCompare.cpp should be extracted into the directory C18.

The last line of a source file contains a triple-slash followed by a colon and a tilde. If the first line has an exclamation point immediately after the colon, the first and last lines of the source code are not to be output to the file (this is for data-only files).

▪ **Note**   If you're wondering why I'm avoiding showing you these tokens, it's because I don't want to break the code extractor when applied to the text of the book

---

The Python program does a lot more than just extract code. If the token {0} follows the file name, its makefile entry will only be set up to compile the file and not to link it into an executable. To link such a file with another source example, the target executable's source file will contain an {L} directive, as in

```
//{L} ../TestSuite/Test
```

This section will present a program in Listing 18-31 to just extract all the code so that you can compile and inspect it manually. You can use this program to extract all the code in this book by saving the document file as a text file (let's call it MFCTC++.txt) and by executing something like the following on a shell command line:

```
C:> extractCode MFCTC++.txt /TheCode
```

This command reads the text file `MFCTC2.txt` and writes all the source code files in subdirectories under the top-level directory /TheCode. The directory tree will look like the following:

```
TheCode/
    C0B/
    C01/
    C02/
    C18/
    C04/
    C05/
    C06/
    C07/
    C08/
    C09/
    C10/
    C11/
    TestSuite/
```

The source files containing the examples from each chapter will be in the corresponding directory.

Listing 18-31. Illustrating Extraction of All the Source Code in the Book

```cpp
//: C18:ExtractCode.cpp {-edg} {RunByHand}
// Extracts code from text.
#include <cassert>
#include <cstddef>
#include <cstdio>
#include <cstdlib>
#include <fstream>
#include <iostream>
#include <string>
using namespace std;

// Legacy non-standard C header for mkdir()
#if defined(__GNUC__) || defined(__MWERKS__)
#include <sys/stat.h>
#elif defined(__BORLANDC__) || defined(_MSC_VER) \
  || defined(__DMC__)
#include <direct.h>
#else
#error Compiler not supported
#endif
// Check to see if directory exists
// by attempting to open a new file
// for output within it.
bool exists(string fname) {
  size_t len = fname.length();
  if(fname[len-1] != '/' && fname[len-1] != '\\')
    fname.append("/");
  fname.append("000.tmp");
  ofstream outf(fname.c_str());
  bool existFlag = outf;
```

```cpp
    if(outf) {
      outf.close();
      remove(fname.c_str());
    }
    return existFlag;
}

int main(int argc, char* argv[]) {
  // See if input file name provided
  if(argc == 1) {
    cerr << "usage: extractCode file [dir]" << endl;
    exit(EXIT_FAILURE);
  }
  // See if input file exists
  ifstream inf(argv[1]);
  if(!inf) {
    cerr << "error opening file: " << argv[1] << endl;
    exit(EXIT_FAILURE);
  }
  // Check for optional output directory
  string root("./");  // current is default
  if(argc == 3) {
    // See if output directory exists
    root = argv[2];
    if(!exists(root)) {
      cerr << "no such directory: " << root << endl;
      exit(EXIT_FAILURE);
    }
    size_t rootLen = root.length();
    if(root[rootLen-1] != '/' && root[rootLen-1] != '\\')
      root.append("/");
  }
  // Read input file line by line
  // checking for code delimiters
  string line;
  bool inCode = false;
  bool printDelims = true;
  ofstream outf;
  while(getline(inf, line)) {
    size_t findDelim = line.find("//" "/:~");
    if(findDelim != string::npos) {
      // Output last line and close file
      if(!inCode) {
        cerr << "Lines out of order" << endl;
        exit(EXIT_FAILURE);
      }
      assert(outf);
      if(printDelims)
        outf << line << endl;
      outf.close();
      inCode = false;
```

```
            printDelims = true;
        } else {
          findDelim = line.find("//" ":");
          if(findDelim == 0) {
            // Check for '!' directive
            if(line[3] == '!') {
              printDelims = false;
              ++findDelim;                    // To skip '!' for next search
            }
            // Extract subdirectory name, if any
            size_t startOfSubdir =
              line.find_first_not_of(" \t", findDelim+3);
            findDelim = line.find(':', startOfSubdir);
            if(findDelim == string::npos) {
              cerr << "missing filename information\n" << endl;
              exit(EXIT_FAILURE);
            }
            string subdir;
            if(findDelim > startOfSubdir)
              subdir = line.substr(startOfSubdir,
                                    findDelim - startOfSubdir);
            // Extract file name (better be one!)
            size_t startOfFile = findDelim + 1;
            size_t endOfFile =
              line.find_first_of(" \t", startOfFile);
            if(endOfFile == startOfFile) {
              cerr << "missing filename" << endl;
              exit(EXIT_FAILURE);
            }
            // We have all the pieces; build fullPath name
            string fullPath(root);
            if(subdir.length() > 0)
              fullPath.append(subdir).append("/");
            assert(fullPath[fullPath.length()-1] == '/');
            if(!exists(fullPath))
#if defined(__GNUC__) || defined(__MWERKS__)
              mkdir(fullPath.c_str(), 0);  // Create subdir
#else
              mkdir(fullPath.c_str());     // Create subdir
#endif
            fullPath.append(line.substr(startOfFile,
                        endOfFile - startOfFile));
            outf.open(fullPath.c_str());
            if(!outf) {
              cerr << "error opening " << fullPath
                   << " for output" << endl;
              exit(EXIT_FAILURE);
            }
            inCode = true;
            cout << "Processing " << fullPath << endl;
            if(printDelims)
```

```
          outf << line << endl;
      }
      else if(inCode) {
        assert(outf);
        outf << line << endl;   // Output middle code line
      }
    }
  }
  exit(EXIT_SUCCESS);
} ///:~
```

First, you'll notice some conditional compilation directives. The mkdir() function, which creates a directory in the file system, is defined by the POSIX standard in the header <sys/stat.h>. Unfortunately, many compilers still use a different header, <direct.h>. The respective signatures for mkdir() also differ: POSIX specifies two arguments, the older versions just one. For this reason, there is more conditional compilation later in the program to choose the right call to mkdir(). I normally don't use conditional compilation in the examples in this book, but this particular program is too useful not to put a little extra work into, since you can use it to extract all the code with it.

The exists() function in ExtractCode.cpp in Listing 18-31 tests whether a directory exists by opening a temporary file in it. If the open fails, the directory doesn't exist. You remove a file by sending its name as a char* to std::remove().

The main program validates the command-line arguments and then reads the input file a line at a time, looking for the special source code delimiters. The Boolean flag inCode indicates that the program is in the middle of a source file, so lines should be output. The printDelims flag will be true if the opening token is not followed by an exclamation point; otherwise the first and last lines are not written. It is important to check for the closing delimiter first, because the start token is a subset, and searching for the start token first would return a successful find for both cases. If you encounter the closing token, you verify that you are in the middle of processing a source file; otherwise, something is wrong with the way the delimiters are laid out in the text file. If inCode is true, all is well, and you (optionally) write the last line and close the file. When the opening token is found, you parse the directory and file name components and open the file. The following string-related functions were used in this example: length(), append(), getline(), find() (*two versions*), find_first_not_of(), substr(), find_first_of(), c_str(), and, of course, operator<<().

Review Session

1. *C++ string objects* provide developers with a number of great advantages over their *C* counterparts. For the most part, the string class makes *referring to strings with character pointers unnecessary*. This *eliminates an entire class of software defects* that arise from the use of uninitialized and incorrectly valued pointers.

2. *C++ strings* dynamically and transparently grow their internal data storage space to accommodate increases in the size of the string data. When the data in a string grows beyond the limits of the memory initially allocated to it, the string object will make the memory management calls that take space from and return space to the *heap*.

3. Consistent allocation schemes prevent memory leaks and have the potential to be much more efficient than *"roll your own" memory management*.

4. The string class member functions provide a fairly comprehensive set of tools for *creating, modifying, and searching in strings*.

5. String comparisons *are always case-sensitive*, but you can work around this by copying string data to *C-style null-terminated strings and using case-insensitive string comparison functions*, temporarily converting the data held in string objects to a single case, or by creating a case-insensitive string class that overrides the character traits used to create the basic_string object.

■ ■ ■

iostreams

You can do much more with the general I/O problem than just take standard I/O and turn it into a class.

Wouldn't it be nice if you could make all the usual "receptacles"—standard I/O, files, and even blocks of memory—look the same so that you need to remember only one interface? That's the idea behind iostreams. They're much easier, safer, and sometimes even more efficient than the assorted functions from the Standard C Library stdio.

The iostreams classes are usually the first part of the C++ library that new C++ programmers learn to use. This chapter discusses how iostreams are an improvement over C's stdio facilities and explores the behavior of file and string streams in addition to the standard console streams.

Why iostreams?

You might wonder what's wrong with the good old C library. Why not "wrap" the C library in a class and be done with it? Sometimes this is a fine solution. For example, suppose you want to make sure that the file represented by a stdio FILE pointer is always safely opened and properly closed without having to rely on the user to remember to call the close() function. Listing 19-1 shows such an attempt.

Listing 19-1. Wrapping the stdio File Class

```
//: C19:FileClass.h
// stdio files wrapped.
#ifndef FILECLASS_H
#define FILECLASS_H
#include <cstdio>
#include <stdexcept>

class FileClass {
  std::FILE* f;
public:
  struct FileClassError : std::runtime_error {
    FileClassError(const char* msg)
    : std::runtime_error(msg) {}
  };
  FileClass(const char* fname, const char* mode = "r");
  ~FileClass();
  std::FILE* fp();
};
#endif // FILECLASS_H ///:~
```

When you perform file I/O in C, you work with a naked pointer to a FILE struct, but this class wraps around the pointer and guarantees it is properly initialized and cleaned up using the constructor and destructor. The second constructor argument is the file mode, which defaults to "r" for "read."

To fetch the value of the pointer to use in the file I/O functions, you use the fp() access function. Listing 19-2 contains the member function definitions.

Listing 19-2. Implementing the header file in Listing 19-1

```
//: C19:FileClass.cpp {O}
// FileClass Implementation.
#include "FileClass.h" // To be INCLUDED from Header FILE above
#include <cstdlib>
#include <cstdio>
using namespace std;

FileClass::FileClass(const char* fname, const char* mode) {
  if((f = fopen(fname, mode)) == 0)
    throw FileClassError("Error opening file");
}

FileClass::~FileClass() { fclose(f); }

FILE* FileClass::fp() { return f; } ///:~
```

The constructor calls fopen(), as you would normally do, but it also ensures that the result isn't zero, which indicates a failure upon opening the file. If the file does not open as expected, an exception is thrown.

The destructor closes the file, and the access function fp() returns f. For a simple example using FileClass, see Listing 19-3.

Listing 19-3. Testing Out the Implementation in Listing 19-2

```
//: C19:FileClassTest.cpp
//{L} FileClass
#include <cstdlib>
#include <iostream>
#include "FileClass.h"
using namespace std;

int main() {
  try {
    FileClass f("FileClassTest.cpp");
    const int BSIZE = 100;
    char buf[BSIZE];
    while(fgets(buf, BSIZE, f.fp()))
      fputs(buf, stdout);
  } catch(FileClass::FileClassError& e) {
    cout << e.what() << endl;
    return EXIT_FAILURE;
  }
  return EXIT_SUCCESS;
} // File automatically closed by destructor
///:~
```

You create the FileClass object and use it in normal C file I/O function calls by calling fp(). When you're done with it, just forget about it; the file is closed by the destructor at the end of its scope.

Even though the FILE pointer is private, it isn't particularly safe because fp() retrieves it. Since the only effect seems to be guaranteed initialization and cleanup, why not make it public or use a struct instead? Notice that while you can get a copy of f using fp(), you cannot assign to f—that's completely under the control of the class. After capturing the pointer returned by fp(), the client programmer can still assign to the structure elements or even close it, so the safety is in guaranteeing a valid FILE pointer rather than proper contents of the structure.

If you want complete safety, you must prevent the user from directly accessing the FILE pointer, as shown in Listing 19-4. Some version of all the normal file I/O functions must show up as class members so that everything you can do with the C approach is available in the C++ class.

Listing 19-4. Hiding File I/O in C++

```
//: C19:Fullwrap.h
// Completely hidden file I/O.
#ifndef FULLWRAP_H
#define FULLWRAP_H
#include <cstddef>
#include <cstdio>
#undef getc
#undef putc
#undef ungetc
using std::size_t;
using std::fpos_t;
class File {
  std::FILE* f;
  std::FILE* F(); // Produces checked pointer to f
public:
  File(); // Create object but don't open file
  File(const char* path, const char* mode = "r");
  ~File();
  int open(const char* path, const char* mode = "r");
  int reopen(const char* path, const char* mode);
  int getc();
  int ungetc(int c);
  int putc(int c);
  int puts(const char* s);
  char* gets(char* s, int n);
  int printf(const char* format, ...);
  size_t read(void* ptr, size_t size, size_t n);
  size_t write(const void* ptr, size_t size, size_t n);
  int eof();
  int close();
  int flush();
  int seek(long offset, int whence);
  int getpos(fpos_t* pos);
  int setpos(const fpos_t* pos);
  long tell();
  void rewind();
```

```
  void setbuf(char* buf);
  int setvbuf(char* buf, int type, size_t sz);
  int error();
  void clearErr();
};
#endif // FULLWRAP_H ///:~
```

This class contains almost all the file I/O functions from <cstdio>. Note that vfprintf() is missing; it implements the printf() member function.

File has the same constructor as in Listing 19-3, and it also has a default constructor. The default constructor is important if you want to create an array of File objects or use a File object as a member of another class where the initialization doesn't happen in the constructor, but sometime after the enclosing object is created.

The default constructor sets the private FILE pointer f to zero. But now, before any reference to f, its value must be checked to ensure it isn't zero. This is accomplished with F(), which is private because it is intended to be used only by other member functions. (You don't want to give the user direct access to the underlying FILE structure in this class.)

This approach is not a terrible solution by any means. It's quite functional, and you could imagine making similar classes for standard (console) I/O and for in-core formatting (reading/writing a piece of memory rather than a file or the console).

The stumbling block is the runtime interpreter used for the variable argument list functions. This is the code that parses your format string at runtime and grabs and interprets arguments from the variable argument list. It's a problem for four reasons.

1. Even if you use only a fraction of the functionality of the interpreter, the whole thing gets loaded into your executable. So if you say printf("%c", 'x');, you'll get the whole package, including the parts that print floating point numbers and strings. There's no standard option for reducing the amount of space used by the program.

2. Because the interpretation happens at runtime, you can't get rid of a performance overhead. It's frustrating because all the information is *there* in the format string at compile time, but it's not evaluated until runtime. However, if you could parse the arguments in the format string at compile time, you could make direct function calls that have the potential to be much faster than a runtime interpreter (although the printf() family of functions is usually quite well optimized).

3. Because the format string is not evaluated until runtime, there can be no compile-time error checking. You're probably familiar with this problem if you've tried to find bugs that came from using the wrong number or type of arguments in a printf() statement. C++ makes a big deal out of compile-time error checking to find errors early and make your life easier. It seems a shame to throw type safety away for an I/O library, especially since I/O is used a lot.

4. For C++, the most crucial problem is that the printf() family of functions is not particularly extensible. They're really designed to handle only the basic data types in C (char, int, float, double, wchar_t, char*, wchar_t*, and void*) and their variations. You might think that every time you add a new class, you could add overloaded printf() and scanf() functions (and their variants for files and strings), but remember, overloaded functions must have different types in their argument lists, and the printf() family hides its type information in the format string and in the variable argument list. For a language such as C++, whose goal is to be able to easily add new data types, this is an unacceptable restriction.

iostreams to the Rescue

These issues make it clear that I/O is one of the first priorities for the Standard C++ class libraries. Because "Hello, World" is the first program just about everyone writes in a new language, and because I/O is part of virtually every program, the I/O library in C++ must be particularly easy to use. It also has the much greater challenge that it must accommodate any new class. Thus, its constraints require that this foundation class library be a truly inspired design. In addition to gaining a great deal of leverage and clarity in your dealings with I/O and formatting, you'll also see in this chapter how a really powerful C++ library can work.

At this point of time, we introduce some Date class files in Listing 19-5.

Listing 19-5. Date Class Files

```
//: C19:Date.h
#ifndef DATE_H
#define DATE_H
#include <string>
#include <stdexcept>
#include <iosfwd>
class Date {
  int year, month, day;
  int compare(const Date&) const;
  static int daysInPrevMonth(int year, int mon);
public:
  // A class for date calculations
  struct Duration {
    int years, months, days;
    Duration(int y, int m, int d)
    : years(y), months(m) ,days(d) {}
  };
  // An exception class
  struct DateError : public std::logic_error {
    DateError(const std::string& msg = "")
: std::logic_error(msg) {}
  };
  Date();
  Date(int, int, int) throw(DateError);
  Date(const std::string&) throw(DateError);
  int getYear() const;
  int getMonth() const;
  int getDay() const;
  std::string toString() const;
  friend Duration duration(const Date&, const Date&);
  friend bool operator<(const Date&, const Date&);
  friend bool operator<=(const Date&, const Date&);
  friend bool operator>(const Date&, const Date&);
  friend bool operator>=(const Date&, const Date&);
  friend bool operator==(const Date&, const Date&);
  friend bool operator!=(const Date&, const Date&);
  friend std::ostream& operator<<(std::ostream&,
                                  const Date&);
```

```
    friend std::istream& operator>>(std::istream&, Date&);
};
#endif // DATE_H ///:~

//: C19:Date.cpp {0}
#include "Date.h"      // To be INCLUDED from Header FILE above
#include <iostream>
#include <sstream>
#include <cstdlib>
#include <string>
#include <algorithm> // For swap()
#include <ctime>
#include <cassert>
#include <iomanip>
using namespace std;
namespace {
  const int daysInMonth[][13] = {
    { 0, 31, 28, 31, 30, 31, 30, 31, 31, 30, 31, 30, 31 },
    { 0, 31, 29, 31, 30, 31, 30, 31, 31, 30, 31, 30, 31 }
  };
  inline bool isleap(int y) {
    return y%4 == 0 && y%100 != 0 || y%400 == 0;
  }
}
Date::Date() {
  // Get current date
  time_t tval = time(0);
  struct tm *now = localtime(&tval);
  year = now->tm_year + 1900;
  month = now->tm_mon + 1;
  day = now->tm_mday;
}
Date::Date(int yr,int mon,int dy) throw(Date::DateError) {
  if(!(1 <= mon && mon <= 12))
    throw DateError("Bad month in Date ");
  if(!(1 <= dy && dy <= daysInMonth[isleap(year)][mon]))
    throw DateError("Bad day in Date ");
  year = yr;
  month = mon;
  day = dy;
}
Date::Date(const std::string& s) throw(Date::DateError) {
  // Assume YYYYMMDD format
  if(!(s.size() == 8))
    throw DateError("Bad string in Date ");
  for(int n = 8; --n >= 0;)
    if(!isdigit(s[n]))
      throw DateError("Bad string in Date ");
  string buf = s.substr(0, 4);
  year = atoi(buf.c_str());
  buf = s.substr(4, 2);
  month = atoi(buf.c_str());
```

```
    buf = s.substr(6, 2);
    day = atoi(buf.c_str());
    if(!(1 <= month && month <= 12))
       throw DateError("Bad month in Date ");
if(!(1 <= day && day <=
    daysInMonth[isleap(year)][month]))
       throw DateError("Bad day in Date ");
}
int Date::getYear() const { return year; }
int Date::getMonth() const { return month; }
int Date::getDay() const { return day; }
string Date::toString() const {
  ostringstream os;
  os.fill('0');
  os << setw(4) << year
     << setw(2) << month
     << setw(2) << day;
  return os.str();
}
int Date::compare(const Date& d2) const {
  int result = year - d2.year;
  if(result == 0) {
    result = month - d2.month;
    if(result == 0)
      result = day - d2.day;
  }
  return result;
}
int Date::daysInPrevMonth(int year, int month) {
  if(month == 1) {
    --year;
    month = 12;
  }
  else
    --month;
  return daysInMonth[isleap(year)][month];
}
bool operator<(const Date& d1, const Date& d2) {
  return d1.compare(d2) < 0;
}
bool operator<=(const Date& d1, const Date& d2) {
  return d1 < d2 || d1 == d2;
}
bool operator>(const Date& d1, const Date& d2) {
  return !(d1 < d2) && !(d1 == d2);
}
bool operator>=(const Date& d1, const Date& d2) {
  return !(d1 < d2);
}
bool operator==(const Date& d1, const Date& d2) {
  return d1.compare(d2) == 0;
}
```

```
bool operator!=(const Date& d1, const Date& d2) {
  return !(d1 == d2);
}
Date::Duration
duration(const Date& date1, const Date& date2) {
  int y1 = date1.year;
  int y2 = date2.year;
  int m1 = date1.month;
  int m2 = date2.month;
  int d1 = date1.day;
  int d2 = date2.day;
  // Compute the compare
  int order = date1.compare(date2);
  if(order == 0)
    return Date::Duration(0,0,0);
  else if(order > 0) {
    // Make date1 precede date2 locally
    using std::swap;
    swap(y1, y2);
    swap(m1, m2);
    swap(d1, d2);
  }
  int years = y2 - y1;
  int months = m2 - m1;
  int days = d2 - d1;
  assert(years > 0 ||
    years == 0 && months > 0 ||
    years == 0 && months == 0 && days > 0);

  // Do the obvious corrections (must adjust days before months!)
  // This is a loop in case the previous month is February, and days < -28.
  int lastMonth = m2;
  int lastYear = y2;
  while(days < 0) {
    // Borrow from month
    assert(months > 0);
    days += Date::daysInPrevMonth(
      lastYear, lastMonth--);
    --months;
  }
  if(months < 0) {
    // Borrow from year
    assert(years > 0);
    months += 12;
    --years;
  }
  return Date::Duration(years, months, days);
}
ostream& operator<<(ostream& os, const Date& d) {
  char fillc = os.fill('0');
  os << setw(2) << d.getMonth() << '-'
```

```
           << setw(2) << d.getDay() << '-'
           << setw(4) << setfill(fillc) << d.getYear();
    return os;
}
istream& operator>>(istream& is, Date& d) {
    is >> d.month;
    char dash;
    is >> dash;
    if(dash != '-')
        is.setstate(ios::failbit);
    is >> d.day;
    is >> dash;
    if(dash != '-')
        is.setstate(ios::failbit);
    is >> d.year;
    return is;
} ///:~
```

Inserters and Extractors

A *stream* is an object that transports and formats characters of a fixed width. You can have an input stream
(via descendants of the istream class), an output stream (with ostream objects), or a stream that does both
simultaneously (with objects derived from iostream). The iostreams library provides different types of such classes:
ifstream, ofstream, and fstream for files, and istringstream, ostringstream, and stringstream for interfacing
with the Standard C++ string class. All these stream classes have nearly identical interfaces, so you can use streams
in a uniform manner, whether you're working with a file, standard I/O, a region of memory, or a string object. The
single interface you learn also works for extensions added to support new classes. Some functions implement your
formatting commands, and some functions read and write characters without formatting.

The stream classes mentioned earlier are actually template specializations, much like the standard string
class is a specialization of the basic_string template. The basic classes in the iostreams inheritance hierarchy
are shown in Figure 19-1.

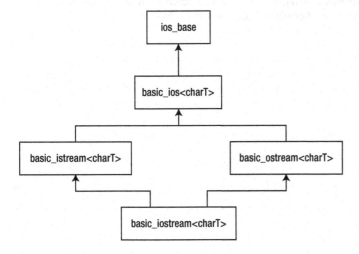

Figure 19-1. *Showing the basic classes in the IOSTREAM inheritance hierarchy*

The ios_base class declares everything that is common to all streams, independent of the type of character the stream handles. These declarations are mostly constants and functions to manage them, some of which you'll see throughout this chapter. The rest of the classes are templates that have the underlying character type as a parameter. The istream class, for example, is defined as follows:

```
typedef basic_istream<char> istream;
```

All the classes mentioned earlier are defined via similar type definitions. There are also type definitions for all stream classes using wchar_t (the wide character type) instead of char. You'll look at these at the end of this chapter. The basic_ios template defines functions common to both input and output, but that depends on the underlying character type (you won't use these much). The template basic_istream defines generic functions for input, and basic_ostream does the same for output. The classes for file and string streams introduced later add functionality for their specific stream types.

In the iostreams library, two operators are overloaded to simplify the use of iostreams. The operator<< is often referred to as an *inserter* for iostreams, and the operator>> is often referred to as an *extractor*.

Extractors parse the information that's expected by the destination object according to its type. To see an example of this, you can use the cin object, which is the iostream equivalent of stdin in C, that is, redirectable standard input. This object is predefined whenever you include the <iostream> header, as in:

```
 int i;
 cin >> i;

 float f;
 cin >> f;

char c;
 cin >> c;

char buf[100];
 cin >> buf;
```

There's an overloaded operator>> for every built-in data type. You can also overload your own, as you'll see later.

To find out what you have in the various variables, you can use the cout object (corresponding to standard output; there's also a cerr object corresponding to standard error) with the inserter <<, as in:

```
cout << "i = ";
cout << i;
cout << "\n";
cout << "f = ";
cout << f;
cout << "\n";
cout << "c = ";
cout << c;
cout << "\n";
cout << "buf = ";
cout << buf;
cout << "\n";
```

This is tedious and doesn't seem like much of an improvement over `printf()`, despite improved type checking. Fortunately, the overloaded inserters and extractors are designed to be chained into a more complex expression that is much easier to *write* (*and read*):

```
cout << "i = " << i << endl;
cout << "f = " << f << endl;

cout << "c = " << c << endl;
cout << "buf = " << buf << endl;
```

Defining inserters and extractors for your own classes is just a matter of overloading the associated operators to do the right things, namely:

- Make the first parameter a nonconst reference to the stream (`istream` for input, `ostream` for output).

- Perform the operation by inserting/extracting data to/from the stream (by processing the components of the object).

- Return a reference to the stream.

The stream should be non-`const` because processing stream data changes the state of the stream. By returning the stream, you allow for chaining stream operations in a single statement, as shown earlier.

As an example, consider how to output the representation of a `Date` object in MM-DD-YYYY format. The following inserter does the job:

```
ostream& operator<<(ostream& os, const Date& d) {
  char fillc = os.fill('0');
  os << setw(2) << d.getMonth() << '-'
     << setw(2) << d.getDay() << '-'
     << setw(4) << setfill(fillc) << d.getYear();
  return os;
}
```

This function cannot be a member of the `Date` class because the left operand of the `<<` operator must be the output stream. The `fill()` member function of `ostream` changes the padding character used when the width of an output field, determined by the *manipulator* `setw()`, is greater than needed for the data. You use a "0" character so that months preceding October will display a leading zero, such as "09" for September. The `fill()` function also returns the previous fill character (which defaults to a single space) so that you can restore it later with the manipulator `setfill()`. I discuss manipulators in depth later in this chapter.

Extractors require a little more care because things can go wrong with input data. The way to signal a stream error is to set the stream's *fail bit*, as follows:

```
istream& operator>>(istream& is, Date& d) {
  is >> d.month;
  char dash;
  is >> dash;
  if(dash != '-')
    is.setstate(ios::failbit);
  is >> d.day;
  is >> dash;
```

```
  if(dash != '-')
    is.setstate(ios::failbit);
  is >> d.year;
  return is;
}
```

When an error bit is set in a stream, all further streams operations are ignored until the stream is restored to a good state (explained shortly). That's why the code above continues extracting even if `ios::failbit` gets set. This implementation is somewhat forgiving in that it allows white space between the numbers and dashes in a date string (because the >> operator skips white space by default when reading built-in types).

The following are valid date strings for this extractor:

```
"08-10-2003"
"8-10-2003"
"08 - 10 - 2003"
```

but these are not:

```
"A-10-2003"  // No alpha characters allowed
"08%10/2003" // Only dashes allowed as a delimiter
```

I'll discuss stream state in more depth in the section "Handling Stream Errors" later in this chapter.

Common Usage

As the Date extractor illustrated, you must be on guard for erroneous input. If the input produces an unexpected value, the process is skewed, and it's difficult to recover. In addition, formatted input defaults to white space delimiters. Consider what happens when you collect the code fragments earlier in this chapter into a single program, shown in Listing 19-6.

Listing 19-6. Illustrating iostream Examples

```cpp
//: C19:Iosexamp.cpp {RunByHand}
// iostream examples.
#include <iostream>
using namespace std;

int main() {
  int i;
  cin >> i;

  float f;
  cin >> f;
  char c;
  cin >> c;

  char buf[100];
  cin >> buf;
```

```
    cout << "i = " << i << endl;
    cout << "f = " << f << endl;
    cout << "c = " << c << endl;
    cout << "buf = " << buf << endl;

    cout << flush;
    cout << hex << "0x" << i << endl;
} ///:~
```

Let's give it the following input:

```
12 1.4 c this is a test
```

We expect the same output as if we gave it

```
12
1.4
c
this is a test
```

The output is, somewhat unexpectedly,

```
i = 12
f = 1.4
c = c
buf = this
0xc
```

Notice that buf got only the first word because the input routine looked for a space to delimit the input, which it saw *after* "this." In addition, if the continuous input string is longer than the storage allocated for buf, you overrun the buffer.

In practice, you'll usually want to get input from interactive programs a line at a time as a sequence of characters, scan them, and then perform conversions once they're safely in a buffer. This way you don't need to worry about the input routine choking on unexpected data.

Another consideration is the whole concept of a command-line interface. This made sense in the past when the console was little more than a glass typewriter, but the world is rapidly changing to one where the graphical user interface (GUI) dominates. What is the meaning of console I/O in such a world? It makes much more sense to ignore cin altogether, other than for simple examples or tests, and take the following approaches.

1. If your program requires input, read that input from a file—you'll soon see that it's remarkably easy to use files with iostreams. iostreams for files still works fine with a GUI.

2. Read the input without attempting to convert it, as just suggested. When the input is some place where it can't foul things up during conversion, you can safely scan it.

3. Output is different. If you're using a GUI, cout doesn't necessarily work, and you must send it to a file (which is identical to sending it to cout) or use the GUI facilities for data display. Otherwise, it often makes sense to send it to cout. In both cases, the output formatting functions of iostreams are highly useful.

Another common practice saves compile time on large projects. Consider, for example, how you would declare the Date stream operators introduced earlier in the chapter in a header file. You only need to include the prototypes for the functions, so it's not really necessary to include the entire <iostream> header in Date.h. The standard practice is to only declare classes, something like this:

```
class ostream;
```

This is an age-old technique for separating interface from implementation and is often called a *forward declaration* (and ostream at this point would be considered an *incomplete type*, since the class definition has not yet been seen by the compiler).

This will not work as is, however, for two reasons.

1. The stream classes are defined in the std namespace.

2. They are templates.

The proper declaration would be

```
namespace std {
  template<class charT, class traits = char_traits<charT>>
    class basic_ostream;
  typedef basic_ostream<char> ostream;
}
```

(As you can see, like the string class, the streams classes use the character traits classes). Since it would be terribly tedious to type all that for every stream class you want to reference, the standard provides a header that does it for you: <iosfwd>. The Date header (see above) would then look something like this:

```
// Date.h
#include <iosfwd>

class Date {
 friend std::ostream& operator<<(std::ostream&, const       Date&);
  friend std::istream& operator>>(std::istream&, Date&);
  // Etc.
```

Line–Oriented Input

To grab input a line at a time, you have three choices.

1. The member function get()

2. The member function getline()

3. The global function getline() defined in the <string> header

The first two functions take three arguments.

1. A pointer to a character buffer in which to store the result.

2. The size of that buffer (so it's not overrun).

3. The terminating character, to know when to stop reading input.

The terminating character has a default value of '\n', which is what you'll usually use. Both functions store a zero in the result buffer when they encounter the terminating character in the input.

So what's the difference? Subtle, but important: get() stops when it *sees* the delimiter in the input stream, but it doesn't extract it from the input stream. Thus, if you did another get() using the same delimiter, it would immediately return with no fetched input. (Presumably, you either use a different delimiter in the next get() statement or a different input function.) The getline() function, on the other hand, extracts the delimiter from the input stream, but still doesn't store it in the result buffer.

The getline() function defined in <string> is convenient. It is not a member function, but rather a stand-alone function declared in the namespace std. It takes only two non-default arguments, the input stream and the string object to populate. Like its namesake, it reads characters until it encounters the first occurrence of the delimiter ('\n' by default) and consumes and discards the delimiter. The advantage of this function is that it reads into a string object, so you don't need to worry about buffer size.

Generally, when you're processing a text file that you read a line at a time, you'll want to use one of the getline() functions.

Overloaded Versions of get( )

The get() function also comes in three other overloaded versions: one with no arguments that returns the next character using an int return value; one that stuffs a character into its char argument using a reference; and one that stores directly into the underlying buffer structure of another iostream object.

▪ **Note** The latter is explored later in the chapter.

Reading Raw Bytes

If you know exactly what you're dealing with and want to move the bytes directly into a variable, an array, or a structure in memory, you can use the unformatted I/O function read(). The first argument for this function is a pointer to the destination memory, and the second is the number of bytes to read. This is especially useful if you've previously stored the information to a file, for example, in binary form using the complementary write() member function for an output stream (using the same compiler, of course). You'll see examples of all these functions later.

Handling Stream Errors

The Date extractor, shown earlier, sets a stream's fail bit under certain conditions. How does the user know when such a failure occurs? You can detect stream errors by either calling certain stream member functions to see if an error state has occurred, or if you don't care what the particular error was, you can just evaluate the stream in a Boolean context. Both techniques derive from the state of a stream's error bits.

Stream State

The ios_base class, from which ios derives, defines four flags shown in Table 19-1 that you can use to test the state of a stream.

Table 19-1. *The Four Flags to Test the State of a Stream*

Flag	Meaning
Badbit	Some fatal (perhaps physical) error occurred. The stream should be considered unusable.
Eofbit	End-of-input has occurred (either by encountering the physical end of a file stream or by the user terminating a console stream, such as with Ctrl-Z or Ctrl-D).
Failbit	An I/O operation failed, most likely because of invalid data (e.g., letters were found when trying to read a number). The stream is still usable. The failbit flag is also set when end-of-input occurs.
Goodbit	All is well; no errors. End-of-input has not yet occurred.

You can test whether any of these conditions have occurred by calling corresponding member functions that return a Boolean value indicating whether any of these have been set. The good() stream member function returns true if none of the other three bits are set. The eof() function returns true if eofbit is set, which happens with an attempt to read from a stream that has no more data (usually a file). Because end-of-input happens in C++ when trying to read past the end of the physical medium, failbit is also set to indicate that the "expected" data was not successfully read. The fail() function returns true if *either* failbit or badbit is set, and bad() returns true *only* if the badbit is set.

Once any of the error bits in a stream's state are set, they remain set, which is not always what you want. When reading a file, you might want to reposition to an earlier place in the file before end-of-file occurred. Just moving the file pointer doesn't automatically reset eofbit or failbit; you must do it yourself with the clear() function, like this:

```
myStream.clear(); // Clears all error bits
```

After calling clear(), good() will return true if called immediately. As you saw in the Date extractor earlier, the setstate() function sets the bits you pass it. It turns out that setstate() doesn't affect any other bits—if they're already set, they stay set. If you want to set certain bits but at the same time reset all the rest, you can call an overloaded version of clear(), passing it a bitwise expression representing the bits you want to set, as in:

```
myStream.clear(ios::failbit | ios::eofbit);
```

Most of the time you won't be interested in checking the stream state bits individually. Usually you just want to know if everything is okay. This is the case when you read a file from beginning to end; you just want to know when the input data is exhausted. You can use a conversion function defined for void* that is automatically called when a stream occurs in a Boolean expression. Reading a stream until end-of-input using this idiom looks like the following:

```
int i;
while(myStream >> i)
  cout << i << endl;
```

Remember that operator>>() returns its stream argument, so the while statement above tests the stream as a Boolean expression. This particular example assumes that the input stream myStream contains integers separated by white space. The function ios_base::operator void*() simply calls good() on its stream and returns the result. Because most stream operations return their stream, using this idiom is convenient.

Streams and Exceptions

iostreams existed as part of C++ long before there were exceptions, so checking stream state manually was just the way things were done. For backward compatibility, this is still the status quo, but modern iostreams can throw exceptions instead. The exceptions() stream member function takes a parameter representing the state bits for which you want exceptions to be thrown. Whenever the stream encounters such a state, it throws an exception of type std::ios_base::failure, which inherits from std::exception.

Although you can trigger a failure exception for any of the four stream states, it's not necessarily a good idea to enable exceptions for all of them. As Chapter 17 explains, use exceptions for truly exceptional conditions, but end-of-file is not only *not* exceptional—it's *expected*! For that reason, you might want to enable exceptions only for the errors represented by badbit, which you would do like this:

```
myStream.exceptions(ios::badbit);
```

You enable exceptions on a stream-by-stream basis, since exceptions() is a member function for streams. The exceptions() function returns a bitmask (of type iostate, which is some compiler-dependent type convertible to int) indicating which stream states will cause exceptions. If those states have already been set, an exception is thrown immediately. Of course, if you use exceptions in connection with streams, you had better be ready to catch them, which means that you need to wrap all stream processing with a try block that has an ios::failure handler. Many programmers find this tedious and just check states manually where they expect errors to occur (since, for example, they don't expect bad() to return true most of the time anyway). This is another reason that having streams throw exceptions is optional and not the default. In any case, you can choose how you want to handle stream errors. For the same reasons that I recommend using exceptions for error handling in other contexts, I do so here.

File iostreams

Manipulating files with iostreams is much easier and safer than using stdio in C. All you do to open a file is create an object—the constructor does the work. You don't need to explicitly close a file (although you can, using the close() member function) because the destructor will close it when the object goes out of scope. To create a file that defaults to input, make an ifstream object. To create one that defaults to output, make an ofstream object. An fstream object can do both input and output.

The file stream classes fit into the iostreams classes as shown in Figure 19-2.

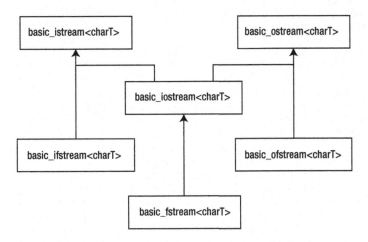

Figure 19-2. *Showing how the file stream classes fit into the iostream inheritance hierarchy*

As before, the classes you actually use are template specializations defined by type definitions. For example, ifstream, which processes files of char, is defined as

```
typedef basic_ifstream<char> ifstream;
```

A File–Processing Example

Listing 19-7 shows many of the features discussed so far. Notice the inclusion of <fstream> to declare the file I/O classes. Although on many platforms this will also include <iostream> automatically, compilers are not required to do so. If you want portable code, always include both headers.

Listing 19-7. Illustrating Stream I/O with Files

```cpp
//: C19:Strfile.cpp
// Stream I/O with files;
// The difference between get() & getline().
#include <fstream>
#include <iostream>
#include "../require.h"          // To be INCLUDED from Chapter 9
using namespace std;

int main() {
  const int SZ = 100;            // Buffer size;
  char buf[SZ];
  {
    ifstream in("Strfile.cpp");  // Read
    assure(in, "Strfile.cpp");   // Verify open
    ofstream out("Strfile.out"); // Write
    assure(out, "Strfile.out");
    int i = 1; // Line counter
     // A less-convenient approach for line input:
    while(in.get(buf, SZ)) {     // Leaves \n in input
      in.get(); // Throw away next character (\n)
      cout << buf << endl;       // Must add \n
      // File output just like standard I/O:
      out << i++ << ": " << buf << endl;
    }
  } // Destructors close in & out
  ifstream in("Strfile.out");
  assure(in, "Strfile.out");
  // More convenient line input:
  while(in.getline(buf, SZ)) {   // Removes \n
    char* cp = buf;
    while(*cp != ':')
      ++cp;
    cp += 2; // Past ": "
    cout << cp << endl;
     // Must still add \n
  }
} ///:~
```

The creation of both the ifstream and ofstream are followed by an assure() to guarantee the file was successfully opened. Here again the object, used in a situation where the compiler expects a Boolean result, produces a value that indicates success or failure.

The first while loop demonstrates the use of two forms of the get() function. The first gets characters into a buffer and puts a zero terminator in the buffer when either SZ-1 characters have been read or the third argument (defaulted to '\n') is encountered. The get() function leaves the terminator character in the input stream, so this terminator must be thrown away via in.get() using the form of get() with no argument, which fetches a single byte and returns it as an int. You can also use the ignore() member function, which has two default arguments. The first argument is the number of characters to throw away and defaults to one. The second argument is the character at which the ignore() function quits (after extracting it) and defaults to EOF.

Next, you see two output statements that look similar: one to cout and one to the file out. Notice the convenience here—you don't need to worry about the object type because the formatting statements work the same with all ostream objects. The first one echoes the line to standard output, and the second writes the line out to the new file and includes a line number.

To demonstrate getline(), open the file you just created and strip off the line numbers. To ensure the file is properly closed before opening it to read, you have two choices. You can surround the first part of the program with braces to force the out object out of scope, thus calling the destructor and closing the file, which is done here. You can also call close() for both files; if you do this, you can even reuse the in object by calling the open() member function.

The second while loop shows how getline() removes the terminator character (its third argument, which defaults to '\n') from the input stream when it's encountered. Although getline(), like get(), puts a zero in the buffer, it still doesn't insert the terminating character.

This example, as well as most of the examples in this chapter, assumes that each call to any overload of getline() will encounter a newline character. If this is not the case, the eofbit state of the stream will be set and the call to getline() will return false, causing the program to lose the last line of input.

Open Modes

You can control the way a file is opened by overriding the constructor's default arguments. Table 19-2 shows the flags that control the mode of the file.

Table 19-2. *Flags Controlling the File Mode*

Flag	Function
ios::in	Opens an input file. Use this as an open mode for an ofstream to prevent truncating an existing file.
ios::out	Opens an output file. When used for an ofstream without ios::app, ios::ate or ios::in, ios::trunc is implied.
ios::app	Opens an output file for appending only.
ios::ate	Opens an existing file (either input or output) and seeks to the end.
ios::trunc	Truncates the old file if it already exists.
ios::binary	Opens a file in *binary mode*. The default is *text mode*.

You can combine these flags using a bitwise *or* operation.

The binary flag, while portable, only has an effect on some non-UNIX systems, such as operating systems derived from MS-DOS, that have special conventions for storing end-of-line delimiters. For example, on MS-DOS systems in text mode (which is the default), every time you output a newline character ('\n'), the file system actually outputs two characters, a carriage-return/linefeed pair (CRLF), which is the pair of ASCII characters 0x0D and 0x0A.

Conversely, when you read such a file back into memory in text mode, each occurrence of this pair of bytes causes a '\n' to be sent to the program in its place. If you want to bypass this special processing, you open files in binary mode. Binary mode has nothing whatsoever to do with whether you *can* write raw bytes to a file—you *always* can (by calling write()). You should, however, open a file in binary mode when you'll be using read() or write() because these functions take a byte count parameter. Having the extra '\r' characters will throw your byte count off in those instances. You should also open a file in binary mode if you're going to use the stream-positioning commands discussed later in this chapter.

You can open a file for both input and output by declaring an fstream object. When declaring an fstream object, you must use enough of the open mode flags mentioned earlier to let the file system know whether you want to input, output, or both. To switch from output to input, you need to either flush the stream or change the file position. To change from input to output, change the file position. To create a file via an fstream object, use the ios::trunc open mode flag in the constructor call to do both input and output.

iostream Buffering

Good design practice dictates that, whenever you create a new class, you should endeavor to hide the details of the underlying implementation as much as possible from the user of the class. You show them only what they need to know and make the rest private to avoid confusion. When using inserters and extractors, you normally don't know or care where the bytes are being produced or consumed and whether you're dealing with standard I/O, files, memory, or some newly created class or device.

A time comes, however, when it is important to communicate with the part of the iostream that produces and consumes bytes. To provide this part with a common interface and still hide its underlying implementation, the Standard Library abstracts it into its own class, called streambuf. Each iostream object contains a pointer to some kind of streambuf.

■ **Note** The type depends on whether it deals with standard I/O, files, memory, and so on.

You can access the streambuf directly; for example, you can move raw bytes into and out of the streambuf without formatting them through the enclosing iostream. This is accomplished by calling member functions for the streambuf object.

Currently, the most important thing for you to know is that every iostream object contains a pointer to a streambuf object, and the streambuf object has some member functions you can call if necessary. For file and string streams, there are specialized types of stream buffers, as Figure 19-3 illustrates.

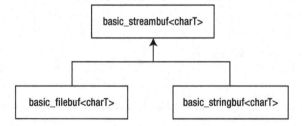

Figure 19-3. *Showing the specialized stream buffers for files and strings*

To allow you to access the streambuf, every iostream object has a member function called rdbuf() that returns the pointer to the object's streambuf. This way you can call any member function for the underlying streambuf. However, one of the most interesting things you can do with the streambuf pointer is to connect it to another iostream object using the << operator. This drains all the characters from your object into the one on the left side of the <<. If you want to move all the characters from one iostream to another, you don't need to go through the tedium (and potential coding errors) of reading them one character or one line at a time. This is a much more elegant approach. Listing 19-8 opens a file and sends the contents to standard output (similar to the previous example).

Listing 19-8. Typing a File to Standard Output

```
//: C19:Stype.cpp
// Type a file to standard output.
#include <fstream>
#include <iostream>
#include "../require.h"
using namespace std;

int main() {
  ifstream in("Stype.cpp");
  assure(in, "Stype.cpp");
  cout << in.rdbuf(); // Outputs entire file
} ///:~
```

An ifstream is created using the source code file for this program as an argument. The assure() function reports a failure if the file cannot be opened. All the work really happens in the statement

```
cout << in.rdbuf();
```

which sends the entire contents of the file to cout. This is not only more succinct to code, it is often more efficient than moving the bytes one at a time.

A form of get() writes directly into the streambuf of another object. The first argument is a reference to the destination streambuf, and the second is the terminating character ('\n' by default), which stops the get() function. So there is yet another way to print a file to standard output, shown in Listing 19-9.

Listing 19-9. Copying a File to Standard Output

```
//: C19:Sbufget.cpp
// Copies a file to standard output.
#include <fstream>
#include <iostream>
#include "../require.h"
using namespace std;

int main() {
  ifstream in("Sbufget.cpp");
  assure(in);
  streambuf& sb = *cout.rdbuf();
  while(!in.get(sb).eof()) {
    if(in.fail())            // Found blank line
      in.clear();
    cout << char(in.get()); // Process '\n'
  }
} ///:~
```

The rdbuf() function returns a pointer, so it must be dereferenced to satisfy the function's need to see an object. Stream buffers are not meant to be copied (they have no copy constructor), so you define sb as a *reference* to cout's stream buffer. You need the calls to fail() and clear() in case the input file has a blank line (this one does). When this particular overloaded version of get() sees two newlines in a row (evidence of a blank line), it sets the input stream's fail bit, so you must call clear() to reset it so that the stream can continue to be read. The second call to get() extracts and echoes each newline delimiter. (Remember, the get()function doesn't extract its delimiter like getline() does.)

You probably won't need to use a technique like this often, but it's nice to know it exists.

Seeking in iostreams

Each type of iostream has a concept of where its "next" character will come from (if it's an istream) *or* go (if it's an ostream). In some situations, you might want to move this stream position. You can do so using two models: one uses an absolute location in the stream called the streampos; the second works like the Standard C Library function fseek() for a file and moves a given number of bytes from the beginning, end, or current position in the file.

The streampos approach requires that you first call a "tell" function: tellp() for an ostream or tellg() for an istream. (The "p" refers to the *put pointer*, and the "g" refers to the *get pointer*.) This function returns a streampos you can later use in calls to seekp() for an ostream or seekg() for an istream when you want to return to that position in the stream.

The second approach is a relative seek and uses overloaded versions of seekp() and seekg(). The first argument is the number of characters to move: it can be positive or negative. The second argument is the seek location/position and is shown in Table 19-3.

Table 19-3. *The Three seek Locations in Any C++ Stream*

ios::beg	From Beginning of Stream
ios::cur	Current position in stream
ios::end	From end of stream

Listing 19-10 shows the movement through a file, but remember, you're not limited to seeking within files as you are with C's stdio. With C++, you can seek in any type of iostream (although the standard stream objects, such as cin and cout, explicitly disallow it).

Listing 19-10. Demonstration of Seeking in iostreams

```
//: C19:Seeking.cpp
// Seeking in iostreams.
#include <cassert>
#include <cstddef>
#include <cstring>
#include <fstream>
#include "../require.h"
using namespace std;

int main() {
  const int STR_NUM = 5, STR_LEN = 30;
  char origData[STR_NUM][STR_LEN] = {
    "Hickory dickory dus. . .",
    "Are you tired of C++?",
```

```
        "Well, if you have,",
        "That's just too bad,",
        "There's plenty more for us!"
    };
    char readData[STR_NUM][STR_LEN] = {{ 0 }};
    ofstream out("Poem.bin", ios::out | ios::binary);
    assure(out, "Poem.bin");
    for(int i = 0; i < STR_NUM; i++)
        out.write(origData[i], STR_LEN);
    out.close();
    ifstream in("Poem.bin", ios::in | ios::binary);
    assure(in, "Poem.bin");
    in.read(readData[0], STR_LEN);
    assert(strcmp(readData[0], "Hickory dickory dus. . .")
        == 0);

// Seek -STR_LEN bytes from the end of file
    in.seekg(-STR_LEN, ios::end);
    in.read(readData[1], STR_LEN);
    assert(strcmp(readData[1], "There's plenty more for us!")
        == 0);

// Absolute seek (like using operator[] with a file)
    in.seekg(3 * STR_LEN);
    in.read(readData[2], STR_LEN);
    assert(strcmp(readData[2], "That's just too bad,") == 0);

// Seek backwards from current position
    in.seekg(-STR_LEN * 2, ios::cur);
    in.read(readData[3], STR_LEN);
    assert(strcmp(readData[3], "Well, if you have,") == 0);

// Seek from the beginning of the file
    in.seekg(1 * STR_LEN, ios::beg);
    in.read(readData[4], STR_LEN);
    assert(strcmp(readData[4], "Are you tired of C++?")
        == 0);
} ///:~
```

This program writes a poem to a file using a binary output stream. Since you reopen it as an `ifstream`, you use `seekg()` to position the get pointer. As you can see, you can seek from the beginning or end of the file or from the current file position. Obviously, you must provide a positive number to move from the beginning of the file and a negative number to move back from the end.

Now that you know about the `streambuf` and how to seek, you can understand an alternative method (besides using an `fstream` object) for creating a stream object that will both read and write a file. The following code first creates an `ifstream` with flags that say it's both an input and an output file. You can't write to an `ifstream`, so you need to create an `ostream` with the underlying stream buffer, as in:

```
ifstream in("filename", ios::in | ios::out);
ostream out(in.rdbuf());
```

You might wonder what happens when you write to one of these objects. Listing 19-11 contains an example.

Listing 19-11. Demonstration of Reading and Writing One File

```cpp
//: C19:Iofile.cpp
// Reading & writing one file.
#include <fstream>
#include <iostream>
#include "../require.h"
using namespace std;

int main() {
  ifstream in("Iofile.cpp");
  assure(in, "Iofile.cpp");
  ofstream out("Iofile.out");
  assure(out, "Iofile.out");
  out << in.rdbuf();
   // Copy file

  in.close();
  out.close();
  // Open for reading and writing:
  ifstream in2("Iofile.out", ios::in | ios::out);
  assure(in2, "Iofile.out");
  ostream out2(in2.rdbuf());

  cout << in2.rdbuf();  // Print whole file
  out2 << "Where does this end up?";
  out2.seekp(0, ios::beg);
  out2 << "And what about this?";
  in2.seekg(0, ios::beg);

cout << in2.rdbuf();
} ///:~
```

The first five lines copy the source code for this program into a file called iofile.out and then close the files. This gives you a safe text file to play with. Then the aforementioned technique is used to create two objects that read and write to the same file. In cout << in2.rdbuf(), you can see the get pointer is initialized to the beginning of the file. The put pointer, however, is set to the end of the file because "Where does this end up?" appears appended to the file. However, if the put pointer is moved to the beginning with a seekp(), all the inserted text *overwrites* the existing text. Both writes are seen when the get pointer is moved back to the beginning with a seekg(), and the file is displayed. The file is automatically saved and closed when out2 goes out of scope and its destructor is called.

String iostreams

A string stream works directly with memory instead of a file or standard output. It uses the same reading and formatting functions that you use with cin and cout to manipulate bytes in memory. On old computers, the memory was referred to as *core,* so this type of functionality is often called *in-core formatting.*

The class names for string streams echo those for file streams. If you want to create a string stream to extract characters from, you create an istringstream. If you want to put characters into a string stream, you create an ostringstream. All declarations for string streams are in the standard header <sstream>. As usual, there are class templates that fit into the iostreams hierarchy, as shown in Figure 19-4.

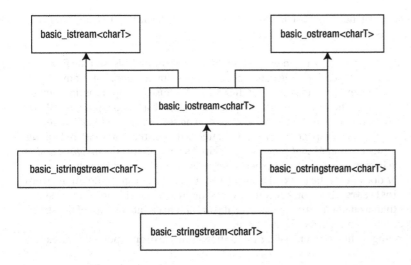

Figure 19-4. *String stream templates in the iostream inheritance hierarchy*

Input String Streams

To read from a string using stream operations, you create an `istringstream` object initialized with the string. Listing 19-12 shows how to use an `istringstream` object.

Listing 19-12. Demonstrating Input String Streams

```
//: C19:Istring.cpp
// Input string streams.
#include <cassert>
#include <cmath>      // For fabs()
#include <iostream>
#include <limits>     // For epsilon()
#include <sstream>
#include <string>
using namespace std;

int main() {
  istringstream s("47 1.414 This is a test");
  int i;
  double f;

  s >> i >> f;        // Whitespace-delimited input
  assert(i == 47);
  double relerr = (fabs(f) - 1.414) / 1.414;
  assert(relerr <= numeric_limits<double>::epsilon());
  string buf2;
  s >> buf2;
  assert(buf2 == "This");
  cout << s.rdbuf(); // " is a test"
} ///:~
```

You can see that this is a more flexible and general approach to transforming character strings to typed values than the Standard C Library functions such as atof() or atoi(), even though the latter may be more efficient for single conversions.

In the expression s >> i >> f, the first number is extracted into i, and the second into f. This isn't the first whitespace-delimited set of characters because it depends on the data type it's being extracted into. For example, if the string were instead "1.414 47 This is a test," then i would get the value 1 because the input routine would stop at the decimal point. Then f would get 0.414. This could be useful if you want to break a floating point number into a whole number and a fraction part. Otherwise, it would seem to be an error. The second assert() calculates the relative error between what you read and what you expected; it's always better to do this than to compare floating point numbers for equality. The constant returned by epsilon(), defined in <limits>, represents the *machine epsilon* for double-precision numbers, which is the best tolerance you can expect comparisons of doubles to satisfy.

As you may already have guessed, buf2 doesn't get the rest of the string, just the next whitespace-delimited word. In general, it's best to use the extractor in iostreams when you know the exact sequence of data in the input stream and you're converting to some type other than a character string. However, if you want to extract the rest of the string all at once and send it to another iostream, you can use rdbuf() as shown.

To test the Date extractor at the beginning of this chapter, Listing 19-13 shows the use of an input string stream.

Listing 19-13. Testing the Date Extractor

```cpp
//: C19:DateIOTest.cpp
//{L} ../C19/Date
#include <iostream>
#include <sstream>
#include "../Date.h"
using namespace std;

void testDate(const string& s) {
  istringstream os(s);
  Date d;
  os >> d;

  if(os)
    cout << d << endl;
  else
    cout << "input error with \"" << s << "\"" << endl;
}
int main() {
  testDate("08-10-2003");
  testDate("8-10-2003");
  testDate("08 - 10 - 2003");
  testDate("A-10-2003");
  testDate("08%10/2003");
} ///:~
```

Each string literal in main() is passed by reference to testDate(), which in turn wraps it in an istringstream so that it's possible to test the stream extractor for Date objects. The function testDate() also begins to test the inserter, operator<<().

Output string streams

To create an output string stream, you just create an `ostringstream` object, which manages a dynamically sized character buffer to hold whatever you insert. To get the formatted result as a `string` object, you call the `str()` member function, as shown in Listing 19-14.

Listing 19-14. Illustrating the Use of ostringstream

```
//: C19:Ostring.cpp {RunByHand}
// Illustrates ostringstream.
#include <iostream>
#include <sstream>
#include <string>
using namespace std;

int main() {
  cout << "type an int, a float and a string: ";
  int i;
  float f;
  cin >> i >> f;
  cin >> ws;              // Throw away white space
  string stuff;
  getline(cin, stuff); // Get rest of the line
  ostringstream os;
  os << "integer = " << i << endl;
  os << "float = " << f << endl;
  os << "string = " << stuff << endl;
  string result = os.str();
  cout << result << endl;
} ///:~
```

This is similar to the `Istring.cpp` example in Listing 19-12 that fetched an `int` and a `float`. A sample execution follows (*the keyboard input is in ITALICS*).

```
type an int, a float and a string: 10 20.5 the end
integer = 10
float = 20.5
string = the end
```

You can see that, like the other output streams, you can use the ordinary formatting tools, such as the `<<` operator and `endl`, to send bytes to the `ostringstream`. The `str()` function returns a new `string` object every time you call it so the underlying `stringbuf` object owned by the string stream is left undisturbed.

Chapter 18 contains a program, `HTMLStripper.cpp` in Listing 18-20, that removed all HTML tags and special codes from a text file. As promised, here is a more elegant version using string streams; see Listing 19-15.

Listing 19-15. Illustrating A More Elegant HTML Stripper using String Streams (the Previous One, you came across in Listing 18-20: Refer to Chapter 18)

```
//: C19:HTMLStripper2.cpp {RunByHand}
//{L} ../C19/ReplaceAll
// Filter to remove html tags and markers.
#include <cstddef>
#include <cstdlib>
```

```
#include <fstream>
#include <iostream>
#include <sstream>
#include <stdexcept>
#include <string>
#include "../ReplaceAll.h"    // To be INCLUDED from Chapter 18
#include "../require.h"
using namespace std;

string& stripHTMLTags(string& s) throw(runtime_error) {
  size_t leftPos;
  while((leftPos = s.find('<')) != string::npos) {
    size_t rightPos = s.find('>', leftPos+1);
    if(rightPos == string::npos) {
      ostringstream msg;
      msg << "Incomplete HTML tag starting in position "
          << leftPos;
      throw runtime_error(msg.str());
    }
    s.erase(leftPos, rightPos - leftPos + 1);
  }

  // Remove all special HTML characters
  replaceAll(s, "&lt;", "<");
  replaceAll(s, "&gt;", ">");
  replaceAll(s, "&amp;", "&");
  replaceAll(s, " ", " ");
  // Etc...
  return s;
}

int main(int argc, char* argv[]) {
  requireArgs(argc, 1,
    "usage: HTMLStripper2 InputFile");
  ifstream in(argv[1]);
  assure(in, argv[1]);
  // Read entire file into string; then strip
  ostringstream ss;
  ss << in.rdbuf();
  try {
    string s = ss.str();
    cout << stripHTMLTags(s) << endl;
    return EXIT_SUCCESS;
  } catch(runtime_error& x) {
    cout << x.what() << endl;
    return EXIT_FAILURE;
  }
} ///:~
```

In this program, you read the entire file into a string by inserting a `rdbuf()` call to the file stream into an `ostringstream`. Now it's an easy matter to search for HTML delimiter pairs and erase them. Listing 19-16 shows how to use a bidirectional (that is, read/write) string stream.

Listing 19-16. Reading and Writing a String Stream

```
//: C19:StringSeeking.cpp {-bor}{-dmc}
// Reads and writes a string stream.
#include <cassert>
#include <sstream>
#include <string>
using namespace std;

int main() {
  string text = "We will hook no fish";
  stringstream ss(text);
  ss.seekp(0, ios::end);
  ss << " before its time.";

  assert(ss.str() ==
    "We will hook no fish before its time.");
  // Change "hook" to "ship"
  ss.seekg(8, ios::beg);
  string word;
  ss >> word;
  assert(word == "hook");
  ss.seekp(8, ios::beg);
  ss << "ship";

  // Change "fish" to "code"
  ss.seekg(16, ios::beg);
  ss >> word;
  assert(word == "fish");
  ss.seekp(16, ios::beg);
  ss << "code";

  assert(ss.str() ==
    "We will ship no code before its time.");
  ss.str("A horse of a different color.");
  assert(ss.str() == "A horse of a different color.");
} ///:~
```

As always, to move the put pointer, you call seekp(), and to reposition the get pointer, you call seekg(). Even though I didn't show it with this example, string streams are a little more forgiving than file streams in that you can switch from reading to writing, or vice versa, at any time. You don't need to reposition the get or put pointers or flush the stream. This program also illustrates the overload of str() that replaces the stream's underlying stringbuf with a new string.

Output Stream Formatting

The goal of the iostreams design is to allow you to easily move and/or format characters. It certainly wouldn't be useful if you couldn't do most of the formatting provided by C's printf() family of functions. In this section, you'll learn all the output formatting functions that are available for iostreams, so you can format your bytes the way you want them.

The formatting functions in iostreams can be somewhat confusing at first because there's often more than one way to control the formatting: through both member functions and manipulators. To further confuse things, a generic member function sets state flags to control formatting, such as left or right justification, to use uppercase letters for hex notation, to always use a decimal point for floating point values, and so on. On the other hand, separate member functions set and read values for the fill character, the field width, and the precision.

In an attempt to clarify all this, let's first examine the internal formatting data of an iostream, along with the member functions that can modify that data. (*Everything can be controlled through the member functions, if desired.*) The manipulators will be covered separately.

Format Flags

The class ios contains data members to store all the formatting information pertaining to a stream. Some of this data has a range of values and is stored in variables: the floating-point precision, the output field width, and the character used to pad the output (normally a space). The rest of the formatting is determined by flags, which are usually combined to save space and are referred to collectively as the *format flags*. You can find out the value of the format flags with the ios::flags() member function, which takes no arguments and returns an object of type fmtflags (usually a synonym for long) that contains the current format flags. All the rest of the functions make changes to the format flags and return the previous value of the format flags, as in:

```
fmtflags ios::flags(fmtflags newflags);
fmtflags ios::setf(fmtflags ored_flag);
fmtflags ios::unsetf(fmtflags clear_flag);
fmtflags ios::setf(fmtflags bits, fmtflags field);
```

The first function forces *all* the flags to change, which is sometimes what you want. More often, you change one flag at a time using the remaining three functions.

The use of setf() can seem somewhat confusing. To know which overloaded version to use, you must know what type of flag you're changing. There are two types of flags: those that are simply on or off, and those that work in a group with other flags. The on/off flags are the simplest to understand because you turn them on with setf(fmtflags) and off with unsetf(fmtflags). These flags are shown in Table 19-4.

Table 19-4. *The On/Off Flags and Effects*

on/off flag	Effect
ios::skipws	Skip whitespace. (For input; this is the default.)
ios::showbase	Indicate the numeric base (as set, for example, by dec, oct, or hex) when printing an integral value. Input streams also recognize the base prefix when showbase is on.
ios::showpoint	Show decimal point and trailing zeros for floating point values.
ios::uppercase	Display uppercase A-F for hexadecimal values and E for scientific values.
ios::showpos	Show plus sign (+) for positive values.
ios::unitbuf	Unit buffering; the stream is flushed after each insertion.

For example, to show the plus sign for cout, you say cout.setf(ios::showpos). To stop showing the plus sign, you say cout.unsetf(ios::showpos).

The unitbuf flag controls *unit buffering*, which means that each insertion is flushed to its output stream immediately. This is handy for error tracing, so that in case of a program crash, your data is still written to the log file. Listing 19-17 illustrates unit buffering.

Listing 19-17. Illustrating the Use of Unit Buffering

```
//: C19:Unitbuf.cpp {RunByHand}
#include <cstdlib>  // For abort()
#include <fstream>
using namespace std;

int main() {
  ofstream out("log.txt");
  out.setf(ios::unitbuf);
  out << "one" << endl;
  out << "two" << endl;
  abort();
} ///:~
```

It is necessary to turn on unit buffering before any insertions are made to the stream. When I commented out the call to setf(), one particular compiler had written only the letter "o" to the file log.txt. With unit buffering, no data was lost.

The standard error output stream cerr has unit buffering turned on by default. There is a cost for unit buffering, so if an output stream is heavily used, don't enable unit buffering unless efficiency is not a consideration.

Format Fields

The second type of formatting flags work in a group. Only one of these flags can be set at a time, like the buttons on old car radios—you push one in, the rest pop out. Unfortunately this doesn't happen automatically, and you must pay attention to what flags you're setting so that you don't accidentally call the wrong setf() function. For example, there's a flag for each of the number bases: hexadecimal, decimal, and octal. Collectively, these flags are referred to as the ios::basefield. If the ios::dec flag is set and you call setf(ios::hex), you'll set the ios::hex flag, but you *won't* clear the ios::dec bit, resulting in undefined behavior. Instead, call the second form of setf() like this: setf(ios::hex, ios::basefield). This function first clears all the bits in the ios::basefield and *then* sets ios::hex. Thus, this form of setf() ensures that the *other flags in the group* "pop out" whenever you set one. The ios::hex manipulator does all this for you, automatically, so you don't need to concern yourself with the internal details of the implementation of this class or to even *care* that it's a set of binary flags. Later you'll see that there are manipulators to provide equivalent functionality in all the places you would use setf().The flag groups and their effects are shown in Table 19-5.

Table 19-5. *The Three Flag Groups and Effects*

ios::basefield	Effect
ios::dec	Formats integral values in base 10 (decimal) (the default radix—no prefix is visible).
ios::hex	Formats integral values in base 16 (hexadecimal).
ios::oct	Formats integral values in base 8 (octal).
ios::floatfield	Effect
ios::scientific	Displays floating point numbers in scientific format. Precision field indicates number of digits after the decimal point.
ios::fixed	Displays floating point numbers in fixed format. Precision field indicates number of digits after the decimal point.
"automatic" (Neither bit is set.)	Precision field indicates the total number of significant digits.
ios::adjustfield	Effect
ios::left	Left-align values; pad on the right with the fill character.
ios::right	Right-align values. Pad on the left with the fill character. This is the default alignment.
ios::internal	Adds fill characters after any leading sign or base indicator, but before the value. (In other words, the sign, if printed, is left-justified while the number is right-justified.)

Width, Fill, and Precision

The internal variables that control the width of the output field, the fill character used to pad an output field, and the precision for printing floating point numbers are read and written by member functions of the same name. See Table 19-6.

Table 19-6. *Width, Fill, and Precision Functions, and Effects*

Function	Effect
int ios::width( )	Returns the current width. Default is 0. Used for both insertion and extraction.
int ios::width(int n)	Sets the width and returns the previous width.
int ios::fill( )	Returns the current fill character. Default is space.
int ios::fill(int n)	Sets the fill character and returns the previous fill character.
int ios::precision( )	Returns current floating point precision. Default is 6.
int ios::precision(int n)	Sets floating point precision and returns previous precision. See ios::floatfield in Table 19-5 for the meaning of "precision."

The fill and precision values are fairly straightforward, but width requires some explanation. When the width is zero, inserting a value produces the minimum number of characters necessary to represent that value. A positive width means that inserting a value will produce at least as many characters as the width; if the value has fewer than width characters, the fill character pad the field. However, the value will never be truncated, so if you try to print 123 with a width of two, you'll still get 123. The field width specifies a *minimum* number of characters; there's no way to specify a maximum number.

The width is also distinctly different because it is reset to zero by each inserter or extractor that could be influenced by its value. It's really not a state variable, but rather an implicit argument to the inserters and extractors. If you want a constant width, call width() after each insertion or extraction.

An Exhaustive Example

To make sure you know how to call all the functions previously discussed, Listing 19-18 calls them all.

Listing 19-18. Illustrating All the Formatting Functions

```
//: C19:Format.cpp
// Formatting Functions.
#include <fstream>
#include <iostream>
#include "../require.h"
using namespace std;
#define D(A) T << #A << endl; A

int main() {
  ofstream T("format.out");
  assure(T);
  D(int i = 47;)
  D(float f = 2300114.414159;)
  const char* s = "Is there any more?";

  D(T.setf(ios::unitbuf);)
  D(T.setf(ios::showbase);)
  D(T.setf(ios::uppercase | ios::showpos);)
  D(T << i << endl;) // Default is dec
  D(T.setf(ios::hex, ios::basefield);)
  D(T << i << endl;)
  D(T.setf(ios::oct, ios::basefield);)
  D(T << i << endl;)
  D(T.unsetf(ios::showbase);)
  D(T.setf(ios::dec, ios::basefield);)
  D(T.setf(ios::left, ios::adjustfield);)
  D(T.fill('0');)
  D(T << "fill char: " << T.fill() << endl;)
  D(T.width(10);)
  T << i << endl;
  D(T.setf(ios::right, ios::adjustfield);)
  D(T.width(10);)
  T << i << endl;
  D(T.setf(ios::internal, ios::adjustfield);)
  D(T.width(10);)
  T << i << endl;
  D(T << i << endl;) // Without width(10)

  D(T.unsetf(ios::showpos);)
  D(T.setf(ios::showpoint);)
  D(T << "prec = " << T.precision() << endl;)
  D(T.setf(ios::scientific, ios::floatfield);)
```

```
  D(T << endl << f << endl;)
  D(T.unsetf(ios::uppercase);)
  D(T << endl << f << endl;)
  D(T.setf(ios::fixed, ios::floatfield);)
  D(T << f << endl;)
  D(T.precision(20);)
  D(T << "prec = " << T.precision() << endl;)
  D(T << endl << f << endl;)
  D(T.setf(ios::scientific, ios::floatfield);)
  D(T << endl << f << endl;)
  D(T.setf(ios::fixed, ios::floatfield);)
  D(T << f << endl;)

  D(T.width(10);)
  T << s << endl;
  D(T.width(40);)
  T << s << endl;
  D(T.setf(ios::left, ios::adjustfield);)
  D(T.width(40);)
  T << s << endl;
} ///:~
```

/* This example uses a trick to create a trace file so that you can monitor what's happening. The macro D(a) uses the preprocessor stringizing to turn a into a string to display. Then it reiterates a so the statement is executed. The macro sends all the information to a file called T, which is the trace file.*/

The output is

```
int i = 47;
float f = 2300114.414159;
T.setf(ios::unitbuf);
T.setf(ios::showbase);
T.setf(ios::uppercase | ios::showpos);
T << i << endl;
+47
T.setf(ios::hex, ios::basefield);
T << i << endl;
0X2F
T.setf(ios::oct, ios::basefield);
T << i << endl;
057
T.unsetf(ios::showbase);
T.setf(ios::dec, ios::basefield);
T.setf(ios::left, ios::adjustfield);
T.fill('0');
T << "fill char: " << T.fill() << endl;
fill char: 0
T.width(10);
+470000000
T.setf(ios::right, ios::adjustfield);
T.width(10);
0000000+47
```

```
T.setf(ios::internal, ios::adjustfield);
T.width(10);
+000000047
T << i << endl;
+47
T.unsetf(ios::showpos);
T.setf(ios::showpoint);
T << "prec = " << T.precision() << endl;
prec = 6
T.setf(ios::scientific, ios::floatfield);
T << endl << f << endl;

2.300114E+06
T.unsetf(ios::uppercase);
T << endl << f << endl;

2.300114e+06
T.setf(ios::fixed, ios::floatfield);
T << f << endl;

2300114.500000
T.precision(20);
T << "prec = " << T.precision() << endl;
prec = 20
T << endl << f << endl;

2300114.50000000000000000000
T.setf(ios::scientific, ios::floatfield);
T << endl << f << endl;

2.3001145000000000000e+06
T.setf(ios::fixed, ios::floatfield);
T << f << endl;

2300114.50000000000000000000
T.width(10);
Is there any more?
T.width(40);
0000000000000000000000000Is there any more?
T.setf(ios::left, ios::adjustfield);
T.width(40);
Is there any more?0000000000000000000000000
```

Studying this output should clarify your understanding of the iostream formatting member functions.

Manipulators

As you can see from Listing 19-18, calling the member functions for stream formatting operations can get a bit tedious. To make things easier to read and write, a set of *manipulators* is supplied to duplicate the actions provided by the member functions. Manipulators are a convenience because you can insert them for their effect within a containing expression; you don't need to create a separate function-call statement.

Manipulators change the state of the stream instead of (*or* in addition to) processing data. When you insert endl in an output expression, for example, it not only inserts a newline character, but it also *flushes* the stream (that is, puts out all pending characters that have been stored in the internal stream buffer but not yet output). You can also just flush a stream like this

```
cout << flush;
```

which causes a call to the flush() member function, as in

```
cout.flush();
```

as a side effect (nothing is inserted into the stream). Additional basic manipulators will change the number base to oct (octal), dec (decimal) or hex (hexadecimal), as in:

```
cout << hex << "0x" << i << endl;
```

In this case, numeric output will continue in hexadecimal mode until you change it by inserting either dec or oct in the output stream.

There's also a manipulator for extraction that "eats" whitespace:

```
cin >> ws;
```

Manipulators with no arguments are provided in <iostream>. These include dec, oct, and hex, which perform the same action as, respectively, setf(ios::dec, ios::basefield), setf(ios::oct, ios::basefield), and setf(ios::hex, ios::basefield), albeit more succinctly. The <iostream> header also includes ws, endl, and flush and the additional set shown in Table 19-7.

Table 19-7. *Manipulators (Additional) Defined in <iostream>*

Manipulator	Effect
showbase noshowbase	Indicates the numeric base (dec, oct, or hex) when printing an integral value.
showpos noshowpos	Shows plus sign (+) for positive values.
uppercase nouppercase	Displays uppercase A-F for hexadecimal values, and display E for scientific values.
showpoint noshowpoint	Shows decimal point and trailing zeros for floating-point values.
skipws noskipws	Skips whitespace on input.
left right internal	Left-align, pad on right. Right-align, pad on left. Fill between leading sign or base indicator and value.
scientific fixed	Indicates the display preference for floating point output (scientific notation vs. fixed-point decimal).

Manipulators with Arguments

There are six standard manipulators, such as setw(), that take arguments. These are defined in the header file <iomanip>, and are summarized in Table 19-8.

Table 19-8. *Manipulators with Arguments Defined in <iomanip>*

Manipulator	Effect
setiosflags(fmtflags n)	Equivalent to a call to setf(n). The setting remains in effect until the next change, such as ios::setf().
resetiosflags(fmtflags n)	Clears only the format flags specified by n. The setting remains in effect until the next change, such as ios::unsetf().
setbase(base n)	Changes base to n, where n is 10, 8, or 16. (Anything else results in 0.) If n is zero, output is base 10, but input uses the C conventions: 10 is 10, 010 is 8, and 0xf is 15. You might as well use dec, oct, and hex for output.
setfill(char n)	Changes the fill character to n, such as ios::fill().
setprecision(int n)	Changes the precision to n, such as ios::precision().
setw(int n)	Changes the field width to n, such as ios::width().

If you're doing a lot of formatting, you can see how using manipulators instead of calling stream member functions can clean up your code. As an example, Listing 19-19 contains the program from the previous section rewritten to use the manipulators. (The D() macro is removed to make it easier to read.)

Listing 19-19. Illustrating the Use of Manipulators

```
//: C19:Manips.cpp
// Format.cpp using manipulators.
#include <fstream>
#include <iomanip>
#include <iostream>
using namespace std;

int main() {
  ofstream trc("trace.out");
  int i = 47;
  float f = 2300114.414159;
  char* s = "Is there any more?";

  trc << setiosflags(ios::unitbuf
          | ios::showbase | ios::uppercase
          | ios::showpos);
  trc << i << endl;
  trc << hex << i << endl
      << oct << i << endl;
  trc.setf(ios::left, ios::adjustfield);
  trc << resetiosflags(ios::showbase)
      << dec << setfill('0');
  trc << "fill char: " << trc.fill() << endl;
```

```
    trc << setw(10) << i << endl;
    trc.setf(ios::right, ios::adjustfield);
    trc << setw(10) << i << endl;
    trc.setf(ios::internal, ios::adjustfield);
    trc << setw(10) << i << endl;
    trc << i << endl; // Without setw(10)

    trc << resetiosflags(ios::showpos)
        << setiosflags(ios::showpoint)
        << "prec = " << trc.precision() << endl;
    trc.setf(ios::scientific, ios::floatfield);
    trc << f << resetiosflags(ios::uppercase) << endl;
    trc.setf(ios::fixed, ios::floatfield);
    trc << f << endl;
    trc << f << endl;
    trc << setprecision(20);
    trc << "prec = " << trc.precision() << endl;
    trc << f << endl;
    trc.setf(ios::scientific, ios::floatfield);
    trc << f << endl;
    trc.setf(ios::fixed, ios::floatfield);
    trc << f << endl;
    trc << f << endl;

    trc << setw(10) << s << endl;
    trc << setw(40) << s << endl;
    trc.setf(ios::left, ios::adjustfield);
    trc << setw(40) << s << endl;
} ///:~
```

You can see that a lot of the multiple statements have been condensed into a single chained insertion. Notice the call to setiosflags() in which the bitwise-OR of the flags is passed. This could also have been done with setf() and unsetf() as in the previous example (Listing 19-18).

When using setw() with an output stream, the output expression is formatted into a temporary string that is padded with the current fill character if needed, as determined by comparing the length of the formatted result to the argument of setw(). In other words, setw() affects the *result string* of a formatted output operation. Likewise, using setw() with input streams only is meaningful when reading *strings*, as Listing 19-20 makes clear.

Listing 19-20. Illustrating Limitations of setw with Input

```
//: C19:InputWidth.cpp
// Shows limitations of setw with input.
#include <cassert>
#include <cmath>
#include <iomanip>
#include <limits>
#include <sstream>
#include <string>
using namespace std;
```

```
int main() {
  istringstream is("one 2.34 five");
  string temp;
  is >> setw(2) >> temp;
  assert(temp == "on");
  is >> setw(2) >> temp;
  assert(temp == "e");
  double x;
  is >> setw(2) >> x;
  double relerr = fabs(x - 2.34) / x;
  assert(relerr <= numeric_limits<double>::epsilon());
} ///:~
```

If you attempt to read a string, setw() will control the number of characters extracted quite nicely... up to a point. The first extraction gets two characters, but the second only gets one, even though you asked for two. That is because operator>>() uses whitespace as a delimiter (unless you turn off the skipws flag). When trying to read a number, however, such as x, you cannot use setw() to limit the characters read. With input streams, use only setw() for extracting strings.

Creating Manipulators

Sometimes you'd like to create your own manipulators, and it turns out to be remarkably simple. A zero-argument manipulator such as endl is simply a function that takes as its argument an ostream reference and returns an ostream reference. The declaration for endl is

```
ostream& endl(ostream&);
```

Now, when you say

```
cout << "howdy" << endl;
```

the endl produces the *address* of that function. So the compiler asks, "Is there a function that can be applied here that takes the address of a function as its argument?" Predefined functions in <iostream> do this; they're called *applicators* (because they *apply* a function to a stream). The applicator calls its function argument, passing it the ostream object as its argument. You don't need to know how applicators *work to* create your own manipulator; you only need to know that they exist. Here's the (simplified) code for an ostream applicator:

```
ostream& ostream::operator<<(ostream& (*pf)(ostream&)) {
  return pf(*this);
}
```

The actual definition is a little more complicated since it involves templates, but this code illustrates the technique. When a function such as *pf (that takes a stream parameter and returns a stream reference) is inserted into a stream, this applicator function is called, which in turn executes the function to which pf points. Applicators for ios_base, basic_ios, basic_ostream, and basic_istream are predefined in the Standard C++ Library.

To illustrate the process, Listing 19-21 is a trivial example that creates a manipulator called nl that is equivalent to just inserting a newline into a stream (i.e., no flushing of the stream occurs, as with endl).

Listing 19-21. Illustrating Creation of a Manipulator

```
//: C19:nl.cpp
// Creating a manipulator.
#include <iostream>
using namespace std;

ostream& nl(ostream& os) {
  return os << '\n';
}

int main() {
  cout << "newlines" << nl << "between" << nl
       << "each" << nl << "word" << nl;
} ///:~
```

When you insert `nl` into an output stream, such as `cout`, the following sequence of calls ensues:

```
cout.operator<<(nl) è nl(cout)
```

The expression

```
os << '\n';
```

inside `nl()` calls `ostream::operator(char)`, which returns the stream, which is what is ultimately returned from `nl()`.

Effectors

As you've seen, zero-argument manipulators are easy to create. But what if you want to create a manipulator that takes arguments? If you inspect the `<iomanip>` header, you'll see a type called `smanip`, which is what the manipulators with arguments return. You might be tempted to somehow use that type to define your own manipulators, but don't do it. The `smanip` type is implementation-dependent and thus not portable. Fortunately, you can define such manipulators in a straightforward way without any special machinery, based on a technique called an *effector*. An effector is a simple class whose constructor formats a string representing the desired operation, along with an overloaded `operator<<` to insert that string into a stream. Listing 19-22 is an example with two effectors. The first outputs a truncated character string, and the second prints a number in binary.

Listing 19-22. Illustrating the Use of Two Effectors (the Former Outputs a Truncated char String while the Latter Prints a Number in Binary Format)

```
//: C19:Effector.cpp
#include <cassert>
#include <limits>  // For max()
#include <sstream>
#include <string>
using namespace std;
```

```
// Put out a prefix of a string:
class Fixw {
  string str;
public:
  Fixw(const string& s, int width) : str(s, 0, width) {}
  friend ostream& operator<<(ostream& os, const Fixw& fw) {
    return os << fw.str;
  }
};

// Print a number in binary:
typedef unsigned long ulong;

class Bin {
  ulong n;
public:
  Bin(ulong nn) { n = nn; }
  friend ostream& operator<<(ostream& os, const Bin& b) {
    const ulong ULMAX = numeric_limits<ulong>::max();
    ulong bit = ~(ULMAX >> 1); // Top bit set
    while(bit) {
      os << (b.n & bit ? '1' : '0');
      bit >>= 1;
    }
    return os;
  }
};
int main() {
  string words = "Things that make us happy, make us wise";
  for(int i = words.size(); --i >= 0;) {
    ostringstream s;
    s << Fixw(words, i);
    assert(s.str() == words.substr(0, i));
  }
  ostringstream xs, ys;
  xs << Bin(0xCAFEBABEUL);
  assert(xs.str() ==
    "1100""1010""1111""1110""1011""1010""1011""1110");
  ys << Bin(0x76543210UL);
  assert(ys.str() ==
    "0111""0110""0101""0100""0011""0010""0001""0000");
} ///:~
```

The constructor for Fixw creates a shortened copy of its char* argument, and the destructor releases the memory created for this copy. The overloaded operator<< takes the contents of its second argument, the Fixw object, inserts it into the first argument, the ostream, and then returns the ostream so that it can be used in a chained expression. When you use Fixw in an expression like this

```
cout << Fixw(string, i) << endl;
```

a *temporary object* is created by the call to the Fixw constructor, and that temporary object is passed to operator<<. The effect is that of a manipulator with arguments. The temporary Fixw object persists until the end of the statement.

The Bin effector relies on the fact that shifting an unsigned number to the right shifts zeros into the high bits. I use numeric_limits<unsigned long>::max() (the largest unsigned long value, from the standard header <limits>) to produce a value with the high bit set, and this value is moved across the number in question (by shifting it to the right), masking each bit in turn. I've juxtaposed string literals in the code for readability; the separate strings are concatenated into a single string by the compiler.

Historically, the problem with this technique was that once you created a class called Fixw for char* or Bin for unsigned long, no one else could create a different Fixw or Bin class for their type. However, with namespaces, this problem is eliminated. Effectors and manipulators aren't equivalent, although they can often be used to solve the same problem. If you find that an effector isn't enough, you will need to conquer the complexity of manipulators.

iostream Examples

In this section, you'll see examples that use what you've learned in this chapter. Although many tools exist to manipulate bytes (stream editors such as sed and awk from Unix are perhaps the most well-known, but a text editor also fits this category), they generally have some limitations. Both sed and awk can be slow and can only handle lines in a forward sequence, and text editors usually require human interaction, or at least learning a proprietary macro language. The programs you write with iostreams have none of these limitations: they're fast, portable, and flexible.

Maintaining Class Library Source Code

Generally, when you create a class, you think in library terms: you make a header file Name.h for the class declaration, and then create a file called Name.cpp where the member functions are implemented. These files have certain requirements: a particular coding standard (the program shown here uses the coding format for this book), and preprocessor statements surrounding the code in the header file to prevent multiple declarations of classes. (Multiple declarations confuse the compiler—it doesn't know which one you want to use. They could be different, so it throws up its hands and gives an error message.)

Listing 19-23 creates a new header/implementation pair of files or modifies an existing pair. If the files already exist, it checks and potentially modifies the files, but if they don't exist, it creates them using the proper format.

Listing 19-23. Testing Files for Conformance

```
//: C19:Cppcheck.cpp
// Configures .h & .cpp files to conform to style
// standard. Tests existing files for conformance.

#include <fstream>
#include <sstream>
#include <string>
#include <cstddef>
#include "../require.h"
using namespace std;

bool startsWith(const string& base, const string& key) {
  return base.compare(0, key.size(), key) == 0;
}
```

```cpp
void cppCheck(string fileName) {
  enum bufs { BASE, HEADER, IMPLEMENT, HLINE1, GUARD1,
    GUARD2, GUARD3, CPPLINE1, INCLUDE, BUFNUM };
  string part[BUFNUM];
  part[BASE] = fileName;

  // Find any '.' in the string:
  size_t loc = part[BASE].find('.');
  if(loc != string::npos)
    part[BASE].erase(loc);  // Strip extension

  // Force to upper case:
  for(size_t i = 0; i < part[BASE].size(); i++)
    part[BASE][i] = toupper(part[BASE][i]);

  // Create file names and internal lines:
  part[HEADER] = part[BASE] + ".h";
  part[IMPLEMENT] = part[BASE] + ".cpp";
  part[HLINE1] = "//" ": " + part[HEADER];
  part[GUARD1] = "#ifndef " + part[BASE] + "_H";
  part[GUARD2] = "#define " + part[BASE] + "_H";
  part[GUARD3] = "#endif // " + part[BASE] +"_H";
  part[CPPLINE1] = string("//") + ": " + part[IMPLEMENT];
  part[INCLUDE] = "#include \"" + part[HEADER] + "\"";
  // First, try to open existing files:
  ifstream existh(part[HEADER].c_str()),
           existcpp(part[IMPLEMENT].c_str());

  if(!existh) { // Doesn't exist; create it
    ofstream newheader(part[HEADER].c_str());
    assure(newheader, part[HEADER].c_str());
    newheader << part[HLINE1] << endl
              << part[GUARD1] << endl
              << part[GUARD2] << endl << endl
              << part[GUARD3] << endl;
  } else { // Already exists; verify it
    stringstream hfile; // Write & read
    ostringstream newheader; // Write
    hfile << existh.rdbuf();

    // Check that first three lines conform:
    bool changed = false;
    string s;
    hfile.seekg(0);
    getline(hfile, s);
    bool lineUsed = false;

    // The call to good() is for Microsoft (later too):
    for(int line = HLINE1; hfile.good() && line <= GUARD2;
        ++line) {
      if(startsWith(s, part[line])) {
        newheader << s << endl;
        lineUsed = true;
```

```
        if(getline(hfile, s))
          lineUsed = false;
      } else {
      newheader << part[line] << endl;
      changed = true;
      lineUsed = false;
      }
    }

    // Copy rest of file
    if(!lineUsed)
      newheader << s << endl;
    newheader << hfile.rdbuf();

    // Check for GUARD3
    string head = hfile.str();
    if(head.find(part[GUARD3]) == string::npos) {
      newheader << part[GUARD3] << endl;
      changed = true;
    }

    // If there were changes, overwrite file:
    if(changed) {
      existh.close();
      ofstream newH(part[HEADER].c_str());
      assure(newH, part[HEADER].c_str());
      newH << "//@//\n"   // Change marker
           << newheader.str();
    }
  }

if(!existcpp) { // Create cpp file
    ofstream newcpp(part[IMPLEMENT].c_str());
    assure(newcpp, part[IMPLEMENT].c_str());
    newcpp << part[CPPLINE1] << endl
           << part[INCLUDE] << endl;
  } else { // Already exists; verify it
    stringstream cppfile;
    ostringstream newcpp;
    cppfile << existcpp.rdbuf();

    // Check that first two lines conform:
    bool changed = false;
    string s;
    cppfile.seekg(0);
    getline(cppfile, s);
    bool lineUsed = false;
    for(int line = CPPLINE1;
        cppfile.good() && line <= INCLUDE; ++line) {
      if(startsWith(s, part[line])) {
        newcpp << s << endl;
        lineUsed = true;
```

```
      if(getline(cppfile, s))
        lineUsed = false;
    } else {
      newcpp << part[line] << endl;
      changed = true;
      lineUsed = false;
    }
  }

  // Copy rest of file
  if(!lineUsed)
    newcpp << s << endl;
  newcpp << cppfile.rdbuf();

  // If there were changes, overwrite file:
  if(changed) {
    existcpp.close();
    ofstream newCPP(part[IMPLEMENT].c_str());
    assure(newCPP, part[IMPLEMENT].c_str());
    newCPP << "//@//\n"  // Change marker
           << newcpp.str();
  }
 }
}

int main(int argc, char* argv[]) {
  if(argc > 1)
    cppCheck(argv[1]);
  else
    cppCheck("cppCheckTest.h");
} ///:~
```

First, notice the useful function startsWith(), which does just what its name says—it returns true if the first string argument starts with the second argument. This is used when looking for the expected comments and include-related statements. Having the array of strings, part, allows for easy looping through the series of expected statements in source code. If the source file doesn't exist, you merely write the statements to a new file of the given name. If the file does exist, you search a line at a time, verifying that the expected lines occur. If they are not present, they are inserted. Special care must be taken to make sure you don't drop existing lines (see the location of the Boolean variable lineUsed). Notice the use of a stringstream for an existing file, so you can first write the contents of the file to it and then read from and search it.

The names in the enumeration are BASE, the capitalized base file name without extension; HEADER, the header file name; IMPLEMENT, the implementation file (cpp) name; HLINE1, the skeleton first line of the header file; GUARD1, GUARD2, and GUARD3, the "guard" lines in the header file (to prevent multiple inclusion); CPPLINE1, the skeleton first line of the cpp file; and INCLUDE, the line in the cpp file that includes the header file.

If you run this program without any arguments, the following two files are created:

```
// CPPCHECKTEST.h
#ifndef CPPCHECKTEST_H
#define CPPCHECKTEST_H
#endif // CPPCHECKTEST_H

// CPPCHECKTEST.cpp
#include "CPPCHECKTEST.h" // To be INCLUDED from above
```

■ **Note**   I removed the colon after the double-slash in the first comment lines so as not to confuse the book's code extractor. It will appear in the actual output produced by cppCheck.

You can experiment by removing selected lines from these files and rerunning the program. Each time you will see that the correct lines are added back in. When a file is modified, the string "//@//" is placed as the first line of the file to bring the change to your attention. You will need to remove this line before you process the file again (otherwise cppCheck will assume the initial comment line is missing).

Detecting Compiler Errors

All the code in this book is designed to compile as shown without errors. Lines of code that should generate a compile-time error may be commented out with the special comment sequence "//!". Listing 19-24 will remove these special comments and append a numbered comment to the line. When you run your compiler, it should generate error messages, and you will see all the numbers appear when you compile all the files. This program also appends the modified line to a special file so that you can easily locate any lines that don't generate errors.

Listing 19-24. Un-commenting Error Generators

```
//: C19:Showerr.cpp {RunByHand}
// Uncomment error generators.
#include <cstddef>
#include <cstdlib>
#include <cstdio>
#include <fstream>
#include <iostream>
#include <sstream>
#include <string>
#include "../require.h"
using namespace std;

const string USAGE =
  "usage: showerr filename chapnum\n"
  "where filename is a C++ source file\n"
  "and chapnum is the chapter name it's in.\n"
  "Finds lines commented with //! and removes\n"
  "the comment, appending //(#) where # is unique\n"
  "across all files, so you can determine\n"
  "if your compiler finds the error.\n"
  "showerr /r\n"
  "resets the unique counter.";

class Showerr {
  const int CHAP;
  const string MARKER, FNAME;
  // File containing error number counter:
  const string ERRNUM;
```

```cpp
    // File containing error lines:
    const string ERRFILE;
    stringstream edited; // Edited file
    int counter;
public:
  Showerr(const string& f, const string& en,
    const string& ef, int c)
  : CHAP(c), MARKER("//!"), FNAME(f), ERRNUM(en),
    ERRFILE(ef), counter(0) {}
  void replaceErrors() {
    ifstream infile(FNAME.c_str());
    assure(infile, FNAME.c_str());
    ifstream count(ERRNUM.c_str());
    if(count) count >> counter;
    int linecount = 1;
    string buf;
    ofstream errlines(ERRFILE.c_str(), ios::app);
    assure(errlines, ERRFILE.c_str());
    while(getline(infile, buf)) {
      // Find marker at start of line:
      size_t pos = buf.find(MARKER);
      if(pos != string::npos) {
        // Erase marker:
        buf.erase(pos, MARKER.size() + 1);
        // Append counter & error info:
        ostringstream out;
        out << buf << " // (" << ++counter << ") "
            << "Chapter " << CHAP
            << " File: " << FNAME
            << " Line " << linecount << endl;
        edited << out.str();
        errlines << out.str();      // Append error file
      }
      else
        edited << buf << "\n";       // Just copy
      ++linecount;
    }
  }
  void saveFiles() {
    ofstream outfile(FNAME.c_str()); // Overwrites
    assure(outfile, FNAME.c_str());
    outfile << edited.rdbuf();
    ofstream count(ERRNUM.c_str());  // Overwrites
    assure(count, ERRNUM.c_str());
    count << counter; // Save new counter
  }
};
```

```
int main(int argc, char* argv[]) {
  const string ERRCOUNT("../errnum.txt"),
    ERRFILE("../errlines.txt");
  requireMinArgs(argc, 1, USAGE.c_str());
  if(argv[1][0] == '/' || argv[1][0] == '-') {
    // Allow for other switches:
    switch(argv[1][1]) {
      case 'r': case 'R':
        cout << "reset counter" << endl;
        remove(ERRCOUNT.c_str());    // Delete files
        remove(ERRFILE.c_str());
        return EXIT_SUCCESS;
      default:
        cerr << USAGE << endl;
        return EXIT_FAILURE;
    }
  }
  if(argc == 3) {
    Showerr s(argv[1], ERRCOUNT, ERRFILE, atoi(argv[2]));
    s.replaceErrors();
    s.saveFiles();
  }
} ///:~
```

You can replace the marker with one of your choice.

Each file is read a line at a time, and each line is searched for the marker appearing at the head of the line; the line is modified and put into the error line list and into the string stream, edited. When the whole file is processed, it is closed (by reaching the end of a scope), it is reopened as an output file, and edited is poured into the file. Also notice the counter is saved in an external file. The next time this program is invoked, it continues to increment the counter.

A Simple Data Logger

Listing 19-25 shows an approach you might take to log data to disk and later retrieve it for processing. It is meant to produce a temperature-depth profile of the ocean at various points. The DataPoint class holds the data.

Listing 19-25. Illustrating A Simple Datalogger Record Layout

```
//: C19:DataLogger.h
// Datalogger record layout.
#ifndef DATALOG_H
#define DATALOG_H
#include <ctime>
#include <iosfwd>
#include <string>
using std::ostream;

struct Coord {
  int deg, min, sec;
  Coord(int d = 0, int m = 0, int s = 0)
  : deg(d), min(m), sec(s) {}
  std::string toString() const;
};
```

```
ostream& operator<<(ostream&, const Coord&);
class DataPoint {
  std::time_t timestamp; // Time & day
  Coord latitude, longitude;
  double depth, temperature;
public:
  DataPoint(std::time_t ts, const Coord& lat,
            const Coord& lon, double dep, double temp)
   : timestamp(ts), latitude(lat), longitude(lon),
       depth(dep), temperature(temp) {}
  DataPoint() : timestamp(0), depth(0), temperature(0) {}
  friend ostream& operator<<(ostream&, const DataPoint&);
};
#endif // DATALOG_H ///:~
```

A DataPoint consists of a time stamp, which is stored as a time_t value as defined in <ctime>, longitude and latitude coordinates, and values for depth and temperature. Note the use of inserters for easy formatting. Listing 19-26 contains the implementation file.

Listing 19-26. Implementing the header file in Listing 19-25 (DataLogger.h)

```
//: C19:DataLogger.cpp {O}
// Datapoint implementations.
#include "DataLogger.h"// To be INCLUDED from Header FILE above
#include <iomanip>
#include <iostream>
#include <sstream>
#include <string>
using namespace std;

ostream& operator<<(ostream& os, const Coord& c) {
  return os << c.deg << '*' << c.min << '\''
            << c.sec << '"';
}

string Coord::toString() const {
  ostringstream os;
  os << *this;
  return os.str();
}

ostream& operator<<(ostream& os, const DataPoint& d) {
  os.setf(ios::fixed, ios::floatfield);
  char fillc = os.fill('0'); // Pad on left with '0'
  tm* tdata = localtime(&d.timestamp);
  os << setw(2) << tdata->tm_mon + 1 << '\\'
     << setw(2) << tdata->tm_mday << '\\'
     << setw(2) << tdata->tm_year+1900 << ' '
     << setw(2) << tdata->tm_hour << ':'
     << setw(2) << tdata->tm_min << ':'
     << setw(2) << tdata->tm_sec;
  os.fill(' '); // Pad on left with ' '
```

```
   streamsize prec = os.precision(4);
   os << " Lat:"     << setw(9) << d.latitude.toString()
      << ", Long:"   << setw(9) << d.longitude.toString()
      << ", depth:"  << setw(9) << d.depth
      << ", temp:"   << setw(9) << d.temperature;

   os.fill(fillc);
   os.precision(prec);
   return os;
} ///:~
```

The Coord::toString() function is necessary because the DataPoint inserter calls setw() before it prints the latitude and longitude. If you used the stream inserter for Coord instead, the width would only apply to the first insertion (that is, to Coord::deg), since width changes are always reset immediately. The call to setf() causes the floating point output to be fixed-precision, and precision() sets the number of decimal places to four. Notice how you restore the fill character and precision to whatever they were before the inserter was called.

To get the values from the time encoding stored in DataPoint::timestamp, you call the function std::localtime(), which returns a static pointer to a tm object. The tmstruct has the following layout:

```
struct tm {
  int tm_sec;        // 0-59 seconds
  int tm_min;        // 0-59 minutes
  int tm_hour;       // 0-23 hours
  int tm_mday;       // Day of month
  int tm_mon;        // 0-11 months
  int tm_year;       // Years since 1900
  int tm_wday;       // Sunday == 0, etc.
  int tm_yday;       // 0-365 day of year
  int tm_isdst;      // Daylight savings?
};
```

Generating Test Data

Listing 19-27 creates a file of test data in binary form (using write()) and a second file in ASCII form using the DataPoint inserter. You can also print it out to the screen, but it's easier to inspect in file form.

Listing 19-27. Illustrating Generation of Test Data (using write( ) and the DataPoint Inserter)

```
//: C19:Datagen.cpp
// Test data generator.
//{L} DataLogger
#include <cstdlib>
#include <ctime>
#include <cstring>
#include <fstream>
#include "DataLogger.h"
#include "../require.h"
using namespace std;

int main() {
  time_t timer;
  srand(time(&timer)); // Seed the random number generator
```

```
ofstream data("data.txt");
assure(data, "data.txt");

ofstream bindata("data.bin", ios::binary);
assure(bindata, "data.bin");

for(int i = 0; i < 100; i++, timer += 55) {
  // Zero to 199 meters:
  double newdepth  = rand() % 200;
  double fraction = rand() % 100 + 1;
  newdepth += 1.0 / fraction;
  double newtemp = 150 + rand() % 200; // Kelvin
  fraction = rand() % 100 + 1;
  newtemp += 1.0 / fraction;

  const DataPoint d(timer, Coord(45,20,31),
                    Coord(22,34,18), newdepth,
                    newtemp);
  data << d << endl;
  bindata.write(reinterpret_cast<const char*>(&d),
            sizeof(d));
}
} ///:~
```

The file data.txt is created in the ordinary way as an ASCII file, but data.bin has the flag ios::binary to tell the constructor to set it up as a binary file. To illustrate the formatting used for the text file, here is the first line of data.txt (the line wraps because it's longer than this page will allow):

```
07\28\2003 12:54:40 Lat:45*20'31", Long:22*34'18", depth:  16.0164, temp: 242.0122
```

The Standard C Library function time() updates the time_t value its argument points to with an encoding of the current time, which on most platforms is the number of seconds elapsed since 00: 00: 00 GMT, January 1 1970 (the dawning of the age of Aquarius?). The current time is also a convenient way to seed the random number generator with the Standard C Library function srand(), as is done here.

After this, the timer is incremented by 55 seconds to give an interesting interval between readings in this simulation.

The latitude and longitude used are fixed values to indicate a set of readings at a single location. Both the depth and the temperature are generated with the Standard C Library rand() function, which returns a pseudorandom number between zero and a platform-dependent constant, RAND_MAX, defined in <cstdlib> (usually the value of the platform's largest unsigned integer). To put this in a desired range, use the remainder operator % and the upper end of the range. These numbers are integral; to add a fractional part, a second call to rand() is made, and the value is inverted after adding one (to prevent divide-by-zero errors).

In effect, the data.bin file is being used as a container for the data in the program, even though the container exists on disk and not in RAM. write() sends the data out to the disk in binary form. The first argument is the starting address of the source block—notice it must be cast to a char* because that's what write() expects for narrow streams. The second argument is the number of characters to write, which in this case is the size of the DataPoint object (again, because of the use of narrow streams). Because no pointers are contained in DataPoint, there is no problem in writing the object to disk. If the object is more sophisticated, you must implement a scheme for *serialization*, which writes the data referred to by pointers and defines new pointers when read back in later.

Verifying and Viewing the Data

To check the validity of the data stored in binary format, you can read it into memory with the read() member function for input streams, and compare it to the text file created earlier by Datagen.cpp. Listing 19-28 just writes the formatted results to cout, but you can redirect this to a file and then use a file comparison utility to verify that it is identical to the original.

Listing 19-28. Scanning and Verifying the Binary Data (Against the Text File Created by Datagen.cpp in Listing 19-27)

```
//: C19:Datascan.cpp
//{L} DataLogger
#include <fstream>
#include <iostream>
#include "DataLogger.h"
#include "../require.h"
using namespace std;

int main() {
  ifstream bindata("data.bin", ios::binary);
  assure(bindata, "data.bin");
  DataPoint d;
  while(bindata.read(reinterpret_cast<char*>(&d),
        sizeof d))
    cout << d << endl;
} ///:~
```

Internationalization

The software industry is now a healthy, worldwide economic market, with demand for applications that can run in various languages and cultures. As early as the late 1980s, the C Standards Committee added support for non-U.S. formatting conventions with their *locale* mechanism. A locale is a set of preferences for displaying certain entities such as dates and monetary quantities. In the 1990s, the C Standards Committee approved an addendum to Standard C that specified functions to handle *wide characters* (denoted by the *type* wchar_t), which allow support for character sets other than ASCII and its commonly used Western European extensions. Although the size of a wide character is not specified, some platforms implement them as 32-bit quantities, so they can hold the encodings specified by the Unicode Consortium, as well as mappings to multi-byte characters sets defined by Asian standards bodies. C++ has integrated support for both wide characters and locales into the iostreams library.

Wide Streams

A wide stream is a stream class that handles wide characters. Most of the examples so far have used *narrow* streams that hold instances of char. Since stream operations are essentially the same no matter the underlying character type, they are encapsulated generically as templates. So all input streams, for example, are connected to the basic_istream class template, as in:

```
template<class charT, class traits = char_traits<charT>>
class basic_istream {...};
```

In fact, all input stream types are specializations of this template, according to the following type definitions:

```
typedef basic_istream<char> istream;
typedef basic_istream<wchar_t> wistream;
typedef basic_ifstream<char> ifstream;
typedef basic_ifstream<wchar_t> wifstream;
typedef basic_istringstream<char> istringstream;
typedef basic_istringstream<wchar_t> wistringstream;
```

All other stream types are defined in similar fashion.

In a perfect world, this is all you'd need to create streams of different character types. But things aren't that simple. The reason is that the character-processing functions provided for char and wchar_t don't have the same names. To compare two narrow strings, for example, you use the strcmp() function. For wide characters, that function is named wcscmp(). (*Remember these originated in C, which does not have function overloading, hence unique names are required.*) For this reason, a generic stream can't just call strcmp() in response to a comparison operator. There needs to be a way for the correct low-level functions to be called automatically.

The solution is to factor out the differences into a new abstraction. The operations you can perform on characters have been abstracted into the char_traits template, which has predefined specializations for char and wchar_t, as discussed at the end of the previous chapter. To compare two strings, then, basic_string just calls traits::compare() (remember that traits is the second template parameter), which in turn calls either strcmp() or wcscmp(), depending on which specialization is being used (transparent to basic_string).

You only need to be concerned about char_traits if you access the low-level character processing functions; most of the time you don't care. Consider, however, making your inserters and extractors more robust by defining them as templates, just in case someone wants to use them on a wide stream.

To illustrate, recall again the Date class inserter from the beginning of this chapter. It was originally declared as

```
ostream& operator<<(ostream&, const Date&);
```

This accommodates only narrow streams. To make it generic, you simply make it a template based on basic_ostream, as in:

```
template<class charT, class traits>
std::basic_ostream<charT, traits>&
operator<<(std::basic_ostream<charT, traits>& os,
           const Date& d) {
  charT fillc = os.fill(os.widen('0'));
  charT dash = os.widen('-');
  os << setw(2) << d.month << dash<< setw(2) << d.day
     << dash<< setw(4) << d.year;
  os.fill(fillc);
  return os;
}
```

Notice that you also have to replace char with the template parameter charT in the declaration of fillc, since it could be either char or wchar_t, depending on the template instantiation being used.

Since you don't know when you're writing the template which type of stream you have, you need a way to automatically convert character literals to the correct size for the stream. This is the job of the widen() member function. The expression widen('-'), for example, converts its argument to L'-' (the literal syntax equivalent to the conversion wchar_t('-')) if the stream is a wide stream and leaves it alone otherwise. There is also a narrow() function that converts to a char if needed.

You can use widen() to write a generic version of the nl manipulator presented earlier in the chapter, as in:

```
template<class charT, class traits>
basic_ostream<charT,traits>&
nl(basic_ostream<charT,traits>& os) {
  return os << charT(os.widen('\n'));
}
```

Locales

Perhaps the most notable difference in typical numeric computer output from country to country is the punctuator used to separate the integer and fractional parts of a real number. In India, a period denotes a decimal point, but in much of the world, a comma is expected instead. It would be quite inconvenient to do all your own formatting for locale-dependent displays. Once again, creating an abstraction that handles these differences solves the problem.

That abstraction is the *locale*. All streams have an associated locale object that they use for guidance on how to display certain quantities for different cultural environments. A locale manages the categories of culture-dependent display rules, which are defined in Table 19-9.

Table 19-9. *Categories of Cultural-Dependent Display Rules Managed by the Locale Associated with the Stream*

Category	Effect
Collate	Allows comparing strings according to different, supported collating sequences.
Ctype	Abstracts the character classification and conversion facilities found in <cctype>.
Monetary	Supports different displays of monetary quantities.
Numeric	Supports different display formats of real numbers, including radix (decimal point) and grouping (thousands) separators.
Time	Supports various international formats for display of date and time.
Messages	Scaffolding to implement context-dependent message catalogs (such as for error messages in different languages).

Listing 19-29 illustrates basic locale behavior.

Listing 19-29. Illustrating the Effects of Locales

```
//: C19:Locale.cpp {-g++}{-bor}{-edg} {RunByHand}
// Illustrates effects of locales.
#include <iostream>
#include <locale>
using namespace std;

int main() {
  locale def;
  cout << def.name() << endl;
  locale current = cout.getloc();
  cout << current.name() << endl;
  float val = 1234.56;
  cout << val << endl;
```

```
// Change to French/France
cout.imbue(locale("french"));
current = cout.getloc();

cout << current.name() << endl;
cout << val << endl;

cout << "Enter the literal 7890,12: ";
cin.imbue(cout.getloc());

cin >> val;
cout << val << endl;

cout.imbue(def);

cout << val << endl;
} ///:~
```

Here's the output:

```
C
C
1234.56
French_France.1252
1234,56
Enter the literal 7890,12: 7890,12
7890,12
7890.12
```

The default locale is the "C" locale, which is what C and C++ programmers have been used to all these years (basically, English language and American culture). All streams are initially "imbued" with the "C" locale.

The imbue() member function changes the locale that a stream uses. Notice that the full ISO name for the "French" locale is displayed (that is, French used in France vs. French used in another country). This example shows that this locale uses a comma for a radix point in numeric display. You have to change cin to the same locale if you want to do input according to the rules of this locale.

Each locale category is divided into number of *facets*, which are classes encapsulating the functionality that pertains to that category. For example, the time category has the facets time_put and time_get, which contain functions for doing time and date input and output respectively. The monetary category has facets money_get, money_put, and moneypunct. (The latter facet determines the currency symbol.)

Listing 19-30 illustrates the moneypunct facet. (The time facet requires a sophisticated use of iterators, which is beyond the scope of this chapter.)

Listing 19-30. Illustrating the 'moneypunct' Facet

```
//: C19:Facets.cpp {-bor}{-g++}{-mwcc}{-edg}
#include <iostream>
#include <locale>
#include <string>
using namespace std;
```

```
int main() {
  // Change to French/France
  locale loc("french");
  cout.imbue(loc);
  string currency =
    use_facet<moneypunct<char>>(loc).curr_symbol();
  char point =
    use_facet<moneypunct<char>>(loc).decimal_point();
  cout << "I made " << currency << 12.34 << " today!"
       << endl;
} ///:~
```

The output shows the French currency symbol and decimal separator:

```
I made Ç12,34 today!
```

You can also define your own facets to construct customized locales. Be aware that the overhead for locales is considerable. In fact, some library vendors provide different "flavors" of the Standard C++ Library to accommodate environments that have limited space.

Review Session

1. This chapter has given you a fairly thorough introduction to the iostream class library.

2. What you've seen here is likely to be all you need to create programs using iostreams.

3. However, be aware that some additional features in iostreams are not used often, but you *can discover them* by looking at the iostream *header files* and *by reading your compiler's documentation on* iostreams.

CHAPTER 20

■ ■ ■

Runtime Type Identification (RTTI)

Runtime type identification (RTTI) lets you find the dynamic type of an object when you have only a pointer or a reference to the base type.

This can be thought of as a "secondary" feature in C++, pragmatism to help out when you get into rare difficult situations. Normally, you'll want to intentionally ignore the exact type of an object and let the virtual function mechanism implement the correct behavior for that type. On occasion, however, it's useful to know the *exact* runtime (that is, most derived) type of an object for which you only have a base pointer. With this information, you may perform a special-case operation more efficiently or prevent a base-class interface from becoming ungainly. It happens enough that most class libraries contain virtual functions to produce runtime type information. When exception handling was added to C++, that feature required information about the runtime type of objects, so it became an easy next step to build in access to that information. This chapter explains what RTTI is for and how to use it.

Runtime Casts

One way to determine the runtime type of an object through a pointer or reference is to employ a *runtime cast*, which verifies that the attempted conversion is valid. This is useful when you need to cast a baseclass pointer to a derived type. Since inheritance hierarchies are typically depicted with base classes above derived classes, such a cast is called a *downcast*. Consider the class hierarchy in Figure 20-1.

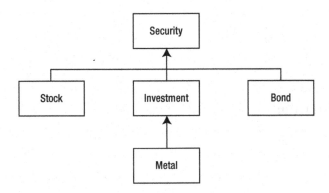

Figure 20-1. *An Investment class hierarchy*

In Listing 20-1, the Investment class has an extra operation that the other classes do not, so it is important to be able to know at runtime whether a Security pointer refers to an Investment object or not. To implement checked runtime casts, each class keeps an integral identifier to distinguish it from other classes in the hierarchy.

Listing 20-1. Checking Casts at Runtime

```
//: C20:CheckedCast.cpp
// Checks casts at runtime.
#include <iostream>
#include <vector>
#include "../purge.h" // SEE ahead in this Section
using namespace std;

class Security {
protected:
  enum { BASEID = 0 };
public:
  virtual ~Security() {}
  virtual bool isA(int id) { return (id == BASEID); }
};

class Stock : public Security {
  typedef Security Super;
protected:
  enum { OFFSET = 1, TYPEID = BASEID + OFFSET };
public:
  bool isA(int id) {
    return id == TYPEID || Super::isA(id);
  }
  static Stock* dynacast(Security* s) {
    return (s->isA(TYPEID)) ? static_cast<Stock*>(s) : 0;
  }
};

class Bond : public Security {
  typedef Security Super;
protected:
  enum { OFFSET = 2, TYPEID = BASEID + OFFSET };
public:
  bool isA(int id) {
    return id == TYPEID || Super::isA(id);
  }
  static Bond* dynacast(Security* s) {
    return (s->isA(TYPEID)) ? static_cast<Bond*>(s) : 0;
  }
};

class Investment : public Security {
  typedef Security Super;
protected:
  enum { OFFSET = 3, TYPEID = BASEID + OFFSET };
public:
  bool isA(int id) {
    return id == TYPEID || Super::isA(id);
  }
```

```
  static Investment* dynacast(Security* s) {
    return (s->isA(TYPEID)) ?
      static_cast<Investment*>(s) : 0;
  }
  void special() {
    cout << "special Investment function" << endl;
  }
};

class Metal : public Investment {
  typedef Investment Super;

protected:
  enum { OFFSET = 4, TYPEID = BASEID + OFFSET };

public:
  bool isA(int id) {
    return id == TYPEID || Super::isA(id);
  }
  static Metal* dynacast(Security* s) {
    return (s->isA(TYPEID)) ? static_cast<Metal*>(s) : 0;
  }
};

int main() {
  vector<Security*> portfolio;
  portfolio.push_back(new Metal);
  portfolio.push_back(new Investment);
  portfolio.push_back(new Bond);
  portfolio.push_back(new Stock);
  for(vector<Security*>::iterator it = portfolio.begin();
      it != portfolio.end(); ++it) {
    Investment* cm = Investment::dynacast(*it);
    if(cm)
      cm->special();
    else
      cout << "not an Investment" << endl;
  }
  cout << "cast from intermediate pointer:" << endl;
  Security* sp = new Metal;
  Investment* cp = Investment::dynacast(sp);
  if(cp) cout << "  it's an Investment" << endl;
  Metal* mp = Metal::dynacast(sp);
  if(mp) cout << "  it's a Metal too!" << endl;
  purge(portfolio);
} ///:~

//: :purge.h
// Delete pointers in an STL sequence container
#ifndef PURGE_H
#define PURGE_H
```

```
#include <algorithm>
template<class Seq> void purge(Seq& c) {
typename Seq::iterator i;
for(i = c.begin(); i != c.end(); i++) {
delete *i;
*i = 0;
}
}
// Iterator version:
template<class InpIt>
void purge(InpIt begin, InpIt end) {
while(begin != end) {
delete *begin;
*begin = 0;
begin++;
}
}
#endif // PURGE_H ///:~
```

The polymorphic isA() function checks to see if its argument is compatible with its type argument (id), which means that either id matches the object's typeID exactly or it matches one of the object's ancestors (hence the call to Super::isA() in that case). The dynacast() function, which is static in each class, calls isA() for its pointer argument to check if the cast is valid. If isA() returns true, the cast is valid, and a suitably cast pointer is returned. Otherwise, the null pointer is returned, which tells the caller that the cast is not valid, meaning that the original pointer is not pointing to an object compatible with (convertible to) the desired type. All this machinery is necessary to be able to check intermediate casts, such as from a Security pointer that refers to a Metal object to an Investment pointer in Listing 20-1.

For most programs downcasting is unnecessary, and is actually discouraged, since everyday polymorphism solves most problems in object-oriented application programs. However, the ability to check a cast to a more derived type is important for utility programs such as debuggers, class browsers, and databases. C++ provides such a checked cast with the dynamic_cast operator. Listing 20-2 is a rewrite of the previous example using dynamic_cast.

Listing 20-2. Modifying Listing 20-1 Using dynamic_cast

```
//: C20:Security.h
#ifndef SECURITY_H
#define SECURITY_H
#include <iostream>

class Security {
public:
  virtual ~Security() {}
};

class Stock : public Security {};
class Bond : public Security {};
class Investment : public Security {
public:
  void special() {
    std::cout << "special Investment function" << std::endl;
  }
};
```

```
class Metal : public Investment {};
#endif                  // SECURITY_H ///:~


//: C20:CheckedCast2.cpp
// Uses RTTI's dynamic_cast.

#include <vector>
#include "../purge.h"
#include "Security.h" // To be INCLUDED from Header FILE above
using namespace std;

int main() {
  vector<Security*> portfolio;
  portfolio.push_back(new Metal);
  portfolio.push_back(new Investment);
  portfolio.push_back(new Bond);
  portfolio.push_back(new Stock);
  for(vector<Security*>::iterator it =
      portfolio.begin();
      it != portfolio.end(); ++it) {
    Investment* cm = dynamic_cast<Investment*>(*it);
    if(cm)
      cm->special();
    else
      cout << "not a Investment" << endl;
  }
  cout << "cast from intermediate pointer:" << endl;
  Security* sp = new Metal;
  Investment* cp = dynamic_cast<Investment*>(sp);
  if(cp) cout << "  it's an Investment" << endl;
  Metal* mp = dynamic_cast<Metal*>(sp);
  if(mp) cout << "  it's a Metal too!" << endl;
  purge(portfolio);
} ///:~
```

This example is much shorter, since most of the code in the original example was just the overhead for checking the casts. The target type of a dynamic_cast is placed in angle brackets, like the other new-style C++ casts (static_cast and so on), and the object to cast appears as the operand. dynamic_cast requires that the types you use it with be *polymorphic* if you want safe downcasts. This in turn requires that the class must have at least one virtual function. Fortunately, the Security base class has a virtual destructor, so we didn't have to invent an extra function to get the job done. Because dynamic_cast does its work at runtime, using the virtual table, it tends to be more expensive than the other new-style casts.

You can also use dynamic_cast with references instead of pointers, but since there is no such thing as a null reference, you need another way to know if the cast fails. That "other way" is to catch a bad_cast exception, as shown in Listing 20-3.

Listing 20-3. Catching a bad_cast Exception

```
//: C20:CatchBadCast.cpp
#include <typeinfo>
#include "Security.h"
using namespace std;

int main() {
  Metal m;
  Security& s = m;

  try {
    Investment& c = dynamic_cast<Investment&>(s);
    cout << "It's an Investment" << endl;
  } catch(bad_cast&) {
    cout << "s is not an Investment type" << endl;
  }

  try {
    Bond& b = dynamic_cast<Bond&>(s);
    cout << "It's a Bond" << endl;
  } catch(bad_cast&) {
    cout << "It's not a Bond type" << endl;
  }
} ///:~
```

The bad_cast class is defined in the <typeinfo> header, and, like most of the Standard C++ Library, is declared in the std namespace.

The typeid Operator

The other way to get runtime information for an object is through the typeid operator. This operator returns an object of class type_info, which yields information about the type of object to which it was applied. If the type is polymorphic, it gives information about the most derived type that applies (the dynamic type); otherwise it yields static type information. One use of the typeid operator is to get the name of the dynamic type of an object as a const char*, as you can see in Listing 20-4.

Listing 20-4. Illustrating use of the typeid Operator

```
//: C20:TypeInfo.cpp
// Illustrates the typeid operator.
#include <iostream>
#include <typeinfo>
using namespace std;

struct PolyBase { virtual ~PolyBase() {} };
struct PolyDer : PolyBase { PolyDer() {} };
struct NonPolyBase {};
struct NonPolyDer : NonPolyBase { NonPolyDer(int) {} };
```

```
int main() {
  // Test polymorphic Types
  const PolyDerpd;
  const PolyBase* ppb = &pd;

  cout << typeid(ppb).name() << endl;
  cout << typeid(*ppb).name() << endl;
  cout << boolalpha << (typeid(*ppb) == typeid(pd))
       << endl;
  cout << (typeid(PolyDer) == typeid(const PolyDer))
       << endl;

  // Test non-polymorphic Types
  const NonPolyDernpd(1);
  const NonPolyBase* nppb = &npd;

  cout << typeid(nppb).name() << endl;
  cout << typeid(*nppb).name() << endl;
  cout << (typeid(*nppb) == typeid(npd)) << endl;

  // Test a built-in type
  int i;
  cout << typeid(i).name() << endl;
} ///:~
```

The output from this program using one particular compiler is

```
struct PolyBase const *
struct PolyDer
true
true
struct NonPolyBase const *
struct NonPolyBase
false
int
```

The first output line just echoes the static type of ppb because it is a pointer. To get RTTI to kick in, you need to look at the pointer or reference destination object, which is illustrated in the second line. Notice that RTTI ignores top-level const and volatile qualifiers. With non-polymorphic types, you just get the static type (the type of the pointer itself). As you can see, built-in types are also supported.

It turns out that you can't store the result of a typeid operation in a type_info object because there are no accessible constructors and assignment is disallowed. You must use it as we have shown. In addition, the actual string returned by type_info::name() is compiler dependent. For a class named C, for example, some compilers return "class C" instead of just "C." Applying typeid to an expression that dereferences a null pointer will cause a bad_typeid exception (also defined in <typeinfo>) to be thrown.

Listing 20-5 shows that the class name that type_info::name() returns is fully qualified.

Listing 20-5. Illustrates RTTI and Nesting

```
//: C20:RTTIandNesting.cpp
#include <iostream>
#include <typeinfo>
using namespace std;

class One {
  class Nested {};
  Nested* n;
public:
  One() : n(new Nested) {}
  ~One() { delete n; }
  Nested* nested() { return n; }
};

int main() {
  One o;
  cout << typeid(*o.nested()).name() << endl;
} ///:~
```

Since Nested is a member type of the One class, the result is One::Nested.

You can also ask a type_info object if it precedes another type_info object in the implementation-defined "collation sequence" (the native ordering rules for text), using before(type_info&), which returns true or false. When you say,

```
if(typeid(me).before(typeid(you))) // ...
```

you're asking if me occurs before you in the current collation sequence. This is useful if you use type_info objects as keys.

Casting to Intermediate Levels

As you saw in Listing 20-2 that used the hierarchy of Security classes, dynamic_cast can detect both exact types and, in an inheritance hierarchy with multiple levels, intermediate types. Listing 20-6 is another example.

Listing 20-6. Illustrates Intermediate Casting

```
//: C20:IntermediateCast.cpp
#include <cassert>
#include <typeinfo>
using namespace std;

class B1 {
public:
  virtual ~B1() {}
};

class B2 {
public:
  virtual ~B2() {}
};
```

```
class MI : public B1, public B2 {};
class Mi2 : public MI {};

int main() {
  B2* b2 = new Mi2;
  Mi2* mi2 = dynamic_cast<Mi2*>(b2);
  MI* mi = dynamic_cast<MI*>(b2);
  B1* b1 = dynamic_cast<B1*>(b2);
  assert(typeid(b2) != typeid(Mi2*));
  assert(typeid(b2) == typeid(B2*));
  delete b2;
} ///:~
```

Note that the following three lines of code

```
Mi2* mi2 = dynamic_cast<Mi2*>(b2);
MI* mi = dynamic_cast<MI*>(b2);
B1* b1 = dynamic_cast<B1*>(b2);
```

may cause the compiler (such as XCode)to issue an "unused variable" warning but the purpose of this example is just to demonstrate the fact that dynamic_cast can detect both exact types and, in an inheritance hierarchy with multiple levels, intermediate types.

This example has the extra complication of *multiple inheritance* (you'll learn more about multiple inheritance later in this chapter). If you create an Mi2 and upcast it to the root (in this case, one of the two possible roots is chosen), the dynamic_cast back to either of the derived levels MI or Mi2 is successful.

You can even cast from one root to the other, as in:

```
B1* b1 = dynamic_cast<B1*>(b2);
```

This is successful because B2 is actually pointing to a Mi2 object, which contains a subobject of type B1.

Casting to intermediate levels brings up an interesting difference between dynamic_cast and typeid. The typeid operator always produces a reference to a static type_info object that describes the dynamic type of the object. Thus, it doesn't give you intermediate-level information. In the following expression (which is true), typeid doesn't see b2 as a pointer to the derived type, like dynamic_cast does:

```
typeid(b2) != typeid(Mi2*)
```

The type of b2 is simply the exact type of the pointer, as in:

```
typeid(b2) == typeid(B2*)
```

void Pointers

RTTI only works for complete types, meaning that all class information must be available when typeid is used. In particular, it doesn't work with void pointers, as you can see in Listing 20-7.

Listing 20-7. Illustrates RTTI and void Pointers

```
//: C20:VoidRTTI.cpp
// RTTI & void pointers.
//!#include <iostream>
#include <typeinfo>
using namespace std;

classStimpy {
public:
  virtual void happy() {}
  virtual void joy() {}
  virtual ~Stimpy() {}
};

 int main() {
  void* v = new Stimpy;

  // Error:
//!  Stimpy* s = dynamic_cast<Stimpy*>(v);
  // Error:
//!  cout<<typeid(*v).name() <<endl;
} ///:~
```

A void* truly means "no type information."

Using RTTI with Templates

Class templates work well with RTTI, since all they do is generate classes. As usual, RTTI provides a convenient way to obtain the name of the class you're in. Listing 20-8 prints the order of constructor and destructor calls.

Listing 20-8. Printing the Order of Constructor/Destructor Calls

```
//: C20:ConstructorOrder.cpp
// Order of constructor calls.
#include <iostream>
#include <typeinfo>
using namespace std;

template<int id> class Announce {
public:
  Announce() {
    cout << typeid(*this).name() << " constructor" << endl;
  }
  ~Announce() {
    cout << typeid(*this).name() << " destructor" << endl;
  }
};
```

```
class X : public Announce<0> {
  Announce<1> m1;
  Announce<2> m2;
public:
  X() { cout << "X::X()" << endl; }
  ~X() { cout << "X::~X()" << endl; }
};

int main() { X x; } ///:~
```

This template uses a constant `int` to differentiate one class from another, but type arguments would work as well. Inside both the constructor and destructor, RTTI information produces the name of the class to print. The class X uses both inheritance and composition to create a class that has an interesting order of constructor and destructor calls.

The output is

```
Announce<0> constructor
Announce<1> constructor
Announce<2> constructor
X::X()
X::~X()
Announce<2> destructor
Announce<1> destructor
Announce<0> destructor
```

Of course, you may get different output depending on how your compiler represents its `name()` information.

Multiple Inheritance

The RTTI mechanisms must work properly with all the complexities of multiple inheritance, including `virtual` base classes, as shown in Listing 20-9 (and discussed in depth in the next chapter—you may want to come back here after reading Chapter 21).

Listing 20-9. Illustrates RTTI and Multiple Inheritance

```
//: C20:RTTIandMultipleInheritance.cpp
#include <iostream>
#include <typeinfo>
using namespace std;

class BB {
public:
  virtual void f() {}
  virtual ~BB() {}
};

class B1 : virtual public BB {};
class B2 : virtual public BB {};

class MI : public B1, public B2 {};
```

```
int main() {
  BB* bbp = new MI;        // Upcast
  // Proper name detection:
  cout << typeid(*bbp).name() << endl;
  // Dynamic_cast works properly:
  MI* mip = dynamic_cast<MI*>(bbp);
  // Can't force old-style cast:
//! MI* mip2 = (MI*)bbp; // Compile error
} ///:~
```

The typeid()operator properly detects the name of the actual object, even through the virtual base class pointer. The dynamic_cast also works correctly. But the compiler won't even allow you to try to force a cast the old way, as in:

```
MI* mip = (MI*)bbp; // Compile-time error
```

The compiler knows this is never the right thing to do, so it requires that you use a dynamic_cast.

Sensible Uses for RTTI

Because you can discover type information from an anonymous polymorphic pointer, RTTI is ripe for misuse by the novice, because RTTI may make sense before virtual functions do. For many people coming from a procedural background, it's difficult not to organize programs into sets of switch statements. They could accomplish this with RTTI and thus lose the important value of polymorphism in code development and maintenance. The intent of C++ is that you use virtual functions throughout your code and that you only use RTTI when you must.

However, using virtual functions as they are intended requires that you have control of the baseclass definition because at some point in the extension of your program you may discover the base class doesn't include the virtual function you need. If the base class comes from a library or is otherwise controlled by someone else, one solution to the problem is RTTI; you can derive a new type and add your extra member function. Elsewhere in the code you can detect your particular type and call that member function. This doesn't destroy the polymorphism and extensibility of the program because adding a new type will not require you to hunt for switch statements. However, when you add new code in the main body that requires your new feature, you'll have to detect your particular type.

Putting a feature in a base class might mean that, for the benefit of one particular class, all the other classes derived from that base require some meaningless stub for a pure virtual function. This makes the interface less clear and annoys those who must override pure virtual functions when they derive from that base class.

Finally, RTTI will sometimes solve efficiency problems. If your code uses polymorphism in a nice way, but it turns out that one of your objects reacts to this general-purpose code in a horribly inefficient way, you can pick that type out using RTTI and write case-specific code to improve the efficiency.

A Trash Recycler

To further illustrate a practical use of RTTI, Listing 20-10 simulates a trash recycler. Different kinds of "trash" are inserted into a single container and then later sorted according to their dynamic types.

Listing 20-10. Simulating a Trash Recycler

```
//: C20:Trash.h
// Describing trash.
#ifndef TRASH_H
#define TRASH_H
#include <iostream>

class Trash {
  float _weight;
public:
  Trash(float wt) : _weight(wt) {}
  virtual float value() const = 0;
  float weight() const { return _weight; }
  virtual ~Trash() {
    std::cout << "~Trash()" << std::endl;
  }
};

class Aluminum : public Trash {
  static float val;
public:
  Aluminum(float wt) : Trash(wt) {}
  float value() const { return val; }
  static void value(float newval) {
    val = newval;
  }
};

class Paper : public Trash {
  static float val;
public:
  Paper(float wt) : Trash(wt) {}
  float value() const { return val; }
  static void value(float newval) {
    val = newval;
  }
};

class Glass : public Trash {
  static float val;
public:
  Glass(float wt) : Trash(wt) {}
  float value() const { return val; }
  static void value(float newval) {
    val = newval;
  }
};
#endif // TRASH_H ///:~
```

The static values representing the price per unit of the trash types are defined in the implementation file (Listing 20-11).

Listing 20-11. Implementing the header file in Listing 20-10 (Trash.h)

```
//: C20:Trash.cpp {O}
// A Trash Recycler.
#include "Trash.h"    // To be INCLUDED from Header FILE above

float Aluminum::val = 1.67;
float Paper::val = 0.10;
float Glass::val = 0.23;
///:~
```

The sumValue() template iterates through a container, displaying and calculating results, as shown in Listing 20-12.

Listing 20-12. Illustrates Recycling using the sumValue( ) Template

```
//: C20:Recycle.cpp
//{L} Trash
// A Trash Recycler.

#include <cstdlib>
#include <ctime>
#include <iostream>
#include <typeinfo>
#include <vector>
#include "Trash.h"
#include "../purge.h"
using namespace std;

// Sums up the value of the Trash in a bin:
template<class Container>
void sumValue(Container& bin, ostream&os) {
  typename Container::iterator tally = bin.begin();
  floatval = 0;
  while(tally != bin.end()) {
    val += (*tally)->weight() * (*tally)->value();
    os << "weight of " << typeid(**tally).name()
       << " = " << (*tally)->weight() << endl;
    ++tally;
  }
  os << "Total value = " << val << endl;
}

int main() {
  srand(time(0)); // Seed the random number generator
  vector<Trash*> bin;

  // Fill up the Trash bin:
  for(int i = 0; i < 30; i++)
    switch(rand() % 3) {
      case 0 :
        bin.push_back(new Aluminum((rand() % 1000)/10.0));
        break;
```

```
      case 1 :
        bin.push_back(new Paper((rand() % 1000)/10.0));
        break;
      case 2 :
        bin.push_back(new Glass((rand() % 1000)/10.0));
        break;
    }

  // Note: bins hold exact type of object, not base type:
  vector<Glass*> glassBin;
  vector<Paper*> paperBin;
  vector<Aluminum*> alumBin;
  vector<Trash*>::iterator sorter = bin.begin();

  // Sort the Trash:
  while(sorter != bin.end()) {
    Aluminum* ap = dynamic_cast<Aluminum*>(*sorter);
    Paper* pp = dynamic_cast<Paper*>(*sorter);
    Glass* gp = dynamic_cast<Glass*>(*sorter);
    if(ap) alumBin.push_back(ap);
    else if(pp) paperBin.push_back(pp);
    else if(gp) glassBin.push_back(gp);
    ++sorter;
  }
  sumValue(alumBin, cout);
  sumValue(paperBin, cout);
  sumValue(glassBin, cout);
  sumValue(bin, cout);
  purge(bin);
} ///:~
```

The trash is thrown unclassified into a single bin, so the specific type information is "lost." But later the specific type information must be recovered to properly sort the trash, and so RTTI is used.

You can improve this solution by using a map that associates pointers to type_info objects with a vector of Trash pointers. Since a map requires an ordering predicate, you provide one named TInfoLess that calls type_info::before(). As you insert Trash pointers into the map, they are automatically associated with their type_info key. Notice that sumValue() must be defined differently in Listing 20-13.

Listing 20-13. Illustrates Recycling using a map

```
//: C20:Recycle2.cpp
//{L} Trash
// Recyling with a map.
#include <cstdlib>
#include <ctime>
#include <iostream>
#include <map>
#include <typeinfo>
#include <utility>
#include <vector>
#include "Trash.h"
#include "../purge.h"
using namespace std;
```

```
// Comparator for type_info pointers
struct TInfoLess {
  bool operator()(const type_info* t1, const type_info* t2)
  const { return t1->before(*t2); }
};

typedef map<const type_info*, vector<Trash*>, TInfoLess>
  TrashMap;

// Sums up the value of the Trash in a bin:
void sumValue(const TrashMap::value_type& p, ostream& os) {
  vector<Trash*>::const_iterator tally = p.second.begin();
  float val = 0;

  while(tally != p.second.end()) {
    val += (*tally)->weight() * (*tally)->value();
    os << "weight of "
       << p.first->name()  // type_info::name()
       << " = " << (*tally)->weight() << endl;
    ++tally;
  }
  os << "Total value = " << val << endl;
}

int main() {
  srand(time(0));              // Seed the random number generator
  TrashMap bin;

  // Fill up the Trash bin:
  for(int i = 0; i < 30; i++) {
    Trash* tp;
    switch(rand() % 3) {
      case 0 :
        tp = new Aluminum((rand() % 1000)/10.0);
        break;
      case 1 :
        tp = new Paper((rand() % 1000)/10.0);
        break;
      case 2 :
        tp = new Glass((rand() % 1000)/10.0);
        break;
    }
    bin[&typeid(*tp)].push_back(tp);
  }

  // Print sorted results
  for(TrashMap::iterator p = bin.begin();
      p != bin.end(); ++p) {
    sumValue(*p, cout);
    purge(p->second);
  }
} ///:~
```

You've modified sumValue() to call type_info::name() directly, since the type_info object is now available as the first member of the TrashMap::value_type pair. This avoids the extra call to typeid to get the name of the type of Trash being processed that was necessary in Listing 20-12.

Mechanism and Overhead of RTTI

Typically, RTTI is implemented by placing an additional pointer in a class's virtual function table. This pointer points to the type_info structure for that particular type.

The effect of a typeid() expression is quite simple: the virtual function table pointer fetches the type_info pointer, and a reference to the resulting type_info structure is produced. Since this is just a two-pointer dereference operation, it is a constant time operation.

For a dynamic_cast<destination*>(source_pointer), most cases are quite straightforward: source_pointer's RTTI information is retrieved, and RTTI information for the type destination* is fetched.

A library routine then determines whether source_pointer's type is of type destination* or a base class of destination*. The pointer it returns may be adjusted because of multiple inheritance if the base type isn't the first base of the derived class. The situation is more complicated with multiple inheritance because a base type may appear more than once in an inheritance hierarchy and virtual base classes are used.

Because the library routine used for dynamic_cast must check through a list of base classes, the overhead for dynamic_cast may be higher than typeid() (but you get different information, which may be essential to your solution), and it may take more time to discover a base class than a derived class.

In addition, dynamic_cast compares any type to any other type; you aren't restricted to comparing types within the same hierarchy. This adds extra overhead to the library routine used by dynamic_cast.

Review Session

1. Although normally you upcast a pointer to a base class and then use the generic interface of that base class (via virtual functions), occasionally you get into a corner where things can be more effective if you know the dynamic type of the object pointed to by a base pointer, and that's what *RTTI* provides.

2. The *most common misuse* may come from the programmer who doesn't understand virtual functions and *uses RTTI to do type-check coding instead.*

3. The philosophy of C++ seems to be to provide you with powerful tools and guard for type violations and integrity, but if you want to *deliberately misuse* or get around a language feature, there's *nothing to stop you.* In this context, it would be worthwhile to mention that sometimes *a slight burn is the fastest way to gain useful experience.*

CHAPTER 21

■ ■ ■

Multiple Inheritance (MI)

The basic concept of multiple inheritance (MI) sounds simple enough: you create a new type by inheriting from more than one base class. The syntax is exactly what you'd expect, and as long as the inheritance diagrams are simple, MI can be simple as well.

However, MI can introduce a number of ambiguities and strange situations, which are covered in this chapter. But first, it is helpful to get some perspective on the subject.

Perspective

Before C++, the most successful object-oriented language was Smalltalk. Smalltalk was created from the ground up as an object-oriented language. It is often referred to as *pure,* whereas C++ is called a *hybrid* language because it supports multiple programming paradigms, not just the object-oriented paradigm. One of the design decisions made with Smalltalk was that all classes would be derived in a single hierarchy, rooted in a single base class (called Object—this is the model for the *object-based hierarchy*). You cannot create a new class in Smalltalk without deriving it from an existing class, which is why it takes a certain amount of time to become productive in Smalltalk: you must learn the class library before you can start making new classes. The Smalltalk class hierarchy is therefore a single monolithic tree.

Classes in Smalltalk usually have a number of things in common, and they always have *some* things in common (the characteristics and behaviors of Object), so you don't often run into a situation where you need to inherit from more than one base class. However, with C++ you can create as many distinct inheritance trees as you want. So for logical completeness the language must be able to combine more than one class at a time—thus the need for multiple inheritance.

It was not obvious, however, that programmers required multiple inheritance, and there was (and still is) a lot of disagreement about whether it is essential in C++. MI was added in AT&T cfront release 2.0 in 1989 and was the first significant change to the language over version 1.0. Since then, a number of other features have been added to Standard C++ (notably templates) that change the way we think about programming and place MI in a much less important role. You can think of MI as a "minor" language feature that is seldom involved in your daily design decisions.

One of the most pressing arguments for MI involves containers. Suppose you want to create a container that everyone can easily use. One approach is to use void* as the type inside the container. The Smalltalk approach, however, is to make a container that holds Objects, since Object is the base type of the Smalltalk hierarchy. Because everything in Smalltalk is ultimately derived from Object, a container that holds Objects can hold anything.

Now consider the situation in C++. Suppose vendor A creates an object-based hierarchy that includes a useful set of containers including one you want to use called Holder. Next you come across vendor B's class hierarchy that contains some other class that is important to you, a BitImage class, for example, that holds graphic images. The only way to make a Holder of BitImages is to derive a new class from both Object, so it can be held in the Holder, and BitImage, as shown in Figure 21-1.

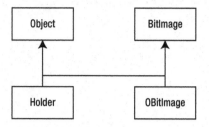

Figure 21-1. *An example illustrating the need for MI to make a container of objects. To make a holder of BitImages, you need MI*

This was seen as an important reason for MI, and a number of class libraries were built on this model. The other reason you may need MI is related to design. You can intentionally use MI to make a design more flexible or useful (or at least seemingly so). An example of this is in the original `iostream` library design in Figure 21-2 (which still persists in today's template design).

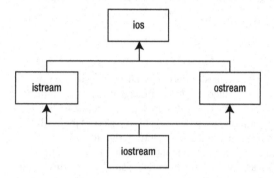

Figure 21-2. *Intentional use of MI to make iostream design more flexible and useful*

Both `istream` and `ostream` are useful classes by themselves, but they can also be derived from simultaneously by a class that combines both their characteristics and behaviors. The class `ios` provides what is common to all stream classes, and so in this case MI is a code-factoring mechanism.

Regardless of what motivates you to use MI, it's harder to use than it might appear.

Interface Inheritance

One use of multiple inheritance that is not controversial pertains to *interface inheritance*. In C++, all inheritance is *implementation inheritance*, because everything in a base class, interface and implementation, becomes part of a derived class. It is not possible to inherit only part of a class (the interface alone, say). As Chapter 14 explains, `private` and `protected` inheritance make it possible to restrict access to members inherited from base classes when used by clients of a derived class object, but this doesn't affect the derived class; it still contains all base class data and can access all non-`private` base class members.

Interface inheritance, on the other hand, only adds member function *declarations* to a derived class interface and is not directly supported in C++. The usual technique to simulate interface inheritance in C++ is to derive from an *interface class*, which is a class that contains only declarations (*no data or function bodies*). These declarations will be pure virtual functions, except for the destructor. Listing 21-1 contains an example.

Listing 21-1. Illustrating Multiple Interface Inheritance

```
//: C21:Interfaces.cpp
// Multiple interface inheritance.
#include <iostream>
#include <sstream>
#include <string>
using namespace std;

class Printable {
public:
  virtual ~Printable() {}
  virtual void print(ostream&) const = 0;
};

class Intable {
public:
  virtual ~Intable() {}
  virtual int toInt() const = 0;
};

class Stringable {
public:
  virtual ~Stringable() {}
  virtual string toString() const = 0;
};

class Able : public Printable, public Intable,
             public Stringable {
  int myData;
public:
  Able(int x) { myData = x; }
  void print(ostream& os) const { os << myData; }
  int toInt() const { return myData; }
  string toString() const {
    ostringstream os;
    os << myData;
    return os.str();
  }
};

void testPrintable(const Printable& p) {
  p.print(cout);
  cout << endl;
}

void testIntable(const Intable& n) {
  cout << n.toInt() + 1 << endl;
}
```

```
void testStringable(const Stringable& s) {
  cout << s.toString() + "th" << endl;
}

int main() {
  Able a(7);
  testPrintable(a);
  testIntable(a);
  testStringable(a);
} ///:~
```

The class Able "implements" the interfaces Printable, Intable, and Stringable because it provides implementations for the functions they declare. Because Able derives from all three classes, Able objects have multiple is-a relationships. For example, the object a can act as a Printable object because its class, Able, derives publicly from Printable and provides an implementation for print(). The test functions have no need to know the most-derived type of their parameter; they just need an object that is substitutable for their parameter's type.

As usual, a template solution is more compact; see Listing 21-2.

Listing 21-2. Illustrating Implicit Interface Inheritance (using templates)

```
//: C21:Interfaces2.cpp
// Implicit interface inheritance via templates.
#include <iostream>
#include <sstream>
#include <string>
using namespace std;

class Able {
  int myData;
public:
  Able(int x) { myData = x; }
  void print(ostream& os) const { os << myData; }
  int toInt() const { return myData; }
  string toString() const {
    ostringstream os;
    os << myData;
    return os.str();
  }
};
template<class Printable>
void testPrintable(const Printable& p) {
  p.print(cout);
  cout << endl;
}

template<class Intable>
void testIntable(const Intable& n) {
  cout << n.toInt() + 1 << endl;
}
```

```
template<class Stringable>
void testStringable(const Stringable& s) {
  cout << s.toString() + "th" << endl;
}

int main() {
  Able a(7);
  testPrintable(a);
  testIntable(a);
  testStringable(a);
} ///:~
```

The names Printable, Intable, and Stringable are now just template parameters that assume the existence of the operations indicated in their respective contexts. In other words, the test functions can accept arguments of any type that provides a member function definition with the correct signature and return type; deriving from a common base class in not necessary. Some people are more comfortable with the first version because the type names guarantee by inheritance that the expected interfaces are implemented. Others are content with the fact that if the operations required by the test functions are not satisfied by their template type arguments, the error is still caught at compile time. The latter approach is technically a "weaker" form of type checking than the former (inheritance) approach, but the effect on the programmer (and the program) is the same. This is one form of weak typing that is acceptable to many of today's C++ programmers.

Implementation Inheritance

As stated earlier, C++ provides only implementation inheritance, meaning that you always inherit *everything* from your base classes. This can be good because it frees you from having to implement everything in the derived class, as shown with the interface inheritance examples earlier. A common use of multiple inheritance involves using *mixin classes*, which are classes that exist to add capabilities to other classes through inheritance. Mixin classes are not intended to be instantiated by themselves.

As an example, suppose you are a client of a class that supports access to a database. In this scenario, you only have a header file available—part of the point here is that you don't have access to the source code for the implementation. For illustration, assume the implementation of a Database class shown in Listing 21-3.

Listing 21-3. Implementing a Database Class

```
//: C21:Database.h
// A prototypical resource class.
#ifndef DATABASE_H
#define DATABASE_H
#include <iostream>
#include <stdexcept>
#include <string>

struct DatabaseError : std::runtime_error {
  DatabaseError(const std::string& msg)
    : std::runtime_error(msg) {}
};

class Database {
  std::string dbid;
public:
  Database(const std::string& dbStr) : dbid(dbStr) {}
```

```
  virtual ~Database() {}
  void open() throw(DatabaseError) {
    std::cout << "Connected to " << dbid << std::endl;
  }
  void close() {
    std::cout << dbid << " closed" << std::endl;
  }
  // Other database functions...
};
#endif // DATABASE_H ///:~
```

/* We're leaving out actual database functionality (storing, retrieving, and so on), but that's not important here. Using this class requires a database connection string and that you call Database::open() to connect and Database::close() to disconnect: */

```
//: C21:UseDatabase.cpp
#include "Database.h"    // To be INCLUDED from Header FILE
                         // above
int main() {
  Database db("MyDatabase");
  db.open();
  // Use other db functions...
  db.close();
}
/* Output:
connected to MyDatabase
MyDatabase closed
*/ ///:~
```

In a typical client-server situation, a client will have multiple objects sharing a connection to a database. It is important that the database eventually be closed, but only after access to it is no longer required. It is common to encapsulate this behavior through a class that tracks the number of client entities using the database connection and to automatically terminate the connection when that count goes to zero. To add reference counting to the Database class, you use multiple inheritance to mix a class named Countable into the Database class to create a new class, DBConnection. Listing 21-4 contains the Countable mixin class.

Listing 21-4. Illustrating the Countable "mixin" Class

```
//: C21:Countable.h
// A "mixin" class.
#ifndef COUNTABLE_H
#define COUNTABLE_H
#include <cassert>

class Countable {
  long count;
protected:
  Countable() { count = 0; }
  virtual ~Countable() { assert(count == 0); }
```

```
public:
  long attach() { return ++count; }
  long detach() {
    return (--count > 0) ? count : (delete this, 0);
  }
  long refCount() const { return count; }
};
#endif // COUNTABLE_H ///:~
```

It is evident that this is not a standalone class because its constructor is protected; it requires a friend or a derived class to use it. It is important that the destructor is virtual, because it is called only from the delete this statement in detach(), and you want derived objects to be properly destroyed.

The DBConnection class inherits both Database and Countable and provides a static create() function that initializes its Countable subobject; see Listing 21-5.

Listing 21-5. Using the Countable "mixin" Class

```
//: C21:DBConnection.h
// Uses a "mixin" class.
#ifndef DBCONNECTION_H
#define DBCONNECTION_H
#include <cassert>
#include <string>
#include "Countable.h"                    // To be INCLUDED from Header FILE
                                          // above
#include "Database.h"
using std::string;

class DBConnection : public Database, public Countable {
  DBConnection(const DBConnection&); // Disallow copy
  DBConnection& operator=(const DBConnection&);
protected:
  DBConnection(const string& dbStr) throw(DatabaseError)
  : Database(dbStr) { open(); }
  ~DBConnection() { close(); }
public:
  static DBConnection*
  create(const string& dbStr) throw(DatabaseError) {
    DBConnection* con = new DBConnection(dbStr);
    con->attach();
    assert(con->refCount() == 1);
    return con;
  }
  // Other added functionality as desired...
};
#endif                                    // DBCONNECTION_H ///:~
```

You now have a reference-counted database connection without modifying the Database class, and you can safely assume that it will not be surreptitiously terminated. The opening and closing is done using the Resource Acquisition Is Initialization (RAII) idiom via the DBConnection constructor and destructor. This makes the DBConnection easy to use, as you can see in Listing 21-6.

Listing 21-6. Testing Out the Countable "mixin" Class

```
//: C21:UseDatabase2.cpp
// Tests the Countable "mixin" class.
#include <cassert>
#include "DBConnection.h"    // To be INCLUDED from Header FILE
                             // above
class DBClient {
  DBConnection* db;
public:
  DBClient(DBConnection* dbCon) {
    db = dbCon;
    db->attach();
  }
  ~DBClient() { db->detach(); }
  // Other database requests using db...
};

int main() {
  DBConnection* db = DBConnection::create("MyDatabase");
  assert(db->refCount() == 1);
  DBClient c1(db);
  assert(db->refCount() == 2);
  DBClient c2(db);
  assert(db->refCount() == 3);
  // Use database, then release attach from original create
  db->detach();
  assert(db->refCount() == 2);
} ///:~
```

The call to DBConnection::create() calls attach(), so when you're finished, you must explicitly call detach() to release the original hold on the connection. Note that the DBClient class also uses RAII to manage its use of the connection. When the program terminates, the destructors for the two DBClient objects will decrement the reference count (by calling detach(), which DBConnection inherited from Countable), and the database connection will be closed (because of Countable's virtual destructor) when the count reaches zero after the object c1 is destroyed.

A template approach is commonly used for mixin inheritance, allowing the user to specify at compile-time which flavor of mixin is desired. This way you can use different reference-counting approaches without explicitly defining DBConnection twice. Listing 21-7 shows how it's done.

Listing 21-7. Illustrating a Parameterized "mixin" Class (using Templates)

```
//: C21:DBConnection2.h
// A parameterized mixin.
#ifndef DBCONNECTION2_H
#define DBCONNECTION2_H
#include <cassert>
#include <string>
#include "Database.h"
using std::string;

template<class Counter>
class DBConnection : public Database, public Counter {
```

```
  DBConnection(const DBConnection&); // Disallow copy
  DBConnection& operator=(const DBConnection&);
protected:
  DBConnection(const string& dbStr) throw(DatabaseError)
  : Database(dbStr) { open(); }
  ~DBConnection() { close(); }
public:
  static DBConnection* create(const string& dbStr)
  throw(DatabaseError) {
    DBConnection* con = new DBConnection(dbStr);
    con->attach();
    assert(con->refCount() == 1);
    return con;
  }
  // Other added functionality as desired...
};
#endif                               // DBCONNECTION2_H ///:~
```

The only change here is the template prefix to the class definition (and renaming Countable to Counter for clarity). You could also make the database class a template parameter (had you multiple database access classes to choose from), but it is not a mixin since it is a standalone class. Listing 21-8 uses the original Countable as the Counter mixin type, but you could use any type that implements the appropriate interface (attach(), detach(), and so on).

Listing 21-8. Testing Out the Parametrized "mixin" Class

```
//: C21:UseDatabase3.cpp
// Tests a parameterized "mixin" class.
#include <cassert>
#include "Countable.h"
#include "DBConnection2.h"          // To be INCLUDED from Header FILE
                                    // above
class DBClient {
  DBConnection<Countable>* db;

public:
  DBClient(DBConnection<Countable>* dbCon) {
    db = dbCon;

    db->attach();
  }

  ~DBClient() { db->detach(); }
};

int main() {
  DBConnection<Countable>* db =
    DBConnection<Countable>::create("MyDatabase");

  assert(db->refCount() == 1);
  DBClient c1(db);
```

```
  assert(db->refCount() == 2);
  DBClient c2(db);

  assert(db->refCount() == 3);
  db->detach();

  assert(db->refCount() == 2);
} ///:~
```

The general pattern for multiple parameterized mixins is simply.

```
template<class Mixin1, class Mixin2, ... , class MixinK>
class Subject : public Mixin1,
                public Mixin2,
                ...
                publicMixinK {...};
```

Duplicate Subobjects

When you inherit from a base class, you get a copy of all the data members of that base class in your derived class. Listing 21-9 shows how multiple base subobjects might be laid out in memory.

Listing 21-9. Demonstrating Layout of Subobjects with MI

```cpp
//: C21:Offset.cpp
// Illustrates layout of subobjects with MI.
#include <iostream>
using namespace std;

class A { int x; };
class B { int y; };
class C : public A, public B { int z; };

int main() {
  cout << "sizeof(A) == " << sizeof(A) << endl;
  cout << "sizeof(B) == " << sizeof(B) << endl;
  cout << "sizeof(C) == " << sizeof(C) << endl;

  C c;
  cout << "&c == " << &c << endl;

  A* ap = &c;
  B* bp = &c;

  cout << "ap == " << static_cast<void*>(ap) << endl;
  cout << "bp == " << static_cast<void*>(bp) << endl;

  C* cp = static_cast<C*>(bp);
  cout << "cp == " << static_cast<void*>(cp) << endl;
  cout << "bp == cp? " << boolalpha << (bp == cp) << endl;
```

```
  cp = 0;
  bp = cp;

  cout << bp << endl;
} ///:~
```

```
    /*Output:

sizeof(A) == 4
sizeof(B) == 4
sizeof(C) == 12
&c == 1245052
ap == 1245052
bp == 1245056
cp == 1245052
bp == cp? true
0
*/
```

As you can see, the B portion of the object C is offset 4 bytes from the beginning of the entire object, suggesting the layout in Figure 21-3.

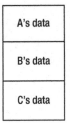

Figure 21-3. *Layout of the output data*

The object C begins with its A subobject, then the B portion, and finally the data from the complete type C itself. Since a C *is-an* A and *is-a* B, it is possible to upcast to either base type. When upcasting to an A, the resulting pointer points to the A portion, which happens to be at the beginning of the C object, so the address ap is the same as the expression &c. When upcasting to a B, however, the resulting pointer must point to where the B subobject actually resides because class B knows nothing about class C (or class A, for that matter). In other words, the object pointed to by bp must be able to behave as a standalone B object (except for any required polymorphic behavior).

When casting bp back to a C*, since the original object was a C in the first place, the location where the B subobject resides is known, so the pointer is adjusted back to the original address of the complete object. If bp had been pointing to a standalone B object instead of a C object in the first place, the cast would be illegal. Furthermore, in the comparison bp == cp, cp is implicitly converted to a B*, since that is the only way to make the comparison meaningful (that is, upcasting is always allowed), hence the true result. So when converting back and forth between subobjects and complete types, the appropriate offset is applied.

The null pointer requires special handling, obviously, since blindly subtracting an offset when converting to or from a B subobject will result in an invalid address if the pointer was zero to start with. For this reason, when casting to or from a B*, the compiler generates logic to check first to see if the pointer is zero. If it isn't, it applies the offset; otherwise, it leaves it as zero.

With the syntax you've seen so far, if you have multiple base classes, and if those base classes in turn have a common base class, you will have two copies of the top-level base, as you can see in Listing 21-10.

Listing 21-10. Demonstrating Duplicate Subobjects

```cpp
//: C21:Duplicate.cpp
// Shows duplicate subobjects.
#include <iostream>
using namespace std;

class Top {
  int x;
public:
  Top(int n) { x = n; }
};

class Left : public Top {
  int y;
public:
  Left(int m, int n) : Top(m) { y = n; }
};

class Right : public Top {
  int z;
public:
  Right(int m, int n) : Top(m) { z = n; }
};

class Bottom : public Left, public Right {
  int w;
public:
  Bottom(int i, int j, int k, int m)
  : Left(i, k), Right(j, k) { w = m; }
};

int main() {
  Bottom b(1, 2, 3, 4);
  cout << sizeof b << endl; // 20
} ///:~
```

Since the size of b is 20 bytes, there are five integers altogether in a complete Bottom object. A typical class diagram for this scenario is shown in Figure 21-4.

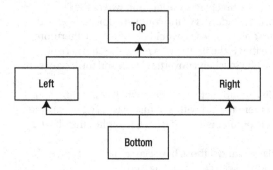

Figure 21-4. *Class diagram for the scenario of diamond inheritance*

This is the so-called "diamond inheritance", but in this case it would be better rendered as in Figure 21-5.

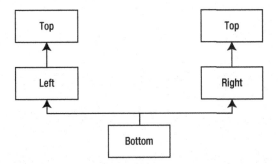

Figure 21-5. *A better class diagram for the same scenario*

The awkwardness of this design surfaces in the constructor for the Bottom class in the previous code. The user thinks that only four integers are required, but which arguments should be passed to the two parameters that Left and Right require? Although this design is not inherently "wrong," it is usually not what an application needs. It also presents a problem when trying to convert a pointer to a Bottom object to a pointer to Top. As shown earlier, the address may need to be adjusted, depending on where the subobject resides within the complete object, but here there are *two* Top subobjects to choose from. The compiler doesn't know which to choose, so such an upcast is ambiguous and is not allowed. The same reasoning explains why a Bottom object would not be able to call a function that is only defined in Top. If such a function Top::f() existed, calling b.f() would need to refer to a Top subobject as an execution context, and there are two to choose from.

Virtual Base Classes

What you usually want in such cases is *true* diamond inheritance, where a single Top object is shared by both Left and Right subobjects within a complete Bottom object, which is what the first class diagram depicts. This is achieved by making Top a *virtual base class* of Left and Right, as shown in Listing 21-11.

Listing 21-11. Demonstrating True Diamond Inheritance

```
//: C21:VirtualBase.cpp
// Shows a shared subobject via a virtual base.
#include <iostream>
using namespace std;

class Top {
protected:
  int x;
public:
  Top(int n) { x = n; }
  virtual ~Top() {}
  friend ostream&
  operator<<(ostream& os, const Top& t) {
    return os << t.x;
  }
};
```

```cpp
class Left : virtual public Top {
protected:
  int y;
public:
  Left(int m, int n) : Top(m) { y = n; }
}

class Right : virtual public Top {
protected:
  int z;
public:
  Right(int m, int n) : Top(m) { z = n; }
};

class Bottom : public Left, public Right {
  int w;
public:
  Bottom(int i, int j, int k, int m)
  : Top(i), Left(0, j), Right(0, k) { w = m; }
  friend ostream&
  operator<<(ostream& os, const Bottom& b) {
    return os << b.x << ',' << b.y << ',' << b.z
              << ',' << b.w;
  }
};
int main() {
  Bottom b(1, 2, 3, 4);
  cout << sizeof b << endl;
  cout << b << endl;
  cout << static_cast<void*>(&b) << endl;
  Top* p = static_cast<Top*>(&b);
  cout << *p << endl;
  cout << static_cast<void*>(p) << endl;
  cout << dynamic_cast<void*>(p) << endl;
} ///:~
```

Each virtual base of a given type refers to the same object, no matter where it appears in the hierarchy. This means that when a Bottom object is instantiated, the object layout may look something like Figure 21-6.

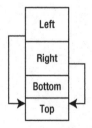

Figure 21-6. The object layout

The Left and Right subobjects each have a pointer (or some conceptual equivalent) to the shared Top subobject, and all references to that subobject in Left and Right member functions will go through those these pointers. Here, there is no ambiguity when upcasting from a Bottom to a Top object, since there is only one Top object to convert to.

The output of the program in Listing 21-11 is as follows:

```
36
1,2,3,4
1245032
1
1245060
1245032
```

The addresses printed suggest that this particular implementation does indeed store the Top subobject at the end of the complete object (although it's not really important where it goes). The result of a dynamic_cast to void* always resolves to the address of the complete object.

Although it is technically illegal to do so, if you remove the virtual destructor (and the dynamic_cast statement, so the program will compile), the size of Bottom decreases to 24 bytes. That seems to be a decrease equivalent to the size of three pointers. Why?

It's important not to take these numbers too literally. Other compilers manage only to increase the size by 4 bytes when the virtual constructor is added. Not being a compiler writer, I can't tell you their secrets. I can tell you, however, that with multiple inheritance, a derived object must behave as if it has multiple VPTRs, one for each of its direct base classes that also have virtual functions. It's as simple as that. Compilers make whatever optimizations their authors invent, but the behavior must be the same.

The strangest thing in the code in Listing 21-11 is the initializer for Top in the Bottom constructor. Normally one doesn't worry about initializing subobjects beyond direct base classes, since all classes take care of initializing their own bases. There are, however, multiple paths from Bottom to Top, so relying on the intermediate classes Left and Right to pass along the necessary initialization data results in an ambiguity—who is responsible for performing the initialization? For this reason, the *most derived class must initialize a virtual base*. But what about the expressions in the Left and Right constructors that also initialize Top? They are certainly necessary when creating standalone Left or Right objects, but must be *ignored* when a Bottom object is created (hence the zeros in their initializers in the Bottom constructor—any values in those slots are ignored when the Left and Right constructors execute in the context of a Bottom object). The compiler takes care of all this for you, but it's important to understand where the responsibility lies. Always make sure that *all concrete (nonabstract) classes* in a multiple inheritance hierarchy are aware of any virtual bases and initialize them appropriately.

These rules of responsibility apply not only to initialization, but to all operations that span the class hierarchy. Consider the stream inserter in Listing 21-11. We made the data protected so we could "cheat" and access inherited data in operator<<(ostream&, const Bottom&). It usually makes more sense to assign the work of printing each subobject to its corresponding class and have the derived class call its base class functions as needed. What would happen if we tried that with operator<<(), as Listing 21-12 illustrates?

Listing 21-12. Demonstrating a Wrong Way to Implement operator<<()

```cpp
//: C21:VirtualBase2.cpp
// How NOT to implement operator<<.
#include <iostream>
using namespace std;

class Top {
  int x;
public:
  Top(int n) { x = n; }
  virtual ~Top() {}
  friend ostream& operator<<(ostream& os, const Top& t) {
    return os << t.x;
  }
};
```

```
class Left : virtual public Top {
  int y;
public:
  Left(int m, int n) : Top(m) { y = n; }
  friend ostream& operator<<(ostream& os, const Left& l) {
    return os << static_cast<const Top&>(l) << ',' << l.y;
  }
};

class Right : virtual public Top {
  int z;
public:
  Right(int m, int n) : Top(m) { z = n; }
  friend ostream& operator<<(ostream& os, const Right& r) {
    return os << static_cast<const Top&>(r) << ',' << r.z;
  }
};

class Bottom : public Left, public Right {
  int w;
public:
  Bottom(int i, int j, int k, int m)
  : Top(i), Left(0, j), Right(0, k) { w = m; }
  friend ostream& operator<<(ostream& os, const Bottom& b){
    return os << static_cast<const Left&>(b)
      << ',' << static_cast<const Right&>(b)
      << ',' << b.w;
  }
};

int main() {
  Bottom b(1, 2, 3, 4);
  cout << b << endl;   // 1,2,1,3,4
} ///:~
```

You can't just blindly share the responsibility upward in the usual fashion, because the Left and Right stream inserters each call the Top inserter, and again there will be duplication of data. Instead you need to mimic what the compiler does with initialization. One solution is to provide special functions in the classes that know about the virtual base class, which ignore the virtual base when printing (leaving the job to the most derived class), as shown in Listing 21-13.

Listing 21-13. Demonstrating a Correct Stream Inserter

```
//: C21:VirtualBase3.cpp
// A correct stream inserter.
#include <iostream>
using namespace std;

class Top {
  int x;
public:
  Top(int n) { x = n; }
```

```
    virtual ~Top() {}
    friend ostream& operator<<(ostream& os, const Top& t) {
      return os << t.x;
    }
};

class Left : virtual public Top {
  int y;
protected:
  void specialPrint(ostream& os) const {
    // Only print Left's part
    os << ',' << y;
  }
public:
  Left(int m, int n) : Top(m) { y = n; }
  friend ostream& operator<<(ostream& os, const Left& l) {
    return os << static_cast<const Top&>(l) << ',' << l.y;
  }
};

class Right : virtual public Top {
  int z;
protected:
  void specialPrint(ostream& os) const {
    // Only print Right's part
    os << ',' << z;
  }
public:
  Right(int m, int n) : Top(m) { z = n; }
  friend ostream& operator<<(ostream& os, const Right& r) {
    return os << static_cast<const Top&>(r) << ',' << r.z;
  }
};

class Bottom : public Left, public Right {
  int w;
public:
  Bottom(int i, int j, int k, int m)
  : Top(i), Left(0, j), Right(0, k) { w = m; }

  friend ostream& operator<<(ostream& os, const Bottom& b){
    os << static_cast<const Top&>(b);
    b.Left::specialPrint(os);
    b.Right::specialPrint(os);
    return os << ',' << b.w;
  }
};

int main() {
  Bottom b(1, 2, 3, 4);
  cout << b << endl;  // 1,2,3,4
} ///:~
```

The specialPrint() functions are protected since they will be called only by Bottom. They print only their own data and ignore their Top subobject because the Bottom inserter is in control when these functions are called. The Bottom inserter must know about the virtual base, just as a Bottom constructor needs to. This same reasoning applies to assignment operators in a hierarchy with a virtual base, as well as to any function, member or not, that wants to share the work throughout all classes in the hierarchy.

Having discussed virtual base classes, let's now illustrate the "full story" of object initialization. Since virtual bases give rise to shared subobjects, it makes sense that they should be available before the sharing takes place. So the order of initialization of subobjects follows these rules, recursively.

1. All virtual base class subobjects are initialized in top-down, left-to-right order according to where they appear in class definitions.

2. Non-virtual base classes are then initialized in the usual order.

3. All member objects are initialized in declaration order.

4. The complete object's constructor executes.

Listing 21-14 illustrates this behavior.

Listing 21-14. Illustrating Initialization Order with Virtual Base Classes

```
//: C21:VirtInit.cpp
// Illustrates initialization order with virtual bases.
#include <iostream>
#include <string>
using namespace std;

class M {
public:
  M(const string& s) { cout << "M " << s << endl; }
};
class A {
  M m;
public:
  A(const string& s) : m("in A") {
    cout << "A " << s << endl;
  }
  virtual ~A() {}
};

class B {
  M m;
public:
  B(const string& s) : m("in B")  {
    cout << "B " << s << endl;
  }
  virtual ~B() {}
};

class C {
  M m;
```

```
public:
  C(const string& s) : m("in C")  {
    cout << "C " << s << endl;
  }
  virtual ~C() {}
};

class D {
  M m;
public:
  D(const string& s) : m("in D") {
    cout << "D " << s << endl;
  }
  virtual ~D() {}
};

class E : public A, virtual public B, virtual public C {
  M m;
public:
  E(const string& s) : A("from E"), B("from E"),
  C("from E"), m("in E") {
    cout << "E " << s << endl;
  }
};

class F : virtual public B, virtual public C, public D {
  M m;
public:
  F(const string& s) : B("from F"), C("from F"),
  D("from F"), m("in F") {
    cout << "F " << s << endl;
  }
};

class G : public E, public F {
  M m;
public:
  G(const string& s) : B("from G"), C("from G"),
  E("from G"),  F("from G"), m("in G") {
    cout << "G " << s << endl;
  }
};

int main() {
  G g("from main");
} ///:~
```

The output of this program is

```
M in B
B from G
M in C
C from G
```

```
M in A
A from E
M in E
E from G
M in D
D from F
M in F
F from G
M in G
G from main
```

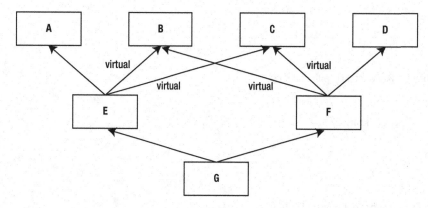

Figure 21-7. *Showing the various classes*

The classes in this code can be represented by Figure 21-7.

Each class has an embedded member of type M. Note that only four derivations are virtual: E from B and C, and F from B and C.

The initialization of G requires its E and F part to first be initialized, but the B and C subobjects are initialized first because they are virtual bases and are initialized from G's initializer, G being the most-derived class. The class B has no base classes, so according to rule 3, its member object M is initialized, then its constructor prints "B from G", and similarly for the C subject of E. The E subobject requires A, B, and C subobjects. Since B and C have already been initialized, the A subobject of the E subobject is initialized next, and then the E subobject itself. The same scenario repeats for G's F subobject, but without duplicating the initialization of the virtual bases.

Name Lookup Issues

The ambiguities illustrated with subobjects apply to any names, including function names. If a class has multiple direct base classes that share member functions of the same name, and you call one of those member functions, the compiler doesn't know which one to choose. The program in Listing 21-15 would report such an error.

Listing 21-15. Illustrating Ambiguous Function Names

```
//: C21:AmbiguousName.cpp {-xo}
class Top {
public:
  virtual ~Top() {}
};
```

```
class Left : virtual public Top {
public:
  void f() {}
};

class Right : virtual public Top {
public:
  void f() {}
};

class Bottom : public Left, public Right {};
int main() {
  Bottom b;
  b.f(); // Error here
} ///:~
```

The class Bottom has inherited two functions of the same name (the signature is *irrelevant*, since name lookup occurs before overload resolution), and there is no way to choose between them. The usual technique to disambiguate the call is to qualify the function call with the base class name; see Listing 21-16.

Listing 21-16. Resolving the Ambiguity in Listing 21-15

```
//: C21:BreakTie.cpp
class Top {
public:
  virtual ~Top() {}
};

class Left : virtual public Top {
public:
  void f() {}
};

class Right : virtual public Top {
public:
  void f() {}
};

class Bottom : public Left, public Right {
public:
  using Left::f;
};

int main() {
  Bottom b;
  b.f(); // Calls Left::f()
} ///:~
```

The name Left::f is now found in the scope of Bottom, so the name Right::f is not even considered. To introduce extra functionality beyond what Left::f() provides, you implement a Bottom::f() function that calls Left::f().

Functions with the same name occurring in different branches of a hierarchy often conflict. The hierarchy in Listing 21-17 has no such problem.

Listing 21-17. Illustrating the Dominance Principle to Resolve Function Name Ambiguities in a Class Hierarchy

```
//: C21:Dominance.cpp
class Top {
public:
  virtual ~Top() {}
  virtual void f() {}
};

class Left : virtual public Top {
public:
  void f() {}
};

class Right : virtual public Top {};

class Bottom : public Left, public Right {};

int main() {
  Bottom b;
  b.f(); // Calls Left::f()
} ///:~
```

Here, there is no explicit Right::f(). Since Left::f() is the most derived, it is chosen. Why? Well, pretend that Right did not exist, giving the single-inheritance hierarchy Top <= Left <= Bottom. You would certainly expect Left::f() to be the function called by the expression b.f() because of normal scope rules: a derived class is considered a nested scope of a base class. In general, a name A::f *dominates* the name B::f if A derives from B, directly or indirectly, or in other words, if A is "more derived" in the hierarchy than B. Therefore, in choosing between two functions with the same name, the compiler chooses the one that dominates. If there is no dominant name, there is an ambiguity.

Listing 21-18 further illustrates the dominance principle.

Listing 21-18. Illustrating the Dominance Principle (again) to Resolve More Ambiguities

```
//: C21:Dominance2.cpp
#include <iostream>
using namespace std;

class A {
public:
  virtual ~A() {}
  virtual void f() { cout << "A::f\n"; }
};

class B : virtual public A {
public:
  void f() { cout << "B::f\n"; }
};

class C : public B {};
class D : public C, virtual public A {};
```

```
int main() {
  B* p = new D;
  p->f(); // Calls B::f()
  delete p;
} ///:~
```

The class diagram for this hierarchy is shown in Figure 21-8.

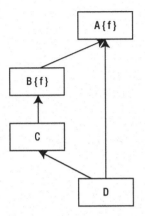

Figure 21-8. *Class diagram*

The class A is a (direct, in this case) base class for B, and so the name B::f dominates A::f.

Avoiding MI

When the question of whether to use multiple inheritance comes up, ask at least two questions.

1. Do you need to show the public interfaces of both these classes through your new type? (See instead if one class can be contained within the other, with only some of its interface exposed in the new class.)

2. Do you need to upcast to both of the base classes? (This also applies when you have more than two base classes.)

If you can answer "no" to either question, you can avoid using MI and should probably do so.

Watch for the situation where one class needs to be upcast only as a function argument. In that case, the class can be embedded and an automatic type conversion function provided in your new class to produce a reference to the embedded object. Any time you use an object of your new class as an argument to a function that expects the embedded object, the type conversion function is used. However, type conversion can't be used for normal polymorphic member function selection; that requires inheritance. Preferring composition over inheritance is a good overall design guideline.

Extending an Interface

One of the best uses for multiple inheritance involves code that's out of your control. Suppose you've acquired a library that consists of a header file and compiled member functions, but no source code for member functions.

This library is a class hierarchy with virtual functions, and it contains some global functions that take pointers to the base class of the library; that is, it uses the library objects *polymorphically*. Now suppose you build an application around this library and write your own code that uses the base class polymorphically.

Later in the development of the project or sometime during its maintenance, you discover that the baseclass interface provided by the vendor doesn't provide what you need: a function may be non-virtual and you need it to be virtual, or a virtual function is completely missing in the interface, but essential to the solution of your problem. Multiple inheritance can be the solution. For example, Listing 21-19 contains the header file for a library you acquire.

Listing 21-19. Illustrating a Vendor-Supplied Class Header

```
//: C21:Vendor.h
// Vendor-supplied class header
// You only get this & the compiled Vendor.obj.
#ifndef VENDOR_H
#define VENDOR_H

class Vendor {
public:
  virtual void v() const;
  void f() const; // Might want this to be virtual...
  ~Vendor();       // Oops! Not virtual!
};

class Vendor1 : public Vendor {
public:
  void v() const;
  void f() const;
  ~Vendor1();
};

void A(const Vendor&);
void B(const Vendor&);
// Etc.
#endif             // VENDOR_H ///:~
```

Assume the library is much bigger, with more derived classes and a larger interface. Notice that it also includes the functions A() and B(), which take a base reference and treat it polymorphically. Listing 21-20 contains the implementation file for the library.

Listing 21-20. Implementing the header file in Listing 21-19 (Vendor.h)

```
//: C21:Vendor.cpp {O}
// Assume this is compiled and unavailable to you.
#include "Vendor.h"    // To be INCLUDED from Header FILE
                       // above
#include <iostream>
using namespace std;

void Vendor::v() const { cout << "Vendor::v()" << endl; }

void Vendor::f() const { cout << "Vendor::f()" << endl; }
```

```
Vendor::~Vendor() { cout << "~Vendor()" << endl; }

void Vendor1::v() const { cout << "Vendor1::v()" << endl; }

void Vendor1::f() const { cout << "Vendor1::f()" << endl; }

Vendor1::~Vendor1() { cout << "~Vendor1()" << endl; }

void A(const Vendor& v) {
  // ...
  v.v();
  v.f();
  // ...
}

void B(const Vendor& v) {
  // ...
  v.v();
  v.f();
  // ...
} ///:~
```

In your project, this source code is unavailable to you. Instead, you get a compiled file as Vendor.obj or Vendor.lib (or, with the equivalent file suffixes for your system).

The problem occurs in the use of this library. First, the destructor isn't virtual. In addition, f() was not made virtual; you assume the library creator decided it wouldn't need to be. You also discover that the interface to the base class is missing a function essential to the solution of your problem. Also suppose you've already written a fair amount of code using the existing interface (not to mention the functions A() and B(), which are out of your control), and you don't want to change it.

To repair the problem, you create your own class interface and multiply inherit a new set of derived classes from your interface and from the existing classes, as shown in Listing 21-21.

Listing 21-21. Illustrates Fixing of the Mess in Listing 21-20 using MI

```
//: C21:Paste.cpp
//{L} Vendor
// Fixing a mess with MI.
#include <iostream>
#include "Vendor.h"
using namespace std;

class MyBase { // Repair Vendor interface

public:
  virtual void v() const = 0;
  virtual void f() const = 0;
  // New interface function:
  virtual void g() const = 0;
  virtual ~MyBase() { cout << "~MyBase()" << endl; }
};
```

```
class Paste1 : public MyBase, public Vendor1 {

public:
  void v() const {
    cout << "Paste1::v()" << endl;
    Vendor1::v();
  }

  void f() const {
    cout << "Paste1::f()" << endl;
    Vendor1::f();
  }
  void g() const { cout << "Paste1::g()" << endl; }

  ~Paste1() { cout << "~Paste1()" << endl; }
};

int main() {
  Paste1& p1p = *new Paste1;
  MyBase& mp = p1p; // Upcast
  cout << "calling f()" << endl;
  mp.f();              // Right behavior
  cout << "calling g()" << endl;
  mp.g();              // New behavior
  cout << "calling A(p1p)" << endl;
  A(p1p);              // Same old behavior
  cout << "calling B(p1p)" << endl;
  B(p1p);              // Same old behavior
  cout << "delete mp" << endl;
  // Deleting a reference to a heap object:
  delete &mp;          // Right behavior
} ///:~
```

In MyBase (which does *not* use MI), both f() and the destructor are now virtual, and a new virtual function g() is added to the interface. Now each of the derived classes in the original library must be recreated, mixing in the new interface with MI. The functions Paste1::v() and Paste1::f() need to call only the original baseclass versions of their functions. But now, if you upcast to MyBase as in main()

```
MyBase* mp = p1p; // Upcast
```

any function calls made through mp will be polymorphic, including delete. Also, the new interface function g() can be called through mp. Here's the output of the program:

```
calling f()
Paste1::f()
Vendor1::f()
calling g()
Paste1::g()
calling A(p1p)
Paste1::v()
Vendor1::v()
```

```
Vendor::f()
calling B(p1p)
Paste1::v()
Vendor1::v()
Vendor::f()
delete mp
~Paste1()
~Vendor1()
~Vendor()
~MyBase()
```

The original library functions A() and B() still work the same (assuming the new v() calls its base-class version). The destructor is now virtual and exhibits the *correct behavior*.

Although this is a messy example, it does occur in practice, and it's a good demonstration of where multiple inheritance is clearly necessary: you must be able to upcast to both base classes.

Review Session

1. One reason *MI* exists in C++ is that it is a *hybrid* language and couldn't enforce a single monolithic class hierarchy the way Smalltalk and Java do.

2. Instead, C++ allows *many inheritance trees to be formed*, so sometimes you may need to combine the interfaces from two or more trees into a new class.

3. If no "diamonds" appear in your class hierarchy, MI is fairly simple (*although identical function signatures in base classes must still be resolved*). If a diamond appears, you may want to eliminate duplicate *subobjects* by introducing virtual base classes. This not only adds confusion, but the underlying representation becomes more complex and less efficient.

4. Multiple inheritance has been called the "*goto of the '90s.*" This seems appropriate because, like a goto, *MI is best avoided in normal programming*, but can occasionally be very useful. It's a "minor" but more advanced feature of C++, designed to solve problems that arise in special situations.

5. If you find yourself using it often, you might want to take a look at your reasoning. Ask yourself, "Must I *upcast* to all the base classes?" If not, your life will be easier if *you embed instances of all the classes you don't need to upcast to*.

Index

D

E

■ F